Praise

"Thanks to Wolff and friends, the cyber-swamp may just have become a little less murky."—*Entertainment Weekly*

"*Net Guide* is the computer world's online *TV Guide*."—*Good Morning America*

"*Net Guide* will keep you from wandering around aimlessly on the Internet, and is full of good ideas for where to pull over."—*Forbes FYI*

"*Net Guide* is the liveliest, most readable online guide yet."—*USA Today*

"What you need to connect."—*Worth Magazine*

"*Net Guide* is the *TV Guide* to Cyberspace!"—Louis Rossetto, publisher/editor, *Wired*

"One of the more complete, well-organized guides to online topics. From photography to the Church of Elvis, you'll find it here."—*PC Magazine*

"The best attempt yet at categorizing and organizing all the great stuff you can find out there. It's the book people keep stealing off my desk."—Joshua Quittner, *New York Newsday*

"It's changed my online life. Get this book!"—Mike Madson, "Computer Bits," Business Radio Network

"My favorite for finding the cool stuff."—*The Louisville Courier-Journal*

"*Net Guide* focuses on the most important aspect of online information—its content. You name it, it's there—from erotica to religion to politics."—Lawrence J. Magid, *San Jose Mercury News*

"Not only did all the existing Net books ignore Cyberspace's entertaining aspects, but they were process-oriented, not content-oriented. Why hadn't someone made a *TV Guide* for the Net? Wolff recognized an opportunity for a new book, and his group wrote *Net Guide*."—Mark Frauenfelder, *Wired*

"Couch potatoes have *TV Guide*. Net surfers have *Net Guide*."—*Orange County Register*

"*Net Guide* is one of the best efforts to provide a hot-spot guide to going online."—*Knoxville News-Sentinel*

"Assolutamente indispensabile!"—*L'Espresso*, Italy

"A valuable guide for anyone interested in the recreational uses of personal computers and modems."—Peter H. Lewis, *The New York Times*

"*Net Games* is a good map of the playing fields of Netdom."—*Newsweek*

"This guide to games people play in the ever-expanding Cyberspace shows you exactly where to go."—*Entertainment Weekly*

"The second book in a very good series from Wolff and Random House."—Bob Schwabach, syndicated columnist

"Hot addresses!"—*USA Weekend*

"Move over Parker Brothers and Nintendo—games are now available online. There's something in *Net Games* for everyone from crossword-puzzle addicts to *Dungeons & Dragons* fans."—*Reference Books Bulletin*

"Whether you're a hardened game player or a mere newbie, *Net Games* is the definitive directory for gaming on the Internet."—*.net*

"A wide and devoted following."—*The Wall Street Journal*

"*Net Money* is a superb guide to online business and finance!"—*Hoover's Handbook of American Business*

"[*Net Chat*] is…the best surfer's guide out there."—*Entertainment Weekly*

"A product line of guidebooks for explorers of the Internet."—*Inside Media*

Instant

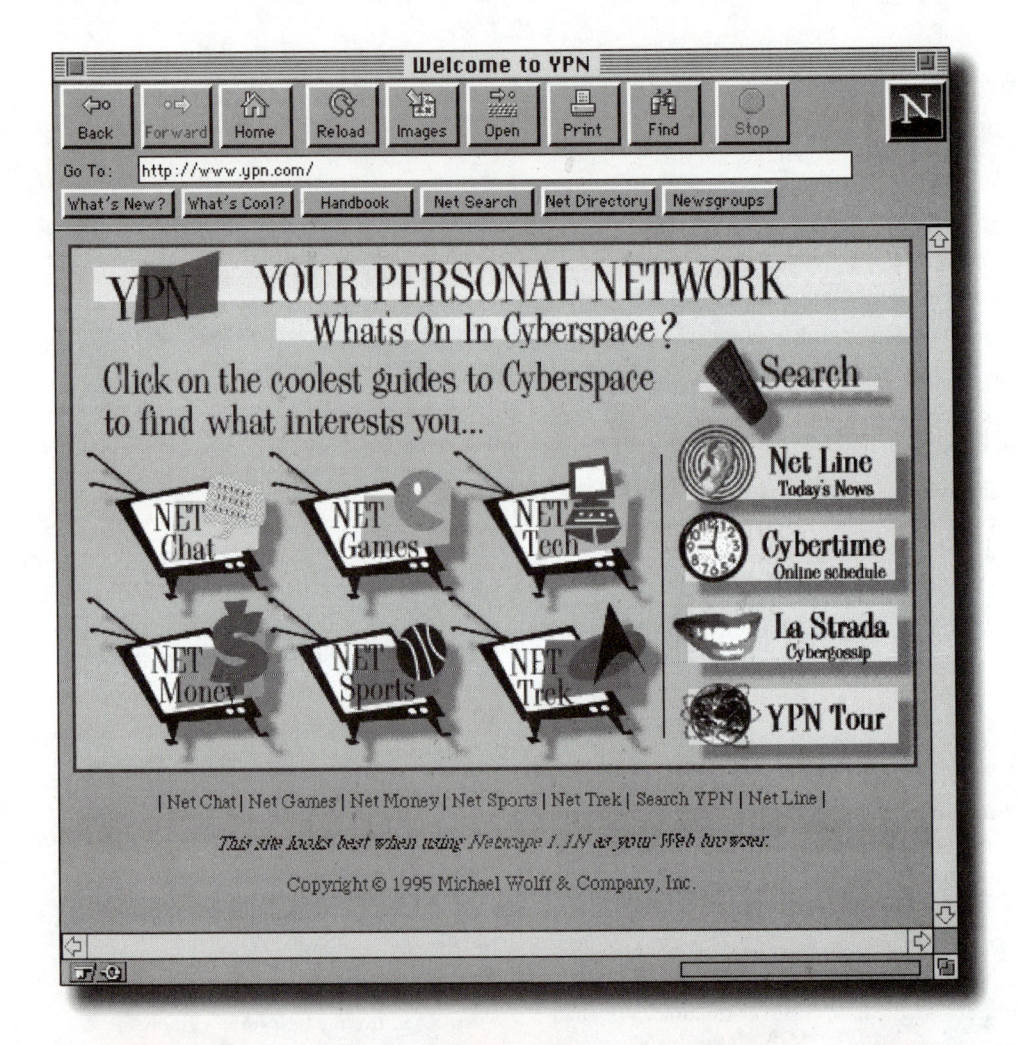

Visit our Web guide at

Updates.

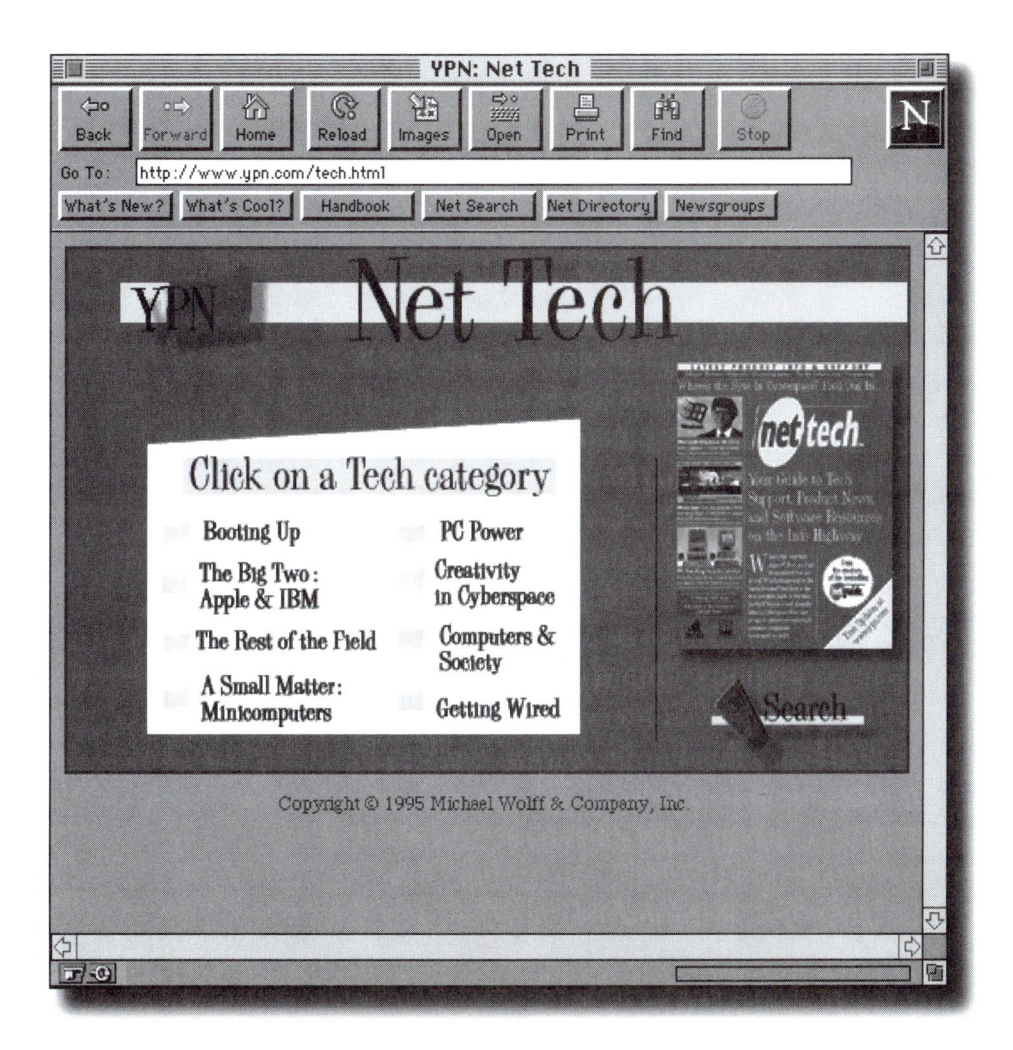

http://www.ypn.com/

Net Books!

netguide

netgames

netchat

netmoney

nettrek

netsports

nettech

Coming soon

netmusic

net tech™

Your Guide to
Tech Support, Product News and Software Resources on the Info Highway

A Michael Wolff Book

Kelly Maloni, Ben Greenman, and Jeff Hearn

For free updates visit our Website at http://www.ypn.com/

RANDOM HOUSE ELECTRONIC PUBLISHING

MICHAEL WOLFF & COMPANY, INC. DIGITAL PUBLISHING

New York

The Net Books series is a co-publishing venture of Michael Wolff & Company, Inc., 1633 Broadway, 27th Floor, New York, NY 10019, and Random House Electronic Publishing, a division of Random House, Inc., 201 East 50th Street, New York, NY 10022.

Net Tech has been wholly created and produced by Michael Wolff & Company, Inc. *Net Games, Net Chat, Net Money, Net Tech, Net Trek, Net Sports,* NetHead, NetSpeak, and CyberPower are trademarks of Michael Wolff & Company, Inc. All design and production has been done by means of desktop-publishing technology. The text is set in the typefaces Garamond, customized Futura, Zapf Dingbats, Franklin Gothic, and Pike.

Copyright © 1995 by Michael Wolff & Company, Inc.

All rights reserved. No part of the contents of this book may be reproduced or transmitted in any form or by any means without the written permission of the publisher.

Published simultaneously in the U.S. by Random House, NY, and Michael Wolff & Company, Inc., and in Canada by Random House of Canada, Ltd.

0 9 8 7 6 5 4 3 2 1

ISBN 0-679-76054-7

The author and publisher have used their best efforts in preparing this book. However, the author and publisher make no warranties of any kind, express or implied, with regard to the documentation contained in this book, and specifically disclaim, without limitation, any implied warranties of merchantability and fitness for a particular purpose with respect to listings in the book, or the techniques described in the book. In no event shall the author or publisher be responsible or liable for any loss of profit or any other commercial damages, including but not limited to special, incidental, consequential, or any other damages in connection with or arising out of furnishing, performance, or use of this book.

All of the photographs and illustrations in this book have been obtained from online sources, and have been included to demonstrate the variety of work that is available on the Net. The caption with each photograph or illustration identifies its online source. Text and images available over the Internet and other online services may be subject to copyright and other rights owned by third parties. Online availability of text and images does not imply that they may be reused without the permission of rights holders, although the Copyright Act does permit certain unauthorized reuse as fair use under 17 U.S.C. §107. Care should be taken to ensure that all necessary rights are cleared prior to reusing material distributed over the Internet and other online services. Information about reuse is available from the institutions that make their materials available online.

Trademarks

A number of entered words in which we have reason to believe trademark, service mark, or other proprietary rights may exist have been designated as such by use of initial capitalization. However, no attempt has been made to designate as trademarks or service marks all personal-computer words or terms in which proprietary rights might exist. The inclusion, exclusion, or definition of a word or term is not intended to affect, or to express any judgment on, the validity or legal status of any proprietary right which may be claimed in that word or term.

Manufactured in the United States of America

New York   Toronto   London   Sydney   Auckland

MICHAEL WOLFF & COMPANY, INC.
DIGITAL PUBLISHING

A Michael Wolff Book

Michael Wolff
President and Editor in Chief

Peter Rutten
Creative Director

Kelly Maloni
Executive Editor

Ben Greenman
Managing Editor

Jeff Hearn
Art Director

Senior Editor: Kristin Miller

Editorial Assistants: Pauline David, Jason Jones, Shaun Witten

Production Assistants: Linda Pattie, Eric Rakov, John Yale

Copy Editors: Jill Rappaport, Julia Curry, Elizabeth Upp

Contributing Writers: Andy Bailey, Vince Bonavoglia, Bill Folsom, Aaron Greenman, Alan Hammes, Allan Hoffman, Richard Kadrey, Anne Kugler, Tristan Louis, Tom Samiljan, Edward Willett, Shaun Witten, David Wood

Illustrations: Eric Rakov

Chief Technology Officer: Stan Norton

Special thanks:
Random House Electronic Publishing—Charles Levine, Tracy Smith, Mark Dazzo, Alison Biggert, Robin McCorry

Alison Anthoine at Kay Collyer & Boose

Peter Ginsberg at Curtis Brown Ltd.

And, as always, Aggy Aed

The editors of *Net Tech* can be reached at Michael Wolff & Company, Inc., 1633 Broadway, 27th Floor, New York, NY 10019, or by voice call at 212-841-1572, fax at 212-841-1539, or email at editors@ypn.com.

For Peter

Contents

Frequently Asked Questions 1

Part 1. Booting Up

Computing hubsites 18
Computing 101 23
Hardware & peripherals 26
Software & CD-ROMs 32
Computer bookstores 35
Shopping 39

Part 2. The Big Two: Apple and IBM

The Apple world 50
Macintosh 52
Apple: other systems 66
The PC world 68
IBMs & clones 75
DOS 79
MS Windows 81
OS/2 88

Part 3. The Rest of the Field

Amiga 94
Atari 98
Sinclair & Acorn 101
Other systems 103

Part 4. A Small Matter: Minicomputers

Portables 110
PDAs & palmtops 113
Calculators 118

Contents

Part 5. PC Power

Word processing 122
Desktop publishing 126
Business and finance 133
Spreadsheets 138
Databases 140
Educational resources 151
Family computing 154
Games & entertainment 156
Programming 162
Utilities 172
Screen savers 177

Part 6. Creativity in Cyberspace

Graphics—picture this 180
Sound & music 194
Hypermedia 209
Multimedia 212

Part 7. Computers & Society

Future tech 224
Security 232
Computer culture 240

Part 8. Getting Wired

Communications 246
Telecommunications 252
Getting online 257
FEATURE: @ the Café 262
Speed surfing 264
The BBS world 268
Real-time chat 271
Navigating the Net 275

Appendices

Company support	292
Internet Providers	320
Shareware BBSs	328
Net Speak	336
Index	340

FAQ

"Frequently Asked Questions" about the Net and Net Tech

1. I have a PC, but I'm not online yet.

You will be. All the things you need to know about your computer—how to fix it, what new products are on the market, how to get the most out of your machine—are on the Net. You'll never need to go to the computer store again, never need to wait for the mailman to bring you another computer magazine or catalogue, never need to suffer through interminable delays on technical support lines.

2. What if I'm not a super techie? Is the Net for me?

Whether you're a dyed-in-the-wool geek trading Perl scripts with friends you met at computer camp, a parent researching the best educational software, a college student panicked because she can't print her final paper, or a restaurant owner downloading inventory databases, you can turn to the Net for the support and resources you need.

Frequently Asked Questions

3. Pardon my ignorance, but what is "the Net," anyway?

The Net is the electronic medium spawned by the millions of computers networked together throughout the world. Also known as Cyberspace, the Information Highway, and the Infobahn, the Net comprises five types of networks—the Internet, a global, noncommercial system with more than 30 million computers communicating through it; the commercial online services, such as America Online, Prodigy, CompuServe, and eWorld; the thousands of local and regional bulletin-board services (BBSs); the discussion groups known as Usenet that traverse the Internet; and other networks of discussion groups, like FidoNet and Smartnet, that are carried out over BBSs. More and more, the Internet unites all the diverse locations and formats that of the Net.

4. For instance, I happen to be looking for a program to compress files so I can have more memory. Can I get it online?

Absolutely. On the Net, there are hundreds and hundreds of sites with programs that can be downloaded free of cost. From graphics converters to sound players, from patches for expensive commercial software to demos of programs not yet

ONLINE SERVICES

America Online:
- 800-827-6364 (voice)
- Monthly fee: $9.95
- Free monthly hours: 5
- Hourly fee: $2.95

CompuServe:
- 800-848-8199 (voice)
- Monthly fees: $9.95, first month free (standard); $2.50 (alternative)
- Free monthly hours: unlimited basic (standard); none (alternative)
- Hourly fee: $4.80 for baud rates up to 14,400
- Email: 70006.101@compuserve.com

Delphi:
- 800-695-4005 (voice)
- Monthly fees: $10 (10/4 plan); $20 (20/20 plan)
- Free monthly hours: 4 (10/4 plan); 20 (20/20 plan)
- Hourly fees: $4 (10/4 plan); $1.80 (20/20 plan), $9 surcharge during prime-time hours
- Setup: $19 (20/20 plan)
- Full Internet access, additional $3/month
- Email: info@delphi.com

eWORLD:
- 800-775-4556 (voice)
- Monthly fee: $8.95
- Free monthly hours: 4
- Hourly rates: $2.95
- Email: askeac@eworld.com

GEnie:
- 800-638-9636 (voice)
- Monthly fee: $8.95
- Free monthly hours: 4

Frequently Asked Questions

released, your software needs are just a download away—and that's true whether you're on a Macintosh, Compaq, Amiga, or Tandy Zoomer.

5. You know, my modem has been hissing like a snake. Can the Net help me fix it?

If it's repair advice you want, it's repair advice you'll get. Whether it's company-monitored message boards on commercial services, BBSs run by software and hardware companies, newsgroups populated by armchair experts, or Websites with the same fact sheets and manuals used by trained technical-support staffs, the Net's technical-support resources will make you into an instant expert. The Net is better than hardware manuals, better than toll-free phone lines. It's never been so easy to empower yourself.

6. I was recently reading about an incredible new color printer, and I'd like to learn more. Where should I go?

Want to do research? Want to compare prices? Why not go to the best computer magazines in the world, and go there online. Most of the major computer magazine publishers have multiple sites, with full-text articles, buyer's guides, links to other technical sites, and even interactive forums that allow users to respond to the recommendations.

- Hourly fees: $3 (off-prime) or $12.50 (prime time) for 2400 baud; $5 (off-prime) or $14.50 (prime time) for 9600 baud
- Email: feedback@genie.geis.com

Prodigy:
- 800-PRODIGY (voice)
- Value Plan I: $14.95/month includes unlimited core services; 5 hours in plus services, which consist of the bulletin boards, EAASY Sabre, Dow Jones Co. News, and stock quotes; additional 'plus' hours cost $2.95 each
- Alternate Plan I: $7.95/month includes 2 hours of core or plus services; additional hours (core or plus) are $2.95/hour
- Alternate Plan II: $19.95/month includes 8 hours of core services; plus services cost an additional $2.95/hour
- Alternate Plan BB: $29.95/month includes 25 hours core and plus services; additional hours are $2.95/hour

Frequently Asked Questions

7. My palmtop just bit the dust. I loved it like a son, and I want to replace it. What about buying computers and peripherals online?

Of course you can. In the past, you've had to hoist yourself out of your chair, get to the telephone, and place a call to one of the national computer mail-order superstores. Now, you can visit a Website, see a picture of the computer you want, place an order, and then sit back and play Marathon until your merchandise arrives.

8. This sounds wonderful, but what will it cost?

Most of the tech sites described in this book have no charge beyond the monthly and hourly fees charged by Internet producers or commercial networks like AOL, Prodigy, eWorld, or CompuServe. Most fees are quite reasonable (10 hours a month on AOL including Internet access costs about $25). But remember to examine costs carefully before plunging into a service. The Net changes.

9. I'm game. What do I need to get started?

A computer and a modem, and a few tricks to find your way around.

Frequently Asked Questions

10. Can you help me decide what computer and modem I'll need?

If you've bought a computer fairly recently, it's likely that it came with everything you need. But let's assume you have only a bare-bones PC. In that case you'll also need to get a modem, which will allow your computer to communicate over the phone. So-called 14.4 modems, which transfer data at speeds up to 14,400 bits per second (bps), have become the latest standard. You should be able to get one for less than $100. (Soon, however, 14,400 bps will feel like a crawl next to faster speeds of 28,800 bps and higher.) Next, you need a communications program to control the modem. This software will probably come free with your modem, your PC, or—if you're going to sign up somewhere—your online service. Otherwise, you can buy it off the shelf for under $25 or get a friend to download it from the Net. Finally, you'll want a telephone line (or maybe even two if you plan on tying up the line a couple of hours per day). And if that's still not good enough, you can contact your local telephone utility to arrange for installation of an ISDN line, which allows data to be transmitted at even higher speeds.

SENDING EMAIL

I'm on a commercial service. How do I send Internet email? Each of the major commercial services offers Internet email with slight variations in form.

From CompuServe
Enter the CompuServe mail area by choosing the **go** command from the menu and typing **mail** (if you don't have CompuServe's Information Manager software, type **go mail**). If you want to send a message to someone on another commercial service, your email will be routed through the Internet, so you must address it with the prefix **internet:**. Mail to John Doe at America Online, for instance, would be addressed "internet:jdoe@aol.com"; to John Doe at YPN, it would be addressed "internet:jdoe@ypn.com".

To CompuServe
Use the addressee's CompuServe ID number. If John Doe's ID is 12345,678, you'll address mail to 12345.678@ compuserve.com. Make sure you replace the comma in the CompuServe ID with a period.

From America Online
Use AOL's Internet mail gateway (keyword: **internet**). Then address and send mail as you normally would on any other Internet site, using the jdoe@service.com address style.

To America Online
Address email to jdoe@aol.com.

From GEnie
Use the keyword **mail** and →

Net Tech 5

Frequently Asked Questions

11. What kind of account should I get?

You'll definitely want to be able to get email; certainly want membership in at least one commercial service; and probably want wide access to the Internet.

Here are some of your access choices:

Email Gateway

This is the most basic access you can get. It lets you send and receive messages to and from anyone, anywhere, anytime on the Net. Email gateways are often available via work, school, or the other services listed here.

Commercial Services

All of the major commercial services have extensive support areas run by computer companies and large archives of technical-support documents. CompuServe is especially impressive, with thousands of vendors, applications, and publications represented, but America Online is also excellent. Commercial services generally require their own special start-up software, which you can buy at any local computer store or by calling the numbers listed in this book. (Hint: Look for the frequent starter-kit giveaways.) AOL, CompuServe, and Prodigy all provide access to many of Usenet's more than 10,000 newsgroups, and through email you can subscribe to any Internet mailing lists. As of spring 1995, the three most popular commercial services—America Online, CompuServe, and Prodigy—took a large step

---

address email to jdoe@service.com@inet#. GEnie's use of two @ symbols is an exception to Internet addressing convention.

To GEnie
Address email to jdoe@genie.geis.com.

From Delphi
Use the command **go mail**, then, at the prompt, type **mail** again. Address mail to Internet "jdoe@service.com" (make sure to include the quotation marks).

To Delphi
Address email to jdoe@delphi.com.

From eWorld
Use the command go email, compose your message, address message to jdoe@service.com, and click on the Send Now button.

To eWorld
Address email to jdoe@eworld.com.

From Prodigy
To send email from Prodigy, first download Prodigy's Mail Manager by using the command **jump: mail manager**. Address mail to jdoe@service.com. Mail Manager is currently available for DOS and Windows only. A Mac version is due soon.

To Prodigy
Address email using the addressee's user ID. For John Doe (user ID: ABCD12A), for example, you would address it abcd12a@prodigy.com.

Frequently Asked Questions

toward the Internet by offering full access to the World Wide Web (WWW).

Internet Providers

There are a growing number of full-service Internet providers (which means they offer email, Usenet, FTP, IRC, telnet, gopher, and WWW access). In practical terms, the Internet enables you to connect with the Microsoft Home Page, the Virtual Shareware Library, HotWired, and AT&T. A dial-up SLIP (serial line Internet protocol) or PPP (point-to-point protocol) account is the most fun you can have through a modem. It is a special service offered by most Internet providers that gets you significantly faster access and the ability to use point-and-click programs for Windows, Macintosh, and other platforms.

BBSs

BBSs range from mom-and-pop, hobbyist computer bulletin boards to large professional services. What the small ones lack in size they often make up for in affordability and homeyness. In fact, many users prefer these scenic roads over the Info Highway. Many of the large Tech BBSs are as rich and diverse as the commercial services. BBSs are easy to get started with, and if you find one with Internet access or an email gateway, you'll get the best of local color and global reach. You can locate local BBSs through the Usenet discussion groups alt.bbs.lists and comp.bbs.misc, the BBS forums of the commercial services, and regional and national BBS lists kept in the file libraries of many BBSs. See the BBS world section in the book for more information. Once you've found a local BBS, contact the sysop to inquire about the echoes (or conferences) you want. These are the BBS world's equivalent of Usenet newsgroups. With echoes, you're talking not only to the people on your particular BBS, but also to

---

IP SOFTWARE

Most "serial" dial-up connections to the Internet treat your fancy desktop computer as a dumb terminal that requires a lot of typed-out commands. An IP connection, whether through a direct hookup like Ethernet or a dial-up over phone lines, turns your computer into a node on the Net instead of a one-step-removed terminal connection. With an IP link, you can run slick point-and-click programs—often many at once. Macintosh users will need MacTCP and, depending on the kind of IP service you're getting, either Interslip or the more advanced MacPPP. Windows users will need the latest version of WinSock. (The latest versions of programs that run over WinSock can be found at ftp.cica.indiana.edu.) Two all-in-one packages of Internet software that you might want to consider for Windows are Chameleon and WinQVT. Your best bet for these programs is to get your online service to give them to you preconfigured, as the IP address can be mind-boggling to set up.

Frequently Asked Questions

everyone else on a BBS that carries the echo (in other words, a universe of millions). Even if the discussion of your choice is not on their board yet, many sysops are glad to add an echo that a paying customer has requested. Many, if not most, local BBSs now offer Internet email, as well as live chat, file libraries, and some quirky database, program, or directory unique to their little corner of Cyberspace.

Direct Network Connection

Look, Ma Bell: no phone lines! The direct network connection is the fast track of college students, computer scientists, and a growing number of employees of high-tech businesses. It puts the user right on the Net, bypassing the phone connections. In other words, it's a damned sight faster.

12. By the way, exactly how do I send email?

With email, you can write to anyone on a commercial service, Internet site, or Internet-linked BBS, as well as to those people connected to the Net via email gateways, SLIPs, and direct-network connections.

Email addresses have a universal syntax called an Internet address. An Internet address is broken down into four parts: the user's name (e.g., jeff), the @ symbol, the computer and/or company name, and what kind of Internet address it is: **net** for network, **com** for a commercial enterprise—as with Your Personal Network (ypn.com) and America Online (aol.com)—**edu** for educational institutions, **gov** for government sites, **mil** for military facili-

---

MAIL READERS

Eudora
(Mac and Windows) If the host for your email supports the POP protocol, you're in luck. Eudora makes email even easier than it already was. The commercial upgrade to the free version includes message filtering for automatically sorting incoming mail, but drops the fun dialog messages (if you start typing without an open window, Eudora beeps, "Unfortunately, no one is listening to keystrokes at the moment. You may as well stop typing.") The Windows version requires an IP connection; the Mac version does not.

Pine
(Unix) Menu-driven, with a full-screen editor and spell check. Support of the MIME "metamail" format means that you can "attach" binary files within an email.

Elm
(Unix, DOS, Windows, OS/2) Programmable "user agent" reader that can also sort, forward, and auto-reply. It does not include its own editor.

Mail
(Unix) As the name suggests, a no-frills mail program.

Frequently Asked Questions

ties, and **org** for nonprofit and other private organizations. For instance, the art director of this company, an epicurean first and Netter second, would be jeff@ypn.com.

13. What about the Web?

The World Wide Web is a hypertext-based information structure that now dominates Internet navigation. The Web is like a house where every room has doors to every other room—or, perhaps more accurately, like the interconnections in the human brain. Words, icons, and pictures on a page link to other pages that reside on the same machine or on a computer anywhere in the world. You have only to click on the appropriate word or phrase or image—the Web does the rest. With invisible navigation, you can jump from the 1995 Robot Olympics to an HTML tutorial to a list of computer magazines online. All the while you've FTPed, telnetted, and gophered without a thought to case-sensitive UNIX commands or addresses.

Your dial-up Internet provider undoubtedly offers programs to access the Web. Lynx and WWW are pretty much the standard offerings for text-only Web browsing. Usually you choose them by typing **lynx** and **www** and then **<return>**. What you'll get is a "page" with some of the text highlighted. These are the links. Choose a link, hit the return key, and you're off.

If you know exactly where you want to go and don't want to meander through the information, you can type a Web page's address, known as a URL (uniform resource locator), many of which you'll find in this book.

14. What about graphical Web browsers? What are these things?

With the emergence of new and sophisticated software like Netscape, the Web is starting to look the way it was envisioned to—pictures,

Net Tech 9

Frequently Asked Questions

icons, and appetizing layouts. Some commercial services, most notably America Online and Prodigy, have even developed customized Web browsers for their subscribers. But Web browsers are more than just presentation tools. Most of them allow Netsurfers to see all kinds of Net sites through a single interface. Want to read newsgroups? Need to send email? Interested in participating in real-time chat? You can do it all with your browser. And many Internet providers, including Prodigy, allow subscribers to build their own Web pages.

15. And these newsgroups?

The most widely read bulletin boards are a group of some 10,000-plus "newsgroups" on the Internet, collectively known as Usenet. Usenet newsgroups travel the Internet, collecting thousands of messages a day from whoever wants to "post" to them. More than anything, the newsgroups are the collective, if sometimes Babel-like, voice of the Net—everything is discussed here. And we mean *everything*. While delivered over the Internet, the Usenet collection of newsgroups is not technically part of the Internet. In order to read a newsgroup, you need to go where it is stored. Smaller BBSs that have news feeds sometimes store only a couple dozen newsgroups, while most Internet providers offer thousands. (If there's a group missing that you really want, ask your Internet provider to add the newsgroup back to the subscription list.)

The messages in a newsgroup, called "posts," are listed and numbered chronologically—in other words, in the order in which

NEWSREADERS

To read the newsgroups, you use a program called a reader, a standard offering on most online services. There are several types of readers—some let you follow message threads; others organize messages chronologically. You can also use a reader to customize the newsgroup menu to include only the newsgroups you're interested in.

Newswatcher
(Mac) Fancy newsreader. Whole newsgroups can be saved locally in a single file, by article or by thread. Multiple binaries can be decoded automatically—making it possible to grab all of alt.binaries.pictures.supermodels with a couple of clicks. Requires an IP connection.

Nuntius
(Mac) Comparable with Newswatcher, except it can multitask. Some people prefer the way Nuntius grabs the full text of threads; others hate waiting to read the first message. Nuntius also stores newsgroup subjects on your computer—this chews up disk space but accelerates searches through old messages. Requires an IP connection.

Trumpet
(Windows) The most popular Windows newsreader. Thread by subject, date, or author. Like in Newswatcher, batch binary extraction. WinNV is also widely used. Requires an IP connection.

→

Frequently Asked Questions

they were posted. Usenet is not distributed from one central location, which means that a posted message does not appear everywhere instantly. The speed of distribution partly depends on how often providers pick up and post Usenet messages. For a message to appear in every corner of the Net, you'll generally have to wait overnight.

You can scan a list of messages before deciding to read a particular message. If someone posts a message that prompts responses, the original and all follow-up messages are called a thread. The subject line of subsequent posts in the thread refers to the subject of the original. For example, if you were to post a message with the subject "Scared of my mouse" in comp.sys.mac.hardware.misc, all responses would read "Re: Scared of my mouse." In practice, however, topics wander off in many directions.

16. Mailing lists?

Mailing lists are like newsgroups, except that they are distributed by Internet email. The fact that messages show up in your mailbox tends to make the discussion group more intimate, as does the proactive act of subscribing. Mailing lists are often more focused, and they're less vulnerable to irreverent and irrelevant contributions.

To subscribe to a mailing list, send an email to the mailing list's subscription address. Often you will need to include very specific information, which you will find in this book. To unsubscribe, send another message to that same address. If the

---

Tin
(Unix) Intuitive Unix newsreader that works especially well for scanning newsgroups. You can maintain a subscription list, decode binaries, and search the full text of individual newsgroups. With its help files and easy-to-use menus, this is our favorite Unix newsreader.

nn (Unix) and rn (Unix)
Complex newsreaders (Network News and Read News) favored by Unix-heads.

trn (Unix)
Maps subjects within newsgroups.

TELNETTING

To telnet, follow this process:

1. Log on to your Internet site and locate the telnet program. Since telnet is a widely used feature, you will most likely find it in the main menu of your Internet access provider. On Delphi, for example, telnet is available in the main Internet menu. Just type **telnet.**

2. Once you've started the program, you should see a telnet prompt (for instance, telnet> or telnet:). Type **open <telnet address>**, replacing the bracketed text with the address of the machine you want to reach. (Note: Some systems do not require you to type **open**. Also, don't type the brackets.) Let's say you want to connect to the Cleveland FreeNet at freenet-in-a.cwru.edu. After the telnet prompt you would type →

Frequently Asked Questions

mailing list is of the listserv, listproc, or majordomo variety, you can usually unsubscribe by sending the command **unsubscribe <listname>** or **signoff <listname>** in the message body. If the mailing list instructs you to write a request to subscribe, you will probably need to write a request to unsubscribe.

Once you have subscribed, messages are almost always sent to a different address than the subscription address. Most lists still send you the address when you subscribe. If not, send another message to the subscription address and ask the owner.

17. And telnet, FTP, gopher? Can you spell it out?

Telnet:
When you telnet, you're logging on to another computer somewhere else on the Internet. You then have access to the programs running on the remote computer. If the site is running a library catalogue, you can search the catalogue. If it's running a BBS, you can chat with others logged on. If it's running a game, you can challenge an opponent.

Anon-FTP:
FTP (file transfer protocol) is a program that allows you to copy a file from another Internet-connected computer to your own. Hundreds of computers on the Internet allow "anonymous FTP" (anon-ftp). In other words, you don't need a

---

open freenet-in-a.cwru.edu, or just **freenet-in-a.cwru.edu**. Some telnet addresses have port numbers; others do not.

3. The telnet program will connect you to the remote computer—in our example, the Cleveland FreeNet. Once you're connected, you'll see a prompt. Type the remote computer's log-in information as listed in the *Net Tech* entry. The prompt may be as simple as **login** followed by another prompt for a password. Oh, and you may be asked about the type of terminal you're using. If you're unsure, vt-100 is a safe bet.

4. You're logged in. Now just follow the instructions on the screen, which will differ with every telnet site.

HOW TO DOWNLOAD

How do I download from a commercial service?

The download command on each of the commercial services may differ slightly depending on the type of computer you use, but in most instances file downloads work as follows:

On **America Online**, once you locate the file you want, you should select the file name so that it's highlighted. After that process, select one of two buttons: **download now**, or **download later**. If you choose **download later**, the file will be added to a list of files, all of which you can down-→

Frequently Asked Questions

unique password to access them. Just type "anonymous" at the user prompt and type your email address at the password prompt. The range of material available is extraordinary—from scripts to free software to pictures to all sorts of trivia lists! More and more, FTP sites are being accessed from the Web, allowing Net users to view documents before retrieving them. FTP addresses are listed as URLs, in the form **ftp://domain.name/directory/filename.txt**.

Gopher:

A gopher is a program that turns Internet addresses into menu options. Gophers can perform many Internet functions, including telnetting and downloading files. Gopher addresses throughout this book are listed as URLs, in the form **gopher://domain.name/**.

18. Any suggestions for first stops on my journey through the world of online tech resources?

Well, you might want to start with the sites listed on the first page of the first section, the hubsites to the online computer universe. Most of these are collections of links, and if you spend some time rooting around you should be able to find a little bit of everything—from PC magazines to programming conferences to printer troubleshooting tips.

---

load when you're done with your America Online session.

On **CompuServe**, if you're browsing a library list (using CompuServe's Information Manager), you can highlight a file you want and select the **retrieve** button to download it immediately. If you want to download it later, select the box next to the file name, then select **yes** when you leave the forum and a window will appear that says download marked files? (If you don't have Information Manager, type **down** and **[return]** at the prompt following the file description.)

How do I download from the Internet?

Web browsers will download for you automatically. Otherwise, use an FTP program and follow these instructions:

1. Log in to your Internet site. Then start the FTP program at that site—in most cases, by typing **ftp** or by choosing it from an Internet menu.
2. Since FTP addresses in this book are displayed as URLs, you will need to break them into the three main parts—domain names, directories, and filenames. This is very easy. For the URL **ftp://ypn.com/pub/mac/demo.zip** the domain name is the part of the URL represented by **ypn.com**; the directory the part represented by **pub/mac**; the filename the part represented by **demo.zip**. Directories may be a single →

Net Tech 13

Frequently Asked Questions

19. So, how does the book work?

If you know what kind of tech information you need, turn to the *Net Tech* index, where every subject and site in the book is listed alphabetically. Of course, you can browse *Net Tech* at your leisure—the book is divided into six sections:

- Booting Up
- The Big Two: Apple and IBM
- The Rest of the Field
- A Small Matter: Minicomputers
- PC Power
- Creativity in Cyberspace
- The Cutting Edge
- Getting Wired

Booting Up collects a variety of cross-platform sites, from online computer primers to online computer stores to the world's largest shareware archives. **The Big Two** lists and describes hundreds of sites with resources for Apple II, Macintosh, DOS, Windows, OS/2, and other Apple, IBM, and clone systems. **The Rest of the Field** covers other platforms and operating systems, from Amiga to Atari to Unix to NeXT. **A Small Matter: Minicomputers** makes a big deal out of portables, PDAs, palmtops, and calculators. **PC Power** spotlights a variety of applications, from word processing to spreadsheets to desktop publishing. **Creativity in Cyberspace** illustrates the aesthetics of computing, with sections on graphics, sound, multimedia, and hypermedia. **The Cutting Edge** keeps a finger on the pulse of high technology. And

step, or a number of steps separated by slashes.
3. When you see the FTP prompt, type **open <domain name>** to connect to the other computer. The Wuarchive Software Archive, for example, is at the domain wuarchive.wustl.edu, so you would type **open wuarchive.wustl.edu**. (By the way, sometimes you'll be asked for just the FTP domain name, which means you wouldn't type **open**.)
4. Most FTP sites offer "anonymous login," which means you won't need a personal account or password to access the files. When you connect to an anonymous FTP machine, you will be asked for your name with the prompt **name:**. Type **anonymous** after the prompt. Next you'll be asked for your password with the prompt **password:**. Type your email address.
4. Once you're logged in to an FTP site, you can change directories by typing **cd <directory name>**. For example, the Wuarchive Software Archive at wuarchive.wustl.edu is in the directory named systems. After login, type **cd/systems** to change to the directory. (To move back up through the directory path you came down, you type **cdup** or **chdirup**.) You must move up one directory at a time.
5. To transfer files from the FTP site to your "home" or "files" directory at your Internet site, use the get command. For example, in the Wuarchive Software Archive, you may run across a

14 Net Tech

Frequently Asked Questions

Getting Wired outlines the basics of Net connection and navigation.

All entries in *Net Tech* have a name, description, and address. The site name appears first in boldface. If the entry is a mailing list, "(ml)" immediately follows; if a newsgroup, "(ng)."

After the description, complete address information is provided. A red check mark (✓) identifies the name of the network—Internet, Usenet, or a commercial service provider. When you see an arrow (→), this means that you have another step ahead of you, such as typing a command, searching for a file, subscribing to a mailing list, or typing a URL, or Web address. Additional check marks indicate that the site is accessible through other networks; an ellipsis indicates another address on the same network; and more arrows mean more steps.

If the item is a Website, FTP site, or gopher, it will be displayed in the form of a URL to type on the command line of your Web browser. If the item is a mailing list, the address will be an email address followed by instructions on how to subscribe (remember—the address given is usually the subscription address; in order to post to the mailing list, you will use another address that will be emailed to you upon subscribing). An entry that includes an FTP, telnet, or gopher address will provide a log-in sequence and a directory path or menu path when necessary.

In a commercial service address, the arrow is followed by the service's keyword (also called go word or jump word), which will take you to the site. Additional arrows indicate that second or third steps are necessary.

IRC addresses indicate what you must type to get to the channel you want once you've connected to the IRC program. The name of a newsgroup entry or BBS echo is also its address.

In addition, there are a few special terms used in addresses. **Info** indicates a supplementary informational address. **Archives** is used to mark collections of past postings for newsgroups and mailings lists. And **FAQ** designates the location of a "frequently asked questions" file for a newsgroup.

---

program to locate a security breach in your office system. Retrieve it by typing the get command and the name of the application, which in this case is **turncoat.zip**. In other words, at the prompt type **get turncoat.zip** and **[return]**. The distinction between the upper- and lowercase in directory and file names is important. Type a lowercase letter when you should have typed uppercase and you'll leave empty-handed.

Frequently Asked Questions

20. What about the huge list of computer vendors in the back of the book?

In the world of computers, technical support is all about the companies—if you know which company programmed your spreadsheet or built your scanner, you're halfway to customer satisfaction. Pick up the box. The name of the company should be displayed prominently. Maybe the company even has a cute logo, like a little man waving or a rising sun. After you've memorized the company name, consult our Computer Vendors appendix, an alphabetical directory of Websites, commercial service forums, and even dedicated BBSs for hundreds of software and hardware companies. We've even gone an extra step and listed a handful of products for each company. Tech support has never been simpler.

21. Even though I'm a computer geek, I have other interests. What else is on the Net?

Try *Net Guide*, *Net Games*, *Net Chat*, *Net Money*, *Net Trek*, and *Net Sports*. Find them in your bookstore right beside *Net Tech*. And keep an eye out for *Net Guide 2* and *Net Music*—they're coming soon.

Part 1

Booting Up

Computing Hubsites Booting Up

Computing hubsites

Even the longest journey must start with a single step, and the extremely long journey through the labyrinth of online computer resources—commercial service forums, Websites, newsgroups, and mailing lists—should begin with a single step toward these sites. Start your trip at America Online's **Computing**, which collects all of AOL's computer services, or the **Virtual Computer Library Spot**, which links to a wealth of Websites devoted to technology. Keep your finger on the pulse of microprocessing issues (and pay tribute to Marvin Gaye) with eWorld's **What's Going On**. And make sure your PC doesn't sicken you with **Computer Ailments**.

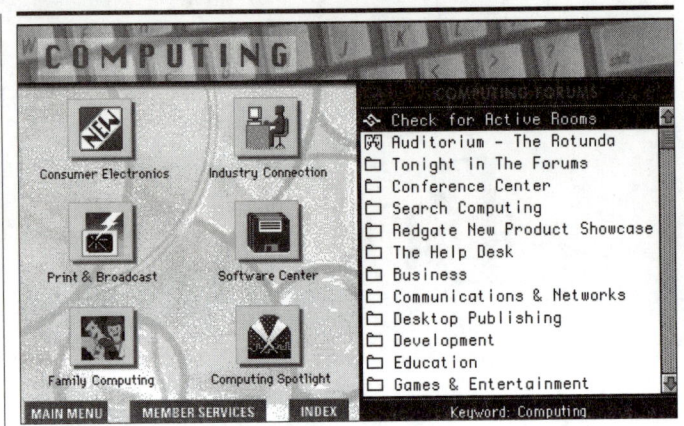

Screenshot—from America Online's Computing area

On the Net

Across the board

Computer Center Humankind was chased out of paradise over an apple, but in return we got eWorld, the Apple-owned online service with so much Apple-related information, news, software, shopping, and support, it should be forbidden. There's a software center for the Mac from ZiffNet. There's so much Apple product support that Mac owners can laugh their 1-800 tears away. There's *MacWeek* and other news mags gone digital. There's a calendar of computer conventions. There's an area for developers. It's too much. They shouldn't have... ✓**EWORLD**→*go* computers

Computers Broadcasting headlines of the day's top computer stories, the main menu for Prodigy's computer offerings links to news stories, computer shopping sites, several computer-oriented bulletin boards, live computer chat, a large PC software download area, and an area sponsored by ZiffNet. The PC orientation should be no surprise; Prodigy, after all, is owned by IBM. ✓**PRODIGY**→*jump* computers

Computers/Technology No commercial service comes close to CompuServe's mega-computer offerings: computing reference guides, hundreds of hardware and software forums (from Hewlett-Packard laser printers to Quark XPress extensions), a software catalog, platform-related forums, gaming forums, computer news magazines, and an extensive range of ZiffNet services. ✓**COMPUSERVE**→*go* computers

Computing A good place to start exploring AOL's computer resources—its software libraries, computer news magazines, vendor support area, family computing center, and many platform-oriented forums. If you are accessing AOL from a Windows machine, the computing menu will focus on PC computing sites (if, for instance, you were to enter the keyword "software," you would move to the PC Software Center). Macintosh users will, on the other hand, see a menu oriented toward Mac computing sites. In either case, you have full access to all sites. (Windows users could enter the keyword "mac software" to get to the Mac Software Center.) The AOL help desk, available from this menu, offers nightly live conferences to help new users. ✓**AMERICA ONLINE**→*keyword* computing

Computing WWW Virtual Library Whether you're looking for an FAQ for the Linux system or a Website that offers a basic overview of the intricacies of artificial

18 Net Tech

Booting Up Computing Hubsites

intelligence, the WWW Virtual Library of Computing should keep you digging for hours. The main index is separated into the following broad categories: Miscellaneous, Specialized Fields, University Computer Science Departments, Institutes, Centers and Laboratories, Other Organizations, Particular Systems, Vendors, and Magazines and Books. ✓**INTERNET**→*www* http://src.doc.ic.ac.uk/bySubject/Computing/Overview.html

U.K. Computing Forum You don't have to live in the United Kingdom to benefit from the many general computing resources this forum offers. Visit the vast software libraries, with thousands of programs for PC, Macintosh, Acorn, Amstrad, NextBase, and Eden Group computers. The place is packed with software and technical support resources you want. Thinking of jumping the pond? The Classified Ads section of the library has loads of listings for "situations vacant" in the European computing community. Browse it over a nice cup of tea. ✓**COMPUSERVE**→*go* ukcomp

Virtual Computer Library If the Net were the New York Public Library, this would be the computing section's card catalog. There are links to thousands of computing resources, from press releases issued by Adobe to animation archives to manuals for Perl scripting to a glossary of computer terms to dozens of computer FAQs to computing magazines like *Boardwatch* and *Computer Shopper*. ✓**INTERNET**→*www* http://www.utexas.edu/computer/vcl/

Chat

Computer BB Stop by for suggestions on using graphics programs or word processors, for help on designing a database or configuring a computer network, or for advice on what financial software or color printer to buy. Just choose the appropriate topic—say, Hardware: Peripherals—post your question, and check back later that day. ✓**PRODIGY**→*jump* computerbb

News

Bits and Bytes Online A weekly e-zine with "One foot in the future, and the other foot, a bit uneasily, in the halls of corporate America." Includes postings from various print and online media relating to the future of computing. This electronic publication prides itself on being "not especially technical" and includes such articles as "Developing a Personal Information Strategy," "Infoliteracy," "How About That Pentium Chip?," and "How to Be Annoying Online." ✓**AMERICA ONLINE**→*keyword* pctelecom→Browse Software Libraries→Computing→Newsletters→Bits and Bytes Online

CMP Publications, Inc. Electronic versions of several popular computer magazines from the Manhasset, N.Y.-based publisher CMP. Read selections from current issues of *NetGuide*, *Interactive Age*, *Windows* magazine, *Computer Retail Week*, *Home PC*, *InformationWeek*, and others. The second address offers a searchable database of all their computer titles. ✓**INTERNET** …→ *www* http://wais.wais.com:80/techweb/ …→ *www* http://techweb.cmp.com/techweb/programs/registered/search/cmp-wais-index.html

Cobb Group Newsletters for the new age. Review tables of contents, selected articles, and back issues of *Inside the Internet*, *Inside OS/2*, and *Inside NewWare*. ✓**IN-**

CYBERNOTES

"To avoid developing Carpal Tunnel Syndrome and Tendinitis:

1) Keep your wrists UP while typing. DO NOT PUT THEM ON THE TABLE! It might seem uncomfortable at first, but you'll get used to it.

2) If you feel your wrists need support in the up position, put a pillow under them.

3) Do not hit the Shift key with the same hand you hit the other key.

4) Try switching your mouse to the left side now and then if you are a righty, and vice versa for lefties.

5) Make sure that the key board is low enough. It should not be too high, so that you would have the temptation to rest your forearm on the table. If the keyboard is too high, put it in your lap.

6) If you experience any pain, ice it and go to the Med Center.

7) If it hurts too much to type, for God's sake, give your hands a rest."

—from **Typing Injury FAQ**

Computing Hubsites Booting Up

TERNET→*www* http://www.cobb.ziff.com/~cobb/

Computer Shopper OnLine You'll probably still have to carry the behemoth print version of *Computer Shopper* around (it's not all online!), but many product reviews, shopping guides ("Seeking the Perfect Hard Drive," May 1995), and magazine features are here. The Website includes hypertext versions of *Computer Shopper*'s top stories and columns as well as links to relevant downloads. It also features a huge national list of BBSs and computer user groups. CompuServe features a forum with message boards and libraries that offer similar content. ✓ **INTERNET**→*www* http://www.ziff.com/~cshopper/ ✓ **COMPUSERVE**→*go* compshopper

Computing Print & Broadcast This is the central location for commercial computer magazines, radio shows, and television shows on AOL. The majority of the publications have their own software libraries, computing tips, and message boards. You can search back issues, renew your subscription, or send a letter to the editor online. The "What's Hot" area offers live conferences and technology news. The news library is nicely designed. You can search for articles by keywords, read late-breaking stories, or download photographs. There's a "Computing Print & Broadcast Tour," that walks you through the collection of available publications, but you're better off browsing on your own. ✓ **AMERICA ONLINE**→*keyword* cp&b

Cowles/SIMBA Media Information Network Media movers and shakers, publishing moguls, and many with a watchful eye on the online world and information industry read the news covered by Cowles/SIMBA. Not only does this site offer daily news reports (neatly divided into folders such as magazines, cable, online services, etc.), it also offers a direct newsfeed, a message board for discussing the news of the day, and a library of Cowles/SIMBA newsletters. ✓ **AMERICA ONLINE**→*keyword* insidemedia

Harvard Computer Review OnLine A monthly review of software, hardware, and computer trends. ✓ **INTERNET**→*www* http://hcs.harvard.edu/~hcr/

I-WIRE (formerly COMPUTE magazine online) A magazine for Windows and MS-DOS users covering the information age, the Internet, interactivity, and individuality (note the reoccurrence of the initial letter "i"). The forum features the requisite chat rooms, message boards, and software libraries. The Internet resource center and the built-in computer lingo dictionary make *I-WIRE* one of the more informative electronic magazines about the Net. ✓ **AMERICA ONLINE** →*keyword* iwire

Industry Insider What's the latest scoop on Power Mac technology? Will Microsoft get sued again? How did Intel's stock react to adverse publicity? This newsletter covers the computer industry from the point of view of one expert analyst. The message boards are lightly visited, but you can post a question directly to the analyst if you wish. There are, however, probably livelier places than this in which to exercise your speculative powers, debate corporate maneuvering, or read up on the latest news. ✓ **AMERICA ONLINE**→*keyword* insider

Information Inc.'s Microindustry News Briefs General information on the microcomputer industry, with daily updates from industry authorities. Start your day off by reading about takeover rumors, company mergers, product upgrades, technical visionaries, and Internet developments. ✓ **EWORLD**→*go* cnb→MicroIndustry News Briefs

InformationWeek Information is sexy and so is this Website. This week's cover story is online, as are product reviews, industry overviews, reports from other Websites, gossip, advice on careers in the info business, and conference announcements. The site is updated daily with industry news. ✓ **INTERNET**→*www* http://techweb.cmp.com:2090/techweb/iw/current/default.html

It's Your Money A magazine dedicated to reviewing PC software. The current issue is online here and back issues may be downloaded from the archives. Reviews from current and back issues are added to a review library and filed alphabetically. In addition, the site features a library of shareware, freeware, and public domain software and a message board for discussing the reviews. ✓ **AMERICA ONLINE**→*keyword* iym

Kim Komando's Komputer Kling Computer advice and tips from a "celebrity" host. Kim Komando offers computer advice, news about software and hardware promotions, the National Computer Exchange listing of used computer systems and related equipment pricing, and demos of popular software programs. ✓ **AMERICA ONLINE**→*keyword* komando

MagNet An index with links to computer magazines around the world. Drop by if you're looking for online versions of popular ti-

Booting Up Computing Hubsites

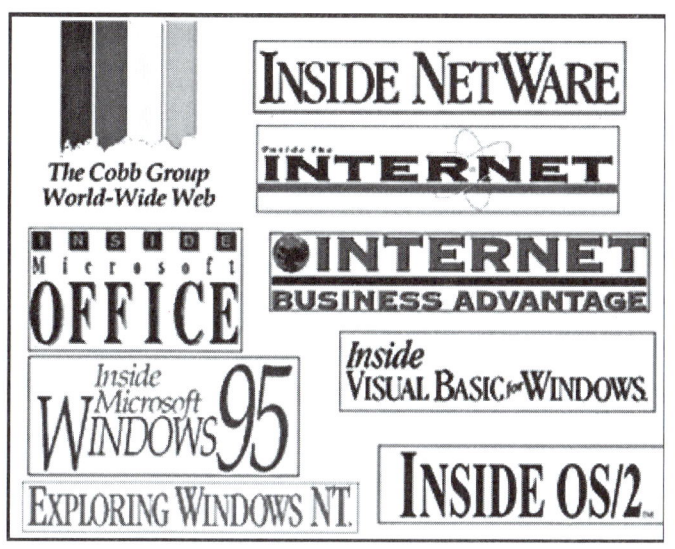

Cobb Group—from http://www.cobb.ziff.com/~cobb/

tles like *Amiga Power, Computer Shopper, Wired, Information Week, Internet Daily News, MacWeek,* and *NetGuide.* ✓ **INTERNET**→*www* http://www.cris.com/~milewski/magnet.html

Newsbytes A daily newswire providing computer and telecommunications reports to busy executives and Internet dilettantes who don't have time to read the newspaper. Get the computer news you need without the lingerie ads. ✓ **AMERICA ONLINE**→*keyword* newsbytes ✓ **COMPUSERVE**→*go* newsbytes ✓ **EWORLD**→*go* newsbytes

What's Going On Keep abreast of the latest developments in the technology and computing industry by dropping by this message board. One of the most popular topics of discussion is the Microsoft Corporation. "Are they unfair and illegal, or just competitive?" asks one eWorlder. It's not only hard to become successful and omnipotent, some people think it's *illegal.* ✓ **EWORLD**→*go* ccr→What's Going On

Emulators

comp.emulators.announce (ng) This moderated message board contains announcements and FAQs about emulators. Not for discussion. ✓ **USENET**

comp.emulators.misc (ng) Q: "When is an operating system not really what it appears to be?" A: "When it's being emulated!" If emulator technology interests you, there are like-minded individuals populating this newsgroup. Even the most obscure systems are being discussed. ✓ **USENET**

Vendors

Computer Corporations An index of hundreds of Net sites sponsored by high-tech companies. ✓ **INTERNET**→*www* http://www.yahoo.com/Business/Corporations/Computers/

Computer White Pages Scan an alphabetical index of links to thousands of computer companies on the Net. ✓ **INTERNET**→*www* http://www.yahoo.com/Business/Corporations/Computers/flat.html

Industry Connection Need support for Claris's FileMaker Pro? Curious about Hewlett-Packard peripherals? A portal to hundreds of forums sponsored by hardware and software companies, the Industry Connection appears to be dominated by Macintosh vendors but still includes a healthy representation of manufacturers and developers of DOS/Windows-based machines and code. Vendor forums usually provide a description of the company, press releases, product information, a customer-support message board, user discussion boards, and libraries of software, the Industry Connection lists companies both alphabetically and by category (product, specialty, etc.). You can also search for vendors using such keywords as "sound and multimedia." ✓ **AMERICA ONLINE**→*keyword* industryconnection

Macintosh Vendor Directory The star of the site is the alphabetical list of authorized Macintosh vendors and consultants, but that's just the beginning. Need repairs? Take a look at the list of local repair shops. Feeling lonely? A long list of Mac user groups is at your fingertips. Bored? Catch up on the latest issue of your favorite Macintosh magazine. More Mac information than you can shake a stick at. ✓ **INTERNET**→*www* http://rever.nmsu.edu/~elharo/faq/vendor.html

Redgate Online Redgate, an interactive marketing company, has put online an easy-to-use, searchable catalogue of close to 8,000 Macintosh products—both hardware and software. For each of the products, Redgate describes its main features and lists retail cost and company address information.

Computing Hubsites Booting Up

In addition, the site features separate directories for Macintosh multimedia and IBM multimedia products, showcases new computer products (often with demos), and archives several Redgate reports and columns on developments in the Macintosh and multimedia worlds. On eWorld, only Macintosh products are featured. ✓**AMERICA ONLINE**→*keyword* redgate ✓**EWORLD**→*go* redgate

Software Phone Directory A list of computer companies and their phone numbers, but what an impressive list it is! ✓**INTERNET** …→*www* http://mtmis1.mis.semi.harris.com/comp_ph1.html …→*www* http://www.mc.utexas.edu/phone-numbers.html

Support Directory Can't figure out how to use that new, expensive program? Not sure which modem to buy? Did you know that more than 800 vendors and organizations offer technical support for their products on CompuServe? You can search this database of on-line vendors via company name, company type, product name, product category, operating system, or language. When you've found the company, link to its forum for product information, updates, and demos, or technical support via the message boards. ✓**COMPUSERVE**→*go* support

tile.NET Vendors You could spend days looking through this enormous listing of computer companies, from the conglomerate to the mom-and-pop computer vendor. You can search by name, product, zip code, state, or area code. Just let your keyboard do the walking any time you need concise vendor information fast. ✓**INTERNET**→*www* http://www.tile.net/tile/vendors/index.html

Virtual Computer Library Vendors A collection of links to hundreds of computer vendors' Websites, from Dell Computer to WordPerfect. ✓**INTERNET**→*www* http://www.utexas.edu/computer/vcl/vendors/

User groups

Computer User Groups on the Web User groups sponsor classes, lectures, get-togethers where users can swap software (if they're so inclined), and job boards where experienced users can advertise their skills. This site brings together contact information about user groups for several computer platforms and products. If a user group has a site online, odds are that this site has a link to it. ✓**INTERNET**→*www* http://www.melbpc.org.au/others/otherugs.htm

User Group Connection A forum with listings of Mac user groups nationwide as well as resources (software, reviews, newsletters, etc.) uploaded by Macitosh user groups. ✓**EWORLD**→*go* ugc

User Groups Forum What do Berkeley, Boston, and the National Association of Quick Printers have in common? They all have active computer user groups in this forum. AOLers visiting the forum can download back issues of electronic newsletters from user groups throughout the country, confer with administrators of local and regional computer user groups, choose from the large collection of shareware, and find contact information about a user group near them. Most of the groups in this forum are Macintosh user groups (a.k.a. MUGs), like the Berkeley Macintosh User Group. ✓**AMERICA ONLINE**→*keyword* ugf

Health

Computer Ailments Does your computer cause you pain? Do you have musculoskeletal problems or blurred vision from sitting in front of your terminal for too long? Do your arms and fingers and wrists ache from that pesky carpal tunnel syndrome? Visit this site, where computer expert Larry Magid is on hand to tell computer users how to keep themselves in the best of health. Those who are paranoid about computer-generated radiation emissions in the workplace or curious about what their rights are when they develop musculoskeletal injuries at work can get answers here. ✓**PRODIGY**→*jump* computerailments

Typing Injury and Keyboard FAQ This is a vaguely fetishistic Website dedicated to alternative types of keyboards. Check out the rather draconian DataHand, a $2,000 device featuring two pods into which you insert your fingers for rapid-fire data entry—it will send your productivity through the roof. The gallery of ergonomic keyboards will bowl you over—some of them seem to involve hydraulics. ✓**INTERNET**→*www* http://www.cs.princeton.edu/grad/dwallach/tifaq/keyboards.html

> "The gallery of ergonomic keyboards will bowl you over—some of them seem to involve hydraulics."

22 Net Tech

Booting Up **Computing 101**

Computing 101

Maybe you have this new next-door neighbor who's kind of, well, weird. He walks with a stoop, eats only berries and bark, sleeps in a cave, and claims he's never seen a computer (well, you think that's what he's claiming, but you can't really make any sense out of the grunting and the pointing). Never fear. You can bridge the gap between you and your local Neanderthal in a jiffy. Just get Mr. Pronounced Eyebrow Ridge acquainted with the Net's introductory computer resources, from Prodigy's **Computer Basics** to **Computer Library Online**. Some of the gizmos in the **Obsolete Computer Museum** may look familiar to him from days of yore. And after a few hours in the **Free On-Line Dictionary of Computing**, he'll be grunting and pointing about hexidecimals, gigs, and VRAM.

Ladies with computer parts—http://ftp.arl.mil/ftp/historic-computers/jpeg/

On the Net

Entry level

Computer Basics This reference guide to computing provides introductory articles on computer topics ranging from operating systems to internal memory to spreadsheet software. Includes a searchable glossary of computer terminolgy. ✓**PRODIGY**→*jump* computer basics

Computer Database Plus Desperately seeking a full-text article on the original line of PowerBooks, or product reviews of Microsoft Word for Windows, version 3.1? Search this database and retrieve articles from more than 200 magazines, newspapers, and journals. ✓**COMPUSERVE**→*go* znt: compdb

Computer Library Online Part of the Ziff/Davis Publishing Group's extensive CompuServe database, this useful site is an information retrieval service designed to provide a complete reference and assistance resource for computer users. It includes three searchable databases: Computer Database Plus, for magazine and newspaper articles related to computers; Computer Buyer's Guide, for those in the market to buy computer hardware, software, or peripherals; and Support on Site, a searchable database for technical support. All these databases specialize in Macintosh- and IBM-compatible products, and the search engines are amazing. ✓**COMPUSERVE**→*go* complib

Indiana University UCS Knowledge Base What is a microchip? How does the Internet work? Will computers ever be able to think like humans? This archive contains more than 3,000 questions and answers on the computer world, ranging from the most basic to the most advanced. Spend some time here, and your PC will be basking in the glow of self-knowledge. ✓**INTERNET**→*www* http://sckb.ucssc.indiana.edu/kb/expsearch.html

The Microsoft Knowledge Base Don't risk being put on

Net Tech 23

Computing 101 Booting Up

hold as your Word document disintegrates. Why wait until the next morning to find out how to fix an Excel report that appears to be corrupted? Microsoft has put several thousand technical articles online with answers and troubleshooting advice for questions about all their products. (On CompuServe, the articles also sometimes refer to software updates and programming aids that can be downloaded from the Microsoft Software Library.) The articles—which CompuServe members can easily search by topic and date and AOL members can search by topic—are the same documents used by Microsoft technical support staff to answer calls. Chances are good that if you've owned a PC for more than a few weeks, you've made one of those calls. ✓**COMPUSERVE**→*go* mskb ✓**AMERICA ONLINE**→*keyword* knowledgebase

Support On Site Keep getting error messages in Microsoft Word 6.0 for Macintosh? Use the search engine to narrow your search down to one or two support documents so that you don't have to sift through a lot of useless information. The site contains support for Macintosh- and IBM-compatible hardware and software. ✓**COMPUSERVE**→*go* znt:onsite

Terminology

Computer Lingo As the online arm of *Compute!* magazine, AOL's I-Wire Forum has a number of resources for the home computer user, including a computer news service, GameWire, and this online glossary of computer terms. While it does cover many important concepts in modern computing—CPUs, sectors, floppies, etc.—this dictionary is not as comprehensive as the other computer references available online, and sometimes it indulges in relatively trivial entries. ✓**AMERICA ONLINE**→*keyword* compute→Computer Lingo

The Free On-Line Dictionary of Computing With more than 300 contributors and thousands of entries, this is the most comprehensive computer dictionary available online. Just remember—comprehensive doesn't always mean convenient, and you may find yourself baffled at the fact that the dictionary includes separate entries for the singular and plural versions of terms, as well as the occasional misspelling. Still, there's no better place to look when you need to find out the proper usage of "nagware" (shareware that reminds you incessantly to register), "My Favorite Toy Language" (the hobbyhorse of an overzealous programmer), or "zigamorph" (Hex FF when used as a delimiter or fence character). Of course, our interns couldn't resist looking for the "sex"-appeal in computers, and a search for the term actually produced the following result: "*Sex:* Software EXchange—a technique invented by the blue-green algae hundreds of millions of years ago to speed up their evolution." Those Brits. ✓**INTERNET**→*www* http://wombat.doc.ic.ac.uk/

Hacker's Dictionary Jargon File Located in Austria, this dictionary lets you speak like a hacker, which is sort of like speaking like a surfer, except that there's no surf. Example: "Hey, dude, be careful that your case and paste doesn't lead to software bloat." Another example: "That magic cookie is one hell of an opaque identifier...or should I say capability ticket." Study this dictionary for a few hours, and your mainframe will never be the same again. ✓**INTERNET**→*www* http://hyperg.tu-graz.ac.at:80/150B0AF9/Cjargon

Webster's Dictionary of Computer Terms Need to learn more about abbreviated addressing? Confused about the history of Arpanet? Just jump right into *Webster's Dictionary of Computer Terms*, available in an easy-to-search format on America Online. From *arrival rate* to *ascending order*, from *daisy-wheel printer* to *data diddling*, Webster's offers clear and concise definitions of thousands of computer words, phrases, and acronyms. And those AOLers on the leading edge of technolinguistics can supplement the dictionary with the special Add-a-Definition function. The area includes a message board for sharing definitions of new and familiar computer terms with America Online members and other newbies. ✓**AMERICA ONLINE**→*keyword* computerterms

History

Boatanchors List (ml) This mailing list is devoted to the discussion of archaic, pre-1970's vintage communications equipment including amateur radio receivers, transmitters, microphones, Morse code keys, military radio equipment, and other out-of-date accessories. People who are interested in and committed to the preservation, restoration, and operation of vintage radio equipment are encouraged to sign up and contribute their knowledge. Wanted ads and items for sale are also encouraged as postings. ✓**INTERNET**→*email* listproc@theporch.com ✎ *Type in message body:* subscribe boatanchors <your full name>

Computer History Association of California This Califor-

24 Net Tech

Booting Up Computing 101

nia-based organization is dedicated to keeping the past alive—and specifically, the digital past. The site contains information and some actual history, and the charter of the group ("The Computer History Association of California, or CHAC, is an educational organization which studies, preserves, protects and popularizes the history of electronic computing in the State of California") will bring a tear to the eye of anyone who has ever labored with vacuum tubes and punch cards. ✓**INTERNET**→*www* gopher://gopher.vortex.com/11/comp-hist

Historic Computer Images
U.S. Army technicians changing tubes on ENIACs. A happy Cray XMP48 flashing its pearly whites. This collection of computer images, some of which date back to the 1950's, is as exciting for the computing community as vintage *Sports Illustrated* swimsuit issues are for lovers of historic swimwear. Here's a vote for the ENIAC maniac. ✓**INTERNET**→*www* ftp://ftp.arl.mil/ftp/historic-computers/

History of Computing
You wouldn't ordinarily think of computing as a science with a history—things happen so fast that a new technology is likely to appear in the time it takes you to down your morning bowl of Cheerios. But this site proves that your thinking machine has a deep past, beginning with counting and shamanistic tradition; working through primitive calendars, abacuses, Pascal, Babbage, Hollerith, and Turing; and then moving on to ENIAC, EDVAC, and John von Neumann's famous Stored Program Concept. Microsoft bigshot Bill Gates even gets a chapter for his role in the birth of BASIC programming. And the beautiful color slides gussy up the sometimes dry material. ✓**INTERNET**→*www* http://calypso.cs.uregina.ca/Lecture/

History of Computing Issues
(ml) Predictably, this Smithsonian mailing list is for all those interested in the history of the computer. ✓**INTERNET**→*email* shothc-l@sivm.si.edu ✍ *Type in message body:* subscribe shothc-l <your full name>

History of Technology Discussion
(ml) Are we really surfing the Third Wave, as Alvin Toffler and Newt Gingrich have so boldly suggested? Here's another Smithsonian discussion group, this time specializing in the history of technology and its implications on man and his surroundings. ✓**INTERNET**→*email* htech-l@sivm.si.edu ✍ *Type in message body:* subscribe htech-l <your full name>

Obsolete Computer Museum
Although tech cynics might argue that the breakneck pace of PC development makes any computer an obsolete computer, this page focuses on the real relics—Spectra-Video, Altair (a religious experience), and the venerable Tandy Model 100. Links include pictures, brief descriptions, and assessments of the dinosaurs; most get high marks for dependability, even if their speed and memory pale next to today's base models. ✓**INTERNET**→*www* http://www.ncsc.dni.us/fun/user/tcc/cmuseum/cmuseum.htm

The Tech Museum of Innovation
Can't make it to San Jose, CA to visit this museum of technology? No sweat. When you finish downloading the digitized photographs of museum exhibits, you'll almost feel as if you're right there in Silicon Valley! Marvel at the Hubble space telescope, a robotics gallery, a photo of the Tech Museum itself, and much more. ✓**EWORLD**→*go* computercenter→Forums→The Tech Museum→An Online Tour→Exhibit Pictures

Unisys History Newsletter
This quarterly publication traces the history of Unisys, one of the largest computer companies in the Jurassic era. If articles with titles like "Univac in Pittsburgh, 1953–63" strike you as thrilling, then dig right in. And if they don't strike you as thrilling, maybe you need to think a little bit about your priorities. ✓**INTERNET**→*www* http://www.cc.gatech.edu/services/unisys-folklore/

Industry profiles

Computer Industry Almanac Online
You just got a job interview at a hot Silicon Valley software company—how much is it worth? Who are the top executives and how much do they make? What are some of the company's job descriptions? How much money can you expect to bring home? What are the opportunities for advancement? Consult this database to find out. And that's not all. Read about events in the computer industry dating back to 3000 B.C. Browse a calendar of upcoming trade shows and conferences in the computer industry. Search a database of computer associations, organizations, consortiums, and national user groups. Drop into the Publications Database for an archive of articles from computer- and technology-oriented magazines, newspapers, periodicals, and newsletters. This is one of the best resources around for both the job hunter and the exec who needs to keep abreast of the computer industry; as long as it stays close at hand, you can be a true computer expert. ✓**EWORLD**→*go* cia

Hardware & Peripherals **Booting Up**

Hardware & peripherals

Software may be the intellectual part of computing, but hardware gives physical form

to machines, and all the programs in the world would be only so much binary babble without CPUs, monitors, printers, disk drives, modems, and scanners. On the Net, hardware novices and vets alike can satisfy their curiosity with dozens of excellent resources. Fight the hardware wars with Prodigy's three large areas—**Hardware: Peripherals, Hardware Support BB,** and **Hardware: Systems.** Learn about the technology of tomorrow with the **CD-ROM FAQ.** And pick up the tricks of the trade (along with a few insider secrets) by perusing the always fascinating **Snake Oil, Miracle Cures, and Monitors.**

On the Net
Across the board

Drive and Controller Guide A directory of hard drives, floppy drives, optical drives, drive controllers, and host adapters. ✓**INTERNET**→*www* ftp://nic.funet.fi/pub/doc/HW/harddisks/theref43.tar.gz

Hardware: Peripherals Problems with the printer? Need advice on choosing a modem? Thinking about adding a CD-ROM drive?

Aeon Sales Department—http://www.aeon.com/aeon.html

Curious about the pros and cons of buying recycled toner cartridges? Or, like Susan, maybe your boss has asked you to buy an external tape drive to back up files at the office and you haven't a clue what brand to get. This board is an informal discussion area where participants regularly ask each other for advice. ✓**PRODIGY**→*jump* computerbb→Choose a Topic→Hardware: Peripherals

Hardware Support BB Bill wants to know "who built the tube and guts" of his GVC 15" Digital monitor. Michael, the MaxTech representative, posted the telephone number of the sales office and suggested Bill give them a call. Acer America, Dell Computer, Maxtech/GVC, Leading Edge, Pionex, Quantex Microsystems, Reveal, and VTech all have their own topics on this message board. Support is given both by company representatives and from other users. ✓**PRODIGY**→*jump* hardwaresupportbb

Hardware: Systems John hates his new Compaq and wants to know if others have problems with theirs. (Yup!) Randy wants to know if there are any reasons why he shouldn't run his 60 MHz Pentium at 66 MHz. And Stuart is ready to buy hardware for his Pentium 120 and has narrowed it down to the Micron or the more expensive Dell. He's posted the advantages of each and wonders what he should do. Post your hardware dilemma and wait for the feedback. ✓**PRODIGY**→*jump* computerbb→Choose a Topic→Hardware: Systems

Snake Oil, Miracle Cures, and Monitors Ever wonder why your new 17" monitor does not actually measure 17" diagonally on the screen? Most consumers don't realize that monitors are not measured in the same way as televisions. This document explains how they're measured and suggests questions to ask when purchasing a new one. The site also features a

Booting Up Hardware & Peripherals

table that translates the display sizes for various resolutions of display as well as a monitor specifications table. ✓**INTERNET**→*www* http://hawks.ha.md.us/hardware/monitors.html

Microchips

Intel Corporation A series of forums offering technical support and information for many Intel products. The libraries in the Processors and About Intel Forum contain product information, technology briefs, data sheets, and technical support documents on Intel's family of CPUs—including the P6, Pentium, OverDrive processors, and Math Coprocessors. The message boards are filled with technical support questions and answers. The Intel Communications and Networking Forum provides information on the company's communications and networking products, including technical documents, troubleshooting tips, and installation information written by support engineers. The Intel Communications and Networking Forum libraries contain the latest drivers, software revisions, test drive kits, product demos, and technology briefs. ✓**COMPUSERVE**→*go* intel

Memory products

Aeon Technology On-Line A Website created by Aeon Technology to offer product support and an online catalogue of the company's optical storage products and memory for Macintosh and IBM-compatibles. Products can be delivered overnight upon confirmation of your order. Includes a toll-free number for technical support and a feedback site where you can give your two cents directly to the company. ✓**INTERNET**→*www* http://www.aeon.com/aeon.html

Impediment, Inc. This company specializes in memory and peripherals for workstation and high-end computer servers. The site includes a product list and a phone number for ordering, and also contains product sheets with links to other company sites. So if you're having trouble with an IBM product, jump to the IBM page and look for help there. ✓**INTERNET**→*www* http://www.impediment.com/

Scanners

Canon Support Forum A forum operated and maintained by the Canon Communications Systems Product Support Staff (aren't you glad you don't answer the phones there?) for owners and operators of Canon products. Post tech support questions on the message boards or browse the libraries for documented support for your Canon laster printer, bubble jet printer, image scanner, color copier, fax system, personal computer, or 35mm camera. ✓**COMPUSERVE**→*go* canon

SCSI

comp.periphs.scsi (ng) A newsgroup revolving around SCSI peripherals, like disk drives and scanners and external CD-ROM players. One denizen of this group was frustrated with his new Quantum Lightning disk drive, which was "fast and cheap, but very loud, like a jackhammer vibrating throughout the room." Someone named Chris came to his rescue in the next thread, recommending the Seagate Hawk2, which he found to be "indeed very quiet." Besides advice, the group includes a lot of product releases. ✓**USENET**

SCSI FAQ Excuse me, but do you know what a SCSI port is for? Known in some circles as a Small Computer Systems Interface and in others as a plain old "scuzzi," it's a standard port for connecting peripherals to your computer. In other words, it's that thing on the back of your computer with a lot of little holes that your SyQuest or CD-ROM drive plugs into. If you have any more questions about the exciting world of SCSI, please refer to this enlightening two-part FAQ. ✓**INTERNET**→*www* http://www.cis.ohio-state.edu/hypertext/faq/usenet/scsi-faq/top.html

Video

comp.sys.ibm.pc.hardware.video (ng) It's Christmas morning and your kids can't wait to play the new *Lion King* CD-ROM Santa left under the tree. Suddenly your video card isn't working. Your kids are in tears, Disney's help lines are closed, and there's no use taking your frustration out on Santa ("How do you like that steel-tipped boot, fat boy?"). What to do? Probably the quickest and most expert solutions will come from this discussion group. ✓**USENET**

Mediatrix A home page for end users of PC sound technology, maintained by a leading manufacturer of high-end PC sound boards. ✓**INTERNET**→*www* http://www.fmmo.ca/mediatrix

Printers

Colorocs View .GIFs and specifications (and prices, of course) for Colorocs copiers and printers. ✓**INTERNET**→*www* http://www.nav.com/colorocs/colorocs.html

comp.periphs.printers (ng) Somebody named Tom is all flustered because the ink cartridge for his HP FaxJet 100 keeps clogging

Net Tech 27

Hardware & Peripherals Booting Up

up. So he posts a query to this newsgroup specializing in printers and fax machines and gets two responses. 1) "Is it one of the 'longer life' cartridges? When we switched to those we found that at least every second one had clogging problems. We just took it back to the store and asked for a replacement." 2) "Did you remember to remove the white and green piece of tape that is along the side and bottom? Failure to do so will shorten the life of the cartridge." People who keep abreast of the printer scene hang out here, so it's a good place to read product updates and swap industry news. ✓**USENET**

High Performance Cartridges This site is a must, if only for the lovely tin of Spam that greets you when you arrive! Otherwise, this is a home page for a company that refurbishes laser toner cartridges and then resells them to clients. Read about how the company goes about recycling used cartridges. ✓**INTERNET**→*www* http://www.netpoint.net/hpcart/hpcart.html

Imagen (ml) Discussion forum for all aspects of Imagen laser printers, including software compatibility, hardware interfacing, LAN attachment capabilities, imPRESS programming, and print spooling. ✓**INTERNET**→*email* list serv@bolis.sf.bay.org ✍ *Type in message body:* subscribe imagen-l <your full name>

Mac Printers & PostScript Having PostScript printing problems on the Macintosh? Need advice on finding printing software and hardware? This active discussion folder includes reviews of PostScript utilities in the Printing Utilities section, guidance for newbies and panicked PostScripters in the Help/Beginner's Corner, and printer reviews from fellow Macintosh users. ✓**AMERICA ONLINE**→*keyword* mdp→Message Boards→Let's Discuss→Printers & PostScript

Printer Works A Website set up by a Hayward, CA-based company specializing in printer sales and repairs. It is also a parts dealer. The company specializes in the repair of NeXT, HP, and Apple laser printers. It also sells its own line of printers. ✓**INTERNET**→*www* http://www.stepwise.com/Vendors/ThePrinterWorks.htmld/

QMS, Inc. QMS, Inc. develops and markets state-of-the-art printing systems and desktop office systems. View images of QMS products, find out where QMS offices are in the U.S. and abroad, get the latest product information and technical support numbers, browse a calendar of QMS trade show appearances, download printer drivers and utilities from the linked FTP site, or check the weather at QMS's home offices or anywhere else in the continental United States. ✓**INTERNET** …→*www* http://www.qms.com/ …→*www* ftp://gatekeeper.qms.com/pub/cts/

Modems

comp.dcom.modems (ng) Modems can be pesky and uncooperative, and so it's nice to have a place where you can vent your frustrations over the little hissing box that helps you get online. Modem users post queries and recommendations on a wide variety of modem-related topics. For instance, did you know that the high voltage of phone lines in Singapore allegedly causes U.S. modems to burn out when they are used over there? ✓**USENET**

comp.sys.ibm.pc.hardware.comm (ng) A newsgroup for PC users who have questions about PC hardware. Modem questions seem to dominate this group, and there are lots of classified ads, including one asking for 80 free modems for churches in Moscow. Another reader is getting strange "crunching noises" from his modem when it's not in operation. If you know what on earth this could mean, he's desperately waiting for your reply. ✓**USENET**

Gateway 2000 Forum A support and discussion forum for Gateway 2000 and its services and products. Technical support sysops and customer representatives monitor the message boards for queries from Gateway users pertaining to the company's line of CD-ROM players, video drivers, hard drives, motherboards, sound cards, and other products. The library has help files for most Gateway products. ✓**COMPUSERVE**→*go* gateway

Global Village Company news and product information are the main focuses of this modem manufacturer's online site, but you can also use the message boards to get technical support from Global Village for your Teleport Silver, Gold, Bronze, or Mercury modem. The software library has product upgrades and text help files to make your online dial-ups more smooth. ✓**AMERICA ONLINE**→*keyword* global

Hayes Online Forum A company-sponsored forum providing technical support and information pertaining to Hayes peripherals, particularly modems and fax products. Visit the News Bulletins section in the forum's library to browse Hayes product and business information or check out the specialized libraries for utilities, upgrades, and help files for your

Booting Up Hardware & Peripherals

modem. Post queries and comments to the company's technical support staff on the message board, or enter the conference room for real-time chat. ✓**COMPUSERVE**→*go* hayes

Line-Link Mailing List (ml) Discussion devoted to the Line-Link 14.4 Modem. ✓**INTERNET**→ *email* listserver@obelisk.pillar.com ✎ *Type in message body:* join

Modem Basics and Setup A handy little primer for people who are just baffled by modems. If you want basic information about everything from modem plugs to DTE rates and initialization strings, this document provides the info in language that you don't have to be a computer geek to understand. ✓**INTERNET**→*www* http://ux1.cso.uiuc.edu/~zinzow/modem.html

Modem FAQs "What features will be in the next generation of ZyXEL modems?" "What exactly is the hardware modification needed for CID/CND and EDR?" If you own a Digicom, NetComm, Practical Peripherals, or ZyXEL modem and you've lost your instruction manual, you can download Usenet FAQs that may answer your questions better than the manual does. ✓**INTERNET**→ *www* http://www.cis.ohio-state.edu/hypertext/faq/usenet/modems/top.html

Modem Tutorial Part one of a three-part report entitled "The Joy of Telecomputing," this article features detailed information for anyone interested in finding out how a modem functions. The writer of this document assumes you already know the basics about going online, so if you're unfamiliar with that process try another resource. But if you're interested in modulation, error control, and data compression protocols, this is a good site to visit. Print out a copy of this informative document and keep it next to your computer and modem for easy reference. ✓**INTERNET**→*www* http://www.racal.com/dcom/modem.tutorial.html

Modem Vendor Forum You can get technical support here if you own a modem fabricated by one of the following companies: Best Data, Boca Research, The Complete PC, Computer Peripherals, Global Village Communications, Megahertz, Multi-Tech Systems, Prometheus, U.S. Robotics, Telebit, Zoom, and ZyXEL. Use the conference room to chat in real-time with a sysop or post a query to the appropriate message board. The libraries contain documented help files as well as utilities programs that work with these modems. ✓**COMPUSERVE**→*go* modemvendor

Practical Peripherals Forum Technical support forums for users and operators of Practical Peripherals products, including low- and high-speed modems, pocket modems, and fax modems. If you're having dial-up problems with your PPI modem and you can still get online, this is a great place to go for real-time help. (On CompuServe just enter the conference room and post your query during business hours. One of the support staff will help you.) You can also post questions and comments on the categorized message boards or visit the Learning Center in the library section for documented help files for PPI products that you can download. AOL's forum is similar. ✓**COMPUSERVE**→*go* ppiforum ✓**AMERICA ONLINE**→*keyword* ppi

RoboWeb The home page for U.S. Robotics carries contact information, product and service information, and company news. ✓**INTERNET** …→*www* http://www.usr.com/ …→*www* ftp://ftp.usr.com/

Rockwell Telecommunications Press releases, modem specifications listings, and online reference manuals for Rockwell modems and related products. ✓**INTERNET**→*www* http://www.tokyo.rockwell.com/

The Village Global Village Communications' Website features a

RoboWeb—from http:// http://www.usr.com/

Hardware & Peripherals **Booting Up**

product catalog, a customer support area (dozens of fact sheets), and its own Internet tour. ✓**INTERNET**→*www* http://www.globalcenter.net/

WH Networks Communications Archive WH Networks Communications specializes in communication products and services. Access its product and price list or product FAQs (e.g., the Digicom modem FAQ). ✓**INTERNET**→*www* http://www.whnet.com/wolfgang/

ZyXEL Home Page This splashy site carries modem brochures, press kits, articles about ZyXel products, and a technical support fact sheet. ✓**INTERNET**→*www* http://www.zyxel.com/

Monitors

Radius Website for this popular manufacturer of monitors. The FTP archive contains documentation and software for Radius products and sales, service, and support contacts. ✓**INTERNET** ...→*www* http://research.radius.com/ ...→*www* ftp://ftp.radius.com/

CD-ROMs

Amiga CD-ROM (ml) Loyal Amigans hellbent on bringing multimedia CD-ROM drives and disks to their desktops come here to discuss logistics. ✓**INTERNET**→*email* cdrom-list-request@ben.com ✍ *Write a request*

CD-I FAQ Okay, so Philips presented the world with another bomb in CD-I, but they're still developing titles. And maybe you bought a player and kind of like it. In fact, you have some good ideas for titles. Where do you sell your CD-I ideas? What system do you need for CD-I authoring? Where do you buy it? Here's some basic info. ✓**INTERNET**→*www* ftp://ftp.cdrom.com/pub/cdrom/cdi/cdifaq.txt

CD-ROM FAQ Looking for a good CD-ROM drive and recommendations for where to buy it? Want to know how to transfer your 10,000-page document onto a CD-ROM? How do you mount an ISO-9660 disc on Sun? Okay, so maybe you just came to find out what CD-ROM stands for ("Compact Disks Read Only Memory"). Whatever the question, from Photo CDs to CD-ROM jukeboxes, you'll probably find the answers here. ✓**INTERNET**→*www* http://www.cis.ohio-state.edu/hypertext/faq/usenet/cdrom-faq/faq.html

CD-ROM Forum CD-ROM central on CompuServe. Although the massive conglomeration of messages and libraries is hard to navigate, the journey is well worth it. Access vendor catalogues or, if you're a retailer yourself, post your own. Discuss the double spin, triple spin, quartic spin till your head spins, and share hints about anything ROM, including installing Club Dead or getting past Day One once you've got it running. And of course, you can get the latest gossip from the interactivity gathering MILIA, or set up

> "Discuss the double spin, triple spin, quartic spin till your head spins, and share anything ROM."

appointments for E3. **COMPUSERVE**→*go* cdrom

CD-ROM Vendor Forums You've got your head up that CD-ROM drive all the time, anyway, so why not give your precious time and hardware to a greater purpose—become a beta tester. You'll get to try out nearly finished CD-ROM titles on your brand-new drive, so that you'll never know if the machine or the title is flawed—but so what: great stuff to talk about into the wee hours. In exchange, you get the beta copy plus a finished copy of the title. Just one of the opportunities you'll find in the CD-ROM vendor forum, a place where creators of CD-ROMs dump demo copies and press releases. If you're really getting ROMantic, and you're considering producing your own disks, talk to the guys who've "been there" and "done that" here—they'll teach you a lesson or two. ✓**COMPUSERVE**→*go* cdven *and* cdvenb

CDPUB (ml) Regardless of your platform persuasion, this discussion covers CD-ROM publishing, desktop CD-ROM recorders, and publishing systems. ✓**INTERNET**→*email* mailserver@knex.mind.org ✍ *Type in message body:* subscribe cdpub <your full name>

comp.publish.cdrom.hardware (ng) Looking for a handheld scanner to interface directly with your parallel port? How about just an adapter to fit your new 4x CD-ROM drive's line-out plugs into your laptop. Whether you're a developer or a consumer, this discussion group provides a forum for questions and answers about the constantly upgradable world of multimedia hardware. ✓**USENET**

30 Net Tech

Booting Up Hardware & Peripherals

comp.sys.ibm.pc.hardware.cd-rom (ng) If choosing your first CD-ROM drive makes you dizzy, come here for advice. If the funny noise your first CD-ROM is making drives you crazy, come here for solace. In fact, this discussion group is populated by many people being driven crazy by the little kinks of their drives. "I have tried EVERYTHING to get this thing going and I'm lost!" ✓**USENET** *FAQ*: http://www.cis.ohio-state.edu/hypertext/faq/bngusenet/comp/sys/ibm/pc/hardware/cd-rom/top.html

Compact Disk Formats What's the difference between CD-ROM, CD-I and Photo CD? They've come a long way since the initial CD revolution more than ten years ago. But compact disks still look the same. And here's where you can find out which play on your computer and which on your television set, and which allow you to record and which don't. You'll also find out that although Philips is publicly pushing CD-I, they seem very involved with the new Video CD format. ✓**INTERNET**→*www* http://cuiwww.unige.ch/OSG/MultimediaInfo/Info/cd.html

Kodak CD Forum "When I open up a PhotoCD image in Photoshop, it always seems to come in at a resolution of 72 dpi no matter which size I choose," writes Jim. The Kodak support staff answers promptly to this and all other technical questions related to the PhotoCD. ✓**COMPUSERVE**→*go* kodak

PHOTO-CD (ml) Official Kodak-sponsored mailing list provides discussion about Photo-CD products and technology (especially Kodak). ✓**INTERNET**→*email* listserv@info.kodak.com ✍ *Type in message body:* subscribe photo-cd <your full name>

Hewlett-Packard

Hewlett-Packard Peripherals Directory Find out about new HP products, keep abreast of related industry news, and review images and product summaries of HP printers, plotters, scanners, faxes, and multi-function machines. Go to the Helping You Choose section to get help on finding the HP printer that best suits your needs. A linked FTP site provides product drivers, utilities, and support information. ✓**INTERNET** …→*www* http://www.dmo.hp.com/peripherals/main.html …→*www* ftp://ftp-boi.external.hp.com/pub/

HP Peripherals Forum Is your Hewlett-Packard DeskJet printer shooting ink onto the walls of your home or office? Use the message board to elicit advice from other users or the technical support staff at Hewlett-Packard. The libraries carry press releases and upgrade information from Hewlett-Packard, as well as documentation on how to clean your HP printer or install a Spanish driver for your new LaserJet color printer. ✓**COMPUSERVE**→*go* hp

Other

IBM ImagePlus Forum An IBM-sponsored forum for owners and users of ImagePlus image processing systems. The forum's message board and library contain documentation from IBM on ImagePlus products and upgrades. Users and prospective buyers can receive technical support directly from Big Blue personnel by posting a query on the message board. ✓**COMPUSERVE**→*go* imagep

Pen Technology Forum Do you get all excited when the Federal Express man comes—so you can marvel at his fancy pen-driven electronic clipboard? If so, you'll love this forum for discussion and files relating to pen systems and portable computing. Although pen-based computing has not been the success that the computer industry was hoping for (remember Apple's original Newton?) there is still a dedicated legion of pentech devotees who can't wait for the day they'll be able to send paperless faxes from a remote location. Remember, the pen *is* mightier than the sword. Join the dream. ✓**COMPUSERVE**→*go* penforum

The Xerox Link Company-sponsored product and support forums for users of Xerox products, including copy machines, software, and other peripherals. The forums provide customers with online product support and technical information, and you can still get online help from a Xerox sysop by posting a message in one of the three specific Xerox product forums: Office Solutions, Production Printing, and Software. ✓**COMPUSERVE**→*go* xerox

> "Do you get all excited when the Federal Express man comes—so you can marvel at his fancy pen-driven electronic clipboard?"

Net Tech 31

Software & CD-ROMs Booting Up

Software & CD-ROMs

No one can function on an empty stomach, and your computer is no different. It needs nourishment, and electronic nourishment comes in the form of software. While naysayers may tell you there's no such thing as a free lunch, shareware buffs know better. Drop in at the **Funet Software Archives**, the **Garbo FTP Archive**, the **UMich Software Archive**, and the **Wuarchive Software Archive** for all the programs your computer can swallow. And if you have been feeding the machine a steady diet of CD-ROMs, make sure that the diet makes the grade with **CD-ROM Reviews**.

On the Net

Across the board

comp.sources* (ng) The source for source code on the Net. There are newsgroups dedicated to most of the big platforms. To stay on top of new shareware programs, follow the group covering the system (e.g., comp.sources.mac) or type of program (e.g., comp.sources.games) you're interested in. The groups are also good places to look for help finding a shareware program: post your requirements and someone will almost certainly suggest a program that meets them, and the place where you'll find it. ✓**USENET**

The Complete FTP Servers List

CD-ROM Today—http://www.future net.co.uk/computing/cdromtoday.html

A hypertext list of hundreds of FTP sites around the world, many of which carry useful software. ✓**INTERNET**→*www* http://www.cs.purdue.edu/homes/veygmamk/ftp-list.html

FTP Software and Support The WordPerfect Corporation and Microsoft have software archives on the Net, as do the University of Michigan and MIT. From one simple menu, this site connects you to more than a hundred archives with DOS, Windows, X-Windows, Apple, OS/2, and Unix software. Includes links to all your favorite Web programs! ✓**INTERNET**→*www* http://mtmis1.mis.semi.harris.com/ftp.html

Funet Software Archives Amid subdirectories for sound clips and graphics programs, there are large archives of software for OS/2, Mac, Windows NT, Unix, and Amiga. ✓**INTERNET**→*www* ftp://ftp.funet.fi/pub/

Garbo FTP Archive Named after the reclusive screen legend from Sweden, this Finnish site carries a huge selection of shareware and public-domain programs for DOS, Windows, Macintosh, Unix, and Linux. And if you don't care about shareware, just come here for that dramatic black-and-white picture of Greta. ✓**INTERNET** …→*www* http://garbo.uwasa.fi/ …→*www* ftp://garbo.uwasa.fi

The Oak Software Repository A large repository of—primarily—DOS shareware. The site both mirrors other big software sites (SimTel, for instance) and carries its own collection. PC owners may have to dig a bit but are almost certain to find what they need. ✓**INTERNET** …→*www* http://www.acs.oakland.edu/oak.html…→*www* ftp://oak.oakland.edu/…→*www* gopher://oak.oakland.edu/

Public Brand Software Applications Forum If you're looking for a specific piece of shareware or freeware but you can't find it anywhere, this forum—which specializes in public-domain software for DOS, Windows, and OS/2-based systems—may be helpful. Use the Ask the Sysops message board-questions about your program, and sooner or later the forum staff will reply. In the meantime, just dig in. The library includes word processors, spreadsheets, database programs, desktop accessories, security software, browsers, and networking tools. ✓**COMPUSERVE**→*go* pbsapps

Shareware Discuss If you

32 Net Tech

Booting Up Software & CD-ROMs

thrive on mining the Net for shareware, you're not alone. Here's a place where shareware buffs and shareware authors trade Net site addresses, get help with compression formats ("How do I unzip the finance program I just downloaded?"), and seek recommendations for programs. Here is a typical message: "I want to learn to write and design a Web page. Anyone know of good software for this?" ✓**PRODIGY**→*jump* computerbb→Choose a Topic→Shareware Discuss

Software BBS software packages and Blake Stone codes, catering software and communications programs, file compression utilities and flight simulators, and label makers and mapping software are all up for discussion in this topic. ✓**PRODIGY**→*jump* computerbb→Choose a Topic→Software

Software Charts Monthly updated lists of the top ten best-selling computer programs in the following categories: Home, Games, Education, Business, Utilities, and the Macintosh. ✓**PRODIGY**→*jump* software charts

Software Guide Detailed descriptions and reviews of thousands of pieces of software. The guide can be searched by title, criteria, or date. ✓**PRODIGY**→*jump* softwareguide

Software Support BB Prodigy's 911 service for people with unsolvable software problems. Often, the support comes from other Prodigy members or from consultants looking to drum up business. Don't look here for the makers of your troublesome code. Nevertheless, the advice appears to be quite valuable—why else would the screams for help continue all through the night? The board is divided into such categories as Business Software and Graphics Programs. ✓**PRODIGY**→*jump* softwaresupportbb

U.K. Shareware Forum A forum catering to both shareware programmers and PC computer users. Interested in learning the ropes of shareware programming? Download the "Shareware Author's Resource Guide (or, Getting Started in Shareware)" from the First Stop library. Otherwise, head straight for the hundreds of shareware programs. Some of the files archived here are geared to the European computing community (get your British football pool coupon-checking program here!), others cater to Netizens from across the global village—a construction-cost estimating and bidding system designed for home improvement and remodeling, a genealogy program that helps you organize the roots of your family tree. You can get technical support for all the programs archived here in the forum message boards. ✓**COMPUSERVE**→*go* ukshare

UMich Software Archive One of the largest repositories of software online, the site has published its own commercial CD-ROM and is mirrored in dozens of sites around the world. Everything's here: games for the Atari, word processors for the PC, databases for the Mac, financial planners for the Amiga, and compilers for Unix, just to hint at some of the offerings. Each operating system has its own directory, which is then broken down into categories such as telecommunications, utilities, games, what have you. ✓**INTERNET**→*www* ftp://archive.umich.edu/

UUNet Archive Large archives of software for more than a dozen operating systems—from Amiga to Windows. ✓**INTERNET**→*www* ftp://ftp.uu.net/systems/

Virtual Shareware Library Carrying more than 60,000 shareware and freeware programs, this mammoth software repository features an excellent search engine that allows you to search both file names and file descriptions in up to six archives at a time. You can also narrow your search to, for instance, programs created after a certain date. The site combines mirrors of the biggest software archives on the Net (from the huge DOS archive, SimTel, to the OS/2 Archive to the giant Info-Mac archive) under one roof. ✓**INTERNET** ...→*www* http://www.fagg.uni-lj.si/SHASE/ ...→*www* http://www.telstra.com.au/cgi-bin/shase

Wuarchive Software Archive Pick a system, any system. This mammoth archive has directories for dozens of operating systems like the Amiga, the PC, the Mac, and OS/2. While the site houses several thousand of its own programs, it also mirrors many of the biggest software archives on the Net. In the Mac directory, for instance, you have the option of accessing the vast resources of the Info-Mac and UMich archives as well as an original Macintosh archive with applications ranging from PostScript programs to virus detectors to education programs. ✓**INTERNET**→*www* ftp://wuarchive.wustl.edu/systems

CD-ROM reviews

Axcess Magazine CD-Rom Reviews Before you shell out fifty bucks for that crappy David Bowie CD-ROM, check out what the techie hipsters at *Axcess* have to say. Besides reviews of the latest

Software & CD-ROMs Booting Up

SNES or Game Boy release, you'll find a section rating gameplay and free multimedia offerings. ✓**INTERNET**→*www* http://www.internex.net:80/axcess/

CD-ROM Reviews Do you want a second opinion before you spend too much money on the CD-ROM version of your favorite dictionary? Here you'll find comprehensive reviews of mostly educational and reference CD-ROMs. ✓**INTERNET**→*www* http://da.awa.com:80/nct/cds/cdlead.html

CD-ROM Today Britain's best-selling CD-ROM magazine. The Website features mostly reviews and an archive of articles from back issues of *CD-ROM Today*. ✓**INTERNET**→*www* http://www.futurenet.co.uk/computing/cdromtoday.html

comp.publish.cdrom.software (ng) If you're looking for a guy who's "willing to do crazy things on a CD-ROM, wear crazy costumes, and even cross-dress," you'll find that here, but mostly you'll find information on multimedia software—from authoring tools to finished titles to information about CD-ROM distributors. Established authors come here to look for prospective agents. ✓**USENET**

Hyper Magazine An Australian online magazine featuring reviews of CD-ROM games. ✓**INTERNET**→*www* http://www.next.com.au:80/games/hyper/

Monster Internet Shareware Sites

Amiga

Aminet Amiga Archive ✓**INTERNET** …→*www* ftp://ftp.luth.se/pub/aminet/ …→*www* ftp://wuarchive.wustl.edu/pub/aminet/ …→*www* http://wuarchive.wustl.edu/pub/aminet/info/www/home.html …→*www* http://src.doc.ic.ac.uk/public/aminet/info/www/home-src.doc.html

Funet Amiga Archive ✓**INTERNET**→*www* ftp://www.funet.fi/pub/amiga/ **Info:** ✓**INTERNET**→*www* http://www.funet.fi:80/pub/amiga/

Apple II

Major Apple 2 Archives ✓**INTERNET** …→*www* file://grind.isca.uiowa.edu/apple2 …→*www* ftp://wuarchive.wustl.edu/systems/apple2/ …→*www* ftp://ftp.cco.caltech.edu/pub/apple2/ …→*www* ftp://apple2.archive.umich.edu/archive/apple2

Linux

Linux Software Archive ✓**INTERNET** …→*www* ftp://sunsite.unc.edu/pub/Linux …→*www* ftp://mrcnext.cso.uiuc.edu/pub/linux

Macintosh

Info-Mac Archive ✓**INTERNET** …→*www* http://cag-www.lcs.mit.edu/HyperArchive.html …→*www* gopher://gopher.archive.merit.edu:7055/11/mac …→*www* ftp://sumex-aim.stanford.edu/info-mac/ …→*www* ftp://mirror.apple.com/mirrors/InfoMac.Archive/

University of Michigan Macintosh Archive ✓**INTERNET** …→*www* http://www.umich.edu/~archive/mac …→*www* ftp://mirror.apple.com/mirrors/mac.archive.umich.edu …→*www* ftp://wuarchive.wustl.edu:systems/mac/umich.edu …→*www* ftp://grind.isca.uiowa.edu/mac/umich

OS/2

Hobbes OS/2 Software ✓**INTERNET** …→*www* ftp://hobbes.nmsu.edu/os2/ …→*www* ftp://ftp-os2.cdrom.com/pub/os2/ …→*www* ftp://software.watson.ibm.com/pub/os2/

PC

CICA Windows Shareware Archive ✓**INTERNET** …→*www* http://alpha.acast.nova.edu/software/windows.html …→*www* ftp://ftp.cica.indiana.edu/pub/pc/win3 …→*www* ftp://ftp.marcam.com/win3/ …→*www* ftp://ftp.cdrom.com/pub/cica …→*www* ftp://ftp.cc.monash.edu.au/pub/win3

Garbo PC Archive ✓**INTERNET** …→*www* ftp://garbo.uwasa.fi/pc/ …→*www* ftp://archie.au/micros/pc/garbo

SimTel MS-DOS Archive ✓**INTERNET** …→*www* http://www.acs.oakland.edu/oak/SimTel/SimTel-msdos.html …→*www* ftp://oak.oakland.edu/SimTel/msdos …→*www* ftp://wuarchive.wustl.edu/systems/ibmpc/simtel/msdos …→*www* ftp:// ftp.uoknor.edu/mirrors/SimTel/msdos …→*www* ftp://ftp.uni-paderborn.de/SimTel/msdos

Windows Shareware Archive ✓**INTERNET**→*www* http://coyote.csusm.edu/cwis/winworld/winworld.html

Booting Up Computer Bookstores

Computer bookstores

Remember when those technology forecasters said that the computer would destroy publishing? Texts would become electric, they said. Books would vanish. The forests of the world would be saved from clearcutting and pulping. As usual, the forecasters were wrong. The computer revolution has tindered a proliferation of new books devoted to technical support and technological issues. Teach yourself everything you always wanted to know about computers but were afraid to ask with the **misc.books.technical FAQ**. Order computer texts from **Compubooks**, **Digital Press**, and **Knowledge in Motion**. And search the vast riches of the Internet with **Macmillan USA Information SuperLibrary**'s Internet Yellow Pages or **Michael Wolff & Company**'s *Net Books* database.

Random House Electronic Publishing—http://www.randomhouse.com

On the Net

Reviews & lists

A Concise Guide to Unix Books Compiled by readers of misc.books.technical, this guide gives author, title, publisher, ISBN number, and brief descriptions for the best of a wide range of Unix books, from general texts like *Unix for Dummies* to advanced programming guides. ✓ **INTERNET** →*www* http://www.cis.ohio-state.edu/hypertext/faq/usenet/books/unix/faq.html

misc.books.technical (ng) While not exclusively devoted to computer books, the group rarely strays too long from the topic. Activity consists of asking for referrals, submitting reviews, and trying to trade reference books. ✓ **USENET**

misc.books.technical FAQ This brief FAQ offers advice on where to get technical books, in and out of print, and how to access Internet library catalogs. Contact information for technical publishers and bookstores is also listed. ✓ **INTERNET**→*www* http://www.cis.ohio-state.edu/hypertext/faq/usenet/books/technical/faq.html

The Unofficial Internet Book List A mammoth list of information about Internet books, including author, publisher, ISBN number, pages, publication date, and a brief description. The list is a hypertext document with links to sites related to the books. ✓ **INTERNET**→*www* http://daffy.cadvision.com/bookstore/Info/booklist.html

Booksellers

Academic Press No, fuzzy logic is not the Contract with America, nor David Hume covered with mold. If you are fascinated by what it really is, this press may have books you want. Choose from titles in C/C++, graphics and imaging, mathematics software, multimedia, networking, windowing, and, yes, texts on artificial intelligence. Order through the UCI Bookstore. ✓ **INTERNET**→*www* http://bookweb.cwis.uci.edu:8042/Books/Academic/index.html

Net Tech 35

Computer Bookstores Booting Up

ACM Press The Association for Computing Machinery, the world's oldest computing society, has its own imprint and an online catalogue entitled "living publication." Its search engine will assist you in locating books in your field of interest. Use the online annotations to choose from *A History of Personal Workstations*, *Database Security*, *Intelligent User Databases*, or hundreds of others. ✓**INTERNET** …→*www* http://www.acm.org/#pubs …→*www* gopher://gopher.acm.org/11gopher_root%3a%5bthe_files.pubs%5d

Albion Books This small San Francisco-based publisher uses its Website to focus on online titles such as *Netiquette* and *Internet Tips and Tricks*. You can order Albion books online through Bookport or Dial-a-Book, or after you take a look at a sample chapter, you can purchase immediate electronic access. If you get the paper edition, the online edition is included. ✓**INTERNET**→*www* http://www.bookport.com/htbin/welcome/albion9501.html

Alpha Books These are the proud purveyors of the "Complete Idiots Guides" to Windows, CD-ROMs, QuarkXPress, the Internet, and many other computer-related subjects. The books are designed for busy folks, newbies, and the computer fearful. (There is a rebate for ordering online.) ✓**INTERNET**→*www* http://www.mcp.com/alpha/

Artech House Features a catalog of titles in communications technology with texts on computer/telephone integration, corporate networks, and cryptology. Artech also has a large selection of software. Order via email. ✓**INTERNET**→*www* gopher://gopher.std.com/11/Book%20Sellers/artech

Benjamin/Cummings Publishing Co., Inc. For Programming 101, snap up *Data Structures and Algorithm Analysis in C*. Taking a class in computer business applications? The fourth edition of *Business Data Communications* could well be required reading. There are also titles in artificial intelligence, databases, operating systems, programming, and engineering. ✓**INTERNET** …→*www* http://www.aw.com/bc/home.html …→*www* ftp://bc.aw.com/bc/ …→*www* gopher://aw.com

CD Publishing Corp CDs are more than indestructible replacements for scratchy Dylan albums. This company offers information on CD-ROM products dedicated to Net topics and resources. ✓**INTERNET** …→*www* gopher://gopher.cdpublishing.com …→*www* http://www.CDPublishing.com *Info:* ✓**INTERNET**→*email* info@CDPublishing.com ✎ Email for automated info

Compubooks Search by platform, subject, or author; this large computer book selection covers a broad range of topics, from word processing tutorials to instruction on mainframe maintenance. Make your selection online and then head for the virtual "checkout" counter. ✓**COMPUSERVE**→*go* cbk

Computer Literacy Bookshops Information Choose from over 35,000 annotated computer-related titles, including such classics as *What You Need to Know to Use Email Effectively* and *Programming WinSock*. This online computer book bonanza features a small button located in each description that pulls up all books on related topics from the vast database. You can order online, or see if the book is in stock in a store near you. ✓**INTERNET** →*www* http://www.clbooks.com/

Digital Press Founded by Digital Equipment Corporation's C. Gordon Bell, the father of the VAX, Digital Press was sold in 1977 and now offers a large selection of technical titles, such as *The Unix Philosophy* and *The Matrix*. Order online through a connection to the Internet Bookshop. ✓**INTERNET**

Hayden Books—http://www.mcp.com:80/adobe/

36 Net Tech

Booting Up Computer Bookstores

...→*www* http://www.bookshop.co.uk/DP/ ...→*www* gopher://gopher.std.com/11/Book%20Sellers/DIGITAL-PRESS

The Electric Bookstore Inc. Need a guide to Quicken or PageMaker? Desperate to learn C++? Entirely devoted to computer books, this easy-to-use site has books on computer applications, computer science theory, engineering and technology, operating systems and platforms, and programming. ✓INTERNET ...→*www* http://www.cadvision.com/bookstore/electric.html ...→*email* books@electric.interlog.com ✍ Send email orders

Elsevier Science (The Netherlands) Peruse the book catalog for science or online titles. Read *The Proceedings of the Third International World-Wide Web Conference* here or search various databases for article abstracts from a wide range of periodicals. ✓INTERNET ...→*www* http://www.elsevier.nl/ ...→*www* gopher://gopher.elsevier.nl

Hayden Books No matter what you are trying to have your Macintosh do for you, this is the place to go for instruction manuals and starter kits. Also get your Apple-authorized books and Adobe-Press publications here. ✓INTERNET →*www* http://www.mcp.com:80/adobe/

Charles River Media Charles River has seen the future, and it is electronic publishing. His Website features books and CD-ROMs, including guides to HTML and 3-D Stereograms. Newbies can "tour" the Net with a CD-ROM simulation of the vast riches of the online world. ✓INTERNET→*www* http://www.algorithm.com:80/crm/

John Wiley & Sons Computer books galore! Each entry has a complete table of contents and a short synopsis. In addition to a wealth of programming and systems management texts, Wiley will soon be placing its *Solutions* and *Insider* series online. ✓INTERNET→*www* http://www.awa.com/wiley/

Knowledge in Motion Send in your text to this formatting company and they'll create a CD for you with Acrobat. They'll even scan hard copy and then mark up the document for a hypertext format. Get complete details on their service from this home page. ✓INTERNET→*www* http://www.fullfeed.com/epub/knowinmo.html

Library Solutions Institute and Press Carries Internet training guides and tutorials. ✓INTERNET→*www* http://www.internet-is.com/library/ *Info:* ✓INTERNET→*email* library@internet-is.com ✍ Email for info

Macmillan Computer Publishing Forum This kind publisher doesn't want to leave you out in the cold after you purchase computer wares. If you don't understand page 46 of *Game Developer*, simply post a message and the author himself will clarify the passage. The staff and frequent visitors are not adverse to giving general help on purchasing hardware, software, and books. Forthcoming Macmillan products are announced here as well. ✓COMPUSERVE→*go* macmillan

Macmillan USA Information SuperLibrary It's a bird, it's a plane, it's Superlibrary. Take a look at what's forthcoming from eight computer-related imprints: Adobe Press (Mac design), Alpha (newbies), Brady (games), New Riders, Que, Que College, Sams, and Sams.net. Choose from 1,000 online titles, many with sample chapters and contents; search the *Internet Yellow Pages*; submit your own home page for inclusion; or indulge in cyberchat on bulletin boards dedicated to Website creation and other computer-related issues. ✓INTERNET→*www* http://www.mcp.com/

McGraw-Hill Online What could be better than a 20 percent discount on new titles, and a guarantee to beat any other Internet bookseller by 5 percent? Most of the books are on computer topics although business, engineering, aviation, and boating/outdoors are represented as well. Ordering online is easy, and don't miss the clearance sale bin for 50 percent off deals. ✓COMPUSERVE→*go* mh

Michael Wolff & Company, Inc. The New York-based book packager Michael Wolff & Company, Inc. has made its name with the Net Books series, beginning with the 1994 best-seller *Net Guide* and continuing on through *Net Games, Net Chat, Net Money, Net Trek, Net Sports, Net Tech,* and the forthcoming *Net Guide 2, Net Music,* and *Net Travel.* All the books are available in hypertext form on the company's Website YPN—Your Personal Network: browse through the pages, use the search engine to find all the Net resources on a topic of your interest, then let YPN take you there with a simple point-and-click. And there's more! Read YPN's daily news feature, which highlights current events and points you to relevant sites across the Internet. Rate tens of thousands of Websites. Submit comments on the Net Books series. Locate the name of a bookstore in your area that carries the Net Books. And keep

Net Tech 37

Computer Bookstores Booting Up

your finger on the pulse of the Net. ✓ **INTERNET**→*www* http://www.ypn.com

Microsoft Press Bookstore Why not go straight to the source? Order Microsoft computer books or a catalog online. Browse titles on Microsoft's most popular products—Excel, Word, Office, PowerPoint, Publisher, Mail, Project, Access, FoxPro, and more. When you're finished, head to the checkout. ✓ **COMPUSERVE**→*go* msp

Morgan Kaufmann Algorithms, ambiguity (in AI, not just life), analogy, and dataprocessing for anesthesiology are just the first four subjects in this online catalog. There is a huge selection of computer science-related books here, some accompanied by concise annotations. Artificial intelligence and human–computer interactive knowledge systems are their specialty. ✓ **INTERNET**→*www* http://market.net/literary/mkp/index.html

NCC Blackwell Computer manuals for all levels of expertise. Nervous newbies will find books on rooting out viruses and imaginative inventors can get help programming artificial intelligence. Order online through the Internet Bookstore. ✓ **INTERNET** …→*www* http://www.demon.co.uk/bookshop/nccat.html …→*www* http://www.bookshop.co.uk/nccat.htm

O'Reilly Mailing List (ml) Updates and information about O'Reilly's latest computer books and software. ✓ **INTERNET**→*email* book-info-request@ora.com ✍ *Write a request*

O'Reilly's Online Bookstore Browse O'Reilly's large selection of computer books—the bookstore's storefront always has the open sign up. O'Reilly, one of the most active publishers online, has its entire book and software catalog available. Most products include a picture of the cover, a brief blurb about the book, an order form, and links to related books. ✓ **INTERNET** …→*www* http://www.ora.com/gnn/bus/ora/catalog/index.html …→*email* nuts@ora.com ✍ *Order a book* **Support:** ✓ **INTERNET**→*email* bookquestions@ora.com

Online Bookstore This online bookshop has a good selection of computer titles from several publishers. Its Internet guide selection is especially good. Ordering online is available. ✓ **AMERICA ONLINE**→*keyword* bookstore

The Online Bookstore (OBS) Perhaps the best bookstore online, this site offers a broad selection of titles, including many computer books. ✓ **INTERNET**→*www* http://marketplace.com/obs/obshome.html **Info:** ✓ **INTERNET**→*email* OBS@marketplace.com ✍ *Email for info*

Random House Electronic Publishing Computer books are currently 20% off in the Random House virtual bookstore. Why not snap up all the Net Books titles? If your interest lies in programming, database management, or even kids and computers there are titles here to please all. CD-ROMs like *Windows Power Tools* and *The Los Angeles Times Electronic Crossword Puzzles* are also available at reduced prices. And don't forget to hit the warehouse sale! ✓ **COMPUSERVE**→*go* random ✓ **INTERNET**→*www* http://www.randomhouse.com/

Resolution Business Press Worried about your kids reading adult material on the Net? Order these family guides to the Internet. This small Pacific Northwest publisher also offers Unix and Internet dictionaries, guides for teachers, and Web design manuals. ✓ **INTERNET**→*www* http://www.halcyon.com/ResPress/

Small Computer Book Club It was bound to happen, a virtual book club. You can order $120 worth of computer books like *CD MOM: The Mother of All Windows Books* for just $3.00 and then you only have to buy one more book…Browse the current selections to see if this is really a deal you can't pass up. ✓ **COMPUSERVE**→*go* bk

Softpro Books Over 4,000 computer-related titles spanning both hardware and software, including the business side of the computer industry, not to mention geek humor (Dilbert cartoon books). ✓ **INTERNET** …→*www* http://plaza.xor.com/softpro/ …→*www* gopher://storefront.xor.com:70/11/Softpro%20Books

Telos This Springer-Verlag imprint specializes in mathematics, visualization and graphics, and scientific computing. The online catalog is supplemented by CD-ROM samples and mathematical graphics. ✓ **INTERNET**→*www* http://www.telospub.com/

Ziff Davis Publishing Ziff Davis is home to the unthreatening, explicatory tomes, *How Computers Work*, *How the Internet Works*, and *How Weather Works*. The featured book this month may be a guide to HTML styling, perfect for Web weavers, and next month it could be a manual for Windows 95. Order online, and don't neglect the bargain table, final resting place of a great number of useful computing guides. ✓ **COMPUSERVE**→*go* booknet

Booting Up Shopping

Shopping

Computers are producers, sure, machines capable of generating equations, texts, sounds, and graphics of impressive complexity. But they are also consumers. From the privacy of your home, your computer can buy books, clothes, CDs, even a lovely floral arrangement that says, "I'm sorry—I didn't mean to sleep with your girlfriend." And computers can also buy other computers. Order your hardware and software from **Computer Express**. Have your favorite programs delivered over the wire with **The Download Superstore**. Stock your office with **OfficeMax Online**. And then take a break from the serious stuff and zoom into Cyberspace with **Mission Control Software**.

Shopping for UNIVAC—downloaded from CompuServe's Bettmann Archive

On the Net

Across the board

Apache Digital Corporation Macintosh aficionados can skip this site—Apache sells system and related software for most of the other major platforms, including NeXTSTEP, Linux/BSD, Unix, Solaris, OS/2, Windows NT, and DOS/Windows. In addition, Apache carries preconfigured Net workstations. Be sure and check out the company mission statement. ✓**INTERNET**→*www* http://www.apache.com/

Catalog.com Almost thirty different hardware and software businesses have set up shop here, from Betacorp (CD-ROM publishers) to Environmental Laser (toner cartridges) to SAGEMusa (ISDN hardware and software) to VirtualNet Consulting (Website designers and consultants). ✓**INTERNET**→*www* http://www.catalog.com/catalog/dir-bus.html

Computer Express Need software in a hurry? Order from this catalog of more then 2,000 titles for both IBM and Macintosh, covering a wide range of computer needs for work or play, including such titles as Doom II, Marathon, and Lotus SmartSuite. ✓**PRODIGY**→*jump* computerexpress ✓**AMERICA ONLINE**→*keyword* computerexpress ✓**EWORLD**→*go* computerexpress ✓**COMPUSERVE**→*go* express ✓**INTERNET**→*www* http://cexpress.com:2700/

Computer Marketplace, Inc. Buy, sell, rent, and lease RISC hardware, RISC software, PC hardware, PC software, workstation equipment, network hardware, network software, new communications hardware, used communications hardware, modems, computer parts, refurbished computer equipment, and other computer hardware and peripheral equipment from Axil, DEC, IBM, Motorola, and Sun Microsystems. ✓**INTERNET**→*www* http://www.mkpl.com/

Computer Recyclers When that IBM-XT or Macintosh SE finally reaches the end of its life, contact Computer Recyclers. Instead of leaving your old computer at the curb for the sanitation engineers, why not minimize its impact on the environment and make a few dollars for yourself at the same time? ✓**INTERNET**→*www* http://

Net Tech 39

Shopping Booting Up

www.utw.com/computer Recycle/cr.html

CyberWarehouse Specializes in discount hardware and software, multimedia peripherals, modems, and printers. ✓**COMPUSERVE**→*go* cyberwareh ✓**PRODIGY**→*jump* cyberwarehouse

Dalco Computer Electronics More than 2,000 computer hardware and accessory items, including modems, motherboards, tools, books, interface cards, monitors, switches, cables, networking items, technical aids, telephone accessories, batteries, and multimedia products. ✓**COMPUSERVE**→*go* da

Internet Mall – THIRD FLOOR: Computer Hardware and Software While you cannot actually purchase anything in this mall, you can find pointers to a wealth of storefronts around the Internet. Hardware and software stores are organized into convenient categories for efficient browsing. ✓**INTERNET**→*www* http://www.mecklerweb.com:80/imall/3-comptr.htm

Internet Shopping Network More than 20,000 products from over 1,000 hardware and software vendors, including but not limited to CPUs, monitors, storage devices, CD-ROMs, and printers. Be sure to check out the Hot Deals page. ✓**INTERNET**→*www* http://www.internet.net/

misc.forsale.computers.discussion (ng) A catch-all group for discussions surrounding the issues of buying and selling computers. Questions range from recovering money from unscrupulous mail-order companies to upgrading hardware and software. ✓**USENET**

misc.forsale.computers.other.misc (ng) The premier Usenet spot for buying and selling computers other than IBM-compatibles or Macintoshes, although the group tends to get postings about the Big Boys as well. ✓**USENET**

misc.forsale.computers.other.software (ng) Looking for word processing software for that Amiga 4000 or Sinclair Palmtop? This is the place to look first. Many off-topic postings end up here though, so bring your filters. ✓**USENET**

misc.forsale.computers.other.systems (ng) The following systems are looking for a new home: Atari, Amiga, HP9000, Sun Sparcstation, Cyber 310, and TRS-80. In fact, just about all types of computers have been listed in this newsgroup at one time or another (except maybe HAL, the computer from *2001: A Space Odyssey*). ✓**USENET**

Paradon Computer Systems Based in Vancouver, Paradon resells a variety of computer peripherals—everything from printers to hard drives to CD-ROMs to back-up systems. The shop also has an extensive software catalog. ✓**INTERNET**→*www* http://islandnet.com/~paradon/paradon.html

PC Catalog A catalog of PC and Macintosh software and hardware, including motherboards, monitors, memory, mice, and modems. ✓**AMERICA ONLINE**→*keyword* pccatalog ✓**COMPUSERVE**→*go* pca ✓**PRODIGY**→*jump* pccatalog

Shareware Club Join the Shareware Club for a small fee and receive a monthly batch of shareware. ✓**PRODIGY**→*jump* shareware-club

Shareware Depot Instead of spending hours downloading megabytes of shareware by modem at a snail's pace, consider purchasing these bundles of shareware for PC and Macintosh in (eek!) diskette form. ✓**COMPUSERVE**→*go* sd ✓**PRODIGY**→*jump* sharewaredepot

Softdisk Superstore Software and accessories for IBM-PCs and Macintoshes, including arcade and puzzle games, graphics packages, and productivity, utility, and education programs. Computer reference books are also sold. Demo programs are available. ✓**AMERICA ONLINE**→*keyword* softdisk ✓**COMPUSERVE**→*go* sp

software.net Over 7,800 products to choose from, including a selection of downloadable products for the Windows, OS/2, DOS, Macintosh, and Unix platforms. In addition to offering free online demos, the company will match any prices advertised elsewhere. ✓**INTERNET**→*www* http://software.net/index.htm

The Branch Mall A wide variety of products and services branch off from the Branch, including consulting/contract programming, ISDN solutions, 3M media products, disk duplication, voice recognition software, ergonomic workstations, used computers, and

> "All types of computers have been listed (except maybe HAL, from *2001: A Space Odyssey*)."

Booting Up Shopping

CD-ROM software and services. ✓**INTERNET**→*www* http://www.branch.com/#computer

PCs

Andataco On-the-Net Andataco specializes in storage for the Unix client/server market. Their products support such Unix platforms as Hewlett-Packard, SPARC, SGI, and IBM RS/6000. On-the-Net allows you to browse Andataco's product line, check out their library of technical documentation, and get information about the company's customer service. Registered users can place orders 24 hours a day. ✓**INTERNET**→*www* http://www.andataco.com/

Bottom Line Distribution Macintosh-compatible accelerators, accessories, cables, components, internals, drives and storage devices, input devices, instructional products, memory products, modems, monitors, network hardware, printers, software, video cards, and even computers. ✓**INTERNET**→*www* http://www.dgr.com/bld/bld_catalog.html

Buying and Selling Macintosh Computers, Software, and Peripherals If you're thinking about buying or selling a Mac, whether online or off, you'd be well advised to peruse this comprehensive set of frequently asked questions. For those thinking about buying new, it answers questions on leasing, superstores, educational discounts, and more. If you're thinking about buying used, you'll learn the logistics of doing so, and find the answer to the question, "How can I avoid being ripped off when I buy something off the Net?" ✓**INTERNET**→*www* http://rever.nmsu.edu/~elharo/faq/wantedfaq.html

Catalink Direct Window shop till you drop on Catalink's product database PECOS with more than 15,000 PC products (available as a Windows 3.1 or 95 application on diskette or CD-ROM; just send a request by email), then tell the program to place an online order for you. "Full-service" Internet ordering is scheduled for fall 1995, says the company. ✓**INTERNET**→*www* http://www.catalink.com/

Ceram Incorporated Specializing in Sun Sparc stations, Ceram carries CPUs, graphics cards and monitors, disk drives, memory, and various flavors of system software. ✓**INTERNET**→*www* http://www.ceram.com/

comp.sys.amiga.marketplace (ng) Amiga's bad marketing and weak distribution system have created a thriving black market; in this newsgroup alone, there are hundreds of classified listings for hardware, software, and peripherals. Whether you're looking for a whole system or just trying to pick up a new bridge board, someone here has got it, and he or she wants to sell it to you. ✓**USENET**

comp.sys.apple2.marketplace (ng) Lots of Apple II goodies for sale here, whether you're looking for old games, a stereo card, a monitor, or just a few old books. You can even salvage old parts at cheap prices. ✓**USENET**

comp.sys.mac.wanted (ng) Sure, you'll find Netheads looking for SIMMs and motherboards here, but you'll also find some strange requests, like the one from Anthony, who wrote, "Does anyone out there have any idea how to make a fish tank out of a compact Mac?" (Victor wrote back, saying, "I'm about to start doing this to a dead old 128 I picked up at a garage sale.") More typically, the Mac fans on this busy group want a mini-dock, a video card, or a complete system. ✓**USENET**

comp.sys.next.marketplace (ng) Buy or sell NeXT-compatible hardware and peripherals. ✓**USENET**

Computer Management Software, Inc. Sure, we have no doubt whatsoever that PC Manager is "the all-purpose tool for keeping track of your hardware usage, tracking how often (or how long) you use your software packages, or maintaining how much time you spend surfing the Internet," and we don't doubt that it's a very useful product, covering topics "from just knowing when it's time to buy

Computer Marketplace—from http://www.mkpl.com/

COMPUTER MARKETPLACE
A PUBLICLY TRADED COMPANY · NASDAQ: MKPL
Delivering Advanced Computer Technology... TODAY!
BUY · SELL · RENT · LEASE

Shopping Booting Up

a bigger hard drive or faster modem, through deciding which old, unused programs to scrap." But isn't there a certain irony in the fact that, after you've read about it online and ordered it online...they snail-mail you a *disk*? ✓**INTERNET**→*www* http://www.cmsoft.com/cms/

Cyberian Outpost Well designed, easily navigable Mac software store with screen and box shots of products. An added feature is the "Celebrity Corner," which lets computer biz luminaries review popular software. ✓**INTERNET**→*www* http://www.cybout.com/

Damark International, Inc. Check out the specs, photos, and accessories available for PCs and laptops from Acer, Packard Bell, and IBM. Then purchase items by clicking on the Shopping Basket button. You will also find office gadgets such as cordless phones, electronic organizers, and fax machines. ✓**INTERNET**→*www* http://www2.pcy.mci.net/marketplace/damark/html/d10000.html

Digital's Electronic Connection While this site is mainly intended for corporate buyers of mainframes and servers, you can also purchase Digital's personal computer, the DECpc XL. ✓**INTERNET**→*www* telnet://order.sales.digital.com/

Digital's PC Store Looking to buy one of Digital's PCs, with the superfast Alpha chip? This is the place; Digital sells a wide range of hardware products, including desktops, monitors, and laptops. ✓**COMPUSERVE**→*go* dd

Exec/Direct *PC World*'s mall, offering a smattering of products ranging from recycled diskettes to the latest CD-ROMs. ✓**COMPUSERVE**→*go* pwm

IBM PC Direct Cut out the middleman and check out IBM's entire line of hardware and peripherals for IBM PCs, including the OS/2 WARP operating system, other software, monitors, printers, modems, memory, and multimedia products. ✓**COMPUSERVE**→*go* buyibm

JDR Microdevices If you like to tinker with the insides of your PC, this is the place for you—VESA local bus products, add-on cards, motherboards, chip accelerators, memory, math co-processors, and more. ✓**COMPUSERVE**→*go* jdr

MacProducts USA Carries Macintosh peripherals including CD-ROMs, chip accelerators, PowerBook upgrades, hard drives, SyQuest drives, tape backup drives, and optical storage drives. ✓**INTERNET**→*www* http://www.dgr.com/mp/planet_mp_l.html

MacWarehouse Macintosh hardware and software clearinghouse—if you don't see it here, it probably does not exist. ✓**COMPUSERVE**→*go* mw

MicroWarehouse Hardware and software for PCs. ✓**COMPUSERVE**→*go* mcw

misc.forsale.computers.mac-specific.cards.misc (ng) Cards and boards of all kinds, whether you're looking for SIMMs for your Quadra, an Asanté network card, or a motherboard for your LaserWriter IINT. ✓**USENET**

misc.forsale.computers.mac-specific.cards.video (ng) Looking for millions of colors? Whatever Mac model you own, you're likely to find someone here selling the video card you need, whether it's the AV card for your Power Mac or a RasterOps card for your SE/30. ✓**USENET**

misc.forsale.computers.mac-specific.misc (ng) It's a virtual Mac bazaar, with Netheads hawking laser printers of all kinds, StyleWriter ink refills, and all brands of mouse. ✓**USENET**

misc.forsale.computers.mac-specific.portables (ng) Want to pick up a PowerBook for under a thou? Well, here's the place to do it. You'll find everything from an old PowerBook 100 to the latest 540C. Some people show up here to salvage parts, like the guy who posted, "Dead PowerBook 100 Wanted." ✓**USENET**

misc.forsale.computers.mac-specific.software (ng) Freehand for $125? Illustrator for $100? What's the deal? "All legal," writes Jonathan, "and includes letter of transfer and original disks." Get all your Mac software here. ✓**USENET**

misc.forsale.computers.mac-specific.systems (ng) "Quadra 660AV system collecting dust" is one of hundreds of posts in this group. Looking for a complete Mac system, or want to sell one and upgrade? Do it here, but expect lots of company. Looks like a buyer's market. ✓**USENET**

misc.forsale.computers.pc-specific.audio (ng) An electronic classifieds for PC audio equipment. There are no discussions here, just advertisements for soundboards and the like. ✓**USENET**

misc.forsale.computers.pc-specific.cards.video (ng) An electronic classifieds for PC video cards. ✓**USENET**

Booting Up Shopping

misc.forsale.computers.pc-specific.misc (ng) "Some junk for sale," announces one of the postings to this diverse message board. If you're browsing for IBM or compatible hardware, then stop off at this electronic garage sale. The offerings include everything from PCMCIA adapters to Elvis Karaoke CD-ROMs to DEAD Pentium chips. ✓**USENET**

misc.forsale.computers.pc-specific.motherboards (ng) An electronic classifieds for PC motherboards. ✓**USENET**

misc.forsale.computers.pc-specific.portables (ng) An electronic classifieds for PC laptops and fax modems. Leather cases are also sometimes advertised. ✓**USENET**

misc.forsale.computers.pc-specific.software (ng) An electronic classifieds for the buying and selling of PC software. Applications range from painting to accounting programs. ✓**USENET**

misc.forsale.computers.pc-specific.systems (ng) An electronic classifieds for complete PC computer systems. Postings advertise both new and used machines. Need a complete 286 system shipped to your door for just $250? Sure you do. And there is even some bartering going on. One person offered to trade comic books for software, and another wanted to exchange his 21-foot trailer for a full Pentium system. ✓**USENET**

misc.forsale.computers.workstation (ng) Power users of workstations should scan this newsgroup for deals on workstations and peripherals from Silicon Graphics, Sun, Hewlett Packard, and NeXTStep. ✓**USENET**

Mr. Upgrade This is a cool site for home handypeople who like to tinker with their PCs. Kick your old PC into the 21st century with cases, CPUs and motherboards, disk drives and controllers, memory, modems, multimedia kits, and video gear. ✓**INTERNET**→*www* http://www.primenet.com/~jimb/mrupgrad.html

Output Enablers Output Enablers is a company that makes clip-on clock-chip accelerators for Macintosh and Power Mac computers. Speed up your Quadra, Centris, or Power Mac by 12-40%, they say. The site includes an FAQ about clock-chipping, a System 7.5 Updater patch for "upclocked" 7100/66 and 8100/100 machines, and utilities such as Mac Benchmarks 2.0, Disk First Aid 7.2, Speedometer 4.0, and MacBench. ✓**INTERNET**→*www* http://www.io.com/user/oe/

PC Catalog 2,000 plus products from over 170 networking, microcomputer, software, and peripheral manufacturers. After making a product selection, you can check out the vendor's location, business hours, phone/fax numbers, technical support offerings, areas of specialty, sales policies, and payment options. ✓**INTERNET**→*www* gopher://pccatalog.peed.com/

PC Software Direct IBM's online software catalog, complete with product descriptions and promotions listed. In addition to OS/2 and AS/400 operating systems, many software resources are here, including languages and development tools, database and transaction management programs, LAN servers, network management and Internet software, workstation applications and productivity tools, and courseware. ✓**INTERNET**→*www* http://www.issc1.ibm.com/pcdirect/

The Download Superstore Shop for and download PC software of all types. Subscribe for a monthly download special. ✓**PRODIGY**→*jump* downloadsuperstore

The Mac Zone You'll find an ever-expanding list of Mac hardware and software here. Check out the Power Macs, PowerBooks, Duos, printers, monitors, RAM upgrades, and the latest Newton Messagepad. ✓**COMPUSERVE**→*go* mz ✓**EWORLD**→*go* maczone ✓**INTERNET**→*www* http://www2.pcy.mci.net/marketplace/mzone/html/2100.html

The PC Zone Computer products for the PC owner. Merchandise is arranged in the following categories: business department, word processing/tools/fonts, communications/modems, computers, educational, entertainment, graphics and design, hardware/accessories, multimedia, music/MIDI/soundcards/speakers, networking, operating systems, programming, software upgrades, and utilities. ✓**COMPUSERVE**→*go* pcz

The PC Zone The online equivalent of the PC Zone's mail-order catalog pushes the envelope for in-

> "One person offered to trade comic books for software, and another wanted to exchange his trailer for a full Pentium system."

Net Tech 43

Shopping Booting Up

teractive shopping, with a well organized graphical interface and logical hyperlinks. In addition to the usual PC clone hardware, you will also find software such as Quicken, WordPerfect, Excel, and QuarkXPress for Windows. ✓INTERNET→*www* http://www2.pcy.mci.net/marketplace/mzone/html/2300.html

Vektron Online An online mall carrying all manner of PC-compatible hardware, software, and peripherals. ✓COMPUSERVE→*go* vek

CD-ROMs

CD-ROM Paradise If you're looking for programming software but don't know what you want, check out the shareware available on CD-ROM Paradise's samplers. Each CD-ROM Paradise sampler contains 3,500 files (or more than 640 megabytes). You'll find graphics, programming, and sound editing programs. Just fill out this site's order form, including your credit card information, and the CD will be mailed to you. If you like what you demo, you can pay the author for the rest. ✓INTERNET→*www* http://www.cdrom-paradise.com/

CD-ROM Network Links to the most boring, ad-like pages of CD-ROM developers, the latest tips on finishing Myst, retailers offering the cheapest price on new titles, and more. ✓INTERNET→*www* http://www.primenet.com/~laig/cdrom.html

CD-ROM World One of the oldest retailers devoted exclusively to CD-ROM software also has one of the best places to shop online. Download the entire catalog, or choose from a selection of CD-ROM-related products: CD-ROM caddies, drives, educational and games titles, graphics, shareware, and programming manuals. ✓INTERNET→*www* http://www.infoanalytic.com/cdrw/index.html

Compton's New Media If you're off to Europe tomorrow and suddenly your CD-ROM edition of *Let's Go* isn't loading properly, this is the place to go. Besides getting information on telephone support and a list of common questions and problems, you can email Compton's help desk directly from here. You'll also find the usual advantages to online catalogs: downloadable demos, MPEG press releases, company history, and a detailed list of the electronic book publisher's titles. ✓INTERNET→*www* http://www.comptons.com/

Computer Data Archival Services (CDAS) Tired of pumping all your archived software back onto your system using multiple floppies or backup tapes? Want a stable storage medium? CDAS specializes in transferring data onto 640MB capacity, recordable CD-ROMs. Even if you want just one copy of the CD, they want your business. ✓INTERNET→*www* http://www.mbnet.mb.ca:80/~cdas/

Compton's New Media—from http://www.comptons.com/

Config.Sys Whether you're looking for the Family Bible Multimedia, Seedy Rom Seventh Heaven, or Fatty Bear's Fun Pack, this is the place to order almost any CD-ROM on the market. An easy-to-use interface allows you to click into 14 categories of CD-ROM listings. Order directly from the site with your credit card or try old-fashioned C.O.D. if that makes you more comfortable. ✓INTERNET→*www* http://dutch.wariat.org:80/1/cdrom/

Discovery CD-ROM If you think that the acclaimed Discovery Channel's CD-ROMs are free of the sensationalism of the blood-and-guts visuals available on many CD-ROM games, then you haven't seen *Sharks*. Check out the first-hand accounts of shark attack victims, with detailed descriptions of their assorted wounds. If this kind of family entertainment is too much for your kids, try the slightly sweeter *In The Company of Whales*. ✓INTERNET→*www* http://www.shopping2000.com/shopping2000/discovery/

Metalogic Metalogic wants to get you in the CD-ROM retailing business. Order 25 copies of the

Booting Up Shopping

same title, pay the wholesale price, design a home page—and suddenly you're in business as a full-service online CD-ROM dealer. ✓INTERNET→*www* http://www.xmission.com/~wwwads/mind/logic.html

MSU Catalog If you know what you're looking for, the MSU catalog is probably the most convenient way to order CD-ROMs online. Click a category and scroll through the list of titles. Select a title, the quantity you want, and click on "Submit order." Your order will be processed on the same day and you'll receive confirmation by email. The only thing you have to do to make this work is become a member. Give MSU your address and relevant credit card information by uh…fax, and you're all set. ✓INTERNET→*www* http://www.datamax.net/msu/catalog.html

The CD-ROM Software Guild Although this is basically an ad for a CD-ROM mail order operation, the site offers decent descriptions of the most popular game, kids', and educational titles on the market. And if you like what you read, just click on a link for a list of mail order and email-order houses ✓INTERNET→*www* http://falcon.cc.

> "If you think that the Discovery Channel's CD-ROMs are free of blood and guts, then you haven't seen *Sharks*."

ukans.edu:80/~dj/

The Voyager Company At last —an online catalog that's better than paper. Just click on a title to summon up a screen with a textual description of a CD-ROM. From here, view screen shots, download a demo, link to related Voyager releases, or purchase online. You can also download free QuickTime "Making of…" movies and get the inside scoop on a title. Finally, you can access Laurie Anderson's Green Room Diaries, written during the Nerve Bible tour. And if all this still isn't enough, you can download Voyager's full-color catalog. Amazing. ✓INTERNET→*www* http:// www.voyagerco.com

Entertainment

Mission Control Software Sells IBM games, CD-ROMs, sound cards, and other accessories. ✓COMPUSERVE→*go* mcs

Graphics & video

ATI Technologoes, Inc. ATI claims they're the "leading supplier of VGA and other graphics products for the PC," including accelerators and video capture boards. Useful resources at this site are the latest updates, drivers, and utilities. Specifically you will find current drivers for Windows 3.1/3.11 and OS/2 2.1/2.11. ✓INTERNET→*www* http://www.atitech.ca/

North American CAD NACAD sells hardware and supplies, specializing in digitizers and plotters, to CAD professionals. It also carries a wide array of printers, monitors, and video boards. ✓INTERNET→*www* http://nacad.com/

Insurance

Safeware Computer Insurance What if Fred MacMurray's character in *Double Indemnity* had sold computers? This agency offers insurance for computer, electronic, and high-tech equipment. ✓COMPUSERVE→*go* saf

Lotus

The Lotus Organizer Store Need to get yourself or your group organized? Maybe Organizer 2.0 will get you on the right track. You can also buy Lotus SmartSuite 3.0. ✓COMPUSERVE→*go* ltm

Magazines

Electronic Newsstand Before you subscribe to any new magazines—computer-oriented or otherwise, be sure and cruise over the the Electronic Newsstand, where you can read entire articles from oodles of publications and then subscribe online. Among the computer magazines represented here are *Byte*, *Dr. Dobb's Journal*, *Internet World*, *Multimedia Week*, *PC World*, and *Virtual Reality World*. ✓INTERNET→*www* http://www.enews.com/

Technology Review *Tech Review*, published continuously since 1899, covers "technology and its implications," focusing on "the practical applications of science, as opposed to laboratory breakthroughs and theoretical abstractions, emphasizing policy issues rather than nuts and bolts." Check out the table of contents of the latest issue, order a sample issue, or scan its online book catalog from this site. ✓INTERNET→*www* http://web.mit.edu/techreview/www/

Ziff Davis Publishing Online Order subscriptions to any of Ziff-Davis's print or CD-ROM publications, including *Family PC*, *PC/Computing*, *PC Magazine*,

Net Tech 45

Shopping Booting Up

MacUser, Computer Shopper, Windows Sources, Computer Life, and *Computer Gaming World.* ✓**COMPUSERVE**→*go* zd ✓**PRODIGY**→*jump* ziffdavis

Multimedia

A2Z Multimedia SuperShop Just what the sign says—oodles of software, both in disk and CD-ROM media, for PCs and Macintoshes. ✓**COMPUSERVE**→*go* mmss ✓**PRODIGY**→*jump* a2z

Alias Alian Nation Alias specializes in digital rendering software, either for personal projects or for developing multimedia software. Products include Alias AutoStudio, Alias Studio, Alias Designer, and Alias StudioPaint. Check out the large gallery of sample images. ✓**INTERNET**→*www* http://www.alias.com/

Multimedia Studio Order CD-ROM titles from this Web store run by IBM. Broadly organized into subject areas of education, entertainment, and information, the service allows you to download screenshots from applications that can be ordered online ✓**INTERNET**→*www* http://www.cdrom.ibm.com/

MultiMedia World Besides the helpful editorial content that includes product news, reviews, a tech clinic, commercial demo software, and shareware, you can also buy related paraphernalia such as CD-ROM racks, clip art collections, and computer reference books. ✓**AMERICA ONLINE**→*keyword* mmworld

Reveal This site specializes in PC multimedia hardware and software, including CD-ROM drives, video and sound cards, and even TV and radio cards ("Now you can watch your favorite TV show, or listen to your daily radio news program from your PC!") ✓**INTERNET**→*www* http://www2.pcy.mci.net/marketplace/reveal/

Networking

A & M Networking Inc. Get your network hardware and software: routers, switches, repeaters, and more. They're authorized resellers of Novell, Firefox, and NetSoft products. ✓**INTERNET**→*www* http://www.bei.net/amni/index.html

FTP Software Sells a full suite of Internet connectivity and client software solutions for Windows and OS/2, including PC/TCP OnNet, PC/TCP Network Software, and Explore OnNet. ✓**INTERNET**→*www* http://www2.pcy.mci.net/marketplace/ftp/

InterCon Systems Before purchasing any new Internet software, download the demos available here for both Windows and Macintosh. TCP/Connect II provides you with terminal, email, news, and gopher client applications. Of particular interest to Mac users is the SLIP freeware package InterSLIP. ✓**INTERNET**→*www* http://www.intercon.com/intercon.html

misc.forsale.computers.net-hardware (ng) This is the place to look for products used to access the Net, whether the Internet or just a small office network. Among the items for sale are ethernet cards, routers, repeaters, switches, Web servers, and cabling. ✓**USENET**

NetManage Windows users dipping their toes into the Net for the first time would do well to check out NetManage's Internet Chameleon software, which includes an all-in-one solution, including applications for surfing the Web, managing email, reading news, and using gopher, FTP, Archie, telnet, ping, finger, and WHOIS. ✓**INTERNET**→*www* http://www.netmanage.com/

Netscape Store "Netscape Communications offers a full line of software to enable electronic commerce and secure information exchange on the Internet and private TCP/IP-based networks." In addition to its Netscape Navigator browser, which is available for Windows, Macintosh, or XWindows operating environments, they carry software for running a business on the Web, including secure server software and IStore, which will help manage your on-line business. ✓**INTERNET**→*www* http://www.netscape.com/netstore/index.html

NSTN Cybermall—Computer Services This site is home to Ashton Architect, which features system and network planning software (downloadable demo available), and Plaintree Systems, which manufactures computer networking products that "improve the performance and simplify the management of local area networks." ✓**INTERNET**→*www* http://www.nstn.ca/cybermall/biz-subject/computer/computer.html

The Internet Adapter Stubbornly sticking—for whatever sad reason—to your Unix shell account? Still haven't seen the colorful version of the World Wide Web? Perhaps you want to stick a toe in the water with these guys: InterMind claims its Internet Adapter (TIA) will convert your shell account into a "pseudo-SLIP" account, allowing you to run those TCP/IP programs everybody's talking about, like Netscape and Eudora. Also downloadable

Booting Up Shopping

from this site is another piece of software they've developed, called EmBarque. It's free. It's an eight-in-one browser (including email, gopher, WWW, and FTP), and—this sounds almost too good to be true—it "automatically" installs WinSock on your PC. ✓**INTERNET**→*www* http://marketplace.com/tia/tiahome.html

Office supplies

OfficeMax OnLine Fax machines, paper shredders, organizers and copiers, and other office equipment and computer hardware. ✓**INTERNET**→*www* http://www2.pcy.mci.net/marketplace/omax/

Staples—The Office Superstore The online equivalent of the office-supply chain. The entire catalog is not here yet, but you will find desktop computers, printers, laser printers, computer audio supplies, memory and data storage, modems, mice and keyboards, tapes, and accessories. Order by fax or toll-free number (sorry, they got rid of the telex machine). ✓**INTERNET**→*www* http://www.staples.com/

Peripherals

AT&T Online Store Modems for desktop or laptop, PC or Macintosh. Special promotions offer long-distance credits with purchase. ✓**COMPUSERVE**→*go* dp

Disk-O-Tape Order 3M storage media, 4mm and 8mm tapes, optical cartridges, and 3.5" floppies, or make use of the disk duplication services. ✓**INTERNET**→*www* http://branch.com/disko/disko.html

JEM Computers All manner of surplus hardware can be found here, including laptops, hard drives, scanners, monitors, desktop systems, etc. The catch is that many items have been refurbished, but if you are willing to take the risk, some great bargains can be unearthed. ✓**INTERNET**→*www* http://www.tiac.net:80/biz/bargains/index.html

Metrostar Computer Center Need cables, diskette labels, or mouse pads? Among the other items listed for sale are joysticks, surge protectors, monitor arms, and a mini-vacuum cleaner. ✓**INTERNET**→*www* http://media1.hypernet.com/metrostar.html

Micro Machines Ever want to trade your puny disk drive in for something roomier? Micro specializes in buying old drives, refurbishing them, and then reselling them. It also sells new drives, laptop drives, controllers, and RAM upgrades. ✓**INTERNET**→*www* http://www.gus.com/emp/microm/microm.html

Mind Logic In addition to the usual assortment of peripherals, including video and sound cards, CD-ROM drives, modems, and multimedia kits, the site features free downloadable utilities. ✓**INTERNET**→*www* http://www.xmission.com/~wwwads/mind/logic.html

Get your mouse pads—from http://media1.hypernet.com/metrostar.html

misc.forsale.computers.memory (ng) No matter how often you upgrade your machine's memory, it never seems to be sufficient, does it? When you need more RAM or storage, this is the newsgroup for bargains. Here's a piece of advice for all those Johnny Mnemonics out there—avoid the deals that seem too good to be true. ✓**USENET**

misc.forsale.computers.modems (ng) Great deals on last year's models, the ones that peak at 14,400 baud (and some that crawl at the snail's pace of 300 baud). Try running your favorite Web browser at that speed! ✓**USENET**

misc.forsale.computers.monitors (ng) Remember when your brand new 14" monitor with 256 colors was the envy of your friends? Not anymore. When you are ready to make the jump to 17" or more, check out the chatter here—people regularly discuss the pros and cons of all makes and models, as well as buying and selling them. ✓**USENET**

misc.forsale.computers.printers (ng) Bubblejets, inkjets, laser, dot-matrix, plotters, thermal transfer, clay tablets—strike that

Net Tech 47

Shopping Booting Up

last one, but you get the idea. This is the place to find every printer ever manufactured, as well as toner and ink cartridges. ✓**USENET**

SNC International Name-brand peripherals at value prices. ✓**INTERNET**→*www* http://www.sncint.com/sncint/home.html

Portables & PDAs

Road Warrior Outpost While this is obviously a commercial site selling anything relating to electronic life on the road (laptops, PCMIA cards, portable hard drives, cellular phones, and PDAs), it also links to information about the laptop newsgroup, an FAQ on portables, and the Road Warrior News, with articles on such topics as increasing battery life. ✓**INTERNET**→*www* http://www.warrior.com/

Other

Access Market Square—Computer Stuff Products offered include Due North Multimedia (learning enhancement software), EFI Power Protection Products, New World Enterprises (do-it-yourself legal software) and NCSS Statistical Software for DOS and Windows. ✓**INTERNET**→*www* http://www.icw.com/map/computer.html

Computer Conversions Hit by catastrophe? Computer Conversions says they "recover lost or damaged data from computer backup tapes and cartridges." Or how about that daily disaster of having three generations of computers in your office, none of them on speaking terms? The company also claims it provides data conversion "for over 2,000 computer systems"—from microcomputers to mainframes to dedicated word processors (remember those?). Finally, these people are also in the business of "disaster recovery planning assistance"—sounds like you could make a TV show out of that, doesn't it? ✓**INTERNET**→*www* http://www.cts.com/browse/cci/

Reviews

BMUG Choice Products Access the know-how of the Berkeley Macintosh Users Group, with this useful archive of Mac and Newton software reviews. You can also download some of BMUG's favorite programs and debate the pros and cons of your favorites in the forums. ✓**EWORLD**→*go* bmugchoice

Computer Buyer's Guide Online computer product information for more than 70,000 hardware and software products, including detailed information about each product's manufacturer. Looking for info about TelePort Mercury modem from Global Village Communications, Inc.? Search by product or manufacturer, but be prepared to pay $1 for each report you download or view. You'll receive product and company specifications, including current retail price, the address and phone numbers of the company, and a listing of the product's features. ✓**COMPUSERVE**→*go* compbg

Computer Buyer's Guide In the market for a new system? Can't decide between a Mac and a PC? Search this database for product reviews from over 200 magazines, newspapers, and journals. Contains a meticulous and easy-to-use search engine that will help you narrow your search down to that perfect machine. The only thing this great resource doesn't do is go out to the computer store and buy the machine for you. ✓**COMPUSERVE**→*go* znt:buyers

Family News Product Reviews Do a little research before you buy. Reviews of computer books, commercial software, and shareware are online here. If you don't find a review for a product, post a request on the message board. ✓**AMERICA ONLINE**→*keyword* familynews→Product Reviews

MacWorld Reviews & Buyers' Tools Find the latest hardware and software for the Macintosh here, as well as an archive of over 300 reviews from the pages of *MacWorld*. Of additional interest are the Comparative Reviews (with lab tests), Bugs & Turkeys (alerts to major flaws), and Streetwise Shopper, which highlights special promotions, rebates, and bundles of note. ✓**EWORLD**→*go* buyerstools

PC Catalog A comprehensive comparision shopping directory, with thousands of listings from hundreds of direct-order vendors. ✓**PRODIGY**→*jump* pccatalog

Redgate Macintosh Product Registry Search over 7,000 listings of Mac products by keyword. ✓**AMERICA ONLINE**→*keyword* redgate ✓**EWORLD**→*go* redgate

Software Guide *Home-Office Computing* magazine provides reviews dating back to April 1988. Reviews of classic and new software are added each month. ✓**COMPUSERVE**→*go* software

ZiffNet Reviews Index The dog ate that article about PDAs in *PC Magazine*? Search this database of over 40,000 Ziff Davis articles by several categories. ✓**COMPUSERVE**→*go* znt:index

Part 2

The Big Two: Apple & IBM

The Apple World The Big Two: Apple & IBM

The Apple world

What would the world be without Apple computers? A far poorer place, no doubt. In the twenty years since Steven Jobs and Steve Wozniak joined forces to produce the first home computer with a graphical interface, Apple has grown from a $6,000 garage business to one of the most powerful corporations in the history of American industry. From early prototypes like the Lisa to the Macintosh revolution, Apple has never fallen far from the tree of success. And now Apple users can access dozens of resources online. Curious about new products? Check out **Apple Information**. Need to research the sound capabilities of your computer? Visit CompuServe's **Apple Technical Information Library**. And don't forget to keep abreast of the latest Apple action with **clari.nb.apple**.

Apple Support & Info Website—http://www.info.apple.com/

On the Net

Across the board

Apple Customer Center A product-related center for people interested in the mechanics of Apple computers. Visit Apple News and Resources for the latest press releases and product updates, or enter the Talk Back message board area to offer feedback on whatever Apple products you use. Can't stand your new PowerBook? Let the company who made it know how you feel. You'll also find direct links to the Quick Answers Technical Support Forum and the Macintosh Development Forum as well as the Apple Cafe, a real-time chat room where special guests drop by to talk about Apple computing. ✓**EWORLD**→*go* acc

Apple Information Need that system software updated? Want to know the specs on the new Quick-Take 150 camera? You'll find them here, along with everything else Apple-flavored, from product descriptions to software updates. The Smorgasbord area includes links to the Apple Virtual Campus, a list of employment opportunities with the company, and an archive of impressive QuickTime movies. ✓**INTERNET**…→*www* http://www.info.apple.com/ …→*www* ftp://ftp.info.apple.com/

Apple Support Forum Want to read about what the Multimedia Tuner's got to offer? Or maybe you're trying to locate a new version of an old favorite—HyperCard, for example? If you're looking for software updates, Apple press releases, or info on how to contact Apple, this is the place. The area includes a comprehensive library of information and software, whether it's for the Newton, the Mac, or the trusty old Apple II. ✓**COMPUSERVE**→*go* aplsup

News

Apple News Clips Avid Technology reports record quarterly revenues. MapInfo introduces a native Power Macintosh version of its desktop mapping software. Apple plans to distribute the beta version of the networking and communications system Apple Open Transport. And that's only a sam-

50 Net Tech

The Big Two: Apple & IBM The Apple World

pling of the kind of news you'll find on this computer newswire; the stories generally center on the business end of the company, with many reports focusing on news of earnings and major promotions. ✓**COMPUSERVE**→*go* applenews

clari.nb.apple (ng) "DayStar Mac Clone Aimed at High-End." "Apple Continues Strong Performance with 2Q Revenues." This moderated group offers Newsbytes (computer-industry news briefs) from the Mac world, with stories about new products and financial fortunes ("revenues up 28% over the same quarter last year"). ✓**CLARINET**

Technical support

Apple Customer Center Quick Answers What do you do when your Mac PC Exchange won't accept DOS disks? Solutions to over 10,000 Apple problems (there are that many?) are archived here, and if these answers are good enough for technical support staff at Apple, they're probably a gold mine for you. ✓**EWORLD**→*go* techinfo

Apple Customer Center Technical Support Search for and download Apple technical support information from this archive. Can't get the CD-ROM drive to work on your new Performa? Visit the Ask Apple message boards and post your query in the Performa area; a member of the Apple technical support staff will post a reply with admirable promptitude. And the massive Apple Tech Info Library contains over 12,000 articles on Apple products culled from various newspapers, magazines, and computer journals, as well as the latest product and support information posted directly from Apple's home office. ✓**EWORLD**→*go* support

Apple Tech Support For starters, this Website contains dozens of arcane details on the Mac operating system, hardware, and software, all cataloged in the Release Notes Archive and Technical Bulletins collection. Check out the Tech Info Library for the down-and-dirty details on everything from zapping the PRAM on your Quadra 630 to achieving the best video-capture rates. And you can even research the radically democratic world of Usenet technical support by perusing the searchable archives of the tech-oriented Mac newsgroups. ✓**INTERNET** …→*www* http://www.support.apple.com/ …→*www* ftp://ftp.support.apple.com/pub …→*www* gopher://ftp.support.apple.com

Apple Technical Information Library If you're looking for your Mac's VRAM requirements or the specs on that speedy new Power PC, head over to this database, which comprises thousands of articles about technical issues. The articles have titles like "System Software: Version and Enabler Matrix" and "IDE Volume Sizes," and they'll provide answers to any and all technical questions you may have about Apple products. ✓**COMPUSERVE**→*go* apltil

The pro's

Apple Worldwide Developers Conference You may have just succeeded in creating an intricate system of aliases but that doesn't quite make you a "developer" yet. On the other hand, you may be so addicted to Apples that you wouldn't miss the tech talk at this conference. Here's everything you need to know about conference registration, schedules, and vendors. ✓**INTERNET**→*www* http://wwdc.carlson.com/

CYBERNOTES

"Keyboard Shortcuts:

Cancel a Print or Copy Job: Command-. (period) keys.

Disable Virtual Memory: Hold down the Command key at startup. Do not release the key until startup is complete.

Activate Easy Access: Without moving the mouse, press the Shift key five (5) times.

Deactivate Easy Access: 1) Without moving the mouse, press the Shift key five (5) times.
2) Press any two modifier keys simultaneously.

Force Quit an Application: Press Command-Option-Esc from within the application.

Rebuild the Desktop: Restart the computer while holding down the Command-Option keys.

Take a Screen Shot: Press the Command-Shift-3 keys.

Dump of Active Window to Imagewriter: Press the Command-Shift-Caps Lock-4 keys."

—from **Apple Information**

Macintosh The Big Two: Apple & IBM

Macintosh

If Macintosh were a haiku, it might go something like this: "Happy, smiling face/Mouse to make it simple/Easy point and click." But it's not a haiku, it's a computer, and not just any computer. Since its debut in 1984, the Macintosh has proven time and time again that anyone can use a computer, and that everyone should. Kick off your personal exploration of the Net's Mac resources by visiting the **Well Connected Mac**, the **Macintosh Clubhouse Forum**, the **Macintosh Directory**, and the **Macintosh Index**. Chat about Mac matters on the **#macintosh** IRC channel. Admit your ignorance by subscribing to **Low End User**. And check in with the most venerable of Mac mags, **MacUser** and **Mac World Online**.

Happy Mac OS screenshot—http://www.austin.apple.com/macos/macosmain.html

On the Net

Across the board

Brian's Repository of Macintosh Information If you want diagrams and specs on monitors and serial ports, this is the place to visit. Brian provides the details in "meticulously constructed (well, almost) technical documents." His pages also offer links to vendors of interest to Mac enthusiasts. ✓**INTERNET**→*www* http://www.cs.wisc.edu/~tuc/mac

Macintosh Clubhouse Forum In the New Products topic, Bill wonders about the advantages of quad-speed CD-ROM drives. In Community Square, Wallace wants advice on using the Mac to put out an in-house newspaper. The Clubhouse offers a place for Mac users to chat, but it also includes libraries containing great Mac sounds, club members' resumés, and such venerable Mac publications as the Info-Mac Digest. ✓**COMPUSERVE**→*go* macclub

The Macintosh Directory Not a modest site. It bills itself as "one-stop shopping for all your Macintosh Internet Resources." What's the truth of the matter? Well, you'll find links to software, publications, vendors, Mac FAQs, and stuff labeled "sites I am not sure where to put," which include Power Macintosh info and links to help you learn AppleScript. ✓**INTERNET**→*www* http://pogo.wright.edu/mac/mac.html

Macintosh Index Like it says, an index—but a detailed and useful one, with good coverage of a wide variety of Net resources. The selection of mailing lists is particularly comprehensive, providing lists on everything from scripting and C programming to Microsoft Word and HyperCard. ✓**INTERNET**→*www* http://ici.proper.com/1/mac

Rob's Mac Page The beauty of the Web is that sometimes the enthusiastic amateurs outdo the corporate pros. Rob's Mac Page is a good example: there's pure and unconditional love in these pages (some of the icons have little apples pasted in them.) There are links to "Apple Computer's

The Big Two: Apple & IBM Macintosh

Stuff"—their websites, archives, gophers, and news section; to several Motorola and IBM PowerPC sites; shareware archives; Macintosh vendor support sites (from Adobe to WordPerfect); news sites (including MacMania by Bubba: "Bill Gates must be the only man alive with more money than brain cells"); and a couple of Macintosh user groups. ✓**INTERNET**→*www* http://www.engr.scarolina.edu/engr/users/rob/robs_mac_home.html

Robert Lentz's Macintosh Resources Check out the Mind Candy section for some entertaining QuickTime movies, Robert's favorite start-up screen ("Intel Outside" on the backdrop of a 68020), and a selection of Macintosh humor ("Apple to Enter Retail Market with Toaster"). On a more practical note, the site offers links to the usual suspects—FAQs, hardware info, etc.—along with an interesting selection of resources related to cross-platform QuickTime issues. ✓**INTERNET**→ *www* http://www.astro.nwu.edu/lentz/mac/home-mac.html

The Well Connected Mac Here you'll find the venerable "Mac Site of the Moment," a periodic review of a cool Mac spot on the Net (nominations accepted). This dynamic, up-to-date clearinghouse for Mac info offers a comprehensive set of links to Mac resources, including periodicals and vendors (more than one thousand listed). ✓**INTERNET**→*www* http://rever.nmsu.edu/~elharo/faq/Macintosh.html

Mac chat

comp.sys.mac.advocacy (ng) Here's where Mac enthusiasts do battle in their effort to have a Supreme Being declare the Macintosh the reigning champ of the personal computing world. This newsgroup has a lot of Windows-bashing, of course, but also a fair amount of introspection about the beloved Mac, with posts like "Why Mac is not as popular as it could be" and "Mac OS logo sucks." Wander around this spot for a while, and you're likely to find a post ending with a signature file prohibiting the Microsoft Network from "redistributing this work in any form, in whole or in part." ✓**USENET**

comp.sys.mac.misc (ng) If you're tired of figuring out where to post that hard-to-categorize Mac question, try this spot. Everything gets discussed here, whether it's the sticky "s" key on Sallie's Duo or Norman's rather embarrassing problems printing envelopes. One lengthy thread focused on "pronunciation trivia": "I'd like to hear, so to speak, how others pronounce Iomega." ✓**USENET**

comp.sys.mac.oop.misc (ng) One guy's complaining about his desk accessories. None of them will open. "I tried shutting virtual memory down," he writes. "No dice. Suggestions, anyone?" As soon as a question on this moderately active newsgroup is asked, the long-distance diagnostics begin. ✓**USENET**

comp.sys.mac.scitech (ng) "I'm looking for any tools which might be used to visualize 4D data," writes Jay. "Something that could render the data as slightly transparent solid volume would work well." Jay received lots of suggestions, as most techies do when asking questions in this newsgroup, where the focus is on science and mathematical issues related to the Mac. The Netheads here talk about software helpful in physics, astronomy, psychology, and other science fields. ✓**USENET**

#macintosh Byrd is talking about T1 lines, while Graphx decides to change his name to GraphX. Izzit's wondering whether he should upgrade to PowerPC. Discuss anything and everything about the Mac on this IRC channel. ✓**INTERNET**→*irc* #macintosh

Macintosh Application Environment-Bugs (ml) Is there a bug in an Apple-created application that has been driving you up the wall? Tell the Apple engineers and programmers on this list. In other words, COMPLAIN! Apple won't guarantee that your submission (or diatribe) will be answered, but stranger things have happened. ✓**INTERNET**→*email* listproc@medraut.apple.com ✎ *Type in message body:* subscribe mae-bugs <your full name>

Instruction

Mac Bible This is not a religious

> "Everything gets discussed here, whether it's the sticky 's' key on Sallie's Duo or Norman's rather embarrassing problems printing envelopes."

Macintosh The Big Two: Apple & IBM

forum—unless you worship your Macintosh. What you'll find here is assistance for Macintosh beginners and information promoting sales of the popular book, *The Mac Bible*. Great for true tyros and anyone needing refresher help in Mac facts. ✓**AMERICA ONLINE**→*keyword* macbible

Mac FAQs "How can I take a picture of the screen?" (Press command-shift-3.) "I think I've found a new virus. What do I do?" (Don't post a report on the Net. Instead, try consulting the local Mac guru.) Answers to thousands of Mac-related questions can be found in these FAQs, including the comp.human-factors FAQ, the Macintosh Duo FAQ, the AppleScript FAQ, the Mac Programmer FAQ, the Macintosh Screensaver FAQ, and many more. ✓**INTERNET**…→*www* http://www.astro.nwu.edu/lentz/mac/faqs/home-faqs.html …→*www* http://ici.proper.com/mac/faqs …→*www* http://www.cis.ohio-state.edu:80/text/faq/usenet/macintoshtop.html

MacAcademy Online Want to go to Macintosh school on the Net? Consult the OnLine Class Schedule and sign up for weekly courses on Macintosh for beginners, System 7.5 features, Mac & DOS/Windows, basic Mac networking, Mac troubleshooting, or Mac desktop publishing. The courses take place in one of the eWorld conference rooms (shortcut "erooms") on various evenings from 6 p.m. to 7 p.m. PST. Good luck trying to get the teacher's attention, though—the courses usually erupt into free-for-alls in which every member of the room demands technical support assistance. ✓**EWORLD**→*go* macacademy →OnLine Class Schedules

Macintosh New Users and

Quadra 650—from http://www.info.apple.com

Help Forum Any question's fair game in this forum, whether you're wondering about switching to System 7.5 or looking for advice on how to recover a mistakenly trashed file. The area is geared to new users, but everyone's welcome. The libraries have an extensive selection of system, disk, and anti-virus tools. ✓**COMPUSERVE**→*go* macnew

Operating systems

comp.sys.mac.system (ng) "System 7.5.1 bugs/weirdness," "Forgot my After Dark password," "My icons have disappeared!" Lots of people with heartbreaking Macintosh problems and questions in this newsgroup, and a few willing to offer solutions. The group's focus is the Mac operating system, but that doesn't mean you won't find interlopers trying to sell a CD-ROM drive or a PowerBook 180. This is an active group, and a good place to visit if you're having problems with desktop patterns, extensions, and the like. ✓**USENET**

Macintosh Operating Systems Forum A meeting place dedicated to the workings of the Mac operating system. The message boards are divided into subgroups, covering topics like "In-

stallations," "General Q & A," and "Hints & Tips." There's also a direct connection to vendors whose products complement the Mac OS. The software library offers downloadable system enabler files, PPD's, and third party software. You'll also find documentation files and conference transcripts ready to download. And the "Critical Files" area contains important new Mac software, such as the latest Laserwriter drivers. Only the "News Update" area is disappointing—it's limited to corportorial materials, press releases put out by Apple. ✓**AMERICA ONLINE**→*keyword* mos

Mac OS and System Software Technologies Home Page Profusely decorated with the Happy Mac face, this site is Apple's official Website for the Macintosh operating system. Offering general information for Mac users, the page also includes technical specifications for the programmer, software updates for the home user, and links to extensive information about System 7.5, 7.5 enhancements, and Copland, a code name for the operating system that will run on the common IBM-Motorola platform due in mid-1996. ✓**INTERNET**→*www* http://www.austin.apple.com/macos/macosmain.html

Macintosh System Software (ml) Get the latest scoop on Mac system software upgrades and related information. Find out how System 7.5 improves upon its predecessor, or discuss Apple's next upgrade. ✓**INTERNET**→*email* listserv@listserv.dartmouth.edu ✍ *Type in message body:* subscribe macsystm <your full name>

Software

alt.sources.mac (ng) Martin

54 Net Tech

The Big Two: Apple & IBM Macintosh

wants the code for a program that generates poems. François offers an attempt at a short, clean, ShowINIT clone: "It compiles with CodeWarrior 5.5, requires System 7, and is as short as possible. Feel free to use it!" Not as active as some other Mac newsgroups, but still a nice place for developers to share source code philosophy, source code secrets, or source code itself. ✓**USENET**

Claris Macintosh Forum A forum for technical questions relating to Claris Macintosh products. Post messages for a Claris representative on one of the message boards (separated into product categories such as ClarisWorks and MacWrite) and then visit the software libraries for software add-ons. The ClarisWorks library includes great add-ons like Grade Sheet (for high school teachers looking to record grades), as well as text files supplementing the ClarisWorks manuals. ✓**COMPUSERVE**→*go* macclaris

comp.binaries.mac (ng) Newsgroup containing long "threads" of binary-encoded utilities files for the Macintosh—a FullWrite upgrader, for instance, or a Quicken update. Decode them with BinHex or uuDecode. ✓**USENET**

comp.sys.mac.apps (ng) An active group for people looking for the right software ("Genealogy software recommendations?"), yearning for a technical mentor ("Can Eudora Open URLs?"), or wondering about new versions of old favorites ("Word 6.01 Upgrade?"). Lots of discussion here, some of it off-topic, like the thread about whether the Mac is the greatest computer ever made ("I think I love my Macintosh more than life itself," claims one poster). ✓**USENET**

Dartmouth College Macintosh Software A repository of freeware and shareware for the Mac, developed at Dartmouth College. Includes vital applications like Fetch, a popular program that lets you download files from remote machines, and provides access to a directory called MedEd which contains a host of Mac applications for medical education. ✓**INTERNET**→*www* gopher://gopher.dartmouth.edu:70/11/ Anon-FTP/pub/mac

Hands on with ZiffNet/Mac Tips, information, and software to help you maximize the use of your Macintosh. The Starter Kits software library has dozens of shareware tool kits and add-ons for your existing system. Want to jump-start your dormant PowerBook before taking it on the road? Download a battery discharger, a keyboard extensions control panel for easier number crunching, and a PowerStrip that displays all the vital stats of your PowerBook (like available RAM and remaining battery power) directly on your desktop. Also check out the large archive of Mac-related FAQ's taken from Usenet newsgroups, or

> "Want to flame a venerable word-processing program? Sure you do! Head to the topic on 'Word 6.0's interface sins.'"

the database of over 1,000 tips and tricks for more productive computing. The site also includes a message board and a chat room for sharing hints on improving the performance of the Macintosh, and for providing help to fellow Mac users. ✓**EWORLD**→*go* handson

Info-Mac Digest (ml) Wondering what's new in Macdom? Find out the latest about the Info-Mac Archive, a massive collection of Mac software. Each issue's got scads of reviews for software of all shapes and sizes. What, you ask? Well, there's Coffee Break 2.1 ("designed to help prevent repetitive stress injuries") and Mazeworld Catacombs 1.0.3 ("a fast-paced arcade-style game"). The Website is great, with a search utility and links to spots where you can download the files you want. ✓**INTERNET**→*email* listserv@ricevm1.rice.edu ✍ *Type in message body:* subscribe info-mac <your full name> *Archives:* ✓**AMERICA ONLINE**→*keyword* mcm→Software Libraries→Info-Mac Digests ✓**INTERNET**→*www* http://dutera.et.tudelft.nl/people/vdham/info-mac/

Info-Mac Archive When Netters think about Macintosh shareware, they think about this site. It's huge. You'll find everything you want here, from fonts to graphics utilities to games to programming utilities to communications software to sound players. The first address offers a searchable archive with brief descriptions of the software. ✓**INTERNET** …→ *www* http://cag-www.lcs.mit.edu/HyperArchive.html …→*www* gopher://gopher.archive.merit.edu:7055/11/mac …→*www* ftp://sumex-aim.stanford.edu/info-mac/ …→*www* ftp://mirror.apple.com/mirrors/Info-Mac.Archive/ …→ *www* ftp://wuarchive.wustl.edu/systems/mac/info-mac/

Net Tech 55

Macintosh The Big Two: Apple & IBM

Mac Applications Forum Want to flame a venerable word-processing program? Sure you do! Head to the topic on "Word 6.0's interface sins," where discussions, somehow, can devolve into strange arguments about British and American cars. Applications of all kinds are covered in this forum, whether you're looking to talk about illustration, page layout, word-processing, or multimedia software. The libraries include a huge archive of tools, utilities, and demos for downloading.
✓**COMPUSERVE**→go macapp

Mac Demos, Shareware & Stuff If you're the type of consumer who prefers to "test drive" a product before buying, then you'll like this library of demos on AOL. The applications are separated into roughly a dozen different categories that range from communications to spreadsheets to games. The majority of the demos allow you to try out the program on a limited basis. If you like what you see, get the complete package using the ordering information provided here. ✓**AMERICA ONLINE**→keyword komando→Software Libraries→Mac Demos, Shareware & Stuff

Mac File Finder Looking for a piece of Mac software, but not sure where to find it? File Finder provides a searchable database of files from CompuServe's Mac forums. It's quick, easy, and a good way to avoid searching through lots of libraries. A search for the keywords "SCSI" and "update," for instance, rapidly located the 630 SCSI Update 1.0, a fix for SCSI problems with the 630 series. ✓**COMPUSERVE**→go macff

Mac Shareware 500 Ever sit up nights wondering what the 500 most popular Macintosh shareware files might be? Not only can you browse through the entire collection here, but if a file piques your interest, you can download it right away. There are also message boards, in case you need some advice or a shareware review. The list is categorized by topics, such as utilities, fonts, and business, but there's a main area that collects the best shareware, as well—it's called "Most of the Best." So what is the most popular shareware file? According to the list, the number one program is "The Standalone Grouch," a freeware program that patches your desktop trash can so that it includes Sesame Street's loveable homeless puppet, Oscar the Grouch. ✓**AMERICA ONLINE**→keyword mac500

Mac Software A vast library of public domain and shareware files is available in this area, and the library is searchable by specific file name or keywords, such as "games and checkers." The Quickfinder feature lets you narrow your search with more complex commands. You can also go directly to smaller libraries which have been organized by subject matter. If you choose to browse, you'll find separate folders for games, desktop publishing, education, and utilities, to name a few. There are even specialty libraries, which offer files recommended by moderators of other forums. The moderators also provide a "Top Downloads" list of the most popular files, as well as a "Downloading Hall of Fame" and a "Weekly New Files" listing. And beginners will thank their lucky stars for the "Downloading Tips and Hints"—if you memorize them, you'll soon be the life of any party. ✓**AMERICA ONLINE**→keyword macsoftware

Mac Software Have a question about Pagemaker, Claris Works,

CYBERNOTES

"Apple needs to be fighting for its life right now. The price of a base-model 6100/66 should be less than $1000; Apple should be flooding the market with low-end PowerPCs and blasting its logo all over everyone's TV screen. Its marketing should be in deficit spending now, with advertisements pointing out that most of the things which Win95 promises were available on Macs five years ago. I've seen Win95, and it is good. Microsoft's marketing, on the other hand, has been revolutionary. Betas of Copland should be in the hands of all major Mac developers NOW. That brings up another interesting point: I hear from various computer-industry pundits that the Mac interface simply looks dated. I don't give a hoot about 3-D buttons and colored menu bars, but apparently a lot of people really do...especially the kind of people who are wandering around Fry's Electronics looking for their first computer."

—from `comp.sys.mac.advocacy`

The Big Two: Apple & IBM Macintosh

FileMaker Pro, Word, or Netscape on the Mac? Post it in this topic, and wait for answers from helpful Mac friends or bossy know-it-alls. Used primarily for specific software questions, the topic is also a good place to keep abreast of new Mac products. ✓**PRODIGY**→*jump* computerbb→Choose a Topic→ Mac Software

Mac Software A basic collection of software sites on the Net, with links to Info-Mac and the University of Michigan archives. Other links provide the latest versions of Disinfectant and UnStuffIt. ✓**INTERNET**→*www* http://alpha.acast.nova.edu/software/mac.html

MacAppli (ml) A mailing list specializing in usage tips about Macintosh applications. List members swap tips and tricks with hundreds of other Mac users. ✓**INTERNET**→*email* listserv@listserv.dartmouth.edu ✎ *Type in message body:* subscribe macappli <your full name>

Macintosh Archives Search The site provides a search interface for Mac files at the University of Michigan and Info-Mac archives—the two biggest Mac software sites online. A handy, quick tool for looking for software. ✓**INTERNET**→*www* http://www.msc.wku.edu/Dept/MSC/Macintosh/search_umich.html

Macintosh OS/System Software Forum On the message board under System Conflicts, you'll find topics such as "Desktop won't rebuild" and "Power Mac system freezes," where users share their woes. The message boards cover lots of system-wide issues, including control panels, utilities, and fonts, and the libraries include an excellent selection of software.

Power Macintosh/Power PC

Home Page

PowerPC Home Page—from http://www.info.apple.com/ppc/ppchome.html

✓**COMPUSERVE**→*go* macsys

Macintosh Software Catalog A hypertext catalog of the University of Michigan's archives of shareware and public domain software. You can browse the catalog, search it, and download files. ✓**INTERNET**→*www* http://web.nexor.co.uk/public/mac/archive/welcome.html

Macintosh Software on the Net A well-organized collection of links to Net spots with Mac software. You'll find the usual suspects, like the archives at the University of Michigan and Info-Mac, but you'll also find links to less well-known sites, like one at the Champaign-Urbana Macintosh User Group and another connected with the comp.binaries.mac newsgroup. ✓**INTERNET**→*www* http://rever.nmsu.edu/~elharo/faq/software.html

MacShareNews (ml) A free electronic publication reporting on shareware and freeware programs for the Macintosh and the Newton. ✓**INTERNET**→*email* steg@dircon.co.uk ✎ *Type in subject line:* MSN-request *Type in message body:* subscribe msn <your full name>

OTS Mac Software Archive SoundMachine 2.1, Moire 4.0.1, JPEGView 3.3.1—you'll find these programs, and many more, at this excellent collection of Macintosh software. You can review the collection by author, date, and product, or you can browse sections devoted to applications, games, graphics, and other topics. The site includes descriptions of programs, contact info, and plenty of files for download. ✓**INTERNET**→*www* http://wwwhost.ots.utexas.edu/mac/main.html

Popular Macintosh Files A collection of popular files for the Mac—StuffIt Lite, Compact Pro, Eudora, Disinfectant, and others. It also provides a basic how-to for file-transfer novices, along with a short review of the best FTP sites. ✓**INTERNET**→*www* http://proper.com:70/1/mac/files

University of Michigan Macintosh Archive Next to the Info-Mac archives, this site carries the most comprehensive collection of Mac shareware online. Applications are divided into a series of directories, including HyperCard, sound, games, graphics programs, utilities, and system extensions. ✓**INTERNET** …→*www* http://www.umich.edu/~archive/mac …→*www* ftp://mirror.apple.com:/mirrors/mac.archive.umich.edu …→*www* ftp://wuarchive.wustl.edu:systems/mac/umich.edu …→*www* ftp://grind.isca.uiowa.edu:mac/umich

ZiffNet/Mac In addition to online editions of popular Ziff publications such as *MacWeek* and *MacWorld*, this area includes a guide to computer buying, an online computer library, and a software support database with the latest advice and software updates for your favorite applications. The

Net Tech 57

Macintosh The Big Two: Apple & IBM

Help Desk search engine for the support database is wonderful—just plug in the name of a program, and it returns the number of related documents in the database. Receiving error messages on Microsoft Word? Simply select the Error Message button. Having installation and setup problems? Click on Getting Started. Then, when prompted, answer diagnostic questions related to your problem and wait as the search responds. In most cases, the engine narrows your query down to one or two highly relevant documents, making this one of the best online support resources for Macintosh users. ✓**COMPUSERVE**→ *go zmac*

ZiffNet/Mac Download Software and Support Forum On CompuServe, the massive software library provides all the latest Internet goodies for the Mac, including Anarchie 1.5.0 and other software you need to "fetch, browse, mark up, finger, and otherwise roll about the Net." Other neat software includes Job Hunt Manager, which sets up mailing and calling campaigns for the harried job seeker, and Coffee Break, a background application that forces you to take breaks from your computer so as to avoid repetitive stress injury and eyestrain. Simply enter the desired amount of work time and break time, and Coffee Break will lock you out of your computer when it's time to cool your workaholic heels. The message boards in these forums provide technical support for each and every application. If you're flummoxed by the online world, visit the Internet Help area—after only a few minutes, you'll realize that you're not the only one whose Netscape constantly freezes up. The eWorld version of the support forum is friendlier and better organized than its CompuServe counterpart, and you'll find the same programs mentioned above in the Software Central shareware library. You can also easily jump to other Ziff/Davis eWorld sites. ✓**COMPUSERVE**→*go* downtech ✓**EWORLD**→ *go* shareware

Hardware

comp.sys.mac.hardware (ng) Markus wants advice on what to do about the dead motherboard in his Color Classic, while Mike wonders if anyone's running the beta version of Windows 95 on a PowerMac 6100 with the DOS card. No matter if you're high-end or low-end, whether you have got a Mac Plus with a single floppy or a super-charged 8100, this is a prime place on the Net to talk Mac hardware. All issues and products are covered at one time or another, but some, like the virtues of Zip versus SyQuest drives, generate frantic debate on the newsgroup. ✓**USENET**

Mac Hardware Don't have enough memory? No one ever does, but if you have a specific question, other Mac users here might be able to help. (No, 4 MB of RAM is not enough to run Photoshop and QuarkXPress at the same time!) The topic covers all facets of Mac hardware, including CD-ROM drives, printers, PowerMacs, hard disks, and even mouses (mice?). This active topic about Macintosh hardware also allows you to ask the wise counsel of Mac experts. ✓**PRODIGY**→*jump* computerbb→ Choose a Topic→ Mac Hardware

Mac Hardware (ml) A mailing list devoted to Macintosh hardware and related peripherals, including Apple scanners, laser printers, and CD-ROM drives.

> "Simply enter the desired amount of work time and break time, and Coffee Break will lock you out of your computer when it's time to cool your workaholic heels."

✓**INTERNET**→*email* listserv@listserv.dartmouth.edu ✍ *Type in message body:* subscribe machrdwr <your full name>

Macav-L (ml) If you've been dreaming of a mailing list that caters to Macintosh Quadra 660AV & 840AV users, wake up and smile—it's here. Get on this list of more than 500 Quadra users, and you'll be able to swap software tips and industry lore to your heart's content. Are high-end Performas really just Quadras with a different name? Where does that leave the Centris? Visit the list to find out. ✓**INTERNET**→*email* listserv @uafsysb.uark.edu ✍ *Type in message body:* subscribe macav-l <your full name>

Macintosh Hardware Forum If you're thinking about purchasing a new modem for your Powerbook, trying to repair a faulty hard drive on a Performa, or merely musing about the latest data storage technologies, you'll find plenty of helpful information in this forum. Besides message boards dedicated to scanners, printers, and

The Big Two: Apple & IBM Macintosh

monitors, the forum also offers direct access to computer industry vendors. The software libraries provide lots of utilities like hard drive formatters, and the "Virus Information Center" collects a series of texts on computer viruses, along with discussion boards and anti-virus tools. And if you want a more social experience, the moderators of this forum host live conferences every Tuesday night at 9 p.m. EST. ✓**AMERICA ONLINE**→*keyword* mhw

Macintosh Hardware Forum Everything's covered here, from questions about using a Mac Plus to connect to the Internet to speeding up the video on a Power Macintosh 7100. There's some talk of upcoming products, but most of the discussion centers around the quirks, both good and bad, of the various existing Macintosh models, along with printers, scanners, and other peripherals. The libraries include info on new product releases and hardware-specific software, like MyBattery, a monitoring utility for PowerBooks. ✓**COMPUSERVE**→*go* machw

Performa Resource Center Performa owners can exchange information about software and hardware or download Performa-specific utilities and files. If you're thinking about purchasing a Performa, there are detailed descriptions of every model in the "Technical Specifications" area. And if you think that a Performa is a new kind of ultra-strong vacuum cleaner, visit the news center, which collects Apple's press releases about the machines. Experienced Performa owners would probably be better off skipping this forum altogether and joining the general Macintosh community instead. ✓**AMERICA ONLINE**→*keyword* performa

History

H-MAC History and Macintosh Society (ml) Devoted to the history of Macintosh, this mailing list selects its members by a complex process of recommendation and approval—exactly the kind of club Groucho Marx would have abhorred. But if H-MAC will have you, you can chew the fat with like-minded historians about the Macintosh and its role in the history of computing. ✓**INTERNET**→ *email* listserv@msu.edu ✍ *Type in message body:* subscribe h-mac <your full name>

News

Ambrosia Times An idiosyncratic and highly interactive Maczine produced by Ambrosia Software, with topics like Rumorcide, Shareware in Jeopardy, and Kudos & Criticism. The zine requires downloading, but once you've got it on your Mac, you'll find a stand-alone document with lots of worthwhile info on Ambrosia products, illustrated with text, photos, and sounds (a guy snoring, for instance). And while the publication is oriented toward the customer, it's lots of fun to peruse, what with all the buttons and graphics. ✓**INTERNET**→*www* http://ats4.colorado.edu/OLM/Ambrosia/AT.html

comp.sys.mac.announce (ng) Infrequent announcements about issues of interest to Mac users, such as the proposed creation of a set of Mac-specific game-related newsgroups. ✓**USENET**

comp.sys.mac.digest (ng) A newsgroup devoted to disseminating the best of the electronic newsletters with a Mac focus, including Mac*Chat, the Info-Mac Digest, and TidBITS. The publications offered here provide scads of useful information on shareware, products, programming, and everything else related to the Mac. ✓**USENET**

Low End User A mag for the "average" Mac user—in other words, those who don't give prime shelf space to *Inside Macintosh*. Issues contain news and rumors ("The Death of NuBus?"), tips and advice ("PowerPC and buying/selling a Mac"), and other sections with info on software bugs, bargains, and product reviews. ✓**INTERNET**→*www* http://ats4.colorado.edu/OLM/LEU/LEU.html

Mac Format Billed as Britain's best-selling Macintosh mag, *Mac Format* carries the latest news, along with features like "Take your Mac into the 21st century." Check out the ultimate Mac add-ons at this electronic version of the publication. Back issues provide descriptions of the contents, but—how annoying—not the articles themselves. Take your *mag* into the 21st century, guys. ✓**INTERNET**→ *www* http://www.futurenet.co.uk/computing/macformat.html

MAC Home Journal Online This magazine for Macintosh users promises to skip all the technical nonsense and get right down to helping you be more productive with your Macintosh. The forum has message boards, software libraries, and chat rooms for homebodies with a Mac. ✓**AMERICA ONLINE**→*keyword* machome

Mac Net Journal Some great articles here, such as "In the Digital Media: The Evolving Face of Multimedia on the Net," along with news and a collection of Mac links. The site contains an archive of past issues; each issue of the publication includes an especially

Net Tech 59

Macintosh The Big Two: Apple & IBM

useful collection of reviews of shareware programs, such as SCSI Probe and Software FPU. ✓**INTERNET**→*www* http://www.dgr.com/web_mnj/

MacHead "Brycian, Bryce-like, KPT Inspired, fractal terrains. These catch phrases and many others like them have germinated in our culture to describe the awesome output of KPTBryce." So begins one review in this small yet growing collection of Mac news and reviews. Other products covered include Fractal Design Dabbler and Square One 2.0. ✓**INTERNET**→*www* http://www.awa.com/nct/software/maclead.html

Macintosh News and Information (ml) Why wait for your *MacWorld* or *MacUser* to arrive by snail mail when you can get all the latest Macintosh computer news sent directly to your emailbox? There are over a thousand subscribers to this mailing list and you can just bet someone here will post the scoop on the latest PowerBook upgrades or the next wave of Mac platforms. ✓**INTERNET**→*email* listserv@yalevm.cis.yale.edu ✍ *Type in message body:* subscribe mac-l <your full name>

The Macintosh On-Line Magazine Database Links to several Macintosh-related e-zines. ✓**INTERNET**→*www* http://ats4.colorado.edu/olm/zines.html

The Macintosh Online Magazine Database Archives of a number of Mac zines, including the *Mac Net Journal*, *Low End User*, *MacSense*, and the *Ambrosia Times*. ✓**INTERNET**→*www* http://ats4.colorado.edu/olm/zines.html

Macintosh Software Update Report A newsletter for Mac network managers, with the electronic version available only to subscribers—though you can check out a sample issue. The publication details the incremental changes being made in software updates. The November '94 issue, for instance, reports on changes to Freehand to speed up the "selection and transformation of an object or a group of objects." The site includes a frequently updated list of Websites for Mac vendors; the data includes tech-support contacts, fax numbers, and even snail mail addresses. ✓**INTERNET**→*www* http://webcom.com/~level6/

MacSense *MacSense* sees its mission as detailing the most significant stories in the world of Macintosh computing and exploring how these developments affect "every-day Mac users." It includes opinion pieces, reviews of a variety of products (the QuickTake 100 camera, the Power Macintosh Upgrade Card, etc.), and info on what's coming soon for Mac computing. ✓**INTERNET**→*www* http://ats4.colorado.edu/OLM/MacSense/MS.html

MacTech Magazine Formerly *MacTutor* magazine, this online journal is for Macintosh programmers and developers and includes product and contact information, outdated message boards, and a software library containing such cryptic items as object method dispatchers and sprocket draggers. Neophytes will find themselves dazed and confused by much of the jargon here. ✓**AMERICA ONLINE**→*keyword* mactechmag

MacUser Selected stories from *MacUser*, like the "Internet Buyer's Guide" and "Niceties on the Net" ("Ten rules of Net etiquette that will keep you from getting flamed,

---

CYBERNOTES

"I'm thinking about upgrading my Quadra 605 with the Power-Card 601, but I'm wondering if it's worth it."

"We've used Apple's PowerPC card (different card) on a Quadra 650 and have had several problems. Given the price of the PowerPC card and the price of a 6100/66, I would honestly suggest selling your 605 and just buying a new machine. The 6100/66 has a 256K Level 2 cache which gives it pretty good performance, immeasurably better than the 50MHz the upgrade card would give you. My only personal complaint about the 6100 is that it only supports 256 colors at 16" and doesn't support 19", two features that my trusty 605 does. I'm in the same situation with my 605, but I'm thinking I'll wait for a low-end 604 machine that should become available and upgrade the entire machine. Apple also might come out with a machine which would provide a motherboard swap for the 605."

—from `comp.sys.mac.hardware`

---

60 Net Tech

The Big Two: Apple & IBM Macintosh

plus help for newbies on how to stay virus-free in your travels"). The site includes columns from the mag, Mac news, a product index, archived articles, contact information, and links to other Mac spots on the Web, as chosen by *MacUser* editors. ✓**INTERNET**→ *www* http://www.macuser.ziff.com/~macuser/

MacUser (European) The European version of *MacUser*, with archived articles and reviews on everything from Netscape Navigator and FrameMaker to Mac clones and making money on the Internet. ✓**INTERNET**→*www* http://www.atlas.co.uk/macuser/macuser.htm

MacUser Forum Articles from this month's issue aren't here yet, but you can post letters to the *MacUser* editors on the message board and download recommended demos or surveys and indices from the libraries. ✓**COMPUSERVE**→ *go* macuser ✓**EWORLD**→*go* MacUser Forum

MacUser Online News, reviews, and feature articles from the popular print monthly as well as Macintosh software libraries, message boards, and conference rooms. ✓**EWORLD**→*go* macuser

MacWeek Download or review this week's news from the current issue of *MacWeek*. ✓**COMPUSERVE**→*go* zmc:macnews

MacWeek Selected articles and information from the latest issue, along with an archive of back issues. The reporting is up to date, with reports on the newest products and goings-on at Apple headquarters. If you're the type who wants the latest on what's happening in the world of the Mac, check out this site weekly for what's new.

MacUser *cover—from http://www.ziff.com:8007/~macuser/*

✓**INTERNET**→ *www* http://www.ziff.com/~macweek/

MacWeek Forum Use this forum to contact the *MacWeek* editors or download articles and product reviews from the libraries (just search by product name). ✓**COMPUSERVE**→*go* macweek

MacWeek Online Online edition of one of the leading industry magazines in the Macintosh computing world. Contains news, reviews, and features from the print version in addition to software libraries, message boards, and weekly conferences with editors and writers from the magazine. Keep on top of Mac happenings before they hit *MacWeek*'s Monday print edition by downloading the top 20 Mac-related stories every Friday evening. ✓**EWORLD**→*go* mac week

MacWorld OnLine This online version of the granddaddy of monthly Mac mags includes feature articles and columns from the print version, as well as software libraries and weekly live events on Thursday and Sunday evenings. A nice graphical interface and a convenient archive of *MacWorld* back issues make this one of the best online magazines. ✓**EWORLD**→ *go* macworld ✓**AMERICA ONLINE**→ *keyword* macworld

Rosenthal on Mac Twice a week Steve Rosenthal, who also writes a New Media column for *MacWeek*, reports on the Macintosh for Prodigy users. Anything Mac goes. He has followed happenings at Apple Corp., told his readers how to clean Macintosh hardware, and prophesied the coming of Mac clones. Prodigy archives more than a year's worth of columns. ✓**PRODIGY**→ *jump* rosenthalonmac

TidBITS Reports on the latest in the world of computers, with an emphasis on Macs. Eclectic content, and well written, too. One issue, for instance, included talk of the Microsoft anti-trust case, a report on the Third International World-Wide Web Conference, and a review of Clifford Stoll's book *Silicon Snake Oil*. If you're serious about your Mac, this is a must-read. ✓**INTERNET** ...→*www* http://www.tidbits.com/tidbits/ ...→*www* ftp://ftp.tidbits.com/pub/tidbits/ ...→*www* http://www.dartmouth.edu/pages/TidBITS/TidBITS.html

ZMac Home of ZiffNet/Mac, an online publishing division of Ziff Communications. The site links to articles from *MacUser* and *MacWeek*, and provides info on the ZiffNet/Mac services available on CompuServe, eWorld, and AppleLink. ✓**INTERNET**→ *www* http://www.ziff.com/~zmac/

Vendors

Buyer's Assistant Great reference site with product reviews, shareware demos, and a message

Net Tech 61

Macintosh The Big Two: Apple & IBM

board for Mac users who want to add hardware or software to their existing system—or buy an entirely new one. Browse the Product Reviews library for articles culled from various Ziff/Davis publications including *MacWeek* and *MacUser*, or check out the Buyer's Basics area for itemized text files on everything from installing your own RAM upgrades to finding the best low-cost scanners. You can also test out various commercial software and shareware demos before you commit to buying them. Ziff/Davis sysops administer the message board, so if you want the scoop on the best 20 monitors directly from the experts, just post away. ✓EWORLD→*go* baz

Macintosh Vendor Forums Wondering whether you can bring your new Zip disk into the desert? Check out the Iomega area, where you'll learn the disk should "live from -40c to 60c, temperature-wise." The vendor forums allow customers to speak with the support staff at companies such as Aladdin Systems, Mirror Technologies, and Daystar Digital. You can offer suggestions, seek advice, or just gripe about a software bug or hardware problem that's giving you a headache. The libraries often include demos and software updates. ✓COMPUSERVE→*go* macaven *and* macbven, *and* maccven *and* macdven

MacWorld Reviews and Buyer's Tools A clearinghouse for featured articles and reviews compiled from back issues of *MacWorld* magazine. The place to go when you need product reviews on everything from word processors to modems to personal digital assistants. Organized and archived into various categories, including Bugs & Turkeys, which keeps you abreast of all the screw-ups and annoyances currently facing Macintosh users, and Editor's Choice, where top picks from *MacWorld* features can be found. ✓EWORLD→*go* buyerstools

Redgate: The Macintosh Product Registry Complete listings of more than 7,000 Macintosh-related products, with an easy-to-use search engine to help you find all the software you'll need to get up and running on the Mac. Need a word processor? Search the database to decide which one is right for you. ✓EWORLD→*go* redgate ✓AMERICA ONLINE→*keyword* redgate

Straight to the Source Dozens of computer hardware and software companies float press releases and software update information here, but it's also a place to go for product demos from companies like Claris, DeltaPoint, and Global Village. Emigré, that cool font dealer from Sacramento, has a program you can download called Now Serving!, which lets you view all the unusual fonts in the Emigré type foundries. ✓EWORLD→*go* stts

PowerMac

comp.sys.powerpc (ng) A freewheeling group for talk of everything PowerPC-related, whether you're looking for the PPC instruction set, wondering about clock chipping, or searching for a cheap price on a PowerMac 6100. Mostly Mac talk, though IBM does get mentioned here and there. ✓USENET

MACPPC-L (ml) This mailing list specializes in all aspects of computing on the PowerPC. Get the latest product updates and industry news delivered right to your e-mailbox and post questions—there are over 500 subscribers on hand to help you out. ✓INTERNET →*email* listserv@yalevm.cis.yale.edu ✍ *Type in message body:* subscribe macppc-l <your full name>

Porting to PowerPC If you're thinking of porting an application to the PowerPC, here's a great set of references to help make the transition as smooth as possible. The resources include an overview of what it takes to make an application native, info from "Inside Macintosh," and lots of other links for PowerPC programming and architecture. ✓INTERNET →*www* http://www.info.apple.com/dev/devinfo/powerpc.html

Power Macintosh Apple's handy home page for the Power Macintosh includes the "Power-Mac White Paper," a comprehensive market and technology overview for third-party developers. The document covers developer benefits ("larger market for your product"), a hardware overview ("why RISC"), and how to get started ("tools for the transition"). The site also includes hardware configurations and a useful list of native PowerMac products currently shipping. ✓INTERNET→*www* http://www.info.apple.com/ppc/ppchome.html

> "Can you bring your Zip disk into the desert? Check the Iomega area. You'll learn it should 'live from -40c to 60c, temperature-wise.'"

The Big Two: Apple & IBM Macintosh

PowerPC News screenshot—from http://power.globalnews.com/

The Power Macintosh Connection This site offers a useful collection of resources related to PowerPC Macs, with links to news about the PowerPC, a clock-chipping homepage, and info for users of the built-in Ethernet on Power-Macs. The site also includes links to spots on the Net with general Apple and Mac info. ✓ **INTERNET**→*www* http://www.phys.unm.edu/~pvg/ppcc/

Power Macintosh Support If you're having some trouble with the transition to PowerPC, visit this spot for advice from the experts. It includes answers to frequently asked questions, info on the latest Power Macintosh software, and tips from Apple's Power Macintosh support team. ✓ **INTERNET**→*www* http://www.info.apple.com/powermac/powermac.html

PowerMac The latest scoop on PowerMac technology waits for you in this AOL forum. Ask questions, speculate on future releases, and exchange practical information with Power Mac owners and software developers. There is even a prominent "Feedback to Apple" message board. The software library offers utilities, patches, and upgrades for popular programs, as well as programs specifically designed to run "native" in the Power Mac environment. There are detailed specs for the different machines, as well as links to archives of press releases pertaining to Power Mac technology. ✓ **AMERICA ONLINE**→*keyword* mhw→Power Mac Center

PowerPC FAQ Seeking answers to basic questions about the future of Macintosh and the PowerPC series of microprocessors? The FAQ answers newbie questions ("What is a PowerPC microprocessor and why is Apple putting it in Macintosh computers?") and those from more experienced techies ("What development environments are available for compiling Mac PPC code?"). ✓ **INTERNET**→*www* http://www.cis.ohio-state.edu/hypertext/faq/usenet/macintosh/PowerPC-FAQ/faq.html

PowerPC News An excellent electronic magazine about everything PowerPC. The mag offers articles on a variety of topics, ranging from IBM's PowerPC plans to the latest on Mac clones. In the Computerwire section, you'll find the latest info industry-wide, whether it's from Microsoft, Intel, Motorola, or other firms. The PowerPC Resources section of the publication points you to the latest and best spots on the Net of interest to PowerPC users. ✓ **INTERNET**→*www* http://power.globalnews.com/

Programming

Apple Developer The site offers a good starting point for both newbies and more experienced developers. It includes info on the current World Wide Web Developers Conference, relevant news ("Apple Files Suit Against Intel and Microsoft"), the Macintosh Developers Guide, and a link to the tech support page for developers (newbies should check out the excellent section labeled "Starting to program Macintosh computers"). A link to the Developer Services FTP site provides tools, documentation, and software for developers. ✓ **INTERNET** …→*www* http://www.info.apple.com/dev/ …→*www* ftp://ftp.info.apple.com/Apple.Supprt.Area/Developer_Services/

comp.sys.mac.oop.macapp3 (ng) "As far as I can tell, everything declared global or accessed like 'fHeapList' is getting flagged as being redeclared (the U<<classname>>.cp files really go nuts)." You understand this, you got yourself a newsgroup to revel in the idiosyncracies of MacApp3—a Macintosh applications developers tool. Don't ask these people how to empty the trash can, but if you're one of them—an ultra tech-head, basically—they're friendly and willing to help you with the troubling aspects of using MacApp. Many posts describe tricky problems, and then end with a query like this one: "Does anyone have any ideas on how to debug this?" More times than not, someone else has had a similar problem—and if not, you've managed to create a whole new class of Mac snafu. ✓ **USENET**

Macintosh The Big Two: Apple & IBM

comp.sys.mac.programmer.codewarrior (ng) A newsgroup for those who favor the highly popular CodeWarrior as a software development system for the Mac, such as the programmer who wrote, "Environment is nice, support is *great*, and our code productivity has gone up." ✓**USENET**

comp.sys.mac.programmer.help (ng) Where Mac programmers look for advice from comrades. The group's regulars range from hackers helping fellow netizens understand C++ to a guy who posted, "Help a stupid newbie?" ✓**USENET**

comp.sys.mac.programmer.info (ng) A moderated newsgroup for posting FAQs, digests, release announcements, contact information, bulletins, and any frequently requested information related to development for the Macintosh. ✓**USENET**

comp.sys.mac.programmer.misc (ng) Anything and everything related to programming for the Mac, whether you're wondering about scripting or Symantec C++. ✓**USENET**

comp.sys.mac.programmer.tools (ng) A group devoted to discussion of various tools for programmers. Typical posts include "Think C oddities" and "Recommendation for GUI builder wanted." ✓**USENET**

Mac Scripting A companion to the MacScripting mailing list, this site is a terrific clearinghouse of info for Mac-hackers using AppleScript, Userland Frontier, or other scripting tools. Links connect you to the Macintosh Scripting FAQ and archives with information specific to the various scripting environments. Does the following error message make sense to you? "Undefined: PutObject (CStream &,CBitMap *)(CBitMapPane.cp)." No? Well, you may not feel at home in this mailing list, where the talk centers on the Think Class Library used by many Mac programmers. Posts typically have titles like "How to get icons bigger than 32 x 32" and "SC++ 8.0 TCL Compile Problems," and include discussion about automated HTML conversion for a local newspaper, editing scripts on a remote machine, or desktop tinkering. *Archives:* ✓**INTERNET** ...→ *www* http://mmm.dartmouth.edu/pages/macscripting/macscripting-home.html ...→*www* http://mmm.dartmouth.edu/pages/macscripting/macscripting-home.html

Mac Technical Notes The site offers errata and addenda for Mac tech issues. You'll find the topics sorted by categories (files, hardware, printing, etc.), and lots of highly technical info useful for the serious developer. ✓**INTERNET**→ *www* http://www.info.apple.com/dev/technotes/Main.html

Macintosh Development Forum A place for Macintosh programmers of all levels of expertise to congregate and chew the fat over the latest in Mac development. Discussion boards are categorized by level of programming experience and contain questions and responses to various programming-related subjects, like cross-platform development and Pascal programming. There are conference rooms for online chat—Developer Exchange caters to the seasoned developer, and professional programmers occupy the room every weekday from 6:30 to 7:00 p.m. PST to provide real-time programming support. The software libraries contain sample code, scripting samples, programming utilities, and more. And the Developer Resources library contains an archive of helpful technical journals and programming books. Novice programmers will want to get their hands on the Macintosh Programming FAQ. ✓**EWORLD**→*go* macdev

Robert Lentz's Programming Resources Finally, a Website for programmers with an eloquent epigraph: "The programmer, like the poet, works only slightly removed from pure thought-stuff. He builds his castles in the air, from air, creating by exertion of the imagination." (The source is *The Mythical Man Month* by Frederick P. Brooks, Jr., just in case you were wondering.) Aside from the erudite celebration of the craft, this site's got heaps of info for programmers, like the AppleGuide Authoring Kit and an intro to RISC technology, along with archives useful for programmers. The section on languages offers links to material on MacPerl, C++, Lisp, and others. ✓**INTERNET**→*www* http://www.astro.nwu.edu/lentz/mac/programming/home-prog.html

TopSoft Home of TopSoft, a nonprofit cyber-organization aimed at bringing free and low-cost software to the Mac. According to the group's FAQ, "We see ourselves both as a user group for developers and a Macintosh software company." The site includes information on membership and ongoing projects. ✓**INTERNET**→ *www* http://www.topsoft.org/

User groups

Arizona Macintosh Users Group A MUG devoted to Macintosh users in Arizona and the Southwest—in other words, don't

The Big Two: Apple & IBM Macintosh

expect to find the riches of the Berkeley Macintosh Users Group. This eWorld site has a few shareware programs and a rather flaccid message board with a couple of Mosaic help requests. The Internet sites offer more, including mirrors of several huge Mac software sight, a tremendous wealth of Newton resources, and information about various user-group activities. ✓**INTERNET** …→*www* http://www.amug.org/index.html …→*www* ftp://ftp.amug.org/ ✓**EWORLD**→*go* amug→

Berkeley Mac User Group BBSs (bbs) Local bulletin boards in Massachusetts and California with software, announcements, and other info generated by the huge Berkeley Mac User Group. ☎→*dial* 617-356-6336/408-777-1720/510-849-2684

BMUG Forum "Does anyone know of a way to use a scanner with a Quadra without disabling the cache?" Consider the message board for the Berkeley Mac User Group a helpline for your Mac, a place to go with questions about your modem, software, or hardware. The rest of the forum—from the library to the monthly calendar—is dedicated to featuring information about the BMUG itself. ✓**AMERICA ONLINE**→*keyword* bmug

BMUG's User Group Forum The world's largest Macintosh user group is located in Berkeley, which is no stranger to grass-roots, nonprofit organizations. The group's motto is "We're in the business of giving away information"—in fact, this forum's software library boasts one of the biggest public domain Macintosh software sites in the world, with itemized sections including PowerPC, Newton, Business, Graphics, and Telecom. There are no slumming trustifarians in BMUG's version of People's Park—the group's message board for posts like "Let's Rebuild Apple!" in which members declare what they would do if they owned Apple Computers, Inc. The BMUG forum also contains links to other BMUG-sponsored services, including BMUG Choice Products, a reference library of all the best hardware and software for the Macintosh and Newton, and the BMUG HelpLine, where you'll find an archive of Mac-related FAQs, not to mention a volunteer-administered message board for technical support questions. One of the most meticulously organized sites anywhere, this is what happens when a bunch of Mac-wielding Berkeleyites band together and announce "We've got Mac power and we're going to use it!" ✓**EWORLD**→*go* bmug

Mac/Chicago The online version of a bimonthly print mag, which bills itself as "The Resource for Chicagoland Macintosh Users." The mag specializes in Chicago Mac resources, like a trade directory and info on local user groups, but it also provides a list of "hot sites" and info on what's in the latest issue. Selected articles include "W3: Weaving the World Wide Web" and a review of "Mosaic Quick Tour for Mac." ✓**INTERNET**→*www* http://www.macchicago.com/home/

New York Macintosh Users Group The cross-coast rival of the Berkeley MUG, this lot bills itself as "the group with the New York attitude." But the NYMUG lacks the togetherness of the Berkeley contingency: the software library is rather bare and the message boards aren't abrasive enough—in fact, they're empty and outdated, as if everyone had fled the city. Like the New York Yankees, this group is ultimately a disappointment—more bravado than actual muscle. What's most interesting about the site, in fact, is its cultural resources, such as the restaurant reviews in the About NYMUG library. Forget computing—let's go out to Chanterelle in Tribeca and have French nouvelle cuisine. ✓**EWORLD**→*go* nymug

User Group Connection Get the scoop on connecting with like-minded MUGS (Mac User Groups) in your area through this networking forum which features a message board and a library full of newsletters and shareware uploaded by the multitude of MUGS on the Net. Want to hook up with Mac users who read the Bible? Or maybe you'd rather hitch your wagon to a group of Mac-toting real estate agents from the Pacific Northwest? Visit the User Groups Online area in the UG Discussions message board and discover how many multifarious Mac militias there are out there in Cyberspace. The UGC Programs & Info area even contains a searchable regional database that will put you in touch with Mac user groups in your part of the country. ✓**EWORLD**→*go* ugc

> "Forget computing—let's go out to Chanterelle in TriBeCa and have French nouvelle cuisine."

Net Tech 65

Apple: Other Systems The Big Two: Apple & IBM

Apple: other systems

Macintosh accounts for the lion's share of Apple business, but there are of course other computers—most notably the Apple II, which livened up suburban basements during the early 80s. And while the Macintosh has largely obliterated its predecessor, there are still thousands of Apple IIs among us. On the Net, Apple IIs still have an estimable presence, with commercial service areas (America Online's **Apple II Forum**) and Websites (the **Apple 2 FAQ**) alike. Get software at **Major Apple 2 Archives**. And programmers of all shapes and sizes are welcome at the **Apple II Programmers' Forum**.

On the Net

Across the board

Apple 2 FAQ Covers all the proverbial bases with regards to computing on the Apple II, including a long list of Net sites with Apple II software, an explanation of various file extensions, the dos and don'ts of hardware configuration ("How about hooking up cheap IDE Hard Drives?"), software advice (graphic conversion programs? BBS echo reading software?) and other Apple hints and tips. ✓**INTERNET** ...→*www* ftp://wuarchive.wustl.edu/systems/apple2/umich.edu/faq ...→*www* ftp://rtfm.mit.edu/pub/usenet-by-hierarchy/comp/sys/apple2 ...→*www* http://www.cis.ohio-state.edu:80/text/faq/usenet/apple2/top.html

The Apple II Forum Software, message boards, and special interest groups—you'll find them all in this active area. The message boards include areas on development, education, hardware, and productivity. The forum includes special interest groups for HyperStudio users and game designers. The libraries include software for development, games, and an Apple II Hall of Fame with the hottest items. ✓**AMERICA ONLINE**→*keyword* a2

The Apple II Info Web Home Page It's not pretty (too many icons), but it brings together a lot of resources for Apple II users—from shareware archives to information on dozens of system and hardware topics (post-patching and GSBug, Apple Superdrive repair, Using a Syquest SCSI on IIes, etc.) to links to other Apple II site on the Internet. ✓**INTERNET**→*www* http://www.ugcs.caltech.edu/~nathan/a2web/Overview.html

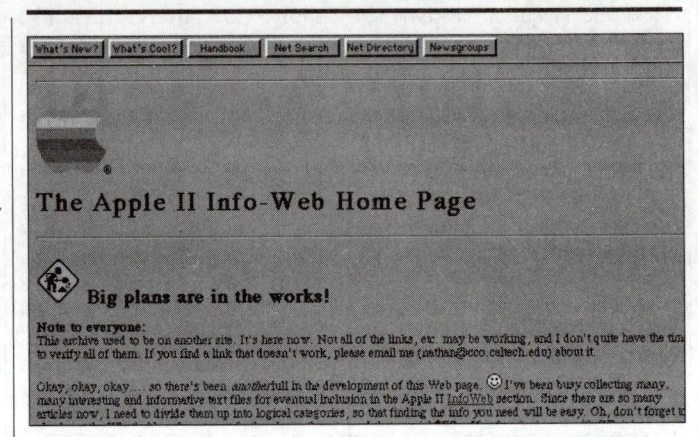

Apple II Info Web—http://www.ugcs.caltech.edu/-nathan/a2web/Overview.html

Apple II Users Forum Edward wants info on installing memory in his IIGS: "How many slots does a GS have? In what combination can I install chips?" And he'll get a quick answer in this active forum, where Apple II users talk about everything from emulators to telecommunications. And users are doing more than exchanging advice; they're also adding programs to the library, which has become a tremendous repository of Apple II programs—some of which are fun (Invaders from Space), some of which are useful (terminal software), and some of which verge on the tasteless (an O.J. and Nicole Brown Simpson morph). And did we mention that some are erotic? There's an R-rated artwork section. ✓**COMPUSERVE**→*go* appuser

Nathan Mates' Apple II Resources Many Websites promise a lot. This page delivers. It carries links to programming resources, Apple II companies, sound and music sites, other Apple II users' home pages, all the relevant news-

The Big Two: Apple & IBM Apple: Other Systems

groups devoted to the computer, a slightly dated list of Apple II BBSs, and dozens of software sites. Nathan's an Apple II developer himself, so look for information about programs he's working on. ✓**INTERNET**→*www* http://www.ugcs.caltech.edu/~nathan/apl2.resource.html

Chat

Apple II Programmers' Forum If you're looking to develop applications for the Apple II, here's an active spot to talk to other programmers. The message sections include areas on Pascal, machine language, and hardware issues. The libraries include a variety of tools to help programmers. ✓**COMPUSERVE**→*go* approg

Apple2-L (ml) This list for Apple's computer-that-isn't-made-anymore provides a forum for almost 400 Apple II owners to discuss hardware and software issues. Stop by to troubleshoot a memory problem, get advice on the best shareware flight simulator for the Apple II, or buy and sell products. ✓**INTERNET**→*email* listserv@brown-vm.brown.edu ✍ *Type in message body:* subscribe apple2-l <your full name>

#appleiigs Need help immediately? Programmers and users of the Apple IIGS hang out here exchanging tips, getting questions answered, and chatting. ✓**INTERNET**→*irc* #appleiigs *Info:* ✓**INTERNET**→*www* http://www.ugcs.caltech.edu/~nathan/appleiigs.html

comp.sys.apple2 (ng) General discussion of the Apple II, from instructions on using peripherals to advice on finding relevant Websites. ✓**USENET**

comp.sys.apple2.usergroups

> "The Apple II Users Forum library is a tremendous repository of Apple II programs, some of which are fun (Invaders from Space), some of which are useful (terminal software), and some of which verge on the tasteless (an O.J. and Nicole morph)."

(ng) User groups for the Apple II dominate discussion here (where to find one, when they're meeting, etc…), but discussion opens up to include a variety of Apple II issues. ✓**USENET**

Programming

comp.sys.apple2.programmer (ng) Discussion of programming the Apple II, whether you're wondering what software to use or looking for a veteran hacker's ideas on how to avoid the errors you're making. ✓**USENET**

Shareware

comp.binaries.apple2 (ng) Filled to the rim with binaries for the Apple II. ✓**USENET**

Major Apple 2 Archives One-stop shopping for the Apple II. Bring a basket (or disk drive) big enough because these University sites have large selections of educational shareware, graphic viewers, communication shareware, programming utilities, games, applications for the Apple IIGS, and utilities. ✓**INTERNET** …→*www* file://grind.isca.uiowa.edu/apple2 …→*www* ftp://wuarchive.wustl.edu/systems/apple2/ …→*www* ftp://ftp.cco.caltech.edu/pub/apple2/ …→*www* ftp://apple2.archive.umich.edu/archive/apple2

Vendors

Apple II Vendor Forum Many companies making Apple II products are here, including Seven Hills Software, Applied Engineering, and InTrec Software. If you're looking for product info, or have a problem or suggestion, post it and wait for an answer. The library is also a good resource for product announcements, updates, and patches. Not the most active spot, but you will find support-staff members willing to help. ✓**COMPUSERVE**→*go* apiiven

Other Apple II stuff

comp.emulators.apple2 (ng) Discussion of programs allowing users to emulate an Apple II on another PC. ✓**USENET**

comp.sys.apple2.gno (ng) Issues related to the GNO multitasking environment for the Apple IIGS. ✓**USENET**

Apple III

Apple3-L (ml) News and general discussion about the Apple III. ✓**INTERNET**→*email* listserv@wvnvm.wvnet.edu ✍ *Type in message body:* subscribe apple3-l <your full name>

Net Tech 67

The PC World **The Big Two: Apple & IBM**

The PC world

Computers weren't always personal. They once filled entire rooms at universities and made slow but steady progress through an endless series of calculations. Now everything is smaller, faster, more personal—tiny chips and processors put the P before the C. Start at **PC Index**, **PCNet**, or **ZiffNet** to gather general information about the world of IBM-compatible PCs. Then visit the **PC New Users Forum** on CompuServe for a refresher course on the basics. Users with more specialized needs should skip directly to the dozens of computer magazines online, and hungry consumers can get their personal purchasing fix with the **PC Vendor Forums**.

On the Net

Across the board

PC Index Looking for an FAQ on PC hardware? A newsgroup on Windows financial applications? A link to the Dell or Compaq Websites? This Web page carries links to many PC resources, including mailing lists, newsgroups, gopher and Web servers, FTP sites, FAQs, and electronic magazines. ✓**INTERNET**→*www* http://ici.proper.com/1/pc

PCNet CompuServe has recently

PC Magazine cover—downloaded from http://www.ziff.com:8001/~pcmag/

begun to link many of its forums together. They've linked Novell's forums, Microsoft's forums, the graphics forums, and even most of the PC-related forums (PCNet). From the PCNet menu, you can go to the PC Communications Forum, the PC Hardware Forum, the PC Applications Forum, the PC Fun Forum, the PC Programming Forum, the PC Utilities/Systems Forum, the PC Bulletin Board Forum, the ASP Shareware Forum, several PC vendor forums, LAN vendor forums, and a file finder that searches several thousand PC files and programs in libraries all over CompuServe. In addition to its role as a jumping pad, PCNet offers its own selection of indispensable software, such as ARC-E (for extracting files from ARC archive files) and VuePrint 3.3 (a fast Windows JPEG/GIF viewer). Veteran users can also test their knowledge in the trivia contest to try and win the prize of the week—an HP 200LX 1MB palmtop, perhaps? ✓**COMPUSERVE**→*go* pcnet

ZiffNet ZiffNet on CompuServe is one cyberspot that PC users should not miss. Several of the large Ziff-Davis magazines have forums here, including *PC Magazine*, *PC/Computing*, *PC Week*, *Computer Shopper*, *Interactive Week*, *Computer Life*, *Computer Gaming World*, *MacUser*, and *MacWeek*. Members can discuss articles or related topics on their message boards and hit the libraries for software and selected articles. In addition, *PC Week*, *MacWeek*, and *Newsbytes* offer full-text daily computer news. To find out the best prices on PCs (and save a tree), read the online edition of *Computer Shopper*. Then do more extensive research in the Computer Library Online (go complib), which gives you access to three databases of computer magazine articles, technical manuals, and detailed product specifications. (Note: the databases in the Computer Library Online carry additional charges.) If you're looking for software (and who in Cyberspace isn't?), all the magazine forums offer libraries of shareware programs, and the ZiffNet Software Center (go center) is a massive searchable library of shareware. Whether you want to download programming utilities, tutorials, Windows and DOS enhancements, games, graphics, or file-management tools, you'll be able to cover most of your shareware shopping needs here. ✓**COMPUSERVE**→*go* ziffnet

ZiffNet ZiffNet has two offers on Prodigy: enroll in a "ZiffNet for Prodigy" plan ($7.50 a month for one hour of access, with additional charges for more time) or choose "ZiffNet Selections for Prodigy" and browse the software listings

The Big Two: Apple & IBM The PC World

for free, but pay for each download (download charges are listed). Enrollment gets you a slightly larger selection of shareware and news features from Ziff-Davis magazines. With either offer, you can select from thousands of applications in categories such as general applications, computing, games, graphics, education, home and hobby, professional, reference, and Windows ("Tools Microsoft Forgot"). All programs are rated by ZiffNet experts. Dig around and you'll find gems like Chores & Rewards (in the Home and Hobby section), which is a system for managing childrens' chores. The organized Stepford Wife can track penalties and rewards and create "automatic allowance reconciliation" for her dutiful, hardworking, and productive little household helpers! ✓**PRODIGY**→*jump* ziffnet

Tutorials & info

Introduction to PC Hardware
Looking to buy a new PC? This site offers down-to-earth advice about CPUs, I/O busses, and SCSI cards, and whether faster is always better—not to mention worth the money! A computer salesman's worst nightmare... ✓**INTERNET**→*www* http://pclt.cis.yale.edu/pclt/pchw/platypus.htm

PC Lube and Tune PCL&T describes itself as "a service station and convenience store at Exit 130.132 on the National Information Highway." The site features tutorials about and explanations of PC topics, including a detailed overview of Ethernet, an introduction to PC hardware, a guide to adding Internet access to Windows machines, and more. The site's weekly newspaper, "Road and Hack," reports on new software releases and other issues relevant to the PC owner. ✓**INTERNET**
→*www* http://pclt.cis.yale.edu/pclt/default.htm

PC New Users Forum Even the personal computing world has its form of the other kind of PC—Political Correctness, that is. The former *PC Novice* forum has been renamed to empower those new to IBMs—they're called *new users* now, and can presumably achieve any level of success from Day One. All the software in this forum has a help facility built in. Don't worry if you have a tough time figuring out file decompression. There's an entire message topic devoted to questions about zipping and unzipping. Feel free to be as computer illiterate as you want to be here. One woman claimed to be "such a dummy [she] didn't even understand the helpful advice [she] was given." ✓**COMPUSERVE**→*go* pcnew

News

IBM InfoLink IBM offers product information and customer service through its Website. Read the company's press releases, review the technical specs of new products and upgrades, or check out the customer testimonials—e.g., J.C. Penney Life Insurance Company loves its IBMs. ✓**INTERNET**→

> "Even the personal computing world has its form of the other kind of PC—Political Correctness, that is."

www http://www.pc.ibm.com/

Larry Majid on PCs Journalist Larry Majid writes a computer column twice a week for Prodigy. His columns cover a wide range of issues, from ISDN to speech recognition to envelope printing. ✓**PRODIGY**→*jump* majid

PC Computing Like its newsstand counterpart, the Website is slick and full of advertising. Or, as they call it, "webvertising." Unlike its newsstand counterpart, the site's content is almost exclusively about the Net; it essentially reports on the online world. Although not even close to being comprehensive, the Web Map on this Website is an amusing effort to "map" the Internet. On CompuServe, the magazine staff maintains a forum where members can post letters to the editor, comment on articles, or access a library of programs, utilities, tools, and macros. ✓**INTERNET** →*www* http://www.ziff.com/~pccomp/ ✓**COMPUSERVE**→*go* pccontact

PC Magazine On-Line Besides a table of contents for the current issue and an excerpt from the cover story, *PC Magazine* publishes online news about Cyberspace and has brought together a significant collection of resources for Web users, including how-to articles, Internet product reviews, and an ambitious, annotated guide to computing resources on the Web (The Computing Trailblazer). The "Downloadable Files Area" also carries utilities from the current and back issues of *PC Magazine*. *PC Magazine* on CompuServe is equally impressive, with links to four forums (one for free utilities from the current issue, one for a huge selection of utilities and tips, one for programming, and one for product reviews and recommenda-

Net Tech 69

The PC World The Big Two: Apple & IBM

tions from the editorial staff), a selection of full-text articles from the current issue, and a computer industry newswire called "Trends Online." ✓ COMPUSERVE→*go* pcmagazine ✓ INTERNET→*www* http://www.pcmag.ziff.com/~pcmag/

PC News What product has just been published? What's being discontinued? What companies are merging? Updated daily, this news service is written exclusively for Prodigy and offers short (approximately 75 words) news briefs about PC hardware and software. ✓ PRODIGY→*jump* pcnews

PC Previews Every day, Prodigy computer writer John Edwards previews a new piece of software, a new CD-ROM, or a new piece of hardware. More than two years' worth of previews are archived. ✓ PRODIGY→*jump* pcpreviews

PC Trends A weekly column on personal-computing industry trends. Columns from the past two years are archived. ✓ PRODIGY→*jump* pctrends

PC Update Online The electronic journal for the Melbourne PC User Group is published and archived on this Website. Each issue features several articles on a personal-computing theme. Past themes include home and family computing, desktop publishing, personal finance programs, communications, and multimedia. ✓ INTERNET→*www* http://www.melbpc.org.au/pcdt/pcupmain.htm

PC Week On-Line Microsoft's overhauling, Borland's debuting, AT&T's reorganizing, and AOL's buying. If not this week then sometime soon, and when they do, *PC Week*, "the national newspaper of corporate computing," will cover the story. *PC Week* has gone online with style. Its Website isn't just a table of contents and one or two stories: staff members add breaking stories daily to the site, and the full text of many of the print publication's weekly columns, lab reviews, profiles, and industry reports is available. In addition, the site provides articles from *Netweek*, a weekly supplement to *PC Week* that covers networking solutions in corporate America, and *PC Week Executive*, a supplement for corporate information-systems leaders. The *PC Week Navigator*, a collection of hypertext articles about the Web, is an added bonus on the Website, with many of the same news stories, Spencer Katt's weekly column of industry rumors, and the *PC Week* price index. On CompuServe, *PC Week* not only has a news feed, it also has a forum where members can discuss PC news or download buyer's guides. On eWorld, there's just the news, but the service has an archive of *PC Week*'s articles going back to May 1994. ✓ COMPUSERVE→*go* znt:pcwonline ✓ INTERNET→*www* http://www.pcweek.ziff.com/~pcweek ✓ EWORLD→*go* pcweek

PC World Online The popular monthly PC computing magazine has put its entire issue online, including an option to download the shareware and utilities featured in the current issue. If that weren't enough, on both CompuServe and AOL you can search more than two years' worth of back issues, download industry press releases, and access a special "Online Exclusive" section with shareware reviews, features on Cyberspace, and other stories. There's also a Consumer Watch section where you can leave messages to the editors about software bugs and product failures; they'll investigate your problem and either post the results online or publish them in the latest print edition of the magazine. On CompuServe, discussions about magazine articles or PC topics in general take place on the message boards of either of the two PC World forums: PC World Online Forum or PC World Entertainment Forum. On AOL, there's a central message board. The forums are also large repositories for shareware—from financial programs to fonts and icons. And on AOL the Top 20 Systems Reviews carry more than a year's worth of computer product reviews. ✓ COMPUSERVE→*go* pcworld

ZD Net Ziff-Davis has put most of its magazine titles online—not the full text but a selection of articles from each current issue, tables of contents, and in many instances, original online content. The staffs of such impressive PC titles as *PCWeek*, *Computer Shopper*, and *Interactive Week* post late-breaking computer stories to the site on a daily basis as well as add to the Website's growing collection of articles about the Net. Also, check out the links to and descriptions of other computer-related sites on the Computing Trailblazer page. Information about ZiffNet services on CompuServe is also provided here. ✓ INTERNET→*www* http://www.ziff.com/

Chat

386-Users (ml) You may wish you owned a Pentium, but if it's a 386 that handles all your computing tasks, this list offers hardware and software support from fellow users. ✓ INTERNET→*email* 386users-request@udel.edu ✍ *Write a request*

comp.sys.ibm.pc.digest (ng) A moderated forum concerning IBM and compatible PCs, including

70 Net Tech

The Big Two: Apple & IBM The PC World

XT and AT models. The topics of discussion are general ones, ranging from software reviews to hard drive configurations. One member needed complicated technical help setting up a modem, while another was just looking for some mouse recommendations. Questions and answers are presented in newsletter form with a table of contents, followed by members' responses. Rather than browse through a sea of message subjects, users access the entire, edited newsletter each time they log on. ✓**USENET**

comp.sys.ibm.pc.misc (ng) A newsgroup covering IBM and compatible PCs. The information here is fairly technical in nature, often concerning bad sectors, questionable clusters, or operating-system glitches. Still, the discussion can sometimes be softer. One popular thread contemplated the steering wheel set-up for the Thrustmaster driving simulator, while another debated how to eliminate fan noise. ✓**USENET**

Info-IBMPC Michael from Germany needs information on serial connections for his old Epson LX86 dot-matrix printer. Chema from Spain is trying to figure out why MS-DOS 6.22 refuses to work under Windows for Workgroups 3.11. Gerhard from the Netherlands suggests that Chema's problem is with a videodriver, not the computer itself. And Paul from the U.S. is looking for the address of Adobe's FTP site. Where technology is concerned—particularly problems with PCs—national boundaries make no difference on this digest. ✓**INTERNET**→*email* listserv@vmd.cso.uiuc.edu ✐ *Type in message body:* subscribe imbpc-l <your full name>

PCTech-L (ml) When the CPU needs upgrading, the hard disk refuses to boot, you don't know where to put the .EXE file, or the cat ate your mouse, you can turn to this list for advice. Join, introduce yourself, and start sharing. ✓**INTERNET**→*email* listserv@trean.bit net ✐ *Type in message body:* subscribe pctech-l <your full name>

PC software

HENSA/Micros IBM PC Section HENSA offers a huge archive of public-domain software and shareware for DOS, Windows, OS/2, and OS/2 WARP systems. There are five different search modes to find the data analysis tool, astrology program, adventure game, or other PC programs that you're looking for. HENSA also provides the decompression programs needed to unpack zipped, tarred, and UUencoded files. ✓**INTERNET**→*www* http://micros.hensa.ac.uk/micros/ibmpc.html

I-Wire Software To capitalize on the increased hipness of technology, the former Compute Online changed its name to I-Wire. Why I? In honor of four hackneyed techno-terms—Information, Internet, Interactivity, and Individuality. I-Wire's online presence includes product reviews (often with direct links to downloadable demos), guides to the Internet, and software help files. If it's software you want, you'll find everything from demos of Theme Park to full-fledged versions of Eudora for Windows. And check out the Games Top 10 Library for the most popular shareware games. As for interactivity, I-Wire sets up regular chat meetings. And even though individuality is just a fancy name for message boards, the postings (over 2,500 at any given time) include folders for DOS, Windows, Multimedia, and Commodore. ✓**AMERICA ONLINE**→*keyword* iwire→Software

IBM Software Solutions Forum "Solutions" in this forum means upgrades or customized software for Windows or DOS systems. IBM offers demos, upgrades, and information on software—from IBM's CSP to BookManager to Software Installers for OS/2 and Windows. ✓**COMPUSERVE**→*go* sofsol

PC Applications Forum Looking for Word memo templates? How about an invoice macro? Maybe you're looking for love. Try downloading the word processor with a built-in poetry writing feature. While it won't write love poems for you, it does include a rhyming dictionary, help features to remember selected rhymes and metric count, and a special screen so you can compose as many drafts as necessary. Romance aside, this forum features utilities, patches, and shareware programs in many catagories: databases, personal-accounting programs, and desktop-publishing programs. ✓**COMPUSERVE**→*go* pcapp

PC Demos, Shareware & Stuff If your Pentium FPU is faulty, there's a patch in this forum that compensates for the problem. But emergency patches aren't the only thing you'll find here. Musicians can download a graphical guitar fretboard for Excel, which marks the location of notes in any key, in 13 scales and modes. Schmoozers can update their version of Symantec Act! 2.01 to 2.03, and jokesters can get their PC to act like a Mac, downloading any number of samples, from Gomer Pyle saying "Shazam!" to a disk-eject sound of a flushing toilet. ✓**AMERICA ONLINE**→*keyword* komando→Software Libraries→PC

Net Tech 71

The PC World The Big Two: Apple & IBM

Demos, Shareware & Stuff

PC File Finder If sorting through dozens of PC-related forums and thousands of files keeps you from taking advantage of the wonders of downloading online, you need to check out the PC File Finder. With eight search criteria, you can execute a wide range of searches, from the general to the witheringly specific. Search by topic, file submission date, forum name, file type, file extension, file name, or submitter's User i.d. Next time someone says CompuServe isn't as user-friendly as AOL, point them to this service. ✓**COMPUSERVE**→*go* pcff

PC Software Center The PC software libraries on AOL offer over 60,000 Windows and DOS shareware files for members to download (Paint Shop Pro and System Checkout/In are two of the most popular). The center has an easy-to-use search engine, and the moderators have also provided a database file for off-line searching (accompanied by the shareware to make it run). If you're looking for a PC program on AOL, this center should be your first stop. ✓**AMERICA ONLINE**→*keyword* pcsoftware

Popular PC Files Simple and straightforward links to some of the most valuable PC programs and archives on the Internet. Software includes many Windows applications, the latest versions of PKZIP (for all your unzipping needs) and Cello (a Windows Web browser), and several anti-virus programs. ✓**INTERNET**→*www* http://proper.com:70/1/pc/files

Query Interface to the PC Software Harvest Broker You can search the descriptions of more than 35,000 PC software files available from six major Internet archives, including the University of Michigan MSDOS Archives and the SimTel Software Repository at Oakland University. ✓**INTERNET**→*www* http://rd.cs.colorado.edu/brokers/pcindex/query.html#archives

Demos

comp.sys.ibm.pc.demos (ng) Since the early 1980s, the demo scene has flourished, with programmers showcasing their skills in flashy animated programs. This newsgroup brings together members of today's PC demo scene for programming support and demo exchange. The exchange centers around coding, but quite a bit of sound and graphics discussion has infiltrated the symposium, to the disgruntlement of veteran members. Amiga coders are here in force too. ✓**USENET**

DemoWeb Partly a very impressive catalogue of demo scene sites on the Internet, partly a tutorial and introduction to demo-ing, and partly an effort to centralize the demo community online. ✓**INTERNET**→*www* http://mind.net/xethyr/demos/

PC Demos Explained For the uninitiated, demos are programs that "display a sound, music, and light show, usually in 3-D," like video games without the interactivity. The site covers the history of the demo scene, provides links to several demo archives, features a selection of impressive demos that "deserve special attention," and gives advice on how to get started coding your own. But be forewarned—getting a plasma cube to bounce through a 3-D landscape is harder than you think. ✓**INTERNET**→*www* http://www.mcs.net/~trixter/html/demos.html

Hardware

Chiplist An extensive list of CPUs and NPXs with clock speeds and other specifications. ✓**INTERNET** ...→*www* http://einstein.et.tudelft.nl/~offerman/chiplist.html ...→*www* http://www.cis.ohio-state.edu:80/text/faq/usenet/pc-hardware-faq/chiplist/top.html ...→*www* ftp://rtfm.mit.edu/pub/usenet/news.answers/pc-hardware-faq/chiplist/

comp.sys.ibm.pc.hardware.chips (ng) "HELP!! I REALLY MESSED UP!" If you have a problem concerning the installation or performance of PC memory chips, this is the place to turn for assistance. This no-nonsense message board also hosts less emotional and far more technical discussions—an analysis of the qualitative difference between Intel and AMD chips, for instance. The postings are filled with technical jargon and alphabet soup references, like "DRAM" and "SRAM." Although almost every query receives a response here, only the truly computer literate will survive. ✓**USENET**

comp.sys.ibm.pc.hardware.misc (ng) A slightly less technical discussion group covering PC hardware topics. "Is it okay to always leave my computer on?" asks one member. Another thread advises a user on how to set up his computer as an answering machine. There are lots of queries and warnings about vendors, so if you're considering a mail-order purchase, you can look for references here. ✓**USENET**

comp.sys.ibm.pc.hardware.storage (ng) This active newsgroup holds discussions on hard drives and other storage devices. The conversation ranges from Stacker questions to partitioning

72 Net Tech

The Big Two: Apple & IBM The PC World

advice, and is relatively technical in nature. One member was looking for a SyQuest driver for Windows 95, and received several helpful suggestions. Another thread addressed mounting hard drives on their sides. There's a lot of interest here in the Iomega Zip drive, with postings about its current uses as well as discussion about the impact it may have upon the future of data storage. ✓**USENET**

comp.sys.ibm.pc.hardware. systems (ng) "Does it make sense to build my own PC?" This newsgroup is for individuals interested in buying or assembling entire PC systems. The discussion covers packages as well as individual components, such as hard drives, monitors, and motherboards. ✓**USENET**

IBM Storage Systems Forum If you're tired of your network crashing and ruining your documents (have you had a file instantly turn to gibberish recently?), look into an automated backup system. Here you'll find information on the ADSTAR Distributed Storage Manager, a high-performance-network-based backup and archive system for workstations and LAN file servers. While the forum is targeted at users with specific questions about the system, prospective clients can download full profiles of ADSM. ✓**COMPUSERVE**→*go* ibmstorage

Intel The PC world has been buzzing with Pentium talk for more than a year now, and this Website carries guides to, and news about, the Pentium chip and the other CPUs developed by the Intel Corporation. In fact, if you own a PC, odds are good—very good—that it's running on an Intel chip. While in many respects the site functions as an electronic product catalog, the interactive PC buying guide takes potential customers through an overview of PCs, helping them to identify what they want in a computer. ✓**INTERNET**→*www* http://www.intel.com/

PC Hardware FAQ More than 100 questions are answered in this five-part PC hardware bible, including "How do I tell how big/fast my SIMMs are?"; "Do I need a CPU fan/heat sink?"; and "Why won't my system boot from the hard drive?" The mammoth document has entire sections devoted to questions about motherboards, controllers and interfaces, storage and retrieval devices, video, diagnostics, and other Internet resources. ✓**INTERNET** ...→*www* http://www.cis.ohio-state.edu:80/text/faq/usenet/pc-hardware-faq/top.html ...→*www* ftp://rtfm.mit.edu/pub/usenet/news.answers/pc-hardware-faq

PC Hardware Forum "Today we have to turn PCs off and on. When you leave a restroom, the toilet flushes automatically," points out Apple CEO Michael Spindler in an issue of RAndY's RumOR RaG, one of the many online journals archived here. For more PC wisdom like this (and slightly more technical insights for seasoned PC users), visit this forum regularly. PC users here give advice on subjects ranging from Pentium problems to vendors to bargain basement PCs for non-profit organizations. ✓**AMERICA ONLINE**→*keyword* pchardware

PC Hardware Forum Do you plan to use your new computer for multimedia applications? If so, what kind of speakers should you buy? If you intend to be online most of the time, what are the best modems. The message boards in this forum offer a place to seek advice—from price comparisons to reviews of the software bundled with new PCs—from other computer shoppers. If you're selling your old system to make way for the new, check out the "What Is Your Equipment Worth?" document in the library's Classifieds folder. Although the site is billed as "everything you need to know about PC hardware," there's a surprising lack of information on sound-related hardware and there are far too many screen savers. ✓**COMPUSERVE** →*go* pchw

Resellers

PC Resellers A list of computer-component dealers accessible via the Internet, including companies selling modems, disk drives, memory, graphics cards, etc. The page

> "'Today we have to turn PCs off and on. When you leave a restroom, the toilet flushes automatically,' points out Apple CEO Michael Spindler in an issue of RAndY's RumOR RaG, one of the many online journals archived here."

The PC World The Big Two: Apple & IBM

contains links to company Net sites, as well as mail and phone/fax numbers. ✓ **INTERNET**→*www* http://mtmis1.mis.semi.harris.com/resellers.html

GEOS

comp.os.geos (ng) The GEOS operating system for PC clones is discussed here. Compatibility issues with Windows is one of the dominant topics. ✓ **USENET**

GEOS FAQ If you've got a low-end machine, you might consider using the GEOS operating system, which "runs on top of MS-DOS or OS/2 and provides a preemptive multitasking, multithreaded, object-oriented environment for any PC-compatible with 640k and a hard drive." Still unsure? Maybe you should see for yourself. Begin with the two-part FAQ here, where you'll find sites for downloading a GEOS demo from the Internet as well as from commercial services. ✓ **INTERNET**→*www* http://www.cis.ohiostate.edu/hypertext/faq/bngusenet/comp/os/geos/top.html

PC GEOS List (ml) Tips, tricks, general information, and more specific technical discussions about PC/GEOS products (GeoWorks Ensemble, GeoWorks Pro, GeoWorks POS). ✓ **INTERNET**→*email* listserv@pandora.sf.ca.us ✍ *Type in message body:* subscribe pcgeo-l <your full name>

Vendors

PC Catalog A quick run-down of more than 2,000 product listings in eight categories: PC systems, modems, monitors, boards, printers, software, storage, and specialty items. The listings give manufacturer, model number, dealer information, price, and other relevant specs. All information is provided by the vendors themselves. If, for instance, you were thinking of purchasing a CD-ROM drive, close to 125 of them are listed here—from $65 to $5,995. Your best bet is to come here after having researched a variety of models. ✓ **AMERICA ONLINE**→*keyword* pccatalog ✓ **INTERNET**→*www* gopher://pccatalog.peed.com/

PC Vendor Forums Technical support and product information from more than 150 PC vendors in 11 forums. The vendors put product patches and manuals in the libraries and monitor message boards to answer customer questions. No problem is too trivial, no question too stupid, and no frustration unwarranted. Find out if the company you're looking for is here by searching CompuServe's index (go index). You'll be given the go word for the appropriate PC vendors forum—"pcven" plus a letter between "a" and "k." ✓ **COMPUSERVE**→*go* pcven <?>

PC User Groups

California State University at Hayward PC Clubhouse ✓ **INTERNET**→*www* http://www.dnai.com/~kenseq/pcc.html

Canberra PC Users Group ✓ **INTERNET**→*www* http://www.pcug.org.au/pcug/

Capital PC Users Group (Washington, D.C.) ✓ **INTERNET** ...→*www* http://cpcug.org/ ...→*www* gopher://cpcug.org/ ...→*www* ftp://cpcug.org/

Central Kentucky Computer Society (bbs) ☎→*dial* 606-233-0154 ✓ **INTERNET**→*www* http://www.mis.net/ckcs/ckcsmain.html

Computer Users of Baltimore (CUB) ✓ **INTERNET**→*www* http://www.clark.net/pub/rjamesd/cub.html

Las Vegas PC Users Group ✓ **INTERNET**→*www* http://www.wizard.com/gibson/lvpcug.html

Long Island PC Users Group ✓ **INTERNET**→*www* http://www.li.net/~lipcug/

Melbourne PC User Group ✓ **INTERNET** ...→*www* http://www.melbpc.org.au/ ...→*www* ftp://www.melbpc.org.au/

New York PC Users Group ✓ **INTERNET**→*www* http://www.catalog.com/nypc/nypc.html

Sierra Vista IBM PC Users Group ✓ **INTERNET**→*www* http://www.primenet.com/~tomheld/svpcug.htm

Tokyo PC Users Group ✓ **INTERNET**→*www* http://shrine.cyber.ad.jp/~jwt/tpc.html

UK PC Users Group ✓ **INTERNET**→*www* http://www.ibmpcug.co.uk/

Vancouver PC Users' Society ✓ **INTERNET**→*www* http://www.wimsey.com/~infinity/vpcus/vpcus_hp.html

Windows Information Network/Manitoba PC Users Group ✓ **INTERNET**→*www* http://www.mbnet.mb.ca/win/winhome.html

The Big Two: Apple & IBM IBMs & Clones

IBMs & clones

When IBM decided to license its PC technology to anybody with a screwdriver, tens of millions of cheap clones—from A (Acer) to Z (ZEOS)—marched out of garage doors into the world and conquered her. Today, there are clone manufacturers with better annual PC sales reports than IBM—not least because of features that the IBM wizards in Bethesda haven't even dreamt of yet. Having trouble with your Compaq? Visit the **Compaq World Wide Web Server**. In a lone star mood? Check in with the **Texas Instruments Forum**. And pay hommage to the desktop revolutionaries of the first hour on the **IBM Home Page**.

On the Net

Acer

Acer Computers "My granddaughter has an Acer 1AG 486 that she wants to sell me. However, she is unable to tell me what the processor speed is. Can you tell me?" Support from Acer representatives is usually quick and thorough in this lively topic about Acer computers and peripherals. ✓**PRODIGY**→*jump* hardwaresupport-bb→Choose a Topic→Acer

Compaq

Compaq Forum Compaq's repu-

Dell Computers Home Page—http://www.us.dell.com/

tation for customer service is generally good, but help lines get overloaded every now and then. If you want to upgrade your two-year-old Contura laptop for multimedia or enhanced online capabilities, this is a good place to begin research. Audio cards, CD-ROM drives, and modems compatible with Compaq computers are fully explained here. And if you still feel you need a real-time, one-on-one, vox phone conversation regarding the issue at hand, the forum includes a list of Compaq support telephone numbers worldwide. "A representative will be with you shortly!" ✓**COMPUSERVE**→*go* cpqforum

Compaq Online Support Online support for Compaq on Prodigy consists of four parts: an FAQ called "Commonly Asked Questions"; a news option that carries Compaq product descriptions; a message board with topics ranging from laptops to printers to desktops; and a download area where Rompaqs, divers, product info, software, and diagnostic programs are archived. ✓**PRODIGY**→*jump* compaq

Compaq World Wide Web Server A pretty slick site. If you're considering buying a Compaq PC or laptop, you'll find full-color images of Compaq gadgets here, with specs and all that, and tables that compare the Presario or ProLinea with the competition. If you already own a Compaq, you'll enjoy the detailed description of the company's warranty policies, the abundance of shareware in the archives, and a few pleasant FAQs (flip through these before you toss the machine out the window). What's missing? Oh…just the list prices, nothing important really. Check the print catalogs before your write the check. ✓**INTERNET**→*www* http://www.compaq.com/

DEC

DEC PC Forum Digital Equipment Corporation certainly has had a rough time over the past decade. Once the kings of the minicomputer and networking, their only successful division these days is their line of PC and notebook computers. If you own one of DEC's more recent PC products, or would like to own one, you'll find plenty of specs, product support, upgrade information, and downloadable games, from flight simulators to PacMan. The forum is run by volunteers and is not affiliated with DEC. ✓**COMPUSERVE**→*go* decpc

DEC Users Network From here you can access five separate DEC forums, broken down by system. The DEC PC Forum caters to users of Digital's successful line of PCs. The DEC Windows NT Forum accepts questions related to running Windows NT on Digital's Alpha AXP platform. The DECPI Forum is aimed at Digital's busi-

Net Tech 75

IBMs & Clones The Big Two: Apple & IBM

ness partners and developers of network integration software. The PDP-11 Forum is dedicated to discussion of the ancient (c. 1970) PDP-11 minicomputer (great place to search for parts). Finally, the VAX Forum is dedicated to discussing DEC's line of VAX 32-bit computer systems, the VMS operating system, VAX applications, and Digital's Unix operating system. ✓**COMPUSERVE**→*go* decunet

Digital Equipment Corporation Server
Servers, firewalls, VAX systems, network adapters, and tape drives are just a few of the products made by Digital. There isn't much mention of their PC products at these Websites. ✓**INTERNET** …→*www* http://www.digital.com/ …→*www* http://www.service.digital.com/

Dell
alt.sys.pc-clone.dell (ng) "My sister's headed off to a graduate program this coming August, and she's in need of a reliable, well-performing laptop. She's giving serious consideration to purchasing the Dell Latitude 475C. Could anyone please give us any opinions on this notebook?" Dell computer owners discuss the pros and cons of…owning a Dell computer. What did you think? ✓**USENET**

Dell The Dell technical support staff checks in at least twice a week to answer questions and respond to complaints from customers. In the interim, other Dell users often have the answers. Ask away. ✓**PRODIGY**→*jump* hardwaresupport-bb→Choose a Topic→Dell

Dell Computer Home Page Comprehensive, fast, and straightforward site with support for Dell's line of desktops, tower systems, and laptops. Color images mean you can drool over your potential computer before you get to the store. If you can't be bothered with the pedestrian task of retail shopping, access a page of vendor links to order by phone or email. Not much in the way of shareware. ✓**INTERNET**→*www* http://www.us.dell.com/

Dell Forum Do you need a replacement for your Dell Pentium processor? Fill out the form in the libraries here and email it back to Dell. Your new processor and/or heatsink kit will be mailed back to you immediately. If you're having problems with your OS/2 for Windows mouse, you'll find a fix-it patch here. All in all, a most user-friendly vendor support forum. ✓**COMPUSERVE**→*go* dell

Epson
Epson Forum Is Microsoft Flight Simulator not working on your Epson EI+? Still haven't found out how to set the clock and date feature? While the lion's share of messages in this forum are about Ep-

> "My granddaughter has an Acer 1AG 486 that she wants to sell me. However, she is unable to tell me what the machine's processor speed is. Can you tell me?"

son's popular Inkjet printer, Epson PCs, laptops, and peripherals are frequently discussed. Both Epson's technical support staff and other Epson users are good sources of information and advice. If you're looking for software, from calendars to fax programs, you'll find plenty to choose from in the Applications/Utilities folder. ✓**COMPUSERVE**→*go* epson

Gateway 2000
alt.sys.pc-clone.gateway 2000 (ng) Of all the PC newsgroups, this one carries the dubious distinction of having the most complaints. It is also the most active. Gateway 2000 owners discuss all aspects of computing with a Gateway 2000, including installing ATI drivers, getting technical support, buying via mail order, running Linux, troubleshooting monitor problems, and more. ✓**USENET** *FAQ:* ✓**INTERNET** …→ *www* http://www.mcs.com/~brooklyn/gatefaq.txt …→ *www* ftp://ftp.sei.cmu.edu/pub/gateway2000/gw2000-FAQ

Gateway 2000 Forum Multimedia, monitors, and motherboards are just of few of the topics that occupy dedicated folders on the message board of this forum, run by the Gateway 2000 technical support staff. Attracting a large cross-section of the community of Gateway owners, the forum is an excellent site for getting advice. The library, on the other hand, is rather sparse. ✓**COMPUSERVE**→*go* gateway

Gateway Users International This rudimentary Website links to a Gateway FAQ, a price list, and technical-support contacts. ✓**INTERNET**→*www* http://www.mcs.com/~brooklyn/home.html

The Big Two: Apple & IBM IBMs & Clones

Hewlett-Packard

HP Systems Forum Your mouse is acting up? Have you checked to make sure it's connected to the mouse port and not the printer port? Aha! Suffering from a "General Protection Fault Error" (the ugliness of which we won't describe here)? Just turn off your computer and restart. Like simple solutions to hair-raising problems? They're here. The forum also carries contact numbers for Hewlett-Packard technical support, new product press releases, and a load of PC software. ✓**COMPUSERVE**→*go* hpsys

IBM

comp.sys.ibm.pc.rt (ng) Discuss the—rather obscure—IBM RT computer and the AIX operating system. ✓**USENET**

comp.sys.ibm.ps2.hardware (ng) A lot of posts from people trying to buy or sell PS/2 equipment. A detailed FAQ about PS/2s is posted regularly. ✓**USENET**

IBM One of the largest computer support areas on Prodigy belongs to IBM. Guess who owns part of Prodigy? The blue-chip company offers its own online store (where you can buy anything from a $300 personal printer to a $3,000 ThinkPad), product information about its entire personal computer line, elaborate product-support areas for owners of both DOS-based and OS/2-based IBM PCs, company news, and even the occasional survey. In the PC Product Support area, you can post about problems on the Info Exchange Board, which is monitored by IBM staff; read a news column with tips and hints for IBM PC users; access a large collection of FAQs about hardware, software,

Compaq Presario—http://www.compaq.com/

Microsoft, DOS, Windows, and OS/2; and download utilities, games, graphics, and other software. ✓**PRODIGY**→*jump* ibm

The IBM Home Page If the guy in your office creates his own home page, your expectations are probably quite moderate. When IBM creates a home page, it's a whole other ball game. And given the high expectations, the site doesn't do too badly. It's corporate, it carries a tremendous amount of product information, company news, and even IBM's current stock price, and it offers profiles of projects and technology the company is currently working on. The Products, Services, and Support link leads to the resources that you probably came for in the first place—e.g., choose the link to the IBM Personal Computers for product descriptions, news, and a file library updated daily with the latest versions of important software. ✓**INTERNET**→*www* http://www.ibm.com/

IBM Online Offers detailed product descriptions, news and press releases about IBM products, an IBM online store, notices about IBM-sponsored conferences and conventions, information on computer training sessions, and a link to PCNet Online (CompuServe's main menu of PC-related forums and services). But the heart of IBM's presence on CompuServe lies with its technical support, which it offers in the 12 OS/2-related forums and services, the six PC-product forums, the 16 software-support forums, and the four "Ultimedia" forums. ✓**COMPUSERVE**→*go* ibm

IBM PS/1 and Aptiva Forum From information on installing games to announcements about educational discounts on PCs, this is a clearinghouse of information about IBM PS/1 and Aptivas. But it's about a lot more than just downloading information or patches. This forum will actually make house calls. The support technicians will call your computer via modem and fiddle with your system remotely. Better dust off that screen! ✓**COMPUSERVE**→*go* ibmps1

IBM PS2 Forum Is your printer spouting gibberish since you installed an additional hard drive on your PS/2? Maybe you have an old PS/2 Model 90 and you want to 'multimediarize'? Whether it's simple solutions you need—like how to print directly to the port to avoid the electronic nonsense—or a full list of SCSI cards and CD-ROM drives, these message boards usually come through with the necessary information. ✓**COMPUSERVE**→*go* ibmps2

IBM Technical Support Bulletin Board (bbs) Information, software patches, files, and online support from the IBM technical support staff. ☎→*dial* 919-517-0001

NCR/AT&T

AT&T-GIS Information Server Specs for and images of the AT&T Globalyst 486 & Pentium desktops, portables, and minitowers.

Net Tech 77

IBMs & Clones The Big Two: Apple & IBM

Five years' worth of postings from the NCR newsgroup may also be searched from this site. ✓**INTERNET**→*www* http://www.ncr.com/

comp.sys.ncr (ng) "Does anyone know anything about upgrading an NCR 3421 machine (386sx, 20mHz, MCA bus) to a 486 processor?" Undoubtedly, someone on this newsgroup does. Get your advice about any NCR (now AT&T) product here. ✓**USENET** *Archives:* ✓**INTERNET**→*www* http://www.ncr.com/pub/comp.sys.ncr/

NCR/AT&T Forum Your True Voice also makes a line of PCs through NCR (purchasing NCR made AT&T the world's seventh-largest computer manufacturer). PC product support and information about AT&T's Globalyst desktops and portables sit alongside telecommunications talk. ✓**COMPUSERVE**→*go* ncratt

Packard-Bell

Packard-Bell Forum Packard-Bell takes the cake for offering affordable multimedia computers for the home user. But where there are multimedia PCs, there are problems. Turn to this forum to get help troubleshooting a problem, whether it's a general complaint about hardware, a question about software compatability, or something more obscure. And if you bought your Packard-Bell a couple of years ago (which makes it ancient) and have no multimedia capabilities, come here for advice about an upgrade. ✓**COMPUSERVE**→*go* packardbell

Packard-Bell Online Although it has all the trappings of a good support center, Prodigy's Packard-Bell Online somehow fails. Besides product information and a download center with drivers, drivers, and more drivers, the site's technical support is essentially a large and detailed FAQ and an option to email the company. ✓**PRODIGY**→*jump* packardbell

Texas Instruments

Texas Instruments Forum Believe it or not, Texas Instruments still makes calculators. Lots of them. But the company also makes computers, and this forum is one of the better collections of public-domain software and "fairware" for TI computers. Download Tetris and Pong, label makers, and terminal emulators. Whether you're talking about BASIC and PASCAL programming or speculating about upgrades, the message boards address your concerns. ✓**COMPUSERVE**→*go* tiforum

> "'I think the hard drive is broken; it just kind of whines. My "authorized factory service center" says they can't get the parts. What should I do?' Responses range from addresses of consumer advocates to religious advice: 'Pray.'"

Toshiba

Toshiba Forum Toshiba is best known for its line of PC portables. Besides offering one of the first multimedia portables with CD-ROM drives, the company recently released the "ultraportable" Pentium Portege 610CT. The forum carries files with answers to many questions about Toshiba PC portables, and what isn't answered in the library documentation can be asked on the message boards. ✓**COMPUSERVE**→*go* toshiba

Zenith

Zenith Forum Although Zenith television sets still suffer from lousy, middle-of-the-road design, Zenith laptops have won critical acclaim and awards for their slick shapes. Is it because Zenith televisions are made in the U.S., while the computer division was sold to Groupe Bull in 1989? Nah. Bull! But design isn't everything, and if you're having problems installing a sound card or silencing a whining hard drive, you might want to ask fellow users here for advice: "I think the hard drive is broken; when I turn it on, it just kind of whines, like the drive is trying to spin and failing…my 'authorized factory service center' says they can't get the parts needed to repair it. What should I do?" Responses range from addresses of consumer advocates to religious advice: "Pray." ✓**COMPUSERVE**→*go* zenith

ZEOS

alt.sys.pc-clone.zeos (ng) The ZEOS technical support staff monitors this low-volume newsgroup, although staff members tend to stay out of the quality debates (and anti-ZEOS rhetoric) that are an ongoing feature of the newsgroup. ✓**USENET**

The Big Two: Apple & IBM DOS

DOS

In the PC world, DOS is like oxygen—it's in everything, and essential to the welfare of most life-forms. On the Net, DOS is also a fact of life, and whether users are commiserating about the operating system's limits in America Online's **DOS Forum** or trying to transcend those limits in **comp.os.msdos.programming**, there's plenty of DOS talk around. And PC people looking for a Halloween costume should visit **SuperDOS**.

Bill Gates—downloaded from http://www.brokaw.com

On the Net

Across the board

DOS Forum An electronic meeting place for users of either the DOS operating system or DOS alternatives. Fittingly, the interface is text based, omitting icons. There is something in this forum for both novices and DOS pros, and the moderators are helpful and conscientious. They answer questions, oversee live forums, and maintain a Tune-up configuration support area to assist users with the CONFIG.SYS and AUTOEXEC.BAT files. The DOS software libraries are split into separate categories, although most of the shareware programs, regardless of the categories they reside in, are utilities. ✓ **AMERICA ONLINE**→*keyword* dos

Microsoft MS-DOS Forum Running DOS 6.2 and out of disk space? Can't delete a file? Have an autoexec.bat file that won't load? Installing, networking, optimizing memory, running software, and other MS-DOS issues are covered in this forum. Documentation and instructions, add-ons, and a fairly large selection of MS-DOS shareware—from soccer games to phone dialers to recipe databases—are available in the library. ✓ **COMPUSERVE**→*go* msdos

Programming

comp.os.msdos.programmer (ng) A meeting place for DOS programmers, featuring answers to sticky code problems and requests for DOS extenders. Not much discussion goes on here, but the FAQ offers an excellent introduction to Net resources for DOS programmers. ✓ **USENET** *FAQ:* ✓ **INTERNET**→*www* http://www.cis.ohio-state.edu:80/text/faq/usenet/msdos-programmer-faq/top.html

4DOS

comp.os.msdos.programmer.turbovision (ng) MS-DOS programmers discuss Borland's Turbovision and share programming tips on this lightly visited message board. ✓ **USENET**

comp.os.msdos.4dos (ng) For programmers writing in 4DOS. ✓ **USENET**

Software

comp.archives.msdos.announce (ng) This message board is used by moderators of DOS FTP sites to make announcements about new uploads or to notify users of changes. Shareware aficionados with MS-DOS systems should regularly scan the group to keep on top of what new programs are available. The newsgroup looks like an FTP directory, with hundreds of message subjects taking the form of a filename and a brief description (e.g., eclogs.zip, Latin poetry with vocabulary and notes; pctrk31.zip, 3-D Earth satellite orbit visualization packet, etc.). The shareware collections at SimTel and Garbo are well represented. ✓ **USENET** *FAQ:* ✓ **INTERNET**→*www* http://www.cis.ohio-state.edu:80/text/faq/usenet/msdos-archives/top.html ...→*www* ftp://rtfm.mit.edu/pub/usenet-by-hierarchy/comp/archives/msdos/announce/ *Info:* ✓ **INTERNET**→*www* http://www.mid.net:80/MSDOS_A/

comp.archives.msdos.d (ng) This unmoderated newsgroup is the companion to the moderated comp.archives.msdos.announce newsgroup. Discussion focuses on the materials available in various MS-DOS archives. The newsgroup features users' reports, questions, and discussions about share-

DOS The Big Two: Apple & IBM

ware programs. And, yes, this is the perfect place to ask: "Does anybody know of any FTP sites that have a Quicktime .MOV file viewer available for download?" ✓USENET

comp.os.msdos.apps (ng) "What does IFSHLP.SYS in CONFIG.SYS do??" and "HELP!! Confused about RAM in MS-DOS 6.2!!" are typical of the posts on this newsgroup. Although the majority of the exchanges here are concerned with where a Netter can find a certain kind of MS-DOS application, anxious pleas for MS-DOS help are quite common. ✓USENET

Downloadable Files for the PC Get the latest version of some of the most popular PC applications here. Offerings include PKZip, Eudora Mail Reader, Trumpet's Winsock, Cello, and a variety of essential anti-virus programs. There are also basic explanations of what FTP is and why it is "anonymous." ✓INTERNET→www http://proper.com:70/1/pc/files

Garbo PC Archive Computer acting funny? Pick up an anti-virus program. Can't find important files? Download a file finder. Hear that the Net is filled with fabulous images and sounds? Get a sound player and a graphics viewer or two and start exploring. And start exploring here—the archive carries hundreds of astronomy .GIFs. Broken down into dozens of directories, from hypertext programs to communications programs to system utilities, Garbo is the other huge DOS archive online besides SimTel. ✓INTERNET …→www ftp://garbo.uwasa.fi/pc/ …→www ftp://archie.au/micros/pc/garbo …→www ftp://wuarchive.wustl.edu/systems/msdos/garbo.uwasa.fi/

MS-DOS Software via FTP An interface that allows the user to search or browse several of the largest MS-DOS archives on the Internet, including SimTel, Garbo, and the UMass-Lowell PC Games Archive. Not only can you use this site to search the archives, you can also download from it. There are instructions on how to retrieve the files you want, and for programmers, instructions on how to submit your wares to the archives. Be sure to scan the "List of Useful Programs," where tech experts review the archived programs; they'll guide you towards the best and keep the clunkers out of your box. Complete indexes of the archives are available here as well. ✓INTERNET→www http://alpha.acast.nova.edu/software/dos.html

SimTel MS-DOS Archive Jason downloaded a cool sports clip and needs an animation player. Ben's writing a novel and would like to develop a hypertext version, but he needs a good program. Kristin, on the other hand, is concerned about her finances and wants a money-management program. She's also planning a vacation to France (cheap, we hope) and is interested in a French tutorial. And Jeff's worried that his computer has a virus. The archive is a huge collection of DOS shareware, large enough to meet a broad range of needs. ✓INTERNET …→www http://www.acs.oakland.edu/oak/SimTel/SimTel-msdos.html …→www ftp://oak.oakland.edu/SimTel/msdos …→www ftp://wuarchive.wustl.edu/systems/ibmpc/simtel/msdos …→www ftp://ftp.uoknor.edu/mirrors/SimTel/msdos …→www ftp://ftp.uni-paderborn.de/SimTel/msdos

Windows Magazine DOS Programs A small collection of programs for DOS users, including a shopping-list generator, an interactive DOS tutorial, a daily planner, and a quiz game/study guide for medical students. ✓AMERICA ONLINE→keyword winmag→Software Libraries→DOS Programs

Wuarchive MS-DOS Site All the great MS-DOS archives on the Internet are mirrored here. All told, the site houses tens of thousands of DOS shareware programs. Each of the mirrors is divided into subdirectories such as astronomy, foreign-language tutorials, modem software, utilities, spreadsheet programs, etc. ✓INTERNET→www ftp://wuarchive.wustl.edu/systems/msdos

Other

PC911/First Aid Cybermedia offers these two utility programs for PCs and Novell networks. First Aid can determine why your newly installed software is not working by checking for invalid INI entries, missing DLLs, and lost application components. PC911 will sort out configuration problems with peripherals, card installations, and multimedia extensions. ✓INTERNET→www http://www.internet-is.com/cybermedia/

SuperDOS Wondering what Carl Jr.'s hamburger restaurants and the Seventh Day Adventist Church have in common? It's their SuperDOS systems, of course. Bluebird Systems has created the SuperDOS platform specifically for business-transaction processing, and its Website describes how it works, how it compares to Ethernet and Unix systems, and why industries will benefit from its applications. ✓INTERNET→www http://www.bluebird.com/superdos.html

The Big Two: Apple & IBM **MS Windows**

MS Windows

Back when Mac had its graphical interface and other computer companies were playing catch-up, most computer industry observers believed that there was a fortune to be made in designing a Mac-like interface for IBM-compatible PCs. But who would make the fortune? Ten years later, we know the answer—Bill Gates, whose Microsoft Corporation's Windows operating system dominates the PC marketplace. Find out more about MS Windows in the **Microsoft Windows Forum** and **comp.os.ms-windows.advocacy**. Then collect information on the groundbreaking update of the operating system by taking the **Hyperlinked Visual Tour of Windows 95**. If you're still not convinced, join the skeptics at **I Hate Windoze**.

Bill Gates again!—downloaded from CompuServe's Photo Gallery Forum

On the Net

Across the board

comp.os.ms-windows.advocacy (ng) Offers lively, spirited discussion about Microsoft Windows. Both the current and future effectiveness of Windows are debated here. This is a true discussion group, with lengthy strings comparing OS/2 WARP, Windows 95, Windows NT, and even the Macintosh operating system. There are strongly voiced opinions posted, along with plenty of unsubstantiated speculation. ✓**USENET**

comp.os.ms-windows.misc (ng) A very active newsgroup with a broad range of questions and discussions about Microsoft Windows. Look for Windows 95 topics to dominate the group. ✓**USENET**

comp.os.ms-windows.setup (ng) Covers issues relating to the installation and configuration of Microsoft Windows. System crashes, file corruption, and drive assignments are all covered. Members will also find some discussion about installing specific programs under Windows. ✓**USENET**

Microsoft Windows Forum Can't install a Windows progam? Want to discuss Microsoft Windows multimedia products like the Mozart CD? This forum is for Windows users seeking news or needing answers to questions on topics ranging from fax software to sound systems to file managers to video display. The library is filled with fonts, printer drivers, video drivers, and screen savers. This is not the place for shareware applications. ✓**COMPUSERVE**→*go* mswin

Windows "Is there a way to load a driver without exiting Windows?" If this is the kind of question that keeps you awake at night (or at least frustrated during the day), head to this topic for help. Screen savers, sound conflicts, mouse questions, memory glitches, and all issues relating to the Windows operating system are covered. Even the most serious Windows issues get addressed: "Can you use icons for the directories shown now as 'houses' in Windows, or must they remain as such?" ✓**PRODIGY**→*jump* computerbb→Choose a Topic→Windows

Windows Forum Features numerous message boards, with separate symposia for Windows NT,

Net Tech 81

MS Windows The Big Two: Apple & IBM

Windows 95, and Visual Basic Windows, as well as workgroups, databases, and multimedia, to name but a few. The software libraries offer thousands of Windows files for users to download. The libraries are separated into categories, so you can easily locate the utility, game, or font you desire. There is a "Top Picks" listing of the most popular downloads, a downloading Hall of Fame listing, and access to feature articles from *Windows Magazine*. The forum has a helpful, friendly atmosphere, with regularly scheduled live chat sessions. ✓**AMERICA ONLINE**→*keyword* winforum

Windows Information Network If you haven't heard enough about Microsoft from the papers, radios, and TV shows, visit WIN's site. The network is a nonprofit organization and PC user group "dedicated solely to the promotion and demonstration of MS Windows, Windows products, and applications," and it has the inside scoop on Windows 95, including reviews, schedules of availability, and where to get the preview version. ✓**INTERNET**→*www* http://www.mbnet.mb.ca/win/winhome.html

Windows User Group Forum Another forum for discussing the Windows environment and applications. Users and developers focus on new products, system configuration, networking, batching and basic tools, multimedia, industry trends, and electronic publishing. The forum hosts a different vendor each month to discuss products. The library carries HTML authoring tools in its electronic publishing section, a large collection of sound players and graphics programs in its multimedia section, tools for application programming in its Batch & Basic section, and more. ✓**COMPUSERVE**→*go* winuser

Microsoft

Microsoft Connection A menu linking to more than 50 Microsoft-sponsored forums and services, 40,000 technical documents, huge archives of software, support journals and publications for Microsoft products, a Windows news services, a sales forum, and a Microsoft bookstore. ✓**COMPUSERVE**→*go* microsoft

Microsoft Internet Servers Omnipresent in offices and homes around the world, Microsoft products range from the word processor Microsoft Word, the database FoxPro, the financial manager Microsoft Money (and, almost but not quite, Quicken), and hundreds of other software titles. The Microsoft Website brings together company and product news, information about getting technical support, product descriptions and sales information, a library of updates and patches, the "Microsoft Knowledge Base," with reports and factsheets addressing thousands of tech support questions, and a Windows 95 Home Page that updates visitors on the progress and features of Windows 95. The FTP site carries the Microsoft Knowledge Base, the software library, product information and updates for hundreds of products, developers' technical notes, and shareholder and financial information. ✓**INTERNET** ...→*www* http://www.microsoft.com/ ...→*www* gopher://gopher.microsoft.com ...→*www* ftp://ftp.microsoft.com/dirmap.htm

Windows (ml) A forum for questions, rumors, and insights about Microsoft Windows, especially Windows 95, which is slated to be released in August 1995. Will Windows 95 become an industry powerhouse or a fiasco? Join in the frenzied speculation with the 1000-odd subscribers to this list, some of whom have already test-driven the beta version and can't wait to tell you all about it. ✓**INTERNET**→*email* listserv@vm1.mcgill.ca ✍ *Type in message body:* subscribe windows <your full name>

Chat

bit.listserv.win3-l (ml/ng) Discussion for users of Windows 3.0 system software who want to swap hints or ask questions of other Win 3.0 users. ✓**USENET** ✓**INTERNET** →*email* listserv@uicvm.uic.edu ✍ *Type in message body:* subscribe win3-l <your full name>

Antipathy

I Hate Windoze If you're past the point of frustration and just think it's funny when your PC crashes for the zillionth time, find some like-minded people here. The flames run the gamut from straight Windows 95 bashing to convoluted rumors about Bill Gates's purchasing the Vatican. Also check out the report about how Microsoft is going to change the name from Windows 95 to the more lyrical WinEver. ✓**INTERNET**→*www* http://www.tach.net/public/personal/scpayne/ihatewin/ihatewin.html

FAQs & info

The Windows FAQ The number of questions and answers in this FAQ is directly proportional to the number of Windows users out there. And that's a lot of questions and answers. There are descriptions of several versions of Microsoft Windows, information

82 Net Tech

The Big Two: Apple & IBM MS Windows

on Windows 95 (previously known as Chicago), links to Windows resources on the Net, information on setting up and configuring Windows systems, hundreds of tips and tricks, and troubleshooting advice for many Windows applications ("uh, oh, PageMaker 4.0 font selection box won't scroll."). ✓**INTERNET**→*www* http://scwww.ucs.indiana.edu/FAQ/Windows/

Windows FAQs This is a repository for Windows FAQs—from the basic Windows FAQ to the Windows Programmers' FAQ. Download them directly from the page or jump to an FTP site and grab them. ✓**INTERNET**→*www* http://www.metrics.com/WinFAQ/index.html

Windows Workshop A collection of well written, easily understood articles with tips, reviews and explanations about Windows-based computing. Need to know the best way to load new programs properly? Curious about the differences between Windows NT and the version you use at home? There are also useful utility reviews, patiently describing the benefits of such products as a spell checker for email and a new macro recorder, and the workshop even contains an excellent overview of rudimentary techniques in the C++ programming language. If you're one of those computer users who has always had a vague understanding of how your system works, but could never find someone to explain it to you completely in detail, then this collection of articles will prove valuable. ✓**AMERICA ONLINE**→*keyword* iwire→Windows→Workshop

News

comp.os.ms-windows.announce (ng) A moderated message board with announcements about Microsoft Windows, including news that comes directly from the Microsoft offices. Releases and updates are trumpeted. A few announcements concerning private programs that run under Windows appear here as well. ✓**USENET**

Microsoft Knowledge Base The Microsoft technical support staff answers thousands of questions a week about its products—often the same questions. The Knowledge Base is a collection of more than 40,000 factsheets and instructions with answers to most of these questions. ✓**INTERNET**→*www* http://www.microsoft.com/pages/kb/kb.htm ✓**COMPUSERVE**→*go* mskb

Microsoft TechNet A well organized repository of product news, technical support documentation, and software updates and demos for Microsoft customers. The service breaks the Microsoft world down into news, BackOffice, personal systems, MS Office and desktop applications (MS Word to MS Access), database and development tools, hardware, planning and implementation, technologies, service and support, the Knowledge Base, conferences, and drivers and patches. This is the online version of Microsoft's TechNet CD-ROM. ✓**INTERNET**→*www* http://www.microsoft.com/pages/services/technet/default.htm ✓**COMPUSERVE**→*go* technet tnforum

Microsoft Windows News Forum When there are changes to an operating system used by more than 30 million people, many PC owners have questions. This forum is devoted exclusively to discussions and news about developments in the Windows operating system, particularly Windows 95.

CYBERNOTES

"TOP 10 THINGS PEOPLE THINK THE 95 IN WINDOWS 95 REALLY STANDS FOR:

10. The number of floppy disks it will ship on;

9. The percentage of people who will have to upgrade their hardware;

8. The number of megabytes of hard disk space required for the operating system;

7. The number of pages in the 'EASY INSTALL' version of the manual;

6. The percentage of existing programs that won't run in the new OS;

5. The number of minutes the operating system takes to install;

4. The number of calls you have to place to tech support before you can get it to run;

3. The number of people who will actually PAY for the upgrade;

2. MHz required for the OS to run;

1. The year it was DUE to ship."

—from **I Hate Windoze**

MS Windows The Big Two: Apple & IBM

There are boards and library sections covering shareware, networking, Internet access, and third-party shareware and hardware news. ✓**COMPUSERVE**→*go* winnews

Windows Magazine Online Have you ever hoarded a stack of magazines because each one contains an article you might want to refer to some day? The problem with that kind of library system is that when you need to find an article, you have to thumb through every issue until you locate what you want! *Windows* Magazine Online has solved that dilemma for you. On AOL and the Internet, you can search the full text of current and back issues while on CompuServe you have to search by month. All the sites also feature press releases and daily late-breaking stories. An extensive collection of "Tips & Tricks," explanatory FAQs, and software is also available (software mentioned in the magazine and the editor's top shareware picks are featured). On both AOL and CompuServe, Netters can turn to the message boards to soak in additional Windows information. ✓**AMERICA ONLINE**→*keyword* winmag ✓**COMPUSERVE**→*go* winmag ✓**INTERNET**→*www* http://www.winmag.com/

Windows News (ml) These press releases, backgrounders, and factsheets come directly from the Microsoft Corporation, so put on your corporate PR filter and read on; it's probably worth wading through the mass of corporate propaganda to read the news about emerging Windows technologies. Back issues of *Win News* electronic magazine are also available, and you can request a subscription to future issues, if you wish. We recommend having the newsletter delivered directly to your mailbox. ✓**AMERICA ONLINE**→

Windows logo

keyword winnews ✓**PRODIGY**→*jump* winnews ✓**INTERNET**→*email* enews @microsoft.nwnet.com ✍ *Write a request*

Windows News Clips Two weeks' worth of news articles about Windows from Dow Jones, UPI, the PR Newswire, and Business Wire. ✓**COMPUSERVE**→*go* winclips

Shareware

CICA Shareware Archive Features the largest and most impressive collection of Windows software, utilities, updates, and add-ons online. Need templates for Excel for Windows? How about ATM or TrueType fonts? Or an adventure game, a screen saver, a programming utility, or a sound clip? Several sites carry this archive. ✓**INTERNET** …→*www* http://alpha.acast.nova.edu/software/windows.html …→*www* ftp://ftp.cica.indiana.edu/pub/pc/win3 …→*www* ftp://ftp.marcam.com/win3/ …→*www* ftp://ftp.cdrom.com/pub/cica …→*www* ftp://ftp.cc.monash.edu.au/pub/win3

comp.os.ms-windows. apps.misc (ng) This "miscella-neous" newsgroup for Microsoft Windows applications truly lives up to its name. The only extended discussion concerns the Windows 95 operating system. Even though Windows 95 is not actually an application, its merits and flaws are energetically debated here. The majority of the other postings are from people looking for shareware or troubleshooting advice. One member asked for a freeware banner-making program, and found it, while another, who had forgotten the password for his startup screen, learned of a trick to clear the password using the WIN.INI file. ✓**USENET**

Microsoft Software Library If your Microsoft program isn't working perfectly, chances are that this library can enhance it significantly. Microsoft's support services offer a huge, searchable library with sample programs, device drivers, patches, software updates, and programming aids—from WordPerfect conversion kits to a tutorial on relational database design. ✓**INTERNET** …→*www* ftp://ftp.microsoft.com/Softlib/ …→*www* gopher://gopher.microsoft.com:70/11%5Csoftlib …→*www* http://www.microsoft.com/pages/kb/softlib/default.htm ✓**COMPUSERVE**→*go* msl

SimTel Windows Archive When Windows users daydream, they dream of a place like this archive, a place where all work needs and entertainment wishes are but a download or two away. And, when they wake up looking for programs to unzip files, take screen shots, teach their kids, edit text, send email, fax documents, track family lineage, view graphics, play music, read newsgroups, and illustrate newsletters, they'd be wise to learn these URLs. ✓**INTERNET** …→*www* http://www.acs.

The Big Two: Apple & IBM MS Windows

oakland.edu/oak/SimTel/SimTel-win3.html ... →*www* ftp://oak.oakland.edu/SimTel/win3 ... →*www* ftp://wuarchive.wustl.edu/systems/ibmpc/simtel/win3 ... →*www* ftp://ftp.uoknor.edu/mirrors/SimTel/win3 ... →*www* ftp://ftp.uni-paderborn.de / SimTel/win3/

Windows Magazine Software Libraries The software libraries of *Windows Magazine* are organized into categories like Drivers & Updates, Fun 'n' Games, and Pictures & Icons. You'll find a nice collection of cartoon voices in the Sounds & Music library and a child's handwriting typeface in the Fonts collection. Regular visitors will appreciate the New Uploads category. ✓**AMERICA ONLINE**→*keyword* winmag→Software Libraries

Windows Shareware 500 There has to be a limit as to the number of shareware files the average person can actually download and use. One publishing company has decided that 500 is an acceptable number, and they've made those 500 files available here, along with generous amounts of promotional material for the accompanying book. The categories are easy to browse through, and include headings like Business, Education, and Utilities. Making the Most of the Best is a collection of the most popular files. Not surprisingly, the most popular download overall appeared to be a game called "Blackjack for Windows." Deal yourself in. ✓**AMERICA ONLINE**→*keyword* win500

Windows Shareware Archive Come and get what you need out of this enormous archive (everything from Bible programs to finance programs), but be forewarned—when last we checked, the graphics were painful! The background wallpaper is a interlacing zigzag mesh with nested pyramidal forms, and the site's logo looks like a blimp that has just caught fire and is about to blow. Makes you extra excited for your new "Wildforest and Sky ScreenPeace" screen saver. ✓**INTERNET**→*www* http://coyote.csusm.edu/cwis/winworld/winworld.html

Windows Shareware Forum Head to the libraries for a jubilee of shareware divided neatly into file utilities and text editors, communications programs, system utilities, networking applications, general Windows utilities, fonts, disk utilities, program managers, finance organizers, PIMS and phonebooks, databases, art and graphics programs, calculators and clocks, education and reference shareware, food and fitness programs, spellcheckers, and programming tools. Not only can you download a fax/modem program and a grocery database, you can also ask questions about them on the message boards or get suggestions for other Windows programs that will probably make your life a little easier and more entertaining. ✓**COMPUSERVE**→*go* winshare

Extensions

Microsoft Windows Extensions Forum Company-monitored forum for users of Microsoft SDK Extensions for Windows. Sysops from Microsoft occasionally administer the message boards, responding to user problems in the following categories of extensions: TAPI, WOSA XRT and XFS, MS Delta, Pen, ODBC, MAPI, and others. Visit the software libraries for programs and documentation related to the above system extensions. ✓**COMPUSERVE**→*go* winexten

Programming

comp.os.ms-windows.programmer.controls (ng) "I've seen how MSVC++ and BC++ have color options for the control fields within a program. How can I do that for a multiline edit control?" This newsgroup for Microsoft Windows programmers answers questions about user interface design, 3-D icons, dialogs, and VBXs. Not much discussion here. ✓**USENET**

comp.os.ms-windows.programmer.drivers (ng) Help for programmers looking for specific Microsoft Windows drivers. This newsgroup is also aimed at programmers writing custom drivers. Advanced programming topics like VXDs and DLLs are discussed. ✓**USENET**

comp.os.ms-windows.programmer.graphics (ng) If you're a Microsoft Windows multimedia programmer with a question that the manuals just won't answer, log on here for some expert advice. Members discuss topics like controlling bitmaps, animation sequences, and remapping color pallets. ✓**USENET**

comp.os.ms-windows.programmer.memory (ng) A lightly populated newsgroup for Microsoft Windows programmers interested in memory management. There's not much discussion here, just questions and answers about creating models and arrays. ✓**USENET**

comp.os.ms-windows.programmer.misc (ng) A newsgroup for amateur Microsoft Windows programmers, with suggestions for books and other sources of information. ✓**USENET**

MS Windows The Big Two: Apple & IBM

comp.os.ms-windows.programmer.networks (ng) A lightly populated newsgroup concerned with network software for Microsoft Windows. ✓USENET

comp.os.ms-windows.programmer.ole (ng) Not much traffic on this newsgroup for programmers who use Microsoft's OLE. There is an ongoing debate here about the benefits of OLE vs. OpenDoc. ✓USENET

comp.os.ms-windows.programmer.tools (ng) A popular meeting place for programmers with questions about tools for programming in Microsoft Windows. ✓USENET

comp.os.ms-windows.programmer.win32 (ng) An active newsgroup for Microsoft Windows programmers working with 32-bit addressing. Think Windows 95. ✓USENET

comp.os.ms-windows.programmer.winhelp (ng) A newsgroup for developers of help files that accompany applications running under Microsoft Windows. ✓USENET

Windows NT

Coast-to-Coast Software Repository The wares available here are divided up into the following categories: Editors, Graphics, Mail, Program Language Tools, and Registry Editors and Tools. And, while the inventory isn't terribly impressive yet, the collection is still under construction. ✓INTERNET →www http://www.acs.oakland.edu/oak/SimTel/SimTel-nt.html

comp.os.ms-windows.nt.misc (ng) General discussion of Windows NT. Topics include compatibility issues, configuration problems, and the future of NT. ✓USENET

comp.os.ms-windows.nt.setup (ng) Answers to questions about configuring and installing Windows NT. Not much discussion here, but a good place to ask your NT troubleshooting questions. ✓USENET

CSUSM Library Technical Services Windows NT Archive There are lots of NT upgrades and applications in this archive, but they're listed alphabetically rather than by category. As a result, you can either scroll through them all or go up to the WinWorld home page and use the search tool located there. ✓INTERNET→www http://coyote.csusm.edu/cwis/winworld/nt.html

Interior Alaska Windows NT User Group Get up-to-the-hour news about NT applications, graphics, and hardware compatibility, or utilize one of the many links to get to an NT FAQ, software archive, or newsgroup. There is also a useful bibliography of NT publications. ✓INTERNET→www http://www.imagi.net/~rmarty/nt.html

Microsoft Windows NT Forum A forum for users of Microsoft Windows NT. Ask questions of Microsoft, report bugs, and discuss the Windows NT operating system. Need to find out what hardware is compatible with Windows NT? Can't achieve modem dial-up within NT? These are just a couple of problems addressed in the message boards. The libraries contain patches uploaded by Microsoft to fix bugs, as well as support tools and documentation you can download or consult when you need technical support. ✓COMPUSERVE→go winnt

Microsoft Windows NT Server If you're in the market to buy a network OS system, it would be well worth your time to check out the product overview and specs available at this site. But if you need NT tech support, visit the other NT sites listed in this book; though Microsoft's page looks as though it might be helpful and informative, it's just a commercial site, with order forms that let you buy tech support from the Seattle software giant. ✓INTERNET→www http://www.microsoft.com/pages/bussys/ntserver/nts00000.htm

Northern California Windows NT Users Group Meeting dates, locations, and agendas for the popular Bay Area user group. ✓INTERNET→ www http://www.actioninc.com/winntug.htm

Rocky Mountain NT Users Group They've got all the links—FAQs, archives, FTP sites, NT Web servers, etc. ✓INTERNET→www http://budman.cmdl.noaa.gov/RMWNTUG/RMWNTUG.HTM

San Diego County Windows NT Users Group The mission of this group is "to promote the use of Windows NT Advanced Server and Workstation, to act as a conduit for the free exchange of information and discussion of NT-related issues, and to be the receiving part for Microsoft and third-party products providing feedback to these vendors on current and future needs of the NT community." Does the group's site satisfy its mission statement? Decide for yourself. ✓INTERNET→ www http://www.bhs.com/sdwntug/

SimTel Windows NT Software Editors, graphics viewers, mail programs, programming

86 Net Tech

The Big Two: Apple & IBM MS Windows

tools, and registry editors for Windows NT users. ✓**INTERNET**→*www* http://www.acs.oakland.edu/oak/SimTel/SimTel-nt.html

University of Karlsruhe Windows NT Support Center Information on NT tools, drivers, hardware compatibility, and other "diverse things." It's about half English and half German, but you'll manage to find your way into the NT directories of the Center for Innovative Computer Applications (CICA) and Microsoft FTP sites. ✓**INTERNET**→*www* http://jerusalem.windows-nt.uni-karlsruhe.de/eng lish.htm

Windows NT Information A good starting point for NT information; it covers the basics like "What is NT?" and supplies links to relevant FAQs, FTP sites, and other NT-related Web servers. Available in German or English. ✓**INTERNET**→*www* http://www.informatik.uni-stuttgart.de/misc/nt/nt.html

Windows 95

A Hyperlinked Visual Tour of Windows 95 Brought to you buy the publisher who puts out *Windows magazine* (not to mention *NetGuide* magazine), this is an illustrated preview of the Windows 95 system. ✓**INTERNET**→*www* http://techweb.cmp.com/tech web/techweb/win95/1.htm

Dylan's Windows 95 Home Page For all its elegance, the page is little more than a collection of links to Net sites carrying Windows 95 information or software. ✓**INTERNET**→*www* http://www.wam.umd.edu/~dylan/win95.html

Frank's Windows 95 Page The site boasts its own "bag o' tips" for Windows 95 (e.g., "icons in control panel are messed up.") and links to other Windows 95 resources, including a page with info on setting up TCP/IP and SLIP. ✓**INTERNET**→*www* http://oeonline.com/~frankc/fjcw95.html

Microsoft Windows 95 Home Page Press releases, newsletters, a reviewer's guide, an FAQ, and information on topics from multimedia to networking. ✓**INTERNET**→*www* http://www.microsoft.com/pages/peropsys/win_news/win95/ms-www/ms-intro.htm

Unofficial Windows 95 Software Archive Small but growing, the archive already carries Internet applications, graphics programs, and animated cursors for Windows 95. ✓**INTERNET**→*www* http://www.netex.net/w95/windows95/

Windows 95 Info Page Besides a work-in-progress FAQ about Microsoft's newest baby, the site links to articles about Windows 95, other Windows 95 home pages, and several guides to configuring TCP/IP in Windows 95. ✓**INTERNET**→*www* http://www2.pcix.com/~snipe/win95home.html

> "There's a fairly wide window of opportunity for those who want to learn more about Microsoft's 1995 update of its immensely popular operating system."

The Windows 95 Page There's a fairly wide window of opportunity for those who want to learn more about Microsoft's 1995 update of its immensely popular operating system. Phil Jones, the creator of this site, has already begun tracking and linking to the best Windows 95 shareware. He is also carrying news about the system, links to several shareware archives with Windows 95 programs, and links to other "interesting sites with Windows 95 information." ✓**INTERNET** →*www* http://biology.queensu.ca/~jonesp/

Vendors

Product Query Form This Web query form can be used to search the "Tools for Windows Buyers' Guide." Select a product category, and within minutes you'll have an extensive list of dealers and manufacturers selling Windows products. ✓**INTERNET**→*www* http://www.mfi.com/msj/wintools/wintprod.html

Tools For Windows Vendor Directory A directory of Windows vendors, listed alphabetically. The information about each vendor includes company name, street address, city, state, zip code, country, phone, and toll-free number. ✓**INTERNET**→*www* http://www.mfi.com/msj/wintools/wintools.html

Windows 3rd Party Applications Forums Eight forums with more than 100 vendors, putting patches, demos, and press releases in the libraries. Vendors range from Asymetrix to ELAN Software to Peachtree Software. How does it work? Substitute the <?> in the address for a letter, a-through-h, or search the CompuServe index (go index) by company name. ✓**COMPUSERVE**→*go* winap <?>

Net Tech 87

OS/2 The Big Two: Apple & IBM

OS/2

In 1987 Bill Gates and IBM signed a joint development agreement for what Gates then described as "the most important operating system, and possibly program, of all time. As the successor to DOS, which has over 10 million systems in use, [OS/2] creates incredible opportunities." Meanwhile Microsoft programmers were working overtime to whip Windows into shape. OS/2 became IBM's first slap in the face and it effectively kept the giant out of the software market. Yet OS/2 has found a small but noticeable group of followers, as these sites prove. Wanna see IBM strike back? Go to **OS/2 Warp vs. Windows95**: "Microsoft has a track record of delivering 'cosmetically advanced' operating systems while ignoring the more important issues like robustness, capacity, and true object-orientation." Ha!

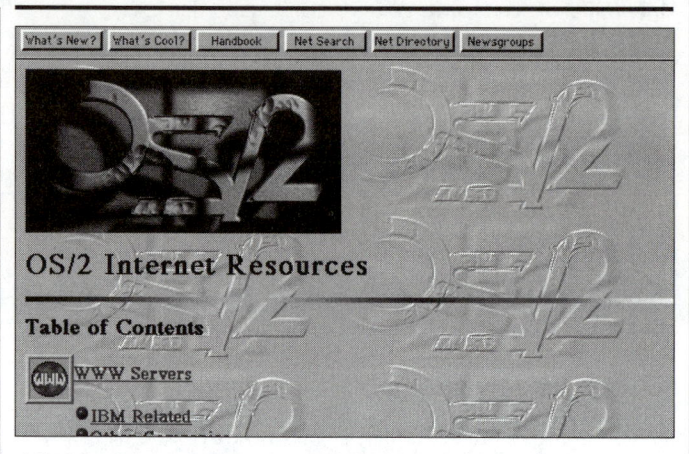

OS/2 Internet Resources—http://www.ccsf.caltech.edu/~kasturi/os2.html

On the Net

Across the board

CalTech's OS/2 Site If you're looking for information about the OS/2 operating system, everything you could ever possibly need is available through this single resource center. This is an exceptionally well-organized Web site, with links to every imaginable Internet resource relating to OS/2, including several different mirror sites for the "OS/2 Pharmacy." You'll find descriptions of, as well as links to, international Web servers, FTP sites, and newsgroups. ✓**INTERNET**→*www* http://www.ccsf.caltech.edu/~kasturi/os2.html

IBM OS/2 Gopher IBM provides this grab bag of OS/2 resources. There are information files, "Tips and Techniques" documents, and an 80-page manual of programming workarounds. Files are accompanied by descriptions. ✓**INTERNET**→*www* gopher://index.almaden.ibm.com/los2info/os2menu.70

IBM OS/2 Users Forum A forum devoted to user questions and comments relating to hardware and software on the OS/2 operating system. Any programming, networking, or gaming queries for any version of OS/2, including WARP, can be addressed through the message boards. Those in search of company-administered technical support should address the IBM OS/2 Support Forum. Be sure and check out the libraries here for help documentation on a variety of topics as well as a large selection of printer drivers and dozens of games for use on any OS/2 system. ✓**COMPUSERVE**→*go* os2users

IBM's OS/2 Site If you're an OS/2 fanatic, you can collect extraneous information about the operating system from this IBM resource center. For example, there's a detailed report about the IBM-sponsored Tour of Italy bicycle race, and a press release concerning OS/2 WARP use in China. You'll also find links to international Websites in Europe, the Middle East, and Japan. There's general information, too, such as IBM corporate promotional material. ✓**INTERNET**→*www* http://www.austin.ibm.com/pspinfo/os2.html

MIT's OS/2 Site The students of the Massachusetts Institute of

The Big Two: Apple & IBM OS/2

Technology (MIT) provide this OS/2 information center. It features some FAQs and links to newsgroups and other Web sites, but nothing you can't find at the more thorough sites. ✓**INTERNET**→*www* http://www.mit.edu:8001/activities/os2/os2world.html

The OS/2 Forum Here's the place to find general information about IBM's OS/2 operating system. One of the best features of this AOL forum is a helpful "Reference Guide," which provides a list of answers to specific frequently asked questions, such as proper OS/2 installation procedures. You can access an extensive list of toll-free telephone numbers that connect you to OS/2 support services, or post a question directly to the message boards, which are conveniently organized. The message board categories include Development, Press Releases, and Tips, as well as separate Q & A's for both OS/2 and WARP. If you're looking for immediate advice, try turning to the live chat conference center. This forum's software libraries are well organized, too. They have been divided into dozens of logical categories, which makes locating the software you need easy. For example, rather than bunching every OS/2 utility into one giant listing, there are separate collections for Printer, Screen, and Patch utilities. Even the Graphics library has ten different categories, ranging from Cartoons to Tools. OS/2 users will appreciate the resources available here. ✓**AMERICA ONLINE**→*keyword* os2

The OS/2 WWW Homepage If it's not linked to this page, it's probably not about OS/2. Besides offering links to major software archives, other OS/2 Web pages, and the OS/2 newsgroups, the site has a large list of OS/2 user group home pages. ✓**INTERNET**→*www* http://web.mit.edu/afs/athena/activity/o/os2/www/os2world.html

UIUC OS/2 Site The University of Illinois provides a collection of somewhat outdated resources for OS/2 at this Web site. The most interesting feature here is "I Heard It/2," a collection of amusing quotations from people like Microsoft's Bill Gates concerning the industry's expectations for OS/2. ✓**INTERNET**→*www* http://www.cen.uiuc.edu/~jt11635/os2/os2.html

Support & info

comp.os.os2.advocacy (ng) Want to discuss the future of computing with a crowd of enthusiastic participants? Then wade on into this heavily populated message board relating to the OS/2 operating system. But, be sure to wear fire-retardant clothing, because among the opinions and speculations there are plenty of energetic flames. Testy message posts like "mentally challenged," "petty WIN95 bashing" and "I thought I would never say this…" liven up the discussions here, and some of the thread lengths run into the hundreds. The discussion is general and informative, focusing mainly upon the various versions of OS/2 and Windows. The marketing, development, and efficacy of WARP, Windows NT, and Windows95 are the hottest topics of conversation. This is not the best place for you to post a specific technical question. Chances are your posting will be either ignored or ridiculed. ✓**USENET**

comp.os.os2.announce (ng) The best way to keep abreast of the latest happenings in the world of the OS/2 operating system is to periodically visit this moderated message board. Featured here are announcements concerning OS/2 news, utilities, and updates. There is no discussion, but you can read press releases, get the dates of user group meetings, and learn the location of a new Internet information site. If you're an OS/2 aficionado, this is definitely worth subscribing to. ✓**USENET**

comp.os.os2.bugs Do you know how on the game show *Jeopardy!* the answers always come before the questions? Well, that's the novel idea behind this informative discussion group for the OS/2 operating system. Users who encounter bugs and glitches report how they went about fixing them here. Happily, the more traditional people can still receive responses to "Help!" messages posted here. One user was experiencing a CD-ROM error message that would not go away, and another had trouble changing drivers under WARP. ✓**INTERNET**

comp.os.os2.misc (ng) "I erased my NoWhere1 folder and now I can't find NoWhere." Like the WARP user who posted this eccentric message, if you can't find a site to answer a specific OS/2 operating system question, try this "miscellaneous" newsgroup. Naturally, the topics are diverse, ranging from OS/2 newsreaders to video cards. Still, there's plenty of traffic here, and someone passing by ought to be able to help you. ✓**USENET**

comp.os.os2.setup "Boot problems" seems to be a key phrase in this newsgroup, and no one's talking about defective footwear, either. The installation and configuration of system software can be an arduous affair. If you're having trouble with OS/2, this well-populated message board

Net Tech 89

OS/2 The Big Two: Apple & IBM

can definitely make your life easier. Besides presenting troubleshooting questions and answers, the group offers some general discussion about WARP and OS/2, along with recommendations about third party software. ✓**INTERNET**

IBM OS/2 Support Forum
Can't get Word for Windows to run on OS/2? Having installation problems with that pesky Warp upgrade? Pay a visit to this IBM-sponsored technical-support forum for users of OS/2 system software. This is a heavily trafficked forum and it usually takes the IBM support staff up to four business days to respond to your OS/2 troubleshooting queries. So you may want to try and catch a fellow OS/2 user in the conference room for more immediate technical support. The libraries contain many technical documents, several of which focus on using fax software from within OS/2 for Windows or DOS. ✓**COMPUSERVE**→*go* os2support

IBM OS/2 Unedited Discussion List (ml) Discuss everything you ever wanted to know about OS/2, but were afraid to ask, at this Dutch mailing list, which comes equipped with an archive search and lots of goodwill toward the popular PC operating system. ✓**INTERNET**→*email* listserv@nic.surfnet.nl ✍ *Type in message body:* subscribe os2-l <your full name>

#os/2 Live discussion with other OS/2 users. Ask questions, exchange advice, and just chat. ✓**INTERNET**→*irc* #os/2

OS/2 FAQ Bring on your OS/2 questions. One FAQ, geared toward the new user, serves as an introduction to the operating system and online resources. The second FAQ, a four-part monstrosity, is targeted at the veteran OS/2 user and reads as a fairly technical and detailed description of this operating system's computing environment. ✓**INTERNET**→*www* http://www.cis.ohio-state.edu:80/text/faq/usenet/os2-faq/top.html

Software

comp.os.os2.apps (ng) Properly configuring the OS/2 operating system to efficiently run commercial applications is a subject which concerns both home users and systems professionals. Memory settings, patches, and glitches are the topics of discussion on this friendly message board. Often a posting that warrants attention gets responses from several people with different opinions, which may be helpful when trying to fix a complex problem. One large thread covers the pros and cons of enlarging the input queue in order to free up memory. Besides general configuration information, the newsgroup also features questions and answers concerning specific software packages, printers, and boards. ✓**USENET**

comp.os.os2.beta (ng) Do you like to be one step ahead of the crowd? Are you the type of person who sneaks into Hollywood movie premieres? Does waiting for the official release of new operating systems drive you batty? Take heart, because Beta testers for OS/2 systems software exchange their impressions of unreleased versions in this newsgroup. The posting with the largest thread is entitled "Advice to IBM," and most of the messages fall into a similar category. Discussion focuses upon the actual characteristics of the Beta version, reporting glitches and problems testers have encountered. If you're interested in becoming a Beta tester, someone here can definitely tell you who to contact. ✓**USENET**

OS/2 FTP Archives An extensive collection of software and information files concerning the OS/2 operating system. In fact, this is probably the largest repository of OS/2 software in the universe. There are 16-bit development tools, 32-bit tools, games, graphics, patches, and drivers. You can also download several years worth of back issues of IBM's Developer Support News Newsletter. ✓**INTERNET** ...→*www* ftp://hobbes.nmsu.edu/os2/ ...→*www* ftp://ftp-os2.cdrom.com/pub/os2/ ...→*www* ftp://software.watson.ibm.com/pub/os2/

Getting Warped with OS/2—http://www.csv.warwick.ac.uk/~phueg/os2/

The Big Two: Apple & IBM OS/2

The OS/2 Shareware BBS (bbs) A pay-for-use shareware board with oodles of OS/2 programs and documentation. ☎→ *dial* 708-895-4042

Software Library—OS/2 A limited collection of OS/2 files and utilities (about 20 in all), accompanied by short file descriptions and release notes. The selection includes REXX Graphics Extensions, an MPEG Video Player, and GIF Viewers. A good starter set. ✓**INTERNET** …→*www* http://www.state.ky.us/software/os2.html …→*www* http://www.state.ky.us/software/windows.html …→*www* http://www.state.ky.us/software/os2.html …→*www* http://www.state.ky.us/software/windows.html

VISION OS/2 Gopher Here's another software library featuring OS/2-related CSDs, drivers, and applications. The best feature of this site is its connection to IBM's Almaden Research Center and the IBM Kiosk for Education. Both are excellent, albeit specialized, Gopher sites. ✓**INTERNET**→*www* gopher://vision.ns.doe.gov/ los2.70

WARP

Bishop University's OS/2 Site Only the most up-to-date version of OS/2 WARP is covered here. There are information files for both OS/2 users and OS/2 programmers, along with a small FTP site. ✓**INTERNET**→*www* http://cyniska.ubishops.ca/os2/os2.html

Get Warped with OS/2! It's nice to encounter Internet sites that can offer serious information and maintain a sense of humor at the same time. The people from this British—aha! that should explain the humor—site offer a thorough listing of FAQ's and system advice pertaining to the OS/2 operating system. However, they also include a "Jokes from the Internet" category featuring Pentium riddles and the "Top 10 Reasons to Buy Windows." There's also a "Groovy Fonts and Bitmaps" category that offers typeface samples and font files for your desktop. And you'll encounter listings of native 32-bit applications along with where they can be found. Plenty of related links here, too. ✓**INTERNET**→*www* http://www.csv.warwick.ac.uk/~phueg/os2/

OS/2 Warp vs. Windows 95 The title for this Website sounds like it's referring to a monster movie, and in many ways it is. Officially known as a "Decisionmaker's Guide," the IBM-sponsored resource center makes comparisons between IBM's OS/2 WARP and Microsoft's Windows 95. Since IBM controls the information here, all of it tends to highlight the benefits of OS/2 and the perceived flaws of Windows 95. The various articles address system architecture, user interfaces, and the availability of third-party software. The language here is very technical, because the information is intended for systems administrators, not home users. In spite of the obvious bias, it's still quite informative. ✓**INTERNET**→*www* http://www.austin.ibm.com/pspinfo/os2vschg.html

The Warp Pharmacy A huge support site for OS/2's latest incarnation—WARP. Walk through a tutorial on hard disk issues or get an update on Avance Logic Video Cards (including drivers). Read notes on Quicken 4.0 under WARP or take the TCP/IP tutorial. Having problems? Browse the Procedures Shelf for advice. ✓**INTERNET**→*www* http://www.zeta.org.au/~jon/WarpPharmacy.html

Programming

comp.os.os2.programmer. misc (ng) Programmers who write code for OS/2 machines gather here to discuss their work. The majority of the postings refer to the C++ and REXX programming languages. Some of the discussion covers OS/2 configurations and where to find OS/2-related books and programming resources. ✓**USENET**

comp.os.os2.programmer.oop (ng) Programming roadblocks and problems in object oriented programming for the OS/2 operating system are the order of the day here. The conversation is highly technical, with source codes thrown in to confuse any beginners who might drop by. If you are an experienced programmer, post your question here. If you're a beginner, you still might want to subscribe, because there are periodic postings concerning support and training resources. ✓**USENET**

comp.os.os2.programmer. porting (ng) If writing ordinary source code for OS/2 system soft-

> "Testy posts like 'mentally challenged,' 'petty WIN95 bashing' and 'I thought I would never say this…' liven up comp.os.os2. advocacy."

Net Tech 91

OS/2 The Big Two: Apple & IBM

ware isn't technical enough to interest you, then maybe your curiosity will be satisfied by this newsgroup dedicated to programming for inter-platform porting software. Naturally, the discussion covers many different operating systems (in relation to OS/2). Many postings do receive responses. ✓USENET

comp.os.os2.programmer.tools (ng) All artists need tools, and computer programmers who work under the OS/2 operating system can find a few of theirs here. The messages in this newsgroup are littered with jargon, so be sure you know your stuff before logging on. You'll find comparisons between programs in the postings, as well as references to where to get programming utilities. ✓USENET

IBM Thomas Watson Research Center OS/2 FTP Server Beta versions of various OS/2 applications are made available by this research branch of IBM. The majority of the offerings are "experimental files," put out by IBM for OS/2 developers. ✓INTERNET→*www* ftp://software.watson.ibm.com/pub/os2

Stupid OS/2 Tricks A popular collection of programming tips and REXX scripts compiled by an Illinois user group. Tips are separated into two different categories, Windows-OS/2 and WARP. The articles address topics such as how to cure a jumpy mouse and methods of opening the "Settings Notebook." You can access this Website from practically every other important OS/2 site on the Internet. ✓INTERNET→*www* http://index.almaden.ibm.com/nonibm/tricks/tricks.html

Team OS/2 Online This is the headquarters for the international electronic user group known as Team OS/2. The group uses this area to announce and report on various OS/2-related events, programming demonstrations, and developers' conferences. There's a searchable membership list, if you're looking for someone in particular. ✓INTERNET ...→*www* http://www.teamos2.org ...→*www* http://www.intac.com/nnjos2/os2web.html

User Groups

Berkeley OS/2 Users' Group ✓INTERNET→*www* http://godzilla.EECS.Berkeley.EDU/os2/

Cleveland OS/2 User's Group ✓INTERNET→*www* ftp://ftp.wariat.org/pub/users/cos2ug.html

Index — OS/2 User Groups from Around the World ✓INTERNET→*www* http://www.halcyon.com/os2_northwest/usergroups.html

Inland Empire OS/2 Users ✓INTERNET→*www* http://krupp.claremont.edu/ieou/ieouwww.html

Mid-Atlantic OS/2 User Group, Virginia Beach, VA ✓INTERNET→*www* http://www.pinn.net/~reaper/maos2ug.html

North Suburban Chicago-Area OS/2 Users' Group (NSCOUG) ✓INTERNET→*www* http://www.mcs.com/~schmidtj/http/nscoug/home.html

Northern New Jersey TEAM OS/2 Web Server ✓INTERNET→*www* http://www.intac.com/nnjos2/nnjos2ug.html

OS/2 Bay Area User Group ✓INTERNET→*www* ftp://ftp.netcom.com/pub/da/daveb/os2baug/main.html

OS/2 User Group at Univ. of Texas ✓INTERNET→*www* http://deputy.law.utexas.edu/os2usersgrp.html

Ottawa OS/2 User's Group ✓INTERNET→*www* http://www.synapse.net/OS2/Welcome.html

Pacific Northwest OS/2 Users Group ✓INTERNET→*www* http://www.halcyon.com/pnwos2ug/pnwos2ug.html

Vendors

IBM OS/2 Vendor's Forum Technical support is provided in these two forums by numerous companies who manufacture software compatible within OS/2-based systems. Just some of the companies offering tech support via the message boards include (in Forum A) One Up, Sundial Systems, DevTech, Hochware, Boca-Soft, GPF Systems, Softronics, JBA, Arcadia Tech, and (in Forum B) PCX, SCA, Carry Associates, MSR Development, ProEngineering, and Softouch Systems. Forum B also has a generic archive of shareware for OS/2, so if you're looking for an alarm clock or a calculator you can get one here. Check the specific company libraries for software upgrades and company news. ✓COMPUSERVE→*go* os2aven *and* os2bven

Part 3

The Rest of the Field

Amiga The Rest of the Field

Amiga

Unlike the senselessly named automobiles that patrol America's streets—Corolla? Gallant? Neon?—Commodore's home computer lives up to its name. Since its introduction, in fact, the Amiga has been a close friend to programmers looking for an affordable alternative to Macintosh and IBM platforms, and it has found special favor with filmmakers and video artists. Online, Amiga culture is alive and well, with chat percolating on the **#Amiga** IRC channel, news bulletins dispatched over **comp.sys.amiga.announce**, and thousands of programs available for downloading at **Aminet**. And don't forget to investigate Commodore commerce at the **Amiga Vendor Forum**.

On the Net

Across the board

#Amiga MAMAbot oversees this hectic Amigan channel; at any given moment there are 15 people coming, 10 leaving, and there's more traffic than on an L.A. freeway. Conversation occasionally focuses on ESCOM's recent purchase of the Amiga product line, or whether the Deep AGA chip works with the A4000, but then the announcement "Vorlon will dine now" comes up, and Mr_ Acne votes to change the subject. Drink a pot of coffee, eat about four candy bars, and then, by all means, jump into the fray. ✓ **INTERNET**→*irc* #amiga

#Amiga IRC Homepage This is the welcome mat of the #Amiga channel; meet MAMA, PAPA, and all the little Amigans—fonkie, drizzit, beachboy, and shadowFox, too. ✓ **INTERNET**→*www* http://www.pitt.edu/~schivins/irc-amiga.html

The Amiga Home Page Tapping into resources across the Net, this page brings together an amazing range of information, support, and software for the Amiga user. The site leads off with the most recent news about the computer and then links to Amiga companies, user groups, software sites, Amiga art projects, news magazines, and other Amiga Websites. ✓ **INTERNET**→*www* http://www.cs.cmu.edu/Web/People/mjw/Computer/Amiga/MainPage.html

Amiga Tech Forum Looking for the latest version of Triton to help you create a graphical user interface? Or maybe you're looking for advice on choosing a C compiler. Here's a forum dedicated to the technical and programming use of Amiga computers, with topics on authoring systems, C programming, system software, and more. ✓ **COMPUSERVE**→*go* amigatech

Amiga User Forum "OK, I'm not stupid, I bought an Amiga," wrote James. "So why can't I get this AmiTCP working?" James got lots of advice in this friendly spot for typical Amiga users (as opposed to the hardcore techies, who've got forums of their own). The message sections have areas focused on issues from communi-

The Rest of the Field Amiga

cations to hardware, while the libraries include utilities, demos, and other files. ✓**COMPUSERVE**→*go* amigauser

The Amiga WWW Resource
The mysterious inner workings of the Amiga cult unveil themselves here: connect to online magazines like "Amiga Power" and "Amiga Link," or access "Her story," a detailed account of how the Amiga OS was developed. First Virtual accounts are accepted at "The Mini-Mall," where the newest Amiga wares and peripherals are available for sale. And for those ready to commit their lives to their A3000, find or seek a position through the Amiga Jobs classified pages. ✓**INTERNET**→*www* http://www.cs.cmu.edu/~mjw/Amiga/

Champagne-Urbana Commodore Users Group This site provides product info on Amiga hard- and software, news updates on the ownership and management of the C=Amiga trademark, and a "Sources" directory of manufacturers and mail-order companies that distribute Amiga-compatible goods. Its links will bring you to Aminet and other shareware archives. ✓**INTERNET**→*www* http://www.prairienet.org/community/clubs/cucug/amiga.html

comp.sys.amiga.advocacy (ng) "I for Amiga, the world for IBM clones" sums up disscussion here. Users discuss the future of C=platforms and suggest ways to expand the Amiga universe. ✓**USENET**

comp.sys.amiga.misc (ng) The computer professionals and Amiga jocks in this newsgroup discuss topics ranging from the best DD/SW68k assembler to the new Scorched Tanks release. It's a great place to get advice if you're having CrossDOS difficulties or can't get your Hawk Board configured right. Be sure to add your Amiga system model number to your .sig file before posting here. ✓**USENET**

Basics

Amiga FAQs Need an introduction to the Amiga? The general Amiga FAQ offers fairly detailed explanations to about 50 questions ranging from "Can I use a 3.5" HD in my A1200?" to "How do I become a developer?" to "Can I run Unix on my Amiga?" ✓**INTERNET**→*www* http://www.cis.ohio-state.edu:80/text/faq/usenet/amiga/top.html

Amiga-Related Books FAQ
Order information and descriptions for dozens of Amiga-related books written on hardware, programming, telecommunications, and other computing topics. ✓**INTERNET**→*www* http://www.cis.ohio-state.edu:80/text/faq/usenet/amiga/books/faq.html

comp.sys.amiga.introduction (ng) If you're just discovering the joys of having a computer that you can plug into your TV, come here for explanations of Amiga's various video modes, SCSI card connectors, and Super Denise. There are also tips on improving your Amiga-to-Internet connectivity. ✓**USENET**

News

AmigaReport Although the lead photo takes a while to download—it's a sort of newsy graphic, a few computers floating above a field of diagonal Amiga logos—this page houses *AmigaReport*, one of the best online sources for information about the Amiga. Want to keep up on the latest peripherals? Curious about how the Bahamian Supreme Court affects the liquidation of Commodore? Every issue of the magazine is here, and you can even donate money to help the page survive. ✓**INTERNET**→*www* http://www.cs.cmu.edu/Web/People/mjw/Computer/Amiga/News/AR/MainPage.html

comp.sys.amiga.announce (ml) Press releases and Amiga-related news items are posted here; recently, the bulk of conversation has been centered on Amiga's new owner, ESCOM Corp., and its plans for expanding the platform. ✓**USENET** ✓**INTERNET**→*email* announce-request@cs.ucdavis.edu ✍ *Write a request*

Imazine You can download this multimedia periodical from their home page and run it from CL1 or Workbench, on any Amiga model, from the A500 up to A4000. Most of the articles are in Polish, but there's an "English Corner" for slower readers. Contributors are encouraged to submit material. ✓**INTERNET**→*www* http://sun10.ci.pwr.wroc.pl/Imazine/

Hardware

comp.sys.amiga.hardware (ng) Bob's looking for a tape backup for his A3000, while Michael wants to know whether he can use his old high-density floppy drive with his A1200. Much of the discussion here centers around the intricacies and quirks of Amiga hardware. An active spot for Amiga-heads. ✓**USENET**

Software

alt.sources.amiga (ng) Users direct one another to particular applications. Generally there are more questions than useful an-

Net Tech 95

Amiga The Rest of the Field

swers. Hint: check out the resources at Aminet before asking about the location of a shareware program; it's probably there. Or try posting to comp.sys.amiga.applications instead. ✓USENET

alt.sys.amiga.demos (ng) It's been pretty quiet here; the sale of Amiga has slowed down the production of new games and applications drastically. Participants remain optimistic though, and rumors about virtual wares abound. ✓USENET

Amiga File Finder Think you saw a file in one of the Amiga-related libraries, but you're not sure where? Well, File Finder's the answer. It provides a searchable database of files from the Amiga forums. You can search by topic, file submission date, forum name, and other criteria. ✓COMPUSERVE→ go amigaff

Aminet The fact that there are thousands of freeware and shareware files available here is a given—it's the largest collection of Amiga files on the Net. But it's the "Recent Uploads" area that is really amazing. Aminet provides its own search tool to make finding files easy, and the "Recent Uploads" area provides a personalized update option so users can view all the files uploaded since the last time they visited. It's hard to believe it's all free. ✓INTERNET ...→www ftp://ftp.luth.se/pub/aminet/ ...→www ftp://wuarchive.wustl.edu/pub/aminet/ ...→www http://wuarchive.wustl.edu/pub/aminet/info/www/home.html ...→www http://src.doc.ic.ac.uk/public/aminet/info/www/home-src.doc.html

comp.sys.amiga.applications (ng) Where the manuals leave off, this newsgroup picks up. If you're having routing problems, need ARexx tips or want Studio II help, query here. ✓USENET

Funet Amiga Archive There's enough software in this archive to make your Amiga stand on its hind legs and bark like a dog. Get new versions of AMOS, fish disks, game demos, business apps, communications programs, and sound and graphics programs here—many have help documents to boot. If you want to browse, be sure to check out the site's index. ✓INTERNET→www ftp://www.funet.fi/pub/amiga/ *Info:* ✓INTERNET →www http://www.funet.fi:80/pub/amiga/

Programming

Amiga Programming A treasure trove for Amiga programmers looking for language code (Perl scripting or Fortran programming, anyone?) or guides to programming. ✓INTERNET→www ftp://www.funet.fi/pub/amiga/programming/

comp.sys.amiga.programmer (ng) If you're seeking beta testers for your new program, looking for help with a "patch problemette," or just want to lurk in a newsgroup full of people talking about programming for the Amiga, then you've found the place. You'll be treated to posts titled "Resource disassembler wanted," "C compiler probs," and many more. ✓USENET

Vendors

Amiga Vendor Forum Here's where you can find Amiga vendors such as NewTek, Softwood, and Utilities Unlimited. Feel free to offer gripes—quite a popular pastime—or even a few suggestions about products. The libraries include release notes, specs, and demos. ✓COMPUSERVE→go amigavendor

comp.sys.amiga.reviews (ng) A moderated newsgroup for reviews of both commercial and shareware Commodore Amiga products. An index to the reviews is usually posted to the newsgroup with new additions highlighted at the top. The group takes its reviews quite seriously, even posting templates and checklists for writers. ✓USENET *Archives:* ✓INTERNET →www ftp://math.uh.edu/pub/Amiga/comp.sys.amiga.reviews/doc

Commodore 64 & 128

The C= Home Page The main focus of this site is DOS emulators: get shareware versions for C64's and PC64's, as well as the Emulator FAQ. Now you can play that old C64 game on your souped-up 486. Links to several other C64 Web and FTP sites are also offered. ✓INTERNET→www http://www.engr.wisc.edu/~conover/c64.html

C64 Emulators Several versions of DOS and Mac emulators are available here, mostly zipped. ✓INTERNET→www ftp://watson.mbb.sfu.ca/pub/c64/emulator/

Commodore 64 Archive From graphics programs to games, archiving utilities to telecommunication software, the site features a wealth of programs for the C64 user. ✓INTERNET→www ftp://www.funet.fi/pub/amiga/misc/c64/

Commodore Application Forum Lots of people looking to sell their Commodore 64 computers in this spot. It's not an especially active area, but it is devoted to those interested in all types of soft-

The Rest of the Field Amiga

ware for Commodore 8-bit computers. If that's your thing, check out the wide range of application in the libraries. ✓**COMPUSERVE**→*go* cbmapp

Commodore Service Forum Having trouble printing? Looking for a way to convert data from your C64 to a Mac? You've come to the right place. Staffed by employees of Commodore Business Machines, this forum provides a spot for Commodore users to seek help from the experts and exchange ideas with fellow users. ✓**COMPUSERVE**→*go* cbmservice

comp.sys.cbm (ng) Where do you go when all your friends have 486's and live for the latest release of the Windows operating system and you're still stuck troubleshooting a problem on your beloved Commodore 128? Take the off-ramp to this newsgroup, where a passionate group of Commodore 8-bit machine owners hang out. And what do "passionate" C64 and C128 owners do? They exchange Commodore jokes, hock printers, query about vendors and file conversion, confer on programming, and advise each other on where to get C64 shareware. Twice a month The Commodore FTP Sites Listing is posted to the newsgroup with updated addresses and descriptions of Net sites with Commodore files. Topics covered in the FAQ include configuring your hard drive, upgrades, emulators, Commodore OSs, how to connect to the Net, DOS compatability, and where to find 8-bit equipment. Coders can get the rundown on recent demos and instructions for tweaking their graphics even further. ✓**USENET FAQ:** ✓**INTERNET**→*www* http://www.msen.com/~brain/faqhome.html

> "Where do you go when your friends have 486's and you're still stuck trouble-shooting a problem on your beloved Commodore 128?"

CP/M Files Thousands of software programs that can run on the C128—from utilities to financial planners to games. ✓**INTERNET** …→*www* ftp://oak.oakland.edu/pub/cpm …→*www* ftp://oak.oakland.edu/pub2/cpm …→*www* ftp://wuarchive.wustl.edu//mirrors/cpm/c128 …→*www* ftp://ftp.demon.co.uk/pub/cpm

Documentation Page Stay away from this page unless you have some idea how to reassemble what you've just learned how to disassemble. There are I/O, ROM, and memory maps available, plus several tricks for making BASIC crash. Discover the secret anti-war message that lies hidden in your C128. ✓**INTERNET**→*www* http://www.hut.fi/%7Emsmakela/cbm/docs/

Jim Brain's CBM 8-bit Computer Home Page Jim will direct you to the Net sites of other Commodore users, newsletters, and the hypertext versions of several CBM-related FAQs. He's also compiled the "Canonical List of Commodore Produced Computer Equipment" and offers visitors a look at his "CBM Snapshot Album," which contains pictures of various Commodore computers and peripherals. ✓**INTERNET**→*www* http://www.msen.com/~brain/cbmhome.html

Major Commodore FTP Site Everyone's doing it. Emulating the C64 on different platforms, that is, and you can get the emulation software here. The site is also home to other Commodore files such as archiving and dearchiving programs, audio files, graphics, utility programs, back issues of a Commodore hacking 'zine, documentation for Commodore computers, and games, games, and more games. ✓**INTERNET**→*www* ftp://ccnga.uwaterloo.ca/pub/cbm

Users

Geographical Amiga Users Home Page Internet List Visit other Amiga users from around the world. Many of them offer Amiga-related FAQs in languages other than English and review games and applications they've encountered. GAUPHIL's "Statistical Diagrams" break up users by nation, presenting perplexing capitalist riddles: how did the Norwegians get so many Amigas? If the birth rate increases in Japan by .34% annually, how many Japanese Amiga users will there be in the year 2041? ✓**INTERNET**→*www* http://namu19.gwdg.de/knoll/GAUHPIL/Main.html

Worldwide Index of Commodore Users Groups From Edmonton to Ireland, from the Pacific Northwest to the deepest reaches of Scandinavia, computer users can't get enough of their Commodores. This page keeps track of user groups, and adds listings regularly. ✓**INTERNET**→*www* http://www.prairienet.org/community/clubs/cucug/usergroups.html

Net Tech 97

Atari The Rest of the Field

Atari

If you know Atari only as a home entertainment system and video games manufacturer, you're partly correct. It's true that Atari stood at the forefront of the video game boom—the company's introduction of Pong in 1972 forever changed the way the world felt about its thinking machines. And since the early eighties, Atari has been producing a variety of microcomputers, known primarily for their cutting-edge graphics and sound capabilities. While Atari's market share in the United States pales in comparison to such companies as Apple and IBM, Atari machines remain extremely popular with certain groups of users, especially musicians. Websurfers with fond memories of Atari's salad days may want to begin their day at the **Central Atari Information Network**; those puzzled by the failure of Atari's Jaguar game system can check out **Jaguar Info**; and everyone should visit the **UMuch Atari Software Archive**.

Unofficial Jaguar Home Page—http://www.bucknell.edu/~svensson/

On the Net

Across the board

Atari Computing Forum The place to go for Atari talk, whether you want to look for advice on a "sick hard drive" or lament what might have been. "The Atari systems were always easy to use and usually represented very good value," wrote Bob. "Unfortunately, we'll never be able to see how far they might have gone." Still, you'll find plenty of like-minded Atari fans in this spot discussing applications, emulators, and anything else Atari. The libraries include graphics software, utilities to convert files for use on other platforms, communication programs, and texts on Atari computing. ✓**COMPUSERVE**→*go* ataricomputing

Atari Web Pages Want a list of FTP sites carrying Atari shareware? Check the Atari FTP List. Need instructions on how to set up a SLIP connection for your Atari ST? Read the Atari ST SLIP FAQ. Unsure which image formats you can read on your Atari? There's an explanation of picture formats here. Looking for a review of Flash 2 (a telecommunications program)? There's a small but growing collection of Atari-related product reviews. This Website also posts news about the Atari world and links to dozens of other Atari Websites. ✓**INTERNET**→*www* http://www.mcc.ac.uk/~dlms/atari.html

Central Atari Information Network CAIN is the CIA of the Atari world; they know everything about all its computing systems, the games and applications still in development in the Atari community, and the Atari Corporation's current stock value. The staff provides tech support for 8-, 16- and 32-bit systems, Portfolio, and Lynx. The Website includes links to the Atari SIG—a forum—on the Cleveland FreeNet. The SIG maintains extensive shareware archives and active message boards—it's known as one of the best Atari spots online. ✓**INTERNET**→*www* http://ace.cs.ohiou.edu/personal/mleair/cain.html

comp.sys.atari.advocacy (ng) People here recognize the fact that Atari completely botched the de-

The Rest of the Field Atari

veloping and marketing of its computer platforms, but they would rather forget about the debate and talk Atari nuts and bolts. Nevertheless, extended Windows rag sessions are ongoing on this newsgroup. ✓ USENET

comp.sys.atari.announce (ng) "June 6, 2004, 11:15 am: Contact with SubStation is lost. In panic, Mitushi's Board of Directors pay the U.S. government an unknown amount of money to lease a 'M.E.M.' (Multi-User Marine) to find out what has happened." That's where you and your friends come in. Get the storylines and press releases for SubStation and other new Atari games here. ✓ USENET

Magazines

ST Beermat Download the most recent issue of this Atari disk magazine to two ST-compatible disks, unzip them, and you've got yourself a Beermat. If you don't know what a Beermat is, run—don't walk—to find out. ✓ INTERNET→ www http://www.cms.dmu.ac.uk/~c1kd/beermat.html

8-bit

#Atari8 Live chat channel for quick responses to questions about Atari 8-bit computers. ✓ INTERNET→ irc #Atari8

8-Bit FAQ Not sure what a .dcm or .arc file is? Want to find the nearest Atari BBS? Then this is the FAQ for you. The section on Atari's custom chips—ANTIC, GTIA, and POKEY—is especially enlightening. ✓ INTERNET→www http://www.cis.ohio-state.edu/hypertext/faq/usenet/atari-8-bit/faq/faq.html

8-Bit Vendors and Develop- **ers FAQ** Companies that produce and distribute Atari 8-bit equipment and applications are listed here, along with addresses, phone numbers, and a brief summary of their products. ✓ INTERNET→www http://www.cis.ohio-state.edu/hypertext/faq/usenet/atari-8bit/vendev/faq.html

Atari 8-Bit Forum If you've got an Atari 8-bit PC or the entertainment-oriented Jaguar, here's a spot to talk telecommunications, utilities, games, and programming. In the "Jag's true potential" thread, you'll find lots of discussion of the virtues and faults of the Jaguar. And in the areas devoted to 8-bit computers, there are quite a few people buying and selling. A great spot for hardcore Atari enthusiasts. ✓ COMPUSERVE→go atari8

The Atari 8-Bit Home Page The Gatekeeper of this page provides all manner of A8 information in the form of documents, WWW links, software, magazines, statistics and a "History of Atari" section. One notable feature of this site is its Pinout offerings, in both .fig and PostScript formats. ✓ INTERNET→www http://www.cs.vu.nl/~ipoorten/Atari.8bit.Homepage/index.html

Closer to Home Atari Archive A mid-size archive for Atari 8-bit computers with games, audio players, utilities, graphics viewers, telecommunication programs, and word processing applications. ✓ INTERNET→www ftp://ftp.xmission.com/pub/users/j/jeking/8bit/

comp.sys.atari.8bit (ng) Participants in this busy newsgroup know their Atari 400/800/XL/XE's inside-out. Learn what they already know—how to re-program joystick ports, optimize an 825 printer, or navigate through applications like Ultima II, Flicker-Term, and Happy 7.1. ✓ USENET

Jaguar

Atari Jaguar This unofficial home page for the Jaguar—"the world's first 64-bit home console video game system"—offers press releases, screenshots, reviews, and secrets for a large selection of Jag wares. The games' plot summaries make for great reading. ✓ INTERNET→www http://www.bucknell.edu/~svensson/

Jaguar Info Jeff, the guy who maintains this site, got hired as a game developer and had to sign a Non-Disclosure Agreement. Consequently, all the juicy bits have been relocated, but the plot synopses and character sketches of games currently in development remain behind. Not thrilling, but interesting enough. ✓ INTERNET→www http://www2.ecst.csuchico.edu/~jschlich/Jaguar/jaguar.html

Atari-ST

comp.sys.atari.st (ng) The inevitable MAC/PC comparisons are plentiful here, but Atari-ST users also get the scoop on new HTML browsers, Linux ST, DigiDesign sound tools, and various remote imaging protocols. ✓ USENET

comp.sys.atari.st.tech (ng) Users investigate the ST's technical universe—ST pinouts, Ghost-Link, TOS Eproms, and what have you. ✓ USENET

Atari 2600

Atari 2600 This site's features include a complete list of all 2600 games and "carts" (cartridges), game manuals, 2600 programming instructions, and specs on Atari-compatible hardware. Get

Atari The Rest of the Field

detailed schematics for building your own composite adapter or learn how to earn Activision patches. And the Pictures of Rare Games section lets you re-live epic moments from classics like Swordquest WaterWorld, Pac Kong, Tooth Protectors, and Space Tunnel—all suitable for framing! ✓**INTERNET**→*www* http://www2.ecst.csuchico.edu/~gchance/2600 Stuff/2600index.html

Software

Atari File Finder Looking for the latest version of Speed of Light, but unsure where to find it? The Atari File Finder provides an easy way to track down all kinds of Atari files. You can search by several criteria, including forum name and topic. ✓**COMPUSERVE**→*go* atariff

Atari Ghostscript Get the full rundown on this freeware, which allows you to preview PostScript (PS) images and documents on your screen, converts PS files for non-PS printers, and creates an "interactive environment" for developing PostScript code. A clear and thorough FAQ explains how to use Ghostscript. ✓**INTERNET**→*www* http://godel.ph.utexas.edu/Members/timg/gs/gs.html

UMich Atari Software Archive With more than 7,500 Atari-related files (including 3,000-plus files for 8-bit computers), this site is a rich resource for Atari owners—shareware heaven, some might say. Sound players, graphic viewers, word processors, spreadsheet programs, programming applications, communications programs, games, compression utilities, it's all here. Read the well-maintained index file in each subdirectory to quickly find what you're looking for. ✓**INTERNET** …→*www* ftp://atari.archive.umich.edu/ …→*www* gopher://gopher.archive.merit.edu:7055/11/atari …→*www* ftp://wuarchive.wustl.edu/systems/atari/umich.edu/

Emagic Logic Though the emphasis here is on Logic, the site contains information on other Amiga products—Notator SL, SoundSurfer/SoundDiver, and Logic Audio. New additions include a Logic tutorial and an Emagic upgrade offer. ✓**INTERNET**→*www* http://www.mcc.ac.uk/~emagic/emagic_page.html

K-Sculpt K-Sculpt is a freeware sound editor and librarian for use with Atari ST and STe systems, and Kawai's K1, K1r, or K1m synthesizers. Use the 64 sound effects that come stored in its memory, or fill it with your own jazzy synth compositions. ✓**INTERNET**→*www* http://web.city.ac.uk/~cb170/ksclpt.html

MiNTOS Distribution and Information Page What is MiNTOS? Well, it's a package of utilities which runs under the MiNT operating system extension and lets Atari ST, TT, and Falcon models operate in a multi-user environment. Get software, documentation, and hardware requirements here. ✓**INTERNET**→*www* http://www.earth.ox.ac.uk/~steve/mintos.html

MultiDialog German-language info on this utility that accommodates multi-tasking on Atari-TOS machines while a dialog box is up (something Atari had forgotten to provide for). ✓**INTERNET**→*www* http://www-users.informatik.rwth-aachen.de/~hn/md.html

Vendors

Atari Vendor Forum Missionware just announced a new release

More Shareware

Atari Archives in Germany ✓**INTERNET** …→*www* ftp://ftp.uni-kl.de/pub/atari/ …→*www* ftp://ftp.fu-berlin.de/pub/atari/ …→*www* ftp://ftp.uni-stuttgart.de/pub/systems/atari/

Atari Archives in the Netherlands ✓**INTERNET** …→ *www* ftp://nikhefh.nikhef.nl/pub/atari/ …→*www* ftp://star.cs.vu.nl/pub/atari/

Atari Archives in the U.K. ✓**INTERNET** …→*www* ftp://micros.hensa.ac.uk/micros/atari/ …→*www* ftp://disabuse.demon.co.uk/pub/atari/

Univ. of Kentucky Atari Archive ✓**INTERNET**→*www* ftp://f.ms.uky.edu/pub2/atari/

The World's Atari Archive ✓**INTERNET**→*www* ftp://ftp.std.com/pub/atari/

---

of Flash II, the popular Atari ST telecommunications program. Here's the place to read about it, to upgrade your old version, or to check out a demo. You'll also find Atari vendors such as DMC Publishing and Lexicor offering support and information. ✓**COMPUSERVE**→*go* atarive

Programming

comp.sys.atari.programmer (ng) "I've been using Laser C for my ST programming, and am quite happy with it, but C++ would be very nice if there is a good compiler for it. Does anyone know what exists and what's good?" Issues related to programming for the Atari are the order of the day on this group. ✓**USENET**

The Rest of the Field Sinclair & Acorn

Sinclair & Acorn

What with Silicon Valley and all, Americans are rather provincial about the computer industry. In fact, we sometimes forget that there are other gigantic English-speaking nations with thriving computer companies. The United Kingdom, for instance. While Sinclair has made some inroads into the U.S. market, it has been most successful in Europe, where it joins such companies as Acorn as industry leaders in British computing. So hop the pond and learn all you can about overseas computing by visiting the **Sinclair WWW Archive**, the **Sinclair Spectrum Home Pages**, the unofficial **Acorn Home Page**, and the **Acorn Computers FTP Server**. And if you're interested in some computer thunder Down Under, plan a stop for the **Australian Acorn Page**. Throw another microprocessor on the barbie, mate!

Unofficial Acorn Home Page—http://www.csv.warwick.ac.uk/-phudv/index.html

On the Net

Sinclair computers

comp.sys.sinclair (ng) Here's the newsgroup where those who can't bear to part with their Sinclair Spectrums come to discuss all things Spectrummy, especially where to find software. (And by the way, if you did part with the old British workhorse, but really miss it, did you know you can get a Spectrum emulator for a Macintosh?) ✓**USENET**

Sinclair Spectrum Home Pages Carries a small but eclectic mix of Sinclair Spectrum ("Speccy") material, including snapshots of Spectrum game screens, technical articles, links to other sites, and, unique to this site, a collection of some of the very strange letters that appeared in *Your Sinclair* magazine—most of which have almost nothing to do with Sinclairs but instead are along the lines of "Send me a badge or my pet fly (enclosed) will bite your head off." Strangely entertaining, in a Monty Pythonesque sort of way. ✓**INTERNET**→*www* http://spodbox.ehche.ac.uk/~rps/speccy/speccy.html

Sinclair WWW Archive This British site tells the story of Sinclair Research, the company that revolutionized the home computer industry in the U.K. by producing the first sub-100-pound computer, the Spectrum, and going on to sell three million of them. Here you can read all about the company (which was bought by Amstrad in 1987), its products, and its personnel, and access other Sinclair information resources available on the Internet. The second address offers enhanced Web pages. ✓**INTERNET** …→*www* http://sable.ox.ac.uk/~tr95006/sinclairtop.html …→*www* http://sable.ox.ac.uk/~tr95006/sincover.html

The Sinclair ZX Spectrum Switchboard It doesn't contain any information about Spectrum computers itself, but it points the way to oodles of other resources: Web pages, FTP and gopher sites, the Sinclair newsgroup and mailing list, and even a Sinclair BBS (in Finland, of all places). ✓**INTERNET**→*www* http://www.mordor.com/nick/spectrum.html

Spectrum Forever This admittedly incomplete Norway-based page contains a grab-bag of Sinclair Spectrum information, in-

Sinclair & Acorn The Rest of the Field

cluding a FAQ, pointers to arcade games and graphic adventures (plus game instructions, screen shots and sound files), and links to a handful of other Sinclair-related sites. ✓ **INTERNET**→*www* http://www.nvg.unit.no/spectrum/

Timex/Sinclair Richard refers to the message board as a Timex/Sinclair ghost town—he's usually the only one here asking questions and a year can pass before there are any new additions to the libraries, but it's still the only place on CompuServe reserved for Sinclair computers. ✓ **COMPUSERVE** …→*go* club→Messages→Timex/Sinclair …→*go* club→Libraries→TS 1000/1500/2068/SP

Acorn computers

Acorn Computers This is a list of links to useful online resources about Acorn Computers—Websites, FTP sites, newsgroups, etc. There's also a link to a "not-so-useful" site: the Trojan Room Coffee Machine viewer, where you can see an up-to-the-second image of a coffee machine at the University of Cambridge—captured by an Acorn Archimedes computer. ✓ **INTERNET**→*www* http://www.cs.bham.ac.uk/~amw/acorn/

Acorn Computers FTP Server This is the official FTP site for Acorn Computer resources, maintained by the manufacturer, Acorn Computers Ltd. in Cambridge, England. It contains the latest information about Acorn computers, plus programs, updates, patches, and utilities. The site is closely monitored, with all software and information uploaded by users screened by the system administrator. ✓ **INTERNET**→*www* ftp://ftp.acorn.co.uk/

Acorn Resources Contains an impressive list of Acorn resources on the Net, including newsgroups, FTP sites, and Web pages. It also features a logo you'll see at several Acorn-related sites: it's the Intel logo with one difference—instead of "Intel inside," it proudly proclaims "Intel outside." ✓ **INTERNET**→*www* http://www.stir.ac.uk/%7Erhh01/Main.html

Acorn-L (ml) The acorn never falls far from the tree, and discussions about the Acorn computer never fall far from this Turkish mailing list, which covers topics ranging from the very general (what is an Acorn?) to the very specific (how can you install new spreadsheet software?). ✓ **INTERNET**→*email* listserv@vm3090.ege.edu.tr ☞ *Type in message body:* subscribe acorn- <your full name>

Australian Acorn Page "Acorn users are some of the world's greatest advocates. Sometimes their fervour for this little machine is greater than the actual machine is capable of," notes Karl "RiscMan" Davis, the math and computer science student at the University of New South Wales in Sydney, Australia, who has authored this page. Here you'll find basic information about Acorn computers and "RiscMan" himself, plus links to Acorn-related Websites and FTP sites and many other sites Davis finds interesting. ✓ **INTERNET**→*www* http://www.geko.com.au/riscman/index.html

comp.sys.acorn (ng) Most of the postings in this newsgroup focus on very specific questions regarding hardware or software for Acorn computers— "700 Upgrade Cards," "ArcWeb 0.22," etc.—but there are always a few ongoing side discussions on broader topics such as "Acorn bashing" and "Software morality." ✓ **USENET**

comp.sys.acorn.advocacy (ng) When last accessed, this newsgroup contained exactly one posting: an announcement (and links to) new Web pages intended for users and potential buyers of the Acorn Risc PC. Presumably this is a newsgroup for avid supporters of Acorn PCs, but it doesn't seem to get much use. ✓ **USENET**

comp.sys.acorn.tech (ng) Just as you'd expect, this newsgroup is full of highly technical postings on such esoteric Acorn Computer-related topics as "exchanging data between 2 A5000's," "Problems with Wimp SpriteOp under RO3.5," and "Producing Acorn CD-ROMs on PCs." It's a hard nut to crack, but worth it for acorn users. ✓ **USENET**

Gerben's Acorn Page Offers a long list of links to Acorn-related resources on the Net, including software, online magazines, basic information, manuals, Acorn-supporting companies, user groups, and more. It also features a large cartoon of Garfield (the famous fat cat drawn by Jim Davis) looking heavenward, with the caption, "Thank God it's not an IBM!"—a sentiment that seems to sum up the Acorn-owners' feelings about their machines. ✓ **INTERNET**→*www* http://www.cs.vu.nl/~gerben/acorn

Unofficial Acorn Home Page An official Acorn Home Page is in the works; in the meantime, here's an unofficial home page listing current Acorn products, complete with prices; technical information; links to Acorn newsgroups, FTP, and WWW sites (including home pages of Acorn users); and even rumors about future Acorn products. ✓ **INTERNET**→*www* http://www.csv.warwick.ac.uk/~phudv/index.html

The Rest of the Field **Other Systems**

Other systems

If you follow the computer world only casually, you may get the impression that there are only a few computer companies in the world (Apple, IBM, Amiga) and only a handful of operating systems (DOS, Windows, the Mac OS). But as any devoted computer user can tell you, this is hardly the case. What about the NeXT, for instance, Steven Jobs's post-Mac brainstorm? It may not be incredibly popular with home users, but it continues to have currency in the **comp.sys.next*** newsgroups. Those dedicated to the Tandy way of life can profess their love for the OS-9 operating system at either **comp.sys.tandy** or **comp.os.os9**. And the millions of Unix diehards in the free world can chatter away on the **Unix Forum** or drop by the **UnixWorld Online Magazine Home Page**.

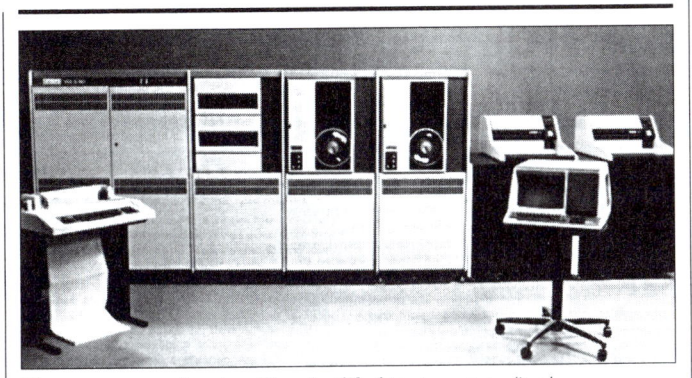

Vintage computer—from http://ftp.arl.mil/ftp/historic-computers/jpeg/

On the Net

Across the board

comp.os.misc (ng) Subscribers to this low-volume newsgroup exchange information about less popular computer operating systems. ✓**USENET**

Tandy & OS9

CoCo—The Tandy Color Computer List (ml) A mailing list devoted to users of the Tandy Color Computer, fondly referred to as CoCo by its devotees. Subscribe to this list for computing tips and tricks. ✓**INTERNET**→*email* listserv@pucc.princeton.edu ✍ *Type in message body:* subscribe coco <your full name>

Color Computer Forum Tandy CoCo enthusiasts in search of a list of software titles—or a document outlining the history of the machine—should visit the reference section of the library. Other sections contain games, graphics, sound players, and telecommunications programs for the CoCo. The barren message boards would suggest, however, that enthusiasm for the Tandy is a road seldom traveled by the multitude. ✓**COMPUSERVE**→ *go* coco

comp.os.os9 (ng) Not a lot of traffic in this newsgroup, but The OS-9 User's Group Sourcebook—an FAQ with information for OS-9ers on how to hook up with user groups, mailing lists, publications, online services, and bulletin boards relating to the rather archaic OS-9 system—is regularly posted to this group. ✓**USENET**

comp.sys.tandy (ng) Welcome to Tandyland, where you can swap user tips and tricks, post a classified ad, or otherwise sound off on Tandy computing. "My cat spit a large amount of water on my model 100," announced one Tandy user. "When I turned it on, the thing was fritzed. I used a hair dryer to dry it off, and in ten minutes, it was fine." Replied a concerned Tandyite in Austin, TX: "Rule one whenever you spill water on a piece of electronic equipment is to NOT TURN IT ON UNTIL IT HAS DRIED OUT. It can kill." Duly noted! This newsgroup also carries fond laments for all the deceased Tandy models—remember the TRS-80 Model III? Ron from the University of Michigan sure does, and he could really use some software for it. ✓**USENET**

DeskMate Forum Before Windows existed, owners of Tandy computers were using the bundled software package Deskmate. Deskmate users, and there are many

Net Tech 103

Other Systems The Rest of the Field

out there, keep abreast of their software's capabilities in this forum. ✓**AMERICA ONLINE**→*keyword* deskmate

OS-9 Forum Support for computing on the OS-9 system, including a library full of bug reports, FAQs, and how-to files, and tutorials on everything from C programming on OS-9 to installing a 3.5" disk drive on your OS-9 system. Also features a message board, but don't rely on it for quick assistance—most of the postings here are from 1994. ✓**COMPUSERVE**→*go* os9

Tandy Corporation Tandy newsletters, product information, and a listing of sites on CompuServe with Tandy and OS-9 resources. ✓**COMPUSERVE**→*go* tandy

CP/M

comp.os.cpm (ml/ng) So what does CP/M really stand for? Is it Control Program for Microcomputers, Control Program for Microprocessors, or Control Program/Monitor? Find out by reading the posts to this newsgroup dedicated to the CP/M operating system. Make sure to get the FAQ—it'll tell you everything you need to know about CP/M, and more. ✓**USENET** ✓**INTERNET**→*email* listserv@vm.its.rpi.edu ✍ *Type in message body:* subscribe cpm-l <your full name> *FAQ:* ✓**INTERNET**→*www* http://www.cis.ohio-state.edu/hypertext/faq/usenet/CPM-faq/faq.html

CP/M Forum A message board, software libraries, and a conference room for users of the CP/M operating system. The forum carries a large selection of word processors, telecommunications utilities, software patches, and program emulators. And if you can't find the software you need in the library, check out the message board for directions to other online sites with CP/M applications. ✓**COMPUSERVE**→*go* cpmforum

X Windows

comp.windows.x (ng) Low-volume newsgroup for users of the X Windows operating system on Intel-based, Unix-supported computers. For prompt attention to any queries try comp.windows.x.i386unix. But the real gem is the six-part FAQ. ✓**USENET** *FAQ:* ✓**INTERNET**→*www* http://www.cis.ohio-state.edu/hypertext/faq/bngusenet/comp/windows/x/top.html

comp.windows.x.announce (ng) This newsgroup is a clearinghouse for announcements pertaining to the X Windows operating system, including information on upgrades, patches, and FTP-sites where you can get X-based software. ✓**USENET**

comp.windows.x.apps (ng) Newsgroup for users of the X Windows operating system. The focus is on running applications on the system. ✓**USENET**

comp.windows.x.i386unix (ng) High-volume newsgroup for users of the X Windows operating system in Intel-based, UNIX-supported computers. If that doesn't make any sense to you, there's an FAQ regularly posted here that should answer all your questions. ✓**USENET**

First Course in X Windows The Curtin University of Technology in Western Australia is offering an introductory class on X Windows. Lecture outlines, assignments, a reading list, and course notes are all available online. ✓**INTERNET**→*www* http://www.cs.curtin.edu.au/units/cg252-502/src/notes/html/

Sources of Information About X Newsgroups, mailing lists, X Windows FAQs, an X Windows bibliography, and source code for X Windows programs. ✓**INTERNET**→*www* http://www.x.org/consortium/x_info.html

Other windows

comp.windows.garnet (ng) A newsgroup for users of Garnet-based systems. ✓**USENET** *FAQ:* ✓**INTERNET** …→*www* http://www.cis.ohio-state.edu/hypertext/faq/bngusenet/comp/windows/x/top.html …→*www* ftp://a.gp.cs.cmu.edu/usr/garnet/garnet/FAQ

comp.windows.interviews (ng) Newsgroup for users of the Interviews operating system. ✓**USENET**

> "This group treats Sun's Network extensible Window System (NeWS), but Microsoft groupies post numerous gossip inquiries here. This outrages NeWS users, who often reply with surly posts."

104 Net Tech

The Rest of the Field Other Systems

comp.windows.misc (ng) Miscellaneous postings related to Windows computing systems other than Microsoft Windows, X Windows, PCGeos, and NeWS. So what's left? How about MGR, 8 1/2, and STDWIN? And newsgroup charters be damned—people on this newsgroup are still talking about Microsoft Windows. ✓USENET *FAQ:* ✓INTERNET→*www* http://www.cis.ohio-state.edu/hypertext/faq/bngusenet/comp/windows/misc/top.html

comp.windows.news (ng) This group is for discussions about Sun's Network extensible Window System (NeWS), but Microsoft groupies post numerous gossip inquiries here (making it a group about news of Microsoft Windows). This outrages NeWS users, who often reply with surly posts. ✓USENET *FAQ:* ✓INTERNET→*www* http://www.cis.ohio-state.edu/hypertext/faq/bngusenet/comp/windows/news/top.html

comp.windows.open-look (ng) A newsgroup catering to users of the OpenLook operating system. ✓USENET *FAQ:* ✓INTERNET→*www* http://www.cis.ohio-state.edu/hypertext/faq/bngusenet/comp/windows/open-look/top.html

comp.windows.suit (ng) A newsgroup for users of the SUIT operating system. ✓USENET

comp.windows.ui-builders.uimx (ng) A newsgroup for users of the UIM/X operating system. ✓USENET

Vintage computers

PDP-8 Lovers (ml) For owners and users of vintage DEC computers, with special emphasis on the PDP-8 series of minicomputers. Discuss hardware, software, and programming techniques with fellow users of vintage terminals. According to the administrators of this mailing list, "Ownership of an 'antique' computer is not required for membership, but flames from people who feel that anything that is not cutting-edge technology is worthless are discouraged." ✓INTERNET→*email* pdp8-lovers-request@mc.lcs.mit.edu ✍ *Type in message body:* subscribe <your full name>

Vintage computer—from http://ftp.arl.mil/ftp/historic-computers/jpeg/

Supercomputers

The Parallel Tools Consortium Though it's highly technical, this site—overseen by researchers working to make parallel tools responsive to user needs—does link to a few interesting papers and projects. For most, though, the computer-science topics (Distributed Array Query? Lightweight Corefile Browser?) will be denser than a white dwarf star, and about as much fun. ✓INTERNET→*www* http://www.llnl.gov/ptools/ptools.html

Supercomputing and Parallel Computing Resources Devoted to the miracle of supercomputing ("it's a bird...it's a plane...it's a supercomputer, running parallel calculations on a series of processors!"), this site is mostly a collection of links to other resources across the Internet. And if you want pictures of Crays, Intels, Fujitsus, and other thinking machines to tape up alongside your pinups of Joey Lawrence and NKOTB, this is the best site around. ✓INTERNET→*www* http://www.cs.cmu.edu/Web/Groups/scandal/www/resources.html

Supercomputing Servers Lists of links to Websites run by institutions and research groups involved with supercomputing and parallel computing. Sites range from Lawrence Livermore National Laboratory to the Cornell Theory Center to the V project in Berlin. ✓INTERNET ...→*www* http://www.umiacs.umd.edu/~dbader/sites.html ...→*www* http://www.ccsf.caltech.edu/other_sites.html ...→*www* http://www-cgi.cs.cmu.

Other Systems The Rest of the Field

edu/afs/cs.cmu.edu/project/scandal/public/www/research-groups.html

Unix

comp.unix.admin (ng) Trying to configure that new tape drive? Wondering what to do when your users' mailspools fill up your hard drives? This group is a good place to start asking questions. Discussions are technical and sometimes intense, dealing with all manner of Unix esoterica, with the occasional job offer or confused newbie thrown in. ✓USENET *FAQ:* ✓INTERNET→*www* http://www.cis.ohio-state.edu/hypertext/faq/bngusenet/comp/unix/admin/top.html

comp.unix.advocacy (ng) Prepare to duel it out in rapid-fire, intricate, and sometimes completely indecipherable technical debates over the merits and shortfalls of every remotely modern operating system. A word of advice: unless you know your GPFs from your core dumps, be wary of entering this fray. ✓USENET

comp.unix.amiga (ng) A newsgroup for Amiga owners running Unix or one of its flavors, including NetBSD. ✓USENET *FAQ:* ✓INTERNET→*www* http://www.cis.ohio-state.edu/hypertext/faq/bngusenet/comp/unix/amiga/top.html

comp.unix.dos-under-unix (ng) "Does anyone happen to know of a place where I could get a copy of the grep command which runs in a DOS/Windows environment?" "Does anybody know the site where I can find the Unix's gzip/gunzip commands for DOS?" In this low-volume newsgroup, questions concern programs that bridge the gap between the worlds of DOS and Unix. ✓USENET

comp.unix.misc (ng) Miscellany abounds. Novices ask how to decode tar files, grad students advertise to share hotel rooms at computer conferences, software and hardware are bought and sold, and many unusual technical issues of as many different Unix-like operating systems as you could think of are picked over. ✓USENET

comp.unix.pc-clone.16bit (ng) Questions and discussion about Unix operating on 16-bit PCs. ✓USENET

comp.unix.pc-clone.32bit (ng) An odd assortment of questions and announcements appear on this newsgroup about PC and Unix systems. ✓USENET

comp.unix.questions (ng) Just about anything goes; whether you're sitting down at your first Unix machine and don't know how to list a directory or you're having trouble compiling that pesky new software package, go ahead and ask the experts. Most questions get a polite and knowledgeable reply. ✓USENET *FAQ:* ✓INTERNET→*www* http://www.cis.ohio-state.edu/hypertext/faq/bngusenet/comp/unix/questions/top.html

comp.unix.shell (ng) Since for most folks, using Unix is all about taming the mighty shell, this is a good place to start conferring with others about your problems. As a result, talk maintains a fairly high altitude. This isn't the best place to ask how to UUdecode an alt.binaries picture, but if you're confused about how to set your prompt or are trying to plumb the mysterious depths of shell scripting, ask away. You will be in good company. ✓USENET

CYBERNOTES

"Sometimes when I send email to friends, I get responses like 'I'm on vacation, your mail has been forwarded to...,' and then the system gives me another email address.

How do I do this with a .forward file (assuming that it's possible?)"

"Have your .forward send the email to the vacation(1) program, or implement an autoresponder yourself (using procmail or some other really nifty mail utility).

For more info, try 'man vacation,' and if your site doesn't have it, threaten your sysadmin with rotten eggs until it's installed. The program is a no-brainer to use and it works fairly well.

Warning: The forwarding program doesn't cover all kinds of correspondence. Be sure to unsubscribe from all mailing lists before signing up for the vacation(1) program, or you'll return to find some very angry letters waiting for you."

—from **comp.unix.questions**

The Rest of the Field Other Systems

comp.unix.wizards (ng) A newsgroup for the most skilled and proficient Unix users and programmers—'wizards,' they call themselves. ✓**USENET**

Unix FAQs A collection of dozens of FAQ documents about Unix. ✓**INTERNET**→*www* http://www.cis.ohio-state.edu/hypertext/faq/bngusenet/comp/unix/top.html

Unix Forum Like the Unix newsgroups, the message board in this forum is broken down into topics such as DOS under Unix, Linux, and New to Unix. The library carries dozens of FAQs on such Unix-related topics as Minix, Xinu, and Unix itself. In addition, the Linux operating system, add-ons, and source code for Unix games and other applications are also available. ✓**COMPUSERVE**→*go* unixforum

UNIX Index An index of links to Unix-related Websites, mailing lists, newsgroups, FTP sites, FAQs, and journals. There are links to companies producing Unix products, Unix tutorials, Unix humor, Unix security discussion groups, source code for Unix programs, and much, much more. ✓**INTERNET**→*www* http://ici.proper.com/unix

Unix Vendors The forum is rather empty at present, but the following Unix vendors offer technical support: Recital, MWC, G.T.R. Data Inc., Thoroughbred, and Acucobol. ✓**COMPUSERVE**→*go* unixaven

UnixWorld Online Magazine Home Page An online publication about Unix topics: product reviews, news columns, etc. The site has a growing archive of Unix-related articles. ✓**INTERNET**→*www* http://www.wcmh.com/uworld/

Linux

comp.os.linux* (ng) Covering the Linux operating system, a flavor of the Unix system, these newsgroups offer a steady stream (actually, a veritable cataract) of Linux advice, programming discussions, and information. Newsgroups range from the incredibly active comp.os.linux.advocacy group (where advocates and naysayers of the operating system discuss Linux) to comp.os.linux.answers (which serves as a repository for several FAQs and software indexes) to the comp.os.linux.setup group (where Linux newbies discuss installing their new system). ✓**USENET** *FAQ:* ✓**INTERNET**→*www* http://www.cis.ohio-state.edu/hypertext/faq/bngusenet/comp/os/linux/top.html

#linux A live channel for Linux questions, insight, and discussions. ✓**INTERNET**→*irc* #linux

Linux Howto & FAQ A collection of Linux instruction manuals and Linux users guides. ✓**INTERNET**→*www* http://yebisu.ics.es.osaka-u.ac.jp/linux/

The Linux Operating System Linux documentation, a searchable archive of Linux software, FAQs, manuals, and even the entire Linux operating system. ✓**INTERNET**→*www* http://www.linux.org/

Linux Software Archive The largest Linux shareware archive on the Net. ✓**INTERNET** ...→*www* http://sunsite.unc.edu/pub/Linux/welcome.html ...→*www* ftp://sunsite.unc.edu/pub/Linux/welcome.html ...→*www* ftp://ftp.tu-graz.ac.at/pub/Linux ...→*www* ftp://mrcnext.cso.uiuc.edu/pub/linux/

MacLinux An FAQ covering Linux on the Macintosh. ✓**INTERNET**→*www* http://nucleus.ibg.uu.se/maclinux/FAQ.txt

NeXT

comp.sys.next* (ng) Several newsgroups where NeXT topics are covered, including debates about the pros and cons of the NeXTSTEP operating system, programming with NeXTSTEP, debugging programs, and buying and selling NeXT products. From comp.sys.next.advocacy to comp.sys.next.announce, from comp.sys.next.sysadmin to comp.sys.next.software, there's a wealth of Usenet information here for the NeXT faithful. ✓**USENET** *FAQ:* ✓**INTERNET**→*www* http://www.cis.ohio-state.edu/hypertext/faq/bngusenet/comp/sys/next/top.html

NeXT Computer, Inc. Product information, job announcements, press releases, and the NeXTanswers database—a searchable database of technical support documents. ✓**INTERNET**→*www* http://www.next.com/

Quick Guide to NEXTSTEP Information on the Internet Links to NeXT newsgroups, NeXT FTP sites, and FAQs. ✓**INTERNET**→*www* http://www.omnigroup.com/Documentation/NEXTSTEP/Guide.html

Stepwise Server A clearinghouse of information (or links to informational sites) on NeXTSTEP and OpenStep, including archives of NeXT electronic journals, information about dozens of NeXTSTEP mailing lists, and information about NeXT products distributed by third-party vendors. ✓**INTERNET**→*www* http://www.stepwise.com/

Net Tech 107

Part 4

A Small Matter: Minicomputers

Portables **A Small Matter: Minicomputers**

Portables

Going mobile? If so, you'll probably want to invest in a laptop computer. While pick-up-and-go computing was unthinkable only five years ago—Apple's purported Macintosh Portable was about as easy to move as Mount Rushmore—today's ThinkPads, PowerBooks, and Omnibooks are the perfect entrées for a movable feast. Begin your quest for the smallest, most powerful machine on the market at **comp.sys.laptops**. Then investigate the theory of the floating office by perusing the pages of **Mobidata: An Interactive Journal**. And if you're loading up your laptop for a three-week trip to the Sahara, be sure to check in with America Online's **Nomadic Computing** message board. Here's a free hint—sand in the drive slot isn't good for anyone.

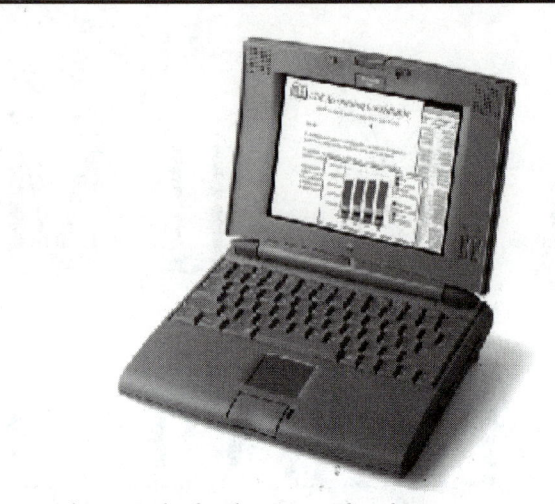

Macintosh PowerBook—from http://www.info.apple.com

On the Net

Across the board

comp.sys.laptops (ng) Although ostensibly geared toward laptop discussion, this newsgroup contains a tremendous amount of buying and selling activity—"My Desktop for Your Laptop." Nonetheless, it's also the place to get answers to questions about upgrades, accessories, and add-ons for your PowerBook, ThinkPad, or one of the less popular laptop models. The majority of the messages are queries from prospective laptop buyers seeking advice regarding which machine to choose. ✓**USENET**

Mobidata: An Interactive Journal If you get beyond how incredibly slow this site is, Mobidata offers the full text of several academic treatises about mobile computing issues (e.g., "Event Delivery Abstractions for Mobile Computing"). Whether it takes longer to read or open is debatable, but at least Mobidata is 'interactive.' Read a paper, post a comment, or read what others thought. If you feel the urge to say more, you can even submit your own paper. ✓**INTERNET**→*www* http://rags.rutgers.edu/journal/cover.html

Mobile and Wireless Computing An index of mobile and wireless computing sites online, including links to relevant online newsletters, computer labs dedicated to the study of mobile computing, and a significant number of mobile computing conference proceedings. ✓**INTERNET**→*www* http://snapple.cs.washington.edu:600/mobile/mobile.html

Mobile Office Sponsored by *Mobile Office* magazine, the site keeps users abreast of news about the portable world with weekly product reviews and industry reports, descriptions of the best mobile products of the year, and links to interesting mobile computing sites online. ✓**INTERNET**→*www* http://www.mobileoffice.com/

Mobile Office Need information on the hottest new notebook computers or the sleekest and slimmest new cellular phones? *Mobile Office*'s AOL site features news and reviews of notebooks, modems, cellular phones, and communica-

A Small Matter: Minicomputers Portables

tions software. Interact with editors and experts in Q&A forums, download shareware and demoware (from Eudora to Fax-Mail), or jump into a live online conference and commiserate with fellow travelers on the perils of laptopping it in business class. ✓**AMERICA ONLINE**→*keyword* mobile

Nomadic Computing Lousy ventilation systems and corporate politics getting you down? Get out of the office! In this forum, you can share tips with successful telecommuters about long trans-Pacific flights or cellular phone companies, download software demos and patches for remote computing and cellular data transfer, and read reviews of wireless pagers and laptops. New technology is always a big topic of conversation. ✓**AMERICA ONLINE**→*keyword* nomadic

Portable Computing Ray has a Kenitech laptop that needs batteries. Where should he buy them? Hey, Ray, ever hear of House of Batteries? Jerry's a big fan of the store: "I had an odd battery that needed replacing. House of Batteries couldn't find one so they made one! There is more than one location. Check it out." David, on the other hand, wants to upgrade the modem for his portable from 2400 bps to 28.8K. He's been told by a salesperson that "no modem over 9600 would work with a normal parallel port because the p. port can't handle the faster speeds," but he thinks it might be a ruse to get him to buy another laptop. The reaction here is mixed. Most members encourage Ray to give it a try, but Martin (after explaining that it's the serial, not the parallel port that is the issue), seems to concur with the salesperson. If you own a portable and need advice on IBM's ThinkPad, PowerBook's track-ball, or portable printers, this is an active and informative topic. ✓**PRODIGY**→*jump* computerbb→Choose a Topic→Portable Computing

Road Warrior Outpost It's true that laptops, email, and modems have made the world a global village. But more often than not, you can't get online. Why? Because you don't have the precise piece of plastic to plug into the local telephone adaptor. Road Warrior offers tips for the mobile computer user in its monthly newsletters archived at the site. It also maintains an FAQ with instructions on how to connect your portable computer's modem to digital phone systems, an explanation of how cellular telecommunications works, and descriptions of battery life and memory. But this site is primarily an online store for portable computing supplies. Check out the PowerBook handcuffs and infrared file-transfer devices or, if you're looking for the basics, consider investing in portable hard drives, battery package replacements, insurance, modems, and Ethernet adaptors. ✓**INTERNET**→*www* http://warrior.com/

comp.sys.mac.portables (ng) Got problems with your 520C freezing up? Wondering about PowerPC upgrades for that Duo? And what do you do if your Duo gets stuck in its mini-dock? If you want to talk about portable Macs, here's the spot. You'll also find computers and memory for sale, info on jacking up your machine to maximum speed, and answers to questions about battery woes, AC adapters, and other PowerBook-related dilemmas. ✓**USENET**

Mac PowerBook Mailing List (ml) For discussions about Mac PowerBooks—including which one to buy, which software to use, and which accessories to add. ✓**INTERNET**→*email* listserv@yalevm.cis.yale.edu ✍ *Type in message body:* subscribe macpb-l <your full name>

PowerBook Army! Japanese journalist and telecommuter Atsushi Iijima spends five hours a day on the train going to and from work. With PowerBook in hand, they're five hours well spent. At this site, which has three separate servers, in Tokyo, Hawaii, and New York (each with localized information), Atsushi passes on tips and tricks for making the most of Mac portables. He has also made the PowerBook utilities and extensions that he's collected available. For instance, if you're getting tired of trying to sort through the miscellaneous icons strewn all over your screen, download the Hover-Bar from this site and watch the icons organize themselves into a perfectly regimented strip. ✓**INTERNET**→*www* http://hisurf.aloha.com:80/PBA/index.html

PowerBooks Compared to

> "More often than not, you can't get online. Why? Because you don't have the precise piece of plastic to plug into the local telephone adaptor."

Portable A Small Matter: Minicomputers

some of the more flashy parts of AOL, this is a simple, straightforward area. The specifications for each computer in the PowerBook line are available, as are press releases covering PowerBook developments. In the software library there are PowerBook tips, FAQs, and utilities (e.g., a utility to fix all Smart-Battery memory-related errors), while the active message board gives PowerBook users a forum to discuss screens, batteries, modems, networking, models, and hundreds of other topics. ✓**AMERICA ONLINE**→*keyword* powerbook

AST Forum If you've got a PC laptop, there's a very good chance it's one of the popular AST models—Bravo, Exec, or Advantage. Although this forum is for support of all AST PCs, there are sections of the message board and library devoted exclusively to its notebooks. ✓**COMPUSERVE**→*go* astforum

HP Omnibook Forum Hewlett-Packard offers this entire forum for support of its line of notebook computers. Technical support staff field questions ("Any news on a lithium ion battery for the 600C? Supposedly this was to be available soon.") and users share tips with one another ("The Fn + screen buttons do not affect screen brightness until one minute has elapsed since the machine was turned on.") on the message boards. For a good selection of downloadable applications and utilities—from daily notes to fax/modem software—check the Apps/Utilities section of the library. ✓**COMPUSERVE**→*go* hpomnibook

IBM ThinkPad Forum If your built-in ThinkPad mouse is giving you problems, Doom isn't running fast enough, or you're awaiting Windows 95 with some trepidation, the message board is filled with users and ThinkPad representatives who can offer wise counsel. The library carries product announcements, FAQs, utilities, and a section where users have uploaded favorite shareware and add-ons. It's a great place to find solutions for everything from basic mouse troubles to dongle difficulties. ✓**COMPUSERVE**→*go* thinkpad

ThinkPad 750 List (ml) For discussions about IBM ThinkPad models 750, 755, and 360. ✓**INTERNET**→*email* tp750-request @cs.utk.edu ✍ *Type in message body:* subscribe

Ultralite List (ml) A mailing list specifically aimed at users or potential users of the older NEC Ultralite PC1701 and PC1702 notebooks (as opposed to the 80X86-based models). ✓**INTERNET**→*email* listserv@grot.starconn.com ✍ *Type in message body:* subscribe ultralite-list <your full name>

Tandy Model 100 Forum There's no question that Tandy laptops are less sexy than Power-Books, but they're helping to keep Radio Shack in business. Intended for owners of TRS-80 Model 100, Tandy 200, NEC portables, Olivetti M-10, Tandy 600, and compatible portables, this forum offers a library with thousands of software programs (games to graphics viewers to calculators), utilities, and how-to files. On the less-used message board, members share tips on which off-the-shelf cable to use (Radio Shack's, no doubt), how to more effectively manage mobile commuting, and what communications programs work best. The message board is also a good place to shop for or sell a portable Tandy. ✓**COMPUSERVE**→*go* tandylaptop

---

CYBERNOTES

"Q: I need to know if any of you have suffered data loss after letting the airport security personnel scan your computer bag with the computer still in it? Do any of you insist that the guards conduct a hand search of the computer luggage instead? Thanks :)

A: I travel every week. My Macintosh PowerBook travels with me, and goes through the scanning and security machines. I have never had a single problem with data loss, and I've been doing the same thing for about four years, maybe more.

I've even been overseas several times, and the only inconvenience I've experienced consistently is that I'm almost always asked to take out the machine and start it up. I assume that this proves to the security officers that my machine is actually a computer, and not some other kind of device disguised as a computer. But that's after it gets scanned. I send disks through too. Never a problem."

—from **Mobile Office Q & A Message Board**

112 Net Tech

A Small Matter: Minicomputers **PDAs & Palmtops**

PDAs & palmtops

Once upon a time, computers filled entire rooms, buildings even, and they huffed and they puffed to execute a simple set of calculations. Now, computers are so small that they can fit into the palm of your hand. How? Simple—40 years of miniaturization. Today's palmtop computers can store immense amounts of data, serve as word processors, and even communicate with other machines through the magic of wireless telecommunications. Learn the basics of palmtops and personal digital assistants (PDAs) by browing the **comp.sys.handhelds** newsgroup. Check in on Hewlett-Packard's latest innovations at the **HP Handhelds Forum**. And prove that computers are sometimes as dumb as people by consulting the **Newton Misspellings Page**.

On the Net

Across the board

comp.sys.handhelds (ng) This lightly populated discussion group focuses on handheld computers, better known as personal digital assistants (PDAs). If you are an experienced PDA user, you probably won't find the conversation very informative. However, there are lots of queries from individuals who are shopping for their first

Newton—from http:// www.info.apple. com/cgi-bin/prodspec-pl?/Newton/

PDA, along with some scattered speculation about the future of handheld computers. ✓**USENET**

comp.sys.palmtops (ng) How many milliamps does a 2.5 PCM-CIA card consume? Which palmtop computers offer a parallel port for connectivity? Experienced users of palmtop computers and personal digital assistants populate this informative message board. The discussions tend to be technical and heady, but if you're a novice with specific questions, you'll also get some answers here. Apple Newton owners will find more extensive resources elsewhere. ✓**USENET**

Mobile Computing and Personal Digitial Assistants Does 3DO live up to its hype? Is the Apple Newton the computer of tomorrow? And can the Tandy Zoomer ever overcome its unfortunate name? Get press releases, reviews, conference transcriptions, and other information on a wide variety of personal digital assistants. ✓**INTERNET**→*www* http:// splat.baker.com/grand-unification-theory/mobile-pda/index.html

Palmtop Forum Whether you're using the Sharp Wizard or LapLink for Windows on your laptop, this is the place to get portable and palmtop computing information and technical support. Product information as well as reviews are maintained here by the Online STReport. If the techno-jargon isn't making your choice any clearer, check out the firsthand reviews from product users in the message boards. ✓**COMPUSERVE**→*go* palmtop

PDA/Palmtop Forum How do you avoid Newton card errors? Looking for tips on Banker/Quicken file transfers? Look to the bulletin boards and software libraries on PDAs in this forum. Every imaginable model of PDA is represented here, from the Newton to the Zaurus. Even older, outdated machines are supported. The well-designed Quick Tips Center is an excellent resource for beginners, offering detailed specs on the various PDAs, software reviews written by forum members, and an extensive collection of FAQs. In addition, there is a development folder for programmers, a formidable collection of electronic books files, and a text-searchable database for quickly locating information. If you'd rather

PDAs & Palmtops A Small Matter: Minicomputers

have real-time help, join the weekly PDA chat every Wednesday evening. Finally, the generous software libraries with demos, patches, and shareware for Newton, Psion, HP, Zoomer, and Magic Cap PDAs will keep your mouth watering. ✓**AMERICA ONLINE**→*keyword* pda

Newton

Apple Newton Wondering how to reset your MessagePad? Looking for the latest system software update? This site is Apple's guide to the Newton, with product information, a customer service area, and info for developers. The link for "Top 10 Answers" provides hints and tips for the questions most frequently asked at the Newton telephone support lines. ✓**INTERNET**→*www* http://www.apple.com/documents/newton.html

Apple Newton Project This site offers links to the Newton newsgroups, the Newton Archives at the University of Iowa, and Apple sites related to the Newton. ✓**INTERNET**→*www* http://www.erg.abdn.ac.uk/projects/pda/newton/

comp.binaries.newton (ng) Not much here, except for some occasional binary files for the Newton. ✓**USENET**

comp.sys.newton.announce (ng) Announcements relevant to Newton users and developers, including information on new software, job openings, and conferences. ✓**USENET**

comp.sys.newton.misc (ng) An active group for Newton users, with posts about encryption programs, modems, handwriting recognition, and anything else related to the MessagePad. ✓**USENET**

comp.sys.newton.programmer (ng) Where Newton programmers swap stories about slinging code. A newbie-friendly group, with plenty of advice on getting started with NTK (Newton Tool-Kit). ✓**USENET**

Mucho Newton Stuff Surf over to this cyberspot and you'll discover an amusing story about Rob, the site's hero/creator, and his Newton obsession. Rob's story includes hypertext links to info on such diverse things as eWorld and the sci-fi series *Red Dwarf*. But the site's not all story; it's also got heaps of Newton stuff—press releases, the Newton FAQ, and links to everything from the user groups to system updates. ✓**INTERNET**→*www* http://rainbow.rmii.com/~rbruce/

NewtNews An e-zine with news about the Newton from such publications as *InfoWorld*, *MacUser*, *MacWeek*, *Information Week*, and the like. The publication includes reviews, an opinions/discussion section, and links to other Newton sites on the Web. ✓**INTERNET**→*www* http://www.ridgecrest.ca.us/NewtNews/NN_top.html

Newton Announce This—slightly incomplete—site provides links to several Newton areas, including the comp.sys.newton.announce newsgroup, mailing list and archive, as well as Newton-related FAQs and FTP sites. ✓**INTERNET**→*www* http://www.oit.itd.umich.edu/Newton-Announce.html

Newton Archive Billed as the premier Newton archive for Newton users and developers, this site is divided into subjects ranging from books and personal finance to programming and games. Aside from the software archives, it offers a well-designed set of links to the Newton newsgroups, Apple's Newton resources, user groups, and software companies. ✓**INTERNET**→*www* http://newton.uiowa.edu/

Newton Developers Forum Maybe you've "bought the book, got the disc, ordered the machine, (can't afford the t-shirt, though), and are ready to start developing," but still can't figure out what a .sit file is. Turn to the PCGUID.TXT files in the library section and you should be on your way. Whether you're an experienced Newton developer or just beginning, this forum is an invaluable resource. ✓**COMPUSERVE**→*go* newtdev

Newton FTP Archive A large selection of materials useful for Apple palmtop developers including Newton sample code, documentation, tools, and technical support articles. ✓**INTERNET**→*www* ftp://ftp.apple.com/pie/newton

Newton Information A selective collection of links to Newton info on the Net—Apple, various

---

"Newton's brilliant misprision of Ezra Pound's 'In a Station of the Metro' ('The opposition of these toiletries / Pedals on a wet bristol brush') is positively literary."

---

114 Net Tech

A Small Matter: Minicomputers PDAs & Palmtops

FTP sites, and some links with Newton News. ✓**INTERNET**→*www* http://www.uth.tmc.edu/newton_info/

Newton Mailing List (ml) For discussion of the entire Newton family—the equipment, that is. ✓**INTERNET**→*email* listserv@datrcms1.dartmouth.edu ✉ *Type in message body:* subscribe newton-l <your full name>

Newton Medical Applications An interesting spot for anyone involved in healthcare, or those interested in the cutting-edge uses of PDA technology. The site is entirely devoted to medical applications of the Newton, such as reference information, patient management, quantitative analysis, and wireless communications. Also includes an archive of Newton medical software. ✓**INTERNET**→*www* http://med-amsa.bu.edu/newton.medical/newton.medical.html

Newton Misspellings Page The Newton reads handwriting. Sort of. Sometimes, those undotted i's and uncrossed t's can throw Newton for a loop. This page collects Newton's most embarrassing errors—how would you like it if you scribbled "stand-up comics are better" and Newton read "standing forks are richer"? And Newton's brilliant misprision of Ezra Pound's imagist landmark "In a Station of the Metro" ("The opposition of these toiletries / Pedals on a wet bristol brush") is positively literary. ✓**INTERNET**→*www* http://htcs1.rit.edu/newton/index.html

Newton Resource Center Newton user software, Newton books, NewtNews (no, no, it has nothing to do with the Speaker of the House), even Newton development software. If you can't meet your Newton needs here, you won't get them met anywhere else. ✓**AMERICA ONLINE**→*keyword* newton

Newton Reviews Reviews of everything Newton, whether it's Name Dropper 2.0 ("a useful little application"), Drop To Do 1.0 ("a good alternative to the Newton's to-do lists"), or Poker 1.0 ("a nice program if you like poker, casinos, or need something to while your time away"). Most of the reviews here concentrate on software, but some deal with accessories and hardware as well. ✓**INTERNET**→*www* http://www.netaxs.com/~archimag/revw.html

Newton Vendor Forum Forum for third-party Newton developers. Besides checking out product information and demo versions of programs developed by third-party vendors—from ActionNames (contact manager) to PocketCall (terminal emulation program)—you can read reviews from the *PDA Developers Journal* online and catch up on the happenings at the most recent PCD Developers Conference. ✓**COMPUSERVE**→*go* newtven

Newton/PIE Forum Central resource center for Newton users. Read NewtNews reviews of the latest software. Download demos of the Newton WWW browser, List-It list manager, Newtris, and Yahtzee. If you want your PDA to burp on command (and who doesn't?), download the charming Newton Boy demo. ✓**COMPUSERVE**→*go* newton

NewtReport This "hypermedia journal" focuses on Newton and other pen-based technology. One issue included articles on BASIC for the Newton, the Newton's development environment, and the Newton's future. It's got material

---

CYBERNOTES

"If you write printed, rather than cursive text, you can improve recognition of the printed letter 'S'. I learned that Newton will usually think that an 'S' is the number '5'. If you write 5's like I do, which is by first drawing the downward stroke and then drawing the top, you can tell Newton not to recognize '1-stroke' 5's, which will make it recognize your S's much better. This, in turn, will improve handwriting recognition. Here are the steps you follow: Open Preferences and choose Letter Styles. Select the number '5'. You will see that there are two ways to write a number '5' that Newton will recognize — with one stroke or with two. I always make my 5's with two strokes — a downward stroke, and then the top of the '5'. Simply select the second type of '5', which is drawn with a single stroke, and click the radio button so that it reads, 'I write this "5" rarely.' You'll see that Newton will now recognize your S's."

—from eWorld's **Apple Customer Center**

PDAs & Palmtops A Small Matter: Minicomputers

for both users and developers. ✓**INTERNET**→*www* http://hgiicm.tu-graz.ac.at/C0A2803F/Cnewtreport

PenWorld-Personal Electronics News The mission of this site is to cover everything related to personal electronics, including pen-based computers, PDAs, cellular phones, videogame machines, and interactive multimedia. Includes articles on hi-tech tools for medical professionals, the government's role in "the technology mix," interviews with industry leaders, and more. A worthwhile place for news and opinions about this growing area. ✓**INTERNET**→*www* http://www.penworld.com/

Thor's Newton Nonsense An idiosyncratic collection of Newton resources, like "the software I think works best and does the most" (Magic App 1.1, Clockwise 2.3, and others), "what I've learned about batteries and the Newton" (renewals work best), and "my take on the whole handwriting recognition issue" (wherein the author offers his opinion: "It just isn't the machine Apple tries to sell on that neat video tape they include with it."). A fun site, largely due to the enthusiastic writing of its creator. ✓**INTERNET**→*www* http://thor.acusd.edu/newton/newtonhomepage.html

University of Michigan Newton Archives Features a small archive of Newton games and utilities, including a version of Master-Mind and a program that lets you set up a garbage collection on your Newton. The site is still "under construction." Just like the Newton, come to think of it! ✓**INTERNET**→*www* gopher://gopher.archive.merit.edu:7055/11/newton

World of Newton Before you

Tech.Net screenshot—from http://www.tech.net/technotes/hplx

throw your Newton against the wall, drop into this forum, filled with product datasheets and discussion forums about Apple's line of personal digital assistants. Keep up on emerging Newton technology in the News & Information area; download clocks, calendars, calculators, and other utilities for your Newton in the Software & Hardware Reference Source. Post your questions (or answers someone else's) on the Newton Discussions message boards. Check out the classified ads area and drop your jaw over the alarming number of people trying to get rid of their Newton 100 and 110 models, at appallingly low prices. And before you leave World of Newton, be sure to pop into the Newton Books area and download a digital copy of Charlotte Bronte's *Jane Eyre*, Mark Twain's *The Adventures of Huckleberry Finn*, or one of the many reference-oriented Newton Books archived here. See, your Newton is still good for something. ✓**EWORLD**→*go* newton

HP 100/200 LX

Eddie New Shareware Archive for HP 100/200 LX. Eddie is a new shareware archive for the Hewlett-Packard 100/200 LX Personal Digital Assistant. Buddy is a shareware program you can download from here with dozens of convenience features and keystroke shortcuts like SmartCaps (automatically produces capital letters where necessary), AutoCalc (automatically activates the calculator when you type in numbers), and preset pathnames for quick opening of frequently used files. You'll also find shareware to connect to a laser printer so you can make a paper copy of documents created on the HP 100/200 LX, among other offerings. And for stress management, try Tetris. ✓**INTERNET**→*www* ftp://eddie.mit.edu/pub/hp95lx/NEW/

HP 100/200 LX FAQ How small is Hewlett-Packard's smallest product? What do you gain from a PCMCIA card? Will miniaturization eventually make the desktop computer an unconscionable waste? Get the answers in this FAQ. ✓**INTERNET**→*www* http://www.cis.ohiostate.edu/hypertext/faq/usenet/hp/palmtops-faq/faq.html

HP 100/200LX Mostly a collection of links, this page offers technical notes on the Hewlett-Packard 100/200 LX models, which remain the anchors of the world's most popular palmtop line. Get news on vertical readers,

A Small Matter: Minicomputers PDAs & Palmtops

video display editors, and transfer programs. You can also subscribe to *The Palmtop Paper*. ✓**INTERNET**→*www* http://www.tech.net/technotes/hplx/

HP Handhelds Forum In the 1970s, the only digital device you could hold in your hand was a pocket calculator—and all it did was add, subtract, multiply, and divide. Nowadays, handheld computers are almost the size of those first toys of the digerati-avant-le-mot. Besides information, product support, and Yahtzee for the calculators Hewlett-Packard still makes, you'll find a full library of shareware and tips for the HP Handhelds. And if you're a prospective HP developer, you'll find a full list of developers conferences, courses, and first-hand feedback. ✓**COMPUSERVE**→*go* hphand

Monash Archive for the HP 100/200 LX. Create individual icons for your database files. Balance your checkbook. Play digitized sounds. These are just a few of the features you can add to your HP PDA by downloading the shareware here. ✓**INTERNET**→*www* ftp://ftp.cc.monash.edu.au/pub/palmtop/

Zip.Com Personal digital assistants do a lot more than just keep track of your appointments and addresses. You can transfer files from your PC and work on them remotely from your PDA or another terminal. This downloadable program is designed for PC-to-PC file transfer and is recommended for the Hewlett Packard 100/200 LX. ✓**INTERNET**→*www* ftp://oak.oakland.edu/pub/msdos/lan/zip172.zip

Zoomer

Zoomer Organized like a Zoomer screen, this site collects technical information, pictures, contact numbers, hardware updates, software reviews, and even Zoomer rumors. What kind of rumors, you ask? How about the one that says that there's a Novell Corsair Client on the way for Tandy's powerful palmtop? Zoomer's ears are burning, no doubt. ✓**INTERNET**→*www* http://www.eit.com/mailinglists/zoomer/zoomer.html

Zoomer List (ml) Discussion and info for current and potential users of Tandy Zoomer PDAs. ✓**INTERNET**→*email* listserv@grot.starconn.com ✎ *Type in message body:* subscribe zoomer-list <your full name>

Magic Link

Sony Magic Link If the Sony Magic Link was an actor, it might be McCauley Culkin—small, lightweight, fun to use, and connected to a multi-billion dollar conglomerate. Get the most out of your personal intelligent communicator with this official Sony site, which will teach you a few palmtop and PDA tricks. ✓**INTERNET**→*www* http://cons1.sel.sony.com/SEL/Magic/

Steve and his Sony Magic Link *Manimal* wasn't a very successful series. Neither was *Supertrain*. And *She's the Sherrif* didn't exactly capture the imagination of America. But Steve and his Sony Magic Link have the potential to run for years, as former Newton owner Steve tries on a new palmtop for size. "I now know five people with Magic Links," says Steve after just one week of his journey. America holds its breath. ✓**INTERNET**→*www* http://www.geeksrus.com/MagicLinkHome.html

> "If the Sony Magic Link was an actor, it might be McCauley Culkin—small, lightweight, fun to use, and connected to a multi-billion dollar conglomerate."

Other

Motorola Envoy If it's Envoy publicity you want, it's Envoy publicity you'll get—a product sheet, specifications, frequently asked questions, software descriptions, press releases, purchase information, and screen shots. Make friends with the computer that brings new meaning to the phrase "Pocket Quicken." ✓**INTERNET**→*www* http://www.motorola.com/MIMS/WDG/Envoy/

Simon Net Those who grew up with the 70's electronic memory game Simon will be thrilled to know that the name has been revived in the Simon PDA. You can do more than play games on this one. Send faxes, send and receive email, import and export files from your computer, and make regular telephone calls. Organize your life with the calendar, address books, to-do list, notepad, sketchpad, clock, and calculator. Here you can read a basic profile as well as request that information be sent to you via email. Yup—it's an ad. ✓**INTERNET**→*www* http://www.chattanooga.net/simon/index.html

Calculators A Small Matter: Minicomputers

Calculators

If you ever went to high school, you probably have some experience with calculators— maybe you used them in trigonometry to calculate sines and cosines, maybe you memorized the square roots of prime numbers to impress the girls, and maybe you learned to type numbers that would look like words when you turned the calculator upside-down. Whatever the case, you can continue your love affair with the calculator on the Net. Visit the **Texas Instruments Home Page**. Stroll the cyberhalls of the **Museum of HP Calculators**. And put a calculator onscreen with **Calc/Stats/Clocks** files.

Calculator—from http://www.teleport.com/adgh/

On the Net

Texas Instruments

Texas Instruments Home Page Before there were home computers, there were pocket calculators—and there still are, although today's powerful devices have features undreamed of in those long-ago four-function days. This is the unofficial home page of Texas Instruments calculators, and it carries links to programs, newsgroups, editors, mailing lists, and even games for Texas Instruments graphing calculators. Each link is identified by a tiny image of the specific model in question. Cute, huh? ✓**INTERNET**→*www* http://dnclab.Berkeley.EDU/~smack/ti.html

Hewlett-Packard

Hewlett-Packard HP48 G/GX Calculators This official HP-sponsored Web page offers software, product information, service, support, and answers to frequently asked questions for the HP48G/GX calculator family. ✓**INTERNET**→*www* http://hpcvbbs.cv.hp.com/

Hewlett-Packard Calculators At this unofficial Hewlett-Packard Calculators home page, you can read about HP calculators, download HP programs, access the HP Art Gallery (a collection of photographs of HP calculators by devoted users), and link to other HP calculator resources on the Internet. And don't forget to look at page author Jeff Thieleke's own collection of HP calculators. ✓**INTERNET**→*www* http://kahless.isca.uiowa.edu/hewlett_packard.html

HP48 FAQ An FAQ document with questions and answers about almost every aspect of HP calculators, plus informative appendices such as "HP48 best programs and where to get them." The page does, however, come with a caveat: "This list contains information which has not necessarily been verified, and is not guaranteed to be correct, or even reflecting reality." ✓**INTERNET**→*www* http://kahless.isca.uiowa.edu/hp/faq/faquindex.html

Jeff Sawdy's HP Pages Despite the apologetic tone ("Most of these are wimpy little links to other people's servers"), this page offers several treats for HP48 users

118 Net Tech

A Small Matter: Minicomputers Calculators

including photographs, games, and nine "goodies disks," each of which contains valuable programs and information for HP48 users. There are also links to other HP48 resources, and the text of the most recent issue of the *Hewlett-Packard Journal*. ✓ **INTERNET**→*www* http://www2.ncsu.edu/eos/users/j/jesawdy/mosaic/hp48.html

John Lueders's HP Page "Welcome to HPLand." Math, science, games, utilities, and other programs are available here, along with links to "Other HP48 Nut Pages" and FTP sites. ✓ **INTERNET** →*www* http://www.mcs.net/~jlueders/HP_Web/hp48.html

The Museum of HP Calculators Remember those early Hewlett-Packard calculators? Sure you do—they appeared throughout the 70's, allowing you, your parents, or your children to add and subtract while wearing bell bottoms and listening to the sounds of the Hughes Corporation. This page contains separate entries for each calculator model; each entry features a very detailed description and photographs. There's also a document entitled "How to Fix HPs" that contains descriptions and pictures of many kinds of repairs to classic HPs. Links to a couple of other HP sites are also provided. ✓ **INTERNET** →*www* http://www.teleport.com/~dgh/hpmuseum.html

SCDI's HP48 Calculators Department SCDI stands for "Society pour la creation et le developpement informatique," which means something like "Computer Creation and Development Society." (It's French, in case you were wondering.) At this Website, you will find an extensive library of HP calculator-related documents and programs (including some beta versions of new programs), plus links to other HP-related sites. ✓ **INTERNET**→*www* http://didecs1-e.epfl.ch/~jcoates/hp48.html

Wayne's HP48 G/GX Calculator Resource Links to online HP resources, including page author Wayne Lee's own FTP-accessible collection of HP files. Why pay tribute to the lowly calculator? "Well," says Wayne, "HP calculators are neat. If you don't have one and are taking a math course above Algebra I go buy one. It is worth it. You can use it as a remote control." ✓ **INTERNET**→*www* http://www.best.com/~waynel/hp48.htm

Shareware

Calc/Stats/Clocks Stock trader clocks. Warp-Speed Calculators. Stopwatches. Astronomy clocks. This library is packed with clocks and calculators in all shapes, sizes, and designs for Windows users. Download, and calculate away. ✓ **COMPUSERVE**→*go* winshare→Libraries→Calc/Stats/Clocks

Macintosh Calculators Mac utilities and applications for calculating everything from test scores, amortization, engineering and programming constants, loan payments, and your take-home pay after withholding. Hint: Take-home pay is usually slightly less than you imagined. ✓ **AMERICA ONLINE**→*keyword* shareware→Utilities Forum→Software Search→calculators

Macintosh Calculators Various calculating programs you can use to determine UPS shipping costs, the value of your 401-K plan, auto leasing payments, and scientific notation. ✓ **COMPUSERVE**→*go* macap→Libraries→*Search by keyword:* calculators

PC Calculators What do you need to calculate? Unless it's something genuinely arcane—the distance between Anthony Quinn's eyebrows, or the number of times per day that someone thinks about Homer Simpson and laughs—you'll find the proper program in this archive. Molecular mass? Body fat? Football spreads? Recipes? Just plug in the necessary numbers. ✓ **AMERICA ONLINE**→*keyword* software→PC Software→File Search→ calculators

SimTel Calculators Calculators for scientists, joggers, students, cooks, bookkeepers, white-collar crooks, and more. The first two addresses are for DOS; the others, Windows. ✓ **INTERNET** …→*www* http://www.acs.oakland.edu/oak/SimTel/msdos/calculat.html …→*www* ftp://oak.oakland.edu/SimTel/msdos/calculat …→*www* http://www.acs.oakland.edu/oak/SimTel/win3/calc.html …→*www* ftp://wuarchive.wustl.edu/systems/ibmpc/simtel/win3/calc …→*www* ftp://ftp.uoknor.edu/mirrors/SimTel/win3/calc

> "HP calculators are neat. If you don't have one and are taking a math course above Algebra I go buy one. It is worth it. You can use it as a remote control."

Part 5

PC Power

Word Processing PC Power

Word processing

Without word processing, you wouldn't be reading this sentence. Or this fragment.

With word processing, though, millions of Americans can write letters, papers, articles, and even books without worrying about typographical errors, pagination problems, or type style concerns. Though message boards like **Word Processors** are dominated by the twin towers of word-processing software—Microsoft Word and WordPerfect—the Net contains dedicated sites for virtually every major program on the market, from the **AmiPro FTP Site** to **MacWrite**.

On the Net

Across the board

comp.os.ms-windows.apps.word-proc (ng) Microsoft Word for Windows, better known in this newsgroup as "WinWord," is the main topic of discussion. How do you create a bibliography in WinWord? Export to HTML? Manage large documents? Create tables? Advice is doled out by MS Word gurus on these and other topics (macro writing, printer drivers, etc.). Computer users looking for hints and advice about WordPerfect, AmiPro, and other Windows word processing programs are also welcome. Take Tom, for instance: "At work there are a ton of form letters and proposals in WordPerfect for Windows 6.1 that I would like to take home and review on my PC in Word 6.0 for Windows. My secretary says there is no good way to do it. There must be some kind of converter or something. Can anyone shed some light?" ✓**USENET**

Mac Word Processing In the world of the Macintosh, word processing usually means Microsoft Word, and, while there is plenty of discussion about Word (including a very active Word 6.0 Nightmare Folder), MacWrite, WriteNow, Nisus, and even WordPerfect for the Mac have their own message folders in this forum. But writers can turn to this forum for more than program support—general advice about word processing and recommendations for dictionaries, file conversion utilities, and index programs are also covered on the message boards. In the libraries, there is an archive of shareware utilities for your Macintosh, including typing tutors, a screenplay formatter, and an HTML convertor that translates Word 6.0 files into text files with hypertext markup language tags. ✓**AMERICA ONLINE** ...→*keyword* mdp→Message Boards→Let's Discuss→Word Processors ...→*keyword* mdp→Software Libraries→Utilities→Word Processors

PC Word Processing The PC Applications Forum has a shareware archive full of software add-ons for word processors, including AmiPro, WordPerfect, and Word for Windows. Need a poetry generating program? Drop into the Utilities area and download PoeTrio, an application that coaches you through the process of writing free verse, cantos, and haiku. How about a bibliography management program (BibLogic 3.02) or the useful Cliché Finder, which scans your document in

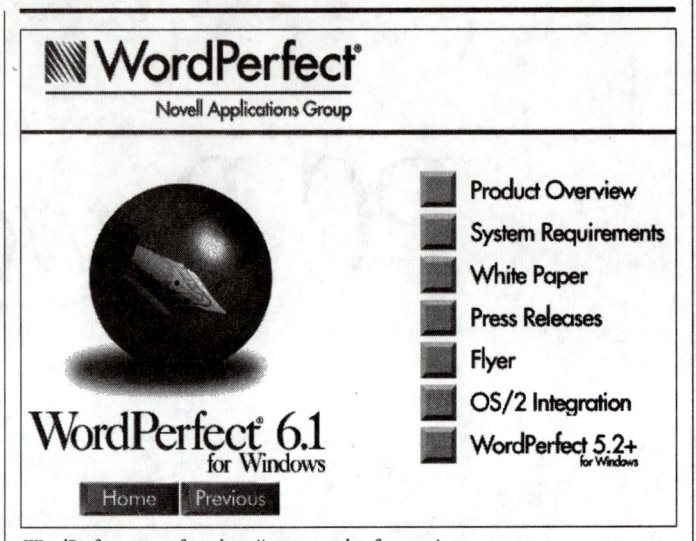

WordPerfect page—from http://www.wordperfect.com/

PC Power Word Processing

search of trite and overused words? The forum also has a message board where word processing and word processing programs are discussed. ✓ **AMERICA ONLINE** ...→*keyword* pcapplications→Browse the Software Libraries→Word Processing ...→*keyword* pcapplications→ Message Boards→Word Processors

PC Word Processing Tips and tricks of that old PC workhorse XWrite ("Is it still breathing?") are exchanged here, as are recommendations for the most powerful Windows word processors, instructions for WordPerfect conversions, and even advice on where to get a Polish-language word processor. The library is a huge repository of shareware word processors, add-ons for popular commercial programs (the WordPerfect Business Correspondence Assistant), and other related programs (a rhyme dictionary, Cyrillic fonts, and tons of thesauri). ✓ **COMPUSERVE**→*go* pcapps→Libraries *or* Messages→Word Processing

Text Processing Directory This directory contains word processing-related software, including filters for graphics programs, converters (to translate WordPerfect documents into Word documents, for example), and text editors. There's even a Braille text editor (Braille 0.6) that translates ordinary text into a Braille format. The text processors are organized by name and filed alphabetically. You can browse a description of the file or download it directly. ✓ **INTERNET** ...→*www* http://hyperarchive.lcs.mit.edu/HyperArchive/Abstracts/text/HyperArchive.html ...→*www* ftp://sumex-aim.stanford.edu/info-mac/TextProcessing ...→*www* gopher://sunsite.doc.ic.ac.uk:70/1/packages/mac-sumex/TextProcessing

Windows Text & Word Programs Need a text editor that lets you drag and drop with ease? Check out SuperEdit. Want to keep a secret diary that no one can access but you? Download My Personal Diary, which features an encryption program and can only be opened with a password. Need to translate Mac files into Windows documents with getting the squigglies? Get yourself Convert 1.01. This library is filled with custom pages like these. ✓ **AMERICA ONLINE**→*keyword* winforum→ Browse the Software Libraries→Applications→Text & Word Programs

Word Processing/DTP For most people—designers aside—the line between word processing and desktop publishing is blurry if not meaningless. The goal, after all, is to produce a business plan, write a resumé, or, perhaps, send a memo. To do the job, you'll use a word processor, fonts, and maybe clip art or scanned images. Located in the Working from Home Forum, this discussion area and library section offer members support, advice, templates, and sample projects to help them flesh out project ideas and troubleshoot problems with word processing and DTP tools. ✓ **COMPUSERVE**→*go* work→Libraries *or* Messages→ Word Processing/DTP

Word Processors Microsoft Word and WordPerfect dominate the discussion of word processing programs here in much the same way they dominate the market. AmiPro also gets a large share of the discussion. In moments of crisis ("Tell me I didn't just lose my whole report!") or times of frustration ("I am having trouble with pagination of a mail-merged form letter in Word 6.0"), the board is a helpful place to pick up word processing tips and advice. ✓ **PRODIGY** →*jump* computerbb→Choose a Topic→Word Processors

AmiPro

AmiPro FTP Site Macros, technical support notes, program updates, and third-party software for AmiPro. ✓ **INTERNET**→*www* ftp://192.216.79.100/pub/desktop/AmiPro/

AmiPro Technical Information Official Lotus information and resources for AmiPro users. Use the search button to retrieve FAQs related to AmiPro or to link directly to the FTP site. ✓ **INTERNET**→*www* http://www.lotus.com/cs&s/htm/css3.htm

LDC Word Processing Forum A company-sponsored forum offering product support for users of Lotus word processing software, including AmiPro, WordPro, LotusWrite, and SmarText. The forum is dominated by AmiPro support and resources, and includes Ami Pro stylesheets, macros, technical notes, and product information and demos. ✓ **COMPUSERVE**→*go* lotuswp

Lotus WordPro A high-tech brochure for Lotus's new group word processor. This site carries video clips demoing the program, press releases, and reviews. ✓ **INTERNET**→*www* http://www.lotus.com/wordpro/wordpro1.htm

MacWrite

MacWrite Claris offers technical support and updates for its Macintosh word processor in this forum. ✓ **COMPUSERVE**→*go* macclaris→Libraries *or* Messages→MacWrite

MacWrite Technical Support Where do you go when you're stumped while word processing in

Word Processing PC Power

MacWrite? The forum carries documentation on the new features of MacWrite Pro, an FAQ file about the program, and program add-ons. And if you've spotted a bug in MacWrite or you're having "goofy spacing problems," the message boards are the place to post questions to the Claris technical support staff. ✓**AMERICA ONLINE**→*keyword* claris→Technical Support→MacWrite

MS Word

bit.mailserv.word-mac (ng) In this discussion group devoted to Microsoft Word for the Macintosh, posts have complained about Word 6.0 (it crashes, it's too slow, it has too many features), asked about how to use Speech Manager with a word processor, or explained how to drop Intellidraw drawings into Word 5.0 documents. Not a lot of traffic, but if you're in search of help you might want to post something here. ✓**USENET**

bit.mailserv.word-pc (ng) A newsgroup devoted to word processing on Microsoft Word for the PC. Having trouble creating footnotes in Word 6.0 for Windows? In search of a converter that will turn Mac text files into WinWord documents? Someone here should be able to point you in the right direction. ✓**USENET**

Microsoft Word for Windows Maximize the features of Word for Windows! The PC Applications Forum carries a software library packed with add-ons—Internet Assistant will turn your copy of Word 6.0 for Windows into a Web browser; ScriptWright is a multi-featured screenplay formatter; PAL is a personal address add-on that creates and maintains a cardfile address list from within Word for Windows; and there are dozens of others. ✓**AMERICA ONLINE**→*keyword* pcapplications→Browse the Software Libraries→Microsoft Applications→Microsoft Word for Windows

Microsoft Word Forum Stop by for a Mac Word screenwriting template, a utility that fixes damaged tables, advice on mail-merging in Word 6.0, or news about the latest patch. The forum offers support, upgrades, templates, and fonts for the Word for Windows and Macintosh Word programs. ✓**COMPUSERVE**→*go* msword

MS Word Directory A huge archive of hundreds of articles about Word from Microsoft's Knowledge Base—each article is a separate file with a distinct file number. Download the index for a brief description of each article (e.g., Word Prints Excel Chart Hairlines as 1-Point Lines). Find the article that best addresses your problem. And download the article with the corresponding number. ✓**INTERNET**→*www* ftp://ftp.microsoft.com/deskapps/word/kb/

SimTel Word for Windows Directory The huge SimTel archive for DOS and Windows files features a directory of add-ons for the Microsoft Word for Windows program. There are programs to help manage files, a tutorial that explains the program, an HTML authoring tool, and other applications that optimize the functionality of the word processor. ✓**INTERNET** ...→*www* http://www.acs.oakland.edu/oak/SimTel/win3/winword.html ...→*www* ftp://oak.oakland.edu/SimTel/win3/winword...→*www* ftp://wuarchive.wustl.edu/systems/ibmpc/simtel/win3/winword ...→ *www* ftp://ftp.uoknor.edu/mirrors/SimTel/win3/win word

---

CYBERNOTES

"This Tip could best be called a back to basics Windows Tip. How many times have you seen a really good clip art image in another program and wished you could pull it into WordPerfect? If you are using WordPerfect for Windows 5.1 or better you can, using the Windows cut & paste features. Simply cut the image in whatever program you're using and then exit that program (if you're tight on RAM) WITHOUT saving the original (that way you don't ruin it).

"Enter the Windows Paintbrush program remove the Pallete and the tools (this gives you a bigger work area) and select Paste from the pull down menu. After the image appears reinstall the pallete and the tools. If you are using one of the older DOS-based versions of Word-Perfect save the image as a PCX file, or if you are a Windows version of WordPerfect save it as a BMP file. This very basic Windows trick works 97% percent of the time."

—from **Wordperfect for Windows**

PC Power Word Processing

...→*www* ftp://ftp.uni.paderborn.de/SimTel/win3/winword

WordPerfect

Novell Inc. Website Novell owns WordPerfect, and Novell's Website includes program brochures and guides, updates, usage tips, and technical documents for the immensely popular program. ✓**INTERNET**→*www* http://www.wordperfect.com/

SimTel WordPerfect Software Although small, this directory for DOS users of WordPerfect includes interesting utilities and information, such as programs to help create HTML documents from text, seven volumes of WordPerfect clip art, macros, a utility to covert .GIF images to WordPerfect.WPG format, a damaged file fixer, and even a tutorial. ✓**INTERNET** ...→*www* http://www.acs.oakland.edu/oak/SimTel/msdos/wordperf.html ...→*www* ftp://oak.oakland.edu/SimTel/msdos/wordperf ...→*www* ftp://wuarchive.wustl.edu/systems/ibmpc/simtel/msdos/wordperf ...→*www* ftp://ftp.uoknor.edu/mirrors/SimTel/msdos/wordperf ...→*www* ftp://ftp.uni-paderborn.de/SimTel/msdos/wordperf

WordPerfect Magazine An online version of the magazine dedicated to the popular word-processing program WordPerfect. Download the Online Access Electronic Magazine Binder to view complete articles with graphics and screenshots. The forum also features software libraries and message boards. ✓**AMERICA ONLINE**→*keyword* wpmag

WordPerfect 5.1 Discussion Group List (ml) Mail-merge on Monday. Address labels on Tuesday. Draft meeting memo on Wednesday. Finalize proposal on Thursday. Create new résumé on Friday. Whatever the task, if you're using WordPerfect in a Windows environment, this is generally a good place to seek advice and get helpful tips. ✓**INTERNET**→*email* listserv@ubvm.cc.buffalo.edu ✍ *Type in message body:* subscribe wpwin-l <your full name>

WordPerfect Center How do I do footnotes? Why won't my image import? I'm having problems merging. What do I do? If you have other things to do besides hang on the phone with the Novell Corporation, visit the WordPerfect Center for tech support. Check the software libraries for WordPerfect add-ons, FAQs, and even special Biblical and military dictionaries. ✓**AMERICA ONLINE**→*keyword* wordperfect

WordPerfect Corporation Products Discussion List (ml) A mailing list for the discussion of WordPerfect products. ✓**INTERNET**→*email* listserv@ubvm.cc.buffalo.edu ✍ *Type in message body:* subscribe wpcorp-l <your full name>

WordPerfect Users Forum If you're having trouble with WordPerfect, look no further—this forum is the Net mecca for technical support. The message boards, which are separated into platform categories and WP software versions, are full of queries and responses to users' problems. The libraries contain a wide range of utilities files—from Haitian and Creole spell-checkers to a supplementary dictionary of drug names that can be added to your built-in WordPerfect dictionary. Never misspell crystal meth again. ✓**COMPUSERVE**→*go* wpusers

WPCorp Files Forum Sponsored by WordPerfect, the forum carries product announcements and press releases pertaining to the WordPerfect word processing program. For a large selection of printer drivers, visit the Printer Drivers library. The message board is for non-technical questions and printer driver queries— more technical support is provided in the WordPerfect Users' Forum ✓**COMPUSERVE**→*go* wpfiles

WriteStar/ WriteNow

Softkey Forum A forum for users of Softkey software, including WordStar for DOS and Windows and WriteNow for the Macintosh. Softkey representatives monitor the message boards, so you can post queries to them in the appropriate software sections. The libraries contain utilities (like grammar-checking programs), text files and patches for WordStar and WriteNow, and even a set of applications that work with other Softkey products. ✓**COMPUSERVE**→*go* softkey→Browse Libraries→WordStar for DOS *or* WS For Windows *or* All Mac Apps

> "Mail-merge on Monday. Address labels on Tuesday. Draft meeting memo on Wednesday. Finalize proposal on Thursday. Create new résumé on Friday."

Desktop Publishing PC Power

Desktop publishing

"Freedom of the press belongs to those who own one." With ever faster, stronger, and cheaper personal computers and printers entering homes and offices everywhere, owning a "press" has become as unremarkable as owning a VCR. Programs like PageMaker and Quark-XPress have not only revolutionized the publishing industry, they have empowered those who for centuries had to rely on the publishing industry. For the pros, converting a book or magazine from whim to finished product once involved a tremendous amount of manpower—now, text can be formatted, graphics prepared, and pages laid out by a single designer. For many businesses and home users, desktop publishing has allowed for the elimination of the designer altogether— "just DTP it" has become synonymous with "do it yourself." It ain't always pretty, but then, freedom seldomly is. Start at the **DTP Internet Jumplist**, which will connect you to dozens of pertinent DTP Websites and newsgroups. Learn to decorate your newsletter at **alt.binaries.clip-art**. Then guess what font this is by dropping by **comp.fonts**.

Macintosh Desktop System—from CompuServe's Bettmann Archive

On the Net
Across the board

Atari DTP Directory A small collection of clip art (flags to teddy bears), fonts, and DTP programs for the Atari. ✓**INTERNET** ...→*www* ftp://wuarchive.wustl.edu/systems/atari/umich.edu/Applications/Dtp/ ...→*www* ftp://atari.archive.umich.edu/Applications/Dtp ...→*www* gopher://gopher.archive.umich.edu:7055/11/atari/Applications/Dtp

Desktop Publishing Perhaps it's a newsletter you're laying out or a sales flyer you're creating, but whatever the design task, you're probably using a computer and DTP software. Prodigy users bring their DTP questions here: "Is Microsoft Publisher a good piece of DTP software and does it import the clip art in MS Power Point?"; "Does anyone know a font for the PC that is comparable to Carlos Roman on the Mac?"; and "I am using Adobe Acrobat on a Windows system and need to print a document which was prepared on a Mac using PostScript fonts; specifically the ones which are causing me trouble are NewCentury-Schlbk fonts." Asked and answered. ✓**PRODIGY** ...→*jump* computerbb→Choose a Topic→Desktop Publishing ...→*jump* softwaresupportbb→Choose a Topic→Desktop Publishing

Desktop Publishing Forum Corrupting fonts? Problems with PageMaker? The message boards are chock-full of advice. Whether you're interested in reminiscing about the glory days of PageMaker 1.2, discussing theories of modular layout, or learning more about the HTML add-ons to Quark, the message boards and real-time conference rooms are great places to confer with professionals. And the

126 Net Tech

PC Power Desktop Publishing

archives are filled with large collections of PC and Mac fonts, clip art, and DTP software. ✓**COMPUSERVE**→*go* dtpforum

DTP Internet Jumplist A hypertext list of resources on the Internet containing links to FAQs, fonts, clip art, and other DTP-related sites. This electronic trampoline lets you search by topic or allows you to jump directly to font and clip art archives or related discussion groups. A good place to start exploring desktop publishing resources on the Internet. ✓**INTERNET**→*www* http://www.cs.purdue.edu/homes/gwp/dtp/dtp.html

Macintosh Desktop Publishing Forum Desktop publishing has revolutionized the publishing industry, and this forum is dedicated to providing designers with the resources, product support, and advice for doing their jobs well. Word processing and typography are extensively covered here, and you'll find font collections, searchable image libraries, tips on formatting text, and message boards with separate discussion folders for popular applications. Special Interest Groups (SIGs) for advertising, legal services, and service bureaus are also directly accessible from this forum. The Industry Connection icon links to many popular vendors, including Adobe (Aldus), Quark, and WordPerfect. ✓**AMERICA ONLINE**→*keyword* mdp

PBS Studio Forum Military clip art? Halloween TrueType font? A moon icon? DTP designers can mine the library here for clip art, icons, fonts, and font tools. ✓**COMPUSERVE**→*go* pbsstudio

PC DTP Resource Center Typefaces, images, and formatting tips for desktop publishers who work in an IBM-compatible environment. And that's just the beginning. Worried about copyright issues on *The X-Files* newsletter you're working on? Turn to the libraries for texts on copyright law or post a question on the message boards. Need to learn the professional lingo? Pick up a glossary of desktop publishing terms. And if you don't know how to convert a GIF to a TIFF, read the graphics file tips. In addition, there are software libraries devoted exclusively to printer support, TrueType Fonts, and DTP utilities. The DTP Classifieds section advertises services and software. You can directly access vendors through the Industry Connection or post questions and observations pertaining to practically every desktop publishing program in the world. ✓**AMERICA ONLINE**→*keyword* pcapplications→DTP Resource Center

Chat

comp.text.desktop (ng) Gossip, opinions, and speculation reign over useful queries and advice in this casual newsgroup dedicated to desktop publishing. In addition to the endless debate pitting Quark against PageMaker, working in an IBM-compatible environment is compared to working in a Macintosh environment, and the merits of hypertext are discussed. Desktop publishing with FrameMaker is also touched upon. Technical questions go unanswered here. ✓**USENET**

DTP General Discussion (ml) A mailing list specializing in general discussion about all facets of desktop publishing. You can also facilitate discussion of the merits of PageMaker vs. QuarkXPress, swap typography lore with fellow font fanatics, or share your knowledge of the best public-domain clip art sites on the Internet. ✓**INTERNET**→*email* listserv@antigone.com ✍ *Type in subject line:* subscribe <your full name>

Typography and Type Design List (ml) A more specialized DTP mailing list catering to typography devotees. This is where you go to voice your opinion on whether serif or sans serif fonts are easier to read, or to inquire whether or not Franklin Gothic is the right font to use in your company's annual report. ✓**INTERNET**→*email* listserv@ir learn.udc.ie ✍ *Type in subject line:* subscribe <your full name>

Basics

DTP Book FAQ A straightforward listing of recommended books and magazines for desktop publishers and graphic designers who use PageMaker. Unfortunately, most of the PageMaker books on this list are about the now-outdated version 4.0. ✓**INTERNET**→*www* http://www.cs.purdue.edu/

> "Want a black and white bunny icon? How about a dead mouse? Perhaps a colored baseball or toilet? Thousands of icons that have passed the Anthony-says-this-is-not-crap test are available here."

Net Tech 127

Desktop Publishing PC Power

homes/gwp/books.faq

DTP Tips FAQ Design tips for desktop publishers on layout, type design, and color manipulation. ✓ **INTERNET**→*www* http://www.cs.purdue.edu/homes/gwp/dtptips.faq

The Scanning FAQ A general, online description of how to capture images with a scanner. Halftones, black and white images, and color scans are covered. ✓ **INTERNET** …→*www* http://www.cs.purdue.edu/homes/gwp/scantips.faq …→*www* http://www.dopig.uab.edu/dopipages/FAQ/The_Scan_FAQ.html

News & magazines

The Desktop Publisher's Journal A DTP-related magazine with a PC slant that "tries to cover all the latest and best graphics and desktop publishing programs." Find out about the best printers and scanners on the market by reading the DPJ's extensive hardware reviews. The magazine also includes software and book reviews and links to other desktop publishing sites on the Net. ✓ **INTERNET**→*www* http://www.awa.com/nct/software/graplead.html

Get Info A free monthly newsletter for DTP professionals looking for tips and tricks. A different topic is addressed each month. The April '95 "Versus" issue compared and contrasted DTP software. PageMaker or QuarkXPress? Illustrator or Freehand? And should you link TIFFs or EPS files? Written and edited by Jeffrey Glover, the newsletter is an insightful monthly resource for the advanced desktop publisher. ✓ **INTERNET**→*www* http://www.winternet.com/~jmg/GetInfo.html

Icons

Anthony's Icon Library Want a black and white bunny icon? How about a dead mouse? Perhaps a colored baseball or toilet? Thousands of icons that have passed the Anthony-says-this-is-not-crap test are available here. And the archives are searchable. ✓ **INTERNET** …→*www* http://www.cit.gu.edu.au/~anthony/icons/ …→*www* http://www.bsdi.com/icons/AIcons/ …→*www* ftp://ftp.cit.gu.edu.au/pub/AIcons/

Daniel's Icon Archive More than 1,300 icons to spruce up Web pages, newsletters, or databases. Need an arrow or a button? How about a cloverleaf? Besides its own huge collection, the site also links to several other icon repositories. ✓ **INTERNET**→*www* http://www.jsc.nasa.gov/~mccoy/Icons/index.html

Icon Editors A collection of programs for creating icons on a Windows machine. ✓ **INTERNET** …→*www* http://www.acs.oakland.edu/oak/SimTel/win3/icon.html …→*www* ftp://oak.oakland.edu/SimTel/win3/icon …→*www* ftp://wuarchive.wustl.edu/systems/ibmpc/simtel/win3/icon …→*www* ftp://ftp.uoknor.edu/mirrors/SimTel/win3/icon …→*www* ftp://ftp.uni-paderborn.de/SimTel/win3/icon

Icons! No guarantees about the quality, but the selection of icons is large and varied—Ferraris, high heels, and O.J. Simpson, to name a few. And if you're looking for something specific, head to the message boards and ask. ✓ **COMPUSERVE**→*go* comart→Libraries *or* Messages→Icons

Windows Icons A great way to customize your Windows desktop

CYBERNOTES

"I'm looking for a desktop publishing program that would suit my needs as a Role-Playing Game designer. I want a program that will allow me to integrate text, a fair number of tables, quite a few graphics, etc. for books of 150-250 pages. I have not ever used FrameMaker, but I was directed to it by various online advice. So here I'm asking you who have experience, would FrameMaker be better suited to this kind of thing than PageMaker, Quark, or another DTP program?

"I also am just getting my masters in English, and will in the forseeable future be returning for my PhD. I was also told FrameMaker was very useful for formatting a dissertation--also a concern. I currently use Word 5.1 and Photoshop (still waffling about Word 6.0). So is FrameMaker more suited to these kind of mostly text documents?"

—from America Online's **Macintosh Desktop Publishing Forum**

PC Power Desktop Publishing

is to incorporate customized icons. This AOL collection provides you with ready-made images in the proper size and format in categories ranging from cartoon and comics to nature and space. In addition, there are separate libraries for icon collections, utilities, and formats. ✓ **AMERICA ONLINE**→*keyword* winforum→Browse the Software Libraries→More...→Icons

Fonts

Adobe Type Manager *Time* magazine owns it. Sony owns it. The neighborhood high school owns it. Deep beneath the system folder of every desktop publisher lurks Adobe Type Manager—the little utility that turns any computer into a publishing machine. ATM, which rastorizes (smooths) PostScript fonts for both display and output, remains hidden to most users—until they need help with it. Turn to the message boards in this forum with questions about ATM ("How high should I set my font cache?") or go to the library for updates, utilities, and documentation. ✓ **COMPUSERVE**→*go* adobea

comp.fonts (ng) Three hundred messages about fonts—every couple of days? And the newsgroup also has an incredibly comprehensive FAQ. Both frustrated computer newbies ("I have some fonts on my hard drive and when I go into the Control Panel and try to load the fonts, they're not shown in the selection window. Help anyone!") and more experienced designers ("Could some kind soul tell me what, if anything, Bitstream Geometric 231 is equivalent to? And if there is a way I could have found this out myself, I'd appreciate knowing how, too.") use the group to confer. The majority of questions involve people trying to locate a font. ✓ **USENET**

comp.fonts FAQ "What's the difference between all these font formats?" "How can I convert my TrueType font to Adobe Type 1 formats?" "Can I Print Checks with the MICR Font?" This monster of an FAQ covers font pronunciation, font formats by computer platform, font utilities, font vendors, typographical history, copyright concerns, and an incredible number of other font issues. ✓ **INTERNET** ...→*www* http://www.cis.ohio-state.edu:80/text/faq/usenet/fonts-faq/top.html ...→*www* http://jasper.ora.com:80/comp.fonts/FAQ/ ...→*www* ftp://jasper.ora.com/pub/comp.fonts/FAQ/FAQ-comp-fonts.txt.tar.gz

The comp.fonts Homepage A well-designed page starts with a well-chosen font. This Website features links to the comp.fonts FAQ (dos, don'ts, and typographical explanations), bibliographic information about typeface designers, several font foundries and service bureaus online, PostScript resources, and electronic publications focusing on typography. A selection of font programs is also available here. ✓ **INTERNET**→*www* http://jasper.ora.com:80/comp.fonts/

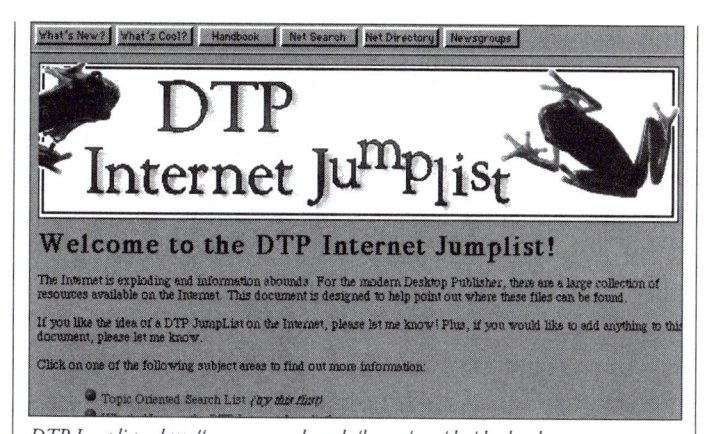

DTP Jumplist—http://www.cs.purdue.edu/homes/gwp/dtp/dtp.html

The Internet Font Archive One man's attempt to collect all of the fonts available on the Internet in a single location. If you're shopping around for new fonts, this is the place to go. Thousands of fonts are archived here, and many commercial sites linked to the archive offer thumbnail previews of selected fonts so you can spy before you buy. ✓ **INTERNET**→*www* http://jasper.ora.com:80/comp.fonts/Internet-Font-Archive/index/html

Jerry's World This graphic arts superstore has thousands of fonts and pieces of clip art. ✓ **COMPUSERVE**→*go* jerry

Mac Shareware Fonts Need a typeface in the shape of armadillos? How about one for creating quick ransom notes for your next kidnapping? Computer users seem to love creating quirky new fonts, and the collection in this library is proof positive. ✓ **AMERICA ONLINE**→*keyword* mac500→Fonts

Windows Shareware Fonts Some of the typefaces in this shareware collection seem practical and worthwhile. Architect, for instance, is a clean "handwriting"

Desktop Publishing PC Power

font. Others, however, sound a bit dubious. Animals is a typeface made up of animal silhouettes, and Trains uses you-know-what to create just 18 characters of the alphabet. There are also a few font utilities scattered throughout this library. ✓**AMERICA ONLINE**→*keyword* win500→Shareware Library →Fonts

Clip art

alt.binaries.clip-art (ng) Need some Buddhist clip art? How about the Kiwanis Club logo? Post your request here. ✓**USENET**

Funet Clip Art Collection A vast archive of clip art including public-domain Amiga, Atari, and Macintosh clip art collections. You'll find everything here, from pictures of garlic and pretzels to those famous universal logos for men's and women's restrooms. ✓**INTERNET**→ *www* http://seidel.ncsa.uiuc.edu/ClipArt/funet.html

Sandra's Clip Art Server Sandra Loosemore searched the Net for public-domain clip art for her own Website and then created a page of links to all the clip art sites on the Web that she found. ✓**INTERNET**→*www* http://www.cs.yale.edu/HTML/YALE/CS/HyPlans/loosemore-sandra/clipart.html

SimTel Desktop Publishing A small collection primarily of clip art and icons for DOS computer users. ✓**INTERNET** ...→*www* http://www.acs.oakland.edu/oak/SimTel/msdos/deskpub.html ...→*www* ftp://oak.oakland.edu/SimTel/msdos/deskpub ...→*www* ftp://wuarchive.wustl.edu/systems/ibmpc/simtel/msdos/deskpub

Vendors

Desktop Publishing Vendors'

Quark Xpress splash screen

Forum For an extensive library of tools and materials—including software upgrade information, non-copyrighted design samples, and assorted tips and tricks—check out this forum, which is visited daily by representatives from several software companies who furnish technical advice and product support online. ✓**COMPUSERVE**→*go* dtpven

DTP Online Want to view or purchase fully licensed, downloadable fonts, clip art, and other software products for your desktop publishing project? You can view GIF file representations of selected fonts and clip art (online through the CompuServe Information Manager Software, or offline through any other GIF viewer) before you buy. Single-image downloads will run you three to four dollars; image packages cost considerably more. ✓**COMPUSERVE**→*go* dtponline

MS Desktop Forum Microsoft's Publisher, Works, PowerPoint, and Project have message boards and library sections in this forum, filled with tips, tricks, add-ons, and patches. ✓**COMPUSERVE**→*go* ms-desktop

QuarkXPress

bit.listserv.quarkxpr (ml) Members share tips for using the powerful DTP program QuarkXPress, heavily favoring the Macintosh version. The list apparently has "official connections" with the folk in QuarkXPress tech support—advice occasionally comes straight from the source. ✓**INTERNET**→*email* listserv@iubvm.ucs.indiana.edu ✍ *Type in message body:* subscribe quarkxpr <your full name>

Quark The most popular professional desktop publishing program is—no doubt—QuarkXPress, and AOL has a resource center dedicated to it. Unfortunately, it is not a particularly impressive one, consisting basically of Xtension libraries, message boards, company information, and press releases for users interested in the desktop publishing industry. ✓**AMERICA ONLINE**→*keyword* quark

Quark FTP Site A complete collection of extensions and utilities for Quark desktop publishing software. There's a downloadable file directory that you can keep for future reference. ✓**INTERNET**→*www*

PC Power Desktop Publishing

ftp://ftp.telalink.net/pub/quark/

Quark On-Line User's Forum Does anyone have any suggestions for why Pantone violet came out dark blue on a press match proof? So goes a typical question. Scripting, the X-data extension, Bit-Stream Fonts, and damaged installation files are all common fare in this forum dedicated to technical support, upgrade information, and user tips and tricks for QuarkXPress. The Quark technical support staff is not just lurking here.
✓**COMPUSERVE**→*go* quark

The XPresso Bar For users who mistakenly log on here looking for mocha information, a couple of links to coffee sites have actually been provided. However, what this Web page really offers is a well-organized collection of Quark tips compiled by a newspaper editor. There are updated categories entitled News, Tips, and Easter Eggs (hidden features). You'll find links to FTP sites, downloadable extensions, and sample scripts. You can also access (or directly subscribe to) the Quark List newsgroup.
✓**INTERNET**→*www* http://www.halcyon.com/bobgale/xpresso.html

FrameMaker

comp.text.frame (ng) How do you create fractions? And does anyone know how to rotate a page? If you're using FrameMaker desktop publishing software, turn to this newsgroup to ask your program questions. Both novices and experts will feel comfortable here.
✓**USENET**

Frame Technology Corporation The makers of FrameMaker provide product update notices, technical support, information about FrameMaker user groups, and company contact information at these sites. ☎→*dial* 408-975-6729 ✓**INTERNET** …→*www* http://www.frame.com/ …→*www* ftp://ftp.frame.com

FrameMaker FAQ What the manual for this popular multi-platform DTP program didn't explain, the FAQ attempts to do—and more. The two-part document features sections on autonumbering and cross-references, page layout, printing, filters, importing and exporting, PostScript, spelling and grammar, bibliographies and endnotes, configuring the program, and templates and clip art.
✓**INTERNET**→*www* ftp://rtfm.mit.edu/pub/usenet/comp.text.frame/

PageMaker

Adobe PageMaker The Adobe Applications forum has message topics and library sections devoted to PageMaker on both the Mac and the PC. PC topics generate the most discussion, with members discussing low-res graphics, memory problems, PageMaker and Windows 95, screen refreshing, and even faxing from PageMaker. The libraries include a smattering of technical notes, FAQs, and demo add-ons. ✓**COMPUSERVE**→*go* adobea

alt.aldus.pagemaker (ng) Desktop publishers congregate at this address to exchange gossip and advice about their favorite desktop-publishing program, PageMaker. There are questions and answers about configuring printer drivers for the Mac, obtaining the native Power Mac version of PageMaker, and installing the program under Windows 95. Many of the postings have words like "Help!" and "Arggg!" in the titles. This is not a panic-free group. The inevitable debate comparing

CYBERNOTES

"With Windows 3.1, Microsoft provides a type manager known as TrueType to compete with Adobe Type Manager (ATM) and other font managers. System 7 on the Mac also has TrueType. ATM has the advantage of a secure base and a large amount of compatible public-domain PostScript fonts. TrueType is marketed by Microsoft to be faster than ATM, but this is very debatable. TrueType fonts also breakdown at higher resolutions (making them the bane of printing bureaus). ATM is likely your best bet, if Adobe keeps its act up.

"Some people have claimed to experience problems using ATM and TrueType simultaneously. The problems range from system crashes to incorrect print-outs. It is not clear how many are actually attributed to having both managers active at once, and how many of those are actually resolvable. My suggestion is to try it out if you need both of them, but just be wary when a problem does arise."

—from **PageMaker FAQ**

Net Tech 131

Desktop Publishing PC Power

PageMaker with the Q-word also surfaces. ✓**USENET**

bit.listserv.pagemakr (ml/ng) With Adobe PageMaker now HTML-capable, this active list hasn't stopped buzzing, but the new Web design features of the program still account for only a fraction of the discussion. "Does anybody know how to get a list of fonts that are used in a document without going thru and looking at each text stream?" asks Christine in a fairly typical "how-to" posting to the group. More than 1,000 people subscribe directly and a significant number more read the newsgroup. ✓**USENET** ✓**INTERNET**→ *email* listserv@indycms.iupui.edu ✉ *Type in message body:* subscribe pagemakr <your full name>

PageMaker FAQ In addition to addressing several dozen questions about PageMaker—from "How can I create drop caps in Page-Maker?" to "How can I import WordPerfect equations?"—the FAQ directs Netters to other DTP resources online and keeps readers up to date with news from Adobe. ✓**INTERNET**→*www* http://www.cs.purdue.edu/homes/gwp/pmfaq.faq ✓**COMPUSERVE**→*go* adobea→Libraries→*Search by file name:* pmfaq.zip

PageMaker FAQ Jumplist Both amateur and professional graphic artists will appreciate this collection of FAQs about Page-Maker. FAQ topics include documented and undocumented keyboard shortcuts, default settings, and the ins and outs of scanning. There are also text files describing the latest version of PageMaker, the results of several mailing-list surveys about the program, and a Desktop Publishing Glossary of Terms. You'll even find a sample syllabus for teaching PageMaker to beginners. ✓**INTERNET**→*www* http://www.cs.purdue.edu/homes/gwp/pagemaker.html

Adobe Font Folio—from http://www.adobe.com

Other programs

Calamus Calamus is a desktop publishing package featuring soft raster-image-processing and outline font technology. The newest version of the program is available here, plus detailed information on all the various graphics modules. ✓**INTERNET**→*www* http://web.city.ac.uk/~cb170/CALAMUS/calamus.html

Microsoft Publisher A collection of templates and information about Publisher desktop publishing software from Microsoft. Business cards, greeting cards, and brochure templates are the most popular downloads here. ✓**AMERICA ONLINE**→*keyword* pcapplications→Browse the Software Libraries→Microsoft Applications→Microsoft Publisher

Publish It! Users of Publish It! software from Timeworks ask questions and exchange tips on the message boards here. There are actually two message boards—one of them is for postings about the fact that Timeworks went out of business. ✓**AMERICA ONLINE**→*keyword* timeworks

Serif PagePlus A promotional site sponsored by the Serif company—the makers of PagePlus, TablePlus, and PhotoPlus desktop publishing software. There's a technical support area, texts on company history, and a few demo software files. ✓**INTERNET**→*www* http://www.serif.com/

Professionals

World List of Desktop Publishers and Freelancers Profiles and portfolio samples from freelance graphic artists around the world. See what the rest of the electronic designing world is doing with their computers; perhaps you can steal a couple of good ideas! ✓**INTERNET**→*www* ftp://ftp.netcom/pub/conus/desktop.txt

132 Net Tech

PC Power **Business & Finance**

Business & finance

You can use your home computer to play space-pilot games, or to record your new baby gurgling happily, but the dirty little secret about PCs is that they are primarily business machines, ways of decreasing workload, increasing productivity, and pushing companies from the red into the black. Online, there are dozens of sites devoted to general business software, from the **Macintosh Business Forum** to the **Microsoft Small Business Center**, and dozens more sites devoted to the virtual office. In the twenty-first century, you see, offices will be no more. Employees will sit at home and send work over the wire. Computer screens will become membranes between interacting parties. Futurologists insist. Skeptical? Check out **Home Office Computing** and the growing popularity of groupware reflected in **Microsoft Workgroup Applications Forum**.

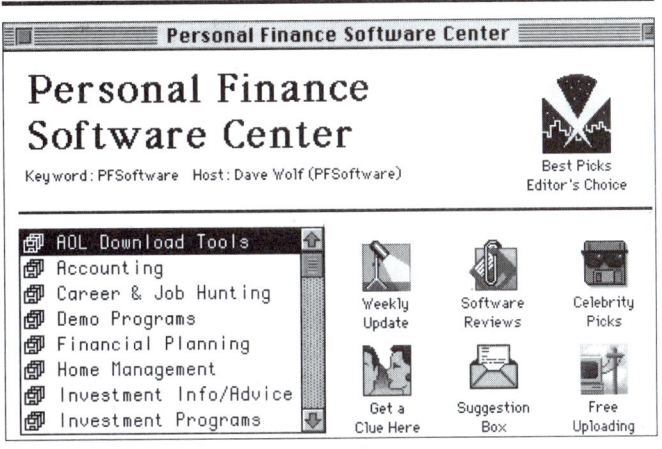

Screenshot—from AOL's Personal Finance Software Forum

On the Net

Across the board

Macintosh Business Forum A forum for people who use a Mac for business-related purposes, including accounting, tax preparation, database maintenance, business presentations, and personal information management. Questions about business software are often posted on the Let's Discuss area of the message boards ("I'm looking for good scheduling software for symphony orchestra musicians. I have to schedule 10-15 groups of different sizes and print calendars with very specific information."). Otherwise, the software library is this forum's glittering prize—it has all the address books, phone number organizers, day planners, calendars, loan payment calculators, and spreadsheet templates you'll need to conduct your business smothly and professionally on the Mac. ✓**AMERICA ONLINE**→*keyword* mbs

Microsoft Small Business Center Whether you already own a small business or are thinking about starting one, you'll find ample assistance here: A message board examines small businesses, home businesses, and consulting opportunities, and a real-time conference room enables you to converse with others about legal issues, marketing and advertising, sales, and women in business. And since this is a Microsoft-sponsored forum, the role of electronics and computers is a central theme. ✓**AMERICA ONLINE**→*keyword* smallbusiness

Office automation

Home Office Computing A monthly online magazine catering to the estimated 34 million Americans who work at home, either as entrepreneurs or telecommuters. Features reviews of hardware, peripherals, office equipment, software, and accessories, as well as tips from business and technology experts. Includes a software library. ✓**AMERICA ONLINE**→*keyword* homeoffice

Office Automation Forum Engage in discussions about office computing issues such as the cost of upgrading equipment, the proliferation of junk email, where to

Net Tech 133

Business & Finance PC Power

find information about getting a Fax-on-Demand system installed, and even the dream of a paperless office. The library is packed with downloadable articles like "10 Brochure Blunders and How to Avoid Them" and nifty software applications that take the place of ordinary sticky notes, desk calendars, and personal organizers. ✓**COMPUSERVE**→*go* oaforum

Office Automation Vendor Forum Where do you go when your scanner by Vertical Tech, Inc., won't scan bar codes or when your word processor by ANGOSS won't format text exactly the way you want it to? This technical support forum is a good bet. It's monitored by a handful of hardware and software companies, including ANGOSS, Synex Systems, ProSoft Corp., Thunder Island, Odesta Systems, Visioneer, Vertical Tech, Inc., and TM MarketWare. ✓**COMPUSERVE**→*go* oavendor

Xerox Office Solutions Forum If you need technical assistance on low-volume Xerox products (i.e., machines that print fewer than 49 pages per minute), turn to the message boards of this forum. Post a message outlining your problem and a Xerox representative will get back to you. And if you're looking for printer drivers for your machine, be sure to visit the Printer Drivers software library. ✓**COMPUSERVE**→*go* xrxoffice

Software support

Business Software A huge message topic with discussions on programs ranging from Excel to Microsoft Access to Manage Your Money (MYM) to MSWorks. The board is at its best when it recommends software. ✓**PRODIGY**→*jump* computersupportbb→Choose a Topic→Business Software

Financial Software Discussion topics for people who are having problems running the financial software that helps them balance their checkbooks. These boards are heavily focused on MECA's software products, particularly MYM. Peachtree, the Mutual Fund Tracker, Quicken, Wealthbuilder, and Tax Cut are also covered. ✓**PRODIGY** ...→*jump* computerbb→Choose a Topic→Financial Software ...→*jump* softwaresupportbb→Choose a Topic→Financial Software

Intuit+ Forum Serves as the largest presence for Quicken on the Net, with support and information on all Intuit products. The libraries are filled with free updates, shareware, archives of message topics, and tech support FAQs, with hundreds of files spread across libraries for Quicken/Mac, Small Business, and Online Services. Most shareware centers around a few main functions: tax planning, incorporating downloaded quotes into Quicken, and converting Quicken files to and from other personal-finance software like Managing Your Money, Dollars & Sense, and Money. Intuit posts new product announcements, feature lists, and demos in the General Information section of

> "What do I do if I damage my data? How do I tell Managing Your Money that I've paid off the mortgage?"

the library. The message boards, divided by platform and program function, are also rich with information. ✓**COMPUSERVE**→*go* intuit

Intuit Online If you need help with an Intuit product, finding it has never been so easy. There's a section where common questions for products such as Quicken or QuickPay are answered, as well as a software download area where members can retrieve tips, troubleshooting guides, instructions, and utilities for the Intuit products of their choice. The Intuit Financial BB is the hub of the area, with a huge message board devoted to member discussions and questions about the products. ✓**PRODIGY**→*jump* intuit

Intuit Personal Tax Preparation Bulletin Board (bbs) Formerly run by ChipSoft (the publisher of TurboTax and MacInTax before the company was bought by Intuit), this BBS offers tech support for tax preparation programs. There is also a library of downloads on subjects like electronic filing and business taxes and a number of conferences for message-based discussions about tax and tax preparation issues. ☎→ *dial* 602-295-3261

MECA Forum What do I do if I damage my data? How do I tell MYM (Managing Your Money) that I've paid off the mortgage? What's internal error #12? Thousands of people use MECA's Taxcut and MYM software packages—and many of them show up on this technical support forum set up by Block Financial Software with questions. ✓**COMPUSERVE**→*go* meca

Microsoft Business Solutions Here's where you'll find a datasheet with the latest informa-

134 Net Tech

PC Power Business & Finance

tion on FoxPro for the Macintosh, a Q&A about Windows 95, and a release on Visual Basic 3.0 for Windows. This library-only forum has news and product fact-sheets with information on Microsoft's OLE Strategy, Windows NT, Windows, development tools, databases, MS Office, and MS BackOffice. ✓**COMPUSERVE**→*go* bizsoln

Microsoft Office Setup Exchange tips and advice on the applications in both the Macintosh and Windows Microsoft Office packages. The forum has separate message boards and libraries for Microsoft Notes, Excel, Word, and cross-application programs. ✓**COMPUSERVE**→*go* msoforum

Quicken Support Archive of more than 50 shareware, free updaters, and freeware downloads for using Quicken under MS-DOS or Windows. Many of these shareware programs facilitate importing downloaded stock quotes into the older version of Quicken (the new version has the capability built in) or make it possible to print checks using Quicken. ✓**AMERICA ONLINE**→*keyword* pcapplication→Browse the Software Libraries→Quicken Support

Simply A forum with updates, demos, and documentation for the various versions of Simply Money, Simply Tax, Simply Accounting, Simply House, and Simply Kids. It's also a place where program users can post suggestions or complaints about the software. ✓**COMPUSERVE**→*go* simply

Timeslips Forum Technical support, company news, and product development information by this manufacturer of managerial software like TimeSheet Professional and TimeSlips Connection. Leave messages for the support staff on the message boards or dig through the software libraries for program upgrades and installation instructions for all Timeslips products. ✓**COMPUSERVE**→*go* timeslips

Workgroups

Microsoft Windows for Workgroups Forum Support for applications on networked Windows offices. The forum features information and discussions about Novell, file and printer sharing, the MSMail and MSSchedule Plus programs, installing Windows for Workgroups, and dialing remotely into the network. Third-party applications are also covered, and the library has a section filled with add-ons, programs, and demos that work in conjunction with Windows for Workgroups. ✓**COMPUSERVE**→*go* mswfwg

Microsoft Workgroup Applications Forum People share gossip, schedule meetings, announce vacation plans, welcome new employees, and bid farewell to old ones via the office electronic mail system. It's become as important to corporate America as the coffee machine. As a result, MS Mail for the PC is the most active topic and packed library section in this forum. Spell-checking, mail configurations, critical errors, password problems, and Internet access are all recurring topics on the message boards, while FAQs on Windows clients, MailCheck demos, and programs to convert cc: Mail messages to MS Mail messages are available for download in the library. The forum also provides technical support for other shared-office applications such as MS Schedule, MS Eforms, and MS Mail Gateways. ✓**COMPUSERVE**→*go* mswga

WFW-L: Microsoft Windows for Workgroups (ml) Questions, answers, and comments from hundreds of users of Microsoft Windows for Workgroups. Help out a fellow user or sound off on whatever is driving you up the wall this week. ✓**INTERNET**→*email* listserv%umdd.bitnet@listserv.net ✍ *Type in message body:* subscribe wfw-l <your full name>

Business software

Amiga Business Software The road to success (or at least greater productivity) may be paved with your Amiga. The Aminet Archives include a large collection of business software. Address databases, invoicing and stock management programs, calendar progams, and home accounting programs are all available. Recipe and movie databases are here as well. ✓**INTERNET** ...→*www* http://src.doc.ic.ac.uk/public/aminet/info/www/dirs/biz.html ...→*www* ftp://wuarchive.wustl.edu/pub/aminet/biz/

Business and Finance Applications Two huge library sections filled with shareware programs that include billing management programs, travel expense converters, business plan applications, loan calculators, employee schedulers, debt analyzers, resumé programs, home budget trackers, and general finance programs. ✓**COMPUSERVE**→*go* winshare→Libraries→General Biz/Finance *and* Personal Finance

Calendars & PIMs You'll never forget a birthday or miss an important business luncheon again after you comb through this archive of personal information managers for Windows machines. Pick and choose from dozens of calendars, address and phone number compilers, client trackers,

Net Tech 135

Business & Finance PC Power

appointment schedulers, and desktop organizers. Then turn your computer into the best secretary you ever had. ✓ **AMERICA ONLINE**→*keyword* winforum→Browse the Software Libraries→Applications→Calendars & PIMs

comp.os.ms-windows.apps.financial (ng) This lightly populated newsgroup is dedicated to problems concerning financial and tax software running under Microsoft Windows. The bulk of the discussion concerns Quicken, with scattered references to Peachtree and Excel. ✓ **USENET**

IBM Applications Forum Various business applications, personal accounting programs, personal information managers, database management systems, and word processors each have their own library section in this massive forum for PC applications. Turn to the message boards to ask for recommendations on, for instance, technical analysis software, a job program, or a mother's PIM (Mom for Windows). ✓ **COMPUSERVE**→*go* ibmapp

Info-Mac Productivity Applications Applications that sound alarms when you're due for an appointment, help you develop a business proposal, calculate your profits (or losses), give you the area code for any street in America, and track your portfolio are just a taste of what's available to the Mac owner looking for finance programs at these sites. Since financial applications are interspersed with other applications, you may want to download the abstracts file to help you identify the programs of interest. ✓ **INTERNET** ...→*www* ftp://ftp.pht.com/mirrors/info-mac/app ...→*www* ftp://ftp.sunet.se/pub/mac/info-mac/app ...→*www* ftp://ftp.funet.fi/pub/mac/info-mac/app

Mac Applications Forum Like its PC counterpart, there are Macintosh libraries for spreadsheets, accounting, databases, general business, and PIM applications. Looking for tax templates, 401k planners, investment managers, auto leasing calculators, or Excel calendars? Drop by. ✓ **COMPUSERVE**→*go* macapp

Mac Shareware Business Keeping track of your business and financial matters on the computer will seem a lot less confusing after you visit this substantive archive of easy-to-use, award-winning business and personal finance shareware for Mac users. Download calendars, envelope creators, personal finance organizers, interest calculators—even a road atlas for people who conduct their business on the road. ✓ **AMERICA ONLINE**→*keyword* mac500→ Business

PBS Business Forum Manage your finances! Write your resume! File your taxes! Organize your workday! An impressive range of applications for both PCs and Macs, from payroll to inventory to address book software to resumé design applications. In the forum's Professional Library, you will find programs for specific careers: home daycare providers, motel and inn owners, firefighters, and bicycle dealers, to name but a few. ✓ **COMPUSERVE**→*go* pbsbusiness

PC Applications The software libraries at this sight are jam-packed with business and financial applications for PCs. In the Productivity Library, there are sections for address and phone applications and desktop and time programs (there's even a Mayan calendar). The Databases library has sections filled with templates and add-ons for major PC database languages including Clipper, dBASE, and Paradox, as well as an entire section devoted to Windows PIMS and Databases. The Finance Library seems endless, with sections devoted to personal finance, investment, Quicken, and Windows. Still browsing for new programs? Head for the Spreadsheets and Word Processing Libraries with templates and utilities. The forum's active message boards make this site even richer, providing a constant flow of questions, answers, and feedback on the applications. ✓ **AMERICA ONLINE** →*keyword* pcapplications→Software Libraries

PC Productivity Software Everyone feels like a sloth now and then, and the nice thing about computers is that there are programs out there that will increase your productivity and make you feel better about yourself. Feeling disorganized? Does your Filofax look like it was invaded by graffiti artists? Check out the Address and Phone library for a large selection of appointment books, business card minders, and time management applications that will help to eliminate the paper trail of business detritus that's taking over your office and home. There's also a printing support archive with dozens of label-makers, envelope-creators, and bar-code-generators that will make your business documents look more professional. ✓ **AMERICA ONLINE**→*keyword* pcapplications→Browse the Software Libraries→Productivity

Personal Finance Software Forum Offers a generous selection of financial software, with hundreds of programs relating to accounting, career and job hunting, financial planning, home management, investment, loan calculation

PC Power Business & Finance

and amortization, organization, portfolio management, real estate, and taxes. AOL provides download assistance and reviews of especially popular programs. A software support section covers more than 50 companies, whose wares range from market analyzers to personal organizers. Each company provides a corporate history and product list, and many have message boards for customers and technical FAQs. ✓**AMERICA ONLINE**→*keyword* pfsofware

PIM/PhoneBk/Dialers How many variations of an electronic address book are there? The collection of personal information managers, calendar programs, and phone books for Windows users in this library alone is incredible. Stop by for a to-do list, the electronic version of Post-It notes, an achievement planner, or even a Christian calendar program. ✓**COMPUSERVE**→*go* winshare→Libraries→PIM/PhoneBk/Dialers

SimTel Finance Software Programs for personal finance and investment management, including bank account managers, loan calculators, stock market analyzers, and business plan workbooks. The first two addresses are for DOS users; the others, for Windows users. ✓**INTERNET** …→*www* http://www.acs.oakland.edu/oak/SimTel/msdos/finance.html …→*www* ftp://oak.oakland.edu/ SimTel/msdos/finance …→*www* http://www.acs.oakland.edu/oak/SimTel/win3/finance.html …→ *www* ftp://wuarchive. wustl.edu/ systems/ibmpc/simtel/wn3/finance …→*www* ftp://ftp.uoknor.edu/mirrors/SimTel/win3/finance

Windows Biz App Forum Exchange recommendations, tips, or troubleshooting advice on the message boards about commercial and shareware business applications—from word processing add-ons to document managers to accounting programs to time management programs. Then, head to the library to choose programs or add-ons that will increase productivity at the office. ✓**COMPUSERVE**→ *go* winbiz

Windows Forum As impressive a collection of Windows financial programs as you're likely to see, online or off. Head to the Applications Library and get ready. There are sections for Excel, Paradox, MS Access, AmiPro, and—hidden in the More folder—huge collections of software in the PIMS & Databases, Quattro, Quicken, Telecom, and Word for Windows sections. And you still haven't heard about the motherlode of financial software: the Forum's collection of business and financial applications. Need programs to track your mutual-fund investments, calculate your child-support payments, keep track of your shoe inventory, or invoice your clients? They're here. ✓**AMERICA ONLINE**→ *keyword* win→Browse the Software Libraries →Applications

Windows Shareware Business Dozens of shareware programs that will help you organize your business and personal finance matters on your PC, including an invoice-generator, numerous time-management programs and appointment books, a stock-tracker, a library-catalog-creator, an auto repair expense monitor, a bar-code-creator, and a handy international clock that will tell you what time it is in Geneva, Frankfurt, Kyoto, Kansas City, or wherever else in the world you do your business. ✓**AMERICA ONLINE**→*keyword* win500→Windows 500 Shareware Library→Business

Windows Shareware Forum If you're in the market for a Windows business or finance application, or, perhaps, a personal information manager to organize your appointments, check out the relevant library sections in this forum. ✓**COMPUSERVE**→*go* winshare→Libraries

Windows Utilities FTP Site Pilgrims go to Mecca. Baseball fans go to the stadium. And aficionados of business and financial software come to this FTP site. One of the largest directories of software on the Net, this gigantic resource is chock-full of finance and business applications for Windows users. One caveat—it's not very well organized, and you may have to wade through pages and pages of listings to find the programs you need. ✓**INTERNET** …→*www* ftp://wuarchive.wustl.edu/systems/ibmpc/win3/util …→*www* ftp://ftp.cica.indiana.edu/pub/pc/win3/util …→*www* ftp://mrcnext.cso.uiuc.edu/pub/win3/util

> "Everyone feels like a sloth now and then, and the nice thing about computers is that there are programs out there that will increase your productivity and make you feel better about yourself."

Net Tech 137

Spreadsheets PC Power

Spreadsheets

Success in life eludes the disorganized. If you only learn one thing, learn that. And once you've learned it, begin your pursuit of perfect organization by getting yourself a good spreadsheet program. Spreadsheets order data, and they can help you do everything—track your business expenses and profits, set interior deadlines for a large project, communicate your ideas clearly and powerfully to an associate. Start with the general discussion found in **comp. apps. spreadsheets**, and then home in on software-specific resources, from the **Microsoft Excel Directory** to the **Lotus Customer Support Web** to the **Novell Quattro Pro Forum**.

On the Net

Across the board

comp.apps.spreadsheets (ng) Whichever spreadsheet you use to crunch your numbers, chances are it's a topic of discussion in this high-traffic newsgroup devoted to software troubleshooting and gossip. The emphasis here is on Microsoft Excel, but there are plenty of posts about Quattro Pro and Lotus 1-2-3. And if you're looking to convert files from one spreadsheet program into another, then this group will serve you well. File conversion appears to be everyone else's quandary, too. ✓**USENET**

Lotus 1-2-3—from http://www.lotus.com/

Spreadsheets Donna drops by to see if Lotus 1-2-3 for Windows has a random number generator function. Rob, who uses Lotus 1-2-3 as well, wants to know how you set up a footer and border at the bottom of each page that shows a subtotal for each page. Mitchell's spreadsheet program of choice is Excel, and he wants to know how to format a cell to automatically add six zeros to every number he types. And Veronica needs to link two spreadsheets—she's using Microsoft Works. Questions rarely go unanswered in this topic. ✓**PRODIGY**→ *jump* computerbb→Choose a Topic→Spreadsheets

Excel

Excel 5.0 to HTML Table Converter Converts Excel 5.0 spreadsheets for Mac and Windows into HTML tables. An FAQ is available at the site as well. ✓**INTERNET**→*www* http://rs712b.gsfc.nasa.gov/704/dgd/xl2html.html

Excel-L (ml) People with gripes about the latest edition of Microsoft Excel would do well to subscribe to this list, which focuses on the ongoing development of the popular spreadsheet program. This list is also a great resource for technical support from fellow users. ✓**INTERNET**→*email* listserv@peach.ease.lsoft.com ✍ *Type in message body:* subscribe excel-l <your full name>

Macmillan Spreadsheet Library Small library of spreadsheet shareware, freeware, and software demos, including a few desktop tools (mostly calendars) and some documented support for Excel 5.0 for Windows. ✓**INTERNET**→*www* http://www.mcp.com/softlib/software.html

Microsoft Excel Features lots of add-on templates and desktop utilities for use with Microsoft Excel for Windows. You'll find a loan payment scheduler, a calculator for depreciation and amortization, a pension-distribution determiner, and even a body-fat calulator. ✓**AMERICA ONLINE**→*keyword* pcapplications→Browse the Software Libraries→Microsoft→Applications→Microsoft Excel

Microsoft Excel Directory What do you do if the page break is appearing in the wrong area? How do you create an XY chart? In Microsoft's FTP directory for Excel, the answers to these and more than a hundred other questions are archived. In addition, the site holds tools, add-ons, and updates for Excel. ✓**INTERNET**→*www* ftp://ftp.microsoft.com/deskapps/excel/

Microsoft Excel Forum The boss is going to a meeting in Zurich on Wednesday, and you need to get her a spreadsheet with

138 Net Tech

PC Power Spreadsheets

all the pertinent financial data—preferably one that implies that the proposal is a good deal. If you're using Microsoft's Excel for Windows or the Macintosh, this Microsoft-sponsored forum not only offers support and advice for using the application, but also features areas for brainstorming on specific projects—and support during moments of crisis. It's Tuesday night. Your report is a mess. The boss is going to gut you with her favorite letter opener. ✓**COMPUSERVE**→*go* msexcel

Lotus spreadsheets

Lotus Customer Support Web Get technical support directly from the source by using the new Customer Support Web for Lotus 1-2-3 and other LDC products. The site links to a downloadable files area containing various desktop utilities, add-on programs, technical notes that work in tandem with Lotus 1-2-3, and FAQs with answers to dozens of questions. ✓**INTERNET**→*www* http://www.lotus.com/

Lotus Spreadsheet Forum It's Sunday afternoon and you've got a figures report due on the big man's desk at 7 a.m. the next morning—why won't the Data Fill work on Lotus 1-2-3 for Windows? Will you be up all night? Head for this technical support forum for speedy help, either from a Lotus sysop or a fellow 1-2-3 user. This forum earns bonus points for offering quick technical support via the message boards—the Lotus sysops usually answer your question within 24 hours. The libraries contain everything from text file troubleshooting files and software translators to printer driver upgrades, so dive in and hope that you'll get an answer before Monday morning. ✓**COMPUSERVE**→*go* lotus

Quattro Pro

Novell Quattro Pro Forum If you're sick of all the steps required for fitting your spreadsheet on the printed page, welcome to macro heaven. Here you can download a macro that makes adjusting column- and row-width as easy as pointing and clicking. How about that other seemingly simple but somehow impossible maneuver, centering a title over several columns? You'll find a macro for that too. Developers can download numerous toolkits to make programming easier. Disgruntled office workers can post complaints in the user comments box. And if you still can't manage to fit that table on an entire page, try posting a help message in the message folder. ✓**COMPUSERVE**→*go* quattropro

Novell Quattro Pro Forum In this technical support forum for users of the Quattro Pro spreadsheet program, the message boards are administered by Novell sysops, so if you're having printing problems (which seems to be the most common problem here) you can get quick assistance. The libraries have almost no software, though each library does contain an FAQ relating to various aspects of working with Quattro Pro, including graphics, printing, and networking. ✓**COMPUSERVE**→*go* quattro

Quattro Carries files related to the Quattro Pro spreadsheet software. There are utilities, FAQs, and ready-made spreadsheet files. For example, one user uploaded a spreadsheet for computing the batting statistics for a softball team. Another created a stand-alone calendar for organizing appointments. The most popular download was "Time Keeper," a worksheet for tracking connect time charges on AOLs. ✓**AMERICA ONLINE**→*keyword* winforum→Browse the Software Libraries→Applications→Commercial Application Add-ons→Quattro

Quattro Pro A flashy Website that includes a product description, flyer, and a demo of the DOS version. ✓**INTERNET**→*www* http://wp.novell.com/qpro/qprotoc.htm

Shareware

Mac Spreadsheet Library The library is home to lots of add-on templates for use with various Macintosh spreadsheet programs, especially Microsoft Excel. Need to calculate stock and option commissions? Want to play around with a prototype of a flat-rate income tax? If you're having trouble organizing a payroll or creating an expense report on Excel, visit the message board in the same forum for technical support and tips and tricks from fellow Macintosh spreadsheet users. ✓**AMERICA ONLINE** …→*keyword* mbs→Browse the Software Libraries→Spreadsheets …→*keyword* mbs→Message Boards→Spreadsheets

PC Spreadsheet Library These software archives contain hundreds of add-on templates for PC-versions of Excel, Quattro Pro, and Lotus 1-2-3, including a simple payroll spreadsheet and a 1995 NFL Football schedule. Also look for programs that work in tandem with your spreadsheet program, like address books and desktop calculators. The message boards contain technical support and user Q&A's for the Big Three spreadsheet programs. ✓**AMERICA ONLINE** …→*keyword* pcapplications→Browse the Software Libraries→Spreadsheets …→*keyword* pc-applications→Message Boards→Spreadsheets

Net Tech 139

Databases PC Power

Databases

We live in an age overwhelmed by data—inventories, statistics, texts. We can't keep track of everything we have and everything we know. We shouldn't even try. But computers can. Need a comprehensive list of the reggae cassettes you own? Just enter the necessary information, and you'll never again have trouble locating Peter Tosh's "Stepping Razor." Whether you're logging recipes or building a family tree, the Net has dozens of database resources to help you organize your information, from the general (**comp.databases**) to the specific (**Borland dBASE 5.0 for DOS**), from the practical (**Claris Support Forum**) to the speculative (**comp.databases.theory**). In fact, if you decide to visit all the data management sites online, you'll probably need a database just to keep track of them.

Oracle Website—http://www.oracle.com/index.html

On the Net

Across the board

comp.client-server (ng) "Any experience with DataEdit?" "Qualix product opinions?" "FORTE anyone?" For the most part, this newsgroup is used as a product review board. Tell the group what kind of database you're developing and the products you're considering using, and sit back. Feedback is on its way. Not that it's only potential consumers who frequent the group. System managers trying to work out the kinks in their office's client-server architecture ("our nastiest PC troubleshooting problems come from finding the wrong version of a DLL") and those with more general and theoretical questions ("What's the difference between peer-to-peer and client-server architecture?") are also here. ✓**USENET** *FAQ:* ✓**INTERNET**→*www* http://www.cis.ohio-state.edu/hypertext/faq/usenet/client-server-faq/faq.html

comp.databases (ng) Do you want to keep track of the programs and movies you have videotaped? Ask members of the newsgroup which database products are best for the job. And speaking of jobs, database consultants and those in need of consulting turn to this newsgroup to find each other. You can also ask questions about specific databases ("Can I define my database structure, relations, reports, forms, and queries in MS-Access and implement my code in its Visual Basic language?"). ✓**USENET**

comp.databases.theory (ng) If you're interested in universal relational models or Codd's theories on relational databases, this is your kind of discussion. Unfortunately, newsgroup activity is quite low. ✓**USENET**

comp.databases.xbase.misc (ng) Are you running dBASE IV 1.1 on a Pentium and getting corrupted indexes? Regulars in this group will tell you that you need to upgrade to version 2.0. Has your boss asked you to transfer data from Rbase to MS-Access? Someone here will walk you through the process. Participants debate the pros and cons of several different dBASE programs, exchange database development advice, and ask specific programming questions. ✓**USENET**

comp.sys.mac.databases (ng) Robert's asking about selecting

PC Power Databases

records in 4D. Stephen's interested in the best way to mail-merge with MS Word and FileMaker. And David's asking about Macintosh databases that (easily) interface with WebStar/MacHTTP. All Macintosh databases are potential topics of discussion here, although FileMaker, FoxPro, and 4th Dimension are the most frequently discussed. Questions occasionally get quite technical, but in general the group has a very practical edge to it—e.g., "Does FileMaker Pro 2.0 have any trouble reading 2.1 files?" A FileMaker Pro FAQ is being developed by the newsgroup readers and upon completion will be posted to the newsgroup. ✓USENET

Database (ml) Discussion forum about databases. Compare products, share design techniques, and ask questions. ✓INTERNET→email listserv@vm1.mcgill.ca ✍ *Type in message body:* subscribe database <your full name>

Database Conference Listings Announcements about database conferences throughout the world are posted to this international message board. Representative countries include Japan, Australia, the Netherlands, Singapore, and India. Announcements are filed under the month the conference is to take place. ✓INTERNET→www http://bunny.cs.uiuc.edu/conferences/

Databases Prodigy has a single database topic where users of Oracle, FileMaker Pro, Paradox, Microsoft Access, and other popular programs gather to share tips, seek instruction, and get design ideas. So whether you're shopping for a database ("4th Dimension or FileMaker Pro?") or programming one ("I am writing Access Basic code and would like to open a record set using SQL and a 'where' condition which uses a field based upon a response from an input box. I would like the result of the input box to be used in the SQL 'where' criteria to open a record set based upon this response"), stop by for advice. ✓PRODIGY→*jump* computerbb→Choose a Topic→Databases

Information Systems Meta-List A Website with links to information system resources (a.k.a. database resources) on the Internet. The collection of links is extensive, ranging from a list of relevant software companies (e.g., Claris) to dozens of links for the programmer (e.g., an FAQ about Visual Basic for Windows). ✓INTERNET→*www* http://www.cait.wustl.edu/cait/infosys.html

Mac Database SIG Information and discussion about the most popular Macintosh database applications, including 4th Dimension ("One of the nicest features of Helix is that you can import whole files from the finder and store them in a field in the database. Is there any way you can do this in 4D?"), FileMaker, Helix, and FoxPro/FoxBase. There are, however, a myriad of less popular programs represented in the forum's "Other Databases" folder. Head to the

> "Are you running dBASE IV 1.1 on a Pentium? Regulars in comp.databases.xbase.misc will tell you that you need to upgrade."

software libraries for technotes on 4D, a FileMaker contacts database, Helix utilities, and other add-ons, templates, and tip sheets. The forum moderators host a couple of live conferences per month, usually on Thursday nights at 9:00 p.m. EST. ✓AMERICA ONLINE→*keyword* database

PC Databases Using a database on a PC? The PC Applications Forum has an entire area of its message board devoted to database discussion ("How do you retrieve a dbf file deleted in error with Approach 3.0?"). And in the forum's library you can download shareware databases for tracking the weather, tracing your family's genealogy, or monitoring your employees' attendance. For Paradox, Clipper, dBASE, and Microsoft Access users, the libraries also carry FAQs, updates, and tools. ✓AMERICA ONLINE …→*keyword* pcapplications→Software Libraries →Databases …→*keyword* pcapplications→Message Boards→Databases

XBase Applications and Programming A collection of links to XBase resources online. Want to discuss FoxPro? Select the link to the FoxPro newsgroup. Before you do, you might want to check out a technical library of FoxPro documents, or the list of Microsoft books on FoxPro—both are linked to this site. Borland's dBase sites and big Clipper site are also a click away. The richness of this page, though, lies in the links to third-party providers and the XBase projects they're working on. ✓INTERNET→*www* http://www.sbtcorp.com/xbase/

News & magazines

Data Based Advisor Forum Sponsored by *Data Based Advisor*

Net Tech 141

Databases PC Power

magazine, the forum is a great place to discuss the major database programs or industry developments in database management systems. Sections of the message board and library have been reserved for the big names in the database world: MS-Access, Clipper, FoxPro, dBASE, Visual Objects, and Lotus Notes. Questions about Borland's dBASE? Post them on the message board and one of the magazine editors might respond. Looking for shareware applications using MS-Access? Check out the library. And if, for instance, you're opening your own restaurant and need a customized inventory program, you can discuss designing one yourself in this forum. Sound scary? If you spend enough time here, you'll find plenty of support, and the library has a great selection of development tools and documentation to aid in your project. If you're not so adventurous, you'll meet countless programmers here willing to do the job. In addition, the "Advisor Pub Files" section of the library carries the source code from each edition of *Data Based Advisor* magazine. ✓ **COMPUSERVE**→*go* dbadvisor

Database Archive An archive of highly technical articles on databases (e.g., "Axiomatization of Dynamic Schema Evolution in Objectbases"). You can search the archive by several criteria, including topic, journal, author, and publication date. ✓ **INTERNET**→*www* http://www.lpac.ac.uk/SEL-HPC/Articles/DBArchive.html

DBMS Forum So you've read the latest issue of *DBMS* magazine and want to try some of the code printed in it? Head to the libraries where all the programming code from each issue is archived. And then stop by the message boards for database discussions. "Anyone know C-tree?" asks a programmer. Whether you're looking for someone who uses C-tree or just for an explanation of C-Tree, you'll find answers here (C-Tree provides an ISAM facility for C programs). ✓ **COMPUSERVE**→*go* dbms

DBMS Magazine *DBMS* is a monthly print magazine devoted to database and client/server solutions. The Website features a selection of full-text articles, the full text of the annual buyer's guide, an industry calendar of events, late-breaking news, the current issue's table of contents, and links to other database resources on the Internet. ✓ **INTERNET**→*www* http://www.dbmsmag.com/

askSam

askSam Systems Home Page A commercial Website from askSam systems that showcases its database programs. The site carries information about the company's product lines and staff, and you can post questions on the site's message board. ✓ **INTERNET**→*www Clipper*http://199.44.46.2/askSam.htm

Clipper

alt.comp.databases.xbase.clipper/comp.lang.clipper (ng) This newsgroup is populated by programmers who use the database programming language Clipper, developed by Computer Associates. Posts range from a job announcement for a Clipper programmer in New York to a first-time Clipper user asking where the data is stored—"There are .dbf, .dbt, and .ntx files. Where is it?" ✓ **USENET** *FAQ:* ✓ **INTERNET**→*www* http://www.xs4all.nl/~junior/HTML/clipper/clipinfo.html

CA-Clipper Forum Source codes, data dictionaries, and speed-search patches are just a few of the downloadable tools available here to make using your Clipper database a little easier. And if you're a Clipper programmer, you'll find new job listings every week in the "Jobs, Vertical Market" folder. Technical support staff from Computer Associates also field user questions. ✓ **COMPUSERVE**→*go* clipper

Clipper Discussion List (ml) Chat about Clipper and other database management systems for the PC. ✓ **INTERNET**→*email* listserv%brufpb.bitnet@listserv.net ✍ *Type in message body:* subscribe clipper <your full name>

Junior's Clippin' Pages The site changes to reflect Clipper resources on the Net. Junior has collected links to archives of the database magazine *Clippings*, a Clipper-related software site, news reports about the Clipper database, the two-part Clipper FAQ, newsgroups, and other Net resources. ✓ **INTERNET**→*www* http://www.xs4all.nl/~junior/

DB2

IBM DB2 Family Basically a sales presentation for IBM's DB2 relational database products. There's ordering information and a "Contact IBM" selection for direct communication with the company. You'll also find links here for DB2-related topics, such as OS/2, HP/UX, and VMS. If you have trouble locating the information you're looking for, there is a "Help" selection to assist you. But unless you're shopping for software, there's not much for you here. ✓ **INTERNET**→*www* http://www.torolab.ibm.com/db2/

PC Power Databases

dBASE

Borland dBASE 5.0 for DOS According to the competitve analysis put up by Borland at this site, 7.1 million people use dBASE 5.0 for DOS (compared to the 800,000 who use FoxPro). A fact sheet highlights the program's major features and specifications, and Borland has put online an extensive "Evaluator's Guide" that serves as a high-tech brochure for the program. ✓**INTERNET**→*www* http://www.borland.com/Product/DB/dBASE/DOSdBASE.html

Borland dBASE 5.0 for Windows An informative advertisement for the Windows version of dBASE. Not only can you download a demo of the program, but you can also read fact sheets, view comparisons with other programs, and click through an impressive evaluator's guide illustrating much of the database's functionality. Bibliographies, conference schedules, and request forms for more information on training and consultants are also available. ✓**INTERNET**→*www* http://www.borland.com/Product/DB/dBASE/WindBASE.html

Borland dBASE Forum Need an algorithm that finds records that fall within a range of ages and an unrelated range of dates of services? Nervous about index files that continue to get corrupted when using dBASE4 1.5? Anxious to develop applications that use AS/400 APPC data but unsure of how to get access? Turn to the message boards with your questions, or to the library for a rich collection of resources that range from instructional documents to handy add-ons that, for instance, convert dBase files into WordPerfect files. There are also hundreds of mini-dBASE programs. Borland representatives run the forum. ✓**COMPUSERVE**→*go* dbasedos

Borland dBASE/Windows Forum Tap into this excellent resource for MS Windows users of Borland's dBASE product and download a home inventory and mail management system designed with dBASE 5.0, a utility to enhance the reports features of the program, or programs to convert CA-Clipper 5.x databases into dBASE for Windows databases. The library is a good place to browse if you know what type of database you want to create; chances are good that someone else has already created a similar database and uploaded templates, documentation, utilities to aid in the creation, or the database itself. And, if you still have questions, Borland representatives and experienced users field a steady stream of queries on the message boards—e.g., "Is there a quick Alert routine like the WAIT WINDOW command in FoxPro?" ✓**COMPUSERVE**→*go* dbasewin

SimTel dBASE Directory A collection of utilities for dBASE on DOS systems. ✓**INTERNET**→*www* http://www.acs.oakland.edu/oak/SimTel/msdos/dbase.html

FileMaker Pro

Claris Support Forum FileMaker isn't the only product featured in these Claris forums, but it's certainly covered extensively. Mac and Windows users can read product descriptions of the database, post technical support questions ,which the Claris support staff will answer on the message boards, search the TechInfo Database for articles and fact sheets about specific FM functions, and plunder the huge FileMaker software li-

---

CYBERNOTES

"Topher's Top Ten (Logical) Tuning Tips

1. Know your data (and how it's accessed)
2. Build an i/o profile
3. Select indexes based on cost
4. Know what the database is doing
5. Re-write problem queries
6. Encapsulate, encapsulate, encapsulate
7. Denormalize and only do things once
8. Understand your optimizer
9. Do a contention diagram
10. Build small transactions

Topher's Top Ten (Physical) Tuning Tips

1. Start with a logically tuned system
2. Watch your data cache
3. Use your contention diagram
4. Believe in controllers
5. Use segments (only where you need to)
6. Multiple databases
7. Consider the effect of mirrors
8. Understand and evaluate the effectiveness of new technology
9. Monitor your system
10. Do ad-hoc queries elsewhere"

—from **Sybase Things**

Net Tech 143

Databases PC Power

braries for sample databases, templates, add-ons, and updates.
✓ **AMERICA ONLINE**→*keyword* claris
✓ **EWORLD**→*go* claris

Claris TechInfo Database
Search a database of thousands of articles and fact sheets on Claris products, including FileMaker Pro. To search, choose FileMaker and the appropriate version in the product name field, the operating system that you are using, and a keyword (e.g., "export") in the document text field. Then, choose "display results" and download the relevant articles. ✓**COMPUSERVE**→*go* clatech

FileMaker for the Macintosh
When someone asks a question here ("Why am I losing records in the middle of the night?"), Claris technical support staff and other diehard FileMaker users weigh in with suggestions. Ghosts? Monsters? Scripts that could be failing because a user is editing a record that a script doesn't have proper access to? But the message boards are not the biggest draw; the library in this forum is packed with templates, add-ons, icons, tips, and FileMaker-created databases (home inventory databases, fantasy football managers, music collection databases, inventory systems, etc.). ✓**COMPUSERVE**→*go* macclaris →Libraries *and* Messages→FileMaker

FileMaker for Windows
"Help, lots of crashes!" "How does one merge the unique data from one version of a database into another?" "I am having a problem getting FMP to run on a Zeos 486/66 PC. Please advise." Far more active than users of FileMaker's Macintosh support board, Windows users here employ the message board to send a steady stream of questions and complaints to Claris's technical-support staff. Visit the library to download FileMaker updates, icons, and user-created databases.
✓**COMPUSERVE**→ *go* winclaris→Libraries *and* Messages →FileMaker

FMPRO-L (ml) If you don't know how to define a field or create a new layout, this list may be too advanced, but if you're concerned about password security, using QuickKeys, importing calculations, creating external scripts, or developing backup procedures, the list has a database-savvy group of regulars willing to share ideas.
✓ **INTERNET**→ *email* listserv@dartcms1.dartmouth.edu ✍ *Type in message body:* subscribe fmpro-l <your full name>

4th Dimension

4th Dimension Run by ACI U.S., the company that developed 4th Dimension, this technical support forum includes a beginner's area for basic troubleshooting (inputting information into a database from a text file) and more advanced areas for those who use 4D servers, compilers, or modules for database programming and development. Look in the libraries for bug fixes, update announcements, and help documentation.
✓**COMPUSERVE**→*go* acius

FoxPro

Colin's FoxPro Page An informative Website dedicated to the FoxPro relational database system. Check the "FoxPro News" feature to read about upcoming conferences and product releases. The "Paper Resources" selection gives overviews of print publications covering FoxPro, along with their prices and subscription information. There are links to FoxPro newsgroups, FTP sites, and Websites if you want more; one of the links takes you to the largest collection of FoxPro software in the world. ✓**INTERNET**→ *www* http://www.state.sd.us/people/colink/fox_page.htm

comp.databases.xbase.fox (ng) Programmers, administrators, and users can get answers to technical questions about the FoxPro database platform in this active newsgroup. One user wanted to speed up the search feature in his program and received several helpful responses. Another poster wanted to know how to change the mouse-pointer into an hourglass icon, and learned of a downloadable utility specifically designed to do the job. ✓**USENET**

#FOXPRO Consultants and users of FoxPro discuss the database in live IRC meetings. The Website offers a schedule of upcoming FoxPro chat, logs of past sessions, and links to IRC software. ✓**INTERNET**→*irc* #foxpro *Info:* ✓**INTERNET**→ *www* http://www.state.sd.us/people/colink/fox_irc.htm

FoxPro FAQ A multi-part FAQ dedicated to describing the FoxPro program, its support resources (both online and offline), and common problems. ✓**INTERNET**→ *www* http://www.cis.ohio-state.edu:80/text/faq/usenet/databases/foxpro/top.html

FoxPro Wish List (ml) Send suggestions, complaints, and compliments to the developers of FoxPro. ✓**INTERNET**→*email* foxwish@microsoft.com ✍ *Write a request*

FoxPro Yellow Pages Let your fingers do the walking through this resource for the FoxPro relational database community. You'll find updated listings of users' conferences, FoxPro-related software,

PC Power Databases

books, and bulletin boards. The listings include addresses, telephone numbers, and contact names. ✓**INTERNET**→*www* http://www.transformation.com/foxpro/

FoxPro-L (ml) Mailing list for users of FoxPro. ✓**INTERNET**→*email* listserv%ukanvm.bitnet@vm42.cso.uiuc.edu ✎ *Type in message body:* subscribe foxpro-l <your full name>

The Fox Software Forum Are you in the market for a database program and think that FoxPro might be suitable? The customer service personnel here will answer any questions you post about the product. Did you buy the application but need advice on programming or configuring the database? The technical support staff will still talk to you. Then, rummage through the library for sample invoices, editors, calendar add-ons, FoxPro updates, patches, and instructions. ✓**COMPUSERVE**→*go* foxforum

The FoxPro I/O Address Reading a manual can be a drag. Why not take the slow route and go through a "Command a Day"? You can also check out the "Function for a Day" and "FoxPro Tip of the Day" pages if you're feeling wimpy (hey, fear of manuals is a serious disease). Next to the manual, the FAQ probably offers the most thorough treatment of the program, and it's linked here. Back issues of the FoxPro newletter are also available at the site, and you can search archives of the FoxPro mailing list from the site as well. If you know the ins and outs of FoxPro, you can annotate your database with report viewers and pop-up calendars in this large archive. ✓**INTERNET**→*www* http://www.hop.man.ac.uk/staff/mpitcher/foxpro.html

Junior's Clippin' Pages—http://www.xs4all.nl/~junior/

Microsoft FoxPro & FoxBase Archive An archive of FoxPro articles and fact sheets, applications, tools, utilities, updates, and drivers. ✓**INTERNET**→*www* ftp://ftp.microsoft.com/developr/fox/

Microsoft FoxPro Products A promotional Website for sales of FoxPro database software. The information here is categorized by system (Macintosh, DOS, Windows, Unix). ✓**INTERNET**→*www* http://www.microsoft.com/pages/sales/foxpro.htm

Montreal FoxPro User's Group Announcements and blurbs about a Canadian FoxPro programming society. ✓**INTERNET**→*www* http://www.transformation.com/mfug/mfug2.html

MS Fox Users Forum A forum for database consultants, users, and third-party developers to gather and discuss FoxPro. The library is filled with ads for FoxPro consultants and demos of third-party products. ✓**COMPUSERVE**→*go* foxuser

Rocky Mountain FoxPro Mailing List (ml) "I have a database with about 3,000 records. I would like to search on last name. Instead of a simple search, I would like to have a browse window open and dynamically move the pointer while I type the name. Does anyone have any sample code that I could look at?" It's for answers to questions like this that members flock to this list. ✓**INTERNET**→*email* FoxPro-L-Request@dsw.com ✎ *Type in subject line:* subscribe

Informix

comp.databases.informix (ng) Need to bounce around ideas on label arrays or cross-platform data migration? Perhaps you're trying to get 12,000 records from an MS-Access table into an Informix table and your PC keeps hanging up (that's with 16 MB of RAM, thank you very much). Beginners and more experienced users flock to this newsgroup to ask questions and share tips (how about breaking up those 12,000 records into four different parts?) about the Informix database. Upgrades are often announced here as well. ✓**USENET FAQ:** ✓**INTERNET**→*www* http://www.garpac.com/informix.html

Net Tech 145

Databases PC Power

Informix Link This is a well-organized promotional Website for the Informix data management corporation. The "What's New" link provides press releases, international jobs listings, and third-party company profiles. Select "Products" to view technical specifications of offerings from Informix's and third-party developers. The "Services" category is for customer support. Corporate information, conference listings, and a listing of international user groups are also provided. ✓**INTERNET** ...→*www* http://www.informix.com/ ...→*www* ftp://ftp.informix.com/

Ingres

comp.databases.ingres (ng) Mike wants to know if anybody knows of "an easy way to identify the differences between two tables." Steve has an idea: "Based on the tables having their columns in the same order (this maybe could be done by inserting into temp tables if it is not the case with the original tables). The simplest way I know is to 1) Copydb '-c' the data to ascii text files, 2) sort (unix sort) the files, and 3) diff the resulting files. This will tell you the differences in your data." It's usually as easy as this to get help with the Ingres relational database on this newsgroup. There are also a few help-wanted ads for Ingres developers. The FAQ offers an excellent overview of Ingres. ✓**USENET FAQ**: ✓**INTERNET**→*www* ftp://ftp.adc.com/pub/ingres/Ingres-FAQ

Ingres Archive Home Page Are you interested in the Ingres relational database management system, in either its commercial or public-domain format? Most of the information, however, is related to commercial Ingres. The Ingres FAQ is here, as well as Ingres conference information. There's also a "Beginner Tutorial," a third-party products page, and links to competing relational database developers such as Oracle, Sybase, and Informix. ✓**INTERNET**→*www* http://www.adc.com/ingres/ing-top.html

Teach Yourself Ingres A hypertext guide to the basics of programming an Ingres database. ✓**INTERNET**→*www* http://wonder.lancs.ac.uk/TeachYourself.html

University Ingres Public-domain (that means free) versions of Ingres for Unix and Linux. ✓**INTERNET**→*www* ftp://s2k-ftp.cs.berkeley.edu/pub/ingres/

Lotus Notes

An Introduction to Lotus Notes Very, very introductory in nature, this site defines groupware and gives a brief overview of the features and capabilities of Lotus Notes. ✓**INTERNET**→*www* http://www-iwi.unisg.ch/delta/notes/index.html

comp.groupware.lotus-notes.misc (ng) This high-traffic newsgroup lets users and administrators of Lotus Notes—a program that helps networked groups of people access, track, share, and organize information—swap tips and respond to each others' questions. ✓**USENET**

LNotes-L (ml) More than 2,000 people subscribe to this discussion list about Lotus Notes. Members offer each other technical support, exchange bug reports and development ideas, and report on program updates. ✓**INTERNET**→*email* lnotes-l-request@atg1.wustl.edu ✉ *Type in message body:* subscribe lnotes-l <your full name>

Lotus Notes Archive While its Website offers a splashy advertisement and several brochures for Lotus Notes, the FTP archive delivers the goods. The site carries a huge directory of Lotus Notes application tools and shareware programs as well as an extensive collection of Lotus technical notes (see the index for brief descriptions of the problems and procedures covered in each). ✓**INTERNET**→*www* ftp://192.216.79.100/pub/comm/notes/

Lotus Notes FAQ It's still a little sketchy, but this FAQ offers programming tips, Lotus Notes administration advice, explanations of how the program works with various platforms and gateways, recommendations for books and magazines, and Net addresses for sites of interest to Lotus Notes users. ✓**INTERNET**→*www* http://www.turnpike.net/metro/kyee/NotesFAQ.html

Lotus Notes Web Page At this official site for Lotus Notes on the Web, Netters can download demos of Lotus Notes programs, browse snazzy brochures, and read press releases and white papers on the product. ✓**INTERNET**→*www* http://www.lotus.com/notesdoc/

Notes FAQs The Lotus corporation has compiled answers to dozens of frequently asked questions about Lotus Notes and made them available here. ✓**INTERNET**→*www* http://www.lotus.com/csswww/faqnotes.htm

Notes-L (ml) Another discussion list for the users and developers of Lotus Notes groupware. ✓**INTERNET**→*email* listserv@vm1.okstate.edu ✉ *Type in message body:* subscribe notes-l <your full name>

PC Power Databases

MS-Access

Access-L (ml) Discussion list for the MS-Access database. ✓**INTERNET**→*email* listserv@peach.ease.lsoft.com ✎ *Type in message body:* subscribe access-l <your full name>

comp.databases.ms-access (ng) In a desperate post, Tim writes: "I give up. I can't persuade MS-Access to read my Paradox table. It keeps insisting that it can't get my user name or Net file." Another user, Gene, is having the same problem and the two of them look to the group for answers. Thorsten from Germany is also panicked. Apparently, after he sorted tables with 4,000 records, the data was scrambled. Any recommendations? Not every question is a matter of life and death. Jim's just curious if it's "possible to use a combo box to specify parameters in the 'Enter Parameter Value Dialogue Box'?" ✓**USENET**

Microsoft Access Database Programming Hints Tom from Texas created this page of helpful hints for MS-Access programmers. To wit: "If you use modules in your programs, and change a field attribute from REQUIRED to NOT REQUIRED, the next time the modules are called, the data in the field that was changed can become scrambled beyond repair. (I speak from experience)." ✓**INTERNET**→*www* http://www.texas.net/users/breid/access.html

Microsoft-Access Archive An archive of MS-Access articles and fact sheets, applications, tools, utilities, updates, and drivers. The MS-Access FAQ put out by Microsoft is one of the more popular downloads. ✓**INTERNET**→*www* ftp://ftp.microsoft.com/deskapps/access/ *FAQ:* ✓**INTERNET**→*www* ftp://ftp.microsoft.com/kbhelp/accfaq.exe

> "Stop by this forum and Bill Gates's staff members (or another user who's already worked through the same problem) will field your questions."

MS-Access A library with a lot of information for users just beginning to learn how to manipulate MS-Access. There are also some MS-Access utilities available for download, such as Win Color 1.0. The libraries carry files ranging from a ham radio logbook to a church parish management program. ✓**AMERICA ONLINE** ...→*keyword* winforum→Browse the Software Libraries→Applications→Commercial Application Add-Ons→MS Access ...→*keyword* pcapplications→Browse the Software Libraries→Microsoft Applications→Microsoft Access

MS-Access If your MS-Access query is misbehaving, the entire database is corrupted, or you're trying to troubleshoot the networking of your database, stop by this forum and Bill Gates's staff members (or another user who's already worked through the same problem) will field your questions. But moments of computing crisis aside, MS-Access users also turn to this forum to exchange tips and tricks, discuss security and presentation issues, and swap modules and forms. ✓**COMPUSERVE**→*go* msaccess

MSACCESS Section A site with close to 50 files related to MS-Access, including code to change printer settings, database tools, and sample databases. There's also an MS-Access tutorial in Win Word format (instruct.zip). ✓**INTERNET**→*www* http://coyote.csusm.edu/cwis/winworld/msaccess.html

Tips for Access Database Users Tips for converts, newbies, and old hacks. Switching from dBASE or Foxbase to Access? Never programmed a day in your life and still want to be able to use MS-Access? Attempting to optimize Access and not afraid to get your hands dirty? The site is filled with tips. ✓**INTERNET**→*www* http://odyssey.apana.org.au/~abrowne/homepage.html

Object-oriented

comp.databases.object (ng) "Does anybody know whether there is any OODBMS (object-oriented database management system) which is able to handle about 3,000 queries per second?" This heady newsgroup is dedicated to the discussion of object oriented programming, and while there are a fair number of task-oriented questions like this one, discussions can also get quite theoretical. Most of the activity in the group, however, involves product comparisons. "Has anyone used Versant or ObjectStore?" You can count on it. ✓**USENET**

comp.soft-sys.powerbuilder (ng) So what can you do with a powerful, object-oriented development tool? That's exactly what members of this newsgroup are constantly trying to figure out. "Does PB4.0 connect and work okay with Oracle 7.1?" "I've been trying to create a table within a powerscript using the EXECUTE

Databases PC Power

IMMEDIATE statement and I found that I can't do this, at least, if my DBMS is Sybase. Any suggestions?" The slightly outdated FAQ might answer some of your questions. ✓USENET *FAQ:* ✓INTERNET→*www* ftp://ftp.powersoft.com/

PowerBuilder Home Page If you're using a version of PowerBuilder to develop databases, this site will link you to an enormous number of online resources, including the PowerBuilder Interactive page, where you can participate in live Web chat about the product; the PowerBuilder newsgroup; the PowerSoft FTP archives; the PowerBuilder Consultant's Page (with a long list of PowerBuilder developers and contact information); and the PowerBuilder Wisdom page for, you guessed it, tips and culled wisdom about the program. ✓INTERNET→*www* http://web.syr.edu/~eastephe/pb.html

The Powersoft Home Page Website for the company that produces the PowerBuilder client/server application development tools. The site features product information and lists of conferences, trade shows, training programs, and PowerBuilder user groups. In the customer-service section there are links to FTP archives with product samples and patches, as well as a link to the PowerBuilder newsgroup. ✓INTERNET …→*www* http://www.powersoft.com/ …→*www* ftp://ftp.powersoft.com/

Oracle

comp.databases.oracle (ng) Hundreds of messages a week flood this newsgroup for discussions about the Oracle database, many of them asking or responding to questions like "So what's wrong with my query?" And who's responding? Not only experienced users, but the Oracle Corporation itself. ✓USENET

comp.databases.rdb (ng) Dedicated to technical discussions of Oracle's relational database software. There's nothing here for home database users. The postings are geared towards database administrators, managers, and engineers who work specifically with Rdb. ✓USENET

DECRDB List (ml) For discussions about the Oracle Rdb. ✓INTERNET→*email* listserv@ccvm.sunysb.edu ✎ *Type in message body:* subscribe decrdb-l <your full name>

JCC's Oracle Rdb Home Page A small collection of resources for Oracle Rdb users, including a short FAQ list (Do you know the difference between RDB and Rdb? The former is an acronym for relational databases; the latter is specific to the Oracle product), Oracle press releases, and information about upcoming Oracle conferences and seminars. The most impressive feature of the site is the engine that will search Oracle-related mailing lists and newsgroups—just plug in your query. ✓INTERNET→*www* http://www.jcc.com/oracle_rdb.html

Oracle The official Website for the Oracle Corporation not only offers online fact sheets and user guides about its products, but it also offers full-featured demos of its databases that you can download directly off the Web. ✓INTERNET→*www* http://www.oracle.com/index.html

Oracle FAQ This document does what every good FAQ does—answers commonly asked questions ("How can I deal with 2000 byte VARCHARs?" and the like). It also lists and describes books written about Oracle database products, and links to other Web and FTP resources covering Oracle. There's a "Free Software" section with import, export, and loader utilities and a fun glossary. For example, a "Data Base Administrator" (DBA) was identified in the glossary as "an aloof bastard totally to blame for poor response times." On the downside, several sections of the FAQ are tagged with notices explaining that they haven't yet been written. ✓INTERNET→*www* http://www.bf.rmit.edu.au/~dtb/orafaq/contents.html

Oracle Forum Robert's heard that the South African Telephone Co. has an Oracle7 database that's 600+ Gb. Anyone with a database that's approaching a Terabyte? Robert's merely curious, but Larry has a serious question: "Can a stored procedure return results set to the client application? In other words, can a SELECT be used in a stored procedure if it returns results, rather than sticking the results in a variable or table?" A day later Larry has an answer: "The dbms packages will do that from SQL*PLUS. In addition, you can return values to PRO*C programs with this. Last month's ORACLE DEVELOPER from Pinnacle publishing had some good examples." In addition to asking questions, you can hook up with an Oracle user group, get recommendations for an Oracle book, or read product announcements from Oracle and third-party developers. The libraries are filled with tutorials, documentation, tools, patches, demos, and forms. ✓COMPUSERVE→*go* orauser

Oracle List (ml) For discussions about Oracle database programs. ✓INTERNET→*email* listserv@ccvm.sunysb.edu ✎ *Type in message body:*

PC Power Databases

subscribe oracle-l <your full name>

Oracle Magazine A promotional home page for *Oracle* magazine, Oracle Interactive, and Oracle Press. You can even download program code from the last issue of *Oracle* magazine. ✓**INTERNET**→*www* http://www.oracle.com/info/magazine/magazine.html

Paradox

Borland Online—Paradox 4.5 for Windows Promotional Website containing fact sheets and electronic brochures for Paradox 4.5 for Windows. The site also includes listings for Paradox books, a link to the Paradox newsgroup, and the option to download a demo of the program. ✓**INTERNET**→*www* http://www.borland.com/Product/DB/Pdox/DOSPdox.html

Borland Paradox 4.5 for DOS Did you know that the latest version of Paradox 4.5 for DOS lets you work with 60 tables (up from 24 in the last version)? Besides a fact sheet and press release, the site also carries a bibliography of Paradox books, an area in which to request assistance locating a consultant or Paradox trainer, and a link to the newsgroup. ✓**INTERNET**→*www* http://www.borland.com/Product/DB/Pdox/DOSPdox.html

Borland Paradox/DOS Forum Charles is looking for templates for organizing recording collections; Roger, who created a database in version 4.5 with four linked tables, is trying to figure out why he keeps getting thrown back to DOS with an error message; and Jeff is downloading an FAQ on beginning programming with PAL. From Paradox programming with DOS to networking to SQL Link, the forum offers areas for discussing Paradox databases and a file library with hundreds of templates, instructions, and utilities. Borland representatives run the forum. ✓**COMPUSERVE**→*go* pdoxdos

Borland Paradox/Windows Forum Can you change fonts in different fields in a report? What files are required to repair damaged tables? And how do you copy data from one TCursor record to another? Windows users share code-writing suggestions, help each other conceptualize databases, and follow product developments. The library has runtime/development tools, an FAQ for SQL Link, Paradox application launchers, forms for building labels, zip-code databases, and hundreds of other helpful files. Borland representatives run the forum. ✓**COMPUSERVE**→*go* pdoxwin

comp.databases.paradox (ng) The Paradox database software manufactured by Borland is the featured topic of discussion in this well-populated newsgroup. To a lesser extent, other Borland products, such as Delphi, are also covered. Participants range from window shoppers ("Is Paradox right for me?") to users with questions ("What is the trick to getting a form to push one of its own buttons?"). Paradox books, training courses, and utilities are also big topics of conversation here. ✓**USENET** *FAQ:* ✓**INTERNET** ...→*www* http://www.cis.ohio-state.edu/hypertext/faq/usenet/paradox-faq/faq.html ...→*www* http://www.lib.ox.ac.uk/internet/news/faq/archive/paradox-faq.html

Paradox A library with files for Paradox database development. The collection includes instructional texts, utility programs, and sample applications to help beginners solve programming problems. ✓**AMERICA ONLINE**→*keyword* winforum→Browse the Software Libraries→Applications→Commercial Application Add-Ons→Paradox

Paradox for Windows (ml) "In Paradox for DOS there was a feature that allowed you to save your reports to text files. I can't seem to duplicate this in Paradox for Windows 5.0." Questions like this are par for the course on this list dedicated to the Windows version of Paradox. ✓**INTERNET**→*email* listserv@tubvm.cs.tu.berlin.de ✍ *Type in message body:* subscribe pdoxwin <your full name>

Paradox Mailing List (ml) Problems with indexing? Need to convert Paradox tables to Lotus 1-2-3? Bring your Paradox questions here. ✓**INTERNET**→*email* listserv%brufpb.bitnet@listserv.net ✍ *Type in message body:* subscribe paradox <your full name>

Pick

comp.databases.pick (ng) A newsgroup dedicated to Pick-like, postrelational database systems. Although the subject matter is somewhat obscure, the discussion here is lively, covering design techniques, administration, and even theory. New Pick products are announced. ✓**USENET** *FAQ:* ✓**INTERNET**→*www* http://www.deltanet.com/users/john/cdpfaq.html

Pick Systems Home Page A company-sponsored Website that does more than just advertise a product. While Pick Systems has product descriptions and company information on the site, it also carries a trade show schedule, back issues of *PickWorld* (the magazine dedicated to Pick databases), and the *Dealer Newsletter*. In addition,

Databases PC Power

the site has three excellent reference manuals in hypertext format for users of Advanced Pick. ✓**INTERNET** ...→*www* http://www.picksys.com/ ...→*www* ftp://ftp.picksys.com/

Shareware

Catalog of Free Database Systems A catalog of database systems available free online. Each database is briefly described, its status noted (e.g., under development), and its Net address listed. The second address allows you to search the list with your criteria. ✓**INTERNET** ...→*www* http://www.cis.ohio-state.edu:80/text/faq/usenet/databases/free-databases/faq.html ...→*www* http://cuiwww.unige.ch/~scg/FreeDB/

Database/Cataloging If your baseball cards and stats need organizing or your CD collection has grown so much that it needs to be recorded and sorted, this Windows library is likely to have databases for just those purposes. There are also video organizers, coin catalogers, book databases, and even sermon databases—if you're in that line of work. ✓**COMPUSERVE**→*go* winshare→Libraries→Database/Catalog

SimTel PC Databases Perhaps you think that the database you need to create is unique. Most likely it's not. Just check out this directory of customized databases of aerobic exercises, airline flights, cocktails, bibliographies, bowling league schedules, baseball stats, coin-collecting info, Net sites, home-repair costs, wedding details, job-interview questions and contacts, sewing cross-stitches, and political-campaign details. And that's just a sampling. All the databases are for DOS systems. ✓**INTERNET** ...→*www* http://www.acs.oakland.edu/oak/SimTel/msdos/database.html ...→*www* ftp://oak.oakland.edu/SimTel/msdos/database ...→*www* ftp://ftp.wuarchive.wustl.edu/systems/ibmpc/simtel/msdos/database ...→*www* ftp://ftp.uoknor.edu/mirrors/SimTel/msdos/database ...→*www* ftp://ftp.uni-paderborn.de/SimTel/msdos/database

Windows Databases Among the jumble of database programs you'll find in this library are a bartenders' database, a doctor's records database, and a personal diary program. As always, there is a healthy selection of address-book and phone-list programs for those who are looking to get organized. ✓**AMERICA ONLINE**→*keyword* winforum→Software Libraries→Applications→Databases

SQL

Microsoft SQL Server A huge advertisement for the Microsoft SQL Server, a relational, client-server database management system. ✓**INTERNET**→*www* http://www.microsoft.com/pages/bussys/sql/sql10000.htm

SQL FAQ Structured Query Language is a standard database query language, and this no-nonsense document answers several questions about it (e.g., "How do you tell what other database objects exist?") and gives sample code as part of the explanation. ✓**INTERNET**→*www* http://epoch.cs.berkeley.edu:8000/sequoia/dba/montage/FAQ/SQL_TOC.html

Sybase

comp.databases.sybase (ng) Csaba is new to Sybase and would like to know if there is a way to read all records in a table from the end of the table. Bill is using "rand( )" to get a unique primary key for inserting new rows, but he's finding that Sybase will "only generate 32k worth or random numbers even though it is a float with 15 digits of precision." And Art is looking for "a good tool to analyze MS SQL Server queries." Follow this group and you'll be Sybase-savvy in no time. ✓**USENET FAQ:** ✓**INTERNET** ...→*www* http://arch-http.hq.eso.org/bfrasmus/db/faq/index.html ...→*www* http://sybase.pnl.gov:2080/Sybase/Sybase_Frequently_ask_questions

The ESO/ST-ECF Sybase Archive Home to several impressive Sybase resources, including the Sybase FAQ, an archive of public-domain Sybase tools, and an article on query optimization. ✓**INTERNET**→*www* http://arch-http.hq.eso.org/bfrasmus/db/

Intro to Sybase A guide to the Sybase software architecture. It begins with a reading list and moves through client-server architecture, Transact SQL, stored procedures, triggers, security and ownership, remote procedure calls, Open-servers, and other topics. The author is a software consultant specializing in Sybase. ✓**INTERNET**→*www* http://www.dgsys.com/~dcasug/sybintro/intro.html

Sybase Inc. Home Page Product overviews and a list of Sybase product distributors, along with Net sites exploring how to make SQL Server data available from WWW pages. ✓**INTERNET**→*www* http://www.sybase.com/

Sybase Things Sybase SQL code, technical newsletters about Sybase, the FAQ, a summary of Sybase C++, and hints for many Sybase processes. ✓**INTERNET**→*www* http://sybase.pnl.gov:2080/Sybase/.Sybase.html

PC Power Educational Resources

Educational resources

No matter what technophobes will tell you—and they'll tell you plenty, beginning with

the claim that microprocessors demand a passive audience that allies personal computing more with television than with literature—computers are supposed to make us smarter. With their help, we can recall more information than ever before, do calculations more quickly, research with greater precision. Turn your brain into a superbrain by surveying the educational resources on the Net, from the **Macintosh Education Forum** to **Windows Educational Software**. Preschoolers struggling to defuse the threat of the alphabet will be weak with relief when they have their passport stamped for entry into **The Magic World of ABC's**. And if you are a child in need of a friend from a foreign land ("Hello, Pyotr…Hello, Elena…Hello, Kentaro"), be sure to grease up your international diplomacy skills and visit **Apple Global Education**.

On the Net

Across the board

Apple Global Education An attempt by Apple Computer, Inc. to connect thousands of students, teachers, parents, and educators around the world. This site is a veritable global village—you can find a pen pal in countries like Finland, Austria, or Saudi Arabia by posting your name and email address on the AGE Bulletin Board, or you can visit the AGE Project Library and download multimedia projects created by students around the world, including "Being a Nordic Child" and "The D-Day Project," about the 50th anniversary of the Normandy Invasion. The software library is full of digital images that you can use for your own multimedia projects, in addition to a World of Age toolkit that contains a HyperCard 2 stack used to produce projects for the library. ✓ **EWORLD**→*go age*

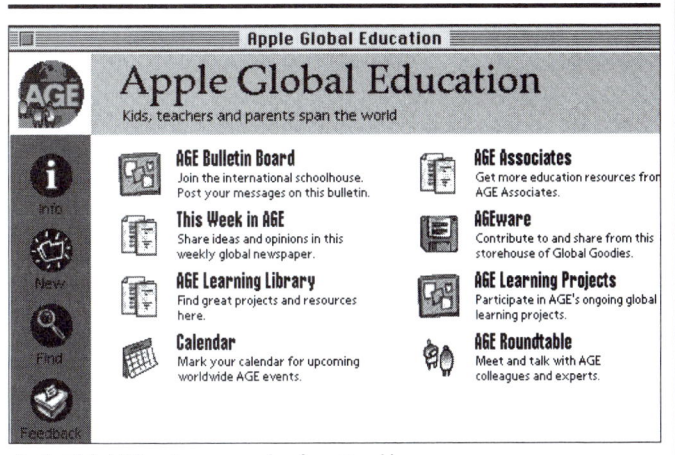

Apple Global Education—screenshot from Eworld

Apple II Education Software Educational software for the Apple II series of computers is divided in this forum into categories, such as math, reading, and social studies. There are some useful tools for teachers in this library, such as computerized grade books and quiz-makers. If you are a Hyperstudio user, there are many stacks available for download. Click on the "Special Interest Groups" icon for live conferences and discussion boards. ✓ **AMERICA ONLINE**→*keyword* a2→Apple II Software Libraries→Education Software

The Children's Software Company Home Page An extensive catalog of educational software for children of all ages (preschool through high school) and all major platforms (Mac and PC). ✓ **INTERNET**→*www* http://www.childsoft.com/childsoft

Cool Software for Kids Prove to Mom and Dad that the computer is an educational tool that benefits us all with this page, which includes software reviews for kids by kids. The Website is primarily a catalog of software. ✓ **INTERNET**→*www* http://www.

Educational Resources PC Power

internet.net/Kidz/index.html

Education & Children's Multimedia Learn how to count. Memorize the ABC's. Study the elements for chemistry class. Practice elementary Spanish. And use the multimedia aids in this library to help you learn quickly. ✓**AMERICA ONLINE**→*keyword* mmwlibrary→Education & Children's

Education/Reference Your two-year-old can learn his ABC's, your 12-year-old can learn the geography of Hungary, and you can explore astrology with the shareware and freeware programs in this library. The collection includes language programs, math tutors, religious quizzes, and even music lessons. ✓**COMPUSERVE**→*go* winshare→Library→Education/Reference

Macintosh Education Forum A forum dedicated to using the Macintosh computer as an educational tool. There are interesting resources here for parents, teachers, administrators, and students. The "Weekly Update" feature fills you in on the latest activities in the forum, including new uploads, live conferences, and updated information files. "Education on the Internet" is a searchable database containing articles, announcements, and information on educational happenings available on the Internet. The "Electronic Books" library includes literary classics like Shakespeare's plays and sonnets, along with science fiction and foreign-language texts. Several Special Interest Groups (SIGs) add to the resources here, including "Apple Classrooms of Tomorrow," and "Pictures of the World," which offers digital photographs of sites around the world that can be downloaded for classroom use. ✓**AMERICA ONLINE**→*keyword* med

SimTel DOS Education Software A large directory of educational shareware for DOS users, including an animated addition and subtraction tutorial, a companion program to *The Diary of Anne Frank*, a coin recognition game, a spelling program, an interactive chemistry game, a beginning Spanish program, a typing training program, and a Russian-English dictionary. ✓**INTERNET** …→*www* http://www.acs.oakland.edu/oak/SimTel/msdos/educatin.html …→*www* ftp://oak.oakland.edu/SimTel/msdos/educatin …→*www* ftp://wuarchive.wustl.edu/systems/ibmpc/simtel/msdos/educatin …→*www* ftp://ftp.uoknor.edu/mirrors/SimTel/msdos/educatin …→*www* ftp://ftp.uni-paderborn.de/SimTel/msdos/educatin

SimTel Windows Education Software A collection of Windows programs for educational purposes, including a student organizer and a multimedia flashcard system. Most programs are for a fairly young crowd. ✓**INTERNET** …→*www* http://www.acs.oakland.edu/oak/SimTel/win3/educate.html …→*www* ftp://oak.oakland.edu/SimTel/win3/educate …→*www* ftp://wuarchive.wustl.edu/systems/ibmpc/simtel/win3/educate …→*www* ftp://ftp.uoknor.edu/mirrors/SimTel/win3/educate …→*www* ftp://ftp.uni-paderborn.de/SimTel/win3/educate

Windows Education Shareware A very small collection of educational software, but practically every one has been downloaded by thousands of users. The two most popular programs are an interactive USA Map and an alphabet tutor, the latter of which uses positive reinforcement to teach the ABC's, and even plays the ABC song at the end of each lesson. ✓**AMERICA ONLINE**→*keyword* mac500→Windows 500 Shareware Libraries→Education

Windows Educational Software Programs for both students and teachers, including a math tutor, a planetarium simulator, and grading organizers, all designed to run under Microsoft Windows. The collection of programs is diverse, with titles ranging from piano instruction to Bible study. Unfortunately, the software has not been organized by category, so you'll have to browse through the listings or use the search engine. ✓**AMERICA ONLINE**→*keyword* winforum→Browse the Software Libraries→Applications→Educational

ABC's

The Magic World of ABC's What letter comes before A? No letter, silly, but there are 25 letters that come after A, and all of them get lavish treatment on this charming educational CD-ROM. For children 4–7, or any kids who show an early tendency for getting hooked on phonics. ✓**INTERNET**→*www* http://www.widdl.com/MediaPro/magic.html

Foreign languages

SimTel Foreign Language Software If you've mastered URLs, Netspeak, and computer commands, you can learn a little French. This site carries dozens of language tutorials, including some on Chinese calligraphy, Japanese grammar, basic German, Italian, and Turkish, for the DOS user. ✓**INTERNET** …→*www* http://www.acs.oakland.edu/oak/SimTel/msdos/langtutr.html …→*www* ftp://oak.oakland.edu/SimTel/msdos/langtutr …→*www* ftp://wuarchive.wustl.edu/systems/ibmpc/simtel/msdos/langtutr

PC Power Educational Resources

…→*www* ftp:// ftp.uoknor.edu /mirrors/SimTel/msdos/langtutr
…→*www* ftp://ftp.uni-paderborn. de /SimTel/msdos/langtutr

Multimedia

Blackberry Creek Become a "Creekie" by joining this creative community for kids and their parents. Learn how to put on a multimedia HyperCard-driven play in the Little Theater, or put together computer-created gifts in the Party & Gift Shoppe. There are message boards for both parents and kids—the Kids' Hangout has postings on such pressing matters as "He doesn't know I exist" and "I hate my cousin." The Parents' Club deals in more concrete issues like "Are Goosebumps books OK for kids?" and "Spanking—good or bad?" Keep your eyes open for new and exciting contests, like the Pet Story Contest: "We've got a winner! It's Justin Alberti from Durham, NC. His 'pet' story was about his dragon, David. (Imaginary pets are fine!) David is a million-year-old, vegetarian dragon. You can even see a picture of David drawn by Justin." And be sure to check out The Exchange, a software repository where you can look at multimedia projects created by Creekies, including Sancho P.'s grade-school report on steroids, as well as download shareware and demos like Kid Pix that will help you create your own multimedia projects. ✓**EWORLD**→*go* blackberry

Carlos' Coloring Book Home Download a Mac coloring program for your own budding van Gogh. Simply choose an image and a color, point and click, and voilá—you're an artist. ✓**INTERNET**→*www* http://robot0.ge. uiuc.edu/~carlosp/color/

ImaginEngine A forum for knowledge-hungry kids and their parents that features an archive of Greak Books for Kids (kids and parents are invited to send in synopses of their favorite kids' books) and a neat interactive game called Intelligent Agent X, which sends kids out into Cyberspace in search of facts that will help them solve a mystery. Meet other "agents" around the world while learning valuable research skills in a game-like environment. ImaginEngine discussions unravel on the bulletin boards and in the live forum. In addition, kids looking for information for school projects (Virginia history? U.F.O.'s?) receive feedback from their cyberpeers by simply posting a question. Multimedia projects created by kids are archived in the software library. ✓**EWORLD**→*go* imagine

MediaPro, Inc. Publishers of the Magic World of ABC's, MediaPro offers a full selection of children's educational games, as well as a link to a catalog of educational toys. All games are published in both English and Mandarin Chinese (perfect for the bilingual tot). ✓**INTERNET**→*www* http://www. widdl.com/MediaPro/

Mountain Lake Software Get free fonts—math fonts, school fonts, kiddo fonts—as well as more general scholastic software geared toward children ages 8–12. ✓**INTERNET**→*www* http://www. woodwind.com/mtlake/index.html

The Multimedia Exchange If there's one field where multimedia applications can make a huge dent, it's education. This library of stackware is designed for teachers interested in exchanging sound samples, graphics, animations, or other media for educational purposes. And teachers won't have to worry about explaining their on-line expenses: the more time you spend downloading, the more free time you get. ✓**AMERICA ONLINE**→ *keyword* tin→The Multimedia Exchange

PBS Education Forum Learn to type or to program a multimedia presentation, to memorize the names of prehistoric animals or to conjugate Spanish verbs, to communicate in sign language or to understand the anatomy of the skull. The shareware libraries here don't require a library card, just a registration fee if you decide to use what you downloaded. Class dismissed. ✓**COMPUSERVE**→*go* pbseducation

Sachi's Icons Though this page is a very slow load, it offers a charming environment for children to display their cybercreativity in. Kids can visit the page to hang an artwork in the online gallery, contribute to the storybook, and download MyRoom and MyBackyard icons for the Macintosh. ✓**INTERNET**→*www* http://www.interport.net:80/~ sachi/

Wierenga Coloring Programs It no longer matters if your little brother scribbles on the dolphin page in your coloring book. Now coloring books are programs online that you can color over and over. Don't like that purple dinosaur? Change it—there's a 48 color pallette! These DOS shareware programs are good for all ages. Choose from African animals, Christmas scenes, dinosaurs, prehistoric animals, whales and dolphins, warbirds (planes), and Rachel's fashion dolls—virtual paper dolls with cool outfits. ✓**INTERNET**→*www* http://www.xmission. com/~wwwads/sharware.html

Net Tech 153

Family Computing **PC Power**

Family computing

The irony of family computing lies in the tension between the two terms. Family, of course, evokes togetherness, interaction, conversation, a low-tech glow. Computing, on the other hand, suggests a cold precision, a doctrine of efficiency in which the human element is willingly sacrificed. The online world is out to reconcile these two apparent opposites with such sites as **The Family Computing Forum**, an AOL area that emphasizes the computer as an addition to the family, sort of like a pet but less cuddly. And the home-management package **DTE Homewise** will organize your chores ("Tuesday: Remember to buy new computer").

The Brady Bunch—http://nick-at-nite.viacom.com/

On the Net

Across the board

Computer Currents Every computer needs a current, if you're talking electricity. And every computer user needs *Computer Currents*, if you're talking convenience. This monthly magazine helps new computer users understand the basics of hardware selection, configuration, and application. ✓**INTERNET**→*www* http://www.onramp.net/~ccurrent/

Computer Life The most general (and in some ways, the most generous) of Ziff's computer magazines, *Computer Life* is oriented toward home and personal computer use. Consult a list of the best products for Macs and PCs. Follow the step-by-step projects to learn more about a variety of computer issues—Ziff will riff on everything from how to upgrade memory to how to do your taxes. And browse back issues to see what computer developments you might have missed ("John, this is Pentium; Pentium, John. I hope you two can be great friends"). ✓**INTERNET**→*www* http://www.ziff.com/~complife/ ✓**COMPUSERVE**→*go* life

DTE Homewise The very definition of a grassroots software success, this program was created by two Ottawa-area entrepreneurs last spring and has blossomed into a flourishing cottage industry. DTE Homewise turns your computer into a home, compartmentalizing basic organizational tasks into bedroom, bathroom, and kitchen tasks. Family members can leave messages for one another. Children can set up individual calendars. Parents can track allowances and chores as well as video rentals. The software, which costs $49.95, can be ordered and registered online. ✓**INTERNET**→*www* http://infoweb.magi.com/~dtes

The Family Computing Forum Splashy graphics and a homey theme are intended to make novice computer users and children comfortable. And, given the targeted audience, it isn't entirely unsuccessful. (More experienced users may wonder if the operative term here isn't family, but "fluff.") Click the Tip-of-the-Day icon for explanations on how to do simple computer tasks like lock files, name Mac folders, or send email.

154 Net Tech

PC Power Family Computing

The Life's Workshop icon links to a dictionary of computer terms, hints on uploading, a dictionary of online terms, and the Novice Playground, where AOLers can practice posting messages and downloading from software libraries without being charged for online time. The '90s family is as concerned about the computing industry as it is about Senate policy, right? Keep informed with the online version of Industry Insider. And for kids, the Rec Room has libraries of gaming software and often sponsors contests; the forum also features holiday-theme activities for kids (make a Mother's Day card, for instance). And what would a home be like without a family room? In this forum's version of that-place-where-parents-and-children-bond, AOLers are invited to get to know each other—chat live, post messages on the Front Porch board, and upload their pictures to what's known here as the Family Photo Album. For both the best and worst of the forum, visit the Computers & Everyday Life area. An archive of utilities for PC and Mac users and a folder of articles about using America Online for important tasks (choosing a college, keeping a diary, making friends, etc.) will be of interest to many forum visitors, but does AOL really need more places like "The Refrigerator Door" and "The Freezer Door," two more silly libraries where children and adults, respectively, can "tack up" their artwork? ✓**AMERICA ONLINE**→*keyword* fc

Family PC On-line With family-tested hardware and software reviews, feature articles relating to home computing and educational software, and a Community Center chat room that lets families swap computer lore, Family PC On-line is where the Brady family would undoubtedly have parked their modem had there been Net access in the seventies. ✓**AMERICA ONLINE**→*keyword* familypc

Home PC Reviews, trends, tips, tricks, and valuable advice on getting the most out of your home computer. The emphasis here is on education, entertainment, and personal productivity; Home PC's online database of kid-tested software is a great resource for parents looking to separate the Mortal Kombats from the Mysts. ✓**AMERICA ONLINE**→*keyword* homepc

Home and Hobby Helpers How can you be organized? Let us count the ways. Here you'll find DOS and Windows programs to organize food purchases and print out grocery lists (The Grocer), track your babysitters (Babysitter), log your jogs (The Runner's Log), and take inventory on your house (Organize Your Home). ✓**AMERICA ONLINE**→*keyword* pcapplications →Browse the Software Libraries→ Homelife and Leisure→Home Management

MS Home Products Forum A forum with support for Microsoft's entertainment and home-finance products. Having problems installing your Microsoft Golf program? Encountering difficulty getting sound from MS Cinemania? Need to import MYM data to your MS Money program? The forum offers updates, add-ons, news, and support for several programs, including Microsoft's games, simulators, Bookshelf, Cinemania, MS Money, MS Kids, and Intuit. ✓**COMPUSERVE**→*go* mshome

Public Brand Software Home Forum A vacuum cleaner? Of course. Responsible babysitters? A must. A PC? What family doesn't need one? More households are relying on software to help them organize their finances, make decisions about dinner or college, and entertain the children. Cost-conscious families buy shareware. The libraries in this forum are packed with wedding planners, patterns for children's crafts, programs to memorize Bible verses, Girl Scout–troop databases, nutrition programs, meal planners, chore to-do lists, and personal-finance programs. Download them. Try them. And if you like them, register them. ✓**COMPUSERVE**→*go* pbshome

The Family Computing Forum—screenshot from America Online

Net Tech 155

Games & Entertainment **PC Power**

Games & entertainment

Sure, computers can make our lives easier. But if we're honest with ourselves, we'll admit that all we really want to do is play games. Doom. Myst. Yahtzee. Checkers. Chess. Tetris. Apache Raid. Rise of the Robots. And the thousands of games yet to be invented. So you can pretend that you care about personal organizers, home finance management, and raytrace utilities. Pretend all you want. But when you want to restore some integrity to your miserably compromised life, you know what to do. **Zarf's List of Interactive Games on the Web. Windows Fun Forum. 3-D Mac Games Homepage.** Don't you feel better already?

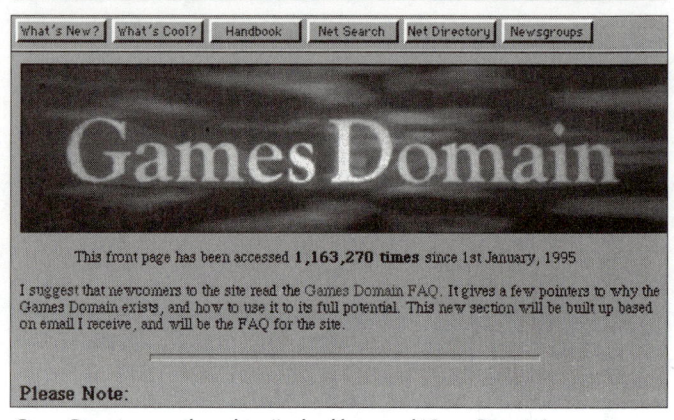

Games Domain screenshot—http://wcl-rs.bham.ac.uk/GamesDomain/

On the Net

Across the board

America Online Games Are you wondering if the SimCity Enhanced CD-ROM is worth purchasing? You might think twice after checking the Interplay message boards. "SIM CITY on CD—A disappointment." "SIM CITY on CD—No sound, load freezes." "SIM CITY on CD stinks—I found it a step back from SC2000." Besides the opportunities for consumer venting and research, you'll find downloadable demos of the latest games, from *Marathon* to *Star Trek the Next Generation: A Final Unity*. And if you're a nonviolent gameplayer, you might want to check out the live word and trivia games that AOL is famous for. ✓**AMERICA ONLINE**→*keyword* games

Disney Software While this is definitely the place to come for help with the *Lion King* CD-ROM that doesn't work, Disney really shines in the download area. Disney isn't the king of animation for nothing, and there are separate folders for official Disney images and sound bytes, from *Little Mermaid* icons to *Lion King* .WAV files. They've also decided to extend the opportunity to create to you. In the animation studio folder, you can upload any computer animation projects you've been working on. Expect this content-rich company to continually fill its folders in the future. ✓**AMERICA ONLINE**→*keyword* disneysoftware

DTF.WWW A group of drunken Swedish students decided to put together this gaming list and it's not half bad. The WWW games list is a selection of Web standards like Hangman, Othello, and Tic-Tac-Toe, but less typical fun and games like the interactive story Drool (where you play a dumb yapping poodle walking along Boston's Charles River) are also on the list. In the real-time department, you'll find links to Chess, Othello, Go, Crossword, Backgammon, and Bridge servers. If you'd rather play by mail, check out the Play-By-Mail Games Homepage or go directly to Battle, Core Wars, and Diplomacy sites. ✓**INTERNET**→*www* http://www.hh.se/home/stud/t/92/mn/c/html/spel.html

Games eWorld doesn't have the largest selection of games in the online world, but they're certainly good for a few laughs. The Inside Games forum has an impressive selection of Mac demos, updates, cheaters, and walkthroughs. The Windows and DOS folders are empty (this is Apple's online service, after all). While you're downloading the Marathon update,

PC Power Games & Entertainment

why not take a cheater as well and edit your saved games. Wolfen Cheat 2.01 highlights hidden doors and saves you time. The scenarios folder offers other people's successful sim cities and modifications to your Marathon game: replace fighters with high-resolution Barneys and Power Rangers. Even those resistant to traditional computer-game play might go for the Yoyodyne forum, filled with games of skill. Solve a riddle and win free pizza; if you think of the most humorous caption for the downloadable cartoon of the week, you'll win a year's subscription to *The New Yorker*. While Electric Adventures interactive role-playing games sound enticing, there aren't many people hanging out in The Forest or The Dungeon. ✓ **EWORLD** →*go* arts→Games

Games CompuServe's gaming services are worth exploring (and probably worth the cost). If you're looking for the latest and greatest, go straight to the 'Hot Games Download Area' for demos of Descent, Dark Forces, Marathon, and Doom II: Hell on Earth. Shareware-heads visiting Epic Megagame's online presence will find full versions of bestsellers such as OverKill, Epic Pinball, Jill of the Jungle, and Zone 66. Those looking to distract their entire office with hot network sessions of Doom II should head for the Modem Games Forum. Not only can you download network versions of games for modem-to-modem play, but CompuServe now offers direct play with others through its MTM Gaming lobby, at considerably cheaper rates than direct dialing. To keep up on the latest game releases, head to the game publishers forum, where LucasArts, InterPlay, and Electronic Arts, among others, make announcements. And if it's Chess, the classic text adventures, or fantasy sports leagues that you're looking for, you can play them here as well. Oh, and did we mention flight sims? ✓ **COMPUSERVE** →*go* games

Games Related Home Pages
You could spend a long, long time chasing down every link and playing every game you find through this list. Teenage and middle-age Doomheads will find at least twelve separate sites where they can learn to kill more efficiently. (Alas, only two Bridge-related sites are listed here.) Whether you're looking for tips on winning new Sony Playstation games or searching for downloadable demos at the Cardiff Video Games Links page, the site is packed with gaming opportunities. ✓ **INTERNET**→*www* http://wcl-rs.bham.ac.uk/GamesDomain/homes.cgi

Interactive WWW Games List
A long list of links to Web games, including Connect 4, Web Yahtzee, at least three Tic-Tac-Toe games, and Find-The-Spam (for serious gamers only). You'll also find links to real-time games like Chess and Scrabble. ✓ **INTERNET**→*www* http://einstein.et.tudelft.nl/~mvdlaan/texts/www_games.html

The Games Domain
A massive site where you can download anything from Doom to its 360-degree clone Descent. If you're FTP-phobic, try the 'Direct Download' section, where games are broken down by category and downloading is as simple as point-and-click. And if you've had enough of sleuthing your way off of Jabba's Barge in Dark Forces, check out the links to game FAQs and walkthroughs. If there's a game on the market, you're sure to find hints for winning it here. ✓ **INTERNET**→*www* http://wcl-rs.bham.ac.uk/GamesDomain/

Virtual Vegas You'll find a representative selection of the real Vegas games in Virtual Vegas. Play blackjack, poker, slot machine, and craps. All you have to do is open a Virtual Vegas online account. The first 500 chips are free. The rest is up to you. If you'd rather socialize, check out the Textual Reality Lounge, a MUSH (a computer-constructed world where participants type-talk to each other) where you don't get free drinks but might have the chance to construct your own ASCII-art Liberace costumes. Cruise down Route 66, where Kickside and Road Attractions include an earthquake in California (QuickTime Movie) and information about opening an international sports wagering account (1-800-I-CAN-BET). ✓ **INTERNET**→*www* http://www.virtualvegas.com/

Zarf's List of Interactive Games on the Web
Believe it or not, you can play ping-pong on the Web. Just make sure you allow for the time delay when moving your paddle around. Links to video and board game favorites—from Tetris to BlackJack to Othello—are also on the list. If you're not all that concerned about winning or losing, check out the Interactive Toys page, where you can build your own virtual robot (you have three criteria to choose from: robot head, torso, and legs) or create your own mad-lib love letter. ✓ **INTERNET**→*www* http://www.cs.cmu.edu/afs/andrew/org/kgb/www/zarf/games.html

News

Computer Gaming World An electronic version of the monthly game guide. Leave a message for

Games & Entertainment PC Power

the editors, browse for gaming tips and secrets, or scan CGW's White Page for online gaming opponents or game-oriented BBSs in your area. ✓**INTERNET**→*www* http://www.ziff.com/~gaming/

MEGAzine & MegaZone Your average 40-year-old can't get through the first hour of Myst. But talk to your average 8-year-old with a multimedia computer and you'll start seeing the state of gameplay 20 years from now. That 8-year-old who knows the ins and outs of Myst isn't a genius, he's a member of the new techno-savvy generation. Finally, a folder for the future generation of gamers in Megazine for kids. If you're a kid and you're stuck somewhere, post a question here: "I was playing HHH and I got to the lake downstairs by the mummy room and I didn't know what to put in the boat. If you know how I can get further than this please respond. Jordan, Age 8 1/2." In other respects, kids today are the same as ever, as in the GigaBrain's Giggles folder, receptacle of hints and jokes: "I know two is company and three is a crowd, but what are four and five? Nine, silly (Jesse, age 7)." ✓**AMERICA ONLINE**→*keyword* magazine→MEGAZone for Kids

Acorn

comp.sys.acorn.games (ng) The Acorn is dead, long live the Acorn! Even though the old 8-bit machine can't compete with today's multimedia powerhouses, you can still play Space Invaders and Brick Out—and discuss them with other loyal Acorn users. ✓**USENET**

Amiga

Amiga Arts Forum Art is a widely defined term in Amiga territory. Here it might mean anything from 3-D fractal images, popular in rave computer-art installations (mostly created on Amigas), to downloadable images of "the very beautiful Ms. Christy" and other nudes. If you're customizing your Amiga's sound emissions, this is the perfect place for a panoply of samples from "It's time for bed" to belching sounds and sinister laughs. And whether games are a new art form or just a break from the digital easel, you'll find plenty of distracting demos here. Rings of Zon is popular, as is the Monopoly freeware game. The Game Hints/Scenario [sic] library has patches, utilities, cheats, and hints. ✓**COMPUSERVE**→*go* amigaarts

Amiga GameZone If you thought that America was filled with magazines devoted to Amiga games, think again. If you've had waking dreams of a newsstand wall papered with covers adorned with Rise of the Robots and Lemmings 3, rein in those runaway fantasies. The truth is that there's only one regularly scheduled publication devoted to Amiga games. Luckily, though, Amiga GameZone is on the Net, which means that it's available to us all. Well, sort of—the site includes subscription information, a games sales list, and brief summaries of recent issues. ✓**INTERNET**→*www* http://uxa.cso.uiuc.edu/~razmataz/agz.html

Aminet Gaming Archive A seemingly endless collection of Amiga shareware, freeware, and demo versions of games. ✓**INTERNET** ...→*www* ftp://wuarchive.wustl.edu/systems/amiga/aminet/game ...→*www* ftp://ftp.doc.ic.ac.uk/aminet/game ...→*www* ftp://ftp.luth.se/pub/aminet/game

Commodore Art/Games Forum If you're a DJ and you want to create a jungle track, this is an ideal place to start. Download bleeps and other *Star Trek*–style sound effects to punctuate the beat. If you're creating the computer-art installation for a jungle rave, you'll find plenty of fractal art images here to play with. And if you're an artist in search of a break, try downloading a game of Pinball or Terminator II. ✓**COMPUSERVE**→*go* cbmart

comp.sys.amiga.games (ng) Discussion of games for the Commodore Amiga, with some nose-thumbing in the direction of far more successful and expensive home computer systems that are not as well suited to graphical action. Also see the related newsgroup for CD-ROM users, comp.sys.amiga.cd32. ✓**USENET**

Apple

Apple II (8-bit) Games Archives Archives of public-domain freeware and shareware games for the old Apple II. Find out what all those elementary and secondary schools ended up using their computers for. Highlights include AppleTrek, an adaptation of the arcade blockbuster Defender, a Wheel of Fortune clone, and a slew of EAMON text adventures. ✓**INTERNET** ...→*www* ftp://apple2.archive.umich.edu/archive/apple2/8bit/games ...→*www* ftp://wuarchive.wustl.edu/systems/apple2/games ...→*www* ftp://grind.isca.uiowa.edu/pub/apple2/games

Apple II Games A huge forum for Apple II gamers: two message boards, software libraries, and its own conference hall. Among the more popular games that are discussed (or that have related files in

PC Power Games & Entertainment

the libraries): Sub Battle Simulator, Zany Golf, Mean 18, Alien Mind, and Task Force. ✓**AMERICA ONLINE**→*keyword* appleii→Games

Apple II Games/Entertainment Not very busy, but there are several downloadable arcade and combat games in the library. ✓**COMPUSERVE**→*go* appuser→Libraries *or* Messages→Games/Entertainment

Atari

Atari Gaming Archive Most Atari-related information on the Net either originates at this mammoth FTP site or filters back into it. There are always large numbers of freeware or shareware games to download—Scrabble to Larn to Breakout to GNU Chess. Start by downloading the index (0index). ✓**INTERNET** ...→*www* ftp://atari.archive.umich.edu/atari/Games ...→*www* ftp://wuarchive.wustl.edu/atari/umich.edu/Games

Atari Gaming Forum Discussion about Atari computer games is sparse, but the libraries carry hundreds of games for Atari users—from NetHack to Oxyd to a Ms. Pacman clone. The Jaguar folders are among the most lively. ✓**COMPUSERVE**→*go* atarigaming

Macintosh

comp.sys.mac.games (ng) Discuss gaming on the Mac—from winning defensive strategies in Spectre tank battles to manipulating bond issues in Sim City 2000. Very lively. ✓**USENET** *FAQ:* ✓**INTERNET** ...→*www* ftp://ftp.rtfm.mit.edu/pub/usenet-by-group/comp.sys.mac.games/comp.sys.mac.games_FAQ ...→*www* http://www.cis.ohio-state.edu/hypertext/faq/usenet/macintosh/games-faq/faq.html

Mac Shareware Fun & Games Shareware heaven for Mac gamers. You'll find standards like Cannon Fodder and Dungeon of Doom, computer versions of classic board games like Risk and Monopoly, and bundles of fun odds and ends in Blob Manager. ✓**AMERICA ONLINE**→*keyword* mac500→Fun & Games

Macintosh Entertainment Forum CompuServe's overall area for discussing games played on the Macintosh. The forum includes message boards with such areas as PML Football Field (to debate what makes one game better than another), Fun on Power Macs (to discuss this nascent gaming world), Adventure Games, Flight Simulation, and Arcade/Action Games (to explore, fly, and kill, respectively). Downloadable game files and tons of sound files from TV shows and movies are in the libraries. ✓**COMPUSERVE**→*go* macfun

Macintosh Games Discuss Mac games on the message boards, participate in live conferences on Fri-

Computer Gaming World cover—from http://www.ziff.com/~gaming/

Games & Entertainment PC Power

day nights at 10 p.m. EST, and download a number of games from the extensive Software Libraries (or the News Files library). Among the more popular games: Quagmire, a robot-to-the-rescue arcade game with six inter-level movies; Zero-G Pinball, a gravity-free pinball game; Macman Classic Pro, a PacMan variation; Ultra Tank; Tron (Kerrigan), based on the arcade game/movie; Monopoly; Risk (II and III); Klondike 5.1, the Mac version of the popular solitaire game; and an '80s classic called Mac vs. IBM, in which you, controlling the Mac at the bottom of the screen, try to destroy the IBM at the top. Uploads of popular magazines, little-known publications, and now-defunct 'zines related to gaming on the Mac are also archived here, including back issues of *Inside Mac Games, Home & School Mac, MacGames Digest, Anti-Matter E-Magazine*, and others. ✓**AMERICA ONLINE**→*keyword* mgm

3-D Mac Games Homepage

Page devoted exclusively to Doom-style 3-D games for the Mac. At present, the selection is limited to demo versions and screen shots of Marathon, Mac-Wolf, and Pathways Into Darkness, with more to follow. ✓**INTERNET**→*www* ftp://ftp.halcyon.com/local/brianf/mac.html

PCs

comp.sys.ibm.pc.games.action (ng) Discuss MS-DOS action and arcade games, classified as such by their emphasis on fast-paced hand-eye reflexes. Stay on the lookout for breakaway newsgroups devoted to the most popular games, such as alt.games.doom and alt.games.mk2. ✓**USENET**

comp.sys.ibm.pc.games.adventure (ng) Discuss adventure games, which originally were text-based exploration and riddle games (the game category is named, in part, for the original interactive treasure story, Adventure) but are now often decorated with graphics and combat sequences. Popular games subjected to heavy analysis include Lost Eden, Alone in the Dark 3, and The Legend of Kryandia. This newsgroup usually eclipses the related newsgroups comp.sys.ibm.pc.hardware.cd-rom and alt.cd-rom. Do check out the classic newsgroups rec.games.int-fiction and comp.sys.ibm.pc.games.rpg for some heavy role-playing. ✓**USENET**

comp.sys.ibm.pc.games.announce (ng) Bottom line: Scan as a backup in case you miss something on the other newsgroups, but don't rely on it for first word of new toys. Regular postings include the PC Games FAQ (twice a month) and a patches list for customizing and cheating at popular games (see FTP Sites for Game Editors and Updates). The two-part PC Games Guide to the Gaming World—with info on an abundance of Internet resources—is the real gem here and recommended background reading before posting to the comp.sys.ibm.pc.games newsgroups. ✓**USENET** *FAQ:* ✓**INTERNET** ...→ *www* http://www.cis.ohio-state.edu/hypertext/faq/usenet/PC-games-faq/top.html ...→*www* ftp://rtfm.mit.edu/pub/usenet-by-hierarchy/comp/sys/ibm/pc/games/announce

comp.sys.ibm.pc.games.flight-sim (ng) An unmoderated group to discuss air- and spaceflight simulation games. Heavy-duty X-Wing discourse, not to mention strategizing over other hits like Aces Over Europe, Air Warrior, Falcon 3.0, and the venerable Microsoft's Flight Simulator. ✓**USENET**

comp.sys.ibm.pc.games.misc (ng) Spillover topics that don't fit the specialized newsgroups dedicated to gaming on the PC. Usually not very lively, except as the unofficial location for discussing sports and puzzle games. Until there's a sports subgroup, come here for games like Links 386 Pro and Formula 1 Grand Prix. ✓**USENET**

comp.sys.ibm.pc.games.rpg (ng) Discussion of role-playing games (RPG) that have descended from the board game Dungeons & Dragons and the text-based computer game Adventure. Popular examples include Dark Sun, Shattered Lands; Lands of Lore; and Ultima VII. For related topics see the often more lively newsgroup comp.sys.ibm.pc.games.adventure. ✓**USENET**

comp.sys.ibm.pc.games.strategic (ng) Discussion of mostly war games that are modeled on the old Avalon Hill historical scenarios and other kinds of strategy-oriented simulations. Popular games that are well covered include Civilization, Master of Orion, and the V for Victory episodes. ✓**USENET**

> "In KillBarn, you hunt down Barney, the infamous purple dinosaur, and burn him to death."

PC Power Games & Entertainment

Games for Windows Downloadable games to play in Windows. The most popular files include Backgammon V.06; Chomp for Windows 3.0, a PacMan-like game; Blitzer, a helicopter shoot-'em-up; Risk for Windows; MJWIN, Mah Jongg for Windows; Lander, a simulation of a Lunar Excursion Module; TetWin, Tetris for Windows; Winpool, Windows Billiards; WSLAM, based on Air Hockey; and KillBarn, where you hunt down Barney, the infamous purple dinosaur, and burn him to death. ✓**AMERICA ONLINE**→*keyword* pcgames→Software Libraries→Other→Windows Games

id FTP Site Unofficial archive of id games in their shareware/demo form, including Keen 4 (Goodbye Galaxy), Wolfenstein 3D, Aliens Ate My Baby Sitter, Keen 1 (Invasion of the Vorticons), Doom, and Spear of Destiny. The home-brew subdirectory contains several related FAQs and screenshots. ✓**INTERNET**→*www* ftp://ftp.uwp.edu/pub/msdos/games/id

PC Games Forum A major hub for discussing games played on the PC, including those for BASIC, DOS, and Windows. File libraries have downloadable shareware games, game add-ons, and game cheats and editors. ✓**AMERICA ONLINE**→*keyword* pcgames

PC Games FTP Sites One of the reasons you got on the Net in the first place—free games! These sites include hundreds of shareware games ranging from Castle Wolfenstein 3D to the satirical Toxic the Groundhog. ✓**INTERNET** ...→*www* ftp://ftp.uml.edu/msdos/Games ...→*www* ftp://msdos.archive.edu/msdos/games ...→*www* ftp://ftp.funet.fi/pub/msdos/games ...→*www* ftp://ftp.funet.fi/pub/msdos/windows/games ...→*www* ftp://wuarchive.wustl.edu/pub/MSDOS_UPLOADS/games

Public Brand Software Arcade Forum A great source for public-domain games for your PC–because everyone gets those darn shoot-'em-up cravings every now and then! Visit the libraries for hundreds of action, adventure, role-playing, strategy, casino, sports, and logic games for Windows, DOS, and OS/2-based systems. And if it's not here, post a request in the Ask the Sysops message board. The sysops can also help out with troubleshooting and hints for when you are stuck trying to solve one of those addictive adventure games like the intriguingly-monikered Dracula in London (which you can also download here.) ✓**COMPUSERVE**→*go* pb-sacrcade

Windows Fun Forum Contrary to popular belief, Windows can be fun. If Gin Rummy for Windows isn't your idea of fun, try Dr. Hell. Maybe you're nuts for natural disasters and you'd have a better time with hurricane-tracking software. There's fun for everyone in the screen savers department, and we do mean everyone. Take your pick among "The Boys of Summer," "Wow! Frauleins!" or the "Bible Story" screen savers. And if your idea of fun is planning out the route for the family excursion to Yosemite, you'll find a wide choice of maps and travel planners. ✓**COMPUSERVE**→*go* winfun

Windows Fun 'n Games Mostly peacenik games like Bricklayer and Blackjack, but you'll also find Atmoids, a popular Asteroids clone. Besides straightforward shareware games, you'll find files like the Mortal Kombat v2 move sheet and other tips and tricks for games not necessarily available here. ✓**AMERICA ONLINE**→*keyword* winmag→Software Libraries→Fun 'n Games

Windows Fun Shareware Forum Windows at the office? Probably. Windows at home? If you're lucky. The library in this forum is filled with slot machines, Jimi Hendrix icons, Scrabble games, birthday clocks, poker games, and even drag-and-drop insect parts. Talk strategy on the message boards and you may even become better at entertaining yourself. ✓**COMPUSERVE**→*go* winfun

Windows Shareware Games Shareware rip-offs like Atmoids (an Asteroids clone), PacMan Remakes, and "Tetris-like games" reign here, along with classics like Yahtzee and Minesweeper. ✓**AMERICA ONLINE**→*keyword* win500→Windows 500 Shareware Libraries→Games

OS/2

comp.os.os2.games (ng) Trying to get Myst to run with WARP? Not many games are developed with OS/2 in mind, and problems finding and running games are part of an OS/2 user's existence. Take the case of one disgruntled OS/2 user talking to an IBM representative: "I asked them if there were plans to develop any native OS/2 games—their answer was 'No, [but] we're fairly sure that these will run in a Win-OS/2 session.'" ✓**USENET**

OS/2 Games Paradise for game-starved OS/2 users. All the blockbusters are here, available in OS/2 specific demo and beta versions: Doom II, SimCity, Tetris. ✓**AMERICA ONLINE**→*keyword* os2→Browse the Software Libraries→Games

Net Tech 161

Programming PC Power

Programming

Programming these days is far removed from the late-seventies two-line BASIC loops ("10 PRINT 'MORON!' / 20 GOTO 10"). In fact, there are more than two thousand programming languages, from FORTRAN to Cobol to C+ to Pascal to Perl, and thousands of programmers working to streamline each of them. Start your trip through the Net's programming resources at **The Language List**, which catalogs all the known computer tongues. If you're interested in C or Pascal, enroll at **Programmer University**. And if you have a burning question about groupware development, post your query on CompuServe's **Software Development Forum**.

On the Net

Across the board

comp.lang.misc (ng) Discussion about and help with any computer language, from C+ to JAVA. ✓USENET

Conlang (ml) List for discussing constructed (a.k.a. artificial) languages. ✓INTERNET→*email* listserv@diku.dk ✍ *Type in message body:* subscribe conlang <your full name>

Developer's Resources A Website for software developers working with MS-DOS, MS-Windows, and OS/2 platforms. The site includes links to source code libraries, FAQs, and other programming-related resources on the Internet. ✓INTERNET→*www* http://www.mind.net:80/jfs/devres.html

Dr. Dobb's Journal This forum is run by the staff of *Dr. Dobb's Journal*, a computer magazine devoted to programming languages, techniques, tools, utilities, and algorithms. The programming code that is published every month in the magazine is uploaded to the forum's library, and the message boards serve as a forum for discussing journal articles and other topics of interest to professional programmers (e.g., Unix, Forth, C++, etc.). Selected journal articles are also available in the library. ✓COMPUSERVE→*go* ddjforum

The Language List A searchable list of more than 2,300 published computer languages. Successful searches return brief explanations of the languages, reference works written about the languages, and online resources related to them. ✓INTERNET→*www* http://cuiwww.unige.ch/langlist

The NetLib Scientific Computing Repository Software and documentation to compute functions, simulations, and algorithms in a variety of programming languages. ✓INTERNET→*www* http://netlib.att.com/

PC MagNet Programming Forum Oriented toward PC users, this forum is a rich resource for programmers and programming students. In the library there are hypertext tutorials for C++, FAQs for BASIC, Pascal source code, tools for Visual Basic, and a wide range of other programming files. The message boards include topics about the philosophy of programming, utilities coding, corporate software development, and C++. The forum is run by Ziff/Davis. ✓COMPUSERVE→*go* program

Programmer University Self-paced introductory, intermediate, and advanced online courses for those interested in learning C or Pascal programming. The courses

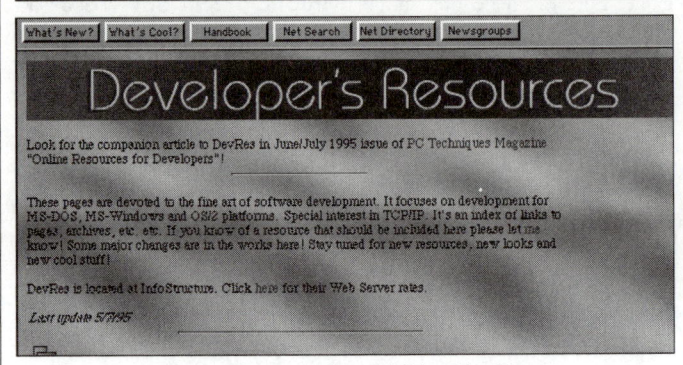

Developer's Resources—http://www.mind.net:80/jfs/devres.html

162 Net Tech

PC Power Programming

consist of weekly online conferences with the instructor and regular programming assignments. ✓**AMERICA ONLINE**→*keyword* programmeru

Programming While it may seem like the Tower of Babel to some, on this topic board, Prodigy members speak of (and in) a broad range of programming languages. Got the Borland C++ blues? Post your programming problems (even part of your program)—maybe someone can help. ✓**PRODIGY**→ *jump* computerbb→Choose a Topic→Programming

Software Development Forum Run by *Software Development* magazine. The message boards carry discussions about object-oriented programming, public domain and shareware, language tools, the ADA language, software development conferences, game development, and other programming topics. The libraries are full of programming instructions and source code, including language FAQs, the source code published in *Software Development* magzine, and public domain software. ✓**COMPUSERVE**→*go* sdforum

WWW Virtual Library's Computer Programming Languages An A-Z hypertext index to programming resources online. The site includes links to an introduction to the ABC programming language, FAQs about Perl, LISP, Dylan, and other languages, source code for C++ programs, and links to more programming sites. ✓**INTERNET**→*www* http://src.doc.ic.ac.uk/bySubject/Computing/Languages.html

Borland

Borland Application Forum Lee doesn't know how to import icons into the Borland Office program. "Click once on the program icon, then use <F>ile <P>roperties, then select Icon—then select an alternate Icon source file," explains the forum's sysop. Besides answering questions about Borland Office, the forum also supports discussions and stores files related to other products and utilities, such as SuperKey, Screenery, Reflex, RapidFile, Applause M, Framework, MultiMate, ObjectVision, Sprint, and the Knowledgebase CD. ✓**COMPUSERVE**→*go* borapp

Borland Development Tools Forum Features support and information about Borland products such as the ReportSmith, Paradox Engine, Borland Database Engine, Brief, and Interbase. ✓**COMPUSERVE** →*go* bdevtools

Computer Associates

CA Visual Objects Forum Run by the technical support staff of Computer Associates, this forum is for CA-Visual Objects users. The message boards are always active with programmers discussing IDE editors, GUI classes, jobs, third-party applications, and Visual Object programming in general. The libraries carry a small selection of utilties and code. ✓**COMPUSERVE**→*go* voforum

Microsoft

Microsoft Developer Services Support and information for programmers using Microsoft development products. CompuServe members must fill out an online registration form before they can get access to many of the services, which include several programming-related forums (e.g., Microsoft Languages Forum, Microsoft Developer Network Forum, Microsoft Windows Multimedia Developer Forum, Windows Components A Forum), a searchable database of thousands of technical articles and tip sheets, a software library with sample code and technical specifications, and an area to file a request for more extensive technical support (at a cost). See the sidebar for a list of these services. ✓**COMPUSERVE**→ *go* msds

Watcom

Watcom Forum Support forum for Watcom's programming products, including Watcom's C and C++ for DOS, Windows, and OS/2; Fortran; SQL; and VX-REXX. The library carries patches and tools for the programs. ✓**COMPUSERVE**→*go* watforum

Watcom International Home Page What company offers product and programming information on languages such as C, C++, SQL, VX-REXX, and Fortran? It's elementary, my dear Watcom. ✓**INTERNET** ...→ *www* http://www.watcom.on.ca/ ...→*www* ftp://ftp.watcom.on.ca/pub

> "What company offers product and programming information on languages such as C, C++, SQL, VX-REXX, and Fortran? It's elementary, my dear Watcom."

Programming PC Power

Programming Languages

ABC

A Short Introduction to the ABC Language ✓ **INTERNET**→*www* http://www.cwi.nl/~guido/ftp/steven/www/abc.html

ABC (ml) List for discussing the ABC language. ✓ **INTERNET**→*email* abc-list-request@cwi.nl ✎ *Type in message body:* subscribe <your email address>

Ada

Ada Frequently Asked Questions ✓ **INTERNET**→*www* http://lglwww.epfl.ch/Ada/FAQ/comp-lang-ada.html

Ada Information Clearinghouse An index for Ada information and resources on the Net. ✓ **INTERNET**→*www* http://sw-eng.falls-church.va.us/AdaIC/

comp.lang.ada (ng) Discussion about Ada programming. Get the FAQs—there are three. ✓ **USENET**

Lovelace Ada Tutorial ✓ **INTERNET**→*www* http://lglwww.epfl.ch/Ada/Tutorials/Lovelace/lovelace.html

Public Ada Library A library of courseware, software, and documentation for Ada programmers. ✓ **INTERNET**→*www* http://web.cnam.fr/Languages/Ada/PAL/

AMOS

AMOS (ml) Mailing list for discussion of programming in AMOS Creator, AMOS Pro, and Easy AMOS for the Amiga computer. ✓ **INTERNET**→*email* amos-request@access.digex.net ✎ *Type in message body:* subscribe <your email address>

APL

APL Discussion and programming tools for the APL language. ✓ **COMPUSERVE**→*go* pcprog→Libraries *and* Messages→APL

APL Frequently Asked Questions ✓ **INTERNET**→*www* http://grover.jpl.nasa.gov/~sam/pub/apl.faq

APL FTP Server ✓ **INTERNET**→*www* ftp://archive.uwaterloo.ca/languages/apl/

comp.lang.apl (ng) Discussion of the APL general-purpose programming language, which is used to create commercial data procession and system design applications, among other things. ✓ **USENET**

IBM Languages Forum Questions, answers, and discussion regarding the APL and APL2 programming languages for IBM computers. ✓ **COMPUSERVE**→*go* ibmlang

BASIC

alt.lang.basic (ng) Discussion about the perennially popular but archaic BASIC programming language. ✓ **USENET**

BASIC Discussion and resources for BASIC programs using a PC. ✓ **COMPUSERVE**→*go* pcprog→Libraries *and* Messages→BASIC

BASIC Development General resource site for BASIC programmers who work on the PC; post questions or download BASIC-related software. ✓ **AMERICA ONLINE** ...→*keyword* pcdev→Message Boards→Languages→BASIC ...→*keyword* pcdev→Software Libraries→BASIC

BASIC Help for the New Programmer Discussion forum for novice BASIC programmers who work on the Mac. ✓ **AMERICA ONLINE**→*keyword* mdv→Message Boards→The Art of Programming→Help for the New Programmer→Programming in Pascal

comp.lang.basic.misc (ng) Discussion about the BASIC programming language. Code is often posted. ✓ **USENET**

Down to BASIC Discussion and resources for BASIC programmers on the Apple II. ✓ **COMPUSERVE**→*go* approg→Libraries *and* Messages→BASIC

Microsoft BASIC Forum Technical support and documentation for Microsoft BASIC. Shareware programs written in MS BASIC arc also available. ✓ **COMPUSERVE**→*go* msbasic

BETA

BETA (ml) Mailing list for BETA programmers. ✓ **INTERNET**→*email* usergroup-request@mjolner.dk ✎ *Type in message body:* subscribe <your email address>

Beta Home Page Includes a FAQ, a link to an FTP archive of related files, a BETA terminology primer, and a Quick Reference Card. ✓ **INTERNET**→*www* http://www.daimi.aau.dk/~beta/

164 Net Tech

PC Power Programming

Programming Languages (cont'd)

comp.lang.beta (ng) Discussion about BETA programming. ✓**USENET**

Mjolner Beta System Home Page Includes a BETA newsletter and a number of tutorials, plus links to other BETA sites. ✓**INTERNET**→*www* http://www.mjolner.dk/

C/C++

An Introduction to C Programming Courseware on programming using the C language. There are 32 modules covering a variety of topics. ✓**INTERNET**→*www* http://www.cit.ac.nz/smac/cprogram/

Ansi C ANSI (American National Standards Institute) created an international standard for the C programming language, and this site describes the language. ✓**INTERNET**→*www* http://www.lysator.liu.se/c/index.html

Borland C++/DOS Forum Support and information about Borland compilers and C++ programming programs including Borland C++, Turbo C++, Turbo C, and Turbo Assembler Turbo Debugger. Questions about Turbo Vision? Here's the place to ask them. ✓**COMPUSERVE**→*go* bcppdos

Borland C++ for Windows/OS2 Forum Support and information about Borland C++, Turbo C++, and Turbo C for Windows. ✓**COMPUSERVE**→*go* bcppwin

C and C++ Discussion and resources for C programmers on the PC. ✓**COMPUSERVE**→*go* pcprog→Libraries *and* Messages→C and C++

C++ Compiler/Lang Discussions and resources for users of Microsoft C++ and Compiler. ✓**COMPUSERVE**→*go* mslang→Libraries *and* Messages→C++ Compiler/Lang

C Compiler/Lang Discussions and resources for users of Microsoft C and Compiler. ✓**COMPUSERVE**→*go* mslang→Libraries *and* Messages→C Compiler/Lang

C Developer Source Code Mac programs created in the C language. ✓**AMERICA ONLINE**→*keyword* mdv→Software Libraries→Developer Source Code→C

C++ Developer Source Code Mac programs created in the C++ language. ✓**AMERICA ONLINE**→*keyword* mdv→Software Libraries→Developer Source Code→C++

C Development Post C programming-related questions. ✓**AMERICA ONLINE**→*keyword* pcdev→Message Boards→Languages→C

C++ Development A place where C++ programmers on the PC can post questions and download software. ✓**AMERICA ONLINE** ...→*keyword* pcdev→Message Boards→Languages ...→*keyword* pcdev→Software Libraries→C++

C Help for the New Programmer A message area for novice C programmers. ✓**AMERICA ONLINE**→*keyword* mdv→Message Boards→The Art of Programming →Help for the New Programmer→Programming in Pascal

C Programming Support for C programming on Amiga. ✓**COMPUSERVE**→*go* amigatech→Libraries *and* Messages→C Programming

The C Programming Language Links to C programming FAQs, a C programming bibliography, code, and other programming texts. ✓**INTERNET**→*www* http://hebb.cis.uoguelph.ca/~deb/27320/C.html

C++ Study Group Run by the editors of *Dr. Dobb's Journal*, the forum has a discussion board and library for C++ programmers. ✓**COMPUSERVE**→*go* ddjforum→Libraries *and* Messages→C++ Study Group

The C++ Virtual Library Though it's relatively difficult to access, this is a good general resource for C++ programmers. ✓**INTERNET**→*www* http://info.desy.de/user/projects/c++.html

C-IBM-370 (ml) Discussion of topics relating to the C programming language on IBM s/370 computers. ✓**INTERNET**→*email* majordomo@pooh.com ✉ *Type in message body:* subscribe c-ibm-370 <your email address>

c2man (ml) Discussion of Graham Stoney's c2man program. ✓**INTERNET**→*email* listserv@research.canon.oz.au ✉ *Type in message body:* subscribe c2man <your full name>

comp.lang.c (ng) Discussion (mostly programming questions, answers, and solutions) about the C programming language. ✓**USENET**

comp.lang.c++ (ng) A large discussion area offering programming tips for C++ in all its flavors:

Net Tech 165

Programming PC Power

Programming Languages (cont'd)

Borland, Symantec, Turbo, Visual, and so on. ✓**USENET**

Introduction to C Programming Tutorials that help you to learn the C programming language ✓**INTERNET**→*www* http://www.iftech.com/classes/c/c0.htm

Introduction to Object-Oriented Programming Using C++ Self-paced course providing an introduction to C++ programming with an emphasis on object orientation. ✓**INTERNET**→*www* http://uu-gna.mit.edu:8001/uu-gna/text/cc/

Pascal and C Discussion and resources for Pascal and C programmers on the Apple II. ✓**COMPUSERVE**→*go* approg→Libraries *and* Messages→Pascal and C

TurboVision (ml) Mailing list for TurboVision programmers who work within C++ and Pascal compilers. ✓**INTERNET**→*email* listserv@vtvm1.cc.vt.edu ⌨ *Type in message body:* subscribe turbvis <your full name>

Understanding C++: An Accelerated Introduction Tutorials offering the fundamental concepts of C++ programming. ✓**INTERNET**→*www* http://www.iftech.com/classes/cpp/cpp0.htm

Watcom's C/C++ Discussion boards and library sections for C programming in DOS, Windows, and OS/2. ✓**COMPUSERVE**→*go* watforum

Cobol

alt.cobol (ng) Discuss the Cobol programming language. Light traffic. ✓**USENET**

Cobol Frequently Asked Questions ✓**INTERNET**→*www* http://www.mfltd.co.uk/FAQ/cobol-faq.html

comp.lang.cobol (ng) Heavily trafficked newsgroup where the Cobol programming language is discussed. ✓**USENET**

comp.compilers (ng) A low-volume newsgroup for discussing compilers and where they can be downloaded on the Net. ✓**USENET FAQ:** ✓**INTERNET**→*www* http://www.cis.ohio-state.edu:80/text/faq/usenet/compilers-faq/faq.html

comp.compilers.tools.pccts (ng) A newsgroup covering PCCTS. ✓**USENET**

Compilers

Compil-L (ml) Mailing list covering compilers in particular and programming language design and implementation in general. ✓**INTERNET**→*email* listserv@american.edu ⌨ *Type in message body:* subscribe compil-l <your full name>

CWarrior (ml) Mailing list where the Metrowerks CodeWarrior set of Macintosh development tools for C, C++, and Pascal are discussed. ✓**INTERNET**→*email* listserv@netcom.com ⌨ *Type in message body:* subscribe cwarrior <your full name>

Think-C (ml) Discuss Think C compilers for the Macintosh. ✓**INTERNET**→*email* think-c-request@ics.uci.edu ⌨ *Type in message body:* subscribe think-c <your email address>

Dylan

Apple Computer FTP Server Archive of files related to Dylan programming. ✓**INTERNET**→*www* ftp://ftp.apple.com/

Apple's Dylan Page An index of Dylan-related programming resources online. ✓**INTERNET**→*www* http://www.cambridge.apple.com/dylan/dylan.html

comp.lang.dylan (ng) Discussion of the Dylan programming language. ✓**USENET**

Dylan Frequently Asked Questions ✓**INTERNET**→*www* ftp://cambridge.apple.com/pub/dylan/faq/dylan-faq.txt

Dylan Home Page Links to a reference manual, an FTP site containing Dylan-related software, and other information about Dylan. ✓**INTERNET**→*www* http://legend.gwydion.cs.cmu.edu:8001/

Eiffel

comp.lang.eiffel (ng) Discussion about the object-oriented Eiffel language. ✓**USENET**

Eiffel Frequently Asked Questions ✓**INTERNET**→*www* http://www.cis.ohio-state.edu/hypertext/faq/usenet/eiffel-faq/faq.html

The Eiffel Page Information and resources relating to the Eiffel language. ✓**INTERNET**→*www* http://www.cm.cf.ac.uk/CLE/

Forth

comp.lang.forth (ng) Discus-

PC Power Programming

Programming Languages (cont'd)

sion about Forth programming. ✓**USENET**

comp.lang.forth.mac (ng) Covers Forth programming for Macintosh users. ✓**USENET**

Forth Rather quiet message board and library for Forth programmers. ✓**COMPUSERVE**→*go* ddjforum →Libraries *and* Messages→Forth

Forth Frequently Asked Questions ✓**INTERNET** ...→*www* http://www.cis.ohio-state.edu/hypertext/faq/usenet/ForthFaq/top.html ...→*www* http://www.cis.ohio-state.edu/hypertext/faq/bngusenet/comp/lang/forth/top.html

Forth Information Group News and information on Forth programming. ✓**INTERNET**→*www* http://taygeta.oc.nps.navy.mil/fig_home.html

Forth Primer An introduction to Forth. ✓**INTERNET**→*www* ftp://taygeta.oc.nps.navy.mil/pub/Forth/Literature/fprimer.zip

Fortran

comp.lang.fortran (ng) Discussions about FORTRAN programming. ✓**USENET**

Fortran 77 Discussion boards and library sections for Watcom's version of Fortran 77. ✓**COMPUSERVE**→*go* watforum

Fortran 90 Software Repository A Website with public Fortran 90 software. ✓**INTERNET**→*www* http://www.nag.co.uk:70/1h/nagware/Examples

Fortran 90 Tutorials Articles on language elements, expressions, procedures, control, array handling, pointer, specifications, intrinsic procedures, and input-output. ✓**INTERNET**→*www* http://asis01.cern.ch/cn/CNTUT/f90/Overview.html

Fortran Development A place for Fortran programmers to post questions and download software. ✓**AMERICA ONLINE** ...→*keyword* pcdev→Message Boards→Languages→FORTRAN ...→*keyword* pcdev→Software Libraries→Other

Fortran Frequently Asked Questions ✓**INTERNET**→*www* http://www.cis.ohio-state.edu/hypertext/faq/usenet/fortran-faq/faq.html

Icon

comp.lang.icon (ng) Discussion about the Icon programming language. ✓**USENET**

ICON Frequently Asked Questions ✓**INTERNET** ...→*www* http://www.cs.arizona.edu/icon/www/faq.html ...→*www* http://www.cis.ohio-state.edu/hypertext/faq/usenet/comp-lang-icon-faq/faq.html

The Icon Programming Language A Website with links to Icon programming resources online. ✓**INTERNET**→*www* http://www.cs.arizona.edu/icon/www/index.html

IDL

comp.lang.idl (ng) Discussions about the Interactive Data Language. ✓**USENET**

comp.lang.idl-pvwave (ng) Discussion about IDL and PV-Wave languages. ✓**USENET**

IDL Frequently Asked Questions ✓**INTERNET**→*www* http://www.cis.ohio-state.edu/hypertext/faq/usenet/idl-faq/faq.html

IDOL

IDOL (ml) Discuss the IDOL programming language. ✓**INTERNET**→*email* idol-group-request@luvthang.ori-cal.com ✍ *Type in message body:* subscribe <your email address>

Linda

Linda (ml) Discussion group for users of Linda-based parallel programming systems (Linda is a set of operators that can be added to conventional programming languages). ✓**INTERNET**→*email* linda-users-request@cs.yale.edu ✍ *Type in message body:* subscribe linda <your email address>

The Linda Group Information about parallel and distributed computing. ✓**INTERNET**→*www* http://www.cs.yale.edu/HTML/YALE/CS/Linda/linda.html

LISP

Association of LISP Users Includes an FAQ, a bibliography of LISP resources, links to various LISP archives, and relevant job listings. ✓**INTERNET**→*www* http://www.cs.rochester.edu/users/staff/miller/alu.html

CMU Common LISP Repository Software and documentation archive for LISP programmers.

Net Tech 167

Programming PC Power

Programming Languages (cont'd)

Also includes a bibliography. ✓**INTERNET**→*www* http://www.cs.cmu.edu:8001/Web/Groups/AI/lang/lisp/html/lisp.html

comp.lang.lisp (ng) Discussion relating to the LISP programming language. ✓**USENET**

comp.lang.lisp.franz (ng) Discussion about the Franz Lisp programming language. ✓**USENET**

comp.lang.lisp.mcl (ng) Discussion on the Common LISP language for the Macintosh. ✓**USENET**

comp.lang.lisp.x (ng) Discussion about the XLISP language system. ✓**USENET**

LISP for the Mac An excellent resource for LISP programs, including FAQs, a 1,030-page guide to Common LISP, utilities, archives of LISP newsgroups, and LISP compilers and interpreters. ✓**INTERNET**→*www* http://www.cambridge.apple.com/other-langs/LISP.html

LISP Frequently Asked Questions Includes an FAQ that outlines LISP FTP sites. ✓**INTERNET**→*www* http://www.cs.cmu.edu/Web/Groups/AI/html/faqs/lang/LISP/top.html

LOGO

comp.lang.logo (ng) Discussion about the LOGO teaching and learning language. ✓**USENET**

Logo Discussion about LOGO. ✓**INTERNET**→ *email* logo-friends-request@aiai.ed.ac.uk ✉ *Type in message body:* subscribe logo-friends <your email address>

Logo Forum Discussion, tutorials, and resources for LOGO programmers. ✓**COMPUSERVE**→*go* logoforum

Logo Frequently Asked Questions ✓**INTERNET**→*www* ftp://cher.media.mit.edu/pub/logo/FAQ

Logo FTP Archive Contains various FAQs, software, and documentation for LOGO programmers. ✓**INTERNET**→*www* ftp://cher.media.mit.edu/pub/logo/

Logo-It's Fun To Program A Web page dedicated to teaching children about programming in the LOGO language. ✓**INTERNET**→*www* http://www.achilles.net/~dsleeth/mw/mainpb.html

Lucid

Lang-Lucid Discuss design issues, implementations, language extensions, bug reports, and fixes relating to the Lucid programming language. ✓**INTERNET**→*email* lang-lucid-request@csl.sri.com ✉ *Type in message body:* subscribe <your email address>

ML

comp.lang.ml (ng) Discussion about the Standard ML, CAML, and Lazy ML programming languages. ✓**USENET**

Information About Standard ML Website for information and resources related to Standard ML programming. ✓**INTERNET**→*www* http://www.cs.cmu.edu/afs/cs.cmu.edu/project/fox/mosaic/sml.html

ML Frequently Asked Questions ✓**INTERNET**→*www* http://www.cs.cmu.edu/afs/cs.cmu.edu/user/jgmorris/web/sml-faq.html

Modula 2

comp.lang.modula2 (ng) Discussions about Modula 2 programming. ✓**USENET**

Modula 2 Frequently Asked Questions ✓**INTERNET**→*www* http://www.cis.ohio-state.edu/hypertext/faq/usenet/computer-lang/Modula2-faq/faq.html

Modula 2 Development For Modula 2 programmers to post questions. ✓**AMERICA ONLINE**→*keyword* pcdev→Libraries *and* Messages→Language→Modula 2

Modula 3

comp.lang.modula3 (ng) Discussion related to Modula 3 programming. ✓**USENET**

Modula 3 Frequently Asked Questions ✓**INTERNET**→*www* http://froh.vlsi.polymtl.ca/m3/m3-faq.html

Modula 3 Hubsite Clearinghouse for Modula 3 programming information and resources. ✓**INTERNET**→*www* http://www.research.digital.com/SRC/modula-3/html/home.html

Oberon

comp.lang.oberon (ng) Discussion about the Oberon language and system. ✓**USENET**

Oberon Development A place

PC Power Programming

Programming Languages (cont'd)

for Oberon programmers to post questions. ✓**AMERICA ONLINE**→*keyword* pcdev→Message Boards→Languages

Oberon Frequently Asked Questions ✓**INTERNET**→*www* http://www.cis.ohio-state.edu/hypertext/faq/bngusenet/comp/lang/oberon/top.html

Oberon FTP Archive An archive of tools and utilities for Oberon programmers. ✓**INTERNET**→*www*ftp://neptune.inf.ethz.ch/pub/Oberon/

Objective-C

comp.lang.objective-c (ng) Discussion related to the Objective-C language and environment. ✓**USENET**

Objective-C Frequently Asked Questions ✓**INTERNET** …→*www* http://www.cis.ohio-state.edu/hypertext/faq/bngusenet/comp/lang/objective-c/top.html …→*www* http://www.symnet.net/~dekorte/Objective-C/objc.html …→*www* http://csld.ucr.edu/NeXTSTEP/objc_faq.html

Pascal

Borland Delphi Forum Support for Borland's version of Pascal. ✓**COMPUSERVE**→*go* delphi

Borland Online—Delphi A Web page devoted to Delphi programming. ✓**INTERNET**→*www* http://www.borland.com/Product/Lang/Delphi/Delphi.html

comp.lang.pascal (ng) Discussions related to Pascal programming. ✓**USENET**

Delphi Development A place for Delphi programmers to post questions. ✓**AMERICA ONLINE**→*keyword* pcdev→Message Boards→Languages→DELPHI

Pascal Developers Source Code Archive of Mac programs created in the Pascal language. ✓**AMERICA ONLINE**→*keyword* mdv→Software Libraries→Developer Source Code→PASCAL

Pascal Development For Pascal programmers to post questions and download software. ✓**AMERICA ONLINE** …→*keyword* pcdev→Message Boards→Languages→Pascal …→*keyword* pcdev→Software Libraries→PASCAL

Pascal Help For the New Programmer Help for novice Pascal programmers. ✓**AMERICA ONLINE**→*keyword* mdv→Message Boards→The Art of Programming→Help for the New Programmer→Programming in Pascal

TurboPascal Development A discussion board where TurboPascal programmers can post questions. ✓**AMERICA ONLINE**→*keyword* pcdev→Message Boards→Languages→TurboPascal

TurboPascal Programmer's Page News, FAQs, documentation, and links to FTP sites for TurboPascal programs. ✓**INTERNET**→*www* http://www.cs.vu.nl/~jprins/tp.html

Perl

comp.lang.perl (ng) Discussions about the Perl language. ✓**USENET**

PERL Language FAQs ✓**INTERNET**→*www* http://www.cis.ohio-state.edu/hypertext/faq/usenet/perl-faq/top.html

PERL Meta-FAQ Includes various FAQs and links to Perl-related FTP sites as well as a bibliography. ✓**INTERNET**→*www* http://www.eecs.nwu.edu/perl/meta-faq.html

Texas Metronet PERL Archive A collection of Perl scripts, source codes, FAQs, and instructional documents. ✓**INTERNET**→*www* http://www.metronet.com/1h/perlinfo

Pop

comp.lang.pop (ng) Discussion on Pop11 and the Plug user group. ✓**USENET**

PostScript

A First Guide to PostScript A primer for beginner PostScript programmers. ✓**INTERNET**→*www* http://www.cs.indiana.edu/docproject/programming/postscript/postscript.html

comp.lang.postscript (ng) Discussion of topics relating to the PostScript Page Description Language. ✓**USENET**

comp.sources.postscript (ng) Source code for PostScript. ✓**USENET**

Internet PostScript Resources Resources on the Internet related to PostScript programming and product development. ✓**INTERNET**→*www* http://yoyo.cc.monash.edu.au/~wigs/postscript/

Net Tech 169

Programming PC Power

Programming Languages (cont'd)

PostScript Frequently Asked Questions ✓**INTERNET**→www http://www.cis.ohio-state.edu/hypertext/faq/bngusenet/comp/lang/postscript/top.html

Prograph

An Introduction to Prograph CPX Primer for novices on programming in Prograph. ✓**INTERNET**→www http://msor0.ex.ac.uk/Prograph_Talk/StartTalk.html

comp.lang.prograph (ng) Lightly trafficked newsgroup for discussion of Prograph programming. ✓**USENET**

Prograph Frequently Asked Questions ✓**INTERNET**→ www http://msor0.ex.ac.uk/Prograph FAQ.html

Prolog

comp.lang.prolog (ng) Discussion about the Prolog computer language. ✓**USENET**

Prolog Frequently Asked Questions ✓**INTERNET** ...→www http://www.cis.ohio-state.edu/hypertext/faq/bngusenet/comp/lang/prolog/top.html ...→www http://www.cs.cmu.edu/Web/Groups/AI/html/faqs/lang/prolog/prg/top.html

Python

comp.lang.python (ng) Discussion of topics related to the Python programming language. ✓**USENET**

Python (ml) Mailing list specializing in the design and use of the object-oriented Python programming language. ✓**INTERNET**→email python-list-request@cwi.nl ✎ Type in message body: subscribe <your full name> <your email address>

Python Frequently Asked Questions ✓**INTERNET** ...→www http://www.cwi.nl/~guido/FAQ.html ...→www http://www.cis.ohio-state.edu/hypertext/faq/bngusenet/comp/lang/python/top.html

Python Language Home Page Website linking to documentation, tutorials, and FTP sites related to Python programming. ✓**INTERNET**→www http://www.cwi.nl/~guido/Python.html

REXX

AREXX Support for REXX programming on the Amiga. ✓**COMPUSERVE**→go amigatech→Libraries and Messages→AREXX

comp.lang.rexx (ng) Discussion about the REXX command language. ✓**USENET**

Ian's REXX Home Page News and links to other REXX-related sites. ✓**INTERNET**→www http://www.comlab.ox.ac.uk/oucl/users/ian.collier/REXX/index.html

REXX Frequently Asked Questions ✓**INTERNET** ...→www http://www.hursley.ibm.com/REXX/REXXfaq.htm ...→www ftp://REXX.uwaterloo.ca/pub/REXXfaq.txt

The REXX Language Various resources, including links to FAQs, FTP sites, and documentation. ✓**INTERNET**→www http://www2.hursley.ibm.com/REXX/

REXX Language Association A tyrannosaurus-size list of resources on the Web for REXX programmers. ✓**INTERNET**→www http://www.pvv.unit.no/REXXLA/index.html

VX-REXX Discussion boards and library sections for VX-REXX, Watcom's version of REXX. ✓**COMPUSERVE**→go watforum

Sather

comp.lang.sather (ng) Discussion about the Sather programming language. ✓**USENET**

Sather Home Page A Web page devoted to the object-oriented language, with tutorials, FAQs, reference materials, instructional texts, and compilers. ✓**INTERNET**→www http://http.icsi.berkeley.edu/Sather/

Scheme

comp.lang.scheme (ng) Discussion about the Scheme programming language. ✓**USENET**

comp.lang.scheme.c (ng) Discussion about the Scheme language environment. ✓**USENET**

The Internet Scheme Repository A Website with source code, documentation, and free implementations for Scheme programmers. ✓**INTERNET**→www http://www.cs.indiana.edu/scheme-repository/home.html

MIT Scheme Hubsite Clearinghouse for Scheme information and documentation. ✓**INTERNET**→www http://www-swiss.ai.mit.edu/scheme-home.html

170 Net Tech

PC Power Programming

Programming Languages (cont'd)

Scheme Frequently Asked Questions ✓INTERNET...→www http://www.cs.cmu.edu/Web/Groups/AI/html/faqs/lang/scheme/top.html ...→www http://www.cis.ohio-state.edu/hypertext/faq/bngusenet/comp/lang/scheme/top.html

Smalltalk

comp.lang.smalltalk (ng) Discussion about the Smalltalk 80 programming language. ✓USENET

Smalltalk Archive An archive of Smalltalk source code. ✓INTERNET→www http://st-www.cs.uiuc.edu/

Smalltalk Development A place for Smalltalk programmers to post questions. ✓AMERICA ONLINE→*keyword* pcdev→Message Boards→Languages

Smalltalk for the Macintosh Programming information and links for Mac Smalltalkers. ✓INTERNET→www http://www.cambridge.apple.com/other-langs/smalltalk.html

Smalltalk Frequently Asked Questions ✓INTERNET→www http://www.cs.cmu.edu/Web/Groups/AI/html/faqs/lang/smalltalk/faq.html

Sources of Smalltalk Information Website with information on all aspects of Smalltalk programming. ✓INTERNET→www http://st-www.cs.uiuc.edu/other_st.html

Verilog

comp.lang.verilog (ng) Discussion of the Verilog and PLC languages. ✓USENET

comp.lang.verilog archive A Website with links to online resources for Verilog programmers. ✓INTERNET→www http://www.cray.com/verilog/archive.html

Verilog Frequently Asked Questions ✓INTERNET→www http://www.cray.com/verilog/verilog-faq.html

VHDL

comp.lang.vhdl (ng) Discussion about the VHSIC Hardware Description Language. ✓USENET

VHDL FTP Archive An archive containing VHDL programming resources. ✓INTERNET→www http://wuarchive.wustl.edu/languages/vhdl/

VHDL International User's Forum A repository of VHDL resources, including archives of the comp.lang.vhdl newsgroups, information from a number of VHDL user groups, and conference schedules. ✓INTERNET→www gopher://gopher.vhdl.org:70/h0/Welcome

Visual Basic

Carl & Gary's Visual Basic Home Page Links to dozens of Visual Basic programming resources online, including newsgroup archives, shareware and utilities, and a list of Visual Basic consultants. ✓INTERNET→www http://www.apexsc.com/vb

CLBV Digest (ml) A newsletter dedicated to Visual Basic programming. ✓INTERNET→*email* clbv-digest-editor@apexsc.com ✍ *Write a request* **Archives:** ✓INTERNET→www http://www.apexsc.com:80/vb/clbv-digest/

comp.lang.basic.visual (ng) A newsgroup covering Visual Basic programming. ✓USENET

comp.lang.basic.visual.announce (ng) Announcements relating to the Visual Basic newsgroups. ✓USENET

comp.lang.basic.visual.database (ng) A small group dedicated to using databases with Visual Basic, including types of engines, do's and don'ts, code. ✓USENET

comp.lang.basic.visual.3rd-party (ng) Advice on where to buy Visual Basic third-party products. ✓USENET

Visual Basic Visual Basic programs and links to other Visual Basic Websites. ✓INTERNET→www http://www.fys.ruu.nl/~zuithoff/Vmain.html

Visual Basic Frequently Asked Questions ✓INTERNET→www http://www.cis.ohio-state.edu/hypertext/faq/usenet/visual-basic-faq/top.html

Visual Basic Programmer's Journal This Windows development magazine hosts a forum for discussing programming with Visual Basic. Selected articles from the magazine are archived in the forum, as are resumés from programmers and sample code and applications. ✓COMPUSERVE→*go* vbpj

Net Tech 171

Utilities PC Power

Utilities

The complexity of a computer's innards gives pause to all but the most expert techies, and when your PC is sick—when it burps and coughs up in the night, when it won't read a disk or claims memory loss—it's hard to diagnose the problem, let alone cure the ailment. That's where utilities come in. An electronic actualization of the old "physician, heal thyself" bromide, utilities allow computers to pinpoint and remedy their afflictions, be they drastic systemic emergencies (hot-zone viruses in the CPU) or minor hygienic concerns (messy desktops). Get medical by platform with **Atari Utilities, Apple II Utilities,** and the **Symantec Central Point Software WinMac Forum.**

MacMania—http://www.europa.com/~bubba/mac/freeshare.html

On the Net

Across the board

PBS Utilities Forum Run by Ziff-Davis staff members, the forum is a gold mine for PC users with questions about utilities ("how do you use the 'regular expression searches' featured in ProFind?") or with utility needs. The library features system, hardware, printer, and file utilities for DOS, Windows, and OS/2 platforms. ✓ COMPUSERVE→*go* pbsutilities

Symantec Central Point Soft-ware WinMac Forum The forum features technical support from the Symantec staff for several of their Windows and Mac utilities, including CP Backup, PC Tools, CPS Anti-Virus for Windows, MacTools, Safe & Sound, Snooper, and Alert! for the Mac. The library carries a large assortment of updaters and FAQs for Symantec programs. ✓ COMPUSERVE →*go* symcpwin

Symantec Norton Utilities Forum Technical support for and product information about Symantec Utilities, including Norton Desktop, Norton Disklock, Norton Backup, Norton Editor, Norton Commander, Norton Utilities, Norton Essentials for PowerBook, pcANYWHERE, and Norton Speedcache+. Norton Desktop and pcANYWHERE take up the lion's share of discussion on the message board, although the Symantec staff answers questions on all the programs. When G. W. couldn't repartition the memory on his hard drive with Norton Utilities—"Does 28,000 files make any difference and if so, what can I do besides partition the hard drive (which is not an option at this time without having another hard drive to put everything on)?"—he turned here for help. And he got it: "Use a sector-translating controller that lies about how many tracks/heads/sectors-per-track are on the disk." The library carries information, updates, and third-party add-ons for all of Symantec's utility programs. ✓ COMPUSERVE→*go* symutil

Trailblazer Utilities *PC Magazine* is compiling links to sites carrying utilities for several computer platforms. Each site is briefly described and rated. ✓ INTERNET→ *www* http://www.ziff.com:8032/~zdi/tblazer/utility.html

Utilities What's your problem? Computer users often need little helpers; utilities are suppose to serve that function. They repair and back up files, clean systems, install other programs, encode and decode, double RAM, protect your screen, and more. So if your

PC Power Utilities

DOS files aren't being backed up and you need advice on which program could do it, or if you can't decide between Uninstall or Quarterdeck's Clean Sweep, members here are willing to recommend programs ✓**PRODIGY**...→ *jump* computerbb→Choose a Topic→Utilities...→*jump* softwaresupportbb→Choose a Topic→Utilities

Utilities and Tools To tackle a world of file extensions (.ARJ, .LHA, .ZOO, .ZIP, .HQX, etc.), savvy computer users come equipped with files to unencode, uncompress, unzip, and convert. This site carries most of the important programs for Mac, Amiga, PC, and Unix users. ✓**INTERNET**→*www* ftp://ftp.tex.ac.uk/pub/archive/tools/

Utilities/Tips Forum The volume of discussion on this forum is quite low. Although sections of the message board have been reserved for posting tips about hardware, software, word processing, spreadsheets, networking, DOS, Windows, and OS/2, most of the discussion concerns troubleshooting utilities. The libraries are huge repositories of utilities—utilities mentioned in *PC* Magazine articles, utilities from the Association of Shareware Professionals, and more utilities for Windows and OS/2 machines. ✓**COMPUSERVE**→*go* tips

Compression

comp.compression.research (ng) A newsgroup for discussing research on data compression and data-compression algorithms. ✓**USENET**

comp.compression/alt.comp.compression (ng) Netters thinking of posting a question on either of these newsgroups should first read the incredibly detailed compression FAQ (good advice in general, but particularly with this newsgroup). The FAQ begins with a list of programs required to open files with specific file extensions and includes the Net addresses for the programs. So, if you download a file with an ".arj" extension, you're on a Mac, and you don't know how to uncompress it, turn to the FAQ; in this circumstance, it recommends the "unarj" program and gives an Internet address where you can download the software. The FAQ also lists addresses for audio and image compression programs, offers explanations of data-compression techniques, and lists image-compression hardware. But not everyone follows good advice, and the newsgroup usually includes several dozen posts from Netters who want to know what programs are required to open their files, what viewing programs read JPEGs or MPEGs, and why their archives are corrupted. Even without the repetitive questions, the group carries a broad range of data compression discussions—from compression algorithms to debates about "the right compression method." ✓**USENET** *FAQ:* ✓**INTERNET** ...→*www* ftp://rtfm.mit.edu/pub/usenet-by-hierarchy/comp/compression/ ...→*www* http://www.cis.ohio-state.edu/hypertext/faq/usenet/compression-faq/top.html

Compression and Encoding Utilities Primarily for DOS and Windows users, this Web page links to several big archives of compression and encoding utilities. ✓**INTERNET**→*www* http://www2.ncsu.edu/bae/people/faculty/walker/hotlist/compress.html

Compression Chart A well-maintained chart of file compression formats, their extensions, computer platforms (DOS, Mac, Unix, VM/CMS, and Amiga), and the programs required to uncompress files. The chart is followed by a list of Net sites carrying compression and decompression programs. ✓**INTERNET**→*www* ftp://ftp.cso.uiuc.edu:/doc/pcnet/compression

HARC-C Compression Technology A home page with information about (and a demo of) the HARC-C compression utility, which can compact an image at variable compression ratios while maintaining a high level of clarity. ✓**INTERNET**→*www* http://www.harc.edu/HARCC.html

UUdeview If you've downloaded a binary from a newsgroup or been emailed an encoded file, you need to decode it. This program decodes all three types of formats (UUencode, MIME, or XX encoding). DOS, Windows, and Unix users may download the program or code directly from this site. It's not available for Mac users, but there are links to other Macintosh decoding programs here. ✓**INTERNET**→*www* http://www.uni-frankfurt.de/~fp/uudeview/

> "The newsgroup usually includes posts from Netters who want to know what programs are required to open their files..."

Net Tech 173

Utilities PC Power

Amiga

Amiga Utilities Need to archive a file or uncompress it? Might your system have a virus? And what time is it anyway? The utilities directories in these archives and libraries are filled with fonts, screensavers, system software patches, virus programs, uncompression utilities, and clocks. ✓**INTERNET** ...→*www* http://ftp.wustl.edu/~aminet/dirs/tree_util.html ...→*www* ftp://wuarchive.wustl.edu/pub/aminet/util/ ...→*www* ftp://www.funet.fi/pub/amiga/utilities ✓**COMPUSERVE**→*go* amiga-user→Libraries

Apple II

Apple II Archivers A small directory of archiving programs, including programs to unzip, de-arc, or archive in a Macintosh format. ✓**INTERNET**→*www* ftp://ftp.cco.caltech.edu/pub/apple2/ARCHIVERS/

Apple II Utilities If files need converting from one Apple II format to another, or uncompressing, bring your wish list to this library, which carries a fairly large selection of Apple II utilities. Have a problem, but uncertain about what utility could help? Visit the message board with your question. ✓**COMPUSERVE**→*go* appuser→Libraries *and* Messages→Utilities

Apple II Utilities A mixed bag of utilities for the ProDos 8 and Apple II-GS computers. If you need a virus detector, a file compressor, a bug reporter, a disk doctor, or a program launcher, you can choose from a number of shareware and freeware applications stored here. There's also an Article & Transcripts folder with archived text files from the message boards that focus on utilities. ✓**AMERICA ONLINE**→*keyword* a2→Apple II Software Libraries→Utilities

Apple II Utilities Shareware and freeware utilities for the Apple II. Not a lot of documentation, but if you know what you're looking for... ✓**INTERNET**→*www* ftp://ftp.cco.caltech.edu/pub/apple2/utils/

Atari

Atari Archivers Need a file converted from ".ARC" to ".LZH," an ".ARJ" file unpacked, or an ".LZH" file converted into a self-extracting file? This is a fairly comprehensive collection of archivers for the Atari. ✓**INTERNET** ...→*www* ftp://wuarchive.wustl.edu/systems/atari/umich.edu/Archivers/ ...→*www* ftp://atari.archive.umich.edu/Archivers ...→*www* gopher://gopher.archive.umich.edu:7055/11/atari/Archivers

Atari Utilities One of the utilities available here changes the date on your computer every day; another copies programs; another makes a file self-extracting; and another finds files on your hard disk. Pillage this directory of more than 600 utilities for applications to optimize your Atari system. ✓**INTERNET** ...→*www* ftp://atari.archive.umich.edu/Utilities ...→*ww* gopher://gopher.archive.umich.edu:7055/11/atari/Utilities ...→*www* ftp://wuarchive.wustl.edu/systems/atari/umich.edu/Utilities/

DOS & Windows

A Few Useful Utilities A very small collection of DOS utilities that includes sound players, a program to divide up large DOS files, a program to convert DOS hex to bin, and a program to ZIP and unZIP files. ✓**INTERNET**→*www* http://www.wood.army.mil/utils.html

comp.os.ms-windows.apps.utilities (ng) This newsgroup deals predominantly with utilities for the Microsoft Windows operating system. Most of the postings are requests by PC owners trying to find utilities to do specific tasks, such as screen capturing, screen saving, or TIFF viewing. It's an easy forum to ask questions on, no matter how rudimentary—e.g., "I just purchased Microhelp's Installer Program and am having trouble getting it installed!" ✓**USENET**

DOS Utilities Hundreds of utilities for DOS users. This archive is easy to navigate—everything is organized into convenient file-type categories, including disk, hardware, and memory utilities. Also check out the Time, Date and Clocks section for chess clocks, event reminders, automatic boot-up schedulers, and other DOS utilities. ✓**AMERICA ONLINE**→*keyword* dos→Software Libraries

EkBackup The Windows program not only restores .ZIP, .ARJ and .LHA files, it also backs up whole directories, fixes damaged .ZIP files, allows you to view files within an archive, and possesses several other features. ✓**INTERNET**→*www* http://www.pvv.unit.no/~gustavf/ekbackup/

Essential Utilities A small collection of Windows utilities that includes an archiver, a file manager, Netscape, a clock, and a text editor. ✓**INTERNET**→*www* http://eohsi.rutgers.edu/personel/jao/index.html

MS-DOS Archive Utilities Before enjoying FTP riches, you may need to find the program tools for

PC Power Utilities

decompressing DOS files; fairly complete collections of these tools can be found at these FTP sites. ✓**INTERNET** ...→*www* ftp: //ftp.uml.edu/msdos/Archivers ... →*www* ftp://ftp. uwp.edu/pub/msdos/arcers ...→*www* ftp://ftp. funet.fi/pub/ msdos/packing ...→*www* ftp://msdos.archive.umich. edu/msdos/compression

PC Compression Software
You never know when you may need to unzip—a compressed file, that is. This software archive includes extraction programs that will turn a little bundle of compacted bytes into a full-fledged, memory-hogging program and then compress programs to get those mnemonic monstrosities back under control. ✓**AMERICA ONLINE**→*keyword* pctelecom→Browse the Software Libraries→Compression

PC Magazine Utiliites Download Area
An archive of all utilities featured in *PC* Magazine's PC Tech section since 1993. In addition, benchmark tests for utilities are featured. ✓**INTERNET**→*www* http://www.ziff.com:8001/~pcmag/download.htm

PC Utilities
Libraries of PC utilities to add functionality to your system. Download file managers, menu systems, backup tools, text editors, copying programs, encryption and password protection applications, file finders, label makers, and more. ✓**AMERICA ONLINE**→*keyword* pchardware→Software Libraries

PC Utilities/Systems Forum
A forum devoted to DOS, Windows, and OS/2 utilities. The library is packed with utilities to manage files, reboot a system, encode and decode files, catalog disks, and make life on a PC easier

VSL—http: //www. acs.oakland.edu/cgi-bin/shase/Form

and more productive (see the large selection of calculators, appointment programs, clocks, etc.) ✓**COMPUSERVE**→*go* pcutil

SimTel Encoding Software
Spend a lot of time hanging out in the erotic binaries newsgroups? If so, you'll need to pick up a decoder. This is a small but useful collection of encoders and decoders for Windows users. ✓**INTERNET** ...→*www* http://www.acs. oakland.edu/oak/SimTel/win3/encode.html ...→*www* ftp://oak. oakland.edu/SimTel/win3/encode...→*www* ftp://wuarchive. wustl. edu/systems/ibmpc/simtel/win3/encode ...→*www* ftp://ftp.uoknor.edu/mirrors/SimTel/win3/encode ...→*www* ftp://ftp.uni-paderborn.de/SimTel/win3/encode

Symantec Central Point Software DOS Forum
Technical support forum for users of Symantec DOS utilities programs like CP Backup, PC Tools, Commute, PC Shell, DiskEdit, FileFix, Mirror, Undelete, Unformat, and DiskFix. The libraries are filled with documentation, press releases, and upgrades. ✓**COMPUSERVE**→ *go* symcpdos

The Windows Bargain Bin
Shareware and freeware utilities, including a squiggly screensaver, a sliding puzzle, an icon manager, and an image viewer. ✓**INTERNET**→*www* http://www.pcug.org.au/~tholland/

Windows Shareware Utilities
Make your Windows system more functional with this award-winning assortment of shareware utilities for Windows users: Trash managers, memory compactors, text editors, program launchers, toolbar replacements, virus scanners, and more. ✓**AMERICA ONLINE**→*keyword* win500→Windows 500 Shareware Library→Utilities

Windows Utilities
A collection of utilities for Windows users, including obscurities like a Hebrew Calendar and a nutrition monitor, and more popular fare like toolbar customizers, audio CD players, expense account managers, and wallpaper extensions. ✓**AMERICA ONLINE**→*keyword* winmag→Software Libraries→Windows→Utilities

Windows Utility Forum
A central repository for Windows utilities, including clocks, file management programs, memory monitors and device drivers, font and printing programs, icon bars, diagnostic programs, and more. The message boards serve as a forum to identify the utilities you're looking for and let you ask questions about how they're used. There's already a section devoted entirely to Windows 95 utilities. ✓**COMPUSERVE**→*go* winutil

Windows Utility Report
This Web report features reviews of shareware, freeware, and public domain utilities and add-ons for Microsoft Windows. If something sounds good, it's yours. Links to the utilities are included. ✓**INTERNET**→*www* http://www.

Utilities PC Power

mindspring.com:80/~dbandlt/report.html

WinZip Home Page A utility to zip and unzip files. The program also works to uncompress files ending with .TAR, .GZIP, .Z, and .GZ. In addition, the Website carries an add-on that makes zipped files self-extracting. Now go out and win one for the Zipper. ✓ **INTERNET**→ *www* http://www.winzip.com/winzip/

ZiffNet Free Utilities Forum An archive of utilities that were advertised or written about in Ziff-Davis's *PC* Magazine. You can also get ZShare, ZiffNet's monthly downloadable newsletter featuring editors' picks of the newest and best in shareware. ✓ **COMPUSERVE**→ *go* freeutil

Macintosh

Mac Shareware DAs, Utilities, Function Keys A small library of award-winning keyware, which is software that allows you to customize your keyboard. Download one of the programs here and you'll be able to put your PowerBook to sleep or insert the date into a word processing document simply by hitting a designated key. Fine-tuning your Macintosh keyboard can save you hours of time. ✓ **AMERICA ONLINE**→*keyword* mac500→DAs, Utilities, Function Keys

Mac Shareware System 7 Utilities Some people just aren't satisfied with Apple's System 7 utilities, so they make their own and then upload them for others to use. In this archive you'll find award-winning utilities like Helium 2.1.1, a control panel extension that allows you to define "Hot Keys" that instantly inflate System 7 Help Balloons without having to choose "Show Balloons" from the Help menu. Those without System 7.5 can get one of those great automatic alias-makers here, too. ✓ **AMERICA ONLINE**→*keyword* mac500→System 7 Utilities

Mac Utilities These sites are rather large clearinghouses of Macintosh utilities that will help to make your computer run more smoothly. Browse these sites for various alias-makers, file compressors, desktop clocks (that display supermodels, no less!), wallpaper, bug checkers, encryption programs, printer drivers, text editors, and more, more, more. ✓ **INTERNET** …→*www* http://hyperarchive.lcs.mit.edu/HyperArchive/Abstracts/util/HyperArchive.html …→*www* ftp://sumex-aim.stanford.edu/info-mac/util/ …→*www* gopher://sunsite.doc.ic.ac.uk:70/1/packages/mac-sumex/Utility …→*www* gopher://sumexaim.Stanford.EDU:70/11/info-mac/util

Macintosh Compression Utilities Download programs for all your Macintosh compression and extracting needs. ✓ **INTERNET** …→*www* ftp://wuarchive.wustl.edu/systems/mac/info-mac/cmp …→*www* ftp://sumex-aim.stanford.edu/info-mac/cmp …→*www* ftp://mac.archive.umich.edu/mac/util/compression ✓ **COMPUSERVE**→*go* macff→Access File Finder→*Search by keyword:* compress *or* extract

Macintosh Utilities Forum Do you know your CDEVs and INITs from your DAs and FKEYs? Well if you do, then you'll love this forum devoted to Mac utilities—those little programs that help to make your computer a more functional and productive machine. ✓ **AMERICA ONLINE**→*keyword* mut

MacMania FreeWare and ShareWare In addition to offering Internet client software for the Mac, this Website links to several Macintosh utilities for viewing graphics, encoding and decoding files, and disinfecting files. ✓ **INTERNET**→ *www* http://www.europa.com/~bubba/mac/freeshare.html

Now Utilities 5.0 More than 70 features make this improved version of Now Utilities essential; they include a button bar with hot-help, unlimited custom menus, a compression option, fast-finds, and much more. Demo versions of the product are available. ✓ **INTERNET**→*www* http://software.net/info/now/utilities.htm/SK:ahikmgjoomlegeej

OS/2

comp.os.os2.utilities (ng) On a mission to acquire the best utilities for your OS/2 machine? To help you find them, join forces with the members of this newsgroup—members like Allen, who wants a PM-based newsgroup decoder; Kevin, who needs a backup utility; and Audrey, who's looking for a utility to convert a PostScript file to text. Also watch for the monthly posting of must-have OS/2 utilities. ✓ **USENET**

OS/2 Utilities After you scour the File/Disk Utilities archive for file finders, encryption programs, compression programs, and disk managers, descend even deeper into this OS/2 archive for printer, screen, and system utilities or for telecommunications helpers (like offline mail readers and terminal emulators) and file decoders that will help you turn binary text into digitized images. ✓ **AMERICA ONLINE**→*keyword* os2→Browse the Software Libraries→File/Disk Utilities *and* MORE…

176 Net Tech

PC Power Screen Savers

Screen savers

Leave the screen on. Don't leave the screen on. An entire industry has been based on the digital-era myth that if you leave something displayed on your monitor for too long *it will burn into the screen*. So protect your monitor with pop-culture animations from **PBS Screen Savers** (Windows), or make new bread out of old wheat with the latest **AfterDark Modules for the Macintosh**. Brighten up your office life with the Teenage Mutant Ninja Turtles, W. C. Fields, O. J. Simpson, Jim Carrey, flying toasters, what have you. Or send the people at the **Ultimate Software Home Page** a picture of your mother, and they'll turn her into an AfterDark module.

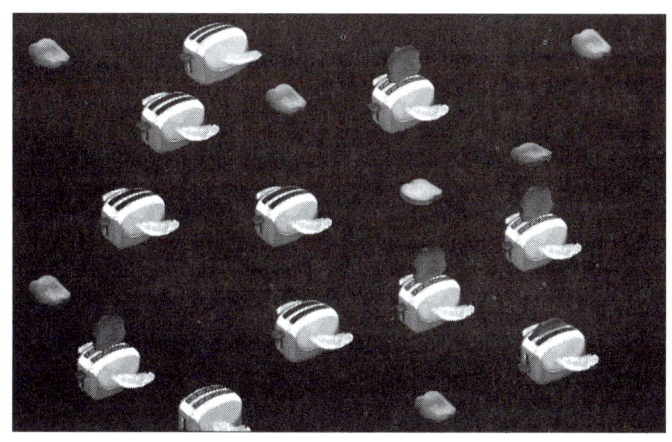

Gleaming Angels of Love—screenshot from After Dark 3.0

On the Net

Windows

Dragon's Eye Software Still under construction at press time, this Texas-based company's site sells customized screen savers for Windows users. Mail them a picture of your favorite girlfriend, boyfriend, household pet, pop star, film star, sports figure, serial killer, whatever, and they'll turn it into a screen saver for you. ✓**INTERNET**→*www* http://rampages.onramp.net/~desoftw/savers.html

PBS Screen Savers First download the Ziff-Davis Animated Screen saver 1.0 for Windows and then grab some of the modules archived here, including W. C. Fields, Bill Gates, Charlie Chan, and others. Customize your computer with these animated screen savers and prevent screen burn-in at the same time. ✓**COMPUSERVE**→ *go* pbsstudio→Libraries→Screen Savers

SimTel Windows Screen Savers Highlights of this fairly small collection of Windows screen savers include the Aerosmith Box of Fire cover, Persian proverbs, and a rollercoaster. ✓**INTERNET** …→*www* http://www.acs.oakland.edu/oak/SimTel/win3/scrsaver.html …→*www* ftp://oak.oakland.edu/SimTel/win3/scrsaver …→*www* ftp://wuarchive.wustl.edu/systems/ibmpc/simtel/win3/scrsaver …→*www* ftp://ftp.uoknor.edu/mirrors/SimTel/win3/scrsaver …→*www* ftp://ftp.uni-paderborn.de/SimTel/win3/scrsaver

Windows Screen Savers An archive of screen saver applications and modules for Windows users. You could download Winsaver 4.0, a program that plays screen saver modules, and collect interesting modules such as *Popeye*, *Jurassic Park*, Bill Clinton, Biblical verses, Contract with America, and O. J. Simpson. ✓**COMPUSERVE** →*go* winfun→Browse Libraries→ Screen Savers

Macintosh

AfterDark Modules for the Macintosh Lots of screen saver modules for AfterDark: Bungee-jumping cows, exploding fireworks, 3-D fractal landscapes, Asian fireflies, bee swarms, and what have you. ✓**COMPUSERVE**→ *go* zmc:download→Libraries→ *Search by file name:* screen

Info-Mac Screen Saver Archive A small collection of screen saver modules and programs for the Macintosh. You can get Dark-

Screen Savers PC Power

Side of the Mac here, which is a freeware screen saver application, as well as numerous savers including The Swarm (bees), ScreenFlip (rotates the contents of your screen), and a special native screen saver for the Power Mac. ✓**INTERNET**→*www* http://hyperarchive.lcs.mit.edu/HyperArchive/Archive/app/ss/screensaver-faq-30.hqx

Macintosh Screen Savers U.K.-based site containing hundreds of interesting screen savers. Yes, they have the famous Beastie Boys screen saver with over 30 animated sequences, but it takes forever to download. Also contains an anti-Barney screen saver and a lot of optical illusions for people who like to hallucinate at their computer terminals. The emphasis here is on AfterDark modules. ✓**INTERNET** …→*www* ftp://sumex-aim.stanford.edu/info-mac/Application/Screen saver …→*gopher* gopher://sunsite.doc.ic.ac.uk:70/1/packages/mac-sumex/Application/Screen saver

Macintosh Screen Savers Contains dozens of AfterDark modules, including Barney Blast 2.0.2 and a hilarious O.J. Bronco saver (you can guess what it does) as well as various other screen saver applications and their modules (including Mighty Morphin Power Rangers, Frank Black, and The Orb). ✓**AMERICA ONLINE**→*keyword* macutilities→Software Libraries→Screensavers & Modules

Ultimate Software Home Page An Iowa-based company that turns your favorite photos and designs into personalized screen savers. The possibilities are virtually limitless—your dog, your cat, your boy-/girlfriend, your girlfriend with her cat, your mother, Alan Greenspan, or you yourself as a snot-nosed kid. Just send the company the required fee ($25 for three to five photos) and the photos, and they'll send you back a customized screen saver that will work on AfterDark or Dark Side of the Mac. ✓**INTERNET**→*www* http://www.netins.net/showcase/ultimate/

University of Michigan Macintosh Screen Saver Archive Nice selection of screen saver modules for AfterDark and Dark Side of the Mac. You name it, they probably have it archived here. ✓**INTERNET** …→*www* http://www.umich.edu/~archive/mac/util/screensaver/ …→*www* gopher://gopher.archive.umich.edu:7055/11/mac/util/screen saver

---

Single-Module Screen Savers

Beastie Deluxe Funky cartoon images of the Beastie Boys' heads bouncing around a basketball court, among other things. In the world of screen savers, this is what'cha, what'cha, what'cha want. ✓**INTERNET** …→*www* http://hyperarchive.lcs.mit.edu/HyperArchive/Archive/app/ss/beastie-boys-screen saver.hqx …→*www* gopher://sunsite.doc.ic.ac.uk:70/1/packages/mac-sumex/Application/Screen saver

Beavis & Butt-head Screen Saver Why would you want to invite MTV's resident morons onto your monitor, especially since they're ugly, offensive, and don't know squat about computers? "He said 'squat'…huh, huh…huh, huh." Enough said. ✓**INTERNET**→*www* http://www.sepc.sony.com/SEPC/Screen Saver/Beavis/BeavisIndex.HTML

Coca-Cola Screen Savers As if Coke weren't ubiquitous enough, now there's a way to put the übersoda on your monitor. And there's even a low-cal version if you're on a diet. ✓**AMERICA ONLINE**→*keyword* macutilities→Software Search→Search by file name: coca-cola ✓**COMPUSERVE**→*go* macbven→Libraries→Search by file name: cocaco.sea *and* dietco.sea ✓**INTERNET**→*www* http://hyperarchive.lcs.mit.edu/HyperArchive/Archive/app/ss/coca-cola-ad.hqx …→*www* http://hyperarchive.lcs.mit.edu/HyperArchive/Archive/app/ss/diet-coke-ad.hqx

Fortune Cookie Windows screen saver with more than 7,000 jokes. Wanna hear one? Oh…maybe not. ✓**INTERNET** …→*www* ftp://ftp.cica.indiana.edu/pub/pc/win3/desktop/jokebag.zip …→*www* ftp://ftp.marcam.com/win3/desktop/jokebag.zip

Madonna Screen Saver She's everywhere else in your life, so why not make her part of your computer? You won't be sorry. ✓**INTERNET**→*www* http://www.st.nepean.uws.edu.au/~ppoulos/madonna/binaries/m-screen.zip

Sugar Screen Saver An AfterDark module with designs by Lou Kregel, from his album-cover artwork for ex-Hüsker Dü guitarist Bob Mould's new band, Sugar. ✓**AMERICA ONLINE**→*keyword* macutilities→Software Search→Search by file name: sugar ✓**INTERNET**→*www* http://hyperarchive.lcs.mit.edu/HyperArchive/Archive/app/ss/sugar-ad.hqx

178 Net Tech

Part 6

Creativity in Cyberspace

Graphics—Picture This **Creativity in Cyberspace**

Graphics—picture this

Remember the days of Koala pads and simple black-and-white drawing programs? Well, as any computer artist can tell you, they were just a sketch for the masterwork to come. Today, computer graphics are full-color, high-resolution marvels. Start in the **alt.binaries.pictures*** hierarchy. With hundreds of new uploads each week, these newsgroups are the .GIFs that keep on giving, and you'll find everything from dogs (**alt.binaries. pictures.animals**) to, well, dogs (**alt.binaries.pictures. erotica.bestiality**). Then drop by **Go Graphics**, CompuServe's massive image bank. And if you want to manipulate existing artwork, there's sure to be a forum for your software of choice, be it **Adobe Illustrator** or **Claris-Draw** and **ClarisImpact**.

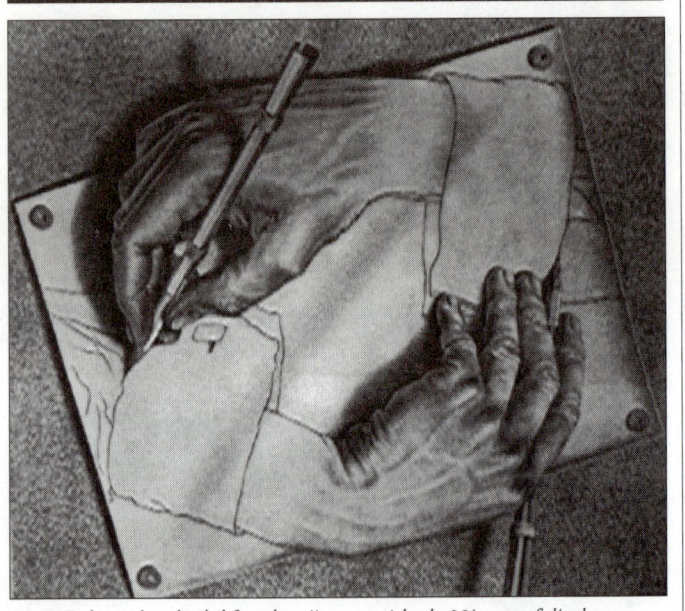

M. C. Escher—downloaded from http://www.umich.edu:80/~mransfrd/escher

On the Net

Across the board

alt.binaries.pictures* **newsgroups** (ng) Get your pictures here! Get your pictures here! In the world of Usenet, there are few groups as well-traveled as the alt.binaries.pictures* hierarchy. Why? Well, it's cool to click on a button and watch your computer retrieve an image of a rocket ship, or Homer Simpson, or Leonard Nimoy. But let's not be naive about this—there's no picture like an erotic picture. Whether your tastes run to bestiality, blondes, nude supermodels, or hairy men, there are plenty of softcore and hardcore pictures online, waiting to be downloaded, unencoded, and viewed to your heart's content. And they said the Net wasn't educational. Groups with a "d" at the end signify a forum for discussing pictures. See the sidebar on page 189 for a list of all the alt.binaries groups. ✓**USENET**

Go Graphics Besides bringing together tens of thousands of images—from weather maps to nude women to news photos—in more than 30 graphics-oriented forums, the site also features an engine to search these forums (Graphics File Finder), a support forum to pick up graphic viewing programs or ask questions about file formats, and even a listing of other CompuServe forums that have graphics. ✓**COMPUSERVE**→*go* graphics

Graphics Design List (ml) What about modular design? Is that still the rage? And how are *RayGun* and other cutting-edge publications affecting Website design? Discuss a wide variety of graphic design concerns on this mailing list. ✓**INTERNET**→*email* listserv@ulkyvm.louisville.edu ✉ *Type in message body:* subscribe graphics <your full name>

Imaging Resource Center A forum concerning the production of digital images on the PC platform. The resource center is a branch of the PC Graphics forum and includes a direct link to that

180 Net Tech

Creativity in Cyberspace Graphics—Picture This

forum's image and utility libraries. Check out the "Pictures of the World" library, which presents its collection of images on-line. The "Featured Library" is an electronic photo gallery of downloadable image files, with thumbnails of the images displayed alongside text-based descriptions. You'll find an extensive explanation of copyright laws and artists' rights here, as well as advice about scanning and manipulating images. You can also access listings of books, software vendors, and hardware manufacturers. The "Imaging Cafe" area is where you can post questions about specific imaging software and techniques. ✓**AMERICA ONLINE**→*keyword* digitalimaging

Chat

comp.graphics (ng) This newsgroup is dedicated to discussions about computer-generated animations and still images. Topics include QuickTime, Photoshop, and cross-platform translations. Not every single question is answered—hey, this is life, not some sort of Utopian fantasy—but board participants are knowledgeable enough to satisfy most of the perplexed. The most popular discussions concern practical problems—function keys for Mediaplayer, image compression protocols, comparisons between painting programs. One user asked for the name of a drawing tablet that could provide "painterly effects" and received several good recommendations. If Pablo Picasso had been able to join an electronic community like this one, he might have made something of himself. ✓**USENET**

Graphics Besides serving as a trading post for .GIFs (post your request and maybe someone will email you the image you want),

these topics are places to get advice on graphics viewers, find information on scanning and illustration programs such as Corel Draw and Adobe Illustrator, and discuss graphics techniques and approaches. The program Print Artist by Maxis has a steadfast group of followers on the first topic, drawing hundreds of messages every few weeks. ✓**PRODIGY** …→*jump* computer bb→Choose a Topic→Graphics …→*jump* softwaresupportbb→Choose a Topic→Graphics

Graphics Developers Forum And what are they developing? Not MacPaint illustrations or home video scans. Instead, this forum is home to graphics developers working with fractals, 3-D stereo images, POV images, and raytraced images. The boards cover discussions about technique; the library sections are filled with graphics programs and images. ✓**COMPUSERVE**→*go* graphdev

Amiga

Amiga Arts Forum Although not limited to the visual (there's an extensive collection of audio programs and MODs), the forum also carries graphics viewers, computer art, and images uploaded by Amiga users. There are libraries dedicated to 3-D images, nudes, animations, and original art. ✓**COMPUSERVE**→*go* amigaarts

Amiga Graphics Archive You could get lost in here. There's that much stuff. The clip art subdirectory alone has hundreds of images, ranging from Christ to a Mercedes—although none of Christ driving a Mercedes—as well as other subdirectories for animation, Amiga images, fractals, raytraces, icons, and more. And for those looking for more than a pretty picture, the site holds documentation

on several graphic file formats, a large selection of graphic and animation viewers, and guides to and instruction in different computer graphic techniques. ✓**INTERNET**→*www* ftp://www.funet.fi/pub/amiga/graphics/

Amiga Viewers Animation players, .GIF and JPEG viewers, image printers, morphing programs, and other graphic utilities for Amiga users. ✓**INTERNET** …→*www* ftp://www.funet.fi/pub/amiga/hypermedia/hypertext/viewers/ …→*www* ftp://www.funet.fi/pub/amiga/graphics/app/ …→ *www* ftp://ftp.wuarchive.wustl.edu/pub/aminet/gfx/ …→*www* http://src.doc.ic.ac.uk/public/aminet/info/www/dirs/gfx.html

comp.sys.amiga.graphics (ng) If you're working on computer graphics for a rave, you're probably using an Amiga. Although ravers may not notice when a fractal movie isn't doing what it's supposed to do, you will. And given Amiga's ultimate marginality in the overall marketplace, this is definitely one of the few places the small, tight-knit community of Amiga users can find graphics help. You will not find very much

> "The clip art subdirectory alone has hundreds of images, ranging from Christ to a Mercedes—although none of Christ driving a Mercedes."

Net Tech 181

Graphics—Picture This Creativity in Cyberspace

design discussion on this message board, but technical problems are well supported. Most of the postings concern cross-platform translations and system configurations. ✓**USENET**

Apple II

Apple II Art & Graphics Animations are the order of the day in the library. Girls morphing, rockets launching, George Washington smiling, Klingon ships cloaking, and balls bouncing are all available for download. Graphics viewers and images are also here. The message board is used primarily to discuss file formats, viewers, and other graphics software. ✓**COMPUSERVE**→*go* appuser→Libraries *and* Messages→Art & Graphics

Apple II Graphics and Art This AOL forum is dedicated to graphics images on the Apple II series of computers. There are healthy clip art collections and StudioWare stacks from which you can download. In addition, text-based conference transcripts are available in their own separate library. Unfortunately, most of the images here are not categorized in any logical fashion, so you'll have to do a lot of browsing to find the ones you need. If photos of pretty girls are what you're looking for, there seems to be an over abundance of them here. ✓**AMERICA ONLINE**→*keyword* a2→Apple II Software Libraries→Graphics and Art

Atari

Atari Graphics If you've been searching the Net for the animation of two birds chasing each other, then look no further: it's here. But what this directory is really known for is its collection of Atari graphics viewers, animation programs, and graphics utilities. ✓**INTERNET** ...→*www* gopher://gopher.archive.umich.edu:7055/00/atari/Graphics/ ...→*www* ftp://atari.archive.umich.edu/Graphics ...→*www* ftp://wuarchive.wustl.edu/systems/atari/umich.edu/Graphics/

Macintosh

comp.sys.mac.graphics (ng) Are you having problems converting a large image file from PC to Mac? Would you like to know where to find freeware/shareware paint programs? Maybe you just want to know if flatbed scanners work well with 35 mm slides. From Adobe Dimensions to Acrobat, you'll find all your Mac graphics questions answered here. ✓**USENET**

Mac Graphics & Clip Art This AOL file library provides graphics applications and images for the Macintosh environment. The library is divided into three categories: Applications, QuickTime Movies, and Clip Art. Unfortunately, none of the categories stands out. It won't hurt to browse here, but you'd be better off moving on to the more extensive graphics collections elsewhere on AOL. ✓**AMERICA ONLINE**→*keyword* mac500→Graphics & Clip Art

MacChat (ml) Production-oriented graphics professionals who do their business on a Macintosh get lonely sometimes. We all do. But while the rest of us have to suffer the indignities of singles bars and food courts, those lucky production-oriented stiffs have their very own mailing list. Discuss business or new technology, or just say hello to the group: Is that Adobe Illustrator, or are you just happy to see me? ✓**INTERNET**→*email* listserv@ulykvm.louisville.edu ✍ *Type in message body:* subscribe macchat <your full name>

Macintosh Graphics Forum A complete resource for graphic designers using the Macintosh. This AOL forum offers access to extensive software libraries and features a convenient, searchable database. If you have specific questions, you can continue on from here to one of the Special Interest Groups (SIGs), such as "Advertising," "3-D," or "Advanced Color Imaging." You'll find a library of Pagemaker templates here, along with helpful text-based descriptions of standard layouts for brochures, newsletters, and flyers. There are message boards, live conferences, and FAQ files, all related to graphic arts. You can also access the interesting "Pictures of the World" area, which provides a library of digital images for both downloading and viewing online. The "Weekly Forum Update" will keep you posted on the latest forum occurrences and save you time spent browsing through the vast store of information that is available here. ✓**AMERICA ONLINE**→*keyword* mgr

Macintosh Graphics Newsletter What would the Mac be without its graphics? A) A powerful computer without graphics. B) A cereal box. C) The subject of another newsletter. Discover the answer to this perplexing question by subscribing to this electronic journal, which keeps its finger on the pulse of Mac visual tech. ✓**INTERNET**→*email* listserv@vm.temple.edu *Type in message body:* subscribe macchat <your full name>

PC

Graphics Programs This AOL file library features graphics shareware programs for Windows. You'll find banner makers, screen capture programs, and graphics

182 Net Tech

Creativity in Cyberspace Graphics—Picture This

viewers, all ready to download. You'll have to do some browsing, however, because the files are all thrown together in one unorganized listing. ✓**AMERICA ONLINE**→*keyword* winforum→Browse the Software Libraries→Applications→Graphics

PBS Studio Forum Need PC programs to play your animation files? A cheap illustration program to edit images? A program to convert PCX files to .GIF files? How about a morph of Johnny Depp turning into Kate Moss? Or a collection of gun clip art? Although the library is not incredibly large, it's worth checking out. ✓**COMPUSERVE**→*go* pbsstudio

PC Graphics Forum Resources and information about CAD, desktop publishing, 3-D modeling, and image scanning in the PC environment. The "Weekly Forum News" update keeps you posted on contest descriptions, file updates, and special events. You'll find a "Graphics Help & Info" area, along with diverse message boards and a "Resource Center" to answer your graphics questions. The "Company Support" center gives you a direct connection to graphics software and hardware manufacturers. Graphics viewing programs can be obtained from the "Recommended Utilities" library, and you can also participate in live conferences about CAD, animation, or general graphic arts almost every night of the week. This is a thorough and useful forum. ✓**AMERICA ONLINE**→*keyword* pcgraphics

SimTel DOS Graphics Viewers Whether you need to convert a JPEG to a .GIF, view PCX files, view BMP files, change image sizes to thumbnails, or convert text screens to PCX files, there is a DOS program here for you. ✓**INTERNET** …→*www* http://www.acs.oakland.edu/oak/SimTel/win3/graphics.html …→*www* ftp://oak.oakland.edu/SimTel/msdos/graphics …→*www* ftp://wuarchive.wustl.edu/systems/ibmpc/simtel/msdos/graphics …→*www* ftp://ftp.uoknor.edu/mirrors/SimTel/msdos/graphics …→*www* ftp://ftp.uni-paderborn.de/SimTel/msdos/graphics

SimTel Windows Graphics Viewers Graphics utilities and viewers for Windows users dying to see uploaded pictures of their favorite bands, porn stars, and IRC friends. ✓**INTERNET** …→*www* http://www.acs.oakland.edu/oak/SimTel/win3/graphics.html …→*www* ftp://oak.oakland.edu/SimTel/win3/graphics …→*www* ftp://wuarchive.wustl.edu/systems/ibmpc/simtel/win3/graphics …→*www* ftp://ftp.uoknor.edu/mirrors/SimTel/win3/graphics …→*www* ftp://ftp.uni-paderborn.de/SimTel/win3/graphics

Windows Graphics & Clip Art A small collection of graphics programs and utilities for Windows. The choices are limited, but they are all top-quality selections. Most of the utilities listed under "Graphics & Clip Art" are for manipulating your Wallpaper images, but the most popular download is

The Last Judgment—from http://www.christusrex.org/www1/sistine/

Graphics—Picture This Creativity in Cyberspace

a freeware CAD program. Under the "Icons" listing you'll find utilities for manipulating icons and installing them onto your desktop, along with an icon library. ✓**AMERICA ONLINE**→*keyword* win500→Windows 500 Shareware Libraries→Graphics & Clip Art→Art *and* Icons

Windows Magazine Pictures & Icons This AOL file library provides graphics images for Windows-based computers. The diverse collection of images includes the Presidential Seal, a photo of the Grand Canyon, and a portrait of a polar bear. The images are not organized in any convenient way, so you might prefer searching by keyword if you know exactly what you want. If you're browsing, many of the text-based file descriptions are accompanied by a helpful thumbnail representation of the image. ✓**AMERICA ONLINE**→*keyword* winmag→Software Libraries→Pictures & Icons

Silicon Graphics

comp.sys.sgi.graphics (ng) This newsgroup discusses general topics concerning the Silicon Graphics computer system. Postings refer to file format conversions (.GIF, MPEG, RGB, etc.), camera orientations, and alpha channel manipulation. The discussion is not too technical, so novice users should feel comfortable posting questions here. One beginner asked how to do texture mapping and received some patient responses from other members of the group. ✓**USENET**

Silicon Surf They're the Ferraris of the desktop computing world: fast and powerful machines coveted by designers and graphic artists around the world. They're Silicon Graphics computers, and this

Silicon Graphics poster—downloaded from http://www.sgi.com/fun/free/

Website not only provides product information about and support for SGI's hardware, software, and other products, it also maintains a "Serious Fun" section which links to a movies and animation theater, an image gallery, graphics newsletters, and "cool freeware." And, yes, it's a lot of fun. ✓**INTERNET**→*www* http://www.sgi.com/

Viewing programs

alt.binaries.pictures.utilities (ng) This newsgroup includes discussions about graphics viewers and utilities. The postings are mostly requests for information, and do not delve into technical jargon. If you're having trouble locating a graphics tool, it's worth your while to log on here. ✓**USENET**

alt.graphics.pixutils (ng) A lightly visited newsgroup concerning image editors, file converters, and other graphics utilities. ✓**USENET**

Graphics Support Forum Frus-

Creativity in Cyberspace Graphics—Picture This

trated that your decoder program won't turn that alphanumeric jumble into a picture of Drew Barrymore? Burning with indignation because your graphic-designer boyfriend won't explain the difference between .GIFs and JPEGs? This forum offers a message board for posting questions about viewing, downloading, converting, and printing graphics. Richard wants "to download a good viewer/converter that handles JPEG, .GIF, and BMP formats (at least) via a Windows interface." "Graphic Workshop," recommends Steve. "Vueprint 3.6," suggests Michael. "ThumbsPlus," pipes in Laura. That was simple. Next? "I'm looking for a full-color scanner to make .GIFs, doesn't need to be a full size as I make many from snap-shot size photos. Looking for something under $500 and I need it to be easy to use, from scan to finished .GIF." Here come the responses… ✓**COMPUSERVE**→*go* graphsup

Graphics Viewers, Editors, Utilities and Info One-stop shopping (except there are no charges) for graphics viewers and related utilities. Want a file explaining file formats? A .GIF viewer? A JPEG viewer? A program that converts JPEGs to .GIFs? A TIFF file program? A QuickTime to MPEG converter? A morphing program? Heavily oriented toward Windows and DOS systems, the site brings the most commonly used graphics programs together on one page. Links to pages with compression and audio utilities are also featured. ✓**INTERNET**→*www* http://www2.ncsu.edu/bae/people/faculty/walker/hotlist/graphics.html

JPEG Image Compression FAQ How do you fit a mountain of images onto your CD-ROM and leave room for music, film, and other assorted multimedia effects? With JPEG, you can compress image files and save memory space. Find out when to use .GIFs and when to use JPEG. ✓**INTERNET**→*www* http://www.cis.ohio-state.edu/hypertext/faq/usenet/jpeg-faq/faq.html

JPEGView A small forum dedicated to the Macintosh graphics viewer that supports JPEGs, PICTs, and .GIFs. Ask questions on the message board ("I can't create new previews anymore.…I used to be able to by clicking the create button, but now it is permanently dimmed, even for files which already have the previews. Help…") or download the latest version of the viewer from the library. ✓**AMERICA ONLINE**→*keyword* jpegview

JPEGView Page Every Mac user should have a JPEG viewer. It's standard fare and this site includes three versions of the latest release of JPEGView—one that runs on standard Macs, another that runs native on PowerPCs, and another that runs on both. ✓**INTERNET**→*www* http://guru.med.cornell.edu/jpegview.html

NIH An archive of images, documentation, Photoshop plug-ins, code, spin-off programs, and copies of the NIH image program itself. What is NIH? It's a public-domain image processing and analysis program for the Mac. ✓**INTERNET**→*www* ftp://zippy.nimh.nih.gov/pub/nih-image/

Viewer Resource Center This is a convenient file library on AOL containing programs and utilities for viewing graphics files and animations. You'll find decoders, translators, and viewers for practically every graphics file type, from

---

CYBERNOTES

"Graphic Formats:

BMP (Bitmap Image File) format, used in Microsoft Windows and OS/2 applications.

PCX file format, used in DOS applications.

TGA (Targa) format, used by many IBM systems that use the Truevision video boards.

ILBM (Interchange File Format), used by the Commodore Amiga.

PICT format, used by Macintosh applications as a common format for importing and exporting graphics.

TIFF or **GIF** format, used when moving graphics from one computer platform to another.

JPEG (Joint Photographic Experts Group compressed file), one popular 'lossy' graphic format used on all computer platforms. JPEG compression economizes data storage and also identifies and discards 'extra' data, that is, information beyond what the human eye can see."

—from **Digital Media Research & Development Center**

Graphics—Picture This Creativity in Cyberspace

JPEG to .GIF. The library is divided into Macintosh and Windows/DOS viewers, to make your search a little easier. A nice feature of this forum is the collection of information files explaining topics such as Wallpapers, Startup Screens, and the PICT file format. ✓**AMERICA ONLINE**→*keyword* viewers

Image compression

Image Compression Information Simple explanations of image dimensions and compression formats such as JPEG and .GIF. While the text is written for users of the OTIS art gallery, the information is relevant to anyone looking for basic image-compression info. ✓**INTERNET**→*www* http://sunsite.unc.edu/otis/notes/otis-compression.html

Adobe

Adobe Applications Forum When you're talking Adobe, you're talking Illustrator, Photoshop, and Persuasion. And when you're talking Adobe, you're also talking Aldus, especially now that the two companies have merged. Discuss the finer points of Freehand—or point out the peccadillos of PageMaker—in the Adobe forum, which not only hosts Adobe chat but also offers free downloads of programs like Acrobat. ✓**COMPUSERVE**→*go* adobea

Adobe Illustrator SIG A branch of the Mac Graphics & CAD forum on AOL, this Special Interest Group (SIG) is devoted to Adobe Illustrator drawing software. You can post questions here about the various versions of Illustrator, or look for a product review. Adobe is not involved with this SIG, so there is no direct connection to the company's message boards. However, you can find chat logs in the Tools Library and sample drawings in the Images Library. This is a good place for a beginner to turn to for Illustrator information. ✓**AMERICA ONLINE**→*keyword* illustrator

Adobe Illustrator (ml) Discussion list for users of Adobe Illustrator that covers all topics, from color extensions to compatibility with other popular graphics software. ✓**INTERNET**→*email* listserv@netcom ✍ *Type in message body:* subscribe illusrtr-l <your full name>

Adobe Photoshop Mailing List (ml) Discussion list for users of Adobe Photoshop. ✓**INTERNET**→*email* listserv@bgu.edu ✍ *Type in message body:* subscribe photoshop <your full name>

Adobe Photoshop & Premiere (ml) For discussion of both Photoshop and Premiere. ✓**INTERNET**→*email* listserv@wsuvm1.csc.wsu.edu ✍ *Type in message body:* subscribe adobeps <your full name>

Adobe Systems A promotional Website featuring information about Adobe Systems software. You can locate technical support phone numbers, software patches,

> "Discuss the finer points of Freehand—or point out the peccadillos of PageMaker—in the Adobe forum."

and application updates. There's also an Acrobat reader available for downloading. The FTP site is thin, featuring some downloadable text files but little else of interest to the Adobe consumer. ✓**INTERNET**...→*www* http://www.adobe.com/ ...→*www* ftp://ftp.adobe.com

Adobe Systems, Inc. This AOL area is a resource for users of Adobe Systems software, on both Macintosh and PC platforms. There are direct links to Special Interest Groups (SIGs) on AOL pertaining to CoSA, Illustrator, and Photoshop. If you visit the Adobe Support Center you'll find pertinent press releases, message boards, and software libraries. The message boards are moderated by representatives of Adobe, and are conveniently categorized by product. And if you're worrying that you might have to leave the area without free downloads, never fear—the software libraries offer a full complement of upgrades, patches, and plug-ins. ✓**AMERICA ONLINE**→*keyword* adobe

Graphic Art Using Photoshop This Website is an electronic photography gallery. There is no information here, just a small collection of Photoshop-created and -enhanced images to view. ✓**INTERNET**→*www* http://www.interport.net/~rexalot/renee.index.html

The Photoshop Archive The next time you take a bad photograph, don't just sit on the steps of your house weeping like a baby. Learn to smooth over your errors and create a better product with the magic of computer technology. This archive contains a wealth of extensions, updates, programming guides, and other info files (tricks for managing fonts, creating a fog effect, reducing graininess, etc.) related to Photoshop. ✓**INTERNET**→

Creativity in Cyberspace Graphics—Picture This

www ftp://export.acs.cmu.edu/pub/PSarch/

Photoshop SIG This AOL Special Interest Group (SIG) is dedicated to Photoshop. You'll find an extensive message board here, with a diverse selection of discussion topics. The software libraries offer Photoshop add-ons, filters, and image manipulation tools. There's also a library of sample illustrations, in case you're interested in what other users are creating. You can also download "KAI's Power Tips," a helpful collection of illustrated text files with advanced Photoshop drawing tricks and techniques. The SIG hosts live Photoshop conference chats every Tuesday at 10:30 p.m. EST in the Mac Graphics & CAD Conference Hall. ✓**AMERICA ONLINE**→*keyword* photoshop

Corel

Corel Applications Forum
Technical support and discussion areas for all Corel products, including CorelDRAW! and Corel-PHOTO-PAINT. ✓**COMPUSERVE**→*go* corel

Corel Ventura Forum
Technical support and software libraries for users of CorelVentura, CorelDraw and VenturaPublisher. Corel customer newsletters are posted to the General Interest library by the Corel Corporation on a monthly basis—they're a great resource for keeping up to date on product upgrades and other company innovations. Plus you can download style sheets and other add-on applications for use within various Corel design programs. Post your technical support queries on the appropriate message board and a Corel sysop will get back to you with answers. ✓**COMPUSERVE**→*go* ventura

The Mask—downloaded from America Online's Hollywood Online

CorelDRAW Resource Center
This AOL forum is dedicated to the CorelDRAW PC-based graphics program. There are direct links to the Desktop Publishing and PC Graphics forums if you want more general information. What you'll find here is a nicely organized "News & Tips" area, well-populated message boards, and categorized software libraries. The software categories include Utilities, Drivers, and Fonts. The "Designs On-line" area can give you the standard specifications for brochures, flyers, and newsletters. There's chat every Thursday night at 9:30 p.m. EST in the Conference Room of the PC Graphics & Animation Forum on AOL. ✓**AMERICA ONLINE**→*keyword* corel

Claris

ClarisDraw and ClarisImpact
A well-organized forum on America Online concerning the Claris Corporation and its products. Even if you don't use Claris software, you ought to visit this area just to experience a truly user-friendly environment. Each category is conveniently divided into folders, providing pertinent information about Claris products. The message boards are monitored by Claris representatives and are uniquely designed to cut down on time-consuming browsing. There is a "Tech Info Database" that allows you to search for technical information by keyword, and a customer service area for direct queries. The software libraries contain useful files and templates, organized by product. There's even a suggestion box, and after visiting this friendly forum, you'll believe that Claris actually listens to customer input. ✓**AMERICA ONLINE**→*keyword* claris

Print Artist

Print Artist Resource Center
This is a promotional area for Maxis' Print Artist and Instant Artist graphics software. Users can download FAQs, clip art collections, and TrueType fonts. There are also Question & Answer message boards and a "Tips and Hints" area. ✓**AMERICA ONLINE**→*keyword* printartist

Other programs

Imagine (ml) "Imagine there's a graphics package / It's easy if you try / Equipped with 3-D rendering capability / Tailored for Amiga and MS-DOS machines." Not as catchy as Lennon's original, perhaps, but no less compelling—es-

Net Tech 187

Graphics—Picture This Creativity in Cyberspace

pecially if you're a professional artist or graphic-effects buff looking for a friendly community of the similarly obsessed. ✓**INTERNET**→*email* imagine-request@email.sp.paramax.com ✎ *Type in subject line:* subscribe

Lexicor Graphics Support List Atari computers may not exactly be industry leaders, but they do have an edge on the competition when it comes to fancy graphics, animation, and VDI programming. The Lexicor list gives fans of the graphically powerful Atari processor a place to discuss their visual needs. ✓**INTERNET**→*email* lexicor-list-request@lexicor.com ✎ *Type in message body:* subscribe <your email address>

Vendors

Computer Graphics and Visualization An annotated list of links to computer graphics organizations and commercial sites, including Web pages for Wavefront Technologies and ACM SIGGRAPH's home page. ✓**INTERNET**→*www* http://www.dataspace.com/WWW/vlib/comp-graphics.html

Graphics Vendor Forums Grasp, STB, Jovian, RIX Softworks, Big_D, Digital Vision, Genus, Pacific Motion, Metagraphics, TEGL, VRLI Inc., Inset Systems, and ATI Technologies are all graphics companies offering support and product information in this forum. ✓**COMPUSERVE**→*go* graphvena

CAD/CAM

alt.cad (ng) This message board is dedicated to general topics concerning CAD software. The majority of the postings here are from newsgroup readers asking where they should post their problems, and as a result discussion tends to be somewhat limited in scope. ✓**USENET**

Autodesk AutoCAD Forum For all your electronic drafting, rendering, and modeling needs, this forum offers message boards and libraries containing text support and shareware for the popular AutoCAD computer-aided design program. Are you stuck trying to create architectural site models on your PC? Simply pop into the Modeling message board and air your query. If you can't wait for a reply, the conference room usually has a few people hanging around—try asking one of them for instant help. Visit the jargon-heavy, technical-oriented message boards here and get tech support from Autodesk staff or other knowledgeable experts. Stick around here long enough and you could become the next I.M. Pei. This forum also offers assistance on AutoCAD-related programs including AutoLISP, AutoSHADE and AutoFLIX. ✓**COMPUSERVE**→*go* acad

Autodesk Multimedia Forum Forum for questions pertaining to Autodesk's Multimedia products, including Autodesk 3D Studio, Autodesk Animator and Animator Pro, Autodesk Multimedia Explorer and Autodesk's Science Series products, CA Lab and Chaos. And break out those funny glasses—the software library contains a huge selection of 3-D and animated image files for downloading. ✓**COMPUSERVE**→*go* asoft

CAD Resource Center This forum is the main AOL resource area for PC-based CAD. A large percentage of files and messages found here pertain to AutoCAD, but other PC-based CAD programs are represented as well. In fact, there is an "Applications" folder which offers a good selection of drawing shareware. You'll also find libraries for drawing utilities, 3-D models, and even background textures. There is an "Industry Connection" area and a "News & Reviews" feature with the latest press releases and news reports concerning CAD. If you want immediate information, you can attend the weekly CAD Conference here each Wednesday night at 9:30 p.m. EST. ✓**AMERICA ONLINE**→*keyword* cad

CAD/Draw/Plot/Engnr A collection of computer-aided design programs for Windows users, including flowchart diagramming programs, illustration programs, mapping programs, and graph builders. ✓**COMPUSERVE**→*go* winshare→Libraries→CAD/Draw/Plot/Engnr

comp.cad.autocad/alt.cad.autocad (ng) These are the newsgroups to turn to with specific questions about using AutoCAD software. The postings refer to printer drivers, software upgrades and 3-D object rotation, to name a few of the topics. You'll also find references to more general CAD subject matter, such as .DXF file specifications, .DWG graphics viewers and even some discussion about room scheduling software. ✓**USENET**

comp.cad.cadence (ng) This newsgroup is dedicated to the discussion of Cadence Design Systems products. ✓**USENET**

comp.cad.compass (ng) A lightly visited newsgroup pertaining to Compass Design Automation EDA tools. ✓**USENET**

comp.cad.pro-engineer (ng) A

188 Net Tech

Creativity in Cyberspace Graphics—Picture This

meeting place for users of Parametric Technology's Pro/Engineer software. ✓**USENET**

comp.cad.synthesis (ng) If you're always delighting your friends with lengthy monologues about "finite state machines" or "fault grading verilog sources," then this is the perfect newsgroup for you. It's dedicated to discussing research and production in the field of logic synthesis. And your friends will be thrilled beyond compare to hear that you've found a way to replenish your scintillating conversational skills.. ✓**USENET**

Raytrace & rendering

3D Rendering Resource Center Visit this AOL forum to discuss 3-D modeling techniques and resources. This area appears to be designed more for the home user than the professional modeler or animator. There's a lot of information here about POV-Trace, a freeware raytrace package. Commercial programs such as Playmation, Silicon Graphics, and Raydream Designer are also represented in the message boards. Nevertheless, the "Industry Connection" seems rather incomplete, with some major omissions. Still, there are useful libraries of textures, 3-D models and utilities, as well as an extensive collection of finished images and animations. The "News & Reviews" board will give you the latest information on modeling packages. ✓**AMERICA ONLINE**→ *keyword* 3d

comp.graphics.raytracing (ng) A well-populated newsgroup on 3-D modeling and rendering. There's a healthy exchange of information here, with postings ranging from lightbulb design to fractal landscape generators. 3-D

experts will enjoy jumping into the conversation, but novices might be better off browsing. ✓**USENET**

comp.graphics.rendering. renderman (ng) This newsgroup serves as a meeting place for users of the Renderman graphics interface and shading language, and while it's not the most popular place in town, it does deliver a steady stream of useful information for those proficient in the software. If you're a fan of Renderman, it's worth an occasional visit. ✓**USENET**

Other graphics

comp.graphics.avs (ng) This programmers' conference deals with problems relating to the Application Visualization System (AVS). ✓**USENET**

comp.graphics.data-explorer (ng) For users of IBM's Visualization Data Explorer, also known as DX. ✓**USENET**

comp.graphics.explorer (ng) Dedicated to the Explorer Modular Visualization Environment (MVE). ✓**USENET**

comp.graphics.gnuplot (ng) A message board pertaining to the GNUPLOT interactive function plotter. ✓**USENET**

comp.graphics.opengl (ng) A newsgroup for users of the OpenGL 3-D application programming interface. A good number of the postings here have been answered. ✓**USENET**

comp.graphics.visualization (ng) A highly technical newsgroup concerning scientific visualization and modeling tools. ✓**USENET**

Graphics Newsgroups

alt.binaries.pictures
alt.binaries.pictures.d
alt.binaries.pictures.misc
ARCHIVE:
  http://web.cnam.fr/
  Images/Usenet/abpm/
  summaries/
alt.binaries.pictures.animals
alt.binaries.pictures.anime
alt.binaries.pictures.ascii
alt.binaries.pictures.astro
alt.binaries.pictures.bruce-lloyd
alt.binaries.pictures.cartoons
alt.binaries.pictures.celebrities
alt.binaries.pictures.erotica
alt.binaries.pictures.erotica.
  amateur.female
alt.binaries.pictures.erotica.anime
alt.binaries.pictures.
  erotica.bestiality
alt.binaries.pictures.erotica.
  blondes
alt.binaries.pictures.erotica.
  bondage
alt.binaries.pictures.erotica.
  breasts
alt.binaries.pictures.erotica.
  cartoons
alt.binaries.pictures.erotica.d
alt.binaries.pictures.erotica.female
alt.binaries.pictures.erotica.fetish
alt.binaries.pictures.erotica.furry
alt.binaries.pictures.erotica.male
alt.binaries.pictures.erotica.
  orientals
alt.binaries.pictures.fine-art.d
alt.binaries.pictures.fine-art.
  digitized
alt.binaries.pictures.fine-art.
  graphics
alt.binaries.pictures.fractals
alt.binaries.pictures.furry
alt.binaries.pictures.girlfriends
alt.binaries.pictures.nudism
alt.binaries.pictures.supermodels
alt.binaries.pictures.tasteless
alt.binaries.pictures.vehicles
alt.binaries.startrek

Graphics—Picture This Creativity in Cyberspace

Graphics Sites

Across the board

Delft Digital Picture Archive If your multimedia project needs generic pictures of landscapes, animals, cars, or Bilbo Baggins, check out this server. Besides saving money on a stock photography house's fee—all pictures available here are taken from Usenet files and are copyright-free—you can try to enter the list of top 50 horny geeks (for those who can't get enough porn pictures), compiled from the server's automatic log. ✓**INTERNET**→*www* http://olt.et.tudelft.nl/fun/pictures/pictures.html

GIFs at UIUC A large collection of photos of the Civil War, *Jurassic Park*, Beavis and Butt-head, Escher's work, animals, movies, *Star Trek*, space (what we've seen prior to the 23rd century), and more. ✓**INTERNET**→*www* http://www.acm.uiuc.edu:80/rml/Gifs/

Kodak Sample Digital Images The Palace at Versailles and the Vancouver skyline, Yellowstone National Park and Bora Bora, and a koala bear and a piggy bank are just a few of the amazing shots available for download from this site advertising Kodak products. ✓**INTERNET**→*www* http://www.kodak.com/digitalImages/samples/samples.shtml

Photos to Go A vast archive of downloadable .GIF and JPEG files that puts a variety of photographic images right at your fingertips. Search the database by typing in any combination of keywords, categories, orientation, or file type relevant to the photo you are looking for, and Photos to Go will display a list of selected photos. You can view thumbnail images free of charge, but any retrieved full-size images will cost you. ✓**COMPUSERVE**→*go* pho-60

Sunet Pictures Looking for a picture of a Pentium or a penny? Actress Katherine Hepburn or physicist Werner Heisenberg? Infant skeletons or the Beatles? Another one of those amazingly rich (and large) collections of images on the Net. Picture categories range from advertisements to historical photos to maps to musicians to raytrace-images to sports to vehicles. ✓**INTERNET**→*www* ftp://ftp.sunet.se/pub/pictures/

Archive Photos Forum This forum, run by a large historical stock photo house, has a selection of pictures of famous figures not easily found elsewhere on the Net. Photos of Miles Davis, Casey Stengel, Elie Wiesel, William Burroughs, and Maya Angelou are just a few of the images you can download for non-commercial home use. ✓**COMPUSERVE**→*go* archive

Graphics Corner Forum Space, vehicles, nature and landscape, pretty women, and more pretty women in less clothing. ✓**COMPUSERVE**→*go* corner→Libraries

Graphics File Finder A powerful tool to search more than 30 picture libraries on CompuServe. This does not search many of the non-graphics-oriented forums (e.g., *Sports Illustrated*) where a wealth of pictures may be found. ✓**COMPUSERVE**→*go* graphicsff

Graphics Gallery Forum What do the Smithsonian, U.S. tourism agencies, and the Wisconsin Historical Society have in common? They've all added to the image collection in these libraries divided into America-oriented topics like the Civil War, Smithsonian Art, NASA, and America (South). ✓**COMPUSERVE**→*go* gallery →Libraries

Graphics Plus Forum The capital building in Pierre, South Dakota, has only had seven downloads from this forum, while captivating Julie in a white bikini has garnered 5,004. Go figure. With a range of images similar to the Graphics Plus Forum (cartoons and fantasy/sci-fi also have sections), the Body Beautiful and Plain Brown Wrapper sections are the big draws here. ✓**COMPUSERVE**→*go* graphplus→Libraries

Photo Gallery Forum CompuServe photographers have uploaded thousands of photos to the libraries here. They've been divided into sections like Birds, Animals, Sports, Seascapes, City Scenes, Still Life, etc. Despite the more arty names of the three "Human Form" library sections, nude women on motorcycles or bikini-wearing "dolls" at the beach are the standard photo fare here. ✓**COMPUSERVE**→*go* photogallery→Libraries

Planet Earth's Images, Icons and Flags Imagine a world where all images were digitized and at your disposal. Planet Earth's site may be the closest you'll get. And what exactly does this virtual paradise offer? Well, it offers gateways (known on the Net as links) to pictures of Japan,

Creativity in Cyberspace Graphics—Picture This

Graphics Sites (cont'd)

space imagery, the Smithsonian Image Archive, flag archives, movie and video imagery, weather images, icons galore, and travel photos. Shall we continue? ✓**INTERNET**→*www* http://www.nosc.mil/planet_earth/images.html

Quick Pictures Forum More than 20,000 CompuServe members downloaded a picture of adult film star Nina Hartley from this forum, where the pictures in Body Beautiful and Plain Brown Wrapper are slightly racier than in the other forums. Ahh, and those sections devoted to cartoons, landmarks, and vehicles are here too. ✓**COMPUSERVE**→*go* qpics→Libraries

The Stock Solution More than 200,000 images strong, this stock photo house has gone online with a searchable database of 200 images. Need a shot of a child eating a watermelon or schoolchildren studying? How about Victorian angels or 19th-century dentistry? ✓**INTERNET**→*www* http://www.xmission.com/~tssphoto/

Sunsite Pictures An eclectic mix of images, with entire subdirectories for old computers, scenes of Israeli and Jewish life, travel photos of Asia, images from the Library of Congress Vatican exhibit, and the OTIS online art gallery. ✓**INTERNET**→*www* file://sunsite.unc.edu/pub/multimedia/pictures/

Wuarchive Graphics Archive The mother of all graphics archives resides at Washington University—and good luck getting in. But if you're looking for a picture (musician? dragon? swimsuit model?) and it's online, it's probably here. Each letter of the alphabet is its own subdirectory filled with images. ✓**INTERNET** …→*www* ftp://wuarchive.wustl.edu/multimedia/images/gif/ …→*www* ftp://wuarchive.wustl.edu/multimedia/images/jpeg/

Wuarchive Image Finder A search engine for the image collection stored at Wuarchive. ✓**INTERNET** …→*www* http://www.cm.cf.ac.uk/htbin/RobH/Images/check_query.pl …→*www* http://wuecon.wustl.edu/other_www/wuarchimage.html

ASCII

ASCII Art Bizarre Fonts, logos, drawings, illustrated stories, maps, and other artworks. Fans of flesh will be sorry to learn that the UAB brass has placed its nudes under lock and key. ✓**INTERNET**→*www* gopher://twinbrook.cis.uab.edu:70/1asciiarc.70

Scarecrow's WWW Link Interested in ASCII art, that art form employing 9-point courier text and a dark screen with bright text? Start with the ASCII Art FAQ and then explore the Scarecrow's own archives—a huge collection of ASCII art created by perhaps the most famous ASCII artist on the Net. ✓**INTERNET**→*www* http://gagme.wwa.com/~boba/scarecrow.html

Net artists

Art on the Net A virtual gallery, with exhibits curated by participating artists. Work changes regularly, but if you're lucky, you may find a painting, sculpture, or photograph that turns your heart into a smoking puddle of love. And don't forget to download soundbytes of artists explaining their works. ✓**INTERNET**→*www* http://www.art.net/

The FineArt Forum Gallery An electronic gallery featuring collections of works by several artists. ✓**INTERNET**→*www* http://www.msstate.edu/Fineart_Online/gallery.html

OTIS The site's acronym-name stands for "Operative Term is Stimulate," and if thousands of images (original works by Net artists) and dozens of links (from the first address) to other arty Net sites don't do the job, maybe you're dead. ✓**INTERNET** …→*www* http://sunsite.unc.edu/otis/otis.html …→*www* ftp://sunsite.unc.edu/pub/multimedia/pictures/OTIS/

Fine art

ArtServe Rubens was almost as prolific as the Net itself, and this page—housed on a server bearing his name—carries on his legacy quite nicely. Overseen by the Australian National University, this art history collection offers access to more than 10,000 images—paintings, prints, architectural photographs, and even a small selection of Islamic monuments. ✓**INTERNET**→*www* http://rubens.anu.edu.au/

Cappella Sistina: the Extended Tour Can you imagine downloading images of the entire Sistine Chapel ceiling and Michelangelo's Last Judgment mural? The site carries more than 300 JPEGs that allow you to do just that. ✓**INTERNET**→*www* http://www.

Graphics—Picture This Creativity in Cyberspace

Graphics Sites (cont'd)

christusrex.org/www1/sistine/0-Tour.html

Dallas Museum of Art Online An electronic guide to the Dallas Museum of Art that includes tours through galleries, bibliographic information, and images. ✓**INTERNET**→*www* http://www.unt.edu/dfw/dma/www/dma.htm

The Escher Gallery Challenge your grasp on reality in this large archive of Escher's work. ✓**INTERNET**→*www* http://www.umich.edu:80/~mransfrd/escher/

Fine Art Forum The libraries feature images of several different forms of art, including sections on Native American art, portraits, modern art, and classical art. ✓**COMPUSERVE**→*go* fineart→Libraries

Leonardo da Vinci Museum The Mona Lisa, of course, and a small collection of other works by da Vinci. ✓**INTERNET**→*www* http://www.leonardo.net/main.html

Monet: the Cyberspace Gallery Dozens of digital reproductions (in JPEG format) of paintings by the famous Impressionist Claude Monet. ✓**INTERNET**→*www* http://magic-box.resnet.cornell.edu/howard/monet.html

The Vatican Exhibit An exhibit about the rebirth of Rome produced by the Library of Congress. Besides huge JPEG images, the exhibit includes extensive descriptions. ✓**INTERNET** ...→*www* http://sunsite.unc.edu/expo/vatican.exhibit/Vatican.exhibit.html ...→*www* file://sunsite.unc.edu/pub/multimedia/pictures/vatican_archives/exhibit

The WebMuseum Network Take an historical tour of Paris. Visit the Famous Paintings exhibition (Baroque, Revolution and Restoration, Impressionism, and Cubism to Abstract Art are the themes). Or view the collection of images from the calendar section of the Très Riches Heures. ✓**INTERNET**→*www* http://mistral.enst.fr/wm/net/

World Arts Resources An impressive effort by The Ohio State University at Newark to compile links to all visual arts information on the Net. Presently, the site links to more than 170 official museums (Luxembourg's National Museum of Art and History, the Online Museum of Singapore Art & History, the National Gallery, etc.), 160 art galleries and exhibitions, 30 art publications, commercial arts resources, antiques catalogs, and more. ✓**INTERNET**→*www* http://www.cgrg.ohio-state.edu/Newark/artsres.html

Pop culture

Classic Movie Posters Posters for the sci-fi, horror, and film noir movie genres. *Double Indemnity, Key Largo, The Maltese Falcon, Frankenstein,* and *Forbidden Planet* are all here. All posters are in JPEG format. ✓**INTERNET**→*www* http://www.best.com/~caddy/posters.html

OscarNet Pictures and sound from Academy Award nominations and winners. Get pictures of Forrest Gump and Bubba, Andie MacDowell in her wedding dress in *Four Weddings and a Funeral,* Susan Sarandon in *The Client,* Travolta and Thurman dancing in *Pulp Fiction,* and more. ✓**INTERNET**→*www* http://ddv.com/Oscarnet/

Sly Stone—Images of the Past Everybody is a star, but Sly's a bigger star. Why? Slurred vocals, outrageous fashions, and a complete mastery of funk. Put a little tickle on the Joneses' head, and visit this archive of classic Sly photos, which follow the erstwhile Mr. Stewart through his days in the spotlight. ✓**INTERNET**→*www* http://www.pathfinder.com/vibe/archive/june94/docs/sly_images.html

Star Trek Pictures *Star Trek* pictures have reached the far corners of the Net, with Kirk, Picard, Dax, and Data surfacing as .GIFs, JPEGs, and screensavers. These are just a few of the big sites carrying images. ✓**INTERNET** ...→*www* http://www.ugcs.caltech.edu/~werdna/sttng/ ...→*www* http://www.ftms.com/vidiot/ ...→*www* ftp://ftp.cis.ksu.edu/pub/pictures/jpg/Startrek ...→*www* ftp://lajkonik.cyfkr.edu.pl/agh/reserve/gifs/startrek ...→*www* ftp://Danann.hea.ie/pub/mirrors/funet-pics/tv+film/StarTrek

Erotic

Erotic Photography Index Take a peek at the fine art of erotic photography. ✓**INTERNET**→*www* http://www.mcs.com/~rune/EroticPhotographyIndex.html

Glamour Paintings and Illustrations Predominantly scantily-clothed women. ✓**COMPUSERVE**→*go* macfun→Libraries→Glamour Paintings *and* Illustrations

192 Net Tech

Creativity in Cyberspace Graphics—Picture This

Graphics Sites (cont'd)

Jef's Nude of the Month A new woman every month. Also links to other erotic image archives. ✓ INTERNET→*www* http://www.well.com/user/jef/nude.html

Nude Images Lots of nude women. ✓ INTERNET→*www* http://www.drag.net:80/images/nudes/

Nude Pictures of Women The name may lack subtlety, but there's no false advertising going on here. This is why your mother didn't want you online. ✓ INTERNET→*www* http://www.umich.edu/~schauber/xxx-nude.html

Penthouse Internet The cover is here and maybe that's enough… ✓ INTERNET→*www* http://www.penthousemag.com/

Playboy Playboy isn't giving it all away, but there are pictures and profiles of the playmates. ✓ INTERNET→*www* http://www.playboy.com/

X-Rated Star Trek Archive Houses roughly two dozen topless shots of Trek women. ✓ INTERNET→*www* ftp://ftp.netcom.com/pub/ev/evansc/pictures

Science

Colorado State Entomology Bugs everywhere! Your source for bug pictures. ✓ INTERNET→*www* http://www.colostate.edu/Depts/Entomology/ent.html#photographs

Bizarre

Lemur Gallery For all your cute, cuddly, marsupial needs, head to this gallery of lemur cheesecake poses. ✓ INTERNET→*www* http://lemur.Stanford.EDU:80/lemurs/

UFO Images This image archive lets you decide. It is a spaceship or a pie plate suspended from an apple tree? Real images of aliens, greys, and crop circles are also online here. ✓ INTERNET→*www* ftp://phoenix.oulu.fi/pub/ufo_and_space_pics/

Horror

Grotesque in Art An exhibit focusing on the anxieties of man—disturbing images depicting fear, paranoia, madness, war, sex, and torture. ✓ INTERNET→*www* http://www.ugcs.caltech.edu/~werdna/grotesque/grotesque.html

Horror Graphics Archive For all your Christmas-card needs, download those unforgettable images: Carrie at the prom and Freddy Kruger after a visit to the manicurist. And don't forget the original *Psycho* movie poster. ✓ INTERNET→*www* http://www.ee.pdx.edu/~caseyh/horror/pics/graphics.html

Space

Astronomy Pretty Pictures An image map of 60 space shots. Just click on a traveling comet or Venus and, voilà, a large image you can download. ✓ INTERNET→*www* http://www.astro.uva.nl/mooie_gifjes/index.html

Space Images at Indiana University Lots and lots of space images. ✓ INTERNET→*www* gopher://enif.astro.indiana.edu:70/11/images

Travel

Art Crimes: The Writing on the Wall Fabulous images of graffiti from cities around the world—from Prague to Bridgeport, CT. ✓ INTERNET→*www* http://www.gatech.edu/graf/index/Index.Art_Crimes.html

Travels with Samantha Photo-heavy online book (215 pages) about an expedition through North America. Gorgeous photos. ✓ INTERNET→*www* http://www-swiss.ai.mit.edu/samantha/

Ships

Age of Sail Clip Art Feel the salt spray in your face as you peruse this attractive collection of tall ship images. If you have rum and danger in your blood, the pirate pictures are perfect. ✓ INTERNET→*www* http://www.cs.yale.edu/HTML/YALE/CS/HyPlans/loosemore-sandra/sail.html

Maps

Historical Map Exhibit Not recommended for navigational purposes, these lovely antiquarian maps do have a certain charm. The ancient seas surrounding Ireland and Turkey are filled with sea monsters, tall ships, and compass roses. ✓ INTERNET→*www* http://www.ee.pdx.edu/~caseyh/horror/pics/graphics.html

These listings constitute only a fraction of the graphics archives in Cyberspace. In fact, pictures are so plentiful that a Website without them is a rarity.

Sound & Music **Creativity in Cyberspace**

Sound & music

Most people think of computers as CPUs with monitors attached. But more and more, the audio capabilities of today's PCs are being exploited. With new sound-encoding technology, computers can reproduce music and sound as crisp as high-end CD players, and home users can learn to edit and manipulate sounds with even the cheapest shareware. Make some noise at the **Audio Engineering Society**, the **Music & Audio Connection**, and the **World of Audio**, and then go in search of sound clips for your specific platform. Need Amiga? There's **Amiga Audio Archives**. Atari? Check out the extensive **Atari Music** site. Those with a hunger for aural sex should visit **alt.sex.sounds**. And Wacko Jacko fans can download clips of HIStory tracks from **Sony Music Clips**.

On the Net

Across the board

Audio Engineering Society More than sound clips and sound players, this site covers audio education and research (visit the announcement for the 1996 IEEE International Conference on Acoustics), audio-related software (including the Director Home Page), and dozens of audio indices. ✓**INTERNET**→*www* http:// www.cudenver.edu/aes/audio_links.html#edures

Audio Virtual Library An index of links to newsgroups, utilities, and support for audiophiles. The sound warehouse features links to great sound clips. ✓**INTERNET**→*www* http://www.comlab.ox.ac.uk/archive/audio.html

The Music & Audio Connection A large collection of links to audio sites, including dozens of newsgroups, MIDI files and software archives, and a mall with audio-related merchandise. Like ear plugs? ✓**INTERNET** ...→*www* http://nor.com/music ...→*www* gopher://nor.com:71/

Sight and Sound Forum A forum for computer graphics and sound aficionados. Contains libraries with software and documentation on animation, graphics, sampling, MIDI programming, and related topics. There are also directories for Amiga, Atari, Macintosh, and IBM-compatible sound players and clips as well as .GIF archives. And while it would be easy and entertaining to get lost in the libraries, the message board is a valuable resource—a place to ask questions, pick up tips and recommendations, and meet others experimenting with sound and graphics on the computer. ✓**COMPUSERVE**→*go* sight

World of Audio Seeking an audio experience? Play that old Yoko Ono album! Just kidding. From

Sound of Music—downloaded from CompuServe's Bettmann Archive Forum

194 Net Tech

Creativity in Cyberspace Sound & Music

the World of Audio, you can explore MIDI software archives, FAQs on audio and electronic music, a database of audio professionals, and dozens of other music and sound sites on the Net. ✓**INTERNET**→*www* http://www.magicnet.net/rz/world_of_audio/woa.html

By platform

Amiga Audio Archives Head to the applications subdirectory for sound players, conversion tools, and trackers for the Amiga. Then, pick up some clips. The site carries a fairly large selection of radio broadcasts, MIDI samples, and other sounds. ✓**INTERNET**→*www* ftp://www.funet.fi/pub/amiga/audio

Apple II Music and Sound A forum dedicated to music composition and sound on the Apple II computer. Download sound players, editors, and converters from the Applications library and then pay a visit to the sound libraries, where you'll find hundreds of archived sounds, including snippets of Hillary Clinton and Ross Perot. There are also libraries for MIDI and MOD programmers, with original compositions by members of the forum. Questions about sound digitizing, music education, and MIDI? Post them on the message boards and get feedback from others who make music on the Apple II. ✓**AMERICA ONLINE**→*keyword* a2→Music and Sound

Atari Music The directory is almost exclusively filled with applications for listening to or manipulating music on the Atari—look elsewhere for sound clips. The range of offerings extends from a MIDI sequencer to a .TUN file player to a MOD player. ✓**INTERNET** …→*www* gopher://gopher.archive.umich.edu:7055/00/atari/Music** …→*www* ftp://atari.archive.umich.edu/Music …→*www* ftp://wuarchive.wustl.edu/systems/atari/umich.edu/Music/

Atari Sounds Can you hear Robocop saying "You have 20 seconds to comply"? How about Homer Simpson yelling "Bart," Clint Eastwood threatening "Make my day," or Robin Williams announcing "Good morning, Vietnam!"? No? Try harder. Still can't? Then get a sound player (there are dozens here), rummage through the clips, take some home, and the sounds will come in loud and clear. What's that silly rabbit saying now? "Toitle shmoitle, I'm the rabbit!" ✓**INTERNET** …→*www* gopher://gopher.archive.umich.edu:7055/11/atari/Sound …→*www* ftp://atari.archive.umich.edu/Sound …→*www* ftp://wuarchive.wustl.edu/systems/atari/umich.edu/Sound/

comp.sys.amiga.audio (ng) "Does anybody know of a MOD-to-MIDI converter program?" asks Dave. The Doomster, on the other hand, is looking for FTP sites with MOD files. And Chris at the University of Washington-Parkside needs help writing a program that converts sequences of DNA to a MIDI file. It's an informative place to bring your questions about Amiga audio format and conversion. ✓**USENET**

Info-Mac Sound Archive An A-Z collection of hundreds of sounds that include lines from the movie *Airplane!*, the original *Star Trek* theme, and—*no, no…go away!*—Zeppelin's "Stairway to Heaven." And, while not quite as big as the collection of clips, the subdirectory of audio utilities is likely to include everything you'll need for audio entertainment on the Mac. There are utilities to convert Amiga IFF (8SVX) sound files to Mac files, convert .WAV files to Mac System 7 files, play MIDI sound files, record voice, translate Suns audio (.au) files into QuickTime movies, and more. ✓**INTERNET**→*www* ftp://sumex-aim.stanford.edu/info-mac/Sound/

Macintosh Music and Sound Forum Want to make music on the Mac? Go to the Macintosh Software Center's Greatest Hits area in the software libraries to download reliable, easy-to-use sound players like SoundMaster and Now Hear This. Attend a weekly conference or engage in real-time chat with a fellow forum member about the technological and aesthetic issues of digital sound. The software libraries are filled with sound files. Use the America Online sounds to customize your AOL software, or explore the world of pop culture with TV samples, music samples, movie samples, cartoon samples, and science fiction samples. Beginners should head to the message boards for some sound advice: "I can't play MIDI files!" screams one post; "Buy a sequencer program that can play standard MIDI files (SMFs)! All the good ones will play SMFs!" shouts back another. ✓**AMERICA ONLINE**→*keyword* mms

OS/2 Music & Sound Utilities This software and sound-clip library in the OS/2 Forum features tools and utilities for listening to sounds (including EZWave, a popular sound player), and a sound-file archive containing WAVE-format clips from cartoons, newsworthy events, games, movies, songs, and TV. Some sound-file gems available here include the geek from *Sixteen Candles* muttering "Very hot, very hot" and radio announcer Casey

Net Tech 195

Sound & Music Creativity in Cyberspace

Kasem bidding his famous fond farewell, "Keep your feet on the ground and keep reaching for the stars." ✓**AMERICA ONLINE**→*keyword* os2→Browse Software Libraries→ More...→Motion and Sound→ More...→Music & Sound Utilites

PC Music and Sound Forum "What is the BEST sound card?" (The general consensus on the message board in this huge forum specializing in music composition and playback on most PC platforms is the Roland Rap-10). Want to continue the discussion in a live forum? Attend one of the weekly conferences, where electronic music aficionados can congregate online to swap industry lore or offer tips and tricks to fellow musicians in real time. Pay a visit to the software libraries and download sound players for MIDI, MOD, and other sound-file formats. Get sound samples in MOD, VOC, or .WAV formats from the Digitized Sounds library. ✓**AMERICA ONLINE**→*keyword* pmu

PC Sounds Satisfy your PC sound-related needs here. The library contains numerous utilities that will play, edit, or convert sound files on your PC. It also features an extensive archive of downloadable music and digitized sounds. ✓**AMERICA ONLINE**→*keyword* pcmultimedia→Software Libraries→Sounds

Tandy Music & Sound Music and sound programs from Tandyland. ✓**AMERICA ONLINE**→*keyword* pmu→Browse Software Libraries→ Tandy

Windows Music & Sound For Windows users, this forum contains sound tools and utilities for playback and composing, including WHAM and GoldWave, two highly recommended, easy-to-use sound editors for .WAV files. The .WAV sound clips archive is organized into the following categories: cartoons, comedians, events, games, historical sounds, interview excerpts, movie and music clips, and radio clips. Scooby Doo fans should head to the cartoons section for dialogue snippets from the old Hanna-Barbera show. ✓**AMERICA ONLINE**→*keyword* winforum→Browse the Software Libraries →More...→Music & Sound

Intro to audio

Audio FAQ This colossal four-part FAQ answers audio-related questions with almost surgical precision. "How can I improve the sound of my stereo?" "Do all amplifiers with the same specifications sound alike?" "What is DAT?" "Do CDs deteriorate with time?" "Where can I read more about speaker building?" These questions and others are clearly and expertly addressed using real-world situations and examples. A better audio information source would be difficult to find. ✓**INTERNET**→*www* http://www.cis.ohio-state.edu/hypertext/faq/usenet/AudioFAQ/top.html

Electronic and Computer Music FAQ A constantly evolving index of frequently asked questions for audiophiles who want to either make or listen to music on their computers. Arranged by topic. ✓**INTERNET**→*www* http://www.cis.ohio-state.edu/hypertext/faq/usenet/music/netjam-faq/faq.html

Macintosh Music Information Center This is an excellent online primer for Mac users who want to experiment with sound and music composition or playback on their computers. Novices can read several texts introducing issues of computer sound and music, including Macintosh Sound Basics, MIDI Basics, Using Downloaded Files, All About MOD Files, and How to Convert Macintosh Sounds into .WAV files. ✓**AMERICA ONLINE**→*keyword* mms→Music Information Center

The Music Studio Linked to the NCT Web Magazine, a computer magazine aimed at small business and home office users, The Music Studio reads like a step-by-step overview of PC sound and music technology. Sequencers, notation and printing software, patch editors and librarians, digital recording and editing, and automated composition are all covered in depth. The best and most value-intensive examples in each category are noted. Manufacturer contact information is also provided. ✓**INTERNET**→*www* http://da.awa.com:80/nct/software/musicled.html

PC Music and Sound InfoCenter Need an FAQ on MIDI sequencing or a rundown of the best sound cards currently on the market? Can't play a MOD file with your SoundBlaster sound card?

> "'How can I improve the sound of my stereo?' 'Do all amplifiers with the same specifications sound alike?' 'What is DAT?' 'Do CDs deteriorate with time?'"

196 Net Tech

Creativity in Cyberspace **Sound & Music**

Turn to this handy reference guide for detailed descriptions of dozens of PC music and sound tapes.
✓**AMERICA ONLINE**→*keyword* pcmusic→PC Music & Sound Info Center

Sound and Music/MultiMedia File Formats on the Internet A good resource for newbies who want to learn about the sound capabilities of their PC. Includes a list of recommended sound players and converters, with links to where they can be downloaded on the Web. Recommended players and converters include Music Sculptor, MOD4Win, GoldWave, Scoptrax, WHAM, and SOX10. ✓**INTERNET**→*www* http://ac.dal.ca/~dong/music.htm

Sound formats

Audio File Formats FAQ This extensive, two-part FAQ is likely to have the answers regardless of your question. Intense, technical dissections of every known audio file format are interspersed with information on hardware, file compression, format conversion, FTP sites, and mailing lists. In short, the most complete and up-to-date guide to computer sound files available on the Net. ✓**AMERICA ONLINE**→*keyword* pcsoftware→File Search→*Search by file name:* audiofm.zip

The Music Studio A Web page dedicated to an emerging multimedia data type for WWW audio distribution. The site features sound clips in both .AU format and NetSound format—for all you Netters to compare the quality. ✓**INTERNET**→*www* http://sound.media.mit.edu/~mkc/netsound.html

Sound utilities

alt.binaries.sounds.utilities (ng) Can't figure out how your

The Music Studio—http://da.awa.com:80/nct/software/musicled.html

sound player or MIDI sequencer works? Post a query in this newsgroup and wait for a cybersound authority to reply with an answer. This is a good place to find out about sound-related software upgrades, too. ✓**USENET**

AMINet Musical Software Archive All the software you'll need to make, play, or edit music on your Amiga computer. Hundreds of downloadable programs indexed by composing software, MIDI software, miscellaneous software, and sound players. ✓**INTERNET**→*www* http://wuarchive.wustl.edu/~aminet/dirs/tree_mus.html

General Audio Information Simple but with many of the right links, this site connects to several popular .AU and .WAV sound players and sound-clip archives. ✓**INTERNET**→*www* http://www2.ncsu.edu/bae/people/faculty/walker/hotlist/audio.html

The ICMA Software Library In an attempt to centralize information concerning noncommercial software available for use by computer researchers and composers, the ICMA has amassed a huge archive of sound-related programs for many platforms. Program categories include sound synthesis, composition, MIDI sequencing, algorithmic composition, interactive performance, granular synthesis, psychoacoustics, and much more. New versions of the library appear every four months. ✓**INTERNET**→*www* http://www.leeds.ac.uk/music/NetInfo/ICMA/icma_cat.html

Mac Shareware 500 This software and sound-file library is based on the *Mac Shareware 500* book from Ventana Press, which reviews and describes the top 500 Mac shareware files. Visit the Sound & Music area and download all the best sound players, editors, and converters for the Mac. (Ventana's editors have tested hundreds of sound players for the Macintosh; SoundMaster 1.7.3 is one of their favorites.) There is also a handy Electronic Music Encyclopedia that will help you when you're stumped on terminology.

Sound & Music Creativity in Cyberspace

Favorite Mac sound clips are archived here as well—some highlights include the Wicked Witch of the West shouting "I'm melting!" and *Saturday Night Live*'s Dan Akroyd shouting "Jane, you ignorant slut!" ✓ AMERICA ONLINE→*keyword* mac500→Sound & Music

Mac Utilities Listen to the sounds of the Net. But before rummaging through archives for clips of presidential speeches, heavy-metal bands, and famous movie lines, get a sound player. This directory has a fairly large selection of sound players and utilities for the Macintosh. ✓ INTERNET→*www* gopher://nic.merit.edu:7055/11/mac.bin/sound/soundutil

Sound & Music Utilities The library carries a Windows drum machine, a .WAV converter, a music-composition program, a dual MIDI and .WAV player, sound editors and conversion programs, and other audio utilities. ✓ AMERICA ONLINE→*keyword* mmw→Library→Sound & Music

Vibe Online Helper Applications Sound players for both the Mac and the IBM. ✓ INTERNET→*www* http://www.pathfinder.com/vibe/soft/helpers.html

Windows Shareware 500 The same features as the Macintosh 500 Shareware forum, but for Windows. There are very few sound players to download, but the selection of sound files is impressive. When, for instance, was the last time you heard the "Where's the Beef?" Wendy's commercial (with Clara Peller, R.I.P.)? And there's a Windows drum machine that you can download and use to annoy the neighbors until they smash your windows. ✓ AMERICA ONLINE→*keyword* win 500→Windows 500 shareware Library→More...→Music & Sound or Utilities

Windows Sound Drivers Sound drivers and updates for both DOS and Windows systems. ✓ AMERICA ONLINE→*keyword* pcmultimedia→More...→Sound Drivers

Sound clips

alt.binaries.sounds.cartoons (ng) Includes popular snippets from *The Simpsons* and *Ren & Stimpy* as well as some obscurities from the *Rug Rats* and the *Gummi Bears*. Post your requests and pray that someone out there made a sound-file recording of MTV's Winter Steel. ✓ USENET

alt.binaries.sounds.d (ng) Newsgroup for any discussion relating to binary sound files on Usenet. This is a great place to post that request for the Japanese National Anthem. Newbies who don't know an .AU file from a .WAV file would be wise to browse the posts here before embarking on a sound-file downloading binge. ✓ USENET

alt.binaries.sounds.misc (ng) Flushing toilets, Dangermouse, and Sheryl Crow. A mixed bag of binary sound files. ✓ USENET

alt.binaries.sounds.movies (ng) A terrific newsgroup and binary sound file archive that specializes in movie dialogue. Contains a variety of cool snippets, including Samuel L. Jackson's classic line from *Pulp Fiction*—"Check out the big brain on Brad!" Also contains the inevitable "My name is Forrest...Forrest Gump." and a lot of bad dialogue from *Saturday Night Live*'s behemoth, Chris Farley. ✓ USENET

alt.binaries.sounds.music (ng) Not as interesting as it sounds, unless you crave binary sound files from Bananarama or Sheryl Crow. Struggling bands also post song samples to this Usenet newsgroup. ✓ USENET

alt.binaries.sounds.tv (ng) All sorts of TV dialogue converted into binary sound files. Includes the obligatory David Letterman and Simpsons snippets as well as some unexpected gems, like *Scooby Doo*'s Shaggy uttering "Zoinks!" ✓ USENET

alt.sex.sounds (ng) Usenet group where you can find binary text files of the horizontal bop. Use a decoder and a sound player to hear people's homegrown orgasms, moans, and phone sex, or just read the replies of satisfied downloaders: "Sounds like you were having great sex, but next time turn off the U2 song in the background." ✓ USENET

Animal Sounds Lions and tigers and bears—oh, my! All the animal sound files you could ever hope to find, including wonderful cat howls. ✓ INTERNET→*www* http://info.fuw.edu.pl:80/multimedia/sounds.animals/

Australian National Botanical Gardens' Bird Sounds The place to go when you feel like listening to the exciting sounds of the currawong or the kookaburra or the exotic spinebill. ✓ INTERNET→*www* http://155.187.10.12:80/sounds/

Cuban Music Samples Excerpts of Cuban music, along with some translations of lyrics into English. ✓ INTERNET→*www* http://itre.uncecs.edu/music/cuban-music.html

HarperAudio! Spoken-word ex-

Creativity in Cyberspace Sound & Music

cerpts from famous novels and plays. From Dickens and Donne to Hemingway and Hansberry. ✓**INTERNET**→*www* http://www.cmf.nrl.navy.mil/radio/harp_ITH.html

Historical Speeches Although it captures only a few moments of history, the Website has excerpts from Martin Luther King Jr.'s 1963 "I have a dream" speech, several Richard Nixon speeches, and speeches made by Joseph McCarthy, Neville Chamberlain, and even the tirades of Adolf Hitler. ✓**INTERNET**→*www* gopher://twinbrook.cis.uab.edu:70/ lasciiarc.70

Internet Underground Music Archive Listen to sound-file snippets from your favorite unsigned band or link to a major label's home page to get all the information on your favorite corporate artists. The site encourages bands to upload samples of their latest demos. Who knows? Maybe you'll be snapped up by DGC. ✓**INTERNET**→*www* http://www.iuma.com/

Movie Sounds Check out this Website with downloadable sound files of movie theme songs from such popular faves as *Back to the Future*, *The Lion King*, *Star Wars*, and *The Wizard of Oz*. Titles rotate on a regular basis, and the page is linked to other sound-related sites on the Web. ✓**INTERNET**→*www* http://www.netaxs.com/people/dgresh/snddir.html

Science Fiction Sound Clips This sound repository contains files of music and dialogue from various science-fiction films, including *Star Wars*, *Star Trek*, and *Dune*. ✓**INTERNET**→*www* http://www.univ-rennes1.fr/ASTRO/sound-e.html

Seinfeld: The Sounds Well-documented sound-file site featur-

> "This Website excerpts speeches made by Joseph McCarthy, Neville Chamberlain, and even the tirades of Adolf Hitler."

ing hundreds of snippets from the beloved NBC sitcom. Can't remember which episode that hilarious Kramer remark about the Junior Mints came from? Fear not, everything is indexed accordingly. Also includes links to other Seinfeld archives. ✓**INTERNET**→*www* http://www.ifi.uio.no/ ~rubens/seinfeld/sounds/index.html

Sites with Audio Clips A Web page with links to digitized sound archives, divided into sounds, music, and voice. ✓**INTERNET**→*www* http://www.eecs.nwu.edu/~jmyers/other-sounds.html

Sony Music Clips Dozens of clips from Sony artists of all ilk, including Godflesh, The London Suede, Terence Trent D'Arby, Basia, and Esa-Pekka Salonen conducting Stravinsky's violin concerto (Cho-Liang Lin, violin). Clips appear in .WAV and .AU formats and are mono (in some sense the Web has set us back approximately 30 years—to the days of "cruising" and AM radio). ✓**INTERNET**→*www* http://www.music.sony.com/Music/SoundClips/ index.html

Sound Bytes: The WWW TV Themes Home Page Hey, is that the theme from *Leave It to Beaver*? *Chicago Hope*? Or the "Coke is it!" commercial? This Website houses an amazing collection of several hundred clips of TV theme music. The clips are in .AU format and divided into several categories: comedy shows, daytime soaps, children's shows, network intros, commercials, etc. Sound players for Windows, DOS, Mac, and Unix systems are linked to the site. ✓**INTERNET**→*www* http://ai.eecs.umich.edu/people/kennyp/sounds.html

Sound Management Downloadable File Listings A huge archive of 250,000 zipped sound files to download and play on your computer. Meticulously indexed by platform and file type. Need we say more? ✓**INTERNET**→*www* http://www.interaccess.com/users/midilink/

Sun Site Sound Files A vast repository of sound files—categories include animals, cartoons, comedy, commercials, Monty Python, screams, and whales. ✓**INTERNET**→*www* gopher://calypso.oit.unc.edu/11/../.pub/multimedia/sun-sounds

Sun-Sounds Movie Themes Page More sound snippets from movies. Indexed alphabetically, this archive runs the gamut from *Aladdin* to *Wayne's World*. ✓**INTERNET**→*www* http://sunsite.unc.edu:80/pub/multimedia/sun-sounds/movies/

Underworld Sound Links A site with links to sound-file archives. ✓**INTERNET**→*www* http://www.nd.edu/StudentLinks/jkeating/links/sound.html

University of Illinois Sound File Archive Huge archive of diverse sound samples that will work on any sound player that reads

Net Tech 199

Sound & Music Creativity in Cyberspace

.AU files. Subdirectories include Beavis & Butt-head, Bill and Ted, Cartoons, Ferris Bueller, Ren & Stimpy, Roger Rabbit, The Simpsons, Star Trek, Star Wars, and Wayne's World. ✓**INTERNET**→*www* http://www.acm.uiuc.edu/rml/Sounds/

VibeLine Preview excerpts of songs from all the latest bands profiled in *Vibe* magazine. See why Massive Attack, Adina Howard, and others are so lauded by *Vibe* critics by downloading samples of their music. It's a nice way to try before you buy—your very own online listening booth. ✓**INTERNET** →*www* http://www.pathfinder.com/vibe/vibeline/open.html

The Vincent Voice Library at Michigan State University This interesting voice archive has recorded utterances of over 50,000 notable persons. There are sound samples of past presidents as well as samples from other luminaries, including aviatrix Amelia Earhart, Sultan of Swat Babe Ruth, and humorist Will Rogers. ✓**INTERNET**→*www* http://web.msu.edu/vincent/index.html

MIDI

The Alf MIDI Site Written with the more advanced MIDI enthusiast in mind, this site's focus is on the MIDI Sample Dump Standard (otherwise known as SDS, a method of transferring sound-sample data between MIDI-equipped devices). Extensive technical documentation, samples, and MS-DOS programs related to SDS are available through an FTP link. There is a small amount of general MIDI information added to satisfy newcomers and a fairly large list of links to other popular MIDI and music-related sites. ✓**INTERNET**→ *www* http://www.uib.no/People/midi/midi.html

alt.music.midi (ng) Need MIDI help? On any given day, the topics here range from heated debates about the best MIDI sequencing software, the hottest and most functional sound cards, keyboard specs, FTP and WWW addresses, and much, much more. ✓**USENET**

alt.music.midi/alt.music.makers.synthesizers (ng) These two newsgroups are frequented by MIDI devotees and electronic music lovers alike. Post your questions and chances are a fellow MIDI aficionado will help you with your sequencing problems. ✓**USENET**

Analogue Heaven The discussion list and its companion, the Website, serve as watering holes for thirsty fans of playing, collecting, designing, repairing, and modifying analog musical gear. A complete archive of the mailing list is available at the Website, along with spotlight features on various subscribers and their musical accomplishments. ✓**INTERNET** …→*email* majordomo@hyperreal.com ✍ *Type in message body:* subscribe analogue <your email address> …→*www* http://www.hyperreal.com/music/machines/Analogue-Heaven/

Atari ST MIDI Software List A list of software and hardware, including prices, to get Atari ST users set up for MIDI programming and playback. ✓**INTERNET**→ *www* http://www.interaccess.com/users/midilink/stsw.html

Digital Guitar Archive This site delivers a comprehensive crash course on the world of digital guitar. Although the site is brimming with such valuable documents as a List of Recommended Recordings Featuring Guitar Synth/MIDI Guitar, back issues of the Digital Guitar mailing list, and an FTP archive, the real star of the show is the brilliant and exhaustive MIDI Guitar FAQ, a primer no self-respecting MIDI mogul can do without. ✓**INTERNET**→*www* http://waynesworld.ucsd.edu/DigitalGuitar/digitar_archive.html

EMUSIC-L Home Page Buying your first keyboard? Setting up a tutorial studio? Building your own drum triggers? Using notation software and dealing with wind-controllers? This site provides a meaty listing of related links, product reviews, essays, and FTP sites. ✓**INTERNET**→*www* http://sunsite.unc.edu/emusic-l/

Ethan Brodsky's Home Page/Learn about Sound Programming A detailed FAQ outlining the ins and outs of sound programming with SoundBlaster 16, useful patches, and plenty of links to other sound-related information and software libraries. ✓**INTERNET**→*www* http://www.xraylith.wisc.edu:80/~ebrodsky/

Future Music Subtitled "Essential listening for all musicians," this home page is the companion site to *Future Music*, the U.K.'s best-selling magazine of hi-tech music and equipment. The content changes monthly, but the high quality of this graphically stunning page is immutable. Past articles have focused on how to get wired for sound via the Internet, forming a virtual band in Cyberspace, and a buyer's guide to desktop MIDI. ✓**INTERNET**→*www* http://www.futurenet.co.uk/music/futuremusic.html

Harmony Central A Website set up at MIT and dedicated to bringing together much of the music and sound-related items that can

Creativity in Cyberspace Sound & Music

be found on the Internet. The software section provides links to sites where you can download sound utilities and applications. Just choose your platform and the link will take you to the proper library. There are also links to sites with patch editors, MIDI tools and utilities, guitar-related software, and commercial software support. The section called "Other Stuff" offers links to FAQs on recording and audio. A separate MIDI section offers information explaining MIDI, where to get MIDI files, info on building your own MIDI interface, and tools for writing MIDI applications. This is one of the best-linked music and sound-related sites on the Internet. ✓**INTERNET**→*www* http://harmony-central.mit.edu/

Internet MIDI Archives An encyclopedic gathering of MIDI programs for all platforms. It includes documentation on several facets of producing digital music—from synthesizer specs to cataloging your compositions, patches for various synths, and a blizzard of various MIDI scores, including Spanish and Latino pieces and selections from popular movies and musicals. ✓**INTERNET**→*www* http://www.ircam.fr/sons/archives/MIDI/index-e.html

Mac MIDI Software List A list of software and hardware for all Mac users interested in MIDI programming and playback. Includes price guides and company information. ✓**INTERNET**→*www* http://www.interaccess.com/users/midilink/macsw.html

MIDI Directory A directory with a fairly large collection of MIDI players for several platforms, patches for synthesizers, and even MIDI song files. ✓**INTERNET**→*www* ftp://ftp.cs.ruu.nl/pub/MIDI

The MIDI Farm The MIDI Farm features links to all the major MIDI software vendors (Twelve Tone Systems, Emagic, Steinberg/Jones, and many more), popular keyboard manufacturers (Korg, Yamaha, Roland, Kurzweil, etc.), examples of digital audio workstations, and best of all, the MIDI Farm bimonthly newsletter, which compiles all the latest news from the world of MIDI and digital audio. ✓**INTERNET**→*www* http://www.PrimeNet.Com:80/~midifrm/

The MIDI Home Page Dedicated to both the budding MIDI enthusiast and the veteran digital composer, the MIDI Home Page has enough information to please even the most jaded Web traveller. Heini Withagen, the author of this remarkable page, has included more data and links than are possible to digest in one sitting. After perusing text files on the history, application, and specifications of the communication protocol, you can advance your MIDI knowledge by following links to other MIDI pages, FTP sites, and related newsgroups. ✓**INTERNET**→*www* http://www.eeb.ele.tue.nl/midi/index.html

MIDI Music Forum Let's say you've just developed an interest in MIDI. In this forum, you could head to the message board and ask for a recommendation for a DOS MIDI player, instructions on how to convert a MIDI file to a .WAV file, or advice on how to get started. And if you're more of an old hand at MIDI, you might engage in a discussion about Motown's treatment of strings, computer-controlled sound systems, or composing jazz MIDI. Each of the major computer platforms (Windows, Amiga, Macintosh, etc.) has its own message and library section. In the huge library, the re-

CYBERNOTES

"How MIDI Works

MIDI translates a pre-defined set of performance events at one instrument, called the master controller, into digital messages that are sent to other devices over a low-speed serial link operating at 31.25 kbps. To make it easy to keep musical information going where it should, these events are encoded on any of 16 independent logical channels within the MIDI data stream. A synthesizer receiving this incoming data stream responds by playing music.

"Imagine playing a series of half-note C major chords on Middle C on a DX7 synth wired to one or more other synths. In this case, the DX7 sends three 'note on' messages, three note numbers, and three 'note off' messages each time you sound the chord--the receiving MIDI device plays a matching chord in perfect synchronization with the DX7. But depending on its settings, the receiving instrument may use a different instrument sound, or 'patch.'"

-from **The ICMA Software Library**

Net Tech 201

Sound & Music Creativity in Cyberspace

sources include MIDI players and editors for several computer platforms, samples, song files, sound card files, and programming guides. ✓**COMPUSERVE**→*go* midiforum

MIDI Software Archives FAQ
A guide to MIDI archives, with addresses for sound utilities and sound clips for several computer platforms. ✓**INTERNET**→*www* ftp://rtfm.mit.edu/pub/usenet-by-hierarchy/comp/sys/amiga/audio/Midi_files_software_archives_on_the_Internet

MIDI Tools and Resources A clearinghouse for MIDI-related information and software for Atari, Macintosh, and IBM computers. Includes documentation, software, and links to other MIDI-related Web pages. ✓**INTERNET**→*www* http://harmony-central.mit.edu/MIDI/

MIDILink Musician's Net A terrific resource for MIDI users of every skill level. Contains links to a huge directory of sound files and a list of bulletin boards that cater to the MIDI programmer. Novices will want to check out the vast archive of help files catering to MIDI on the Macintosh, IBM, and Atari. ✓**INTERNET**→*www* http://www.interaccess.com/users/midilink/

Sound Constructors An offshoot of the graphically arresting Arne's Nethole, this fledgling netzine is dedicated to "exposing the artists on and off the Net that use electronic means for the production of their music" through intense study and discussion of their techniques, tips, and musical toys. Check in frequently for Arne's ever-changing array of articles, reviews, columns, and technical babble targeting electronic music

Jukebox—from http://www.music.sony.com/Music/TheVault/index.html

in all its various manifestations. ✓**INTERNET**→*www* http://isl-garnet.uah.edu/claassen/sc.html

The TidBITS Guide to MIDI and the Macintosh A thorough and painstaking tutorial on MIDI for the Mac, this page progresses from an extensive introduction to MIDI (covering what it is, how it works, general MIDI specs, and a list of additional sources for further perusal) through a course on application software and hardware specifications. The authors also offer valuable advice for beginners, and a few tips and tricks that may raise the eyebrow of a seasoned professional. ✓**INTERNET**→*www* http://www.leeds.ac.uk/music/MacMIDI/Contents.html

World of Audio MIDI Page If there were ever a contest for the best MIDI-related Web page, this one would definitely be in the running. There isn't much missing from this page. For the novice, there's an Introduction to MIDI, a MIDI Overview Chart, the Usenet MIDI Primer, a Bibliography of Electronic Music, and much, much more. Add a comprehensive list of MIDI archive sites, links to Internet MIDI resources, and professional MIDI software vendors, as well as a staggering archive of Mac and PC files. *Crème de la crème*, as they say in the land where Midi was invented—the hemline, that is. ✓**INTERNET**→*www* http://www.magicnet.net/rz/world_of_audio/midi_pg.html

MIDI clips

alt.binaries.sounds.midi (ng) UUencoded binary MIDI files (*.MID) of every musical genre are the focus of this newsgroup. Where else would you expect to find discussions and examples of the work of Elton John, Mozart, Yanni, and Nine Inch Nails (to name but a few) in the same group? Most of the regulars are open to requests, too. So if you don't see your favorites right off the bat, ask. Open the files you are interested in, save them to your hard disk and then decode them with a freeware program called uuDecode. ✓**USENET**

Classical MIDI Archives Presented by ID Logic, this page is host to the most extensive collection of classical music in MIDI format found anywhere on the Web. Hundreds of files, from Barber to Wagner, are available for downloading, or (if your Web browser supports it) immediate online listening. If you are using Windows and find your browser lacking this feature, the authors have graciously provided Midi Gate, a Web browser helper application that automatically plays MIDI sequences. Yes, they have Rachmaninov's Third Concerto for the Piano. ✓**INTERNET**→*www* http://www.hk.net/~prs/midi.html

The SoundCanvas Users Group Made up of users of the Roland SoundCanvas family of synths, this group's goal is to com-

Creativity in Cyberspace Sound & Music

pile an archive of original works by a wide variety of composers creating with the SoundCanvas. To quote the author, "...anything that can be played back on a SoundCanvas correctly is fair game." A detailed FAQ and FTP access to the archive site are also provided. ✓**INTERNET**→*www* http://www.eeb.ele.tue.nl/midi/scgroup/index.html

MIDI software

Cakewalk Home Page Cakewalk Pro from Twelve Tone Systems, Inc. is the most complete and functional MIDI sequencer available for the PC. Catering to both long-time and potential Cakewalk Pro users, this home page provides dump-request macros, instrument-patch names, instrument definitions, latest version demo software, and more. A large selection of shareware and freeware MIDI programs is also provided. ✓**INTERNET**→*www* http://www.isvr.soton.ac.uk/People/ccb/Cakewalk/

The Emagic Users Page Assembled with the present and future users of Emagic software in mind, this page takes the concept of product support to new and unprecedented levels. The emphasis here is on Logic (formerly known as Notator Logic), but you can also find timely information on Notator SL, SoundSurfer/SoundDiver, and Logic Audio. It's all here—the Logic-Users Mailing List and archive, a Logic tutorial, Emagic upgrade offers, distributor information, and the usual file and FAQ collections. ✓**INTERNET**→*www* http://www.mcc.ac.uk/~emagic/emagic_page.html

Opcode Opcode Systems, pioneers in MIDI for over ten years, produce a vast array of software (Mac and PC) for recording, editing, and cataloging MIDI and SMPTE format music. Their entire product catalogue is featured here as well. ✓**INTERNET**→*www* http://www.rahul.net/opcode/products.html

MIDI vendors

Electronic Music Software Price Guide Encyclopedic in its scope, this list is the absolute last word in music-related software. The guide covers the total sound spectrum, itemizing everything from sequencers and notation programs to educational tools and recording programs—as well as a host of other software—in a straightforward and logical manner. Equal coverage is given to retail, shareware, and freeware programs (noting special upgrade and trade-up offers). ✓**INTERNET**→*www* http://oingomth.uwc.edu/~whizkid/emspg.txt

The KAT Home Page Delve into the world of electronic percussion through the "high-tech, high-touch" array of products from KAT, Incorporated. Friendly and inviting, this page takes you on an expansive tour of the KAT catalogue and in the process explains a great deal about MIDI drumming. ✓**INTERNET**→*www* http://mozart.mw3.com:80/kat/

MIDI Controllable Analog Synthesizers A nonstop barrage of facts, figures, and specifications, this page is a MIDI technophile's dream come true. Comprehensive stats on every MIDI controllable analog synth from AKAI to Waldorf (and then some) are provided along with subjective interpretations of each synth's strengths and weaknesses, availability, and price ranges. The authors have also included translation options for all those pesky acronyms that inevitably pop up. ✓**INTERNET**→*www* http://www.me.chalmers.se/~thed/analog.html

MIDI Vendor Forums Four large forums containing utilities and support for various MIDI-related software and hardware. Companies post press releases and upgrade information here so you can keep abreast of all that is happening in the ever-changing world of MIDI programming and composing. The forums are also a good resource for downloading sound utilities that work with individual companies' products. The organization is chaotic because the four forums are not alphabetized by company. But search and you will find. If you're looking for the Roland Corp. files, go straight to library C. This happens to be a good location for freeware MIDI players and editors that work with Roland synthesizers—give Multi-MIDI Player and SongCanvas a shot. There are also FAQs for various Roland products. The General Library of each vendor forum contains a master index of all the files available within each individual forum. This eliminates a lot of unnecessary searching. ✓**COMPUSERVE**

> "Hundreds of files, from Barber to Wagner, are available for downloading or (if your Web browser supports it) immediate online listening."

Sound & Music Creativity in Cyberspace

→*go* midi

Music and Gear This page is your direct link to the major manufacturers of electronic musical instruments and software. A large portion is devoted to all things Roland: an introduction to their sampler owner's group (sgroup) mailing list, sgroup sample libraries and utility archives, FTP sites, an equipment FAQ, and the all-important SoundCanvas Archive. Blend in healthy doses of Ensoniq, Turtle Beach, and Twelve Tone Systems information and you have a data-rife concoction that's very hard to top. ✓**INTERNET**→*www* http://www.halcyon.com/mdf/sound/sound.htm

Music Machines This page is host to more raw data on synthesizers, drum machines, and effects than should be allowed by law. The focus here leans toward true synthesists' electronic tools rather than acoustic instruments or preconfigured sound boxes. Wade through a vast collection of images, patches, product descriptions and reviews (conveniently organized by manufacturer), money-saving price lists, do-it-yourself hints and tips, and detailed schematics. A veritable ocean of information. ✓**INTERNET**→*www* http://www.hyperreal.com/music/machines/

Musical Address List Having a problem getting in touch with Twelve Tone Systems? Need the address to Audio Lighting and Technologies? Check out this sweeping compendium of music-industry manufacturers, service providers, software publishers, and professionals. Complete stats, including fax numbers and email addresses, are provided for each entry. In light of the ever-changing nature of the music industry, each address is accompanied by a confirmation date. ✓**INTERNET**→*www* http://www.halcyon.com/mdf/sound/company.list

Roland SoundCanvas Products Compared How do the SC-55, SC-155, SC-7, Boss Dr. Synth, and SCC-1 sound modules compare? These and other questions are fully answered in this sound FAQ, which comprises the entire suite of products using the Roland SoundCanvas. Discover exactly why the SoundCanvas became famous, prompting Roland to design an entire line of products around its architecture. ✓**INTERNET**→*www* http://www.pitt.edu/~cjp/Reviews/rol.canvas

USA New Gear Price List Maintained by Casey Palowitch, this list is an invaluable resource for anyone in the market for new and used electronic music equipment. The list of items covered includes keyboards, controllers, MIDI modules, drum machines, MIDI interfaces, patchbays, synchronizers, timecoders, tuners, recording and signal processing devices, sound pickup, computer cards, amplification, music-related internals, and much more. Everything is listed alphabetically by manufacturer for easy retrieval, too. Thanks to Usenet, most of the prices are up-to-the-minute calculations based on national averages; you shouldn't have to resort to guesswork when buying gear. ✓**INTERNET**→*www* http://www.pitt.edu/~cjp/newgear.html

The Wavestation Home Page An invaluable page for users of the Korg Wavestation, featuring back issues of the Wavestation mailing list (currently inoperable), Effects Parameter Documentation, Developer Hints 'n Tricks, a Wavestation SR Developer Overview, and

CYBERNOTES

"How does a computer play sound/music?"

"The sound or music that a computer can play is digitalized sound or music. It can be classified into two types: synthesized sound and sound data.

Synthesized sounds are produced through a synthesizer called MIDI (Music Instrument Digital Interface).

When notes are played, a MIDI command is sent to a synthesized chip, which then produces the sound specified. Because synthesized sounds are stored as simple commands, they require much smaller space than wave-form audio.

Sound data is digital representation of an analog signal, which is typically represented as continuous waveform. When sound is digitally recorded, samples of waveform are captured at fixed intervals. The more samples that are taken, the more information stored for each sample, the higher quality the sound has."

—from **Sound and Music/Multimedia File Formats on the Internet**

Creativity in Cyberspace Sound & Music

the usual FAQs. A generous supply of MIDI and other sound-related links is also provided. ✓**INTERNET**→*www* http://anjovis.tky.hut.fi:80/~ws/

MOD

alt.binaries.sounds.mods (ng) This is supposed to be a newsgroup for MOD sound files, but there are a lot of questions and answers about MOD players, programmers, and converters. A good place to go and post questions you need to have answered. ✓**USENET**

Amiga Music for the PC Everything you need to play or create MOD-format music on the Amiga. The Players and Utilities section includes MOD players (the most popular one here seems to be MODPLAY). There are also hundreds of alphabetized MOD sound files, many of which are original compositions posted by AOL members. ✓**AMERICA ONLINE**→*keyword* pmu→Browse Software Libraries→Amiga Music for the PC

AMInet MOD Music Archives Hundreds of MOD sound files for the Amiga, conveniently indexed by subject. This archive is part of the largest site of Amiga-related documentation and software on the Internet. ✓**INTERNET**→*www* http://ftp.wustl.edu/~aminet/dirs/tree_mods.html

AMINet Subdirectory of MODS After you've chosen a sound player for your Amiga computer, visit this huge archive of digital sound modules. Indexed into numerous subcategories—including dreamy and atmospheric music, jazzy and funky music, techno, rock & roll and pop music, and piano music—the site also features subdirectories of MOD composers. So, if you get hooked

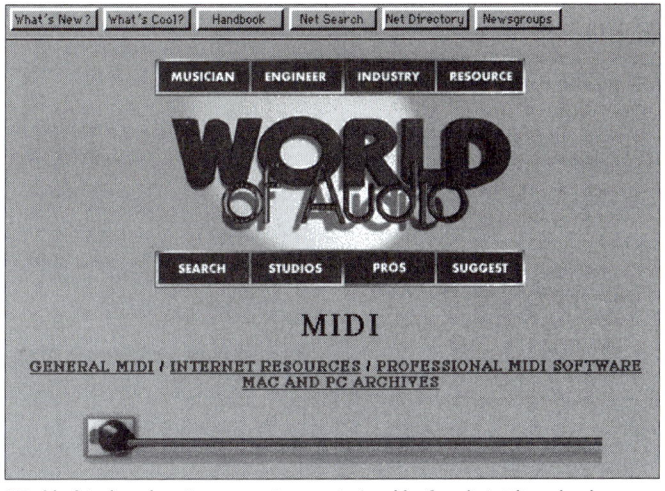

World of Audio—http://www.magicnet.net/rz/world_of_audio/midi_pg.html

on somebody's creations you can access their collected works here. ✓**INTERNET**→*www* http://ftp.wustl.edu/~aminet/dirs/tree_mods.html

MOD FAQ Everything you could possibly want to know about digital music modules (a.k.a. MODs) in one handy little document. The FAQ outlines a brief history of the MOD file, describes similarities and differences between MOD and MIDI files, and lists the best MOD editors and players. ✓**AMERICA ONLINE**→*keyword* pcsoftware→File Search→*Search by file name:* modfaq12.zip ✓**COMPUSERVE**→*go* sight→Libraries→*Search by file name:* modfaq.txt

The MOD Page A good general resource on MOD files and how they work. Includes instruction on programming and playing back MOD files on PCs as well as links to MOD-related sites on the Web. ✓**INTERNET**→*www* http://www.eskimo.com/~future/mods.htm

Sound cards & boards

Advanced Gravis Forum A support forum for users of the Gravis UltraSound sound card. Features product lists and updates, a message board for questions and answers, and a software library that houses various utilities that work with Gravis products. ✓**AMERICA ONLINE**→*keyword* gravis

comp.sys.ibm.pc.soundcard.advocacy (ng) All sorts of advice and comments on buying or using a sound card in your IBM computer. ✓**USENET**

comp.sys.ibm.pc.soundcard.games (ng) Where do you go when the sound won't work on your favorite computer game? Here, for starters. ✓**USENET**

comp.sys.ibm.pc.soundcard.misc (ng) Will it be a Gravis UltraSound or a Turtle Beach sound card? What's the best sound card that will convert recorded phone calls into .WAV files? And does anyone out there have a Roland daughterboard they want to get rid of? This newsgroup specializes in questions, answers, and advice for PC users with sound cards. ✓**USENET**

Sound & Music Creativity in Cyberspace

comp.sys.ibm.pc.soundcard.music (ng) This newsgroup is devoted to sound cards and music composition on PC platform computers. ✓**USENET**

comp.sys.ibm.pc.soundcard.tech (ng) Technical questions and answers related to sound cards and music composition on the PC. ✓**USENET**

Creative Labs Forum Company-sponsored support forum for users of Creative Labs software products, including the popular line of SoundBlaster audio cards. If you own one and are having technical problems, this forum offers you direct access to a company representative. It also includes product- and software-upgrade information and MOD and MIDI sound utilities in the library. ✓**COMPUSERVE**→*go* blaster

The Linux Sound HOWTO A HOWTO document intended as a quick and painless reference detailing everything you need to know to install, configure, and troubleshoot sound support under Linux. Topics such as configuring the kernel, creating the device files, and testing the installation offer a complete, step-by-step walkthrough, leaving very little to chance. The primary focus of the document is on sound cards. Frequently asked questions are answered and references to additional sources of information on a variety of sound-related topics are also supplied. ✓**INTERNET**→*www* http://sunsite.unc.edu/mdw/HOWTO/Sound-HOWTO-2.html

MediaVision Forum Company-sponsored forum offering technical support, information on new products and upgrades, and software libraries with utilities and sound files that will work with MediaVision products. Includes a message board for questions and answers. ✓**COMPUSERVE**→*go* mediavision

PC Sound Cards Frequently Asked Questions An assemblage of Usenet FAQs pertaining to sound cards for IBM compatibles. Included here are FAQs for the Aria, IBM PC Generic, Gravis UltraSound, and Turtle Beach sound cards. ✓**INTERNET**→*www* http://www.cis.ohio-state.edu/hypertext/faq/usenet/PCsoundcards/top.html

Soundboards Part of the Music Studio, this introduction to the world of computer audio and sound boards will probably prove invaluable to the burgeoning audiophile. Highlights include a tutorial on understanding audio terminology and specs, tips on choosing the right speakers, and an unflinching critical overview of the many sound boards available. The all-encompassing soundboard reviews include technical specs, installation tips and tricks, performance ratings (if the board is substandard, they'll be sure to

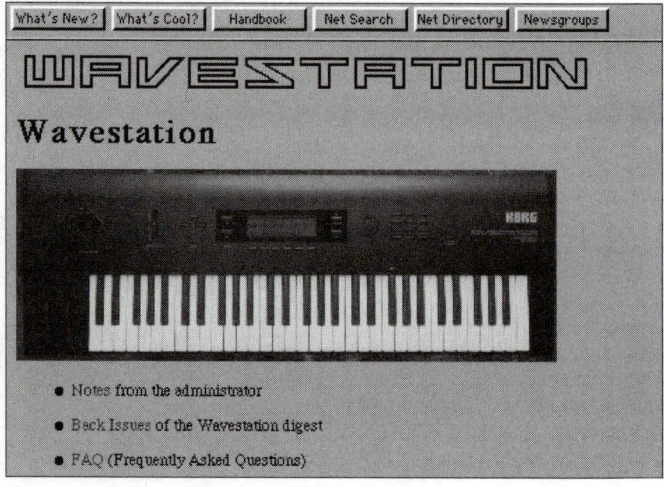

Wavestation—http://anjovis.tky.hut.fi:80/~ws/

let you know), prices, and manufacturer contact information. ✓**INTERNET**→*www* http://da.awa.com:80/nct/hardware/sondlead.html

Other resources

Center for Computer Research in Music and Acoustics To quote the author, the CCRMA is "a multi-disciplinary facility where composers and researchers work together using computer-based technology both as an artistic medium and as a research tool." Highlights include access to the Catgut Acoustical Society Research Library, software available through the CCRMA, and a current chronicle of CCRMA workshops and upcoming events. ✓**INTERNET**→*www* http://ccrma-www.stanford.edu/

Music Resources on the Internet A hypertext list of hundreds of music sites online, ranging from the home page for the School of Music at Acadia University to the Conductors Home Page to the Sony Music Page. ✓**INTERNET**→*www* http://www.music.indiana.edu/misc/music_resources.html

Creativity in Cyberspace Sound & Music

Sound players

AMOS Audio Tool Download this software tool for presentation and manipulation of sound on Sun Sparc workstations. AMOS lets you mix audio data on your computer just like you would mix tracks in a recording studio. A graphical interface shows you exactly what you're doing to the audio file. ✓INTERNET→*www* http://este.darmstadt.gmd.de:5000/dimsys/amos/aat.html

MP2 Audio Playback Freeware for playing MPEG Layer 2 audio files under Windows 3.1. Requires an audio playback adapter/sound card. ✓**AMERICA ONLINE**→*keyword* pcsoftware→File Search→*Search by file name:* mpgaudio ✓**COMPUSERVE**→*go* sight→Browse Libraries→Library 8→*Download a file:* MPGAUDIO.ZIP

Now Hear This! 2.1 for the Mac A simple, easy-to-use program that lets you play sounds from sound suitcases, System 7 sound files, applications, HyperCard stacks, SoundEdit or SoundWave files, Windows .WAV files, and most of the files with digitized sounds. Its editing feature lets you fine-tune or customize your sound-file collection. ✓**AMERICA ONLINE**→ *keyword* macsoftware→Search the Libraries→Search all Forums→*Search by file name:* nowherethis.sit

Real Audio Sometimes sounds can be so aggravating. They take hours to download, and then you have to move them through a sound player. Or at least you had to. Now, though, the waiting is over. With Real Audio, sounds play as they download—your computer merely creates a buffer file that it deletes after the entire sound is played. Download a Real Audio test version and link to pages with Real Audio sounds, from NPR's Morning Edition to college radio. ✓INTERNET→*www* http://www.realaudio.com

SoundHandle 1.0.2 for the Macintosh Record, play, display, analyze, modify, and save sound samples with this sound-player program for any Macintosh that runs on System 7. This program also lets you generate waveforms, read "snd" resources from other applications, save sounds as System 7 sound files, and convert sounds to and from ASCII text files. A modification feature lets you alter the frequency or amplitude of sound files. Won't work on Power PCs. ✓**AMERICA ONLINE**→ *keyword* macsoftware→Search the Libraries→Search all Forums→*Search by file name:* soundhandle 1.0.3

Ultra Recorder 2.1 for the Mac A shareware sound utility for the Mac that lets you play, record, and convert AIFF and other types of sound files. An easy-to-use program for anyone who wants to play or record sound files. A new feature of Ultra Recorder will allow you to play sounds at up to 600% of their normal playback volume. Blow away your coworkers with Fugazi snippets! Record Maria Callas onto your start-up disk! Also plays .WAV sound files. ✓**AMERICA ONLINE**→*keyword* macsoftware→Search the Libraries→Search all Forums→*Search by file name:* ultrarecorder 2.1

Windows Play Any File, V1.1 Play any sound file through a Windows 3.1 audio device. ✓**AMERICA ONLINE**→*keyword* pcsoftware →File Search→*Search by file name:* wplany v1.1 ✓**COMPUSERVE**→ *go* sight→Libraries→*Search by file name:* WPLANY.ZIP

Sound editors

Balthazar 1.5.1 A sound utility that converts Microsoft Windows' .WAV sound files into System 7 sounds or vice versa. ✓**AMERICA ONLINE**→*keyword* mms→Software Libraries→Software Search→*Search by file name:* balthazar 1.5.1 ✓**COMPUSERVE**→*go* macff→*Search by file name:* balthz.sea

MPEGAud 1.0a7 An MPEG audio conversion program for the Mac that converts MPEG audio files to or from AIFF files. Download a separate version for your Power PC, or for your Mac with-

Composing on the computer—from http://www.rrruni-koeln.de/wiso-fak/wisotatsem/

Sound & Music Creativity in Cyberspace

out a floating point unit coprocessor. ✓**AMERICA ONLINE**→*keyword* mms→Software Libraries→ Software Search→*Search by file name:* mpegaud 1.0a7

SoundBuilder A multi-featured sound editor for Macintosh users that recognizes SND, AIFF, .WAV, and VOC formats. Requires System 7.x. ✓**AMERICA ONLINE**→*keyword* mms→Software Libraries→ Software Search→*Search by file name:* soundbuilder 2.0.2

SoundEffects 0.9.1 A powerful sound editor that will run on any Mac. The program lets you manipulate and enhance your favorite sounds. ✓**AMERICA ONLINE**→*keyword* mms→Software Libraries→ Software Search→*Search by file name:* soundeffects0.9.1

SOX10 (SOund eXchange) A converter that allows you to translate sound files from one format to another. Supports .AU, .HCOM, .RAW, .SF, VOC, .AUTO, .CDR, .DAT, .WAV, AIFF, SND, and other file formats. ✓**INTERNET**→ *www* ftp://ftp.cwi.nl/pub/audio/ sox10dos.zip

WaveWindow v2.5 A software oscilloscope that displays sound visually on your screen in real time. In other words, you can sing into your computer and watch your lovely voice turn into wild visual imagery. ✓**AMERICA ONLINE** →*keyword* mms→Software Libraries →Software Search *Search by file name:* wavewindow v2.5

WHAM (Waveform Hold and Modify) A freeware application for Windows 3.1 that allows you to manipulate digitized sound. WHAM also lets you create or play Windows sound files. ✓**INTERNET**→*www* ftp://ftp.cic.net/pub/ Software/pc/www/viewers/ wham131.zip

Winjammer V2.30 A full-featured MIDI sequencer that runs in Windows 3.1. This program reads and writes standard MIDI Files (.MID), so the resulting sequences can be played almost anywhere. Requires a Windows MIDI interface or sound board. ✓**AMERICA ONLINE**→*keyword* pcsoftware→File Search→*Search by file name:* winjammer v2.30

MIDI players

MIDI Gate for Windows Features a program that automatically starts MIDI sequences linked to a Web page, and also functions as a stand-alone MIDI player. The page includes a link to the Classical Music Archives, which feature MIDI sequences from hundreds of composers. ✓**INTERNET**→*www* http://www.hk.net/~prs/midigate.html

Midi Machine V1.21 Downloadable jukebox and sound-file manager for Windows 3.1+. This sound player features a drag-and-drop auto-play function and can merge sound files and moving images. ✓**COMPUSERVE**→*go* sight→ Browse Libraries→Library 8→ *Download a file:* MM121.ZIP

MOD players

MODFiler An easy-to-use MOD player for DOS machines. ✓**AMERICA ONLINE**→*keyword* pmu→ Browse Software Libraries→Programs & Utilities→ *Download a file:* modfiler

Mod4Win V2.10 A MOD player for Windows that supports sample rates between 11 and 48 KHz, 8- and 16-bit sample depth, and mono and stereo. ✓**AMERICA ONLINE**→*keyword* pcsoftware→File Search→*Search by file name:* mod4win v2.10

CYBERNOTES

"The Net: Music Format of the Future?

So is it feasible to download music via the Net at the moment? Well, yes and no. Downloading complete, CD-quality tracks is not an option as far as most people are concerned, simply because the size of the files is too large to make it practical. Even low-bandwidth clips take time-for instance, 5 minutes and 20 seconds to download a 42-second, 8kHz mono sample from The Rolling Stones' 'Love Is Strong,' off their Web server. Yeah, even the Stones are on the Internet!

"So record companies selling and distributing music via the Internet isn't a practical proposition at the moment. However, the Net does provide one way to check out tracks before you head off to a record shop - though it hardly competes with radio! All manner of musical life is on the Net, represented by newsgroups, mailing lists, file archives, and Websites."

—from **Future Music**

Creativity in Cyberspace **Hypermedia**

Hypermedia

Traditional media—texts, movies, and records—demand linear processing; readers must move from Point A to Point B, and from Point B to Point C. But with hypermedia, all straight lines are thrown out the window. Readers can jump from the beginning of a text to the end, and from the end back into the middle; in fact, notions like "beginning," "middle," and "end" hover on the brink of extinction. With one foot in future-tech, another in multimedia, and a third in post-structuralist criticism, hypermedia is the most exciting media development in the last four centuries. Visit **alt.hypertext**. Then jump to **Hyperedu**. Then career from the **HyperCard Forum** to **Hyperbole** like a pinball. Did someone say "Ted Nelson?" Don't worry. You'll link into him.

On the Net

Across the board

alt.hypertext (ng) "You really think that Cyberspace would have happened without visionaries like Ted Nelson?" The debate among these digital revolutionaries is quite interesting. Also get your technical hyper fix here, and check the schedule for hypermedia seminars. ✓**USENET**

The Epub Center The Electronic

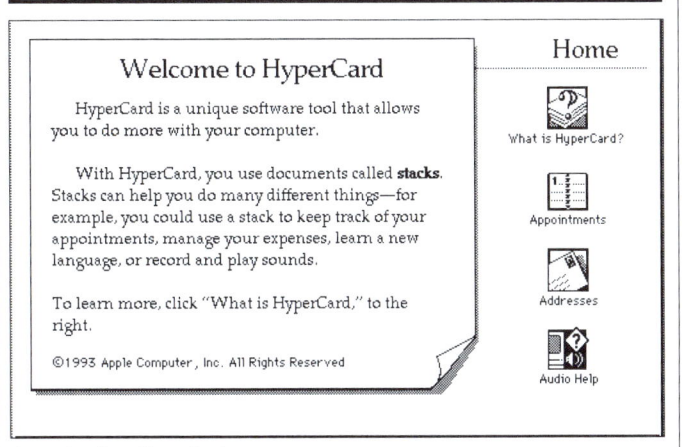

Screenshot from HyperCard

Publishing and Hypertext Reference Center offers instruction and tools for creating electronic books, zines, hypertext documents, and other texts. While the collection of HTML software, the multi-part Hypertext Reference Guide (from an article on hyperlinking to an overview of hypertext terms), product news and information, and the message boards for sharing tips and asking questions are indispensible, the forum is at its best in its libraries, which collect newsletters, magazines, books, and multimedia presentations. ✓**AMERICA ONLINE**→*keyword* epub

HT_Lit (ml) Stuart Moulthrop, Michael Joyce, Robert Coover, and other giants of hypertext fiction get frequent mention on this mailing list, which also gives props to Jorge Luis Borges, Thomas Pynchon, Julio Cortazar, Roland Barthes, Jacques Derrida, and virtually every author, philosopher, or semiotician who has followed a link, path, or *morceau*. Long live nonlinear narratives. ✓**INTERNET**→ *email* subscribe@journal.biology.carleton.ca ✍ *Type in message body:* subscribe ht_lt <your email address>

Hyperedu (ml) Could this be the greatest teaching invention since chalk? Hundreds of educators explore applications of hypertext in the classroom on this list. ✓**INTERNET**→*email* listserv%itocsivm.bitnet@listserv.net ✍ *Type in message body:* subscribe hyperedu <your full name>

Information about Hypermedia Hypertext forerunner Vannevar Bush's 1945 paper "As We May Think" is available at this site, as are dozens of other documents—histories of this young medium, general programming resources, and basic guides to HTML. ✓**INTERNET**→*www* http://www.lawrence.edu/www/hypertext.html

Macintosh Hypertext Forum

Hypermedia Creativity in Cyberspace

Macintosh hypermedia takes a number of forms. There's HyperCard, for one, which remains a powerful means of manipulating text, images, and sound. And then there are zillions of other hypertext editors and protocols. This forum ranges from discussion of the theory of hypertext to specific tips and tricks. Click here for more. ✓ **COMPUSERVE**→*go* hyper

SimTel Hypertext Software A small directory of hypertext authoring systems, browsers, and tutorials for DOS computer users. ✓ **INTERNET** …→*www* http://www.acs.oakland.edu/oak/SimTel/msdos/hypertxt.html …→*www* ftp://oak.oakland.edu/SimTel/msdos/hypertxt …→*www* ftp://wuarchive.wustl.edu/systems/ibmpc/simtel/msdos/hypertxt …→*www* ftp://ftp.uoknor.edu/mirrors/SimTel/msdos/hypertxt

State of the Art Review on Hypermedia Issues and Applications All about hypertext and issues in hypertext programming, including implementation, interfaces, and information retrieval issues. Perhaps not surprisingly, the review itself is in hypertext. ✓ **INTERNET** →*www* http://www.isg.sfu.ca/~duchier/misc/hypertext_review/index.html

History

A Short History of Hypertext In 1945, Vannevar Bush invented a machine called the Memex that retrieved information from translucent cards. In 1965, Ted Nelson coined the term "hypertext," using it to refer to any system of information arranged in a nonlinear fashion that permits multiple linkages between individual blocks of information. Fifty years after Bush, thirty years after Nelson, the computer world is still struggling with the implications of hypertext, trying to situate it in the larger framework of artificial intelligence, Internet design, and French post-structuralist criticism. Find out a little bit about the history of this technology, and then marvel at the irony of a hypertext history without links. ✓ **INTERNET** …→*www* http://www.w3.org/hypertext/History.html …→*www* http://epics.aps.anl.gov/demo/guide/www.guide.app.a.html

Terminology

Hypertext Terminology Anchors, annotation, authoring, buttons, nodes, and so many other hypertext terms that Ted Nelson will have to take notes. ✓ **INTERNET** →*www* http://www.w3.org/hypertext/WWW/Terms.html

HyperCard

comp.sys.mac.hypercard (ng) Serious devotees of HyperCard hang out here, talking about ways to make the most of this relatively simple authoring system. The talk is detailed and, at times, painstakingly technical, with lots of discussion about scripting and "XCMDs," but not everyone's an expert, and newbies looking to construct their first stack will get friendly advice. ✓ **USENET**

Heizer Software Heizer is one of the industry leaders in helper applications for Apple scripting programs like HyperCard, and the company's Website includes a program index, demos, updates, and press releases. ✓ **INTERNET**→*www* http://www.webcom.com/~heizer/

HyperCard Forum A HyperCard resource center, including a message board for swapping stacks, stories, and programming tips with other users and developers. The software library contains a lot of useful homemade HyperCard stacks, like an email address organizer and a runner's log. Drop into the education software folder and download HyperCard reference books on subjects ranging from philosophy and architecture to world capitals and the JFK assassination. ✓ **EWORLD**→*go* hypercard

HyperCard Forum This user-friendly scripting tool has been around almost as long as the Macintosh, and it enjoys continued popularity in this AOL forum. Resources are conscientiously presented here so that beginners will not be deterred. In the message board area there are categories for learning HyperCard, programming HyperTalk, and reading stack reviews. There is also a special beginner's corner where you can ask those "basic" questions you might hesitate to place elsewhere. Advanced users will find plenty of information about scripting, including a separate Special Interest Group (SIG) devoted to X-command developers. The software libraries really ought to be called "Stack Libraries," because, for the most part, that's what they contain. You can search for what you need using keywords,

> "In 1945, Vannevar Bush invented a device called the Memex that retrieved information from translucent cards."

Creativity in Cyberspace *Hypermedia*

or browse through the collections on your own. Learning stacks and information files dominate the listings, but there are business tools, scripting tools, and development tools as well. Regular visitors can check the weekly "New Files" area to save themselves some time. Live HyperCard conferences take place on Friday nights at 9 p.m. EST. ✓**AMERICA ONLINE**→*keyword* mhc

HyperCard Mailing List (ml) Discussions about HyperCard for Macintosh. ✓**INTERNET**→*email* listserv@purccvm.bitnet ✍ *Type in message body:* subscribe hypercrd <your full name>

Mac Shareware HyperCard A small, unimpressive collection of HyperCard stacks. Files are not organized by subject matter, so you'll have to open up each description to discover what it really is. The most popular download is a stack entitled "Birthday," a database that lists the winners of annual awards, such as Pulitzers, Nobel Prizes and Oscars, for the year you were born. Don't lie! ✓**AMERICA ONLINE**→*keyword* mac500→HyperCard

Software

Hyperbole Hyperbole is a flexible hypertext information-retrieval system developed at Brown University. It allows buttons to be embedded within structured and unstructured files, mail messages, and even news articles, all of which come in handy if you're trying to set up a Website with fluid content. And that's no exaggeration. Get the latest on Hyperbole here. ✓**INTERNET**→*email* hyperbole-request@cs.brown.edu ✍ *Type in subject line:* add <your full name> <your email address> to hyperbole

---

The Language of Hypertext

"Authoring—A term for the process of writing a document.

Browser—A program which allows a person to read hypertext.

Client—A program which requests services of another program.

Cyberspace—This is the 'electronic' world as perceived on a computer screen.

Daemon—A program which runs independently of a browser.

Document—A term for a node or a collection of nodes on related topics.

External—A link to a node in a different database.

Hypermedia/Hypertext—Text which is not constrained to be linear.

Link—A relationship between two anchors, stored in the same or different database.

Navigation—The process of moving from one node to another through the hypertext web.

Node—A unit of information. Also known as a frame or card.

Path—An ordered set of nodes which represent a sequence in which a web can be read.

Server—A program which provides a service to another, known as the client.

Versioning—The storage and management of previous versions of a piece of information.

VRML (Virtual Reality Modeling Language)—a logical markup format for non-proprietary platforms.

Web—A set of nodes interconnected by links."

—from **Hypertext Terminology**

Multimedia **Creativity in Cyberspace**

Multimedia

When Konrad Zuse built Z3, the first machine to work on a binary system, in 1941, he
used perforated strips of discarded movie film—a hole in the film represented a 1, no hole represented 0. Little did the German know that half a century later, zeroes and ones would become the stuff that movies are made of. Today, everyone from rock musician Todd Rundgren to Hollywood's special-effects experts can attest to the versatility of binary code. Talk about the way that technology assists art in **comp.multimedia**. Become a PC Scorsese with **How to Make MPEG Movies**. Brush up on the latest theories and practices at the **NYU Center for Digital Multimedia**. And then download some stock footage of locomotives, or a few classic Buster Keaton routines, at CompuServe's **Archive Films Forum**.

Man with camera—from http://www.panix.com/~rayh/artcar/artcar.html

On the Net

Across the board

Desktop Video Forum Whether you're working with MPEG, QuickTime, or Video for Windows, this is the place to find sofware and hardware reviews and to compare notes with other digital-video developers. Also noteworthy are the discussions regarding A/V equipment, 3-D video, and Interactive Television as well as the back-and-forth regarding the continuing saga of multimedia standards. ✓ **COMPUSERVE** ›*go* dtvforum

Digital Media Research & Development Center What's an audio format? What does .WAV stand for? If reading your first multimedia FAQ makes you dizzy, check out this multimedia glossary for short and sweet definitions of 50-plus basic multimedia terms. In addition, you'll find downloadable artwork and graphics from the Minneapolis College of Art, resources for 2-D graphics, 3-D modeling, digital video, digital audio, and authoring, and tons of other exciting multimedia-related information. ✓ **INTERNET**→*www* http://shenzi.cc.missouri.edu/

Index to Multimedia Information Sources A well-organized resource for multimedia information, featuring an extensive FAQ collection with topics ranging from Amiga to Computer Speech. There is also a multimedia events calendar, a large software collection, and a long list of useful multimedia links. ✓ **INTERNET**→ *www* http://viswiz.gmd.de/MultimediaInfo/#CurrentEvents

Macintosh Multimedia Forum Looking for a way to convert your movies created with Premiere for Windows into Macintosh QuickTime? Contemplating the development of a CD-ROM title for both Windows and Macintosh? Save on a multimedia consultant's fee and ask your questions here. If you can't wait for a forum reply, try attending one of the live multimedia conferences. Multimedia in general is discussed on Monday evenings at 9 p.m. EST, and more

Creativity in Cyberspace Multimedia

specific discussions about the authoring program HyperCard are discussed on Friday evenings. And did we mention the vast libraries of Macromedia Director movies, QuickTime movies, and sound clips? ✓**AMERICA ONLINE**→*keyword* mmm

MS Windows AV Forum Make your Windows machine sing, play movies, and, well, entertain. Listen to Newt on Larry King, Beavis & Butt-head, the Monty Python Camelot song, or a clip from the JFK inaugural speech. Then, watch as a David Letterman guest performs a stupid human trick or a woman morphs into a werewolf. The forum's library has huge archives of movie and TV sound clips, music sound clips, multimedia presentations, and MIDI files. The applications needed to run these files, such as sound and movie players and graphics programs, are also available here. ✓**COMPUSERVE**→*go* winav

Multimedia Jeff wants to create a training video and would like suggestions for authoring software. Other Prodigy users respond with reviews of Macromedia Director 4.0, IconAuthor, and Quest. Susan is interested in finding entertaining QuickTime movies for the Mac. And Jack's asking about screensavers and converting JPEGs to GIFs. These topics include a lot of how-to advice for those exploring the visual and audio capabilities of their computers as well as a fair amount of specific product advice. ✓**PRODIGY** …→*jump* computerbb→Choose a Topic→Multimedia & CD-ROM …→*jump* software supportbb→Choose a Topic→Multimedia

Multimedia Forum Whether you're looking for recommendations on a new sound card or advice on how to market a finished multimedia title, this forum covers most multimedia bases. Access Usenet FAQs, brush up on copyright issues in the Multimedia Law Primer, or post your resumé in the classifieds section. You can download files ranging from screensavers to GIFs to Adobe Acrobat Reader 2.0. ✓**COMPUSERVE**→*go* multimedia

Multimedia World Online Can't get sound on AOL? Ask Dr. Multimedia, just one of several features in what is definitely an online improvement over the print edition of *Multimedia World*. Download demo versions of new games and software, clip media, 3-D graphics, and other shareware, or attend online discussions with multimedia luminaries like The Fat Man (composer of music for Wing Commander, 7th Guest, and Ultima Underworld). If you're feeling the urge to upgrade your present system or stock up on CD-ROM titles, an entire database of Buyer's Guides from the past three years is at your disposal. And if all this still isn't enough, you can save the five bucks you'd spend at your local newsstand and read the contents of MW's latest issue. ✓**AMERICA ONLINE**→*keyword* multimediaworld

Navy Multimedia Page Leave it to the Navy to construct this no-nonsense launching pad into all essential corners of multimedia-related Cyberspace. From here you can link to the multimedia and image-processing newsgroups, the nebulous euro-babble of EC multimedia commission documents, or the very practical "How to Make MPEG Movies." ✓**INTERNET**→*www* http://netlab.itd.nrl.navy.mil/MM.html

PC Multimedia Forum Probably the best and biggest multimedia forum available on any commercial service. Start off with the Multimedia Reference Guide, where you can read up on sound cards and their specific applications in multimedia, or copyright law, or the common problem of hooking up a CD-ROM drive. Tuesdays and Wednesdays, you can join in on live chat sessions about multimedia. Why even bother going to the store? You can download Windows drivers, multimedia utilities, and movie and CD-player software directly from the software library, not to mention the vast collection of sounds, images, and the ubiquitous fractal movies. ✓**AMERICA ONLINE**→*keyword* pcmultimedia

The Video Interest Group A meeting place for Macintosh users interested in computer-generated video. Topics include capture boards, editing tools, and production techniques. The forum's message boards are separated into two categories—hardware and software. Several manufacturers of digital video products, including Radius and RasterOps, are represented in the software library with

> "And if all this still isn't enough, you can save the five bucks you'd spend at your local newsstand and read the contents of *Multimedia World*'s latest issue."

Multimedia Creativity in Cyberspace

their own folders. The company folders include message boards, product descriptions, and software. ✓**AMERICA ONLINE**→*keyword* videosig

Chat

comp.multimedia (ng) Discussion group covering all aspects of multimedia. This is a great place to look for job listings if you're a game developer or a Macromedia Director consultant. Also, if you're an aspiring Lingo programmer but can't figure out Macromedia Director's instruction manual (you're not alone!), this is where you'll find useful recommendations. And of course, there are plenty of reviews of the latest multimedia titles. ✓**USENET**

comp.os.os2.multimedia (ng) Are you feeling alone and confused when installing multimedia applications on your OS/2 machine? "If I try a selective install of my sound card and move the mouse around a lot during the install, my swapper.dat file fills up and the whole shebang crashes.... Is this a known issue?" Come here, OS/2ers, for feedback on such topics as MPEG, Web browsers, MIDI, and QuickTime. ✓**USENET**

comp.sys.amiga.multimedia (ng) You've heard you can play QuickTime movies on an Amiga, but you have questions. Bring them here. If you're in Europe, where Amiga boasts a much larger market share, this is also a good place to come hunting for bargains. ✓**USENET**

MACMULTI (ml) For all discussions relating to multimedia and the Macintosh. ✓**INTERNET**→*email* listserv%fccj.bitnet@listserv.net ≤ *Type in message body:* subscribe macmulti <your full name>

Multimedia Mailing List (ml) Multimedia free-for-all discussion list. ✓**INTERNET**→*email* listserv @vmtecmex.bitnet ≤ *Type in message body:* subscribe mmedia-l <your full name>

News

Digital Currency Excerpts from the monthly publication *Digital Currency*, which provides the latest information on developments in the interactive media industry. ✓**INTERNET**→*www* http://www.primenet.com/~laig/digital.html

Go Digital *Go Digital* bills itself as "*Wired* meets *Playboy*," a mixture of technology stories, multimedia and music reviews, and video pictorials of nude women on CD-ROM. While you won't get instant video from the magazine's Web version, you will get a few stills, plus a selection of cybersavvy links: the EFF, Timothy Leary sites, LucasArts, and the Funk Page. ✓**INTERNET**→*www* http://www.godigital.com/

Multimedia World Catering to those enjoying multimedia on a PC, this online companion to the print publication *Multimedia World* features news and reviews, a shareware library, a message board, and a software testing area. ✓**AMERICA ONLINE**→*keyword* multimediaworld

Rosenthal on Multimedia Twice a week Steve Rosenthal, who also writes a new media column for *MacWeek*, reports on multimedia for Prodigy users. Heavily oriented toward products, Rosenthal often reviews CDs, multimedia equipment, and industry directions. Prodigy archives more than a year's worth of columns. ✓**PRODIGY**→*jump* multimedia

---

CYBERNOTES

"Graphic Formats:

BMP (Bitmap Image File) format, used in Microsoft Windows and OS/2 applications.

PCX file format, used in DOS applications.

TGA (Targa) format, used by many IBM systems that use the Truevision video boards.

ILBM (Interchange File Format), used by the Commodore Amiga.

PICT format, used by Macintosh applications as a common format for importing and exporting graphics.

TIFF or **.GIF** format, used when moving graphics from one computer platform to another.

JPEG (Joint Photographic Experts Group compressed file), one popular 'lossy' graphic format used on all computer platforms. JPEG compression economizes data storage and also identifies and discards 'extra' data, that is, information beyond what the human eye can see."

—from **Digital Media Research & Development Center**

Creativity in Cyberspace Multimedia

Synapse—Multimedia Journal of the Eclectic Download an image-processing learning program or a full version of The Complete Morph, a new image-morphing application; read reviews of the latest PC hardware and software; and pick up some tricks and tips for designing game music. Synapse is a new CD-ROM magazine produced by hardcore hackers. ✓ **INTERNET**→*www* http://www.tricon.net/Comm/synapse/index.html

CD-ROMs

comp.publish.cdrom.multimedia (ng) So you're jumping into the multimedia production business and you can't choose between Macromedia Director or MediaVerse's Authorware. This is a good place to come for help. And what if you want a job? Listings for everything from summer intern to multimedia programmer to assistant producer are posted on this newsgroup. You only want to shop? Many online retailers post lists of the titles they stock. If you're lucky, you might catch a liquidation sale and pick up Fatty Bear's Birthday Surprise for nine bucks. ✓ **USENET**

Animation/MPEGS

comp.graphics.algorithms (ng) This highly technical newsgroup discusses algorithms used in manipulating computer graphics. Topics include texture mapping, cloud generators, and blurring filters. ✓ **USENET**

comp.graphics.animation (ng) A meeting place for advanced computer animators. The discussion covers programming code, system configurations, and A/V development packages. There are also a number of "Help Wanted"

Laurie Anderson's Puppet Motel— *from http://www.voyagerco.com*

postings here. ✓ **USENET**

comp.graphics.packages.alias (ng) A highly technical newsgroup dedicated to the Alias animation package. ✓ **USENET**

comp.graphics.packages.lightwave (ng) This well-populated newsgroup discusses the Lightwave animation package (for all platforms) as well as the animation industry in general. ✓ **USENET**

G-Web G-Web is an electronic journal that covers the computer-animation industry: interviews with leading animation professionals, links to the Websites of prominent animation companies (Adobe, Electric Image, Fractal Design, Apple, Advanced Media Productions, etc.), and a database of schools that teach computer animation (with contact information and links to the schools). ✓ **INTERNET**→*www* http://www.cinenet.net:80/GWEB/index.html

How to Make MPEG Movies An explanation of the ins and outs of making MPEG movies on a Unix system—in layman's language. Find out about image data files, converting to YUV, and where to download MPEG display programs. ✓ **INTERNET**→*www* http://www.arc.umn.edu/GVL/Software/mpeg.html

MPEG FAQ JPEG? MHEG? MPEG 1, 2, 3, 4? What's the difference? The FAQ gives you the lowdown on digital video and audio compression. In other words, if you want high-quality video for your multimedia project, you'd better start here. You can also find out exactly what the "Moving Pictures Experts Group" (MPEG) is and how to get involved. ✓ **INTERNET**→*www* http://www.crs4.it/HTML/LUIGI/MPEG/mpegfaq.html

MPEG Movie Archive Listing of Animations The Dallas Cowboys win the NFC Championship. Lisa Simpson inspects her braces. And the Starship *Enterprise* travels through space. These and a small but stellar collection of other MPEG animations are available here. ✓ **INTERNET**→*www* http://peace.wit.com/surrealism/movies/anim/

MPEG Technical Info Most of the technical information here concerns converting QuickTime movies into MPEG on either a Mac or a Unix machine, or using both. The site offers very precise instructions with links to FTP sites whenever a piece of software or shareware is recommended. ✓ **INTERNET**→*www* http://www.eit.com/techinfo/mpeg/mpeg.html

SimTel Animation Utilities A small collection of animation generators and players for DOS computers. ✓ **INTERNET** ...→*www* http://www.acs.oakland.edu/oak/SimTel/msdos/animate.html ...→*www* ftp://oak.oakland.edu/SimTel/msdos/animate ...→*www*

Net Tech 215

Multimedia Creativity in Cyberspace

ftp://wuarchive.wustl.edu/systems/ibmpc/simtel/msdos/animate...→*www* ftp://ftp.uoknor.edu/mirrors/SimTel/msdos/animate...→*www* ftp://ftp.uni-paderborn.de/SimTel/msdos/animate

Education

The Multimedia Exchange If there's one field where multimedia applications can make a difference, it's education. This library of stackware is designed for teachers interested in exchanging sound samples, graphics, animations, and other media for educational purposes. And teachers won't have to worry about explaining their on-line expenses: the more time you spend downloading, the more free time you get. ✓ **AMERICA ONLINE**→*keyword* tin→The Multimedia Exchange

NYU Center for Digital Multimedia Carries the curriculum catalog for New York University's Center for Digital Multimedia, including general program information, course descriptions, faculty bios, and registration information. Also available are links to the Media Lab's research projects (take control of a robot from your Web browser), as well as the home pages of affiliated groups. ✓ **INTERNET**→*www* http://found.cs.nyu.edu/CAThome_new.html

QuickTime

Apple's QuickTime Online Anyone working with both the Mac and Windows versions of QuickTime knows the endless nightmares involved. Serious programmers will find a few cross-platform development tips here, as well as information about the Apple Multimedia Development Program, which offers professionals tools, tips, a development channel, and discounts on software. If you want to teach yourself QuickTime, check out the FAQ. Novice multimedia explorers can see what the QT hype is all about by downloading digitized excerpts from Madonna, REM, and Tom Petty videos. You can also preview the latest developments in QuickTime technology, such as QuickTime VR—360-degree views of real-world scenes. ✓ **INTERNET**→*www* http://quicktime.apple.com/

QuickTime Swish! A basketball flies into the hoop. Pop! A college student's head explodes. Yikes! A space-age rollercoaster rides with no tracks. Whether it's a QuickTime clip of ten seconds on New York's Broadway or instructional tips for Quark, this Mac-based forum is a huge QuickTime file repository. ✓ **AMERICA ONLINE**→*keyword* mmm→Software Libraries

QuickTime 2.0 Download Area For $9.95 (billed to your CompuServe account), you can download the latest version of QuickTime for Mac, Power Mac, or Windows. ✓ **COMPUSERVE**→*go* qtime

QuickTime 2.0 Download Area (Internet) If you have a First Virtual account, you can download QuickTime 2.0 for Windows or Mac for only $9.95. If you need an account, click the First Virtual icon and fill out the application form. Call a toll-free number with your credit card information and you're in secure business. ✓ **INTERNET**→*www* http://quicktime.apple.com/ordering-qt.html

QuickTime FAQ Squash any fears you may have about working with QuickTime. Check out tips on better digitization. Need sound advice? You'll find plenty of information on music, MIDI, and sound tracks for QuickTime. And if none of the above takes care of inevitable last-minute glitches, you'll find a list of online support and resource outlets to help you out of a jam. ✓ **INTERNET**→*www* http://www.mcs.net:80/~cwiltgen/www/quicktime/quicktime.html

Clips

alt.binaries.multimedia (ng) In this newsgroup, multimedia

The QuickTime Continuum—http://quicktime.apple.com

216 Net Tech

Creativity in Cyberspace Multimedia

means movies and TV video bytes. Download your favorite Sega commercials, scenes from the Simpsons, and even part of *Naked Gun 33 1/2* (costarring the most famous Simpson, O.J.). ✓ **USENET**

alt.binaries.multimedia.erotica (ng) Straight guys and lesbians get erotic video ya-yas here, where MPEG B-movie shower scenes and files called "Gigantic Breasts" are the order of the day. You can even download all forty parts of "The Nurse" or the single file "Ex-Wife with Bottle in Butt." If your porn tastes match the above, you'll have a field day here. ✓ **USENET**

Archive Films Forum One-stop shopping for trains, planes, and automobiles, not to mention natural disasters. The film archive consists of over 14,000 hours of stock footage, plus classic silent and talkie films. The best gems are to be found in the "Technology Gone Bad" file, featuring filmed interviews with the Klaatu-like Westinghouse Moto-Man and GIFs of Goggle Wipers. While you may not be able to use this material for commericial purposes without permission, it's still a great place to see what's available, or to dazzle guests at your next dinner party. ✓ **COMPUSERVE**→*go* arcfilm

Contemporary Motion Images Forum Are you looking for ultra-generic footage for a public relations CD-ROM? Here you'll find lowest-common-denominator QuickTime clips of tractors plowing fields and pretty models wading in the surf. ✓ **COMPUSERVE**→*go* energy

Entertainment Drive Forum Miss May 1994 is in the *Playboy* section, and *Baywatch* bathing beauties are in the section devoted entirely to that show. An excerpt from Nirvana's "Smells Like Teen Spirit" is in the .WAV section, while *Batman Forever* QuickTime movies reside in the Warner Brothers section. The site is packed with sounds and images from the entertainment world. ✓ **COMPUSERVE**→*go* eforum→Libraries

Entertainment Drive: Multimedia and More CompuServe's flagship entertainment arena contains a few QuickTime clips promoting new movies. If you want Travolta and Thurman dancing on your desktop monitor, Entertainment Drive will do nicely. ✓ **COMPUSERVE**→*go* emedia

FOOTAGE.net Looking for footage but don't feel like flipping through a mound of stock footage–company catalogues? Run a "Zap request." Enter a key word for the type of footage you're looking for and search the archives of over 150 stock-footage companies. You'll get an instant list of those companies that have the sort of footage you're looking for. If you're confused about copyright issues, read the downloadable Library of Congress copyright handbook. You can also connect to the Library of Congress's Motion Picture, Broadcast, and Sound Division or read up on the latest trends in the stock archival and footage industries. While you can't download any actual footage from here, it's still a top source for footage finding. ✓ **INTERNET**→*www* http://www.footage.net:2900/

Fractal Movie Archive Throwing a rave party? Here you'll find plenty of fractal movie clips, in MPEG and .FLI formats, to accompany techno/ambient soundtracks. From "Very Strange Waves of Smoke" to "Fast Fly Through a Fractal Generated Canyon," the

> "The best gems are to be found in the 'Technology Gone Bad' file, featuring filmed interviews with the Klaatu-like Westinghouse Moto-Man and GIFs of Goggle Wipers."

computer-generated art films found here are guaranteed to get any desktop rave going. ✓ **INTERNET**→*www* http://www.cnam.fr/fractals/anim.html

Hollywood Online Forum Need a picture of "Smokin' Lori Petty" or "Liam Neeson in a Kilt"? These are just a few of the .GIFs you can download from the multimedia film preview files at this site. If you want celebrity-packed sound bytes for your computer, try Ethan Hawke's third-person confession to Julie Delpy that "he's crazy about her!" And if that isn't enough for you, try a sound-and-vision-packed QuickTime clip of Jim Carrey's morphing *Mask*. The QuickTime program and Run-Time modules are available here as well. ✓ **AMERICA ONLINE**→*keyword* hollywoodonline ✓ **EWORLD**→*go* hollywood ✓ **COMPUSERVE**→*go* flicks ✓ **INTERNET**→*www* http://hollywood.com/

Multimedia Maniacs Looking for Monty Python samples? "Stairway to Heaven"? Maybe you're a

Net Tech 217

Multimedia Creativity in Cyberspace

UK-based techno god and the Amiga is your music-making tool of choice. Multimedia Maniacs offers several pages with a variety of music, sound, and video samples, plus access to the Hungarian Amiga Home Page, a resource center for those making rave art and music. ✓**INTERNET**→*www* http://MM.iit.uni-miskolc.hu/

Rob's Multimedia Lab From this wide range of easy-to-find multimedia samples for professional and private use, you could choose between Jeff Spicoli's "Hey Bud, what's your problem" and Butt-head's "Huh, huh, huh." But that's just the beginning. Download Richard Nixon's "I am not a crook" speech, the Banana Splits theme, or Krusty the Clown's laugh. And for film and video fans, you can get clips of everything from Bjork to Indiana Jones to more computer-generated fractal movies. Finally, you'll find a range of still images worthy of any stock-photography house, from twee tiger photos to *Simpsons* animations to natural distasters. ✓**INTERNET**→*www* http://www.acm.uiuc.edu/rml/

The Screening Room Looking for experimental digital cinema or just old stock footage of a hangglider? Here you'll find both, plus the usual space and computer-generated film archives. Perhaps the best thing about this collection of links is its organization. Each archive is put into a category and summed up in a paragraph—no more checking out each link to see if it has what you need. ✓**INTERNET**→*www* http://gnn.interpath.net/gnn/special/drivein/screening.room.html

Sunsite Multimedia Information Good place to find MPEG animations of generic bicycles, aliens, and airplanes. You'll also find a selection of greeting card–variety .GIFs, from orchids to cats to Miami Beach. But the real reason to check out this site is its wide range of interesting film- and video-oriented links. ✓**INTERNET**→*www* http://sunsite.sut.ac.jp/multimed/multimed.html

UNC Multimedia Archive If you're looking for distinct audio, video, and photographic samples, welcome to paradise. Download current Chinese pop hits, Gang of Four favorites, or Beijing Opera. In the pictures directory, you'll find a stylish set of vintage 1950s computer photos, complete with magnetic tape reels and hole-punch cards. And if you're lucky enough to get into the video archives (this is a very busy site), you'll find a random selection of "little MPEG movies," from scenes of Genoa to monitor stress tests. ✓**INTERNET**→*www* gopher://sunsite.unc.edu:70/11/../.pub/multimedia

3D moviegoers—from http://www.pathfinder.com

Programming

Autodesk Multimedia Forum All Autodesk products are discussed here. You'll find the latest press releases on Animator Studio and Autodesk 3D Studio, hardware information, and solutions for perfecting the Pac Man morph (getting his mouth to chomp without creating a fold in the back of his neck). First-hand tips for professionals. ✓**COMPUSERVE**→*go* asoft

Autodesk Showcase Forum If you're an Autodesk ace, this is where you flaunt it. In the library sections, you'll find hundreds of .GIFs, TIFFs, and JPEG files featuring 3-D models of Los Angeles, Space Stations, and "Running Wooden Heads." If you want to find out how some of these were made, post a query and maybe the creator will answer. ✓**COMPUSERVE**→*go* ashowcase

AWARE—Authorware Mail-

Creativity in Cyberspace Multimedia

ing List (ml) Discussion list for developers using Authorware Professional. ✓**INTERNET**→*email* listserv@ccl.kuleuven.ac.be ✍ *Type in message body:* subscribe aware <your full name>

comp.os.ms-windows.programmer.multimedia (ng) Looking for information on writing MCI drivers? Do you feel like comparing cross-platform tips with colleagues? Maybe you're looking for a job. Here's a discussion group geared towards multimedia programmers authoring in Windows. ✓**USENET**

EMASHE/Establishing Multimedia Authoring Skills in Higher Education Looking for aids to teach yourself multimedia authoring? Based at the University of Glasgow, the EMASHE project develops and builds multimedia training packages. Although you might want to skip the pedagogical treatises on multimedia in education, you can find out how to order the latest EMASHE tutorial CD-ROM and print manuals. ✓**INTERNET**→*www* http://www.info.apple.com/dev/

General DOS Game Programming Material/Directory Need information about writing source code for DOS sound programming? How about a review of the latest mapmaking software for game programming? If you're willing to dig, this massive DOS game-programming directory is likely to have the answers. You can also download basic game-programming utilities, from font editors to fractal-generation programs. ✓**INTERNET**→*www* ftp://x2ftp.oulu.fi/pub/msdos/programming/

HSC Software Mailing List (ml) For discussion about Kai's Power Tools, KPT Bryce, KPT Convolver, Live Picture, and other HSC Software products. ✓**INTERNET**→*email* listserv@netcom.com ✍ *Type in message body:* subscribe kpt-list <your full name>

Macromedia Not only is this forum a product-support and promotion center for Macromedia's authoring programs, but it's an extensive multimedia archive as well. Download 3-D characters named Billy or third-party utilities and patches for Director, Authorware Professional, and Action! Read up on the latest Macromedia developments in the news folder or find out how to get technical support. ✓**AMERICA ONLINE**→*keyword* macromedia

Macromedia Director for Macintosh and Windows (ml) For discussions about Macromedia Director for both Macintosh and Windows. ✓**INTERNET**→*email* listserv@uafsysb.uark.edu ✍ *Type in message body:* subscribe direct-l <your full name>

Macromedia Director Page Macromedia Director may have become the near standard for CD-ROM authoring, but its use has by no means become perfected. Here you'll find an entire page of archives featuring first-person tips on mastering everything from Lingo programming to authoring on Macs to Sprites and Puppets. You can also download add-ons for Director and XObjects. ✓**INTERNET**→*www* http://www.mcli.dist.maricopa.edu/director/

Microsoft Windows Multimedia Developer Forum Are you looking for programs for authoring in Windows? Check out demos, FAQs, and patches for Wintoon, Video for Windows, MediaVision, and others in the library. If you're looking for tips, exchange away in the message boards. ✓**COMPUSERVE**→*go* winmm

MMDEVX A discussion list for developers interested in cross-platform multimedia development tools, particularly Apple Media Kit and Keleida ScriptX. ✓**INTERNET**→*email* Mail-Server@knex.mind.org ✍ *Type in message body:* subscribe mmdevx <your full name>

Multimedia Authoring Page Central source of information for most major multimedia authoring languages. You'll find links to the pages for Authorware, Director, HyperCard, SuperCard, and ToolBook. Looking for information on the latest authoring developments? Check out the Multimedia Development Centers list, which will take you everywhere from the Apple Developers page to the Yale Center for Advanced Instructional Media. There is also a list of addresses for multimedia mailing lists. ✓**INTERNET**→*www* http://www.mcli.dist.maricopa.edu/authoring/

Preparing Media for Director

> "If you're lucky enough to get into the video archives, you'll find a selection of 'little MPEG movies,' from scenes of Genoa to monitor stress tests."

Net Tech 219

Multimedia Creativity in Cyberspace

Online manual featuring some tips on preparing media for authoring with Macromedia Director. To what size should you crop images? How do you best implement changing palettes? Is it better to import a file as a linked .PIC file or just import the whole thing? Reading through this document might not only make your multimedia project look great and run smoothly, but also most likely reduce your all-nighter quotient. ✓**INTERNET**→*www* http://www.peg.apc.org/~firehorse/mmedia/pmedia.html

ToolBook Mailing List (ml) Discussions about Asymetrix ToolBox and OpenScript. ✓**INTERNET**→*email* listserv@uafsysb.uark.edu ✍ *Type in message body:* subscribe toolb-l <your full name>

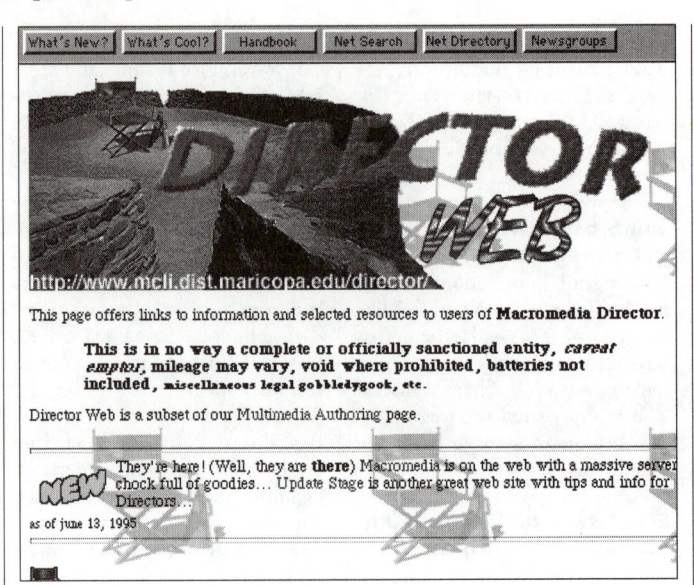

Director Web—http://www.mcli.dist.maricopa.edu/director/

Production companies

Fry Multimedia Let's say you work for a mail-order retailer and want to put your catalogue on CD-ROM. Or that you want to launch a CD-ROM magazine. Maybe you want a kiosk as well. Here you'll find all the information you need to get Fry Multimedia working on digitizing your print products. ✓**INTERNET**→*www* http://www.frymulti.com/

Interact Multimedia Although the site is primarily a place to advertise Interact Multimedia's production services, it also reports on multimedia developments. ✓**INTERNET**→*www* http://www.datanet.net/interact/interact.htm

Magnet Interactive Studios Products and service information from an interactive media company that says it develops products ranging from role-playing and action games for the consumer market to Dow Jones CD-ROMs for the business market. ✓**INTERNET**→*www* http://www.magnet.com/

Millennium Communications Looking to move beyond the simple slide show or flip-chart presentation? Using QuickTime movies, sound, and animation, Millennium, along with thousands of other companies (but are they on the Web?), will help you create a flawless business presentation. ✓**INTERNET**→*www* http://www.webcom.com/~milcom/

Multimedia Vendor Forums Looking for more information on Turtle Beach sound cards? What new titles are being released by Voyager? Here you'll find a market for multimedia software developers and companies to show off their products. Besides FAQs, on-line catalogues, and company bios, you can target a specific company to see if they've got any job offers. ✓**COMPUSERVE**→*go* multiven *and* multibven *and* multicven

New Media Associates Offering multimedia services for corporate clients, this company publishes CD-ROMs for clients, develops interactive presentations, consults on computer-based training, and sets up touch-screen kiosks for businesses. ✓**INTERNET**→*www* http://www.ip.net/NMA/

Time Warner Interactive Having problems getting through Hellcab alive? Graphics scratch during the Noah's Ark slide show in the New Family Bible? Check out the Hints and FAQs library. Or get advice from users on the message board. But TWI's presence isn't just to promote their products. Comments and feedback are encouraged, and many customers exercise their rights liberally. On Rise of the Robots: "I found a way to beat almost every robot flawlessly. I don't even use the cyborg's special moves! I spent $60 on a game hyped this much to enjoy it for only six hours! Come on, guys—you could be a little bit more creative." ✓**AMERICA ONLINE**→*keyword* twi

Creativity in Cyberspace Multimedia

Voyager Voyager, the company that sets the standards for the CD-ROM industry, is now setting standards on the Web. With elegance and simplicity, Voyager has placed its entire catalog online. Each CD-ROM title has its own page, with detailed descriptions, screenshots, QuickTime demos, and recommendations for other titles that might be of interest. In its Criterion Collection pages, *every* movie title has a downloadable clip and essay and is cross-referenced with other films by director, country, and year. With a forms-capable Web browser, you can order online. ✓ **INTERNET**→*www* http://www.voyagerco.com

Voyager Whether it's Laurie Anderson's stunning *Puppet Motel* or the overrated *People* magazine CD-ROM, you can order it here. Find out about the latest Voyager releases and download demo products. If you've still got your laserdisc player, order selections from the Criterion Collection, the impeccably annotated laserdiscs that were Voyager's original claim to fame. ✓ **AMERICA ONLINE**→*keyword* voyager

Software

SimTel Multimedia Directory If your Windows-based PC is roarin' to go, but you still can't find the courage and the software necessary to make multimedia magic, drop by this massive collection of Windows shareware, which includes everything from MIDI, .WAV, and .AVI players to simple authoring systems to multimedia file players. ✓ **INTERNET** …→*www* http://www.acs.oakland.edu/oak/SimTel/win3/multimed.html …→*www* ftp://oak.oakland.edu/SimTel/win3/multimed …→*www* ftp://wuarchive.wustl.edu/systems/ibmpc/simtel/win3/multimed …→*www* ftp://ftp.uoknor.edu/mirrors/SimTel/win3/multimed …→*www* ftp://ftp.uni-paderborn.de/SimTel/win3/multimed

More Production Companies

AApex Software Corporation ✓ **INTERNET**→*www* http://io.com/user/aapex/

ACT Advanced Cultural Technologies Inc. (ACT) is developing software products and services integrating multimedia data with high-speed computer networks. ✓ **INTERNET**→*www* http://www.ACTinc.bc.ca/

Amiga World Wide Web Resource ✓ **INTERNET**→*www* http://www.cs.cmu.edu/Web/People/mjw/Computer/Amiga/MainPage.html

Children's Software Company ✓ **INTERNET**→*www* http://www.childsoft.com/childsoft

Computers At Large ✓ **INTERNET**→*www* http://www.aimnet.com/cal/

Creative Labs, Inc. ✓ **INTERNET**→*www* http://www.creaf.com/

Due North Multimedia Multimedia tools for education. ✓ **INTERNET**→*www* http://www.icw.com/duenorth/duenorth.html

IVI Publishing ✓ **INTERNET**→*www* http://www.seattle.ivi.com/ivi/

JUTASTAT ✓ **INTERNET**→*www* http://www.os2.iaccess.za/jutastat/index.htm

Kaleida Labs ✓ **INTERNET**→*www* http://www.kaleida.com/

MediaTools Online ✓ **INTERNET**→*www* http://www.firmware.com.au/

Multimedia Central European Creative Labs site. ✓ **INTERNET**→*www* http://www.demon.co.uk:80/cluk/

Optimus ✓ **INTERNET**→*www* http://www.csn.net:80/~ravaldez/

Pacific Hi-Tech Corp. ✓ **INTERNET**→*www* http://www.pht.com/

Pro-CD Phone books on CD-ROM. ✓ **INTERNET**→*www* http://www.procd.com/

QRZ (Ham Radio CD-Rom, Beer CD-Rom, etc.) ✓ **INTERNET**→*www* http://www.qrz.com/

Rocket Science ✓ **INTERNET**→*www* http://www.rocketsci.com/

Rocky Mountain Digital Peeks Home Page ✓ **INTERNET**→*www* http://www.csn.net/malls/rmdp/

Sega ✓ **INTERNET**→*www* http://www.segaoa.com/

Starwave ✓ **INTERNET**→*www* http://www.starwave.com/corp/about.html

Timestream ✓ **INTERNET**→*www* http://www.timestream.com/~ts/

Part 7

Computers & Society

Future Tech **Computers & Society**

Future tech

Laurie Anderson once sang, "Paradise is exactly like where we are right now / Only much, much better." The same can be said of the future, which for years has been touted as the only cure for the ills of the present. Need to eradicate a deadly disease? Want to be transported to work through molecular rearrangement? Obsessed with the possibility of virtual sex? Wait until the future—they'll figure out how to do all that, and more. The Net emphasizes the speculative and spectacular aspects of future tech. Mailing lists like **Alife** and **AI-Nat** wonder whether computers can one day think as intelligently as human beings (some scientists believe they've already surpassed Dan Quayle). The **NCSA Virtual Reality Lab** brings the latest in 3-D modeling and navigable environments to the Net. And the **1995 International BEAM Robot Olympics** proves that even machines feel competitive urges.

Boy and robot—downloaded from CompuServe's Bettmann Archive Forum

On the Net

Artificial intelligence

AI FAQs Interested in speech recognition, natural language processing, genetic algorithms, cellular automata, music and AI, neural nets, and fuzzy logic? Aside from answering many basic questions about the nature of AI and its various forms, the FAQ provides extensive bibliographies and addresses for FTP resources. ✓**INTERNET**→ *www* http://www.cs.cmu.edu/ Web/Groups/AI/html/faqs/ai/ai _general/top.html

AI-Nat (ml) When computers start to figure out how to apply themselves to real-world problems, all heaven will break loose. We'll have more efficient natural resource management, more productive mining technologies, and national defense arsenals entirely free of human decision-making. Sounds positively Utopian, doesn't it? ✓**INTERNET**→*email* majordomo @adfa.oz.au ✍ *Type in message body:* subscribe ai-nat <your email address>

Alife (ml) No, artificial life isn't a

224 Net Tech

Computers & Society Future Tech

new field devoted to studying the Michael Jackson–Lisa Marie Presley marriage. It's a cutting-edge discipline that cross-pollinates computer science, mathematics, medicine, and traditional developments in artificial intelligence. And it's the subject of this mailing list. ✓**INTERNET**→*email* alife-request @cognet.ucla.edu ✍ *Write a request*

Artificial Intelligence Resources There's a vast amount of AI-related information on this site, including conference announcements, calls for papers, job listings, journals, tech reports, and bibliographies. ✓**INTERNET**→*www* http://ai.iit.nrc.ca/ai_point.html

CMU Artificial Intelligence Repository If you've had enough of the abstract theorizing and are ready to plunge into the workings of AI, get software and documentation about Prolog, LISP, and SCHEME here. An HTML version of the entire book, "Common LISP: the Language" is available for downloading. ✓**INTERNET**→ *www* http://www.cs.cmu.edu/ Web/Groups/AI/html/repository. html

comp.ai* (ng) We all know that computers can rip through algorithms and calculate at blazing speed, but can they think? Can they understand a complex human facial expression or rhyming slang? Can they make decisions with shifting risks and rewards? Can they write a poem? Can they read Pynchon and understand it? The comp.ai hierarchy deals with artificial intelligence in all its complex glory—while the main group treats issues ranging from associative structure systems to symposia and journal publications, the more specific newsgroups narrow the focus. Interested in fuzzy logic? Try comp.ai.fuzzy. Curious about neural nets? Visit comp.ai.neural-nets. The Journal of Artificial Intelligence Research (JAIR) divides its editorial content into two groups, one for announcements and the other for articles. And comp.ai.philosophy moves from God to Goedel, from Turing to capital-t Truth. Get lost in the muddle, and explain to your computer that you are merely trying to bridge the gap between you and it. And remember—artificial intelligence is better than none at all. See the sidebar at right for AI newsgroup names. ✓**USENET**

Fuzzy-Mail (ml) What's fuzzy logic? Someone once told us that it has something to do with teaching computers to factor intangibles into complex decisions, but our memory is a little hazy. Check this mailing list for more details. ✓**INTERNET**→*email* listserver@ vexpert.dbai.tuwien.ac.at ✍ *Type in message body:* subscribe fuzzy-mail <your full name>

Journal of Artificial Intelligence Reports created by research teams studying how to do things like teach computers the English past tense, digitize human notetaking, and add decision-making elements to a computer are published here. ✓**INTERNET**→*www* http://www.cs.washington.edu/ research/jair/home.html

Neural Net FAQ Learn the difference between an ANN and a statistical model, or how exactly an FAM (Fuzzy Associative Memory) works. Development software like NeuFuz4, Neurowindows, and Neuroforecaster is available for downloading. ✓**INTERNET**→ *www* http://www.cs.cmu.edu/ Web/Groups/AI/html/faqs/ai/ neural/faq.html

AI Newsgroups

```
comp.ai
comp.ai.alife
comp.ai.edu
comp.ai.fuzzy
comp.ai.genetic
comp.ai.jair.announce
comp.ai.jair.papers
comp.ai.nat-lang
comp.ai.neural-nets
comp.ai.nlang-know-rep
comp.ai.philosophy
comp.ai.shells
comp.ai.vision
```

SEL-HPC Article Archive This archive is broken into 11 topic areas including: high-performance computing (1,163 articles), vision and image processing (373), neural networks (179), and functional programming (984). Researchers can add their papers to the site, or modify information they have already posted there. ✓**INTERNET**→ *www* http://www.lpac.qmw.ac.uk/ SEL-HPC/Articles/index.html

SRI Artificial Intelligence Center If you found HAL unnerving (*2001: A Space Odyssey*, remember?), this site will scare your pants off. The intelligent computing systems being developed here have applications like "diagnosis and decision support; emergency response planning and action; autonomous vehicle control; military planning and scheduling." Yikes. ✓**INTERNET**→ *www* http://www.ai. sri.com/aic/

Virtual reality

alt.cyberpunk.tech (ng) Devoted to information and debates over the technical aspects of Cyberspace, magnetic-powered weapons, monomolecular blades, etc. There is also a fair amount of information and discussion of VR,

Future Tech Computers & Society

including announcements of Virtual Reality Modeling Language demonstrations at the Electronic Cafe in Los Angeles. The punk, outlaw edge of the group often causes discussions to degenerate into flame wars. If you're faint of heart or easily offended, skip this newsgroup. ✓**USENET**

ARI Virtual Reality Research Virtual reality research is almost certainly being conducted at the Army Research Institute. While you won't read any military secrets on this page, the site does list VR-environment research centers; a link to the Simulator Training Research Advanced Testbed for Aviation (STRATA), their jet simulation training site; software sites; and other research centers. ✓**INTERNET**→*www* http://alex-immersion.army.mil/default.html

Cardiff VR Pages This University of Cardiff–based site contains a dozen links to pages on VR, including information on restricted and special-interest pages, private sites, and bios of people involved with VR, as well as software, hardware, and documentation pages. ✓**INTERNET**→*www*http://www.cm.cf.ac.uk/User/Andrew.Wilson/VR/index.html

Cyber Forum In a topic designated for virtual beginners, Gabriel is looking to get VR for less than $300 on a 486 with 4MB of RAM. Elsewhere on the message board, Ryan's trying to motivate other members to help him build a virtual city; Richard's describing the advances made by the University of Chicago in holographic VR; and Andrew's analyzing the financial report released by the Virtuality Group. Whether it's nanotechnology (see the library for a Nanotechnology FAQ and .GIFs of nanotech atoms) or issues related to computers and society (see the library for the text on VR and the law), the library and message board in the forum are great places to explore issues of virtual reality. ✓**COMPUSERVE**→*go* cyberforum

Cybermind (ml) Remember Robocop? How about the Six Million Dollar Man? And what about the Borg? They're all fearsome combinations of man and machine, and they're also our future. Yes, that's right—in the next few years our arms will turn into flippers, our legs will shrink to the size of gherkins, and our very flesh, cooked to putrefaction by the many-years worth of toxic waste dumped into our drinking water, will be replaced by rubber, spandex, or pleather. Get a handle on the disappearance of humanity and the rise of the superbrain by subscribing to this list, which tends toward philosophical, psychoanalytic, and social inquiry. ✓**INTERNET**→*email* majordomo@jefferson.village.virginia.edu ✍ *Type in message body:* subscribe cybermind <your email address>

The Encyclopedia of Virtual Environments Short articles on VR technologies, applications, and terminology. ✓**INTERNET**→ *www* http://www.cs.umd.edu/projects/eve/eve-main.html

Gadget Mania For those obsessed with consumer electronics and high-tech gadgetry, Gadget-Don and GadgetBob Brown review the news on gadgets and consumer electronics in the monthly *Gadget Gazette* magazine—and they don't just tell you about them, they gush over them. ✓**EWORLD**→*go* gadgets

The Homebrew-VR Homepage This page is essential surf-

CYBERNOTES

"Please excuse my ignorance, but would a holodeck, such as the one in Star Trek: The Next Generation series, be feasible?"

"For one Dan... What you say is about 5 to 10 years BEHIND the rest of the world. I have been researching virtual reality and found that a holodeck (interactive, with no physical objects) IS possible! If you talk to Whirlpool (yeah the dishwasher people) they have a new Kitchen 2000 with a revolutionary new holographic projector that projects real-time 3D holographic images that can't be distinguished from the real thing...yes it's for displaying food in your recipe, but still it's there. Secondly, with high resolution walls, this system can be used to project believable images and holographics along with it. I have many great ideas stored in my head for the application of the advances I have found... Hope I didn't put down your VR lab too much ;-)."

—from **sci.virtual-worlds**

Computers & Society Future Tech

Lawnmower Man—downloaded from http://www.ee.pdx.edu/~caseyh/horror/pics/

ing for anyone interested in setting up their own home-based VR system. You'll find all the basic data you need to get started, plus lists of recommended gear. ✓**INTERNET**→*www* http://www.acm.uiuc.edu/homebrew/

Jaron Lanier's Homepage You've probably seen Jaron Lanier, the sleepy-eyed, dreadlocked VR visionary, on TV or in magazines like *Time* or *Newsweek*. Not only did he found the first VR company, VPL, but he coined the phrase "virtual reality." While Lanier's homepage gives plenty of background on his involvement with VR, it also includes information on his interests in visual art, writing, and music. From his site, you can download one of his MIDI software experiments, the Infinite Opera program. You can also find a video clip of a VR musical-instrument performance. A linked page with information on his acoustic album, *Instruments of Change*, contains downloadable sound clips from each track. ✓**INTERNET**→*www* http://www.well.com/Community/Jaron.Lanier/index.html

NASA VR lab The VR lab at NASA's Johnson Space Center is primarily geared toward using the technology as a training aid and carries, for instance, information on the environment simulators used to train the astronauts who repaired the Hubble Space Telescope. There are also detailed descriptions and selected images of NASA's VR equipment. ✓**INTERNET**→*www* http://www.jsc.nasa.gov/cssb/vr/vr.html

NASA's Web Stars Housed in NASA's High Energy Astrophysics Science Archive Research Center, this is NASA's guide to sites on the Net, including some very hot VR pages. ✓**INTERNET**→*www* http://guinan.gsfc.nasa.gov/WebStars.html

NCSA Virtual Reality Lab Set up and run by the National Center for Supercomputing Applications (NCSA), this site lets you track VR experiments and explore how virtual environments can help navigate information, mostly employing the CAVE system. Goggles and gloves aren't used in this VR system, but CAVE has a wraparound movie-type projection screen and surround-sound system. ✓**INTERNET**→*www* http://www.ncsa.uiuc.edu/VR/VR/VRHomePage.html

Open Virtual Reality Testbed Home Page A no-frills page from The National Institute of Standards and Technology (NIST), a government group dedicated to setting standards and promoting the development of VR. The site has links to research papers, technical proposals, and images, most of which describe how various companies and organizations such as NASA use VR. There are also VR demo MPEGs and lots of links to other VR research sites. ✓**INTERNET**→*www* http://nemo.ncsl.nist.gov/~sressler/OVRThome.html

PowerGlove FAQ There is no obsolete technology anymore, just technology that's moved on to other jobs. The Mattel PowerGlove was originally a video game–input device that fit over your hand. Since then, it's been hacked by artists and techies to serve a variety of VR purposes. This FAQ gives you the basic technical and resource info you need to remake the PowerGlove into something weird and new. ✓**INTERNET**→*www* http://gopher.well.com:70/1/hacking

sci.virtual-worlds (ng) "Could anybody email me a fast-fill polygon algorithm?" This moderated newsgroup serves people working in VR research and interested amateurs, and includes requests for information, job postings, product and conference announcements, and ongoing arguments over topics such as "...would a holodeck, such as the one in the Next Generation Star Trek series, be feasible?" (So far the consensus is "No," but it's been suggested that something

Future Tech Computers & Society

almost as cool might be possible using techniques for directly computing the wavefield of light, a technique developed at the MIT Media Lab). If you're serious enough about VR to want to join the moderated Usenet group sci.virtual-worlds, you should read the Meta-FAQ first. Updated monthly, this document gives you not only the history of sci.virtual-worlds, but a rundown on the major players, the posting process, etiquette, a suggested reading list, and archive information. ✓**USENET FAQ:** ✓INTERNET→*www* http://www.cis.ohio-state.edu/hypertext/faq/usenet/virtual-worlds/meta-faq/faq.html

Virtual City Network Project This ongoing project is sort of a Cyberspace real-estate development, but one designed to include people, not exclude them. While it's still in its infancy, you can check out the proposed city's map, construction timeline, and notes about future plans and developments. ✓INTERNET→*www* http://www.virtual.net/VirtualCity/

Virtual Reality Overburdened by an introduction that defines virtual reality as a field so new it can't yet be defined, this forum is a rich collection of virtual-reality resources—graphics, demonstrations, animations, simulations, fractals, and more cybersurprises. Ostensibly an extension of the PC graphics forum, this area lets you get a glimpse of tomorrow's buzzword today. ✓**AMERICA ONLINE**→*keyword* virtualreality

The Virtual Reality Alliance of Students and Professionals Even if you're not a member of VRASP (the Virtual Reality Alliance of Students and Professionals), its Web page is a good place to know about. The VRASP "Virtual Reality on the Net" index is a good overview of VR links and resources across the Net, and the announcements section contains up-to-date info on VR conferences. ✓**INTERNET***www* http://www.vrasp.org/vrasp/

Virtual Reality Modeling Language (VRML) While most big-time computer applications are developed deep in security-heavy labs and industrial parks, the team developing Virtual Reality Modeling Language (VRML) has chosen another strategy. They're encouraging interested people to pitch in and help design the 3-D VR systems we will eventually use to navigate the Net. The page includes general data on the project—including the draft specifications—as well as archives of the VRML mailing list. ✓**INTERNET**→*www* http://vrml.wired.com/

Virtual Reality on Network Based on information culled from the sci.virtual-worlds Usenet group and other Websites, this Japanese page organizes VR links by subject. These include other VR indices, online papers about virtual reality, VR groups and labs, FTP sites, and journals. ✓**INTERNET**→*www* http://www.star.rcast.u-tokyo.ac.jp/VR-on-net.html

Virtual Reality Resource List Willing to buy into this virtual reality thing? You can find information about the prices, availability, and specs on a wide variety of VR gear, from Sega game systems all the way up to $60,000 professional systems. ✓**INTERNET**→*www* http://enuxsa.eas.asu.edu/~rutledge/vrstuff.html

Virtual Reality Roller Coaster Part of Georgia Tech's Interactive Visualizer Project, the page includes a description of Mach IV, a rollercoaster virtual environment. The page also holds four different demo MPEGs of the coaster ride. ✓**INTERNET**→*www* http://www.ce.gatech.edu/Projects/IV/coaster.html

The Virtual Reality Society The homepage of the Virtual Reality Society (VRS), an international special-interest group, won't let you read the group's magazine without joining. You can, however, check their site for VR events and links to other U.K. VR pages. ✓**INTERNET**→*www* http://web.dcs.hull.ac.uk:80/VRS/

Virtual Reality Update Though this page is relatively prosaic—no fancy graphics, no special effects—it contains a frighteningly exhaustive list of scholarly articles and a smaller list of popular articles and books about VR. There are also a number of interesting links to other Net sites, including commercial VR companies around the world. ✓**INTERNET**→*www* http://www.hitl.washington.edu/projects/knowledge_base/vru/

Virtual Reality Web Pages You can't get much simpler than this U.K.-based page: it's a long list of around 230 links to VR sites across the Net. ✓**INTERNET**→*www* http://tin.ssc.plym.ac.uk/vr.html

VR at Banff The Banff Center for the Arts in Canada produced eight performance pieces that used VR in a purely creative and artistic way. You can get the background on these projects and see some images on its Virtual Environments Project page. The companion page, Other Virtual Reality Projects, looks at recent and ongoing art-oriented VR projects. ✓**INTERNET**→*www* http://www-nmr.banffcentre.ab.ca/

228 Net Tech

Computers & Society Future Tech

VR Metropolis "Where VR enthusiasts can learn about and explore VR worlds online." The VR Bytes department features weekly news bulletins about developments in virtual reality. ✓**INTERNET**→*www* http://www.mecklerweb.com:80/mags/vr/vrm/newvrm.htm

VR World The text-only online version of *VR World* magazine carries short news items, product announcements, reviews, and a Q&A forum. There are also selected articles from the current issue of *VR World* and an archive of articles from recent issues. If Fox's new *VR.5* series doesn't satisfy your thirst, then this Website surely will. All the latest news, reviews, and trend analysis for those who like to strap on that helmet and freejack into the electronic stratosphere. ✓**INTERNET**→*www* http://www.mecklerweb.com/mags/vr/vrhome.htm

VR-SIG This British VR special-interest group provides you with links to demo versions of PC and Mac software, images of VR systems and virtual environments, information about VR events around the world, and links to Usenet VR groups and the European Virtual Reality Society. ✓**INTERNET**→*www* http://www.crg.cs.nott.ac.uk/ukvrsig/vr-sig.html

Robotics

1995 International BEAM Robot Olympics Events run along the lines of: robot Sumo (400 lb. robots?), aquavore, aerobot, solaroller, the Legged Race, nanomice, etc. Competition rules are available, as well as pictures of last year's champs. ✓**INTERNET**→*www* http://sst.lanl.gov/robot/

A Mathematical Introduction to Robotic Manipulation Get the abstract, table of contents, and some of the source code that Murray, Li, and Sastry used to formulate their theories on kinetics, dynamics, and control of robot manipulators. ✓**INTERNET**→*www* http://avalon.caltech.edu/~murray/mls/

Arrick Robotics Product specifications from this manufacturer of motor controllers, positioning tables, and mobile robots. ✓**INTERNET**→*www* http://www.robotics.com/

Australian Telerobot This site features an ASEA 6-axis industrial robot that you can control from your couch. Grabby, grabby, grabby. ✓**INTERNET**→*www* http://telerobot.mech.uwa.edu.au/

comp.robotics (ng) Robotics professionals and Radio Shack hobbyists populate this newsgroup. Learn how to make your Mac control your bot, or how to optimize a miniboard's resonators. ✓**USENET**

comp.robotics FAQ Whether you're looking for a brief overview on robotics or trying to get the specs on new microprocessors for your Puma Manipulator, look here first. The FAQ offers extensive reference lists for publications and periodicals, competitions, conferences, university programs, manufacturers, and other Net resources. ✓**INTERNET**→*www* http://www.frc.ri.cmu.edu:80/robotics-faq

Eurobots An archive "devoted to the storage of mobile robot and Intelligent Autonomous Vehicle related information." Its extensive holdings originate from software developers, research groups, and robotics companies. There's also a Robot Gallery where you can check out all the real-life R2D2's.

CYBERNOTES

"I've been toying with the idea of actually building a movable robot to drive around indoors. So far I've looked briefly at design, and of course positioning. I have not built anything yet, and don't plan to for a long time to come. First, the programming issues must be resolved. I'd like to use this to let the robot build an image of the world it is in, and to determine how much it has moved since last stop (for simplicity I assume that measures are taken while no drive-motors are running). So far I've built a simulator program, with a robot that I can run through two rooms separated by a door and with some smaller objects around that generate shadows. I then recorded the sequence and animated it in another program. The differences between two subsequent scans are not that enormous, at least not to the human viewer. What I basically need is a pattern-matching program to identify elements in the scan, be they corners or long flat sections or something else."

—from **comp.robotics**

Future Tech Computers & Society

✓**INTERNET**→*www* http://hp1.essex.ac.uk/Eurobots/

Info-Robo (ml) This moderated electronic discussion list addresses issues related to robotics. Commercial robot providers are not welcome. ✓**INTERNET**→*email* info-robo-request@spie.org ✍ Write a request

International Aerial Robotics Competition Watch out—this one is for unmanned flying vehicles performing predefined tasks. ✓**INTERNET**→*www* http://cwis.usc.edu/dept/robotics/other/avsarc/auvsarc.html

IS Robotics Corporation ISR specializes in all-terrain microrobots which function autonomously and utilize "behavioral software." For just under $15,000, Genghis II, Pebbles III, or the deluxe Hermes can be yours. Get their specs here. ✓**INTERNET**→*www* http://isr.com/~isr

JPL Robotics/NASA JPL is working on a variety of projects for NASA and other U.S. governmental agencies. Preview projects involving rovers for lunar terrain, remote surface inspection, robot-assisted microsurgery, and more. ✓**INTERNET**→*www* http://robotics.jpl.nasa.gov/

Mercury Robot USC's Tele-Excavation Project was completed in March 1995, but it's still well worth a visit to read about this research project. A robot controlled by Net users would dig up objects from its sandy environment; all the objects were derived from a particular novel, and users had to figure out which novel by unearthing all the props. We're not telling! ✓**INTERNET**→*www* http://www.usc.edu/dept/raiders/story/index.html

North Carolina State University Walking Machine Project Each year NCSU brings together a team of 12 engineers and programmers to develop a new breed of walking machine, with the goal of increasing the current bot record for standing linear velocity by two meters/second. This is evolution in the works, folks. ✓**INTERNET**→*www* http://2.ncsu.edu/eos/info/sae_info/WMP/cyberspace/wmp01.html

NYU's LabCam The telerobot here will show you around NYU's lab with the magic of point-and-shoot video. All the robots seem to be eying one another in a funny, kind of suspicious way. ✓**INTERNET**→*www* http://found.cs.nyu.edu/

Robot Web The page links to many of the large university sites and provides an up-to-date guide to who's doing what where in the world of robotics research. ✓**INTERNET**→*www* http://www.sm.luth.se/csee/ra/sm-roa/RoboticsJump.html

> "The telerobot here will show you around NYU's lab with the magic of point-and-shoot video. All the robots seem to be eying one another in a funny, kind of suspicious way."

Robotics Internet Resources Although this site provides a brief overview of the projects under way at UMASS's Laboratory for Perceptual Robotics, it serves primarily as a directory of other bot sites. It's organized by format, with listings for the Web, FTP, gopher, MPEG videos, and software. The comp.robotics FAQ can be found here, as well as a "Grad Students Who's Who in Robotics." ✓**INTERNET**→*www* http://piglet.cs.umass.edu:4321/robotics.html

Robotics, Learning, Chaos Virtual courses in robotics, with separate lessons for programmers, mechanical engineers, and electronic engineers, as well as a list of robotics supply houses. ✓**INTERNET**→*www* http://lenti.med.umn.edu/~mwd/robot.html

Stiquito Colony The goal of this ambitious project is to build a colony of robots in order to study cooperative behavior among the artificially intelligent. They will be connected to and viewable from the Net. ✓**INTERNET**→*www* http://www.cs.indiana.edu/robotics/projects.html

Survival Research Lab San Francisco's bad boys have infiltrated the halls of Berkeley, and they're coming up with even sicker beasts. Check out the Intellidex robotic arm customized for "postmortem veterinary manipulations." ✓**INTERNET**→*www* http://robotics.eecs.berkeley.edu/~paulos/SRL/

University of Rochester Micro-Mouse Robot Contest In addition to contest guidelines and maze specs, this site holds lots of information on building Micro-Mice. ✓**INTERNET**→*www* http://ceas.rochester.edu:8080/ee/users/weisberg/mouse.html

University Robotics Labs & Research Institutes

Boston University ✓INTERNET→*www* http://robotics.bu.edu/lab.html

California Institute of Technology ✓INTERNET→*www* http://robby.caltech.edu/resources.html

Caltech Robotics Laboratory ✓INTERNET→*www* http://robby.caltech.edu

Cambridge University Speech Vision Robotics Group ✓INTERNET→*www*http://svr.www.eng.cam.ac.uk

Center for Automation Research (CfAR) ✓INTERNET→*www* http://www.cfar.umd.edu

Cornell CSRVL ✓INTERNET→*www* http://www.cs.cornell.edu/Info/Projects/csrvl/csrvl.html

ETHZ—Institute of Robotics IfR ✓INTERNET→*www* http://www.ifr.mavt.ethz.ch

Georgia Institute of Technology ✓INTERNET→*www* http://www.cc.gatech.edu/ai/robot-lab/prj-uav.html

Georgia Tech Mobile Robot Laboratory ✓INTERNET→*www* http://www.cc.gatech.edu/aimosaic/robot-lab/MRLHome.html

Harvard Robotics Lab ✓INTERNET→*www* http://hrl.harvard.edu/

Heriot-Watt University—Ocean Systems Lab ✓INTERNET→*www* http://anchovy.cee.hw.ac.uk

Johns Hopkins Robotics Lab ✓INTERNET→*www* http://montezuma.me.jhu.edu

JPL Telerobotics ✓INTERNET→*www* http://robotics.jpl.nasa.gov

NASA Telerobotics Program ✓INTERNET→*www* http://ranier.oact.hq.nasa.gov/telerobotics_page/telerobotics.html

Queens University (Ontario)—Robotics and Perception Lab Index ✓INTERNET→*www* http://quail.qucis.queensu.ca:9000/index.html

Robotics and Control at Boston University ✓INTERNET→*www* http://robotics.bu.edu

Robotics Integration & Analysis Section ✓INTERNET→*www* http://lego.jsc.nasa.gov

Stanford Aerospace Robotics Laboratory Home Page ✓INTERNET→*www* http://sun-valley.stanford.edu

Stanford Dextrous Manipulation Lab ✓INTERNET→*www* http://cdr.stanford.edu/html/Touch/touchpage.html

Stanford Robotics Laboratory ✓INTERNET→*www* http://robotics.stanford.edu

Stanford University ✓INTERNET→*www* http://sun-valley.stanford.edu/projects/helicopters/helicopters.html

The Triangle Virtual Reality Group ✓INTERNET→*www* http://trinet.com/trivr.html/

UCLA Mobile Robotics ✓INTERNET→*www* http://muster.cs.ucla.edu:8001

Univ. of Tokyo Jouhou System Kougaku Laboratory ✓INTERNET→*www* http://www.jsk.t.u-tokyo.ac.jp

University of Amsterdam Robotics and Neurocomputing ✓INTERNET→*www* http://carol.fwi.uva.nl/~smagt/neuro/index.html

Univ. of Delaware—Rehabilitation Robotics Program ✓INTERNET→*www* http://www.asel.udel.edu/robotics/robotics.html

University of Genova—Laboratory for Integrated Advanced Robotics ✓INTERNET→*www* http://afrodite.lira.dist.unige.it:81

University of Illinois UC Robotics and Automation Laboratory ✓INTERNET→*www* http://uxh.cso.uiuc.edu/~gedept/ge/facilities/robot_lab.html

University of Maryland at College Park: Autonomous Mobile Robots Lab ✓INTERNET→*www* http://www.cs.umd.edu/projects/amrl/amrl.html

University of Massachusetts Laboratory for Perceptual Robotics ✓INTERNET→*www* http://piglet.cs.umass.edu:4321/lpr.html

University of Utah—Robotics ✓INTERNET→*www* http://www.cs.utah.edu/projects/robot

Virtual Environments Research at Delft ✓INTERNET→*www* http://dutiws.twi.tudelft.nl/TWI/IS/vr-overview.html

Security **Computers & Society**

Security

"I understand that computers make things easier, but I'm not sure I like the idea of having all that information about me publicly accessible. I mean, what if someone breaks into my bank's databanks and reads my balance, or accesses my home system and reads my personal correspondence. Can this happen? And what can I do to protect myself?" If you've been asking yourself these kinds of questions, you're not alone; insecure information goes out over the wires millions of times each day. Learn about hacking and cracking issues from **Security-Related Net-pointers**. Find out how you can protect yourself from Big Brother by lurking on **alt.privacy**. And phreak out with **alt.2600**.

Access denied—from http://www.lfbs.rwth-aachen.de/pix/pix/science/compute/sun/

On the Net

Across the board

Cliff Stoll's Performance Art Theater and Networking Security Revue "And now for something completely different..." Cyber-comic Cliff Stoll is featured here in a series of still photographs and audio clips from the Cisco NetWorkers '94 conference, recounting how the discovery of a 75-cent accounting error led to the world-wide online chase of a hacker, ultimately uncovering a KGB spy ring. This was, of course, a very serious matter, as is indicated by section titles such as "Buy this book," "Steal this camera," and "Decaf versus Jolt." ✓**INTERNET**→*www* http://town.hall.org/university/security/stoll/cliff.html

COAST Project COAST stands for Computer Operations, Audit, and Security Technology. It's a computer security research project at Purdue University focused on "real-world needs and limitations." Here you can find out more about COAST and access what the page claims is "the largest single Internet-accessible collection of security-related papers and tools." Among the goodies here is the source code for the controversial SATAN scanning tool, which detects weaknesses in network security. ✓**INTERNET**→*www* http://www.cs.purdue.edu/coast/coast.html

Computer Security Research Lab The Computer Security Research Lab is at the University of California in Davis. Its Website offers information about the lab, recent papers and presentations developed at the laboratory, other security-related links, and "Security Lab Fun," which features pictures of the computer science department's recent rafting trip. ✓**INTERNET**→*www* http://everest.cs.ucdavis.edu

Computer Technologies Security Center The CTSC, located at Lawrence Livermore National Laboratory, serves the security needs of the Department of Energy and other federal agencies. Its WWW page links to an extensive

232 Net Tech

Computers & Society Security

variety of computer and network security resources, including a program called Courtney, designed to warn administrators when their system is being scanned by SATAN—computer security jargon is taking on a rather apocalyptic air, no? This site also offers information about CTSC, of course, including weather and transit information should you want to visit in person. ✓**INTERNET**→*www* http://ciac.llnl.gov/cstc/CSTCHome/html

The Cypherpunks The Cypherpunks are computer science students at the University of California at Berkeley. Their Website links to security information and tools, "rants," newspaper clippings, and security-related resources. ✓**INTERNET**→*www* http://www.csua.berkeley.edu/pub/cypherpunks/Home.html

Electronic Commerce Standards for the WWW If the World Wide Web is to be truly useful, the data traveling its strands has to be secure from prying eyes. Spyglass, Inc. has posted its December, 1994 proposal to use extensions to the existing HyperText Transfer Protocol to enhance Web security. Links to documents about other security schemes are included. ✓**INTERNET**→*www* http://www.spyglass.com/techreport/stdsec.htm

FIRST FIRST is the catchy acronym for "Forum of Incident Response and Security Teams." It's a coalition of government and private-sector organizations from around the world that exchange information and coordinate responses to security threats to computer systems and networks. This page provides information about FIRST, links to many home pages of its members, and other resources. ✓**INTERNET**→*www* http://csrc.ncsl/nist/gov/first/

The Internet Underground Links to resources for those interested in computer and telephone security. Resources range from the full text of Bruce Sterling's *The Hacker Crackdown* (Bantam, 1992) to a tutorial about PGP to archives of hacker-related text and software. ✓**INTERNET**→*www* http://www.engin.umich.edu/~jgotts/underground.html

PC Security For a full selection of PC anti-viral programs, check out this library. Most are written by fellow computer users and include custom features unavailable in more commercial programs. In the fast-track world of viruses, it pays to have the latest anti-viral programs just to stay afloat. You'll also find file encryption programs and password makers. Scared your electronic love letters to your mistress will be intercepted by your system administrator and publicized? Find out how to prevent your private life from getting posted on the Net, Congressman. ✓**AMERICA ONLINE** ...→*keyword* pctelecom→Browse Software Libraries→Security ...→*keyword* pctelecom→Message Boards→Security

Security Reference Index This is an Australian (Telstra Corporation Ltd.) index of network and computer security resources. It includes several FAQs, plus links to an online document archive, security advisories, WWW and FTP sites, newsgroups, mailing lists, other security indexes, product vendors, and even "Canned Firewall: A Beginner's Guide to Building an Internet Firewall." ✓**INTERNET**→*www* http://www.telstra.com.au/Info/security/html

Security-Related Net-pointers An extensive list of pointers to security-related information on the Net culled by Bennet Yee, a post-doctoral researcher in Carnegie Mellon University's computer science department. ✓**INTERNET**→*www* http://www.cs.cmu.edu:8001/afs/cs.cmu.edu/user/bsy/www/sec.html

WWW-Security A relatively quiet list (just a handful of messages a week) on which subscribers discuss all kinds of security issues related to the Web, including problems with security, proposals to enhance it, and specific cryptography schemes. ✓**INTERNET**→*www* http://asearch.mccmedia.com/www-security.html

Privacy

alt.privacy (ng) If the newsgroup had a motto, it might be "Big Brother is watching, and we don't like it!" The misuse of computer information about individuals, especially through the disclosure of Social Security numbers, is a common topic, but polygraph tests, urine tests, automatic callback on telephones, and many other privacy-related issues are debated as well. ✓**USENET** *FAQ:* ✓**INTERNET**→*www* ftp://rtfm.mit.edu/pub/usenet-by-hierarchy/alt/privacy/

alt.security.misc (ng) Discussions about all aspects of computer security, including the Pretty Good Privacy and Ripem programs, and distribution of public encryption keys. Common topics include where to get the latest versions of programs, the problems associated with them, and the regulations forbidding the export of some of these programs. ✓**USENET**

Anonymity A collection of articles appearing in major print pub-

Net Tech 233

Security Computers & Society

lications (e.g., *Time* and *The L.A. Times*) about anonymity online. ✓**INTERNET**→*www* http://www.clas.ufl.edu:80/~avi/NII/anonymity.html

Anonymous Remailer FAQ A brief overview of anonymous remailers, computer services that let Netters send anonymous email or post anonymously to newsgroups. ✓**INTERNET**→*www* http://www.cs.berkeley.edu/~raph/remailer-faq.html

comp.society.privacy (ng) Posts to this generally low-volume newsgroup range from questions about privacy online—"Can someone monitor my downloads from a newsgroup?"—to summaries of court decisions affecting computer privacy. ✓**USENET**

Remailer List A list of sites offering remailing services, followed by links to other online remailer resources. ✓**INTERNET**→*www* http://www.cs.berkeley.edu/~raph/remailer-list.html

Your Privacy A collection of links to Internet resources related to privacy issues—from a link to the home page for Privacy International, an organization that monitors government abuse of privacy, to links to newsgroups covering privacy issues. ✓**INTERNET**→*www* http://draco.centerline.com:8080/~franl/privacy/

Security

comp.risks (ng) A moderated newsgroup focusing on risks to the public from computers and related systems. Topics range from legal cases involving computer use and abuse to the risks posed by patrol-car computers, online documentation, and online catalogs. Messages are compiled in a weekly digest posted to the newsgroup or uploaded to the Website and FTP site. ✓**USENET** ✓**INTERNET**→*www* http://catless.ncl.ac.uk/Risks *Archives:* ✓**INTERNET**→*www* ftp://ftp.unix.sri.com

comp.security.announce (ng) Distributes announcements of known security problems and their solutions. ✓**USENET**

comp.security.misc (ng) Another newsgroup for discussing computer security topics, including SATAN and other programs, firewalls, and viruses. Rumors and security jokes ("How many crackers does it take to screw up a lightbulb?") are quite common. ✓**USENET**

comp.security.unix (ng) Discussions and queries about security problems for Unix platforms. Firewalls and network security are big topics. ✓**USENET**

Compromised Security FAQ An FAQ with suggestions on what to do if your Unix network has been compromised by an intruder. ✓**INTERNET**→*www* http://www.cis.ohio-state.edu/text/faq/usenet/computer-security/compromise-faq/faq.html

Mac-Security (ml) How would you feel if someone broke in and desecrated that smiley face that opens every Mac session? Pretty glum, probably. With System 7.0's information-sharing features, Mac privacy and security are more complicated than ever. This mailing list hosts discussions on Mac security—everything from existing security programs to potential problems in hardware. ✓**INTERNET**→*email* mac-security-request@world.std.com ✍ *Write a request*

misc.security (ng) A newsgroup dedicated to discussion about all issues of security, from computers to telephones to homes. ✓**USENET**

Security FAQ Internet Security Systems, Inc., in Norcross, Georgia, maintains this index of FAQs, aimed primarily at system administrators. There's information about and links to many of the big software and hardware vendors, patches for various systems, checklists to follow when security is compromised, an FAQ on sniffing (intercepting messages intended for other machines), and information on how to set up a secure anonymous FTP site. ✓**INTERNET**→*www* http://iss.net/~iss/faq.html

Firewalls

BorderWare–Internet Firewall Server The BorderWare Internet Firewall Server (formerly the JANUS Firewall Server), marketed by the California company NetPartners, combines a router, a firewall, and a server into a single, easy-to-use-and-install device, according to the promotional information at this site. Also offered: a program to help system administrators calculate the amount of storage space they'll need for Usenet Newsgroups. ✓**INTERNET**→*www* http://lykos.netpart.com/janus/

> "How would you feel if someone broke in and desecrated that smiley face that opens every Mac session?"

234 Net Tech

Computers & Society Security

Checkpoint Checkpoint Technologies' Firewall-1 security system is highlighted here, complete with color illustrations. Firewall-1 routes all traffic between an organization's internal network and the Internet through a filtered gateway to ensure that security remains tight. ✓**INTERNET**→*www* http://www.checkpoint/com:8000/firewall-1.html

Firewalls FAQ Answers to 20 frequently asked questions about firewalls, those Cyberspatial barriers designed to keep local networks safe from outside intruders while still allowing access to the Internet. ✓**INTERNET** ...→*www* http://www.cis.ohio-state.edu/hypertext/faq/usenet/firewalls-faq/faq.html ...→*www* ftp://ftp.greatcircle.com/pub/firewalls/FAQ

Firewalls List (ml) A discussion forum for administrators of Internet firewalls. Topics include design, software, and administration. ✓**INTERNET**→*email* majordomo@greatcircle.com ↳ *Type in message body:* subscribe firewall <your email address> *Archives:* ✓**INTERNET**→*www* ftp://ftp.greatcircle.com/pub/firewalls/

GFX-94 Family of Internet Firewalls Here is everything you wanted to know about Global Technology Associates' GFX-94 family of Internet firewalls, which, this site informs you, uses a unique double-wall design: if the outer firewall is compromised, the inner firewall isolates the system before the intruder can gain access. ✓**INTERNET**→*www* http://www.gta.com/firewall/html

Internet Security Firewalls Tutorial Information about a tutorial on firewall construction offered by Brent Chapman, a consultant in the San Francisco Bay Area specializing in Unix networks and manager of the Firewalls Internet mailing list. The tutorial is offered in cities across the U.S. and Canada, with new dates and locations posted here on a regular basis. ✓**INTERNET**→*www* http://www.greatcircle.com/gca/tutorial/main.html

Security software

Livermore Software Livermore Software Laboratories, Inc., in Houston, offers a downloadable Firewall and Network Security tutorial at this site. By clicking on tiny images of bananas (for reasons never explained) you can also access other Internet security resources and download Courtney, the program that detects SATANic activity. An added bonus: quirky paintings by quirky rocker Robyn Hitchcock. ✓**INTERNET** →*www* http://www.sccsi.com/lsli/lsli.homepage.html

Netscape's SSL Protocol Latest info from Netscape about its SSL (Secure Sockets Layer) protocol, designed to allow client and server computers on the Internet to communicate without danger of anyone else eavesdropping. ✓**INTERNET**→*www* http://www.netscape.com/info/SSL.html

Terisa Systems Terisa Systems, launched in 1994 to develop technologies that make secure Internet transactions possible, offers the latest information about its products here. Terisa's security toolkits may soon become the industry standard: the company recently received major investment from America Online, CompuServe, IBM, and Netscape. By the summer of 1995, the company hopes to introduce a toolkit combining the two major security protocols on the market today, Secure HTTP and SSL. ✓**INTERNET**→*www* http://www.terisa.com/

Commerce & security

Commerce An index of documents and links pertaining to business on the Internet. There's information on network payment mechanisms, marketing information, an out-of-date history of the commercialization of the Internet, and a list of commercial sites. ✓**INTERNET**→*www* http://gopher.econ.lsa.umich.edu/EconInternet/Commerce.html

Network Payment Mechanisms A collection of documents and links to Internet resources about schemes for transferring money over the Net. You can also download several papers and articles published by David Chaum, the "father of digital cash." ✓**INTERNET**→*www* http://ganges.cs.tcd.ie/mepeirce/project.html

Clipper Chip

About the Clipper Chip This page provides dozens of links to information about—in the words of its author, Francis Litterio—"the U.S. government's attempts to restrict the privacy of its citizens via the Escrowed Encryption Standard (EES), a.k.a. 'the Clipper Chip.'" A collection of papers, statements, and letters representing both sides of the issue is linked here. ✓**INTERNET**→*www* http://draco.centerline.com: 8080 /~ franl /clipper/about-clipper.html

E-Privacy Home Page This is a bare-bones page with a small number of links to privacy-related resources, including several articles dealing with the Clipper Chip. Information is also provided on how to add your name to the Comput-

Security Computers & Society

er Professionals for Social Responsibility petition opposing the Clipper Chip. ✓ **INTERNET**→*www* http://www.cs.cmu.edu:8001/afs/andrew.cmu.edu/usr25/jbde/www/matrix/clipper/clipper.html

Fight for Your Right to Electronic Privacy! As befits a site about maintaining online privacy, you'll need a username and password to access this archive of Clipper Chip information maintained by *Wired* magazine. Use "cypherpunk" for both and you'll find yourself looking at an image of a blood-red fist clenching two lightning bolts, along with the slogan, "Cyber rights now!" Following an introduction accusing the "national security state" of attempting a "stealth strike on our rights," you'll find information and links to other resources about privacy issues, including the Communications Decency Act, the Wiretap Bill, and, of course, the Clipper Chip, "a last-ditch attempt by the United States, the last great power from the old Industrial Era, to establish imperial control over Cyberspace." There is also information about organizations fighting for online privacy, and suggestions of what readers can do to fight the government's plans. ✓ **INTERNET**→*www* http://www.wired.com/clipper/

PGP

alt.security.pgp (ng) A very active newsgroup covering Pretty Good Privacy issues: where to get it, problems with it, information about it and, of course, discussions (often heated ones) of the export restrictions placed on it. Several FAQs have been created to answer frequently asked questions about the Pretty Good Privacy encryption program and to list where Netters can get the latest versions of PGP. ✓ **USENET** *FAQ:* ✓ **INTERNET** …→*www* ftp://rtfm.mit.edu/pub/usenet-by-hierarchy/alt/security/pgp/ …→*www* http://www.cis.ohio-state.edu/hypertext/faq/bngusenet/alt/security/pgp/top.html

Cryptography—from http://bibd.unl.edu/~stinson/CTAP.html

Info-PGP (ml) Discuss PGP, the public key encryption program for MS-DOS, Unix, SPARC, VMS, Atari, Amiga, and other platforms. The mailing list includes a mirror of alt.security.pgp and related articles on sci.crypt. ✓ **INTERNET**→*email* info-pgp-request@lucpul.it.luc.edu ✍ Write a request

The International PGP Home Page Besides carrying the latest version of PGP, the site also includes information on the program, the legal issues surrounding PGP, and links to other PGP resources on the Web. ✓ **INTERNET**→*www* http://www.ifi.uio.no/~staalesc/PGP/home.html

MIT Distribution Site for PGP MIT maintains current versions of PGP, programs to integrate PGP with other Net programs, and an FAQ about PGP. ✓ **INTERNET**→*www* http://web.mit.edu/network/pgp.html

PGP: A Nutshell Overview A reference guide to the PGP program. ✓ **INTERNET**→*www* http://www.engin.umich.edu/~jgotts/underground/pgp-nutshell.html

PGP—Pretty Good Privacy A repository of information, news, and documentation (from PGP user guides to PGP quick reference charts) about PGP. The home page also links to sites that carry the PGP program and utilities. ✓ **INTERNET**→*www* http://draco.centerline.com:8080/~franl/pgp/pgp.html

PGP Quick Reference You won't find Pretty Good Privacy here, but if you've already got it, you might find this list of commands useful. ✓ **INTERNET**→*www* http://draco.centerline.com:8080/~franl/pgp/pgp-2.6.x-quickref.html

Pretty Good Privacy Primarily a long list of links to sites carrying the PGP program, the page also links to an article explaining the legal issues surrounding PGP. ✓ **INTERNET**→*www* http://www.mantis.co.uk/pgp/pgp.html

S/KEY

S/KEY This FTP site contains an archive of documents, patches, and information maintained by Bellcore for the convenience of users of its S/KEY authentication system. Copies of the S/KEY program for Macintosh, DOS, and Unix machines are also available here. This directory also contains the archives of the S/KEY-users mailing list. ✓ **INTERNET**→*www* ftp://ftp.bellcore.com/pub/nmh/

Computers & Society Security

Viruses

Anti-Virus Resource Center On this page, the software company Symantec offers Symantec anti-virus products and warnings about widespread viruses. A section under construction promises hints for implementing anti-virus protection on networks. ✓**INTERNET**→*www* http://www.symantec.com/virus/virus.html

comp.virus (ng) Keeping computers virus-free (and healing those already infected) is the solemn pledge of this newsgroup, which serves as the Center for Disease Control of the computer world. The relative merits of antiviral programs, information on specific viruses, warnings about new viruses, and questions about the best ways to prevent viral infection are common topics. ("How many anti-viral programs does it take?" asks one writer plaintively; the not-terribly-reassuring answer: three should cover you "reasonably well.") Although Mac users aren't specifically excluded, almost all messages concern PCs. ✓**USENET**

Computer Viruses & Security This page from the Einet Galaxy database of Net resources is subtitled "An introduction to nasty things that go bump in the night." Maintained by David B. Hull, assistant professor of computer science at National University, it contains a complete seminar by the author on "Safe Hex for the 90s," links to security documents, Web pages and newsgroups about viruses and anti-viral software, plus jokes, hoaxes, and, as an added bonus, "a complete listing of all the weirdos in Cyberspace." ✓**INTERNET**→*www* http://www.einet.net/galaxy/Engineering-and-Technology/Computer-Technology/Security/david-hull/galaxy.html

Data Fellows Ltd. On this page Data Fellows Ltd. provides information about its F-PROT anti-virus and data security programs. A link is provided to Data Fellows' FTP server, which contains demos, virus information, and a place to upload virus reports and virus samples. ✓**INTERNET**→*www* http://www.datafellows.fi/

Look Software This page supports and promotes Look Software's Virus Alert anti-viral software and includes a "slide show" of actual screen shots of the program in action. You can also order a copy of the program online. ✓**INTERNET**→*www* http://www.globalx.net/look/

Macintosh Virus Information Center Apparently if you get an email message about a virus called "Good Times," you should delete it immediately without even reading it, if you know what's good for you. So what do you do about the 55 messages in the "Good Times" folder here? Enter at your own risk. But you can safely enter the "barfing/coughing" folder and discuss the virus which made one user's Mac IIci "make random coughing noises when starting up and vomiting sounds when ejecting floppies." Besides panicked calls for feedback and help, you'll find anti-viral software in the libraries. And if you just can't get enough virus gossip, check out the Virus Discussion Archive, for information about viruses of yesteryear. ✓**AMERICA ONLINE**→*keyword* virus

McAfee Associates Offers detailed (in a sales-brochure kind of way) descriptions of McAfee Associates' anti-virus products Virus-Scan, RomShield, and NetShield, as well as its network management software. A link is provided to McAfee Associate's FTP site, from which you can download the latest software updates and related information. ✓**INTERNET**→*www* http://www.mcafee.com/

McAfee Associates Shareware versions of the world's most popular anti-virus programs are available here. Try them for five days. If you like the the products, purchase the license directly from McAfee. If you're not satisfied, delete the files from your hard drive. VirusScan, VirusShield, and NetShield are available here, plus gossip about the latest viruses—from Michelangelo to New York Boot. ✓**AMERICA ONLINE**→*keyword* mcafee

McAfee Virus Forum Is your computer telling you it's about to erase the contents of your hard drive? Maybe it's got the DOOM II Death Virus. Huh? Go to the Q&A message folder, where experts in computer virology will not only tell you the origins of a virus, but how dangerous it might be. The forum carries information about and offers support for McAfee's anti-virus programs. Shareware versions of Windows, DOS, and OS/2 VirusSCAN programs, or NetShield, are available in the libraries. You'll also find a full range of press releases describing McAfee's business dealings and new products. ✓**COMPUSERVE**→*go* virusforum

NCSA InfoSecurity Forum If, while working on your UCLA graduate thesis, THE BIG ONE hits, you'll find information in the "Disaster Recovery" folder about the latest methods for securing computer files in the event of earthquakes, bombings, and the like. If you don't happen to live in a natural disaster zone and the most you fear is a debilitating computer virus, the forum library carries standard anti-viral pro-

Net Tech 237

Security Computers & Society

grams and security information. ✓ **COMPUSERVE**→go ncsaforum

NCSA Virus Vendor Forum If you're looking for security programs and either can't decide or can't tell the difference between Dr. Solomon's Anti-Virus tool and Thompson's Doctor Anti-Virus system, this forum might be helpful. You can ask questions on the message boards or download information about viruses from the libraries. Even though this forum is a showcase for vendors of security products, general discussions about encryption, privacy, computer ethics, LAN security, Internet security, and viruses are quite common. ✓ **COMPUSERVE**→go ncsaven

Symantec AntiVirus Forum Not all viruses are created equal, and most cause no more than minor annoyance; some even get a chuckle. Take the Oprah Winfrey virus, for example, in which your 200 MB shrinks down to 80 MB and then expands back to 200 MB, or the AT&T virus, which tells you every three minutes what great service you're getting. For descriptions of these viruses and more, real or otherwise, check out the virus discussion folder here. Since this forum is run by Symantec, it also contains technical support and information about the company's products, particularly Norton Anti-Virus. ✓ **COMPUSERVE**→go symvirus

Virus FAQ This large document addresses frequently asked questions about computer viruses. It is divided into seven sections: sources of information and anti-viral software; definitions (i.e., "What is a Trojan Horse?"); tips on detecting and eliminating viruses; tips on preventing infections; "Facts and Fibs" ("Can a virus infect data files?"); answers to miscellaneous questions ("What is the plural of virus, anyway?"); and information about specific viruses and anti-viral programs. Although the preface indicates that this document is supposed to be constantly changing, it hasn't been updated since November 18, 1992. ✓ **INTERNET** ...→*www* http://www.umcc.umich.edu/~doug/virus-faq.html ...→*www* http://www.cis.ohio-state.edu/hypertext/faq/usenet/computer-virus-faq/faq.html ...→*www* ftp://rtfm.mit.edu/pub/usenet-by-hierarchy/comp/virus/

Hacking

alt.2600 (ng) *2600 Magazine* was named after the 2600Hz tone that was used by phone phreaks (or phreakers) in the 80's to hack the phone system, and this newsgroup was named after the magazine. Always very active, the group is a forum for discussing both the how-to and the ethics of computer and telephone hacking. Writes one hacker to the newsgroup: "Okay, let's get one thing nice and sparkling clear. If you use stolen credit cards to to buy things, you are not a hacker. You are a criminal. If you use a redbox or stolen calling cards to make a call, you are not a phreaker. You are a criminal. And, of course, if you break into someone else's computer system without permission, you guessed it, you are not a hacker.

> "If you use stolen credit cards to buy things, you are not a hacker. You are a criminal."

You are a criminal. I was always into the hack/phreak thing for the knowledge." While debates are common and flaming par for the course, the newsgroup is primarily a place for technical discussions of hacking and phreaking. The FAQ not only addresses many of the most common questions about hacking (e.g., how do I crack Unix passwords?) but also maintains an extensive listing of online resources about hacking and viruses. ✓ **USENET** *FAQ:* ✓ **INTERNET**→*www* http://www.engin.umich.edu/~jgotts/underground/hack-faq.html

alt.hackers (ng) Hacking isn't just for computers anymore. Here you'll find not only scripts for hacking your way into computer networks, but also ways to wire your television for free cable: "About a month ago my mother called the cable company to fix her cable because of lousy reception (No!!!!!!!). To my dismay, the 'repair' man removed all my wiring between the TV, VCR, and cable box...So now I come home to find my work lying on the floor and have to reconnect all the wires... And there was a really good porn flick on that night. So....digging up some wires I had lying around I 'built' audio-video cables and only missed the first 10 minutes or so. I was so proud I was almost tempted not to replace them." ✓ **USENET**

Hack-L (ml) If you want a monthly report on hacks and hoaxes on the Net, subscribe to this newsletter, which carries the Hack Report. ✓ **INTERNET**→*email* majordomo@alive.ersys.edmonton.ab.ca ✎ *Type in message body:* subscribe hack-l <your email address> ✓ **AMERICA ONLINE**→*keyword* pctelecom→Browse the Software Libraries→Newsletters→The Hack Report

238 Net Tech

Computers & Society Security

Hacker Links A long list of links to hacker-related Websites, gophers, FTP sites, and newsgroups. ✓ **INTERNET**→*www* http://www.primenet.com/~kludge/haqr.html

John's Boxing Page A collection of articles about "boxes" and phone gadgets used by "phreakers" to defraud phone companies. ✓ **INTERNET**→*www* http://www.engin.umich.edu/~jgotts/underground/boxes.html

Phrack An electronic magazine with a hacker's sensibility and attitude, *Phrack* reports on computer and telephone technology for hard-core hackers. ✓ **INTERNET** …→*email* phrack@well.com ✍ *Write a request* …→*www* http://freeside.com/phrack/pread.html

Cryptography

Applied Cryptography Bruce Schneider's book *Applied Cryptography* includes an offer for disks containing cryptography-related documents and software packages. Much of that material is already available on the Internet; this page links to the appropriate FTP archives. ✓ **INTERNET**→*www* http://www.openmarket.com/info/cryptography/applied_cryptography.html

Cryptography Archive Two slightly altered Intel logos, one labeled "big brother inside" and the other "big brother not inside," illustrate this Web page. The site links to dozens of cryptography-related documents and resources on the Net, ranging from tech reports to magazine editorials to the Clipper Chip newsgroup. ✓ **INTERNET**→ *www* http://www.cs.umbc.edu/~mohan/Work/crypt.html

Cryptography Export Control Archive This page links to documents related to the State Department's efforts to control the export of cryptography, including the regulations under which that control is exerted and detailed information about specific cases and court challenges. ✓ **INTERNET**→*www* http://www.cygnus.com/~gnu/export.html

Cryptography Theory and Practice What is *Cryptography Theory and Practice*? It's a textbook by Doug Stinson, a professor of Computer Science and Engineering. This page includes the table of contents, a photograph of the cover, and solutions to some of the book's exercises. ✓ **INTERNET**→ *www* http://bibd.unl.edu/~stinson/CTAP.html

CypherWonks (ml) Serious discussions for the "technically adept" about the development of Cyberspace, with an emphasis on trendy Internet topics such as cryptography and digital cash. ✓ **INTERNET**→ *email* majordomo@lists.eunet.fi ✍ *Type in message body:* subscribe cypherwonks <your email address>

Macintosh Cryptography At this page, a sinister figure in fedora and trenchcoat welcomes you to "the wonderful world of cryptography." But this site is wonderful only for Mac users, for whom it provides answers to frequently asked questions, links to other cryptography-related FTP sites, add-ons for the Mac version of Pretty Good Privacy, and PGP public keys. ✓ **INTERNET**→*www* http://www.utexas.edu/~grgcombs/htmls/crypto.html

sci.crypt (ng) A forum for discussing the how-to's of data encryption, including the pros and cons of encryption programs and the science of cryptology. Programming code is often posted. ✓ **USENET**

More Hacking

Hacking BBSs

Apocalypse 2000
☎→*dial* 708-676-9855

Hacker's Haven ☎→*dial* 303-343-4053

Independent Nation ☎→*dial* 315-656-4179

Rune Stone ☎→*dial* 203-832-8441

Hacking on IRC

#2600 ✓ **INTERNET**→*irc* #2600

#hack ✓ **INTERNET**→*irc* #hack

#phreak ✓ **INTERNET**→*irc* #phreak

#warez ✓ **INTERNET**→*irc* #warez

---

sci.crypt.research (ng) A moderated discussion of encryption technology. Essays, algorithms, and program announcements often appear on this low-volume newsgroup. ✓ **USENET**

talk.politics.crypto (ng) Debate the political implications of cryptography. Take a side on the Clipper debate or the distribution of RC4 on this newsgroup. ✓ **USENET**

Today's Cryptography Although this FAQ is slightly outdated (perhaps it should be titled "Last Night's Cryptography"), it's still an excellent resource, brought to the online world courtesy of Paul Fahn from the RSA Laboratories. ✓ **INTERNET**→*www* ftp://rtfm.mit.edu/pub/usenet-by hierarchy/alt/security/ripem/

Net Tech 239

Computer Culture Computers & Society

Computer culture

In the movies, computers have either been tools to help man lead a better life (*The Jetsons* springs to mind) or monstrous machines that run amok with dystopian fury (*Total Recall*, *War Games*, and the *Terminator* series, to name just a few). In real life, computers rarely permit that strict a Manichean division—more often, they are devices that expose the equivocal nature of progress. To find out who's holding the knife in today's cutting-edge technologies, read **Upside Online** and **HotWired**. Probe electronic copyright and privacy legislation with the resources provided by **Computer Professionals for Social Responsibility** and the **Electronic Frontier Foundation**. And join the cyberfeminist revolution with **Geekgirl**.

Johnny Mnemonic—from http://hollywood.com

On the Net

Info age news

Information Week Interactive An electronic version of the print trade magazine for managers who use information technology. There are links to other information technology sites, including a calendar of trade shows and conferences relating to the digital age. ✓ INTERNET→*www* http://techweb.cmp.com:2090/techweb/iwk/

InfoWorld Online A selection of articles and columns from the current issue of the print world's weekly bible of the information age. ✓ INTERNET→*www* http://www.infoworld.com/

Technology Review It's been in print since 1899, and now this respected magazine dedicated to "technology and its implications" has a Website. Published by the Massachusetts Institute of Technology, its subjects range from biological warfare on the farm to federal subsidies for the Internet. The site includes the full text of a few articles from the current issue and an expanding archive of articles from back issues—back to 1994, not 1899. ✓ INTERNET→*www* http://web.mit.edu/afs/athena/org/t/techreview/www/tr.html

Upside Online Mainly for the technology executive, this e-zine features "provocative, insightful analyses of the individuals and companies leading the digital revolution." *Upside*, whose site also includes an archive of back issues, is hardly as jargon-heavy as one would expect. In fact, it features some of the most entertaining business and technology-related writing around. ✓ INTERNET→*www* http://www.upside.com/upside/upside.html

ZD Europe Find out what's happening in the European world of computing. *PC Professionell* offers industry happenings in German, *PC Expert* gives you the score in French, and *Computer Life UK* and *PC Magazine UK* let you in on the PC scene in the United Kingdom. ✓ INTERNET→*www* http://www.ziff.com/~zdeurope/

Wired

alt.wired (ng) It's the kind of newsgroup where some people debate about whether Kurt Cobain was a genius or an overrated jerk, others consider Einstein's theory that a fully functional brain could

240 Net Tech

Computers & Society Computer Culture

do fifty times the work that he did, and still others trade back issues of *Wired* magazine. Occasionally, Wired itself posts announcements to this unofficial and unmoderated newsgroup. ✓**USENET**

HotWired An innovative electronic "magazine" produced by the *Wired* organization. It's hip, well-designed, and packed with original editorial content. The site features a continuously changing mix of features like the recent profile of independent record labels using the Web (with sound clips of their musicians), a Net Surf column highlighting new sites, a gossip column called Flux about the online medium and the media, Club Wired for live symposiums with special guests, and much more. And did we mention that it's completely free and that the "cover" changes each time you access it? Send our regards to Chip if you visit. ✓**INTERNET**→*www* http://www.hotwired.com/

HotWired Mailing List (ml) A moderated list with news about *Wired*, *HotWired*, and the digital frontier. ✓**INTERNET**→*email* info-rama@ wired.com ✍ *Type in message body:* subscribe hotwired

The WIRED Info-rama An automated mail server with archives of all *Wired* articles. Sending the command in the address will return instructions on how to use the server and an index of articles. ✓**INTERNET**→*email* info-rama@ wired.com ✍ *Type in message body:* get help get master. index

WIRED Online One of the pleasures of reading the print version of *Wired* magazine is holding that sexy paper stock in your hands. But *Wired*'s AOL site is the next best thing: Browse or download the full text of back issues or .GIFs of *Wired* covers, discuss *Wired*-related issues (censorship to techno-music) with AOL members and the magazine's staff, or visit an auditorium or chat room and give your two cents on the latest techno-topics at hand. ✓**AMERICA ONLINE**→*keyword* wired

Society

comp.society (ng) Not a whole lot of traffic, but there are always a few interesting ideas floating around here about the social implications of computing. Sandra A. is doing research on artificial intelligence and wants to elicit opinions on the social and ethical concerns of machine-driven thinking. Brett B. has uploaded some excerpts from a Camille Paglia interview in which "The Pirate Queen of Cultural Discourse" makes the following cri de coeur about sex on the Internet: "So if we're getting sex now on the Internet, that's good, because we've overdeveloped our rational side. That is one part of the brain that is being stimulated by Internet communications. So it is crucial to get more sex on the Internet in order to activate the body. I often talk about creative duality. When we feel our culture drifting too far in one direction, it's like yin/yang. We have to compensate; we have to work to regain our balance." Brett waits for comments, and Ms. Paglia probably loves all the attention. ✓**USENET** *FAQ:* ✓**INTERNET**→*www* http://www.cis.ohio-state.edu/hypertext/faq/bngusenet/comp/society/top.html

comp.society.development (ng) Are computers contributing to or detracting from our social development? James T. votes for the former, and he can't wait for cable TV–access to the Internet because "Knowledge should be accessible to all." A different James posts a *New York Times* story about connecting Vietnam to the Internet—the government worries about opening up channels to dissident voices and pornography but also seeks the connection to the modern world. Announcements for conferences about computer technology and development are also posted to this low-traffic newsgroup. ✓**USENET**

comp.society.futures (ng) Futuristic predictions are the order of the day in this philosophical newsgroup that addresses technological advances and their implications on society. "I'm conducting research pertaining to society's battle with its modern 'conveniences,'" announces Nick M., who is clearly a journalist in disguise. "Read *Islands in the Net* by Bruce Sterling or *Neuromancer* by William Gibson," replies a somewhat disgruntled Craig N. "Read them, look around you, and come up with some of your own answers." John S. was kind enough to post an article he found in *Cybernautics Digest* called "Kiss Your Branch Bank Goodbye," in which interactive banking takes the place of bank tellers. No more free lollipops! ✓**USENET**

Computers and Society ARPA Digest (ml) Administered by the government's Advance Research Projects Agency, which was instrumental in the evolution of the Internet circa 1969, the list provides a forum for discussing issues of computing and society. And, yes, ARPA is the central research and development organization of the Department of Defense. Think Mulder and Scully know? ✓**INTERNET**→*email* listserv@american.edu ✍ *Type in message body:* subscribe comsoc-l <your full name>

Computer Culture **Computers & Society**

Computers and Society Articles Collection These articles were compiled for a university course, but don't let the academic tone scare you off. There are interesting musings on subjects such as encryption, gender issues and computing, electronic democracy, the social life of the Internet, law and order on the digital frontier, and privacy in the age of free information. ✓ **INTERNET**→*www* http://cec.wustl.edu/~cs142/articles.html

Hotwired—from http://www.hotwired.com

Ethics-L (ml) Add your two cents' worth to discussions about ethics-related computer issues. How do you feel about artificial intelligence? And speaking of artificial intelligence, do you agree with Newt that everyone should be issued a laptop for equal-opportunity access to the Net? ✓ **INTERNET**→ *email* listserv@vm.poly.edu ✍ *Type in message body:* subscribe ethics-l <your full name>

The Netizens and the Wonderful World of the Net: An Anthology An online book about the history of Usenet and how it helped to create wholly new academic and scientific fields and disciplines, not to mention a clearinghouse for free information for netizens around the world. Anyone interested in the sociological implications of the Internet should check out chapters 7 (The Impact the Net Has on People's Lives) and 10 (The Computer as Democratizer). ✓ **INTERNET** →*www* http://www.cs.columbia.edu/~hauben/netbook/

The Society for Electronic Access This group believes that the world of computers and the communications links that bind users together should be open to everyone. And as a result, it is SEA's mission to "work to educate people about computer networks and how to use them to find information and to communicate with one another." The site includes an archive of information about SEA as well as documents on issues of electronic privacy, government and policy (check out the government Internet resources file), and telecom law. SEA also hopes, through its online efforts, to bring Cyberspace to those who may not have the resources to access it. ✓ **INTERNET**→ *www* gopher://gopher.panix.com/11/SEA

Activism

comp.org.eff.talk (ml/ng) Whether censorship, child pornography, data security, or digital cash is the civil liberties debate-of-the-moment in Cyberspace, this electronic soapbox known as a newsgroup carries some of the most iconoclastic and passionately argued opinions. Writes one anti–gun control advocate: "...I'm a radical libertarian. I'm willing to accept the risks that go with widespread firearms possession just as I'm willing to accept the frightening risk of terrorists and pedophiles on the Net, as a small practical price to pay for adherence to a principle." Other hot topics of late include the transmission of child pornography over the infobahn. Should anyone be prosecuted? If so, should it be the system administrators? Should it be the Internet carrier? Cases are sometimes discussed in painful detail. ✓ **USENET** ✓ **INTERNET**→*email* listserv@eff.org ✍ *Type in message body:* subscribe comp-org-eff-talk <your full name>

Computer Professionals for Social Responsibility (ml) Eschewing the belief that technology alone will improve our world, CPSR, an organization of computer scientists founded in 1981, goes after government organizations hellbent on tapping your telephone or raiding your computer's database. Take the case of the Clipper Chip, an encryption device for the next generation of telephones that makes it impossible for amateur techno-voyeurs to tap your phone but opens a back door for eavesdropping secret service and military agencies. The CPSR Website has an automated letter of protest against the Clipper Chip that users can send to the White House. The heart of the site, however, is its archive of academically oriented texts on computing responsibility in such areas as computer crime, the Freedom of Information Act, privacy and encryption, MUDs and MOOs, and more; it's a good clearing-

242 Net Tech

Computers & Society Computer Culture

house for information on the sociology of the online world. CPSR also maintains a list of 20-plus mailing lists covering specific issues from security in the workplace to Bay Area CPSR member concerns. ✓**INTERNET** …→*www* http://www.cpsr.org/dox/home.html …→*email* listserv@cpsr.org ✎ *Type in message body:* subscribe cpsr-announce <your full name>

EFFector Online (ml) A biweekly newsletter focusing on legislation affecting the online world, particularly issues of censorship and security. ✓**INTERNET**→*email* listserv@eff.org ✎ *Type in message body:* subscribe effector-online <your full name>

The Electronic Frontier Foundation Do you believe in freedom of expression and the right to privacy on the Internet? The EFF was founded in 1990 to ensure that "the principles embodied in the Constitution and the Bill of Rights are protected as new communications technologies emerge." Find out what's pushing the EFF's buttons this week by reading the Action Alerts available at these cybersites—the group has recently gone to court to try and overturn cryptography restrictions. EFF also has some choice things to say about the proposed Exon/Gorton Communications Decency amendment and efforts by the Church of Scientology to censor Usenet newsgroups. The sites offer archives of the EFF newsletter, action alerts, Internet guides, and, on AOL and CompuServe, message boards and live chat areas for discussing cyber-rights issues. ✓**INTERNET** …→*www* http://www.eff.org/ …→*www* ftp://ftp.eff.org ✓**AMERICA ONLINE** →*keyword* eff ✓**COMPUSERVE**→*go* effsig

Humor

alt.folklore.computers (ng) In response to the tongue-in-cheek, anything-goes attitude of alt.folklore.computers, an official newsgroup, comp.society.folklore, was created several years ago to discuss the history and legends of computers and the Net. The official group still exists but rarely gets any messages. On the other hand, this newsgroup is thriving. Discussions break out around rumors, insults, and trivia. "What was the longest newsgroup thread ever?" was a recent topic of discussion and, not so surprisingly, it was a relatively long discussion. "What's the computer with the most RAM on the planet?" was another topic. "An SGI Challenge L with 2Gb of RAM!," pipes in one reader with a serious answer. But then came the ever-so-typical digression: "The biggest computer in the world _was_ _The Earth_, until the Vogons blew it up to make way for a hyperspace bypass." And with that reference to *The Hitchiker's Guide to the Galaxy*, the topic spun off to a debate over which computer came up with the number 42. Then someone made a Microsoft joke and the topic took another twist. And so it goes. ✓**USENET**

Law

alt.politics.datahighway (ng) Sign an online petition to stop the Communications Decency Act, read the latest issue of EFFector Online (a newsletter published by the Electronic Freedom Foundation), or read someone's rant about the new Website maintained by the Christian Coalition. Tap into the group for insight on how the online masses feel about electronic legislation and its implications. ✓**USENET**

CYBERNOTES

"The Ten Commandments of Computer Ethics:

1. Thou shalt not use a computer to harm other people.

2. Thou shalt not interfere with other people's work.

3. Thou shalt not snoop in other people's files.

4. Thou shalt not use a computer to steal.

5. Thou shalt not use a computer to bear false witness.

6. Thou shalt not copy or use proprietary software for which you have not paid.

7. Thou shalt not use other people's resources without authorization.

8. Thou shalt not use other people's output.

9. Thou shalt think about the consequences of the program you are writing.

10. Thou shalt use a computer in ways that insure consideration for your fellow humans."

—from **Computer Professionals for Social Responsibility**

Computer Culture **Computers & Society**

comp.society.cu-digest (ng) Holding tanks for the irreverent, in-your-face *Computer Underground Digest*, which is dedicated to sharing information among computerists and to "the presentation and debate of diverse views." Issue #40 is devoted entirely to Scientology, especially its declaration of war on the Internet and on Usenet newsgroups: "Internet users are finding out something that writers and journalists have known for years: the Church of Scientology doesn't take kindly to people who write negative things about it." Issue #39, on the other hand, addresses the Federal government and its efforts to stifle computer hackers in the United States. Can you say CONSPIRACY THEORY??!!? ✓ **USENET Archives:** ✓ **INTERNET**→ *www* http://www.soci.niu.edu:80/~cudigest/

The Crypto Anarchist Manifesto A spirited tract about how innovations in encryptographic digital transmission will alter the face of government as we know it. ✓ **INTERNET**→ *www* http://www.quadralay.com/www/Crypt/Crypto-Anarchist/crypto-anarchist.html

Cyberlaw/Cyberlex Each month, important legal issues related to computer technology from Microsoft's antitrust case to the Scientology suit—are reported at these sites. In the form of either short news briefs (Cyberlex) or long features (Cyberlaw), the reports describe both the rulings and their implications. ✓ **AMERICA ONLINE**→ *keyword* cyberlex ✓ **INTERNET**→ *www* http://www.portal.com/~cyberlaw/cylw_home.html

Liquid Mercury Soup Let's say you scan a copyrighted photograph and alter it digitally for your CD-ROM's interface. Are you in violation of copyright law? You bet, and you could be sued for up to $100,000 dollars. To avoid such complications in the nebulous world of multimedia rights, read the Multimedia Law Primer here (excerpted from the *Multimedia Law Handbook*). For more detailed information, you can order the book. But copyrights aren't the only unresolved issues in the burgeoning, confused world of multimedia. For example, how do you make money? Where should you sell your multimedia product? While this site may not have all the answers, it provides brief speculations on marketing strategies for multimedia, basically teasers so you'll go ahead and order books from this retailer/publisher. ✓ **INTERNET**→ *www* http://www.primenet.com/~clancy/soup/liquid.mercury.soup.html

Women

ACM SIGMOD University computer science departments are still overwhelmingly male, but not for much longer if these women have their way. The site features suggestions, warnings, and information, to help women break into the boys club. ✓ **INTERNET**→ *www* http://bunny.cs.uiuc.edu/funding/academic-Careers.html

Geekgirl What is cyberfeminism? "An intimate and possibly subversive element between women and machines—especially the new intelligent machines—which are no longer simply working for man as women are no longer simply working for man." So says Dr. Sadie Plant of the University of Birmingham. This hip online journal combines cyberculture and a feminist attitude. Learn about the chromo-phallic patriarchal code or electronic salons for women only. The campy illustrations make this site a lot of fun. ✓ **INTERNET**→ *www* http://www.next.com.au/spyfood/geekgirl

TAP: The Ada Project Computing women and other scientists will find professional support in this page's listings of conferences, fellowships, and job opportunities. The page is a huge collection of links; it's a site with links to Systers-out for lesbian programmers, the Los Alamos Women in Science group, historical profiles of women in computing, and much more. ✓ **INTERNET**→ *www* http://www.cs.yale.edu/HTML/YALE/CS/HyPlans/tap/tap.html

Women and Computer Science Read up on women's progress in the male-dominated computer field with this collection of online articles. Get in touch with other female Netheads too. Or just click on Nerd Songs and hum along to "Girls Just Wanna Defun." ✓ **INTERNET**→ *www* http://www.ai.mit.edu/people/ellens/gender.html

Women Web-sters' Net-work The image of women as Web weavers is as old as Arachne, and this site carries on that proud tradition as women build a Web for women in Cyberspace. Although many of its links are to generic women's interest sites, the Web-sister in charge has made a special effort to provide networking links for women in the information industry. Visit, for instance, the Geekgirl or the Electric Anima page, or find a new fellowship or job at the ADA Project. The women's computing societies at Stanford, Berkeley, and Carnegie Mellon are also just a keystroke away. ✓ **INTERNET**→ *www* http://lucien.berkeley.edu/women_in_it.html

Part 8

Getting Wired

Communications **Getting Wired**

Communications

No man is an island, of course, and no computer is either. While computers of the past were isolationists, computers of the present talk to each other all the time. Visit Prodigy's **Communications** topic or the **Computer and Communications Home Page** to find out the basics—you'll be communicating without even knowing it—and then drop by industry publications like **CommunicationsWeek** and even new-tech-meets-old-tech sites like **The Internet Fax Server**.

Switchboard operator—from CompuServe's Bettmann Archive

On the Net

Across the board

Communications Buying a modem, configuring a communications program, setting up an Ethernet connection, faxing via the Internet, using ISDN, and video conferencing are just a few of the communications issues that Prodigy members fret about in this topic. It's also a good place to discuss other online services and Internet providers. ✓**PRODIGY**→*jump* computer bb→Choose a Topic→Communications

Communications & Telecommunications A straightforward but incredibly extensive list of communications and telecommunications sites on the Internet. The home page for the Institute of Electrical and Electronics Engineers merits a link, as does the BBC, HotWired, *Telecommunications Magazine*, an historical overview of the Irish Telecomm system, and others. Like an international telephone network, it stretches on and on. ✓**INTERNET**→*www* http://www.analysys.co.uk/commslib.htm

Computer and Communications Home Page In part, the site serves as a central repository of information about upcoming computer and telecommunications conferences. In part, it's a guide to technology-related media online—go straight to the Ziff-Davis page or take a left turn at Albuquerque and flip through *Digital Biscuit* (the hip, hyped underground techno magazine from Tokyo). It is also a good place to explore academic and employment opportunities in the computer and communications field. Finally, you'll find basic information on everything from ATM to Virtual Reality Modeling Language (VRML). ✓**INTERNET**→ *www* http://www.atp.llnl.gov/atp/telecom.html

Information Sources: the Internet and Computer-Mediated Communication A huge, well-organized guide to Internet resources on computer-mediated communication. Computer-mediated communication? Could be just about anything, it seems, and this is indeed a huge guide, with links to hundreds of Websites and discussion groups that range from histories of the Internet, maps of the Web, HTML tutorials, search engines, and dense technical documents about Internet protocols. ✓**INTERNET**→*www* http://www.rpi.edu/Internet/Guides/decemj/icmc/top.html

UK Communications Forum A forum with hundreds of shareware

246 Net Tech

Getting Wired Communications

programs and patches for modems, remote-access programs, and other communications software. The libraries and message boards are filled with announcements for U.K. BBSs and Internet services, as well as information and discussion about communications topics in general. ✓**COMPUSERVE**→ *go* ukcomms

News

CommunicationsWeek The weekly print publication about data communications and computer networking is now online, with full-text articles on communication trends, product tests, and industry gossip. ✓**INTERNET**→*www* http://techweb.wais.com/techweb/cw/

Cowles/SIMBA When the *Village Voice* and *L.A. Weekly* announced the launch of their bicoastal online nightlife guide, Cowles/SIMBA had a story on it the next day. When AT&T announced a series of consumer products and billing options merging telephone and computer technologies, Cowles/SIMBA covered it. And when Prodigy announced that its members could create home pages…well, you can probably guess the rest. Each weekday, new stories about online media are added to both the Internet and AOL sites. On AOL, the forum offers coverage of other media as well, including magazines, newspapers, book publishing, broadcast and cable, and advertising. ✓**INTERNET**→*www* http://www.mecklerweb.com/simba/internet.htm ✓**AMERICA ONLINE**→*keyword* cowles

Inter@ctive Week The electronic counterpart to the weekly magazine that covers the interactive computing and telecommunications industries. Keep abreast of the latest movements of the Big Three online services, or find out how the Baby Bells will affect the way you receive information. Back issues of this bible for the fast-paced telcom world are also archived here. ✓**INTERNET**→ *www* http://www.ziff.com/~intweek/

Interactive Age Home Page If you're trying to follow developments in the online industry, this is one of the best places to start. The several full-text articles from the current issue of the biweekly print edition of *Interactive Age* are a wonderful resource, and that's not the only draw of this site. It also has an electronic daily version of the magazine, several news briefs about the online industry, and a comprehensive hotlist that links to all sites mentioned in the current issue. ✓**INTERNET**→*www* http://techweb.cmp.com:80/techweb/ia/current/

The Journal of Computer-Mediated Communication A new electronic journal that publishes essays and research reports on communications networks, electronic privacy, the sociology of the information infrastructure, and the educational benefits of computer-mediated communication. ✓**INTERNET**→*www* http://shum.huji.ac.il/jcmc/jcmc.html

Faxing

comp.dcom.fax (ng) Does anyone use a traditional fax machine anymore? You wouldn't think so by reading the posts in this newsgroup. Netters here are concerned with faxing via modem and over the Internet. David is looking for fax software for his PC; Petras, who has tried BitFax Pro for Windows and WinFax, wants advice on why his Class 2 Internal Fax/Modem keeps hanging up in the middle of transmitting a fax; and Ed needs to find an email-to-fax remailer service that works in the Chicago area. The newsgroup's FAQ functions as an instructional primer, answering both what-can-I-do and how-can-I-do-it questions as well as providing an excellent overview of faxing equipment and software. Ed, who's looking for the remailer, should definitely read the FAQ. ✓**USENET** *FAQ:* ✓**INTERNET**→*www* http://www.faximum.com/faqs/fax

How Can I Send a Fax from the Internet? Perhaps unsurprisingly, this document addresses how to send a fax on the Internet, and includes Net addresses for both free and pay-for-use fax services. ✓**INTERNET**→*www* ftp://rtfm.internet-services/fax-faq

The Internet Fax Server Need to fax Hong Kong, Greece, Boston, New York City, Washington, D.C., or San Francisco? It's free and incredibly easy on the Internet. Just fill out the fax form on this Web page and send. The fax number is constructed in the following way: <country code or 1><area code and telephone number>.iddd.tpc.int. Don't use spaces or dashes in the number. The service sends faxes to many U.S. and international destinations; check the sites for a list of area codes and cities covered. ✓**INTERNET**…→*www* http://town.hall.org/fax/ →*www* http://www.balliol.ox.ac.uk/fax/faxsend.html *FAQ:* ✓**INTERNET**→*www* http://town.hall.org/fax/faq.html

Wireless

Mobile and Wireless Computing A large hypertext index of mobile and wireless computing sites on the Internet. The index is organized into categories such as

Net Tech 247

Communications Getting Wired

conferences, journals, providers and services, and laboratories. One of the links, Columbia University's mobile-computing laboratory, leads to academic papers on mobile computing, while another link, *Mobilis: the mobile lifestyle magazine*, leads to an electronic journal that features product reviews, tutorials, and even ads. ✓**INTERNET**→*www* http://snapple.cs.washington.edu:600/mobile/mobile_www.html

Wireless Communications The forum caters to both consumers and industry types. News bulletins covering the latest developments in the wireless communications industry are fed daily into the forum from BusinessWire and PRNewswire. While some of these read like press releases (many are), the latest announcements on corporate mergers, expansion plans, stock-market developments, and other information of interest to wireless industry types are available. The message boards offer separate discussions for different types of wireless-communication devices: cellular phones, pagers, and PDAs, to name a few. The libraries contain back issues of *Wireless Digest*, for those interested in a more probing analysis of industry developments. ✓**AMERICA ONLINE**→*keyword* wireless

Wireless Communications Forum Are you on the road so much that you're out of touch with important matters? Maybe you need to go wireless. You can send commands to your Mac from anywhere on the road if you have a wireless communications device and U-Page 4.0, available in this forum's libraries. If you need vendor support or product information (from the Air Communications mobile telephone to vendors selling third-party products for your Motorola paging device), there are message folders and libraries with info. ✓**COMPUSERVE**→*go* wireless

Amigas

Amiga Datacommunication Archives Internet tutorials for newbies, SLIP and PPP software for Amiga Netters needing fast connections, terminal software for those plugging away on dial-up connections, and Net software clients—and that's only the beginning of what's available in this Amiga directory. The site also carries programs and manuals for a broad range of datacommunication needs. ✓**INTERNET**→*www* ftp://www.funet.fi/pub/amiga/datacomm/

Amiga Networking FAQ All aspects of networking with the Amiga are covered in this FAQ, from using Novell Netware to configuring email to learning network parallel programming. ✓**INTERNET**→*www* http://www.cis.ohiostate.edu:80/text/faq/usenet/amiga/networking-faq/top.html

AmigaNOS FAQ An FAQ for the Amiga program that allows hams to run AX25 and TCP/IP over packet radio modems, Ethernet, and serial lines. ✓**INTERNET**→*www* http://www.cis.ohiostate.edu:80/text/faq/usenet/amiga/AmigaNOS-faq/faq.html

The Aminet Communications Archive A large collection of terminal programs, mail applications, news readers, BBS software, TCP/IP programs, and other Amiga-related communications files. ✓**INTERNET**…→*www* ftp://wuarchive.wustl.edu/pub/aminet/comm/…→*www* http://src.doc.ic.ac.uk/public/aminet/info/www/dirs/comm.html

---

CYBERNOTES

"I am going to replace my current communications program with one more up to date—a Windows programs capable of fax and 28.8 data. I would also like to have additonal tools for BBSs and graphics downloads. I understand there is a new ProComm version out which may even have some Internet capabilities. I would like to buy next week so your help is much appreciated."

"I have Procomm + 2.11. I use it for both fax and data. In fax, it will only import in .bmp files for customizing coversheets (if that is important to you), also it still does not have OCR capabilities. According to tech support they are working on it but who knows when it will arrive. For faxing, I like Faxworks Pro 3.0, but it has many shortcomings besides the fact that it is only a fax program. I have heard some good things about the Delrina communications suite. Don't know if I helped or just goofed you up."

—from Prodigy's **Communications**

---

248 Net Tech

Getting Wired Communications

comp.sys.amiga.datacomm (ng) Have you spent the past three weeks unsuccessfully trying to get on the Web with AMosaic and AmiTCP? Dry your eyes. Take your head off the desk. Put that whiskey back in the cabinet and take George Jones's "If Drinkin' Don't Kill Me (Her Memory Will)" out of your tape player. And then join a support group. This newsgroup might be a good choice; it's filled with Webheads with Amigas who are usually quite helpful. Besides TCP/IP connections, the newsgroup also covers modems, modem software, and other data-communications issues. ✓**USENET**

Apple II

Apple II Telecommunications Features a collection of communications software (terminal programs to BBS software), networking guides, and software documentation for Apple II users. The message board topic is always fairly active with members asking about sending email, using Lynx, setting up modem scripts, and other communications issues. ✓**COMPUSERVE**→*go* appuserc→Libraries

comp.sys.apple2.comm (ng) Questions about image viewers, modem hardware and software, and Web browsers are par for the course in this newsgroup on communications issues relating to the Apple II computer. ✓**USENET**

Atari

Atari Networking How do you build an Ethernet card for the MegaST? See the directions in the Ethernet directory. If you want to use a graphical Web browser to navigate the Internet, you'll need software to handle the SLIP and PPP protocols. You can get it here, along with the necessary source code. But, hell, maybe you just want to connect two Atari computers at home. Try the Duet program. Although the site fails noticeably in its attempt to build an archive of SLIP client programs for the Atari (Web browsers, gopher programs, etc.), its holdings are impressive enough that it's still worth a trip. ✓**INTERNET** …→*www* gopher://gopher.archive.umich.edu:7055/00/atari/Network …→ *www* ftp://atari.archive.umich.edu/Network… →*www* ftp://wu-archive.wustl.edu/systems/atari/umich.edu/Network/

Atari ST SLIP FAQ A detailed explanation of installing and using a SLIP connection on an Atari ST. ✓**INTERNET**→*www* gopher://gopher.archive.umich.edu:7055/00/atari/Network/tcpip.faq

Atari Telecommunications A modest, well-organized collection of simple communications programs and mail readers for the Atari. ✓**INTERNET** …→*www* gopher://gopher.archive.umich.edu:7055/00/atari/Telecomm…→*www* ftp://atari.archive.umich.edu/Telecomm …→*www* ftp://wuarchive.wustl.edu/systems/atari/umich.ed/Telecomm

Macintosh

comp.sys.mac.comm (ng) Maybe you're having trouble with your computer's voice-mail answering system. Perhaps you're having less luck than you had hoped configuring your Mac TCP account. Or are you just worried about using your portable U.S. modem in Italy? Macintosh users visit this newsgroup for data communications advice and discussion. The newsgroup's FAQ is an excellent reference for Mac users trying to make a data connection; there are sections devoted to modems and cables, file formats and conversion, file transfers, AppleTalk, TCP/IP networking, email, Usenet newsgroups, and much more. ✓**USENET** *FAQ:* ✓**INTERNET**→*www* ftp://rtfm.mit.edu/pub/usenet-by-hierarchy/comp/sys/mac/comm/

Info-Mac Communications Directory Looking for an AppleTalk chatting program? No sooner said than done; choose between EZChat or ChatNet. The large communications directory also includes add-ons for AppleShare servers, network management tools, Ethernet card drivers, and a number of other Mac communications programs, such as MacPager 1.0, which automatically lets you know about an incoming call while on the road. ✓**INTERNET** …→*www* ftp://sumex-aim.stanford.edu/info-mac/comm/ …→ *www* gopher://sumex-aim.Stanford.EDU:70/11/info-mac/Communication …→*www* gopher://sunsite.doc.ic.ac.uk:70/1/packages/mac-sumex/comm

Mac Communication Software A gold mine of Mac communication software. Need an Apple Remote Access script for your new modem? No problem. You can download the appropriate scripts for Hayes, Global Village, Teleport, US Robotics, and several other brands. You'll also find some of the latest email software accessories, such as E-mail Buddy, which allows you to copy and paste email addresses into another program, and PageNOW!, which sends messages from any Mac to pagers or Apple Newtons. ✓**INTERNET**→*www* http://hyperarchive.lcs.mit.edu/HyperArchive/Abstracts/comm/HyperArchive.html

Communications Getting Wired

Mac Shareware Communications & Connectivity Can you figure out what MacWoof is? Besides sending and receiving mail automatically from FidoNet, it wins the award for most goofy title in the enormous Mac 500 shareware archive. If MacWoof isn't what you're looking for, try the Termulator bug fix, which lets you create elaborate front ends and split your terminal screen. And if all you need is ZTerm or MacKermit, just point, click, and retrieve. ✓**AMERICA ONLINE**→*keyword* mac 500→Communications & Connectivity

Macintosh Communications Forum Are you distressed because your Supra 14.4LC modem worked flawlessly and the upgrade to Supra 28.8 modem is unreliable? "Use the ft & ai setup string," says one fellow 28.8 convert. While the message board is a valuable resource for advice about data communications on the Mac, the forum is also a great place to download communications software, patches, and demos from MacKermit to ZTerm. ✓**AMERICA ONLINE**→ *keyword* mcm

Macintosh Communications Forum Before you consign fax machines to the graveyard of mid-80s technology, remember that the facsimile machine is still the data communications standard in offices worldwide. Faxes haven't gone anywhere, but they've been absorbed by modem and Internet technology, and cybersavvy faxers meet in this CompuServe forum to discuss fax technology. But faxing talk is only a small part of the traffic here. The forum also includes Mac-related information on how to configure settings for terminal emulation, phone numbers for local BBSs, the newest version of CIS Navigator, and discussion about the Internet. The Internet topic looks to be the busiest for the foreseeable future. ✓**COMPUSERVE**→*go* maccomm

DOS & Windows

Communications/FAX Applications Simple and sophisticated communications programs for Windows systems, ranging from a program to fax from your Word application to a program that uses Caller ID to unmask all incoming modems. ✓**COMPUSERVE**→*go* winshare→Libraries→Comm/FAX/App-Utils

comp.os.ms-windows. apps.comm (ng) Setting up the popular email program Eudora can be a daunting task, especially when dealing with Microsoft Windows. Add Windows 95 to the recipe and you can expect to see even more frustrated PC datacom chefs. MS Windows users can turn to this newsgroup for support and advice about Eudora and other communications applications. ✓**USENET**

comp.sys.ibm.pc.hardware. comm (ng) Modem hardware dominates the discussion. John is posting to find out if his new modem is defective or if he's just hooking it up incorrectly. Karen upgraded to a 28.8 and is trying to sell her 14.4. Duncan wants to know how fast he can run a modem over a phone line. And Bill is trying to find out if anyone else who uses the serial ports on the Promise 2300+ is getting comm overruns in Trumpet Winsock. ✓**USENET** *FAQ:* ✓**INTERNET**→*www* ftp://rtfm.it.edu/pub/usenet-by-hierarchy/comp/sys/ibm/pc/hardware/comm/

PC Communications Forum While you can get into a discus-

CYBERNOTES

"I have Netscape and MacTCP and PPP, but I can't connect to the Web. I can connect with my terminal emulation software to my provider but then I don't have a graphical interface. With the Netscape browser, I feel that I'm not dialing anywhere? Is this whole Internet thing more difficult than the pop media would have us think? Please point me in the right direction thanks."

"Do you have all your ISP info plugged into MacTCP and MacPPP? If that is all setup, you should be able to lauch Netscape, and if memory serves me, Netscape is set to default to their Web site (you'll want to change that in the Preferences). It will activate MacTCP and dial your ISP. You'll probably want the MacPPP control panel open so you can shutdown. That's about all there is to it! Get the little control panel here on CompuServe called PPPfloater. It will help you control MacPPP?"

—CompuServe's **Macintosh Communications Forum**

250 Net Tech

Getting Wired **Communications**

sion about the most minute details of ISDN, SLIP, and PPP on the message boards of this forum, you might also want to go to the library, print out "How to E-mail," and give it to a cyberphobic friend—it's far more fun being online if you have friends in Cyberspace. Besides cybertalk about datacommunications, the forum also carries a large selection of PC communications software, from basic modem software to graphical Web browsers, as well as guides and documentation to help you communicate with your PC. ✓**COMPUSERVE**→ *go* pccom

PC Telecom & Networks Forum Is your office's networked Marathon game affecting productivity? Find ways to entice workers back to work in the LAN and Network message boards. Are you stuck with nothing to do, but have full access to four 486 computers and a Lantastic network? Sounds like your office could use a little Doom or PacWars distraction action. The forum has how-to instructions on getting started. Maybe you just want to start up a small peer-to-peer network for your office. Turn to the message boards for advice. ("All you need is an Ethernet connection, Windows for Workgroups 3.11, and a couple of low-end 486's with 8 MB of RAM"). Resources and discussion for both PC networking and datacommunications issues are included in this forum. ✓**AMERICA ONLINE**→*keyword* pctelecom

SimTel Communications Programs A small directory of Windows communications programs, including Procomm Plus, a program to calculate phone costs when on a modem, an image viewing program, and others. ✓**INTERNET** …→*www* http://www.acs.oakland.edu/oak/SimTel/win3/

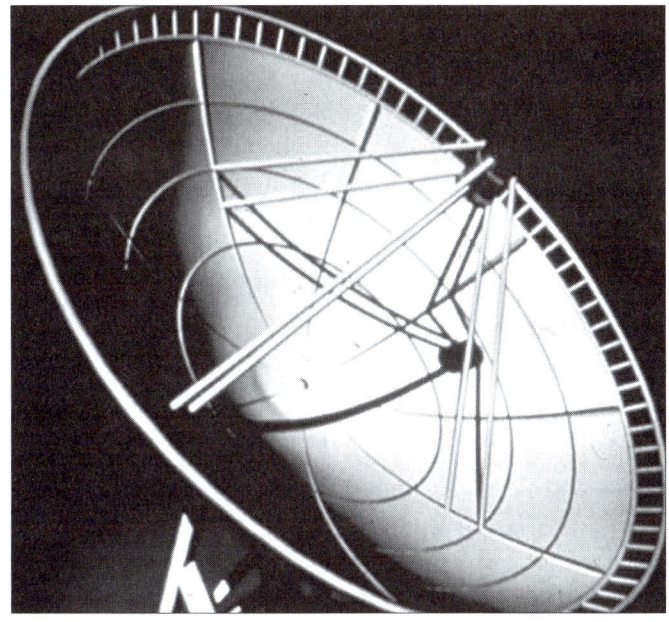

Satellite dish—from http://www.artn.nwu.edu/phsc/

commprog.html …→*www* ftp://oak.oakland.edu/SimTel/win3/commprog …→*www* ftp://wuarchive.wustl.edu/systems/ibm-pc/simtel/win3/commprog …→*www* ftp://ftp.uoknor.edu/mirrors/SimTel/win3/comm prog …→*www* ftp://ftp.uni-paderborn.de/SimTel/win3/commprog

Windows Connectivity Forum Whether connecting to coworkers on the office network, logging into BBSs via modems, dialing into computers remotely, or surfing the Net, MS Windows users are getting connected, and this forum offers advice and discussion about Windows connectivity. The message board features sections on modems, WinSock applications, groupware, client-server applications, and the Web. The library is filled to the gills with email shareware packages, BBS shareware packages, remote-dialup tools, and fax/modem programs. ✓**COMPUSERVE**→*go* wincon

Windows Shareware Communications & Connectivity Some of the most popular Windows telecommunications shareware programs are archived at this site, including the Kermit terminal emulation program, E-mail for Windows, WinQVT, etc. ✓**AMERICA ONLINE** →*keyword* win 500→Windows 500 Shareware Library→Communications & Connectivity

Windows Telecom Programs With the right software, your PC can answer calls, identify the caller, or page you remotely. You can even carry on a conversation with another human voice over the Internet using the program Megaphone. This library carries a selection of downloadable shareware to turn your desktop into a powerful multitasking telecommunications tool. ✓**AMERICA ONLINE**→*keyword* winforum→Browse the Software Libraries→Applications→Telecom

Net Tech 251

Telecommunications **Getting Wired**

Telecommunications

Since Alexander Graham Bell bellowed for Watson, the telephone has been one of the threads of the loom of modern life. And since the first computers were networked over phone lines, the field of telecommunications has been inseparable from the computer industry. Drop a dime on the gigantic **Telecom Information Resources on the Internet** to learn how computers and telephones can join forces to build a better tomorrow. Talk toll-free numbers and intercontinental networks on **alt.dcom.telecom**. Then visit the **AT&T Home Page**, the **MCI** site, and the **Sprint Home Page**. And remember—if you tell your friends and family about these sites, there may be big savings right around the corner.

Get Smart—downloaded from CompuServe's Bettmann Archive

On the Net

Across the board

Keith O'Brien's Telecom Info Home Page Keith has compiled and organized a large number of links to telecommunications resources, such as trade magazines and journals, vendors, newsgroups, MCI's headline news, and telecom carriers. ✓**INTERNET**→*www* http://www.castle.net/~kobrien/telecom.html

National Telecommunications & Information Administration It's not very exciting but it is the official online presence of the U.S. government's NTIA. ✓**INTERNET**→*www* http://www.ntia.doc.gov/

{Tele}Communications Information Sources A large collection of links to telecommunications sites online, including sites for Australian telecom policy papers, the United States National Telecommunications & Information Administration, several telephone companies in Finland, Ameritech, the Bells, and many others. ✓**INTERNET**→*www* http://www.telstra.com.au/info/communications.html

Telecom Information Resources on the Internet Holy touch-tone, Batman! It's the nerve center of the globe! There are over 350 links to "information sources relating to the technical, economic, public policy, and social aspects of telecommunications. All forms of telecommunication, including voice, data, video, wired, wireless, cable TV, and satellite, are included." Read the FAQ on usage-based pricing for Net providers, research papers on digital currency, or a Freenet how-to guide. You can find out whether MBONE is a viable form of commercial broadcast or get in touch with the League for Programming Freedom, an organization that opposes software patents and interface copyrights. Plus, there are plenty of juicy bits

252 Net Tech

Getting Wired Telecommunications

for all the phreaks. ✓**INTERNET**→*www* http://www.ipps.lsa.umich.edu/telecom-info.html …→*www* http://ippsweb.ipps.lsa.umich.edu/telecom/telecom-info.html

Telecommunications Forum Living overseas and tired of paying inflated telephone rates to the U.S.A.? Maybe you should look into using a telephone reseller—ask questions about resellers on the message boards or download information about long-distance plans from the library. Did someone just recommend an ISDN hookup? There's an ISDN FAQ in addition to the ABC Guide to ISDN, an ISDN catalog, and hundreds of other documents and guides to ISDN in the library—more than enough info to bring you up to speed. If you're afraid of hackers' or the federal government's tampering with your computer files, read up on encryption systems and firewalls on the message boards. Voice, email, and paging software are also heavily discussed here. So whether you're curious about new area codes, interference on your portable phone, or serious discussions about network security, this forum covers the gamut of telecommunications issues. ✓**COMPUSERVE**→*go* telecom

Telephone Industry Information Page Browse alphabetically or by category through an online edition of the Yellow Pages for toll-free numbers—and that's just one link from this index of telecommunications sites on the Internet. There are also links to the FCC and other governmental agencies, comparative price charts on long-distance carriers, and FAQs from telecom-related newsgroups. And, you can be sure, there's a mainline to the AT&T "you will," "you will," "you will"

psychotrope. ✓**INTERNET**→ *www* http://www.teleport.com/~mw/cc/tii.html

WilTel This telecom giant operates a nationwide fiber-optic network, and provides data, voice, and video communications services. Its Website publishes a weekly newsletter called "Keeping Up with the Industry." The newsletter carries dozens of synopses from articles about the telecom industry, articles that are reprinted from magazines such as *PC Magazine*, *Computer Reseller News*, *InformationWeek*, and the *Telecommunications Alert*. The Website's library has one of the most significant collections of telecom references and research online, including a searchable glossary of telecommunications terms; listings of telecom conferences; archives of the *Telecom Digest*, the *Long Distance Digest*, and *Telecomreg*; and three years' worth of articles on telecommunications. ✓**INTERNET**→ *www* http://www.wiltel.com/wilhome.html

Chat

alt.dcom.telecom (ng) Did you know the supply of 800 numbers is being reduced by 30,000 per week? At this rate, there won't be any new 800 numbers left by March of 1996. As a result, a new 888 toll-free area code is in development. Follow industry trends on the most user-friendly of the telecom discussion groups. ✓**USENET**

comp.dcom.telecom (ng/ml) What the fax line was to the '80s, the modem line is to the '90s. One thing remains constant—the increasing requests for phone lines are wreaking havoc on the formerly rigid and clear system of area codes and prefixes. One phone enthusiast on this discussion group wonders if it would be possible to have an outgoing line with no number or capacity to receive incoming calls, thereby conserving phone numbers. Another discussion thread debates the ways in which the former Soviet Union will start splitting up its area code system now that their number of phone lines is on the rise. Occasionally, the group digresses into talk of telecommunications history (how did people make long-distance calls from pay phones in 1942?). The telecommunications talk on this moderated newsgroup, which is also available as the *Telecom Digest*, is pitched at a relatively high level and is one of the oldest continuing discussion groups on the Internet—14-plus years. It's not that the discussions are too technical, they're just less chatty and noisy than most. Many of the posts read like newspaper reports about the industry, and there appears to be a significant number of professionals who work in the telecommunications industry online here—job announcements are quite common. The FAQ covers questions ranging from "What frequencies do touch tones use for which numbers?" to "What is

> "Did you know the supply of 800 numbers is being reduced by 30,000 per week? At this rate, there won't be any left by March of 1996."

Net Tech 253

Telecommunications Getting Wired

Bellcore?" The extensive archives include the hundreds of book reviews that have been published in the *Telecom Digest* over the years, essays, and information and articles about several frequently discussed topics (cellular, area codes, carriers, Minitel, security fraud, etc.). ✓**USENET** ✓**INTERNET**→*email* telecom-request@eecs.nwu.edu ✍ *Write a request Archives:* ✓**INTERNET**→*www* ftp://lcs.mit.edu/telecom-archives / *FAQ:* ✓**INTERNET**→*www* http://www.wiltel.com/telecomd/tele_faq.html

comp.dcom.telecom.tech (ng) Leo from Portugal wants to know what "911" is. Kimmo from Finland answers with a chart of emergency numbers in countries all over the world. Need the police in Singapore? Dial 999. In Israel? 100. In Portugal? It's 112. (But Leo probably already knew that.) In general, posts are about T1s, cellular networks, and fiber lines. ✓**USENET**

Info-Fibers List (ml) Find out why your transatlantic phone connection sounds as good as a local call by learning all about fiber optics. If you're a fiber-optics professional, bring questions and concerns to the discussion table. ✓**INTERNET**→ *email* info-fibers-request@spie.org ✍ *Type in message body:* subscribe info-fibers <your email address>

Long-Distance Digest Share information about and discuss long-distance services and providers: resellers, carriers, aggregators, wholesalers, and agents. In the FAQ, discover how the effects of the 1984 antitrust suit against AT&T are still rippling outward. It's an intensely competitive market, and you can benefit from the telecom industry's internecine strife. ✓**INTERNET**→*email* telconet@aol.com ✍ *Type in subject line:* subscribe digest <your email address> *FAQ:* ✓**INTERNET**→*www* http://www.wiltel.com/ldd/faq.html *Archives:* ✓**INTERNET**→*www* http://www.wiltel.com/ldd/ldd.html

Telecom Regulations (ml) Unmoderated discussion of telecommunications regulation and deregulation, including cable television and telephony. With European telecoms deregulating faster than you can say "1998" (the year the EC has mandated for deregulation), there should be a lot of interesting discussion here in the next few years. ✓**INTERNET**→*email* listserv@relay.adp.wisc.edu ✍ *Type in message body:* subscribe telecom-reg <your full name>

News & reference

Peter W. Huber Home Page A Website featuring excerpts and tables of contents from several books and reports about the telecommunications industry written by lawyer-author-engineer Peter Huber. ✓**INTERNET**→*www* http://www.telecoms-mag.com/tcs.html

The Telecommunications Glossary If you know your RBOCs (regional Bell operating companies) from your BCCs (Bellcore Client Company) and your BERs (bit error rate), you might not need this service. But for most, this glossary of hundreds of telecommunications terms provides clear definitions of the lingo used in one of the most important industries in the world. ✓**INTERNET**→*www* http://www.wiltel.com/glossary/glossary.html

Telecommunications Online Registering is a truly painful process, but, once registered, a user has access to tables of contents and selected articles from

---

CYBERNOTES

"Q: What is ISDN?

A: Simply speaking, ISDN provides the customer with the 64k bit/sec that PCM (Pulse Code Modulation) digital representation of speech occupies, but doesn't insist that it be used for speech. The simplest connection you can buy offers `2B+D' (BT's ISDN-2, or `basic-rate' ISDN), which is 2x64k bit/sec with a 16k bit/sec signalling channel. You can send rather wimpy video with 128k bit/sec, but it would have to be highly compressed, at low resolution and with a low frame rate (like in a picture-phone).

Q: Say I want to access my university computer from home, using an ISDN connection, in order to get fast terminal access and file transfer. What would I need to connect a PC?

A: You will need a terminal adaptor at the Unix end, and a PC card in the PC. Software is dependent upon what you wish to run over the link."

—from the **UK.telecom FAQ**

Getting Wired Telecommunications

Telecommunications Magazine (e.g., "Making the Frame Relay Decision: User Criteria," April 1995), schedules for telecommunications conferences, and the magazines' media planner. ✓ **INTERNET**→*www* http:// www.telecomsmag.com/tcs.html

Services

The AmeriCom Long Distance AREA DECODER Enter the city, state, and country. The service returns area codes. ✓ **INTERNET**→*www* http://www.xmission.com/~americom/aclookup.html

AT&T 800 Directory A searchable directory of businesses with AT&T 800 service numbers. Search the directory by company name, category, city, and/or state. ✓ **INTERNET**→*www* http://www. xmission.com/~americom/aclookup. html

The big players

AT&T Home Page Summaries of calling plans, residential ISDN information, the AT&T multimedia catalog of products and services, the consumer product catalog (cordless phone, anyone?), an option to order an AT&T Universal Calling Card online, a directory of 800 numbers for businesses, descriptions of AT&T business and international services, and networking solutions. The On the Net page links to interesting AT&T sites online and other telecommuting sites. The second address links to the Bell Laboratories Research Server, which carries papers on electronic privacy and payment, seminar schedules, and an FAQ on the Global MBONE. And, as you move through the pages on the AT&T server, you can almost hear an echo: You will…you will…you will. ✓ **INTER-**

AT&T Home page—from http://www.att.com/

NET…→*www* http://www.att.com/ …→*www* http://www.research. att.com/

MCI Info about MCI telephone and Internet services and an archive of company press releases. The highlight of the site is the MCI lab (a.k.a., glorified press release), which links to infomation about MCI's future plans. ✓ **INTERNET**→*www* http://www.mci. com/

Sprint Home Page Candice Bergen is its spokesperson, AT&T and MCI are its chief competitors, and telecommunications is its business. We're talking about Sprint, of course. Sprint's Website provides an overview of all the services offered. ✓ **INTERNET**→*www* http://www.sprint link.net/

International

ITU WWW Server In Geneva, Switzerland, the International Telecommunications Union coordinates telecommunications networks and services worldwide. Its online Website houses thousands of documents on telecommunications standardization, radio communication, and telecom development. The site also features an extensive collection of links to other telecommunications sites online and information on annual TELECOM conferences. ✓ **INTERNET**→ *www* http://www.itu.ch/

Ministry of Posts and Telecommunications, Japan Reports, news, and press releases about communications services and objectives in Japan, including status reports on Nippon Telegraph and Telephone Corp. ✓ **INTERNET**→*www* http://www.mpt. go.jp/index.html

PTC Web! The Pacific Telecommunications Council organizes conferences and seminars, and publishes magazines and newsletters about telecom topics in the Pacific Rim area. Its Website lists conference schedules and prints publication abstracts. ✓ **INTERNET**→ *www* http://www.ptc.org/

U.K. Telecom FAQ A Website with a collection of questions and answers about the U.K. telecom system, including its telephone service and data line provision services. ✓ **INTERNET**→ *www* http:// www.tecc.co.uk/public/uk-telecom/

Telecommunications Getting Wired

Worldwide Telecommunications Companies

AT&T ✓ INTERNET→www http://www.att.com/

BCTEL ✓ INTERNET→www http://www.bctel.com/

Bell Atlantic ✓ INTERNET→www http://www.bell-atl.com/

Bell Canada ✓ INTERNET→www http://www.bell.ca/

Bellcore ✓ INTERNET→www http://www.bellcore.com/

BellSouth ✓ INTERNET→www http://www.bst.bls.com/

British Telecom ✓ INTERNET→www http://www.bt.net/

CallAmerica ✓ INTERNET→www http://www.callamer.com/callamer.html

Cellular One Mobile Communications ✓ INTERNET→www http://www.elpress.com/cellone/cellone.html

Cook Communications Telephone resellers. ✓ INTERNET→www http://www.elpress.com/cellone/cellone.html

Deutsche Telekom ✓ INTERNET→www http://www.telekom.de

France Telecom Network Services ✓ INTERNET→www http://www.transpac.se/

GTE Laboratories ✓ INTERNET→www http://info.gte.com/

Helsinki Telephone Company ✓ INTERNET→www http://www.hpy.fi

InfoNet ✓ INTERNET→www http://info.gte.com/

KDD ✓ INTERNET→www http://www.kddlabs.co.jp

Korea Telecom ✓ INTERNET→www http://melon.kotel.co.kr/ktrl/koreatelecom.html

LDDS Communications ✓ INTERNET→www http://www.wiltel.com/ldds/ldds.html

McCaw Cellular ✓ INTERNET→www http://www.cellular.com

MCI ✓ INTERNET→www http://www.mci.com/

MFS Datanet ✓ INTERNET→www http://www.mfsdatanet.com/

MinitelWeb: France Telecom Intelmatique ✓ INTERNET→www http://melon.kotel.co.kr/ktrl/koreatelecom.html

NTT (Nippon Telegraph and Telephone Corporation) ✓ INTERNET→www http://www.ntt.jp/

Pacific Bell ✓ INTERNET→www http://www.pacbell.com/

Pacific Telesis ✓ INTERNET→www http://www.pactel.com/

PHP (Lahti Telephone Company) Lahti, Finland ✓ INTERNET→www http://www.php.fi/php/php.html

Post & Telecom Iceland ✓ INTERNET→www http://www.simi.is/pti.html

Singapore Telecom ✓ INTERNET→www http://www.singnet.com.sg/singnet/singtel/singtel.html

Slovenian Telekom ✓ INTERNET→www http://www.abm.si/~dalibor/telekom/telekom.html

Southwestern Bell ✓ INTERNET→www http://www.sbc.com

Sprint ✓ INTERNET→www http://www.sprintlink.net/

Swiss PTT Telecom ✓ INTERNET→www http://www.vptt.ch/

Tampere Telephone Company (Finland) ✓ INTERNET→www http://www.tpo.fi/

Telecom Eireann ✓ INTERNET→www http://www.broadcom.ie/telecom/dupjmc/teprofile.html

Telecom Finland ✓ INTERNET→www http://www.tele.fi/

Teleglobe ✓ INTERNET→www http://www.teleglobe.ca/

Telekom Malaysia ✓ INTERNET→www http://ittm.com.my/telekom/tmsia.html

Telkom (Indonesia) ✓ INTERNET→www http://pusren01.telkom.go.id/

Telstra ✓ INTERNET→www http://www.telstra.com.au/

Turku Telephone Company (Finland) ✓ INTERNET→www http://www.ttl.fi/

US West ✓ INTERNET→www http://usw.interact.net/

WilTel ✓ INTERNET→www http://www.wiltel.com/

Getting Wired **Getting Online**

Getting online

All your friends are online. Your parents refer to you as "my child, the holdout." Even your grandparents ask you when you're going to stop living that crazy mixed-up life and get the Net. But you're confused. You're conflicted. You're cowed by your own ignorance. Take hold of yourself. You don't have to be afraid any longer. Read **alt.internet.access.wanted** to meet others who share your secret shame (how they're posting on newsgroups without Internet access will remain one of the great mysteries of the century). Consult **FreeNets & Community Networks** to learn about organizations that are making the Net a low-cost dream. And then shop for a commercial service, using such resources as **CompuServe's Web Home Page**, **alt.online-service.genie** and **alt.aol-sucks**.

On the Net

Across the board

alt.online-service (ng) Many of the postings in this newsgroup are cross-posted from the other service-specific newsgroups. Postings range from rumors about AOL runaways to debates about the pros and cons of eWorld to advertisements from Internet providers. ✓**USENET**

The road less travelled—downloaded from AOL's Macintosh Graphics Forum

Internet providers

alt.internet.access.wanted (ng) The newsgroup carries a few hundred messages per week from Netters trying to find local Internet access or providers advertising their services. The FAQs describe Internet access options in Australia, the U.K., and New Zealand. ✓**USENET** *FAQ:* ✓**INTERNET**→*www* ftp://rtfm.mit.edu:/pub/usenet/alt.internet.access.wanted/

CRISP Directory A directory of Internet providers along the coasts of the Pacific Ocean—from California, Oregon, Washington, and Hawaii to China, Singapore, and several regions of Australia. Information includes email addresses, BBS numbers, URLs, and links to other Internet provider lists. ✓**INTERNET**→*www* http://sensemedia.com/crisp/crisp

How to Select an Internet Provider A short guide that outlines the issues in choosing an Internet provider. ✓**INTERNET**→*www* http://sensemedia.com/crisp/crisp

Internet Access Providers List A simple list of providers by area code. Email address and a voice number are included with most listings. ✓**INTERNET**→*www* http://www.umd.umich.edu/~clp/i-access.html

Internet Service Providers Catalog A list of Internet providers around the world—country codes are provided. ✓**INTERNET**→*www* http://www.netusa.net/ISP/

The Lips' List of IAP's Internet Access Providers Around the World What if you need Internet access for an upcoming visit to Argentina or Israel? This is an excellent directory to help you find local Internet access providers anywhere on the planet. Start by selecting a region: Africa, Central or South America, Asia, Australia, Central Europe, Eastern Europe, Western Europe, or the Middle East, then pick your country. Several FAQs explain what to do next. ✓**INTERNET**→*www* http://www.best.be/iap.html

Lists of Internet Providers An index to Internet provider lists, occasionally by "region"—from New York City to Delaware Valley to the United Kingdom. ✓**INTERNET**→*www* http://www.tagsys.com/Provider/ListOfLists.html

U.S. Internet Service Providers List An alphabetical list of Inter-

Net Tech 257

Getting Online Getting Wired

net providers. Each listing includes an explanation of the type of access, a description of the fee structure, a voice, fax, and modem number, an email address, and a URL. The document also lists Internet providers by area code. ✓**INTERNET** ...→*www* http://www.primus.net/providers/ ...→*www* ftp://ftp.primus.com/pub/providers/isp-list

FreeNets

alt.online-service.freenet (ng) Is there a FreeNet in Vancouver? How about the U.K.? The newsgroup is primarily used by Netters looking for information about FreeNets in their area although more philosophical discussions about the future of FreeNets have popped up here from time to time. ✓**USENET**

FreeNets & Community Networks Get the scoop on the continuously-evolving world of public access computing by consulting this list of FreeNets in the U.S., Canada, and abroad. ✓**INTERNET**→*www* http://herald.usask.ca/~scottp/free.html

Gateway to FreeNets and Community Networks via the World Wide Web A hypertext list of FreeNets by country as well as links to articles and other online information about FreeNets. ✓**INTERNET**→*www* http://freenet.victoria.bc.ca/freenets.html

International FreeNets Listing A hypertext list of FreeNets organized by country. ✓**INTERNET**→*www* http://www.uwec.edu/info/freenets.html

The NPTN FreeNet List Information about FreeNets in the U.S. and other countries, including FreeNets still being organized.

Listings often include modem numbers, telnet addresses, email addresses, voice numbers, and contact names. The list is also posted weekly to alt.online-service.freenet. ✓**INTERNET**→*www* gopher://nptn.org:70/00nptn/npn.affil-organ.list

America Online

alt.aol-sucks (ng) AOL may be the most successful of the commercial services, but it also breeds the most resentment among the Internet crowd. AOL bashers post hundreds of postings a week to this newsgroup, primarily about AOL censorship, the terms of service, and online costs. The newsgroup also includes its fair share of rumors about viruses that erase hard drives and cyberimpersonators of AOL President Steve Case. ✓**USENET** *FAQ:* ✓**INTERNET**→*www* http://www.en.com/users/tfinley/aol-sux/resources.html

alt.online-service.america-online (ng) Gossip, ask questions, and vent about America Online. ✓**USENET**

America Online The largest of the online services, AOL rose to the top by providing its users with an easy-to-navigate and attractive interface, a hugely successful live chat area, a wide range of offerings, and forums sponsored by big-name media players like *Time* magazine. (All those free AOL disks wrapped up with magazines didn't hurt either.) Over the course of the past year, AOL has given its users more and more access to the Internet (*keyword* internet). AOLers can now send email, read Usenet newsgroups, download from FTP and gopher sites, and navigate the Web with AOL's own custom Web browser. Recently, AOL purchased the WebCrawler

and GNN, an Internet search engine and directory, to expand upon the Internet resources it provides its members. The one criticism consistently levied against AOL is that it censors the comments and activities of its members. For more information, voice call 800-827-6364 or visit the service's Website. ✓**INTERNET**→*www* http://www.blue.aol.com

America Online Sucks Home Pages Feeling a profound dislike for the family filters on AOL's People Connection? Share your rage. Although slightly different, both pages offer lists of reasons to dislike AOL and links to places to vent, including alt.aol-sucks and the email address of AOL Presi-

> "Once upon a time, the Delphic Oracle would answer questions about the fate of men. Now, the alt.online-service.delphi newsgroup answers questions about the current status of Delphi. The more things change, the more they stay the same. Or something like that."

258 Net Tech

Getting Wired Getting Online

dent Steve Case. ✓**INTERNET** ...→ *www* http://www.cloud9.net/~jegelhof/ ...→*www* http://www.iglou.com/members/will.html ...→*www* http://www.en.com/users/tfinley/aol-sux/aol-sux.html

CompuServe

alt.online-service.compuserve (ng) Gossip, ask questions, and vent about CompuServe. ✓**USENET FAQ:** ✓**INTERNET**→*www* ftp://rtfm.mit.edu/pub/usenet-by-hierarchy/alt/online-service/compuserve/

CompuServe's Web Home Page CompuServe's Website is simple and functional. Not only can a Netter subscribe to CompuServe and find a local access number, but the Website is designed both to entertain visitors and to give them a clear idea about what CompuServe has to offer. The main page leads off with a short list of new forums and CompuServe events. A "Hot" section links to hundreds of descriptions of Internet and CompuServe sites. The "Find" area lets visitors search CompuServe for descriptions of relevant forums and services or search the Internet for links to relevant Websites. Like its Website, CompuServe tends to be very service-oriented. The online service has excellent business and periodical databases, travel resources, and an extensive selection of support forums for computer hardware and software. That doesn't mean it's a killjoy. *Sports Illustrated*, *People* magazine, the Human Sexuality Forums, and live chat on the CB Bands are all big draws. In addition, CompuServe offers full Internet access and several forums devoted to Internet topics (*go* internet). For Web access, members may use the CompuServe network with their own browser. If you're looking for information about subscribing to the service but don't have access to the Internet, voice call 800-848-8199. ✓**INTERNET**→*www* http://www.compuserve.com/

Delphi

alt.online-service.delphi (ng) Once upon a time, the Delphic Oracle would answer questions about the fate of men. Now, the alt.online-service.delphi newsgroup answers questions about the current status of Delphi. The more things change, the more they stay the same. Or something like that. ✓**USENET**

Delphi Drop-Outs Club A diatribe against Delphi that links to the Delphi Home Page and the Delphi newsgroup. ✓**INTERNET**→*www* http://edge.edge.net/~rdouglas/delphi_drop-outs.html

Delphi Internet Home Page At one point, Delphi was the only online service to offer full Internet access, and despite the rather slim pleasures of its other services, large numbers of subscribers began to sign up. Once the other services began to offer Internet access, Delphi quickly lost its ace, and it's trying desperately to regain ground. Delphi's new Website is not so much "about" the online service as it is a new version of the service. The home page highlights interesting topics (a blockbuster movie, a popular musician, a sporting event, etc.) and then links to Delphi Web pages about these topics. For information about joining, voice call 800-695-4005. ✓**INTERNET**→*www* http://www.delphi.com/

GEnie

alt.online-service.genie (ng) Gossip, ask questions, and vent

---

CYBERNOTES

"ISDN was supposed to be blindingly fast. Here's the catch: the actual data transfer rates are excruciatingly slow. MacTCP Watcher says there are huge numbers of 'retransmits', and the stats' window on MacPPP shows VERY high numbers of "CRC Errors" and "Framing Errors". Any help would be appreciated!"

"John got caught in the ISDN trap. ISDN will never be 'blindingly FAST' until all the components on the Net are 'blindingly FAST'. The telcos of the world have convinced us that ISDN is the way of the future. It may not be. ISDN at its fastest will be only half as fast as localtalk and localtalk is certainly not 'blindingly fast'. The transmission speed of the Net is a problem. ISDN is only a small part of the answer. So is the speed of Netscape, the speed of the network hardware, the amount of traffic, etc. Is ISDN worth the investment? I am skeptical!:-)"

—from **Apple Internet Providers**

Getting Online Getting Wired

about GEnie. ✓ **USENET**

GEnie Services Home Page
GEnie's new front-end software gives the struggling service a fresh new look, but it's still several steps behind the big three—Prodigy, America Online, and CompuServe—in content, membership, and Internet access. GEnie members have only recently been given access to telnet, FTP, gopher, and Lynx (a text Web browser), and its newsgroup service was still under construction at the time of this writing. Those loyal to the service are usually involved with one of GEnie's more popular RoundTables, such as the mammoth Sci-Fi RoundTables. From the Website, visitors can download the latest version of the GEnie software, read the current issue of GEnie's multimedia magazine *GEnie LiveWire*, or tap into the gopher for information about GEnie's services. For more information about joining, voice call 800-638-9636. ✓ **INTERNET** ...→*www* http://www.genie.com ...→*www* gopher://gopher.genie.com/

Prodigy

alt.online-service.prodigy
(ng) Gossip, ask questions, and vent about Prodigy. ✓ **USENET**

Prodigy's AstraNet Although AstraNet links to information about Prodigy and even features an option to download the latest Windows version of Prodigy software, it is primarily an Internet directory. There are sections of this directory for investors, news buffs, businessmen, Internet novices, and those with other interests such as shopping and entertainment—and the entire Internet community has access. Each listing has a brief description and is linked to the actual site. Prodigy's Website,

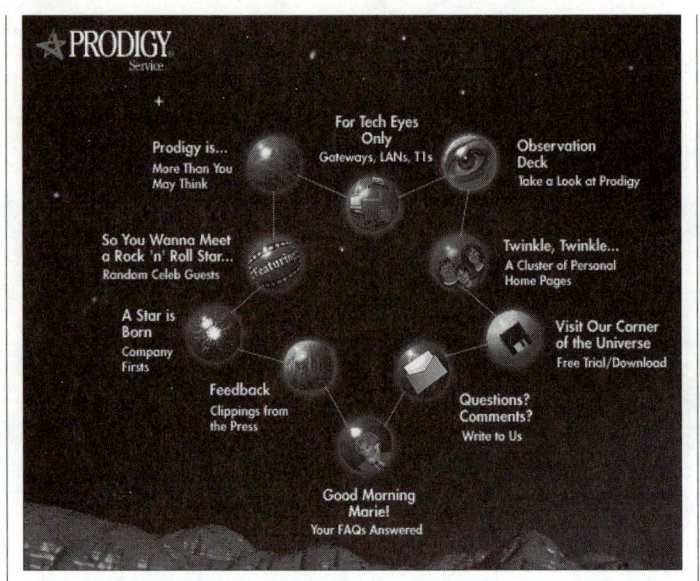

Prodigy on the Web—http://www.prodigy.com/welcome1.htm

like the service itself, emphasizes business and investment. The Prodigy service prides itself on having extensive personal finance services, and has attempted to strengthen its position in the on-line market by developing a chat room area similar to AOL's and by offering its members Usenet and Web access in addition to Internet email. Windows users can download a browser from Prodigy and even design their own Web pages. ✓ **INTERNET**→ *www* http://www.astranet.com/

Other services

alt.online-service.imagination (ng) Gossip, ask questions, and vent about the Imagination Network. ✓ **USENET**

eWorld Web Central A low-key Website with information about the service, back issues of an eWorld newsletter, and job advertisements. Apple's eWorld service itself is anything but low-key. Its urban theme is illustrated with snappy graphics and traffic noises; unfortunately, the honking cars constitute most of the traffic on this service—it's still rather empty here. While the subscribers have yet to come in droves, eWorld has a rich selection of forums and services for Mac users. Eventually, eWorlders will have access to email, Usenet, the Web, and FTP. ✓ **INTERNET**→*www* http://www.eworld.com/

For providers

Apple Internet Providers (ml) Very active list for those providing Internet service on Apple computers. ✓ **INTERNET** →*email* listproc@abs.apple.com ✍ *Type in message body:* subscribe apple-internet-providers <your full name>

Internet Access Provider FAQ How to become an Internet service provider. ✓ **COMPUSERVE**→*go* inetresources→Libraries→*Search by file name:* inaccs.zip ✓ **INTERNET**→ *www* http://amazing.cinenet.net/faq.html

Getting Wired Getting Online

FreeNets

Big Sky Telegraph Sign on as "bbs." ☎→*dial* 406-683-7680 ✓**INTERNET**→*telnet* Bigsky.bigsky.dillon.mt.us

Buffalo FreeNet Sign on as "freeport." ☎→*dial* 716-645-6128 ✓**INTERNET**→*telnet* freenet.buffalo.edu

CapAccess Sign on as "guest" with the password "visitor." ☎→*dial* 202-785-1523 ✓**INTERNET**→*telnet* cap.gwu.edu

Chebucto Community Net Sign on as "guest." ☎→*dial* 902-494-8006 ✓**INTERNET**→*telnet* cfn.cs.dal.ca

CIAO! Sign on as "guest." ☎→*dial* 604-368-5764 ✓**INTERNET**→*telnet* ciao.trail.bc.ca

Cleveland FreeNet Select #2 at first menu. ☎→*dial* 216-368-3888 ✓**INTERNET**→*telnet* freenet-in-a.cwru.edu

Columbia Online Information Network Sign on as "guest." ☎→*dial* 314-884-7000 ✓**INTERNET**→*telnet* bigcat.missouri.edu

Dayton FreeNet Sign on as "visitor." ☎→*dial* 513-229-4373 ✓**INTERNET**→*telnet* 130.108.128.174

Denver FreeNet Sign on as "guest." ☎→*dial* 303-270-4865 ✓**INTERNET**→*telnet* freenet.hsc.colorado.edu

EnviroFreeNet Sign on as "visitor." ✓**INTERNET**→*telnet* envirolink.org

Heartland FreeNet Sign on as "bbguest." ☎→*dial* 309-674-1100 309-438-2300 ✓**INTERNET**→ *telnet* heartland.bradley.edu

Lorain County FreeNet Sign on as "guest." ☎→*dial* 216-366-9721 ✓**INTERNET**→*telnet* freenet.lorain.oberlin.edu

Los Angeles FreeNet Select #2 for visitor. ☎→*dial* 818-776-5000 ✓**INTERNET**→*telnet* lafn.org

MidNet Sign on as "visitor." ✓**INTERNET**→*telnet* dasher.csd.scarolina.edu

National Capital FreeNet Sign on as "guest." ☎→*dial* 613-564-3600 ✓**INTERNET**→*telnet* freenet.carlton.ca

Ocean State FreeNet Sign on as "visitor." ☎→*dial* 401-831-4640 ✓**INTERNET**→*telnet* 192.207.24.10

Ozark Regional Information-al On-Line Network Sign on as "guest." ☎→*dial* 417-869-6100 ✓**INTERNET**→*telnet* ozarks.sgcl.lib.mo.us

Prairienet Sign on as "visitor." ☎→*dial* 217-255-9000 ✓**INTERNET**→*telnet* prairienet.org

Rio Grande FreeNet Sign on as "visitor." ☎→*dial* 915-775-5600

Prairienet—http://www.prairienet.org

✓**INTERNET**→*telnet* rgfn.epcc.edu

Saskatchewan FreeNet Sign on as "guest." ✓**INTERNET**→*telnet* broadway.sfn.saskatoon.sk.ca

SEFLIN FreeNet Sign on as "visitor." ☎→*dial* 305-765-4332 ✓**INTERNET**→*telnet* bcfreenet.seflin.lib.fl.us

SEND-IT Sign on as "bbs" with the password "sendit2me." ✓**INTERNET**→*telnet* sendit.nodak.edu

Tallahassee FreeNet Sign on as "visitor." ☎→*dial* 904-488-5056 ✓**INTERNET**→*telnet* freenet.fsu.edu

Tristate Online Sign on as "visitor." ☎→*dial* 513-579-1990 ✓**INTERNET**→*telnet* tso.uc.edu

Vancouver Regional FreeNet Sign on as "guest." ☎→*dial* 604-257-8778 ✓**INTERNET**→*telnet* freenet.vancouver.ca.ca

Victoria FreeNet Sign on as "guest." ☎→*dial* 604-479-6500 ✓**INTERNET**→*telnet* freenet.victoria.bc.ca

Youngstown FreeNet Sign on as "visitor." ☎→*dial* 216-742-3072 ✓**INTERNET**→*telnet* yfn2.ysu.edu

@ the Café **Getting Wired**

@ the Café

Cyberspace à la carte

You're travelling abroad and miss the Web. You have a date, but you're expecting an important email; perhaps you don't even have a PC. Now, you're in luck! Around the world in large cities and small towns, cybercafes are blooming. What's a cybercafe? In Toronto, it's Eek-a-Geek; where you can have a cappucino, chat with friends, and appreciate art—either hanging on the walls, or in the many galleries of the Web via Netscape. Perhaps you'll IRC with a new acquaintance at Syberia Netc@fe in Reykjavik, Iceland. Visit Eek-a-Geek at 460 Parliament Street, or at http://www.io.org/~eek. Cyberdiners at the cafes include total Netheads who can't pry themselves from their terminals, shy novices still afraid of mouses, the unaware who haven't noticed that PCs have mushroomed in the dining room, and all in between. The atmosphere is generally congenial; no one need feel unwelcome for lack of Net savvy (At worst, you could just have the salad). The cafes tend to be located in or near college campuses, giving them a more spirited atmosphere than you'd expect in a room full of computers. Ask about instruction; either formal or informal classes are held—and it's often appropriate to seek technical support from your waiter.

Cafes serve every level of need, from being your local access provider, supplying a simple email account, browsing that cool website you found in *Net Trek*, or dishing out hazelnut pie. @Cafe in New York's East Village will provide you with great food, while proprietor Glenn helps you design your own Web page. At Cybersmith in Cambridge, MA, you can explore the Web, view that new CD-ROM, or have a Virtual Reality "experience." The Internet Cafe in Seattle has free Internet intro classes on weekends: test out your new skills afterwards. Cyberia, with branches in

Outside the @ Café—East Village, New York City

Getting Wired @ the Café

Greater London and the UK is poised to become the first Internet cafe chain Absolutely no Nestle cocoa is served at Web13 in Edinburgh; find out why at http://www.presence.co.uk/. To find out if there's a cafe in your neck of the woods, http://www.easynet.co.uk/pages/cafe/ccafe.htm lists those which are currently open, or opening soon. Or post a message in alt.cybercafes, which often includes listings of special cyberevents—new cafe openings, video link-ups between them, maybe even the URL (or catch) of the day.

The Zap—Brighton, England

The following is a partial list of cafes. Bon Appetit!

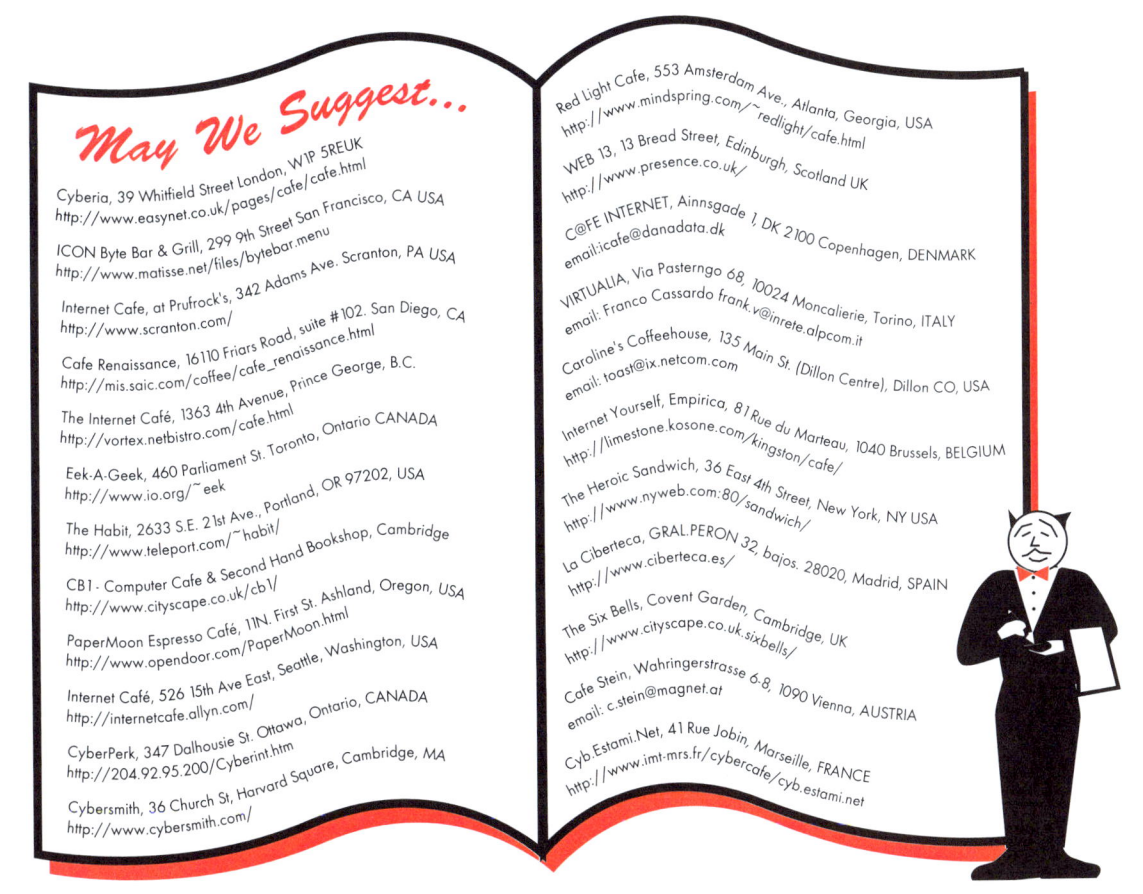

May We Suggest...

Cyberia, 39 Whitfield Street London, W1P 5REUK
http://www.easynet.co.uk/pages/cafe/cafe.html

ICON Byte Bar & Grill, 299 9th Street San Francisco, CA USA
http://www.matisse.net/files/bytebar.menu

Internet Cafe, at Prufrock's, 342 Adams Ave. Scranton, PA USA
http://www.scranton.com/

Cafe Renaissance, 16110 Friars Road, suite #102. San Diego, CA
http://mis.saic.com/coffee/cafe_renaissance.html

The Internet Café, 1363 4th Avenue, Prince George, B.C.
http://vortex.netbistro.com/cafe.html

Eek-A-Geek, 460 Parliament St. Toronto, Ontario CANADA
http://www.io.org/~eek

The Habit, 2633 S.E. 21st Ave., Portland, OR 97202, USA
http://www.teleport.com/~habit/

CB1 - Computer Cafe & Second Hand Bookshop, Cambridge
http://www.cityscape.co.uk/cb1/

PaperMoon Espresso Café, 1IN. First St. Ashland, Oregon, USA
http://www.opendoor.com/PaperMoon.html

Internet Café, 526 15th Ave East, Seattle, Washington, USA
http://internetcafe.allyn.com/

CyberPerk, 347 Dalhousie St. Ottawa, Ontario, CANADA
http://204.92.95.200/Cyberint.htm

Cybersmith, 36 Church St, Harvard Square, Cambridge, MA
http://www.cybersmith.com/

Red Light Cafe, 553 Amsterdam Ave., Atlanta, Georgia, USA
http://www.mindspring.com/~redlight/cafe.html

WEB 13, 13 Bread Street, Edinburgh, Scotland UK
http://www.presence.co.uk/

C@FE INTERNET, Ainnsgade 1, DK 2100 Copenhagen, DENMARK
email: icafe@danadata.dk

VIRTUALIA, Via Pasterngo 68, 10024 Moncalierie, Torino, ITALY
email: Franco Cassardo frank.v@inrete.alpcom.it

Caroline's Coffeehouse, 135 Main St. (Dillon Centre), Dillon CO, USA
email: toast@ix.netcom.com

Internet Yourself, Empirica, 81 Rue du Marteau, 1040 Brussels, BELGIUM
http://limestone.kosone.com/kingston/cafe/

The Heroic Sandwich, 36 East 4th Street, New York, NY USA
http://www.nyweb.com:80/sandwich/

La Ciberteca, GRAL.PERON 32, bajos. 28020, Madrid, SPAIN
http://www.ciberteca.es/

The Six Bells, Covent Garden, Cambridge, UK
http://www.cityscape.co.uk.sixbells/

Cafe Stein, Wahringerstrasse 6-8, 1090 Vienna, AUSTRIA
email: c.stein@magnet.at

Cyb.Estami.Net, 41 Rue Jobin, Marseille, FRANCE
http://www.imt-mrs.fr/cybercafe/cyb.estami.net

Net Tech 263

Speed Surfing **Getting Wired**

Speed surfing

When Keith Richards sang "Connection, connection," he wasn't talking about the Net.

But in today's breakneck online world, you're measured by the speed of your connection. Still on a 9600 bps modem? You'll be mocked as a throwback by fellow members of the Wired Generation. Having trouble with your ISDN? If you can't stand the strong currents, get out of the bitstream. But before you do, spend some time researching point-to-point and single-line protocols (that's PPP and SLIP to those in the know), and learning to configure TCP/IP software for your particular operating system. Start at the **PPP FAQ**, **The Consummate Winsock Apps List**, and **comp.dcom.isdn**. And pay attention. Otherwise, you may be stuck on a slow boat to cyber-enlightenment.

Rushing into the future—from http://www.ee.pdx.edu/~caseyh/horror/pics/

On the Net

Across the board

Charm Net Personal IP Page From the MacTCP FAQ to the Winsock Beginners Guide, from the PPP FAQ to PPP software, the site is a good place to find information and software for cruising the Net with a SLIP or PPP connection, or over a T1. ✓**INTERNET**→*www* http://www.charm.net/ppp.html

comp.protocols.ppp (ng) Golden Richard is "having a weird problem getting PPP going between a Linux box with a direct Internet connection and a 28.8K modem and [his] home machine." Al recommends checking the BPS rate and using the flow-control and asyncmap options. Netters post requests about PPP software, ask for advice configuring their PPP, and troubleshoot conflicts with client software. Oh, and you won't find any FAQs here. Instead, you'll find "Frequently Wanted Information." Those darned PPP people have different terms for everything. ✓**USENET** *FAQ:* ✓**INTERNET** ...→*www* http://www.cis.ohio-state.edu:80/text/faq/usenet/ppp-faq/top.html ...→*www* ftp://rtfm.mit.edu/pub/usenet/comp.protocols.ppp/

comp.protocols.tcp-ip (ng) Warren is a programmer who is "trying to locate some information on developing software to work with Apple's MacTCP driver." Paul is perplexed: "I have a 486-66MHZ dx2 with 8 megabytes of memory. Windows tells me that it doesn't have enough memory to run Winsock. Approximately how much memory does the application Winsock require?" As large numbers of Netters start buying SLIP and PPP connections, they're also becoming intimately acquainted with TCP/IP protocols. And

264 Net Tech

Getting Wired Speed Surfing

this newsgroup has become a resource for those with questions or problems. ✓**USENET**

comp.protocols.tcp-ip.domains (ng) "I need an IP address. How are they obtained?" "Is there a straightforward way to configure a single machine as a Web server for two domains?" Discuss the ins and outs of customizing an Internet address and domain. The newsgroup is particularly useful for companies in the process of setting up a presence on the Internet. ✓**USENET**

Introduction to TCP/IP Beginning with an account of how the U.S. Army developed TCP and IP, the document includes both a history and an explanation of the two protocols. ✓**INTERNET**→*www* http://www.rtd.com/pcnfsfaq/faq.html

The PC-Mac TCP/IP & NFS FAQ List An incredibly comprehensive FAQ covering TCP/IP and related protocols for the two major platforms—Mac and PC. The hypertext document links to information about setting up TCP/IP, defines many of the most common TCP/IP terms, and describes and links to shareware and public-domain versions of email packages, Web browsers, newsreaders, FTP clients, and finger servers. ✓**INTERNET**→*www* http://www.rtd.com/pcnfsfaq/faq.html

PPP FAQ It isn't pretty, but there's a lot of technical information about PPP in this FAQ. The document includes an introduction to PPP, a description of PPP's features, a glossary of terms, configuration questions and answers, as well as Net addresses for PPP. ✓**INTERNET**→ *www* ftp://ftp.merit.edu/internet.tools/ppp/documents/pppfaq-3.9

Amigas

AmiTCP Networking Software This Web page contains a brief explanation of AmiTCP/IP—the first publicly available TCP/IP protocol for the SANA-II interface—and the software itself. ✓**INTERNET**→*www* http://insti.physics.sunysb.edu/AMosaic/about-amitcp.html

AmiTCP/IP FAQ For every Amiga owner who's wanted to break out of his dial-up access to the Net and start SLIPping, this document offers how-to instructions on using TCP/IP on the Amiga. The FAQ is also posted semimonthly to most major Amiga newsgroups. ✓**INTERNET** …→*www* http://insti.physics.sunysb.edu/AMosaic/about-amitcp.html …→*www* http://www.cis.ohio-state.edu:80/text/faq/usenet/amiga/AmiTCP-faq/faq.html

Windows & DOS

alt.winsock A clearinghouse for announcements about new Winsock applications and a place to ask questions about setting up, running, and programming the applications. ✓**USENET** *FAQ:* ✓**INTERNET**→ *www* http://www.well.com/user/nac/alt-winsock-faq.html

bit.listserv.ibmtcp-l (ng/ml) Low-volume discussion of IBM TCP/IP. ✓**USENET** ✓**INTERNET** *email* listserv@pucc.princeton.edu ✍ *Type in message body:* subscribe ibmtcp-l <your full name>

comp.os.ms-windows.networking.tcp-ip (ng) Having problems getting a response from Netscape while in a PPP connection? Maybe it's your Trumpet Winsock software. Or perhaps you're getting your email, but Netscape doesn't work. Have you properly set up the protocol? "Take a look at what protocols you have enabled. You probably want ONLY TCP/IP and not IPX or NETBEUI." Microsoft Windows users pool minds to troubleshoot problematic TCP/IP connections. ✓**USENET**

comp.protocols.tcp-ip.ibmpc (ng) Dave needs to set up Winsock to use from behind a firewall. Chris needs to build a script that updates his home page to say he's online whenever he logs on. Both turn to this newsgroup for suggestions. Discuss protocol problems and issues relating specifically to TCP/IP connections for the IBM PC. Each week a list of new Winsock shareware applications is posted to the newsgroup. ✓**USENET**

The Consummate Winsock Apps List An extensive collection of the most current versions of Winsock applications and utilities, including Web browsers, mail clients, newsreaders, gopher clients, WAIS programs, and FTP clients. Rated descriptions of the applications are linked to shareware or demo versions and, when applicable, company home pages. New additions to the site are posted weekly on many of the TCP/IP newsgroups. ✓**INTERNET**→*www* http://uts.cc.utexas.edu/~neuroses/cwsa.html…→ http://homepage.eznet.net/~rwilloug/stroud/cwsapps.html

The DOS Internet Kit A prepackaged selection of Internet programs for DOS users that's been billed by its author as "a (fairly) painless way to install the basic parts that will permit a PC running Windows to take advantage of some of the new software." Files include Trumpet Winsock, Mosaic for Windows, a telnet and

Speed Surfing Getting Wired

FTP program, an image viewer, and an unzip program. The "kit" includes ample documentation and instructions for installing the software. ✓**INTERNET**→*www* http://tbone.biol.scarolina.edu/~dean/kit/kit.html

E-Znet's Winsock Archive An archive of Winsock applications, including gopher, finger, FTP, email, IRC, telnet, Web browser, Archie, and newsreader programs. ✓**INTERNET**→*www* ftp://ftp.eznet.net/pub/win/winsock/

EtherPPP Software that emulates an Ethernet-class packet driver and allows PCs running DOS systems to serve as a host on the Internet, thus enabling the use of graphical Internet clients. ✓**INTERNET**→*www* ftp://ftp.merit.edu/internet.tools/ppp/dos/

Keith's Best Of List of Winsock Apps You can't download applications from the site (in fact, the list doesn't even give full Net addresses), but it's a good—albeit highly subjective—overview of Internet Winsock applications. "News Express is the only Newsreader I've been willing to use from Windows. Some people like WinVN or TrumpetNews, but I don't. In particular, neither of these handle threading well, or at all." ✓**INTERNET**→*www* http://www.nmt.edu/~kmellis/netapps.html

The Official Windows Sockets Web Page Hypertext overview of Windows Sockets (Winsock) and the program specifications, as well as an archive with several versions of Winsock and dozens of Internet applications. ✓**INTERNET**→*www* http://sunsite.unc.edu/pub/micro/pcstuff/ms-windows/winsock/

Trumpet Winsock for Windows If you're running a graphical Web browser on a Windows machine, odds are very high that you're using Winsock, a popular TCP/IP stack grouped together with a WINSOCK.DLL file that allows Microsoft Windows users to run many Internet applications. ✓**INTERNET** …→*www* ftp://garfield.scbe.edu.on.ca/library/INTERNET/TWSK20B.ZIP …→*www* ftp://oak.oakland.edu/SimTel/win3/winsock/twsk20b.zip

Ultimate Collection of Winsock Software A very large collection of Winsock software that includes Archie clients, drivers, HTML editors, Web browsers, finger programs, TCP/IP stacks, IRC programs, gopher clients, movie viewers, sound players, email programs, and more. ✓**INTERNET**→*www* http://gfecnet.gmi.edu/Software/index.html

The Windows 95 TCP/IP Set-up HOW-TO/FAQ A hypertext document that explains how to install and set up TCP/IP stacks in Windows 95. ✓**INTERNET**→*www* http://www.aa.net/~pcd/slp95faq.html

Windows and TCP/IP for Internet Access Clear and detailed descriptions of several Windows Internet applications, including Trumpet Winsock, WSGopher, Eudora, WS_FTP, Cello, Mosaic, Netscape, WinWeb, and several telnet clients. Descriptions include contact information, links to the software, and installation instructions. ✓**INTERNET**→*www* http://www.nmt.edu/~kmellis/netapps.html

Windows Internet SLIP Software Peter Faris maintains a collection of Windows software for Internet surfing—e.g., Netscape, Cello, CU-SeeMe, etc. Each program that is listed links to a short description and several sites from which the program may be downloaded. ✓**INTERNET**→*www* http://tbone.biol.scarolina.edu/~dean/kit/kit.html

#Winsock Web browser not working? Mail reader acting buggy? Can't set up your IRC client? The channel is for live discussions about Winsock and related Internet applications. ✓**INTERNET**→*irc* #Winsock *FAQ:* ✓**INTERNET**→*www* http://mars.superlink.net/user/mook/winfaq.html

Winsock-L (ml) Questions about Winsock under Windows 95, messages describing problems running Chameleon with internal SLIP, and posts about trouble with Trumpet allocating network buffers are typical fare on this active mailing list dedicated to Winsock and related applications. ✓**INTERNET**→*email* listadmin@papa.indstate.edu ✉ *Type in message body:* subscribe winsock-l <your full name> *Archives:* ✓**INTERNET**→*www* http://papa.indstate.edu:8888/mailindex.html

> "In comp.dcom.isdn, you'll find cost breakdowns, comments on the PPP/SLIP vs. ISDN debate, and even some vituperative Baby Bell bashing ('Nynex Sucks!')."

Getting Wired Speed Surfing

OS/2

comp.os.os2.networking.tcp-ip (ng) A high-volume newsgroup for asking questions about TCP/IP, locating programs on the Net, and keeping up to date on TCP/IP issues for OS/2 systems. ✓**USENET**

Macintosh

Info-Mac Communications Software A repository for practically every Mac shareware program that uses a TCP/IP or SLIP connection (Web browsers to newsreaders). The files required to set up a SLIP or PPP connecting on a Mac are also archived here. ✓**INTERNET** ...→*www* ftp://mirror.apple.com/mirrors/Info-Mac.Archive/_Communication/ ...→*www* ftp://ftp.tidbits.com/pub/tidbits/tisk/ ...→*www* ftp://wuarchive.wustl.edu/systems/mac/info-mac/_Communication/ ...→*www* http://hyperarchive.lcs.mit.edu/HyperArchive/Abstracts/comm/HyperArchive.html

InterNet Directory An archive of Internet programs that run on Macs with SLIP or PPP connections. Download Homer for chatting on IRC, CU-SeeMe for live video conferencing, Newswatcher for reading Usenet newsgroups, TurboGopher for navigating gophers, Eudora for monitoring mail, Anarchie for retrieving files, NCSA Telnet for logging on to other computers, and Netscape, Mosaic, or MacWeb for Web surfing. The archive has many programs, but they're not always the most current versions. ✓**INTERNET**→*www* ftp://mirror.apple.com/mirrors/Info-Mac.Archive/_Communication/

Internet Tools and the Mac You've just configured a SLIP or PPP account and you want to surf the Net with software that works via point-and-click commands, not Unix. Start your "shopping" in this collection of Macintosh Internet applications that includes Eudora, Fetch, TurboGopher, MacWAIS, NCSA Telnet, Anarchie, PPP, MacTCP Watcher, and other programs. ✓**INTERNET**→*www* http://gfecnet.gmi.edu/Software/index.html

Macintosh Internet Software Both AOL and CompuServe have large libraries of Internet software, FAQs, and other information for Macintosh users with a SLIP or PPP connection. The standard programs such as MacWeb, TurboGopher, and CU-SeeMe are available. ✓**AMERICA ONLINE**→*keyword* mcm→Software Libraries→Internet Cafe ✓**COMPUSERVE**→*go* inetresource→Libraries→*Search by file name:* Mac Internet S/W

MacPPP MacPPP is software that allows a Macintosh to act as an Internet host, thereby allowing end users to operate graphical Internet clients such as the popular Web browser Netscape or the mail program Eudora. MacPPP may be downloaded from these sites. ✓**INTERNET** ...→*www* ftp://ftp.merit.edu/internet.tools/ppp/mac/ ...→*www* http://www.sys.uea.ac.uk/macsupporters/RemoteAccess.html ...→*www* ftp://ftp.mxm.com/Pub/Macintosh/InterNet/MacPPP/ ✓**COMPUSERVE**→*go* inetresource Libraries→Libraries→*Search by file name:* macppp2.hqx

ISDN

comp.dcom.isdn (ng) Now that an ISDN hook-up has become an affordable option in most places, many people are reevaluating their PPP/SLIP accounts. Silent and slick, ISDN provides a fast connection to the Net. Depending on your usage levels, ISDN may well be cheaper than using a phone line. Here you'll find cost breakdowns, comments on the PPP/SLIP vs. ISDN debate, and even some vituperative Baby Bell bashing ("Nynex Sucks!"). ✓**USENET**

How to Upgrade to ISDN A brief overview of ISDN costs and installation issues. ✓**INTERNET**→*www* http://pclt.cis.yale.edu/pclt/comisdn/isdn.htm

ISDN FAQ What is ISDN and should you get it? How much does it cost? The multi-part FAQ offers detailed answers to the most basic ISDN questions, complete with ASCII diagrams. And if all these acronyms are confusing, check out the section titled "What do all these acronyms mean?" ✓**INTERNET** ...→*www* http://alumni.caltech.edu/~dank/isdn/ ...→*www* http://www.cis.ohio-state.edu:80/text/faq/usenet/isdn-faq/top.html ✓**COMPUSERVE**→*go* inetresources→Libraries→*Search by file name:* isdn.faq

ISDN-High Speed On-ramp to the Digital Highway Although the site serves as an advertisement for Pacific Bell's ISDN services, it also offers ISDN info, including a User's Guide. ✓**INTERNET**→*www* http://alumni.caltech.edu/~dank/isdn/

ISDN Informationbase A mix of ISDN information and resources that include descriptions of ISDN telephones, fax machines, and modems, downloadable Linux device drivers, links to ISDN vendors and suppliers, information about three major ISDN Internet providers, an ISDN glossary, and an ISDN reading list. ✓**INTERNET**→*www* http://igwe.vub.ac.be/~svendk/

The BBS World Getting Wired

The BBS world

Long before the rise of the World Wide Web, before the information superhighway was a catchphrase, the on-line world was ruled by bulletin board systems (BBSs), computers configured to accept incoming calls from other computers and transmit information over phone lines. There are thousands of BBSs devoted to hundreds of specific topics, from pornographic photos to party politics, sports to sci fi. Visit **alt.bbs** to learn about software and new boards; drop by the **Bulletin Board Systems Corner** to talk to other sysops and subscribers; and then go to the **Computer Shopper BBS and User Groups** list to find the numbers in your area.

Boardwatch Magazine Cover—from AOL's BBS Corner

On the Net

Across the board

alt.bbs (ng) Both the most popular and the most generic of the BBS newsgroups. Despite the fact that there is a separate newsgroup for BBS ads, many of the posts here are advertisements: "If you are looking for a BBS in Germany, check out the National Data Service—06783-1785"; or "Call (914) 477-0264 for the newest and nudest celebs available!" BBS users also compare long-distance plans, sysops compare BBS software, and everyone discusses the legal issues in the BBS world. ✓ **USENET**

alt.bbs.internet (ng) Sysops discuss Internet software and issues of becoming an Internet provider. BBS users can also scan the group for announcements about BBSs with Internet access. ✓ **USENET FAQ:** ✓ **INTERNET**→*www* ftp://rtfm.mit.edu/pub/usenet-by-hierarchy/alt/bbs/internet/

The BBS Page A brief introduction to BBSs that links to a list of BBSs in the 206 area code, several big BBSs which have telnet addresses, and other resources about the BBS world. ✓ **INTERNET**→*www* http://www.eskimo.com:80/~future/bbs.htm

Bulletin Board Systems Corner In a little electronic corner on AOL, sysops and BBS callers have assembled a wide range of information about the BBS world. The small forum has a folder of FAQs that answer questions such as "What is a BBS?" and "How do I connect to a BBS?" To provide sysops with support, several BBS software and hardware vendors have set up areas on the message boards and in the libraries. In addition, the libraries carry hundreds of BBS lists and advertisements, BBS software (so you can start your own BBS), extensions and externals for jazzing up a BBS with sound or games, and the large BBS Database, which is the reason most visitors drop by the forum: you can search for a BBS by area code, location, or interest. Looking for BBSs in the 212 area code? BBSs that run games? BBSs with a religious theme? Just search the database. Besides vendor support, the message boards have sections covering *Boardwatch* Magazine, sysop concerns, and general topics ranging from "sysops under 20" to "starting a BBS." The Sysop message folder is broken down by BBS software—Major BBS, TBBS, NovaLink, etc. ✓ **AMERICA ONLINE**→*keyword* bbs corner

comp.bbs.misc (ng) BBS callers use the newsgroup to get recommendations for QWK readers, to find BBSs running good Tradewars games, and to collect advice to help them navigate the BBS world. Sysops, who are responsible for the majority of posts, use the newgroup to troubleshoot BBS programs, get advice on how to improve their services, and, of course, advertise. ✓ **USENET**

Mac BBS Systems Which Mac boards are carrying scores for soccer matches? Anyone know the BBS number for the Tulsa MUG? And why won't Bob's PowerBook modem connect to a First Class BBS? The message board gets a

Getting Wired The BBS World

random mix of BBS questions from both sysops and users and the library is a mix of BBS programs, utilities, BBS guides, and hundreds of BBS lists. ✓**COMPUSERVE**→*go* maccomm→Libraries *and* Messages→BBS Systems*Mac BBS Systems*

PC Bulletin Board Forum Allen is desperate. He wants to download files from local BBSs, but keeps winding up in the same loops without getting the files he's after: "The software isn't the problem, it's me. I'm not experienced with downloading files from BBSs." Christopher writes back with a detailed explanation of downloading. Another caller is compiling a list of Christian BBSs and is looking for leads. And still another is looking for the best program to set up a BBS on the Web. She's in luck. Many companies have representatives that monitor this forum and they can feed her all the info she's looking for. And while the message boards are great information resources, the libraries are packed with BBS programs, lists and lists of BBS numbers, doors and utilities to enhance a BBS (with clocks, quotes, games, news, etc.), programs for BBS users to read QWK messages, and information about topical BBS networks—from UFO BBS networks to adult networks. ✓**COMPUSERVE**→*go* pcbbs

News

Boardwatch Magazine The print magazine that began as a list of BBS numbers has expanded its coverage to include Internet and the commercial services. The monthly has columns on legal issues in Cyberspace, reviews of communications hardware and software, spotlights on BBSs and Websites, features on Cyberspace trends, and profiles of the personalities behind the Net. This isn't *Wired* magazine or a 'zine with slick virtual reality hype, it's a nuts-and-bolts guide to the online world aimed at users and sysops. The full text of every issue is available at these sites. In addition, the Website has a search engine that traces articles back through the October 1994 issue. In addition, the magazine continues to maintain BBS lists that you can access from these sites. ☎→*dial* 303-973-4222 ✓**INTERNET** …→*www* http://www.boardwatch.com …→*www* ftp://boardwatch.com/bbs/tips/files/ …→*telnet* telnet://boardwatch.com

BBS lists

alt.bbs.ads (ng) Post after post of BBS advertisements. If it's porn you're after, there's no shortage of BBSs advertising their erotic wares. Music and movie BBSs and systems with Internet access are also big draws. ✓**USENET**

alt.bbs.lists (ng) BBS culture has thrived on the lists that BBS callers pass around—lists of favorite boards, boards by area codes, boards by topic, porn boards, etc. In the spirit of that culture, this newsgroup was created for BBS users and sysops to post lists. ✓**USENET** *FAQ:* ✓**INTERNET**→*www* ftp://rtfm.mit.edu/pub/usenet-by-hierarchy/alt/bbs/lists/

The BBS Listing Home Page Updated often, this is an extensive list of BBSs that offer telnet access. Each BBS is briefly described, and subscription information is included if it is known. ✓**INTERNET**→*www* http://kbt.com/bbs/bbslist.html

BBS Numbers A topic filled with advertisements for all varieties of BBS, primarily organized by area code. ✓**PRODIGY** →*jump* computer bb→Choose a Topic→BBS Numbers

Computer Shopper BBS and User Groups *Computer Shopper* has one of the largest BBS lists available. Besides names and data numbers, the BBS listings include very brief descriptions. Organized by state, area code, and then alphabetical order, the list is so large that the print version of *Computer Shopper* features one half of the list one month and the other half the next. Online BBS callers may access the entire BBS list at the Cyber-locations posted here. The Website is updated most frequently. *Computer Shopper* also lists the data numbers of user groups. There's one other difference between the two sites: On the Website, these listings are integrated with the BBS listings, while on CompuServe, BBS callers must download a separate file. ✓**INTERNET**→ *www* http://www.ziff.com:8009/~cshopper/bbs/ ✓**COMPUSERVE**→*go* compshopper→Libraries→Connections:Online

Guide to Select BBSs on the Internet A guide to more than 250 BBSs that provide Internet access. Several versions of the guide are available, including a "quick guide" with names and addresses only, a full-text guide with address and subscription information, and a hypertext version of the guide called the "Guided Tour." ✓**INTERNET**→*www* http://dkeep.com/sbi.htm

The Vicious Book of BBS's A long list of BBSs and Free-Nets with Internet gateways. Not only does the document list names and telnet addresses, it describes and reviews many of the BBSs. Unfortunately, the book, while vicious, isn't very current, and listings

Net Tech 269

The BBS World Getting Wired

aren't updated as often as most BBSs aficionados would like. ✓ **INTERNET**→*www* http://www.dsv.su.se/~mats-bjo/bbslist.html

Sysop info

alt.bbs.allsysop (ng) Dedicated to that class of devoted electronic citizens known as sysops (BBS system operators), this newsgroup covers a broad range of topics, from technical discussions about software and doors to announcements about new BBS networks. ✓ **USENET**

alt.bbs.first-class (ng) Support and discussion for sysops running first-class BBSs. ✓ **USENET**

alt.bbs.gigo-gateway (ng) Support and discussion for sysops running Gigo BBSs. ✓ **USENET**

alt.bbs.pcboard (ng) Support and discussion for sysops running PCBoard BBSs. ✓ **USENET**

alt.bbs.renegade (ng) Support and discussion for sysops running Renegade BBSs. ✓ **USENET**

alt.bbs.tribbs (ng) Support and discussion for sysops running TriBBSs. ✓ **USENET**

alt.bbs.unixbbs (ng) Support for sysops running Unix BBS programs. ✓ **USENET** *FAQ:* ✓ **INTERNET**→*www* ftp://rtfm.mit.edu/pub/usenet-by-hierarchy/alt/bbs/unixbbs/

alt.bbs.watergate (ng) Support and discussion for sysops running Watergate BBSs. ✓ **USENET**

alt.bbs.wildcat (ng) Support and discussion for sysops running Wildcat BBSs. ✓ **USENET**

comp.bbs.majorbbs *and* **alt.bbs.majorbbs** (ng) Very active support and discussion groups for sysops running Major BBSs, a BBS software package which is so popular that it cannot be contained by a single newsgroup. ✓ **USENET**

comp.bbs.tbbs (ng) Support and discussion for sysops running TBBS BBSs. ✓ **USENET**

comp.bbs.waffle *and* **alt.bbs.waffle** (ng) Break out the syrup. These newsgroups offer support and discussion for sysops running Waffle BBSs. ✓ **USENET** *FAQ:* ✓ **INTERNET**→*www* ftp://rtfm.mit.edu/pub/usenet-by-hierarchy/comp/bbs/waffle/

FidoNet Archive FidoNet documentation and software for Macintosh, DOS, and Unix systems. The software is designed for BBS owners and operators, not BBS callers. A current copy of the nodelist (a complete list of all FidoNet BBSs) is also archived at this FTP archive, and it is updated regularly. *Archives:* ✓ **INTERNET**→*www* ftp://ftp.psg.com/pub/fidonet/

Opus Technical information, a product history, and contacts for the Opus-CBCS BBS software, which runs on a PC. The site also links to a FidoNet nodelist and various Opus utilities. Need a QWK mail door? Say no more. ✓ **INTERNET**→*www* http://www.global.org/opus/

RBBS-PC A freely distributed bulletin board service for IBM PCs and compatible computers. The Website describes the software and links to RBBS files, including the source code for the program. ✓ **INTERNET**→*www* http://www.infinet.com/~chip/rbbs/

BBS Home Pages

Almac BBS ✓ **INTERNET**→*www* http://www.channel1.com/

The Annex On-Line ✓ **INTERNET**→*www* http://204.74.67.50/top.htm

Atlanta Windows BBS ✓ **INTERNET**→*www* http://www.atlwin.com/atl/atl.htm

Back Alley BBS ✓ **INTERNET**→*www* http://athenet.net/~gutt/index.html

Black Gold BBS ✓ **INTERNET**→*www* http://www.tulsa.com/bgbbs.htm

Burn This Flag BBS ✓ **INTERNET**→*www* http://www.btf.com/

Channel 1 ✓ **INTERNET**→*www* http://www.channel1.com/

The Dragon's Lair BBS ✓ **INTERNET**→*www* http://www.hacks.arizona.edu/hacks/bbs.html

Event Horizons BBS ✓ **INTERNET**→*www* http://www.ingress.com/ims/eh.html

Exec-PC ✓ **INTERNET**→*www* http://www.execpc.com/

Eye Contact ✓ **INTERNET**→*www* http://www.eyecon.com/

The Male Box BBS ✓ **INTERNET**→*www* http://166.93.11.77/

SonicNet ✓ **INTERNET**→*www* http://www.sonicnet.com/

Trilogy Online Service ✓ **INTERNET**→*www* http://www.trilogy.net/

Getting Wired Real-Time Chat

Real-time chat

Want to make new friends on the Internet? Looking for love in all the wired places? Join the online chat revolution. Newsgroups and message boards are fine, but they can't compare to the thrill of real two-way communication. Most of the real-time chat on the Internet occurs on IRC channels; visit **They May Be Beautiful or Ugly—They Are On IRC** to see who's on the other end of the line. Then confabulate to your heart's content on CompuServe's **CB Bands** or America Online's **People Connection**.

On the Net

IRC

alt.irc* (ng) College students flood the hundreds of IRC channels for live talk about politics, sports, computers, culture, and sex, sex, sex—along with a small minority of those without college affiliation. The IRC newsgroups are used by Netters to figure out how to IRC, where to get client software to make IRCing easier, and, for the more advanced IRCers, how to set up their own IRC server. Alt.irc and alt.irc.questions get the most traffic, while the newsgroups for specific channels such as alt.irc.42, alt.irc.hottub, and alt.irc.jeopardy are much quieter. IRC operators (those who run the servers) use the alt.irc.opers newsgroup. There are two main FAQs about IRC: the Un-

Øystein Homelien—http://www.powertech.no/IRCGallery/Norway/edison/

dernet FAQ and the regular IRC Frequently Asked Questions. Both list popular IRC servers (sites carrying IRC channels) and FTP sites archiving client software, give overviews of IRC, compare IRC clients, and outline basic commands, but the two-part Undernet FAQ is far more comprehensive. It covers both the standard IRC network and a second network of channels—Undernet. ✓**USENET FAQ:** ✓**INTERNET** ...→*anon-ftp* ftp://rtfm.mit.edu/pub/usenet-by-hierarchy/alt/irc/...→*www* http://www.cis.ohio-state.edu/hypertext/faq/usenet/irc/

IRC and Undernet Channels A collection of links to home pages for many IRC and Undernet channels. Most include channel descriptions, links to personal home pages of some of the regular channel visitors, schedules of upcoming events, and logs of IRC sessions. ✓**INTERNET**→*www* http://www2.undernet.org:8080/~cs93jtl/IRCChan.html

IRC Connections It should be a last resort—telnetting for IRC access. But if you can't run client software and your Internet provider does not offer IRC access (did you try typing "irc" at the prompt?), then you can telnet to one of the sites on this list. ✓**INTERNET**→*www* http://alpha.acast.nova.edu/irc/connect.html

IRC—Internet Relay Chat Another good resource for IRC users, this Finnish Website links to FTP sites with client and server software, manuals and protocol explanations, pictures of European IRCers, and home pages for some IRC channels. ✓**INTERNET**→*www* http://www.funet.fi/~irc/

The IRC Library Sometimes IRC users enjoy the anonymity; other times they want to see their IRC friends, enemies, and love interests. The Gallery has become a popular IRC photo album. IRCers can submit a .GIF or snail mail a picture, and the site owners will scan the picture and add it to the gallery. ✓**INTERNET**→*www* http://www.powertech.no/IRCGallery/

IRC-Related Resources on the Internet Though it doesn't have the most thrilling name imaginable, this Website may feature the

Gurmundur Fertram Sigurjónsson —http://www.powertech.no/IRCGallery/

Real-Time Chat Getting Wired

"Playmate" (IRC handle)—http://www.powertech.no/IRCGallery/

most comprehensive listing of IRC resources online. All the basics are here (FAQs, manuals, primers, history, etc.), and that's just the beginning. Essays on IRC sociology, articles on IRC events, links to home pages of many IRC channels, links to telnet IRC clients, logs of big IRC events (the 1992 Russian revolution, the 1994 California earthquake, various online weddings, etc.), and links to other IRC Web pages and FTP sites are just some of the resources at this site. ✓**INTERNET**→*www* http://urth. acsu.buffalo.edu/irc/WWW/ircdocs.html

They May Be Beautiful or Ugly—They Are on IRC Perhaps the largest collection of IRC user images. IRC nicknames appear next to each image. ✓**INTERNET**→*www* http://www-stud.enst.fr/~tardieu/irc/

The Undernet Directory IRC is known to be addictive, but if you're willing to risk being drawn into a world of chat channels that run 24 hours a day, then you need to get equipped. After you've secured an Internet connection that gives you IRC access, take a trip to this directory. Beginners can pick up the well-regarded IRC primer, an IRC history, and the IRC and Undernet FAQs. Netters with an Internet connection that lets them run client software (SLIP, PPP, ISDN, etc.) should download clients and manuals. Client programs (e.g., mIRC for Windows and Homer for the Mac) are available for several operating systems, including the Amiga, Mac, Windows, OS/2, and DOS. Running a client makes following and participating in IRC discussions much easier and usually more fun. This directory also stores images of IRC chatters, code for IRC servers, documents on IRC netiquette, and more. ✓**INTERNET** ...→*anon-ftp* ftp://ftp.undernet.org/irc/ ...→*www* http://www2.undernet.org:8080/~cs93jtl/Undernet.html

Videoconferencing

comp.dcom.videoconf (ng) What's the best videoconferencing technology for a PC? How come CU-SeeMe doesn't work? A low-volume newsgroup covering videoconferencing technology. ✓**USENET**

CU-SeeMe A small Website for CU-SeeMe novices that links to a very brief tutorial, an FAQ, a list of reflectors, and archives with versions of CU-SeeMe for both the PC and the Mac. ✓**INTERNET**→*www* http://magneto.csc.ncsu.edu/Multimedia/Classes/Spring94/projects/proj6/cu-seeme.html

CU-SeeMe FAQ "What is CU-SeeMe?" "What do I need to receive video?" "What is a reflector?" From CU-SeeMe etiquette to a list of CU-SeeMe reflector sites, the FAQ gives a brief, how-to overview of the popular form of videoconferencing. ✓**INTERNET**→*www* http://www.wpine.com/cuseeme.html

CU-SeeMe & White Pine Software While Cornell University originally developed CU-SeeMe and will continue to distribute a free version, White Pine Software company is developing an enhanced commercial version. White Pine's Website offers product information and links to other CU-SeeMe sites and resources. ✓**INTERNET**→*www* http://www.wpine.com/cuseeme.html

I-TV List (ml) Discuss two-way videoconferencing and its uses in educational and community development. ✓**INTERNET**→*email* majordomo@zilker.net ✍ *Type in message body:* subscribe i-tv <your email address>

MUDs

Doran's Mudlist Although Cardiff's MUD Page offers links to some of the other major MUD Web pages, its raison d'être is to provide a searchable interface to Doran's Mudlist, the most comprehensive list of MUDs, MOOs, and MUSHes in Cyberspace. Search the list by the type of MUD server or its name, or by theme. The second and third sites

ALT.IRC.*

alt.irc (ng)	✓USENET
alt.irc.announce (ng)	✓USENET
alt.irc.42 (ng)	✓USENET
alt.irc.hottub (ng)	✓USENET
alt.irc.jeopardy (ng)	✓USENET
alt.irc.opers (ng)	✓USENET
alt.irc.questions (ng)	✓USENET
alt.irc.recovery (ng)	✓USENET

Getting Wired Real-Time Chat

are hypertext versions of Doran's list. ✓**INTERNET** …→*www* http://www.cm.cf.ac.uk/User/Andrew.Wilson/MUDlist/ …→*www* http://www.eskimo.com/~tarp3/muds.html …→*www* http://shsibm.shh.fi/mud/Mudlist.html

The MUD Archive Lauren Burka's archive traces the history of MUDs from Richard Bartle's first MUD to the present incarnations. The site carries a timeline, an FAQ, MUD gossip and legends, and essays and articles on MUDs. ✓**INTERNET**→*www* http://www.ccs.neu.edu/home/lpb/muddex.html

MUD FTP Site An archive with servers, clients, and numerous MUD-related documents. Includes manuals for playing on Pern MUSH and TinyTim, a general guide to MUSHes, client software for MUDding, code for creating your own MUD, lists of MUDs, the three-part FAQ, and much more. ✓**INTERNET**→*www* ftp://caisr2.caisr.cwru.edu/pub/

The MUD Resource Collection Lydia Leong (known in the MUSH world as Amberyl) is one of the most prominent personalities in the MUSH online culture. Not only has she helped to run several MUSHes, she is also one of the major developers of the MUSH code. This Website is an extensive collection of MUD resources that include the three-part rec.games.mud* FAQ, a user's manual to MUSHing, links to Web pages about specific types of MUDs, links to FTP sites carrying code and clients, and links to Usenet newsgroups dedicated to MUDding. Leong also maintains "Amberyl's Almost-Complete List of MUSHes," a fabulous and frequently updated list of MUSHes with descriptions and addresses.

Have you visited Camelot or Pern today? ✓**INTERNET**→*www* http://www.cis.upenn.edu/~lwl/mudinfo.html

Welcome to MUDdom… The site pieces together a history of MUDdom, offers a how-to explanation of MUDding, explains the different types of MUDs (do you know your DikuMUDs from your TinyMucks?), describes the role of characters in and the social aspects of MUDding, and looks ahead to the future of MUDdom. ✓**INTERNET**→*www* ftp://caisr2.caisr.cwru.edu/pub/ftp/caisr2.caisr.cwru.edu/pub/

On the Web

Cybersight: Real-Time Conversations "Joubert, I need a boyfriend. How old are you and where are you netting from?" Live on the Web, this is a simple chatting site for those with a Web browser that supports forms. Just type your message and press the submit button. To follow the conversation, press the "reloading" button. Listen: someone's telling an urban legend. ✓**INTERNET**→*www* http://cybersight.com/cgi-bin/cs/ch/chat

Talker Hey, is that a monkey and

Eric G. V. Fookes—http://www.powertech.no/IRCGallery/Switzerland/

a rubber ducky talking to each other? Pick an animal, a cartoon character, or a texture pattern. Then click the "Let me talk" button. Choose one of the public rooms listed or create a private room to go to with a special someone. When you "speak" (type in the text box and click the talk button), your comments appear next to the image you have chosen. ✓**INTERNET**→ *www* http://www2.infi.net/talker/

WebChat A real-time chatting environment on the Web that allows users to include .GIFs of themselves in their messages, provided that they have a Web browser that supports forms. Everyone in the Main Hallway chooses a room (e.g., the watercooler, the twilight zone, tech talk) and joins in the discussions. There's an option to see who's here, a picture and icon library to illustrate messages, and even mailing lists to keep up to date on the site's development. ✓**INTERNET**→ *www* http://www.irsociety.com/webchat/webchat.html

Commercial services

CB Bands While most of CompuServe is rigidly broken down into forums and services on specific topics, the CB channels, especially those in the General Band, are anything but focused, and members like them that way. People hop from channel to channel with handles like City Slicker, Fire Bear, Ridicula, and Princess Lily, enjoying the company of CB friends who mix a little bit of serious chat with a whole lot of silliness—laughing, exchanging hugs and kisses, and bopping each other over the head. The CB area is divided in three separate bands with 36 channels in each: the General Band, Adult Band I, and Adult

Real-Time Chat Getting Wired

Bjarke Dahl Ebert—http://www.powertech.no/IRCGallery/

Band II. None of these channels permit obscene or sexually explicit language; monitors lurking in the background will escort offenders and bashers off channels, but these monitors don't seem very obtrusive. Part of the fun is in joining or forming private group discussions. You may even find yourself involved in multiple private discussions at once! The "Welcome Newcomers" (channel 2) in the General Band offers assistance to CB newbies. On CompuServe, the CB bands are by no means the only live chat areas. Each forum also has its own topic-related real-time conference areas, and members in the same forum may page each other at any time. ✓**COMPUSERVE**→*go* cb

People Connection Several thousand people pass through the chat rooms each night in AOL's version of a Cyberspace hotel. After entering through a lobby, AOLers choose from among assorted conference rooms. People Connection's chat sites come in three varieties: Public Rooms, which range from broad mixers (The Flirts Nook, The Meeting Place) to directed discussions (Thirtysomethings, Over Forty, Trekkies); Member Rooms, which cater to narrower tastes (Gay in Texas, F Seeking F Mistress, Tennessee Studs, Female Amputee); and finally Private Rooms, created by users for on-site, impromptu use. Each room holds up to 23 people, and users may send private messages to any other chat-zone participant at any time. Live chat is a strange experience, certainly, full of strategies and aliases and disheartening stabs at seduction ("hey, baby, want to butter my cyber-roll?"). But the mix of alienation and intimacy is both thrilling and chilling, and users looking for like-minded chat pals—or even a one-net stand—shouldn't hesitate to set up at People Connection and let their fingers do the talking. ✓**AMERICA ONLINE**→*keyword* people

Prodigy Chat Modeled after the very successful AOL chat system, the Prodigy chat area has rooms in areas like Astrology/New Age, Business/Finance, Medical Support, Sports-ESPNET, PSEUDO (think sex), and Women Online. Enter a room with up to 24 other people, make friends, and type-talk in real time. Make predictions about the market in the Fundamental Analysis room. Get help navigating the Web in the Internet Help room. Or liven up your Saturday night in the Married and Flirting room. Prodigy members can also create their own public and private rooms. Prodigy has tried to bring some degree of organization to the chaos of live chat; when you first enter the chat area, there's a calendar of chat events, transcripts of chat sessions with famous guests, a bulletin board for posting chat questions, chatting guidelines, and even a how-to explanation. ✓**PRODIGY**→*jump* chat

IRC Channels

Amiga Home page for the Amiga channel. ✓**INTERNET**→*www* http://www.pitt.edu/~schivins/irc-amiga.html

AppleIIGS Home page for the Apple IIGS channel. ✓**INTERNET**→*www* http://www.ugcs.caltech.edu/~nathan/appleiigs.html

HP48 Home page for the HP48 calculator channel. ✓**INTERNET**→*www* http://twws1.vub.ac.be/studs/tw45639/hp48.htm

Linux Home page for the Linux channel. ✓**INTERNET**→*www* http://weber.u.washington.edu/~roland/irc/irc.html

Macintosh Home page for the Macintosh channel. ✓**INTERNET**→*www* http://www.disserv.stu.umn.edu/~thingles/PoundMac/

OS/2 Home page for the OS/2 channel. ✓**INTERNET**→*www* http://venus.ee.ndsu.nodak.edu/os2/curtis/irc/os2irc.htm

root Home page for the root channel. ✓**INTERNET** …→*www* http://www.ksu.edu/~strat/irc-root.html …→*www* http://www.seas.upenn.edu/~mengwong/irc.root.html

unix Home page for the Unix channel. ✓**INTERNET**→*www* http://www.seas.upenn.edu/~mengwong/irc.unix.html

WWW Home page for the WWW channel. ✓**INTERNET**→*www* http://www.ugcs.caltech.edu/~kluster/ircwww.html

Getting Wired **Navigating the Net**

Navigating the Net

Once you've arrived at the Internet—whether it's via the World Wide Web or through an

older protocol like gopher or telnet—you will be amazed by the wealth of resources, by the millions of sites, documents, services, and secret treasures. How does a newcomer get around? With a tremendous amount of help. Need to search for specific sites? Ask **Yahoo**, or **WebCrawler**, or **Lycos**, and ye shall receive. Curious about the ins and outs of newsgroup etiquette? Visit **alt.usenet.culture**. Confused? Back up and read **A Brief Introduction to the Internet**. Bored? Drop by the **Cool Site of the Day**. And then memorize **The Internet Index** so that you can amaze and amuse your friends with your grasp of the statistical specifics of the online world.

Munch's Scream—*from http://www.ee.pdx.edu/~caseyh/horror/pics/graphics.html*

On the Net

Across the Internet

Internet Prodigy has done almost everything it could do to prevent its members from making Internet blunders. At every turn, there are tutorials, netiquette guides, FAQs, and glossaries. From the main Internet screen, members can link to newsgroups, email, or (if they are on a Windows system) the Web. All Prodigy members may use the Internet Support BB (*jump* internet bb) to explore Net topics—porn on the Web, getting President Clinton's email address, downloading photos from Usenet—in the safety of a Prodigy bulletin board. ✓ **PRODIGY**→*jump* internet

Internet Cafe A wonderful, nononsense collection of Internet instructional guides and software. Download files like TurboGopher, "Setting up a WWW Home Page," and even the "Internet Downloading Guide." ✓ **AMERICA ONLINE**→*keyword* mcm→Software Libraries→Internet Cafe

The Internet Connection "Can I play MUDs through AOL?" "Can anyone help me find a mailing list for people who have an interest in Shakespeare?" "Hi, all—I'm trying to find a program called MacPing. Any help would be

Net Tech 275

Navigating the Net **Getting Wired**

greatly appreciated." Questions from AOLers about a wide range of topics flood the Internet Message Board. And while fellow AOLers share a fair amount of information about the Internet with one another, AOL itself has spent extra efforts to arm its members with information. Next to the newsgroup reader, for instance, are instructions and guidelines for reading and posting to newsgroups. AOL has also tried to make the Internet more user-friendly, with searchable databases of mailing lists, FTP sites, and gophers. Currently, AOLers can telnet, FTP, send email, read newsgroups, use gopher and WAIS clients, and, with a special AOL browser, access the Web. ✓**AMERICA ONLINE**→*keyword* internet

Internet Files and Utilities If you're seeking information about the Internet, this library has quite an extensive collection of resources, including FAQs about TCP/IP, the World Wide Web, and Internet providers. Besides that, there's no shortage of Internet software here for PC users. ✓**AMERICA ONLINE**→*keyword* pctelecom→Browse the Software Libraries→Networks→Internet Files and Utilities

Internet Services From within CompuServe, members can telnet, FTP, and read newsgroups. The main Internet menu also links to a trio of active Internet forums where netters discuss all facets of the Internet. In the New Users Forum (*go* inetforum) novices are introduced to Internet Web browsers, email, telnet programs, IRC channels, FTP, and CompuServe via PPP connections. They can ask questions on the boards or turn to the libraries to download Internet guides, tutorials, and software. More experienced surfers should head straight for the Internet Resources Forum (*go* inetresource) for more technical discussions of Internet software and navigational tools. The strength of the Resources Forum lies with its libraries, which are packed with FAQs on Net topics such as TCP/IP, firewalls, and cryptography, as well as lists of mailing lists, and lists of Web browsers and HTML editors, telnet and gopher clients, and much more. The third forum, the Internet Publishing Forum (*go* inetpub), is exclusively for CompuServe members interested in Web design and creating home pages. ✓**COMPUSERVE**→*go* internet

Internet 101

A Brief Introduction to the Internet Just what the title says. Includes descriptions of the major Internet tools: email, FTP, gopher, Usenet, telnet, and the World Wide Web. ✓**INTERNET**→*www* http://www.sigma.unb.ca/sigma/intro.htm

alt.newbie/alt.newbies/ news.newusers.questions/ comp.unix.questions (ng) Newsgroups created especially for Internet novices to post questions. The FAQ directory includes guides to email, FTP, Internet access providers, signature files, and newsgroups. ✓**USENET** *FAQ:* ✓**INTERNET**→*www* http://www.cis.ohio-state.edu/hypertext/faq/bngusenet/news/newusers/questions/top.html

Desktop Internet Reference This 1800-page guide offers an easy-to-use index to some of the most famous documents about and available on the Internet. It's a virtual encyclopedia of the Internet that should be on every PC user's list. The document is available for download in DOS and Windows formats. ✓**INTERNET**→*www* http://www.clark.net/pub/listserv/dir1.html

EFF's Extended Guide to the Internet A very basic primer on the Internet. The guide covers Internet providers, email programs and email addresses, Usenet culture and newsreaders, mailing lists, telnet instructions and sites, FTP instructions and sites, gophers and sites, IRC and MUDs, netiquette, the EFF, and much more. ✓**INTERNET** ...→*www* http://www.eff.org/papers/eegtti/eegttitop.html ...→*www* http://www.eff.org/pub/Net_info/EFF_Net_Guide/netguide.eff ...→*www* ftp://ftp.lib.ncsu.edu/pub/stacks/guides/big-dummy/bdg_toc.html ✓**COMPUSERVE**→*go* inetforum→Libraries→*Search by file name:* ntgd31.zip

Entry Level Internet Sometimes the online world feels like another country, except they don't take your passport at the border. To alleviate that culture shock, *Internet World* editor Andrew Kantor has written a series of articles for novices about the Internet, and Mecklermedia has published them online. Article topics range from getting on the Internet to using encryption programs. "Entry Lev-

> "Sometimes the online world feels like another country, except they don't take your passport at the border."

Getting Wired Navigating the Net

el: Baby Steps" offers a good first look at what one needs to become an upstanding Netizen. ✓**INTERNET** →*www* http://www.mecklerweb.com/webguide/entry.htm ✓**COMPUSERVE** →*go* iworld→Libraries→Entry Level/Newbies

Internet Foreplay Strange. Very strange. The title would suggest that this was one of those sites on the Net where men go to download dirty pictures. Instead, it's an Internet tutorial that explains FTP, offers statistics on Web usage, gives modem recommendations, and offers advice on choosing a provider. ✓**INTERNET**→*www* http://www.easynet.co.uk/pages/forepl/forepl.htm

The Online World A guide to the online world that is revised every two months. It covers the Internet extensively and also offers information about commercial services such as CompuServe and BBS networks like FidoNet. It offers both how-to explanations and Net site recommendations. Not tremendously well written. ✓**INTERNET**→*www* http://login.eunet.no/~presno/index.html

Zen and the Art of the Internet Among Internet manuals, this is one of the most venerated. Generations of Internet users started with this compact reference, which covers topics ranging from Archie file searching to the Internet domain name system. ✓**INTERNET** …→*www* http://www.cs.indiana.edu/docproject/zen/zen-1.0_toc.html …→*www* ftp://ftp.internic.net/pub/internet-doc/zen.txt ✓**AMERICA ONLINE**→ *keyword* internet→Zen & the Art of Internet

Net news
alt.internet.media-coverage

Why did the *Wall Street Journal* predict the demise of Usenet? Is *Internet World* being compromised by AOL advertising dollars? This is a moderated newsgroup that monitors the media that monitors the Internet. **FAQ:** ✓**INTERNET** …→ *www* http://www.dorsai.org/~tristan/AIMC/ …→*www* http://www.cais.com/jdfalk/html/aim-c.html

Connect A bimonthly telecomputing magazine for modem users. *Connect* specializes in Net navigation instruction, and its message boards and libraries are good resources for Net newbies. ✓**AMERICA ONLINE**→*keyword* connect

Globetrotter An electronic start-up magazine specializing in online culture and technology, *Globetrotter* promises not just to report on the electronic frontier, but to report from it. Submissions are welcome from prospective writers who can write with authority on Net culture and its implications. ✓**INTERNET**→*www* http://www.dungeon.com/~globe

In, Around and On-line A weekly digest reporting on events in the online world, with heavy emphasis on what's happening at the Big Three services (America Online, Prodigy, and CompuServe). The Website also includes links to other online magazines on the Web. ✓**INTERNET**→*www* http://www.clark.net/pub/robert/home.html

Internet World A monthly magazine that reports on the Internet—sites, new Internet software, and trends. Written for the Net user, not the network administrator, the magazine repeatedly runs simple, how-to Internet articles in addition to its Net surfing coverage. The Web version features arti-

Internet World *cover—from http://www.mecklerweb.com/*

cles from the print version, an archive of articles from back issues, and a link to other sites from the Mecklermedia publishing group. On CompuServe, articles from back issues are archived in the libraries and timely Internet news and discussions take place on the message boards. ✓**INTERNET**→*www* http://www.mecklerweb.com/mags/iw/iwhome.htm ✓**COMPUSERVE**→*go* iworld

Net Day Very brief, daily summaries of news about the Net. A terrific resource for busy professionals or Net junkies who crave one-stop Internet information. ✓**INTERNET**→*www* http://www.mecklerweb.com/netday/newsmenu.htm

.net—The Internet Magazine Online edition of the glossy print magazine that covers the Internet from a pop culture viewpoint. Typical articles explore topics ranging from the financial possibilities of Webvertising to the perils of credit card cruising in electronic malls. This Website is a glorified table of contents for the print version; don't come here expecting full-text articles. ✓**INTERNET**

Net Tech 277

Navigating the Net Getting Wired

→*www* http://www.mecklerweb.com/netday/newsmenu.htm

NetGuide On-line What sites are worth visiting? Who's making news on the Net? And what tips would make your Net life a lot easier? The monthly print magazine is pitched to answer exactly these questions. Its online counterpart includes listings of all the Websites reviewed in the Cyberguide (reviews and live links are available online) as well as the full texts of a selection of articles from the current issue. ✓**INTERNET**→ *www* http://www.wais.com:80/techweb/ng/current/default.html

Netsurfer Digest (ml) A weekly guide reporting news in the online world and describing dozens of Net sites—Websites, newsgroups, FTP archives, IRC channels, etc. ✓**INTERNET** ...→*email* nsdigest-request@netsurf.com ✎ *Type in message body:* subscribe nsdigest-html ...→*www* http://www.netsurf.com/nsd/index.html

Online Today A CompuServe-sponsored area for news about the computer industry. The service includes product announcements, book reviews, articles from *CompuServe Magazine*, and daily news reports. Much of *Online Today*'s content is about the Net. ✓**COMPUSERVE**→*go* olt

WebWeek The electronic version of Meckler's print weekly, *WebWeek* serves the growing community of technical, financial, and creative Web developers. Visit the WebWatch forum for information on overcoming fear of HTML programming, or read the latest industry news about the World Wide Web and its emerging role in today's telecommunications world. ✓**INTERNET** →*www* http://www.mecklerweb.com/mags/ww/wwhome.htm

Powersurfing

All-in-One Search Page A Web page with more than 100 search tools. You can take advantage of Lycos and Yahoo search engines at this page, but you can also search a database of mailing lists, the largest software archives on the Net, a weather database, CMP's technical articles, the full text of Shakespeare's plays and sonnets, a movie database, White House documents, the Bible, and a thesaurus. ✓**INTERNET** →*www*http://www.albany.net/~wcross/all1srch.html

Clearinghouse for Subject-Oriented Internet Resource Guides Netters are incredibly generous with information—and their time. This collection of subject guides cataloguing Internet resources testifies to that generosity. David Brown has created a guide to children's literature on the Web; Michele Pfaff and David Bachman have authored a guide to resources on individual rights; and Tricia Segal and Julie Lea have authored a guide to women's health issues. More than a hundred of these guides—with information on newsgroups, Websites, mailing lists, and FTP and gopher sites—are available here in hypertext or ASCII format. ✓**INTERNET**→*www* http://www.lib.umich.edu/chhome.html

comp.internet.net-happenings (ng) When new Websites go up, they're often announced here. It's a good group for surfers to keep an eye on. ✓**USENET**

Email basics

comp.mail * What's your email address? Knowing an address is

CYBERNOTES

"Widely Used Smileys

(-: User is left handed.

%-) User has been staring at a green screen for 15 hours.

:*) User is drunk.

8-) User is wearing sunglasses.

8:-) User is a little girl.

:-)-8 User is a Big girl.

:-{) User has a mustache.

:-{} User wears lipstick.

{:-) User wears a toupee.

}:-(Toupee in an updraft.

:-[User is a vampire.

:-7 User just made a wry statement.

:-* User just ate something sour.

:-~) User has a cold.

:'-(User is crying.

-:-) User is a punk rocker."

-from **EFF's (Extended) Guide to the Internet**

278 Net Tech

Getting Wired Navigating the Net

only the first step. Netters then need to navigate mail readers. Several of the most common mail readers have their own newsgroups—e.g., comp.mail.elm—where users can post questions about how to filter, attach signatures, forward messages, and even compile the program. The comp.mail* newsgroup FAQs collect the wisdom of email users and system operators, answering hundreds of questions such as "What does the 'Precedence' header mean?" and "How can I get a 'Reply-To' header in all of my messages?" There are also newsgroups for multimedia mail and mailing-list owners. *FAQ:* ✓**INTERNET** …→*www* http://www.cis.ohio-state.edu/hypertext/faq/bngusenet/comp/mail/top.html …→*www* ftp://rtfm.mit.edu/pub/usenet-by-hierarchy/comp/mail/

E-Mail Web Resources Equip yourself with email know-how and software at this Web page, which links to email FAQs, email servers, and archives of email software. ✓**INTERNET**→*www* http://andrew2.andrew.cmu.edu/cyrus/email/email.html

Searching for people

College Email Address FAQ This FAQ explains how to track down people in undergraduate and graduate schools. From short descriptions of Net tools such as finger and Netfind to a school-by-school descripton of userid constructions, this multi-part FAQ is also a good primer for finding people on the Internet in general. ✓**INTERNET** …→*www* http://www.qucis.queensu.ca/FAQs/college-email/college.html …→*www* ftp://rtfm.mit.edu/pub/usenet/news/answers/college-email ✓**COMPUSERVE** →*go* inetforum→Libraries→*Search by file name:* colleg.txt

Four11 Directory Services (SLED) A directory service for the entire Internet. Success finding someone through this service is dependent upon netters' having registered their own addresses. ✓**INTERNET**→*www* http://www.four11.com

How to Find People's E-mail Addresses An excellent reference guide that describes how to locate people on the Internet. If the method isn't described in this FAQ, it's probably not worth using. ✓**INTERNET** …→*www* ftp://rtfm.mit.edu/pub/usenet/news.answers/finding-addresses …→*www* http://www.cis.ohio-state.edu/hypertext/faq/usenet/finding-addresses/faq.html ✓**COMPUSERVE** →*go* inetforum→Libraries→*Search by file name:* netfnd.zip

Member List Looking for that long-lost uncle from Detroit who you heard had a Prodigy account? Unless your uncle has "registered" himself on this screen, he won't be listed—this is not an inclusive list of all Prodigy members. But it's worth a shot. ✓**PRODIGY**→*jump* Member List

Netpages Though this service has a lot to offer, it's plagued by lack of participation, and it's recommended only if you've tried everything else (including calling the person). If you do drop by, don't forget to add your info to the database. ✓**INTERNET**→*www* http://www.aldea.com

The RTFM Mail Server Probably the quickest and easiest way to find people on the Internet, the RTFM mail server searches all recent Usenet postings and matches an address to a name. *Caveat emptor:* RTFM will only return addresses of people who have posted to Usenet. ✓**INTERNET** …→*www* wais://rtfm.mit.edu:210/usenet-addresses …→*email* mail-server@rtfm.mit.edu ✍ *Type in message body:* "send Usenet-addresses/name"

soc.net-people (ng) Don't know where your friend is—physically or in Cyberspace? Post to soc.net-people to see if someone has met him online. ✓**USENET** *FAQ:* ✓**INTERNET**→*www* http://www.cis.ohio-state.edu/hypertext/faq/bngusenet/soc/net-people/top.html

Mailing lists

The List of Lists This is by far the most comprehensive tool to search for mailing lists on the Internet. Comprising over 6,000 entries and revised on a weekly basis, it's the quickest way to find a good mailing list. ✓**INTERNET**→*www* http://alpha.acast.nova.edu/cgi-bin/lists

Publicly Accessible Mailing Lists Fossils or felines? Tolkien or Africa? Bonsai plants or MUDs? Pick a discussion from a huge and diverse list of mailing lists. The first address allows netters to sort by subject or list name. ✓**INTERNET** …→*www* http://www.neosoft.com/internet/paml/ …→*www* ftp://rtfm.mit.edu/pub/usenet/news.answers/mail/mailing-lists …→*www* http://www.cis.ohio-state.edu/hypertext/faq/usenet/mail/mailing-lists/top.html

Tile.Net ListServ Lists It's late in the evening and you have a craving to discuss underwater basket-weaving. Why not join a mailing list? Tile.Net has catalogued thousands of ListServ mailing lists that are run by a ListServ program. The site lets you search by subject or list name and sort alphabetically or by number of sub-

Navigating the Net Getting Wired

scribers. (In case you were interested, David Letterman's top ten list has the most subscribers, with more than 66,000.) ✓**INTERNET**→ *www* http://www.tile.net/tile/listserv/index.html

Elements of e-style

A Beginner's Guide to Effective email An explanation of the difference between writing email and snail mail. The more unique features of email (emoticons, etc…) are covered. ✓**INTERNET**→*www* http://alpha.acast.nova.edu/cgi-bin/lists

Signature, Finger, & Customized Headers FAQ Instructions for using the finger program, attaching signatures to email, and customizing mail headers. ✓**INTERNET** …→*www* http://www.cis.ohio-state.edu/hypertext/faq/usenet/signature_finger_faq/faq.html …→*www* ftp://rtfm.mit.edu/pub/usenet/news.answers/signature_finger_faq

Email services

International E-mail Accessibility To send an email to France, append "fr" to the end of the email address. A message with "ca" at the end is from Canada. This document matches countries with their country codes. ✓**INTERNET**→ *www* http://alpha.acast.nova.edu/cgi-bin/inmgq.pl

The Internetwork Mailguide A program that translates a FidoNet, CompuServe, Prodigy, or America Online address into an Internet address. Definitely one of the best email tools directly available on the Net. The principles of translating these addresses are spelled out in the document at the second location. ✓**INTERNET** …→ *www* http://alpha.acast.nova. edu/cgi-bin/inmgq.pl …→*www* http://www.cis.ohio-state.edu/hypertext/faq/usenet/mail/internetwork-guide/faq.html

Remailers!!! Have a hot tip about your company but don't want people to know who you are? Want to post to an alt.sex* group without anyone else knowing? Use an anonymous remailer, a controversial program that lets you send email without people's knowing where or whom it's coming from. ✓**INTERNET**→*www* http://electron.rutgers.edu/~gambino/anon_servers/anon.html

Web basics

alt.www.culture (ng) With a slightly less geeky atmosphere than the comp.infosystems.www.* newsgroups, netters here recommend and discuss interesting Web pages. Strong opinions have led to flame wars in the past, and while this group isn't for the faint of heart, it's well worth a regular visit if you want to stay up-to-the-minute with the Web. ✓**USENET**

BrowserWatch The site reports on and reviews Web browsers. It also links to online sites carrying the browsers. ✓**INTERNET**→*www* http://www.ski.mskcc.org:80/browserwatch/index.html

comp.infosystems.www.* (ng) Gather in the Webaholics Anonymous section of Usenet— the comp.infosystems.www.* newsgroups—to get technical support on using a browser, designing a Web page, or running a Web server. Look for announcements of new Websites in the comp.infosystems.www.announce newsgroup. ✓**USENET** *FAQ:* ✓**INTERNET**→*www* http://www.cis.ohio-state.edu/hypertext/faq/bngusenet/comp/infosystems/www/top.html

Easy Mosaic and Introductory Web Surfing While you won't find specific help on using Mosaic for Windows or the Mac here (the title refers to Mosaic for X-Windows), the site provides a basic introduction to the Web and links to help you begin surfing the Net. ✓**INTERNET**→*www* http://www.lm.com/~lmann/docs/easymosaic.html

Entering the World Wide Web: A Guide to Cyberspace Cyberspace and the Web are not synonymous, no matter what this site says. But, that mistake aside, this online guide offers a good overview of Web technology, describes the Web's place in Internet history, and features a timeline of the history of hypertext. ✓**INTERNET**→ *www* http://www.hcc.hawaii.edu/guide/www.guide.html

Starting to Use the WWW If you need to get up to speed on the Web quickly, this site defines essential Web terms and concepts, and also offers a basic guide to coding Web documents. There are also links to other Web authoring resources. ✓**INTERNET**→*www* http://www.sils.umich.edu/~fprefect/inet/using/html.html

The World Wide Web Inititative A central repository for software and information about the Web. The site links to documents about HTML programming, Web browsers for several platforms, resources on Web security, Web development tools, and links to other Web resources. ✓**INTERNET**→ *www* http://www.w3.org/

World Wide Web Tools Besides information about Web browsers, *PC Week* has organized a good collection of links to information about Web authoring—an HTML style guide, coding standards,

280 Net Tech

Getting Wired **Navigating the Net**

HTML writing tools, and more. ✓ **INTERNET**→*www* http://www.ziff.com:8002/~pcweek/navigator/webtools.html

WWW FAQ A valuable resource about the Web. The FAQ describes and links to Web browsers, guides to writing HTML, HTML editors, and documents about designing a home page. ✓ **INTERNET** ...→*www* http://sunsite.unc.edu/boutell/faq/www_faq.html ...→*www* http://www.cis.ohio-state.edu/hypertext/faq/usenet/www/faq/faq.html

Web directories

Aliweb When the system administrator of the Nexor site saw his computer taken over by a Web Wanderer (a robot gathering information about the Web), he decided to create his own robot. Aliweb was born and quickly expanded into a great search engine. ✓ **INTERNET**→*www* http://www.nexor.co.uk/public/aliweb/aliweb.html

CUSI A reference desk for the Internet, this site carries several search engines and databases on one Web page. Not only does it feature Web search tools, it also offers tools for searching mailing lists, FAQs, and email addresses. ✓ **INTERNET**→*www* http://pubweb.nexor.co.uk/public/cusi/cusi.html

Einet Galaxy Search the Web, gopher, Hytelnet, and Einet's own Web pages for up to 240 listings at a time. Einet has also created its own topical index of the Web. ✓ **INTERNET**→*www* http://www.einet.net/

Harvest Homepage Broker The Harvester provides you with a highly detailed, easy-to-use search page. Not only can you define what you're looking for, you can also choose different display formats for the results. ✓ **INTERNET**→*www* http://rd.cs.colorado.edu/brokers/www-home-pages/query.html

InfoSeek A newcomer to the search-tool scene, Infoseek lets you search and receive up to 100 links on the Web for free; after the gratis period, you pay a modest fee. You can search WWW pages, Usenet news, over 50 computer magazines, newswires and press releases, company profiles, medical and health information, movie reviews, and technical support databases. ✓ **INTERNET**→*www* http://www.infoseek.com

Jumpstation Another site for searching Web pages. The Jumpstation and its brother, Jumpstation II, are not as rigorously updated as other sites. ✓ **INTERNET**→*www* http://www.stir.ac.uk/jsbin/jsii

Lycos Hailed as the best search tool on the Internet, Lycos claims over 3.5 million Web pages in its database. Unfortunately, its popularity often means you have to resend your search several times. While recent server reconfiguration has made Lycos more convenient, searches during daylight hours can still be frustrating. ✓ **INTERNET**→*www* http://lycos.cs.cmu.edu

NetSearch Aimed mainly at businesses, this search engine also provides quick descriptions of the links it finds. Note that businesses must pay for the privilege of being listed here. ✓ **INTERNET**→*www* http://www.ais.net/netsearch/

Planet Earth Organized like a library, complete with rooms and floor plans, Planet Earth is one of the easiest sites to surf. Pick an "aisle" to browse, or use the search engine to find sites. ✓ **INTERNET**→*www* http://www.nosc.mil/planet_earth/everything.html

W3 CUI Search Engine At one time, this was the only place to search for Web resources, and it continues to be one of the major search engines online. ✓ **INTERNET**→*www* http://cuiwww.unige.ch/meta-index.html

WebCrawler An incredibly quick, no-frills search engine. ✓ **INTERNET**→*www* http://webcrawler.cs.washington.edu/WebCrawler/

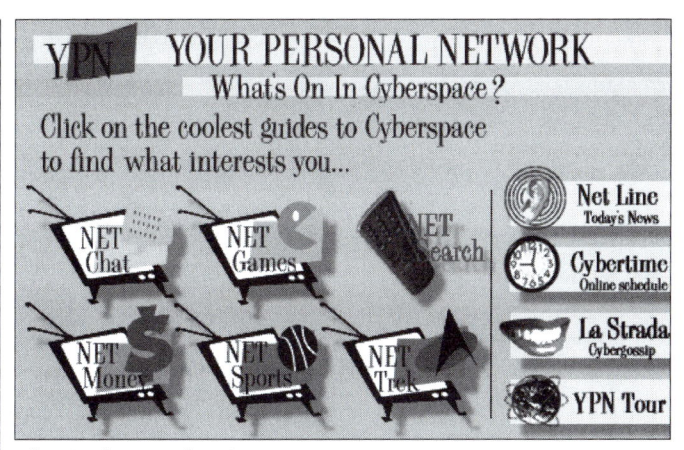

The YPN directory—http://www.ypn.com/

Navigating the Net Getting Wired

WebQuery.html

The Whole Internet Catalog An entertaining database of Net resources based on the seminal book by Ed Krol. ✓**INTERNET**→ *www* http://www.gnn.com/wic/newrescat.toc.html

The World Wide Web Worm Nominated Best of the Web in 1994, the Worm lets you choose between a quick and dirty search or a long and detailed one. ✓**INTERNET**→ *www* http://www.cs.colorado.edu/home/mcbryan/WWWW.html

Worldwide Yellow Pages Look up information on thousands of companies in this online database, which bills itself as "The Yellow Pages for the Next 100 Years." Listings often include direct links to company home pages or technical support sites. Others simply list the company's address, phone number, or email address. ✓**INTERNET**→*www* http://www.yellow.com/

The WWW Virtual Library It's the first Web directory, and still one of the largest, with comprehensive coverage of online resources concerning subjects ranging from chemistry to wireless computing. Unfortunately, the breakdown by subject areas is not hierarchical and there are a clutter of topics on the first page. ✓**INTERNET**→*www* http://www.w3.org/hypertext/DataSources/bySubject/Overview.html

Yahoo Features a well organized subject hierarchy, a powerful search function, and a huge collection of Websites. For a long time, the site has reigned as the Web directory of choice for most serious netters. Those surfing the Net on slow modems will appreciate the absence of large graphics. ✓**INTERNET**→ *www* http://www.yahoo.com/

YPN—Your Personal Network Search the collection of sites listed and described in the Net Books series, including sites from *Net Guide*, *Net Games*, *Net Chat*, *Net Money*, *Net Trek*, *Net Sports*, and *Net Tech*. Unlike the other online directories, YPN includes coverage of the commercial services and BBS world as well as the Internet. The site also features a daily news story with links to relevant Net sites. ✓**INTERNET**→ *www* http://www.ypn.com/

Web picks

The Awesome List Internet trainer John Makulowich has compiled a list of more than one hundred Net sites to illustrate the wide range of cyber-offerings. Start with the Academic Physician and Scientist home page, stop by the Electronic Newsstand, head over to the Global Network Navigator, and then drop by the Tulsa County Sheriff's Office. ✓**INTERNET**→*www* http://www.clark.net/pub/journalism/awesome.html

Cool Site of the Day Recent winners include the Geek Chic page and the World Wide Web Dating Game. ✓**INTERNET**→*www* http://www.infi.net/cool.html

Spider's Pick of the Day An incredibly popular site for Net surfers, Spider's Pick features a new Website everyday. Past Spider picks have included a tour of the Sistine Chapel, *People* Magazine online, a Frisbee page, a page dedicated to Timothy Leary, and a gallery of space shots. ✓**INTERNET**→ *www* http://gagme.wwa.com/~boba/pick.html

URouLette Random sites for jaded surfers who can't find anything new or interesting. Get whisked off to the farthest reaches of the Net on this roulette wheel to Net sites—where the wheel stops, no one knows! ✓**INTERNET**→*www* http://kuhttp.cc.ukans.edu/cwis/organizations/kucia/uroulette/uroulette.html

Web HotSpots: No 404's! Fred Langa, the Editorial Director for CMP's Personal Computing Group, recommends a unique or interesting site each day. ✓**INTERNET**→*www* http://www.winmag.com/flanga/hotspots.htm

What's Hot and Cool Operating with a pseudo-democratic approach, this site solicits suggestions from its readers, and then writes short-descriptive reviews of its favorites. ✓**INTERNET**→*www* http://kzsu.stanford.edu/uwi/reviews.html

Newsgroups

alt.usenet.culture (ng) Which newsgroups are embroiled in flame wars? Who's been ostracized? Which threads should you put in your kill file? This newsgroup is primarily filled with gossip about the activities on various newsgroups. ✓**USENET**

Internet Newsgroups A hypertext list of newsgroups with very short descriptions. ✓**INTERNET**→ *www* ftp://ftp.uu.net/uunet-info/newsgroups.gz

KILL File FAQ The Usenet solution to idiocy and annoying individuals is a kill file. Put a name or email address in a "kill file" and you can erase the pest from your virtual sight. Poof! This FAQ describes how it's done. ✓**INTERNET**→ *www* http://www.cis.ohio-state.

Getting Wired Navigating the Net

edu/hypertext/faq/usenet/killfile-faq/faq.html

Mercury News Gopher Is your provider missing newsgroups? This site provides read-only access via gopher to thousands of newsgroups. ✓**INTERNET**→*www* gopher://gopher.msu.edu:3441/

MG's Fabulous News Page A collection of links to newsgroup FAQs, lists of newsgroups, newsgroup archives, and the Web pages of some newsgroups. ✓**INTERNET**→ *www* http://sunsite.unc.edu/usenet-i/home.html

news.admin.hierarchies (ng) Primarily questions from administrators about adding newsgroup hierarchies to newsfeeds. ✓**USENET**

news.admin.misc (ng) A mix of postings related to administering newsgroup sites, creating newsgroups, debating Usenet scandals and abuses, and outing Usenet troublemakers. FAQs about Usenet are frequently posted here. ✓**USENET** *FAQ:* ✓**INTERNET**→*www* http://www.cis.ohio-state.edu/hypertext/faq/bngusenet/news/admin/misc/top.html

news.admin.net-abuse.announce (ng) Spamming, posting the same message to an excessive number of newsgroups, is a serious offense in the Usenet community and several netters have acquired programs that cancel these spams. This newsgroup reports on abuses and on the number of posts cancelled. ✓**USENET** *FAQ:* ✓**INTERNET**→*www* http://www.cis.ohio-state.edu/hypertext/faq/bngusenet/news/admin/net-abuse/announce/top.html

news.admin.net-abuse.misc (ng) Court is now in session! Whereas news.admin.net-abuse.

Can o' SPAM—from http://www.acm.uiuc.edu/rml/Gifs/

announce merely reports on the abuse and the attempts to curb it, this group is filled with netters debating censorship and issues of free speech, malicious intent, and the future of Usenet. ✓**USENET** *FAQ:* ✓**INTERNET**→*www* http://www.cis.ohio-state.edu/hypertext/faq/bngusenet/news/admin/net-abuse/misc/top.html

news.admin.policy (ng) Have a gripe against someone on Usenet? Bring it here. (Airing gripes is certainly not in the newsgroup charter, but quite a few people apparently think it is.) In general, it's a noisy group with lots of off-topic discussions mixed in with accusations of Net abuse and reports about Usenet trends. ✓**USENET**

news.admin.technical (ng) A moderated newsgroup for technical discussions about administering newsgroup sites. ✓**USENET**

news.announce.important (ng) A low-volume newsgroup where important announcements about Usenet issues are posted. ✓**USENET**

news.announce.newgroups (ng) What new newsgroups are on the horizon? Follow this moderated newsgroup where calls for votes (CFV) on starting new newsgroups, and the results of the votes, are posted. The FAQs cover the process of creating a newsgroup and include lists of newsgroups. ✓**USENET** *FAQ:* ✓**INTERNET** →*www* http://www.cis.ohio-state.edu/hypertext/faq/bngusenet/news/announce/newgroups/top.html

news.announce.newusers (ng) There are two kinds of computer users: those who read the manuals and those who don't. The former should drop by this newsgroup where the updated versions of Usenet's "manuals" are kept. Postings include Hints on Writing Style for Usenet, the Anonymous FTP FAQ, and even FAQs about FAQs. ✓**USENET** *FAQ:* ✓**INTERNET**→ *www* http://www.cis.ohio-state.edu/hypertext/faq/bngusenet/news/announce/newusers/top.html

news.answers (ng) The Chocolate FAQ, the Fat-Free Vegetarian Resource List, the alt.polygamy FAQ, and the MPEG FAQ are a few of the hundreds of posts in this newsgroup that serves as a repository for FAQs. ✓**USENET**

news.groups (ng) Partly for discussing the creation of new newsgroups, partly a place to go to get recommendations for newsgroups, and partly a collection of Usenet-related FAQs. ✓**USENET**

news.groups.questions (ng) A newsgroup to help netters find the right newsgroup. "Is there a newsgroup for WordPerfect?" (bit.listserv.wpcorp-l) "Is there a newsgroup for new parents?" (alt.parenting*) "Who built the Egyptian pyramids?" (soc.culture.egyptian, sci.archaeology, or alt.mythology) ✓**USENET** *FAQ:* ✓**INTERNET**→*www* http://www.cis.ohio-state.edu/hypertext/faq/bngusenet/news/groups/questions/top.html

Net Tech 283

Navigating the Net Getting Wired

news.groups.reviews (ng) A moderated and very low-volume newsgroup for reviews of newsgroups. ✓USENET *FAQ:* ✓INTERNET→ *www* http://www.cis.ohio-state.edu/hypertext/faq/bngusenet/news/groups/reviews/top.html

news.lists (ng) Several different lists of newsgroups: Top-40 newsgroups by popularity, top-40 newsgroups by amount of cross-posting, lists of moderators for Usenet newsgroups, lists of active newsgroups, lists of alternative newsgroups, lists of Usenet mailing lists, etc. ✓USENET *FAQ:* ✓INTERNET→ *www* http://www.cis.ohio-state.edu/hypertext/faq/bngusenet/news/lists/top.html

news.misc (ng) Another newsgroup devoted to discussions or announcements about Usenet. ✓USENET

news.newusers.questions (ng) Hundreds of messages each week from netters trying to find newsgroups that their providers don't carry, looking for good off-line news readers, and seeking answers to a slew of other Usenet- and Internet-related questions. ✓USENET

news.software* (ng) Five newsgroups where users can ask questions and share hints about news reader software: news.newusers.questions; news.software.anu-news; news.software.b; news.software.nn; news.software.nntp; news.software.readers The FAQ directory includes tutorials and guides to several newsreader programs. ✓USENET *FAQ:* ✓INTERNET→ *www* http://www.cis.ohio-state.edu/hypertext/faq/bngusenet/news/software/top.html

Reading Usenet News Besides FAQs about Usenet culture and news reading, the Web page also links to lists of newsgroups, lists of newsgroup moderators, information on posting anonymously, and guides to several news reader programs. ✓INTERNET→ *www* http://www.ocf.berkeley.edu/help/usenet/

Stanford Netnews Filtering Service Sorts through thousands of Usenet newsgroups, and emails you newsgroup articles based on a specified criteria. The key to the service is defining a good search phrase. News will be emailed to you as often as you choose. ✓INTERNET ...→ *www* http://woodstock.stanford.edu:2000/ ...→ *email* netnews@db.stanford.edu ✍ *Type in message body:* help

Tile.Net News View newsgroups and descriptions by hierarchy, by name, or by whether or not they are moderated. Netters may also search newsgroup descriptions from this site. ✓INTERNET→ *www* http://www.tile.net/tile/news/

Usenet Info Center Launch Pad The Website walks visitors through a Usenet education, programming a tutorial that includes more than a dozen FAQs and primers on Usenet. The site also links to central archives of Usenet groups, a news filtering service, a collection of several hundred newsgroup FAQs, newsgroup software, and more. ✓INTERNET→ *www* http://sunsite.unc.edu/usenet-i/home.html

UUNET's List of Newsgroups A "complete" list of newsgroups. ✓INTERNET→ *www* ftp://ftp.uu.net/uunet-info/newsgroups.gz

FAQs

List of USENET FAQs Links to the hypertext versions of hundreds of Usenet FAQs, from the Atlanta Olympics FAQ to the ZyXEL U 1496 series modem resellers' FAQ. ✓INTERNET→ *www* http://www.cis.ohio-state.edu/hypertext/faq/usenet/

MIT FAQ Repository If an FAQ is "official" (read: approved by the FAQ-maintainers committee), it will be archived here. ✓INTERNET ...→ *www* ftp://rtfm.mit.edu/pub/usenet ...→ *www* ftp://ftp.uu.net/usenet/news.answers

Usenet Newsgroup Hierarchy with Searchable FAQ Archive Organizes FAQs by category and by newsgroup and includes a feature to search all FAQs by keyword. There are annotated links to both the FAQs and the newsgroups. ✓INTERNET→ *www* http://www.lib.ox.ac.uk/internet/news/

FTP

Anonymous FTP FAQ How do I use the FTP program? What is Archie? How do I automate FTP sessions? The guide features fairly detailed instructions for FTPing. ✓INTERNET→ *www* http://www.cis.ohio-state.edu:80/text/faq/usenet/ftp-list/faq/faq.html

Anonymous FTP Site List A listing of more than 2300 FTP sites. Each listing includes an FTP address, information about the institution where the site is located, and a brief description of the FTP site's contents. Use one of the first two addresses if you want to search the list. ✓INTERNET ...→ *www* http://www.mid.net/FTP-LIST/ ...→ *www* http://www.info.net/Public/ftp-list.html ...→ *www* ftp://rtfm.mit.edu/pub/usenet-by-hierarchy/news/answers/ftp-list/sitelist/ ...→ *www* http://www.cis.ohio-state.edu:80/text/faq/usenet/ftp-list/sitelist/top.html

Getting Wired Navigating the Net

Archie on the Web Looking for software or an electronic copy of Joseph Conrad's *Heart of Darkness*? Search several hundred FTP sites on the Internet by a string of characters ("conrad" or "heart") that are likely to appear in the names of files you would be interested in. ✓**INTERNET** ...→*www* http://www.lerc.nasa.gov/Doc/archieplexform.html ...→*www* http://hoohoo.ncsa.uiuc.edu/archie.html ...→*www* http://www.sco.com/Third/archie.html ...→*www* http://www.funet.fi/funet/archie/ archieplex-form.html ...→*www* http://www.csi.nb.ca/archgate.html

Gopher

comp.infosystems.gopher (ng) Will the Web kill off gopher servers? How can a gopher be compiled so it uses free WAIS? Can HTML documents be converted to gopher menus? How do you download from a gopher? Both site administrators and gopher users turn to this newsgroup with questions. Gopher developers also announce new sites here. ✓**USENET** *FAQ:* ✓**INTERNET** ...→*www* ftp://rtfm.mit.edu/pub/usenet/news.answers/gopher-faq ...→*www* http://www.cis.ohio-state.edu/hypertext/faq/bngusenet/comp/infosystems/gopher/top.html

Navigating the Net: Lets Go Gopherin' Twenty-three lessons designed to teach Netters how to use the gopher program. ✓**COMPUSERVE**→*go* inetforum→Libraries→*Search by file name:* gopher.zip

Veronica The Web has many good search engines. The gopher world has one—Veronica. This powerful tool searches most public gopher-server menu titles and file names. ✓**INTERNET** ...→*www* gopher://futique.scs.unr.edu/11/veronica ...→*www* gopher://info.psi.net:2347/7 ...→*www* gopher://veronica.utdallas.edu:2348/7 ...→*www* gopher://empire.nysernet.org:2347/7 ...→*www* http://www.einet.net/gopher/gopher.html

Veronica FAQ How do you search gophers with a wildcard? Can you define the type of file you want (e.g., text)? Consult this guide to searching with Veronica. ✓**INTERNET**→*www* gopher://gopher.scs.unr.edu/00/veronica/veronica-faq ✓**COMPUSERVE**→*go* inetforum→Libraries→*Search by file name:* veroni.zip

Gopher—from http://www.infop.com/photo/

WAIS

comp.infosystems.wais (ng) Where can I find a list of WAIS servers? What is the best way to use WAIS to index HTML documents? How can I design a WAIS search form that only searches certain sites? A forum primarily for the WAIS-related technical questions that programmers have, although end users with client software questions also use the group. ✓**USENET** *FAQ:* ✓**INTERNET** ...→*www* ftp://ls6-www.informatik.uni-dortmund.de/pub/wais/FAQ ...→*www* http://www.cis.ohio-state.edu/hypertext/faq/usenet/wais-faq/freeWAIS-sf/faq.html

Wais-Discussion (ml) A moderated discussion about electronic publishing and WAIS ✓**INTERNET**→*email* listproc@wais.com ✉ *Type in message body:* subscribe wais-discussion <your full name>

Wais-Talk (ml) An unmoderated but highly technical discussion for WAIS developers and implementors. ✓**INTERNET**→*email* listproc@wais.com ✉ *Type in message body:* subscribe wais-talk <your full name>

Internet numbers

The Internet Index Inspired by Harper's Index, each bimonthly issue of the Internet Index offers a collection of online trivia (e.g., "Number of Norwegian television shows with a WWW home page: 4.") ✓**INTERNET**→*www* http://www.openmarket.com/info/internet-index/index.html

Statistics on Internet Usage Statistics on several facets of Internet usage, from World Wide Web to telneting to a state-by-state breakdown of Internet traffic. ✓**INTERNET**→*www* http://www.tig.com/IBC/Stats/Stats.html

Software

Netsurfer Tools (ml) A hypertext guide to new Net tools and software. Each listing in the guide includes a product description and a URL linking to a Website for the product. ✓**INTERNET** ...→*www* http://www.netsurf.com/nst/ ...→*email* nstools-request@netsurf.com ✉ *Type in message body:* subscribe nstools-html

Net Tech 285

Navigating the Net Getting Wired

Surfing programs: the clients

Archie (Mac)

Archie ✓**INTERNET** ...→*www* http://sumex.stanford.edu/info-mac/_Communication/_MacTCP/archie-10.hqx ...→*www* ftp://ftp.tidbits.com/pub/tidbits/tisk/_MacTCP/archie-10.hqx

Archie (PC)

Trumpet Archie ✓**INTERNET**→ *www* http://gfecnet.gmi.edu/Software/Files/winapps2.zip

WS Archie ✓**INTERNET** ...→*www* ftp://ftp.demon.co.uk/pub/ibmpc/winsock/apps/wsarchie/wsarch07.zip ...→*www* http://gfecnet.gmi.edu/Software/Files/wsarch07.zip

Email (Mac)

Eudora 1.5.1 for Mac ✓**COMPUSERVE**→*go* inetresource→ Libraries→*Search by file name:* eudora.sea ✓**AMERICA ONLINE**→*keyword* mcm→Software Libraries→*Search by file name:* Eudora 1.5.1 .sit ✓**INTERNET**→*www* ftp://ftp.tidbits.com/pub/tidbits/tisk/_MacTCP/mail/eudora-151.hqx ...→*www* ftp://nic.switch.ch/mirror/info-mac/_Communication/_MacTCP/mail/eudora-151.hqx ...→*www* ftp://ftp.sys.uea.ac.uk/Macintosh/Eudora 1.5.sea.hqx

Eudora for Mac Sys6 ✓**INTERNET**→*www* ftp://ftp.qualcomm.com/mac/eudora/1.3/Eudora1.3.1.sea.hqx

Eudora for Mac Sys7 ✓**INTERNET**→*www* ftp://ftp.qualcomm.com/mac/eudora/1.4.1/Eudora1.4.1.sea.hqx

Eudora Manual (for Macintosh) ✓**COMPUSERVE**→*go* inetresource→Libraries→*Search by file name:* eudman.sea ✓**AMERICA ONLINE**→*keyword* mcm→Software Libraries→Software Search→*Search by file name:* man151-word.sit ✓**INTERNET**→*www* ftp://ftp.tidbits.com/pub/tidbits/tisk/_MacTCP/mail/eudora-151-docs.hqx ...→*www* ftp://nic.switch.ch/mirror/info-mac/_Communication/_MacTCP/mail/eudora-151-docs.hqx

Email (PC)

Connectsoft ✓**INTERNET**→*www* http://www.connectsoft.com/

Eudora ✓**INTERNET** ...→*www* ftp://ftp.qualcomm.com/quest/eudora/windows/1.4/eudor144.exe ...→*www* ftp://sunsite.unc.edu/pub/micro/pc-stuff/ms-windows/winsock/apps/eudora14.exe ...→*www* http://gfecnet.gmi.edu/Software/Files/eudor144.zip ...→*www* http://www.acs.oakland.edu/oak/SimTel/win3/eudora.html ✓**COMPUSERVE**→*go* inetresource→Libraries →*Search by file name:* eudman.exe

MAIL-IT ✓**INTERNET** ...→*www* http://uts.cc.utexas.edu/~neuroses/mailit.html ...→*www* http://gfecnet.gmi.edu/Libraries/mailit.html

NETcetera ✓**INTERNET**→*www* ftp://ftp.airtime.co.uk/netcetera/netcetra.zip

Pegasus Mail ✓**INTERNET** ...→*www* ftp://risc.ua.edu/pub/network/pegasus/winpm2b4.zip ...→*www* http://gfecnet.gmi.edu/Software/Files/winpm2b4.zip ✓**COMPUSERVE**→*go* inetresource→Libraries→*Search by file name:* winpm.zip

Pronto IP ✓**INTERNET** ...→*www* ftp://ftp.best.com/pub/schaft/Internet_Apps/ip103.zip ...→*www* http://gfecnet.gmi.edu/Software/Files/prontoip.zip

FTP (Mac)

Anarchie ✓**INTERNET** ...→*www* ftp://ftp.mxm.com/Pub/Macintosh/InterNet/FTP/Anarchie-150.sit ...→*www* ftp://ftp.tidbits.com/pub/tidbits/tisk/_MacTCP/anarchie-15.hqx ✓**AMERICA ONLINE**→*keyword* mcm→Software Libraries→Software Search→*Search by file name:* Anarchie-140.sit ✓**COMPUSERVE**→*go* inetresource→Libraries→*Search by file name:* anarch.sit

Fetch MacTCP FTP client. ✓**INTERNET** ...→*www* ftp://ftp.tidbits.com/pub/tidbits/tisk/_MacTCP/fetch-212.hqx ...→*www* ftp://nic.switch.ch/mirror/info-mac/_Communication/_MacTCP/fetch-212.hqx ✓**AMERICA ONLINE**→*keyword* mcm→ Software Libraries→Software Search→*Search by file name:* Fetch 2.1.2.sit ✓**COMPUSERVE** →*go* inetresource→Libraries→*Search by file name:* fet212.sit

FTPd Mac FTP and Gopher server. ✓**INTERNET** ...→*www* ftp://ftp.tidbits.com/pub/tidbits/tisk/_MacTCP/ftpd-24.hqx ...→*www* ftp://nic.switch.ch/mirror/info-mac/_Communication/_MacTCP/ftpd-24.hqx ...→*www* ftp://src.doc.ic.ac.uk/packages/mac/umich/util/comm/ftpd2.2.sit.hqx

XFerIt FTP client. ✓**INTERNET** ...→*www* ftp://ftp.tidbits.com/pub/tidbits/tisk/_MacTCP/xferit-15b4.hqx ...→*www* ftp://src.doc.

Getting Wired **Navigating the Net**

Surfing programs: the clients (cont'd)

ic.ac.uk/packages/mac/umich/util/comm/xferit1.5b4.cpt.hqx ...→*www* ftp://nic.switch.ch/mirror/info-mac/_Communication_/_MacTCP/xferit-15b4.hqx

FTP (PC)

Cute FTP ✓INTERNET ...→*www* ftp://oak.oakland.edu/SimTel/win3/winsock/ctftp12.zip ...→*www* http://gfecnet.gmi.edu/Software/Files/ctftp12.zip

WS-FTP For Windows. ✓INTERNET ...→*www* ftp://ftp.usma.edu/pub/msdos/ws_ftp.zip ...→*www* http://gfecnet.gmi.edu/Software/Files/ws_ftp.zip ✓COMPUSERVE→*go* inetresource→Libraries→*Search by file name:* ws_ftp.zip

WS-FTP 32 Bit For Windows 95 and Win-NT. ✓INTERNET→*www* http://gfecnet.gmi.edu/Software/Files/ws_ftp32.zip ✓COMPUSERVE→*go* inetresource→Libraries→*Search by file name:* ws_ftp32.zip ✓AMERICA ONLINE→*keyword* pcsoftware→File Search→*Search by file name:* WS_FTP32.ZIP

WSN-FTPC ✓INTERNET ...→*www* ftp://rmii.com/pub2/mclouden/WSNWUTIL.ZIP ...→*www* http://gfecnet.gmi.edu/Software/Files/wsnwutil.zip

Gophers (Mac)

Gopher Surfer Lite (for 68K Macs) ✓INTERNET→*www* ftp://src.doc.ic.ac.uk//computing/document/formatting/tex/uk-tex/tools/gopher/Mac_server/GopherSurfer1.0b8_68K.sea.hqx

Gopher Surfer Lite (For Power PCs) ✓INTERNET→*www* ftp://src.doc.ic.ac.uk//computing/document/formatting/tex/uk-tex/tools/gopher

Turbo Gopher ✓INTERNET ...→*www* ftp://ftp.tidbits.com/pub/tidbits/tisk/_MacTCP/turbo-gopher-20.hqx ...→*www* ftp://ftp.sys.uea.ac.uk/Macintosh/TurboGopher2.0.sea.hqx ...→*www* ftp://ftp.mxm.com/Pub/Macintosh/InterNet/Gopher/TurboGopher2.0b5.sit ✓AMERICA ONLINE→*keyword* mcm→Software Libraries→Software Search→*Search by file name:* TurboGopher2.0b6.sit ✓COMPUSERVE→*go* inetresource→Libraries→*Search by file name:* tgophervr.sea

Gophers (PC)

BC Gopher ✓INTERNET ...→*www* ftp://ns.uam.es/pub/ms-windows/comm/bcg08ba3.exe ...→*www* http://gfecnet.gmi.edu/Software/Files/bcg08ba3.zip ...→*www* ftp://sunsite.unc.edu/pub/micro/pc-stuff/ms-windows/winsock/apps/bcgopher.zip

HGopher ✓INTERNET ...→*www* ftp://ftp.ccs.queensu.ca/pub/msdos/tcpip/winsock/hgoph24.zip ...→*www* ftp://sunsite.unc.edu/pub/micro/pc-stuff/ms-windows/winsock/apps/hgopher2.3.zip ...→*www* http://gfecnet.gmi.edu/Software/Files/hgoph24.zip

WS Gopher ✓INTERNET ...→*www* ftp://dewey.tis.inel.gov/pub/wsgopher/wsg-12.exe ...→*www* http://gfecnet.gmi.edu/Software/Files/wsg-12.zip

IRC (Mac)

Homer ✓INTERNET ...→*www* ftp://mrcnext.cso.uiuc.edu/pub/info-mac/comm/MacTCP/homer-0934.hqx ...→*www* ftp://ftp.tidbits.com/pub/tidbits/tisk/_MacTCP/homer-0934.hqx ...→*www* ftp://ftp.mxm.com/Pub/Macintosh/InterNet/IRC/Homer0.93.4.sit ✓AMERICA ONLINE→*keyword* mcm→Software Libraries→Software Search→*Search by file name:* Homer_.94.sit ✓COMPUSERVE→*go* inetresource→Libraries→*Search by file name:* Homer_.94.sit

IRC (PC)

IRCle ✓INTERNET→*www* ftp://ftp.tidbits.com/pub/tidbits/tisk/_MacTCP/ircle-20f4.hqx ✓AMERICA ONLINE→*keyword* mcm→Software Libraries→Software Search→*Search by file name:* ircle-1.5.5.sit

IRC 4 Windows ✓INTERNET ...→*www* ftp://winftp.cica.indiana.edu/pub/pc/win3/winsock/irc4win.zip ...→*www* http://gfecnet.gmi.edu/Software/Files/irc4win.zip

mIRC ✓INTERNET ...→*www* v ...→*www* http://gfecnet.gmi.edu/Software/Files/mirc32.zip ✓COMPUSERVE→*go* inetresource→Libraries→*Search by file name:* mirc31.zip

WS-IRC ✓INTERNET ...→*www* ftp://oak.oakland.edu/SimTel/win3/winsock/wsirc14g.zip ...→*www* http://gfecnet.gmi.edu/Software/Files/wsirc14g.zip

News readers (Mac)

NewsWatcher ✓INTERNET ...→*www* ftp://ftp.tidbits.com/pub/tidbits/tisk/_MacTCP/newswatcher-20b26.hqx ...→*www*

Navigating the Net Getting Wired

Surfing programs: the clients (cont'd)

ftp://nic.switch.ch/mirror/info-mac/_Communication/_MacTCP/news-watcher-20b26.hqx ...→*www* ftp://src.doc.ic.ac.uk/packages/mac/umich/util/comm/usenet/newswatcher2.0b20.sit.hqx ...→*www* ftp://ftp.mxm.com/Pub/Macintosh/InterNet/Newsgroups/Newswatcher/NewsWatcher.sit ✓AMERICA ONLINE→*keyword* mcm→Software Libraries→Software Search→*Search by file name:* NW 2.0b22 _.sit

Nuntius ✓INTERNET ...→*www* http://guru.med.cornell.edu/~aaron/nuntius/nuntius.html ...→*www* ftp://ftp.tidbits.com/pub/tidbits/tisk/_MacTCP/nuntius-203.hqx ...→*www* ftp://nic.switch.ch/mirror/info-mac/_Communication/_MacTCP/nuntius-203.hqx ✓COMPUSERVE→*go* inetresource→Libraries→*Search by file name:* nuntiu.cpt ✓AMERICA ONLINE→*keyword* mcm→Software Libraries→Software Search→*Search by file name:* Nuntius 1.2 Folder.sit

News readers (PC)

Free Agent ✓INTERNET ...→*www* ftp://ftp.forteinc.com/pub/forte/agent055.zip ...→*www* http://gfecnet.gmi.edu/Software/Files/agent055.zip

NewsXpress ✓INTERNET ...→*www* ftp://ftp.best.com/pub/schaft/Internet_Apps/nx10b3.zip ...→*www* http://gfecnet.gmi.edu/Software/Files/nx10b3.zip

QNews ✓INTERNET ...→*www* http://www.magi.com/~rdavies/qn09a5.zip ...→*www* http://gfecnet.gmi.edu/Software/Files/qn09a5.zip

Trumpet News ✓INTERNET ...→*www* ftp://ftp.cyberspace.com/pub/ppp/windows/utils/wt_wsk.zip ...→*www* http://gfecnet.gmi.edu/Software/Files/wt_wsk.zip ✓COMPUSERVE→*go* inetresource→Libraries→*Search by file name:* wtwsk1.zip

WinVN 16-bit ✓INTERNET ...→*www* ftp://ftp.ksc.nasa.gov/pub/winvn/win3/wv16_99_05.zip ...→*www* http://gfecnet.gmi.edu/Software/Files/wv16_99_05.zip

Ping (Mac)

MacPing ✓AMERICA ONLINE→*keyword* mcm→Software Libraries→Software Search→*Search by file name:* MacPing3.0DEMO .sit

MacWatcher ✓AMERICA ONLINE→*keyword* mcm→Software Libraries→Software Search→*Search by file name:* MacTCPWatcher-112.sit

Ping (PC)

NS-Lookup ✓INTERNET→*www* http://gfecnet.gmi.edu/Software/Files/nslookup.zip

Trumpet Ping ✓INTERNET→*www* http://gfecnet.gmi.edu/Software/Files/winapps2.zip

WS-Ping 16-bit ✓INTERNET→*www* http://gfecnet.gmi.edu/Software/Files/ws_ping.zip ✓COMPUSERVE→*go* inetresource→Libraries→*Search by file name:* wsping.zip

Telnet (Mac)

NCSA Telnet 2.6 ✓INTERNET ...→*www* ftp://ftp.ncsa.uiuc.edu/Mac/Telnet ...→*www* ftp://src.doc.ic.ac.uk/packages/mac/umich/util/comm/ncsatelnet2.6.sit.hqx ...→*www* ftp://ftp.tidbits.com/pub/tidbits/tisk/_MacTCP/ncsa-telnet-26.hqx ✓AMERICA ONLINE→*keyword* mcm→Software Libraries→Software Search→*Search by file name:* Telnet.2.6.1d4(68k).sit ✓COMPUSERVE→*go* inetresource→Libraries→*Search by file name:* telnet.sit

Telnet (PC)

CommNet for Windows ✓INTERNET ...→*www* http://www.radient.com/ ...→*www* http://gfecnet.gmi.edu/Software/Files/cmnet10e.exe

EWAN Telnet and terminal emulation program. ✓INTERNET ...→*www* http://www.lysator.liu.se/~zander/ewan.html ...→*www* http://gfecnet.gmi.edu/Software/Files/ewan1052.zip ...→*www* ftp://sunsite.unc.edu/pub/micro/pc-stuff/ms-windows/winsock/apps/ewan105.zip ✓COMPUSERVE→*go* inetresource→Libraries→*Search by file name:* ewan1.zip

NCSA Telnet ✓INTERNET→*www* http://gfecnet.gmi.edu/Software/Files/wintelb3.zip

QWS3270 Extra Terminal emulation. ✓INTERNET ...→*www* ftp://ftp.eznet.net/pub/win/winsock/telnet/qws3270e.zip ...→*www* ftp://sunsite.unc.edu/pub/micro/pc-stuff/ms-windows/winsock/apps/qws3270.zip ...→*www* http://gfecnet.gmi.edu/Software/Files/qws3270.zip

Trumpet Telnet Telnet client.

Getting Wired Navigating the Net

Surfing programs: the clients (cont'd)

✓INTERNET ...→*www* ftp://ftp.eznet.net/pub/win/winsock/telnet/ttel0_07.zip ...→*www* http://gfecnet.gmi.edu/Software/Files/winapps2.zip ✓**COMPUSERVE**→*go* inetresource→Libraries→*Search by file name:* ttelo.07.zip

UWTerm Telnet client. ✓**INTERNET** ...→*www* ftp://ftp.uni-trier.de/pub/pc/win3-koeln/tcpip/uwterm.zip ...→*www* http://gfecnet.gmi.edu/Software/Files/uwterm.zip

WinQVT 16-bit Telnet, mail, newsreader and ftp client. ✓**INTERNET** ...→*www* http://gfecnet.gmi.edu/Software/Files/qvtws398.zip ...→*www* ftp://biocserver.bioc.cwru.edu/pub/windows/qvtnet/qvtws398.zip

WAIS (Mac)

MacWAIS ✓**INTERNET** ...→*www* ftp://src.doc.ic.ac.uk/packages/mac/umich/util/comm/macwais1.25.cpt.hq ...→*www* ftp://ftp.tidbits.com/pub/tidbits/tisk/_MacTCP/mac-wais-129.hqx ✓**AMERICA ONLINE**→*keyword* mcm→Software Libraries→Software Search→*Search by file name:* MacWAIS 1.29.sit

WAIS (PC)

ElNet winWais ✓**INTERNET** ...→*www* ftp://ftp.einet.net/einet/pc/EWAIS204.EXE ...→*www* http://gfecnet.gmi.edu/Software/Files/ewais204.zip

WAIS for Windows ✓**INTERNET** ...→*www* ftp://ridgisd.er.usgs.gov/software/wais/wwais24.exe ...→*www* http://gfecnet.gmi.edu/Software/Files/wwais24.zip

Web browsers (Mac)

AOL Browser ✓**AMERICA ONLINE**→*keyword* aolpreview→Download Now→Enter Software Library

Mac Web ✓**INTERNET**→*www* http://galaxy.einet.net/ElNet/MacWeb/MacWebHome.html ✓**AMERICA ONLINE**→*keyword* mcm→Software Libraries→Software Search→*Search by file number:* macweb1.00A3.2.68K.sit

Mosaic ✓**INTERNET**→*www* http://www.ncsa.uiuc.edu/SDG/Software/MacMosaic/MacMosaicHome.html

Netscape ✓**INTERNET** ...→*www* ftp://ftp.netscape.com/netscape1.1/mac/netscape-1.1N.hqx ...→*www* ftp://ftp2.netscape.com/netscape1.1/mac/netscape-1.1N.hqx ...→*www* ftp://server.berkeley.edu/pub/netscape/mac/10N/netscape.sea.hqx

Web browsers (PC)

AirMosaic Express 1.1 ✓**INTERNET** ...→*www* http://www.spry.com/sp_prod/airmos/amosdown.html ...→*www* http://gfecnet.gmi.edu/Software/Files/amosdemo.zip

AOL Browser ✓**AMERICA ONLINE**→*keyword* aolpreview→Download Now→Enter Software Library

Cello ✓**INTERNET** ...→*www* http://www.law.cornell.edu/cello/cellotop.html ...→*www* http://gfecnet.gmi.edu/Software/Files/cello.zip *FAQ:* ✓**AMERICA ONLINE**→*keyword* pc software→File Search→Search by File Name→cello.zip

I-Comm Graphical WWW browser which doesn't require SLIP/PPP account. ✓**INTERNET** ...→*www* http://www.mcs.com/~jvwater/trial.html ...→*www* http://gfecnet.gmi.edu/Software/Files/icm100b5.zip

Mosaic ✓**INTERNET** ...→*www* http://www.ncsa.uiuc.edu/SDG/Software/WinMosaic/HomePage.html ...→*www* http://gfecnet.gmi.edu/Software/Files/mos20b4.zip ✓**AMERICA ONLINE**→*keyword* pc software→File Search→*Search by file name:* mos20b4.exe

Netscape ✓**INTERNET** ...→*www* ftp://ftp.netscape.com/netscape1.1/windows/ ...→*www* ftp://ftp2.netscape.com/netscape1.1/windows/ ...→*www* ftp://server.berkeley.edu/pub/netscape/windows/10N/InternetWorks ...→*www* http://www.booklink.com/ ...→*www* ftp://ftp.megaweb.com/beta/setup23b.exe

Slipknot ✓**INTERNET** ...→*www* http://www.interport.net/slipknot/slipknot.html ...→*www* http://gfecnet.gmi.edu/Software/Files/slnot110.zip

Spry Mosaic-CompuServe Edition ✓**COMPUSERVE**→*go* NetLauncher→Download NetLauncher

WinWeb ✓**INTERNET** ...→*www* http://www.einet.net/ElNet/WinWeb/WinWebHome.html ...→*www* http://gfecnet.gmi.edu/Software/Files/winweb.zip

World Wide Web Browser ✓**PRODIGY**→*jump* world wide web

Net Tech 289

Appendices

Company support
alphabetical by company

3+

3Com AutoLink and Transcend. ☎→*dial* 408-980-8204 ✓**COMPUSERVE**→*go* askforum ✓**INTERNET**→*www* http://www.telebit.com/ ...→*www* http://www.3com.com/

7th Level CD-ROM game publishers including the Monty Python series. ✓**COMPUSERVE**→*go* cdven→Messages *and* Libraries →7th Level

A

A T & T Bell Laboratories Dataport Express Modem, desktop and portable computers, servers, and telephones. ✓**COMPUSERVE**→*go* ncratt ✓**INTERNET**→*www* http://www.att.com/ ...→*www* http://www.paradyne.att.com/

Aatrix Software, Inc. Checkwriter Pro, TimeCard, Paycheck, Ultimate Payroll, and Checkprint. ✓**AMERICA ONLINE**→*keyword* aatrix

Abacus Concepts, Inc. Computer software and books, Becker-Tools, NoMouse, StatView, and Fast-CD. ☎→*dial* 616-698-8106 ✓**COMPUSERVE**→*go* winapc→Messages *and* Libraries→Abacus

Abaton Technology InterFax. ☎→*dial* 510-226-9694

Abbate Video, Inc. Video ToolKit products. ✓**AMERICA ONLINE**→*keyword* abbate ✓**INTERNET**→*www* ftp://ftp.abbate.com/publ

About Software Corporation 5PMPRO. ☎→*dial* 408-725-4252 ✓**EWORLD**→*go* about ✓**INTERNET**→*www* ftp://ftp.ascus.com/

Abstract Software WSI fonts. ✓**INTERNET**→*www* http://www.abstractsoft.com/Abstract/index.html

Abstract Technologies The abXgraphic adapter series. ✓**INTERNET**→*www* http://www.abstract.co.nz/

Access Software Under a Killing Moon (UKM), and other games. ☎→*dial* 801-364-7449 ✓**AMERICA ONLINE**→*keyword* accesssoftware ✓**COMPUSERVE**→*go* gambpub→Messages *and* Libraries →Access Software

Accolade Brett Hull Hockey, Barkley: Shut Up, Jam, Hardball, Jack Nicklaus Golf, Pele Soccer, Unnecessary Roughness, Elvira, Test Drive, and other games. ☎→*dial* 408-296-8800 ✓**AMERICA ONLINE**→*keyword* accolade ✓**COMPUSERVE**→*go* gamapub→Messages *and* Libraries→Accolade

Acculogic Corporation Linux. ☎→*dial* 714-454-8124

Acecad AceCAD. ☎→*dial* 408-655-1988

Acer America Acer Note, Acer Acros PC, Acer Power PC, Acer Altos, Acer View, Acer Fax, Pionex, Quantex, Maxtech/GVC, and VTech. ✓**AMERICA ONLINE**→*keyword* acer ✓**COMPUSERVE**→*go* pcvenf→Messages *and* Libraries →Acer America ✓**PRODIGY**→*jump* hardware support bb→Choose a Topic→Acer America

ACI US, Inc. 4th Dimension, 4D Runtime, FileForce, 4D Compiler, 4D Write, 4D Calc, Graph 3D, 4D Draw, 4D xRef, 4D Mover, and Object Master. ✓**COMPUSERVE** →*go* acius

Acorn Computers Computers such as the Risc PC, the A4000, the A3020, the A3010, Spectrum, and the Pocketbook. ✓**INTERNET**→*www* ftp://ftp.acorn.co.uk/ ...→*www* http://www.csv.warwick.ac.uk/~phudv/

Activision Shanghai I and II, Return to Zork, Simon the Sorcerer, Pitfall, Sargon V, World Class Chess, and other games. ✓**AMERICA ONLINE**→*keyword* activision ✓**COMPUSERVE**→*go* gampub→Messages *and* Libraries→Activision

Adaptec Full line of host adapters including AVA, the AHA series, and other products for portable and desktop computers. ☎→*dial* 408-945-7727 ✓**INTERNET**→*www* http://www.adaptec.com/ ...→*www* ftp://ftp.adaptec.com/pub/BBS

Adaptek Systems Kurzweil Voice. ✓**INTERNET**→*www* http://branch.com/adaptek/adaptek.html

ADC Telecommunications Homeworx, Soneplex, NetStar, Logix, FiberBase, FiberWatch, HDSKL, and QFLC. ✓**INTERNET** →*www* http://www.adc.com/

Adobe Systems & the Aldus Corporation PageMaker, PhotoShop, Premiere, Illustrator, Acrobat, After Effects, Mac type Twister, TrapWise, Color Central, Home Publisher, Intellidraw, and

Company Support

Fetch. ☎→*dial* 206-623-6984 ✓**AMERICA ONLINE**→*keyword* adobe ✓**COMPUSERVE**→*go* adobe ✓**INTERNET**→*www* ftp://ftp.adobe.com/pub/adobe/ ...→*www* http://www.adobe.com/

Advanced Gravis Computer Ultrasound series, MouseStick II, Phoenix, Firefall, GamePad, Eliminator, and Analog Pro Joystick. ☎→*dial* 604-431-5927 ✓**AMERICA ONLINE**→*keyword* advancedgravis ✓**COMPUSERVE**→*go* pcvenb *or* macdven→Messages *and* Libraries→Advanced Gravis ✓**INTERNET**→*www* http://www.st.nepean.uws.edu.au/pub/pc/ultrasound/ ...→*www* http://www.nacamar.net:8080/companies/Gravis

Advanced Logic Research Express VL, Evolution X, and the Revolution series. ☎→*dial* 714-458-6834 ✓**INTERNET**→*www* http://www.alr.com/

Advanced Micro Devices Microprocessors, CPUs, desktop and portable PCs. ✓**INTERNET**→*www* http://www.amd.com/

Advanced Software, Inc. DocuComp, InTouch, QuickTools, and DataView. ✓**AMERICA ONLINE**→*keyword* advancedsoftware

Aeon Technlogy Storage and memory products. ✓**INTERNET**→*www* http://www.aeon.com/aeon.html

Affinity Microsystems Ltd. Tempo II and Affinifile. ✓**AMERICA ONLINE**→*keyword* affinity

The AG Group, Inc. EtherPeek. ☎→*dial* 510-937-6704 ✓**EWORLD**→*go* aggroup ✓**INTERNET**→*www* ftp://ftp.aggroup.com/ ...→*www* http://www.aggroup.com/

Agfa Compugraphics Arcus II, FotoTune, FotoLook, and StudioScan II. ☎→*dial* 508-694-9577 ✓**COMPUSERVE**→*go* dtpbven→Messages *and* Libraries→Agfa

AI Expert Vortex, Turbo PROLOG, and PIE2. ✓**COMPUSERVE**→*go* aiexpert

Aladdin Systems, Inc. Aladdin Desktop Tools including Shortcut, SpeedBoost, Viewer, Unstuffed, Makeover, Magic Tools, and Secure Delete. ✓**AMERICA ONLINE**→*keyword* aladdin ✓**COMPUSERVE**→*go* maccven→Messages *and* Libraries→Aladdin Systems ✓**EWORLD**→*go* aladdin ✓**INTERNET**→*www* ftp://ftp.netcom.com/pub/le/leonardr/aladdin/

Alden Electronics, Inc Thermal printers. ✓**INTERNET**→*www* http://www.alden.com/

Alisa Systems, Inc. AlisaMail. ✓**INTERNET**→*www* http://www.alisa.com/

Allpen, Inc. Allpen and Earthquake. ✓**EWORLD**→*go* allpen

Alpha Software A5 and Alpha 4x4. ☎→*dial* 617-229-2915 ✓**COMPUSERVE**→*go* pcvene→Messages *and* Libraries→Alpha Software

Alta Technology Transputer Toolset, a series of compilers, and NodeView DeBugger. ✓**INTERNET**→*www* http://www.xmission.com/~altatech/

Altsys Corporation EPS Exchange, Fontographic, and Metamorphosis. ✓**AMERICA ONLINE**→*keyword* altsys ✓**COMPUSERVE**→*go* macbven→Messages *and* Libraries→Altsys Corporation

Alysis Software, Corp. eDisk, Superdisk, Resource Compressor, and Complete Delete. ✓**AMERICA ONLINE**→*keyword* alysis ✓**COMPUSERVE**→*go* maccven→Messages *and* Libraries→Alysis ✓**EWORLD**→*go* alysis

Ambrosia Software, Inc. Aperion, Chiral, ColorSwitch, Eclipse, Maelstrom, Oracle, BombShelter, and Snapz. ✓**AMERICA ONLINE**→*keyword* ambrosia ✓**COMPUSERVE**→*go* macdven→Messages *and* Libraries→Ambrosia Software ✓**EWORLD**→*go* ambrosia

Amdek Corportion Monitors. ☎→*dial* 408-922-4400

American Megatrends IBM PC hardware. ☎→*dial* 404-246-8780 ✓**INTERNET**→*www* ftp://ftp.megatrends.com/

Amstrad NextBase, Eden.

Andyne Computing Limited GQL and PaBLO. ☎→*dial* 613-548-1032 ✓**COMPUSERVE**→*go* winape→Messages *and* Libraries→Andyne Computing ✓**INTERNET**→*www* ftp://bbs.andyne.on.ca/ ...→*www* http://bbs.andyne.on.ca/

Animated Software P11, The Engine Of Life, and Viper PCI card. ✓**AMERICA ONLINE**→*keyword* animatedsoftware ✓**COMPUSERVE**→*go* graphbven→Messages *and* Libraries→Animated Software

Another Company What's In That Box?, PCX.EXE, Puzzle.EXE, Large Speech Library, Writer's Dream, Pascal Magic, 583 C Magic, BGI Draw, and the Educational series. ✓**AMERICA ONLINE**→*keyword* anothercompany

Apogee Software Mystic Towers, Hocus Pocus, Raptor:Call of the Shadows, Duke Nukem II, Blake Stone:Aliens of Gold, Hal-

Net Tech 293

Company Support

loween Harry, Bio Menace, Monster Bash, Major Stryker, Wolfenstein 3-D, and more. ☎→*dial* 508-365-2359 ✓**AMERICA ONLINE**→*keyword* apogee

Appian/ETMA Plato and Renegade. ✓**COMPUSERVE**→*go* graphbven→Messages *and* Libraries→Appian

Apple Computers, Inc QuickDraw, Powerbook, MacIntosh, QuickTime, PowerBook, SimpleText, SNAps, Quadra, StyleWriter, PhotoFlash, AppleShare, and many more. ✓**COMPUSERVE**→*go* aplsup ✓**EWORLD**→*go* apple ✓**INTERNET**→*www* http://www.apple.com/ …→*www* ftp://ftp.support.apple.com/

Applicom Software Industries TeamConference. ✓**INTERNET**→*www* http://www.applicom.co.il/

Arabesque Software Ecco Professional. ☎→*dial* 206-881-0905

Arcada Software QBackUp and BackUpExec. ✓**COMPUSERVE**→*go* pcvenh→Messages *and* Libraries→Arcada Software ✓**INTERNET**→*www* http://www.arcada.com/

Archtek America Corp. SmartLink. ☎→*dial* 818-912-3980

Argosy Software, Inc. RunPC/Network, RunPC/Remote, and Software Bridge. ✓**AMERICA ONLINE**→*keyword* argosy

Ariel Publishing QDFx, CDEF City Volumes I-II, Menu Mill, and Odd I/O. ✓**AMERICA ONLINE**→*keyword* ariel

Arion Software, Inc. MasterCook software. ☎→*dial* 512-327-9814 ✓**INTERNET**→*www* ftp://ftp.arion.com/ …→*www* http://www.arion.com/

Arrick Robotics Mobile robots. ✓**INTERNET**→*www* http://www/robotics.com

Articulate Systems, Inc. PowerSecretary, PowerLaw, ASI Voice Record, and Voice Navigator. ✓**AMERICA ONLINE**→*keyword* articulate ✓**COMPUSERVE**→*go* macaven→Messages *and* Libraries→Articulate Systems

Artifice, Inc. DesignWorkshop. ✓**AMERICA ONLINE**→*keyword* artifice

Artisoft LanTastic Product series. ✓**INTERNET**→*www* http://www.artisoft.com

Artist Graphics PCI Graphics Board, MicroStation, Flexicon, and WinSprint. ☎→*dial* 612-631-7669 ✓**AMERICA ONLINE**→*keyword* artistgraphics ✓**COMPUSERVE**→*go* artist

Asante Technologies AsanteView, MacConi, MacRing, NetDock, and NetExtender. ✓**EWORLD**→*go* asante ✓**INTERNET**→*www* ftp://ftp.asante.com/ …→*www* http://www.asante.com/

Ascend Communications, Inc. Multiband series, Pipeline 50 series, and MAX series. ☎→*dial* 508-814-2302 ✓**INTERNET**→*www* http://www.internex.net/ascend/home.html …→*www* http://www.ascend.com

Ascom Timeplex Express Routing/Switching products including ST-1000, IAN, ARISO, BNP, and RouterBridge. ✓**INTERNET**→*www* http://www.timeplex.com/

askSam Systems Database software. ☎→*dial* 904-584-8287 ✓**COMPUSERVE**→*go* winapf→Messages *and* Libraries→askSam Systems ✓**INTERNET**→*www* http://199.44.46.2/askSam.htm

ASLAN Computer SK-4145DE, SK-4230DE, TK-4230DE, and TK-4330DE. ✓**INTERNET**→*www* http://www.gus.com/emp/aslan/aslan.html

ASP Safpak, Skymap, Scanex, and War 2000. ✓**COMPUSERVE**→*go* aspforum

AST Research Advantage, Ascentia, Bravo, Manhattan, Premmia MX, and GRiD. ☎→*dial* 714-727-4723 ✓**PRODIGY**→*jump* ast ✓**COMPUSERVE**→*go* astforum

Asymetrix Asymetrix Digital Video Producer, ToolBook, 3DF/X, InfoModeler, and MediaBlitz!. ☎→*dial* 206-451-1173 ✓**AMERICA ONLINE**→*keyword* asymetrix ✓**COMPUSERVE**→*go* winapa→Messages *and* Libraries→Asymetrix

Atari Lynx game series, Jaguar game series, and Atari 8-bit series. ✓**COMPUSERVE**→*go* atarigaming

ATI Technologies ATI Pro Turbo Mach 64, ATI Mach 32, and drivers. ☎→*dial* 905-764-9404 ✓**COMPUSERVE**→*go* graphaven→Messages *and* Libraries→ATI Technologies ✓**INTERNET**→*www* http://www.atitech.ca/

Attachmate NetWizard, Visual Basic, Visual REXX, and PowerBuilder. ☎→*dial* 206-649-6660 ✓**COMPUSERVE**→*go* attachmate ✓**INTERNET**→*www* http://www.atm.com/

Atticus Software Christmas Lights, Super 8, Vista, and RAMDiskSaver. ✓**AMERICA ONLINE**→*keyword* atticus ✓**COMPUSERVE**→*go* macdven→Messages *and* Libraries→Atticus

Company Support

Audio Electric Systems Boy Scout RecordKeeper. ✓EWORLD→*go* aes

Auspex Systems, Inc Specializes in Netservers such as the NS 7000/200 series, NS 7000/500 series, and NS 7000/600 series. ✓INTERNET→*www* http://www.auspex.com/

auto*des*sys, Inc. form*Z. ✓AMERICA ONLINE→*keyword* formz

Autodesk Inc. AutoCAD, 3-D Studio, Animator, Multimedia Explorer, Science series, Chaos. ☎→*dial* 415-507-5921 ✓COMPUSERVE→*go* acad ✓INTERNET→*www* ftp://ftp.autodesk.com/

AutoMap, Inc. AutoMap. ☎→*dial* 206-646-9130 ✓EWORLD→*go* automap

Avalon Engineering PresenterPad. ✓EWORLD→*go* avalon

Avid Technology, Inc. VideoShop and Media Suite. ✓AMERICA ONLINE→*keyword* avid

Avocat Systems, Ltd. Law Office Manager. ✓AMERICA ONLINE→*keyword* avocat ✓EWORLD→*go* avocat

B

Baseline Publishing Init Manager, Talking Moose, Vantage, Thunder 7, and WINspool. ✓AMERICA ONLINE→*keyword* baseline ✓COMPUSERVE→*go* winapd <or> maccven→Messages *and* Libraries→Baseline Publishing ✓EWORLD→*go* baseline

BaseView Products, Inc. WireManager, QTools, IQUE, ClassManager Plus, and ClassFlow. ✓AMERICA ONLINE→*keyword* baseview

Bentley Systems CAD products including: MicroStation, MicroStation Modeler, MicroStation Review, MicroStation Field, MicroStation, and PowerDraft. ☎→*dial* 610-458-5353 ✓AMERICA ONLINE→*keyword* bentley ✓INTERNET→*www* http://www.bentley.com/ …→*www* ftp://ftp.bentley.com/

Berkeley Software Design BSD/OS. ✓INTERNET→*www* http://www.bsdi.com/info/

Berkeley Systems, INc. After Dark, Expresso Calendar, Address Book, and Launch Pad. ✓AMERICA ONLINE→*keyword* berkeley ✓COMPUSERVE→*go* winapc *or* macbven →Messages *and* Libraries→Berkeley Systems ✓EWORLD→*go* berkeley

Best Data Modems. ✓COMPUSERVE→*go* modemvendor→Messages *and* Libraries→Best Data

Best!Ware MYOB. ✓AMERICA ONLINE→*keyword* myob ✓COMPUSERVE→*go* accounting→Messages *and* Libraries→MYOB

Bethesda Softworks Elder Scroll, Delta-V, NCAA Basketball, Terminator 2029 series, and other games. ☎→*dial* 301-990-7552 ✓AMERICA ONLINE→*keyword* bethesda ✓COMPUSERVE→*go* gamapub→Messages *and* Libraries→Bethesda Softworks

Beyond! Inc. PatchRules, Beyond Mail, Winrules, and Zoomit. ✓AMERICA ONLINE→*keyword* beyond ✓COMPUSERVE→*go* pcvenc →Messages *and* Libraries→Beyond! Inc.

Binary Software SquareOne. ✓EWORLD→*go* binary

Bit Jugglers KidsWorld and UnderWare. ✓AMERICA ONLINE→*keyword* bitjugglers

Bitstream, Inc. A full line of fonts. ✓COMPUSERVE→*go* dtpaven →Messages *and* Libraries→Bitstream ✓INTERNET→*www* http://www.bitstream.com/

Black Diamond Software Multimedia devices including Display/Graphics boards, printers, and keyboards. ✓INTERNET→*www* http://blackdiamond.com/

Blue Sky Softwarel, Inc. RoboHelp and WinMaker Pro. ✓INTERNET→*www* http://www.blue-sky.com/

Blueridge Technologies OPTIX, Printer Plug In, and OCR.. ✓EWORLD→*go* blueridge ✓INTERNET→*www* http://www.blueridge.com/

Boca Research Sound Blaster Pro, Boca Modem, and FAXWorks. ☎→*dial* 407-241-1601 ✓COMPUSERVE→*go* modemvendor →Messages *and* Libraries→Boca Research

Borland International ReportSmith, InterBase, Delphi, Turbo Pascal, Paradox, dBASE, Brief, and ObjectVision. ☎→*dial* 408-439-9096 ✓COMPUSERVE→*go* borland ✓INTERNET→*www* ftp://ftp.borland.com/pub …→*www* http://www.borland.com/

Bowers Development AppMaker. ✓AMERICA ONLINE→*keyword* bowers

Brainstorm Products Accelerators. ✓AMERICA ONLINE→*keyword* brainstorm

Brightwork Development NetWare. ☎→*dial* 408-988-4004

Net Tech 295

Company Support

Broderbund Software CD-ROM children's series including: Ancient Art of War, Lode Runner, The Print Shop, Geometry, The Toy Shop, Jam Session, Calculus, Physics, The Print Shop Paper Pack, The Toy Shop Refill Pack, the Carmen Sandiego series, Kid Pix series, and Prince of Persia series. ☎→*dial* 415-883-5889 ✓ AMERICA ONLINE→*keyword* broderbund ✓ COMPUSERVE→*go* bb

Buerg Software Encoding and decoding programs. ☎→*dial* 707-778-8944

Bungie Software Marathon, Minotaur, Pathways Into Darkness, and other games. ✓ AMERICA ONLINE→*keyword* bungie

Business Sense Business Sense. ✓ AMERICA ONLINE→*keyword* businesssense

Byte By Byte, Corporation Sculpt series and Soft F/X. ☎→*dial* 512-795-0032 ✓ AMERICA ONLINE→*keyword* bytebybyte ✓ COMPUSERVE→*go* anvena→Messages *and* Libraries→Byte By Byte

ByteWorks ORCA languages. ✓ AMERICA ONLINE→*keyword* byte

C

Cabletron Systems, Inc. DNI card series, ethernet products such as Ether Switch, token rings, WAN Products, SPECTRUM, and Specialty MIMs such as TP-mim. ☎→*dial* 603-335-3358 ✓ COMPUSERVE→*go* ctron ✓ INTERNET→*www* ftp://ctron.com/

Caere Corporation PageKeeper, OmniPage Direct, OmniPage, and OmniPage Pro. ☎→*dial* 408-395-1631 ✓ AMERICA ONLINE→*keyword* caere

Calamus Calamus. ✓ INTERNET→*www* http://web.city.ac.uk/~cb170/CALAMUS/calamus.html

Calera Recognition Systems OCR software. ☎→*dial* 408-773-9068 ✓ COMPUSERVE→*go* winape→Messages *and* Libraries→Calera

Caligari Corporation trueSpace and viewSpace. ✓ AMERICA ONLINE→*keyword* caligari ✓ COMPUSERVE→*go* grvenc→Messages *and* Libraries→Caligari

Callisto Corporation Spin Doctor, Super Mines, Super Maze Wars, and other games. ✓ AMERICA ONLINE→*keyword* callisto

Cambridge Scientific Computing, Inc. Software including CS ChemDraw and CS ChemOffice. ✓ INTERNET→*www* ftp://ftp.camsci.com/ ...→*www* http://www.camsci.com/

Campbell Services Time management software. ☎→*dial* 810-559-6434 ✓ COMPUSERVE→*go* winapc→Messages *and* Libraries→Campbell Services

Canon LaserBeam printers, Bubble Jet printers, and LBP 860 printers. ✓ COMPUSERVE→*go* canon ✓ INTERNET→*www* http://www.cre.canon.co.uk/index.html

Capstone Software Legend of Zorro, Trump Castle 3, Terminator 2:Chess Wars, Operation Body Count, Discoveries of the Deep, Corridor 7, Grandmaster Chess, and other games. ☎→*dial* 305-374-6820 ✓ AMERICA ONLINE→*keyword* capstone

Captain's Software Jigsaw Deluxe and Puzzle Collection. ✓ EWORLD→*go* captsoftware

Cardinal Technologies SNAP-plus, PCMCIA high speed modems, VGA800, and WARP Speed. ☎→*dial* 717-293-3074 ✓ AMERICA ONLINE→*keyword* cardinal

Carnation Software NetCruiser software, MacTopic, MacTopic Plus, SBMac, and LinksToMac. ✓ INTERNET→*www* ftp://ftp.netcom.com/pub/ca/carnation/ ...→*www* http://www.netcom.com/

Casa Blanca Works, Inc. Drive7, DriveCD, Blue Parrot, DriveShare, and Manager7. ✓ AMERICA ONLINE→*keyword* casablanca

Casady & Greene, Inc. Snap Mail, Conflict Catcher, Quickdex, Crash Barrier, Fluent Laser Font Library, Crescendo, and Glastnost; games such as Crystal Crazy, Spaceway 200 Paradena, Mission Thunderbolt, and more. ✓ AMERICA ONLINE→*keyword* casady ✓ COMPUSERVE→*go* maccven→Messages *and* Libraries→Casady & Greene ✓ EWORLD→*go* casady ✓ INTERNET→*www* http://www.casadyg.com/

CASE Asymetrix, IEF, Excelerator 2, and DOM102. ✓ COMPUSERVE→*go* caseforum

Castelle Fax Server, LANpress, and JetPress. ☎→*dial* 408-496-1807 ✓ COMPUSERVE→*go* lanven→Messages *and* Libraries→Castelle

Cayman Systems, Inc. GatorAccess series, including: GatorStar iHR, GatorRoute iR, GatorAccess, GatorBox CS, GatorStar GX, GatorLink, GatorShare and GatorPrint. ✓ INTERNET→*www* ftp://ftp.cayman.com/ ...→*www* http://www.cayman.com/CaymanHomePage.html

Company Support

CBIS, Inc. Network OS, CD Connection, and Desk-to-Desk. ☎→*dial* 404-446-0485

cc:Mail cc:Mail Mobile, cc:Mail Desktop, cc:Mail Pager Gateway, cc:Mail Link, cc:Mail View, and cc:Router. ☎→*dial* 415-691-0401 ✓**INTERNET**→*www* http://www.ccmail.com:8001/

CE Software QuickMail, QuicKeys, TimeVision Network Scheduler, CalendarMaker, and ProKey. ✓**AMERICA ONLINE**→*keyword* cesoftware ✓**COMPUSERVE**→*go* macaven→Messages *and* Libraries→CE Software ✓**EWORLD**→*go* ce ✓**INTERNET**→*www* http://www.cesoft.com/

Central Point PC Tools for IBM and MacIntosh. ☎→*dial* 503-690-6650

Certus Novi. ☎→*dial* 503-484-6669

CH Products FlightStick, ProPedals, and Trackball. ☎→*dial* 619-598-3224 ✓**AMERICA ONLINE**→*keyword* chproducts

Charles River Analytics Open Sesame. ✓**AMERICA ONLINE**→*keyword* opensesame ✓**COMPUSERVE**→*go* macdven→Messages *and* Libraries→Charles River Analytics ✓**EWORLD**→*go* sesame

CheckMark Software, Inc. Payroll, Cash Ledger, and Multi Ledger. ✓**EWORLD**→*go* checkmark

Chena Software InfoDepot. ✓**EWORLD**→*go* chena

Cheyenne Software, Inc. ARCServe, Monitrix, FAXserve, and InocuLAN. ☎→*dial* 516-484-3445 ✓**COMPUSERVE**→*go* ncsaven→Messages *and* Libraries→Cheyenne InocuLAN ✓**INTERNET**→*www* http://www.chey.com/...→*www* ftp://ftp.chey.com/

Chinon America CD-ROM and floppy disk drives. ☎→*dial* 310-320-4160

Chipcom Corp. OnLine, OnDemand, OnCore, Onsemble series, and more. ✓**INTERNET**→*www* http://www.chipcom.com/

Cisco Systems LAN2LAN product line. ✓**INTERNET**→*www* http://www.cisco.com/

Citizens America Corp Series of dot-matrix printers. ☎→*dial* 310-453-7564

Citrix Systems A Plus Server. ☎→*dial* 305-346-9004

Clarion Software TopSpeed. ☎→*dial* 305-785-2594 ✓**COMPUSERVE**→*go* clarion

Claris Corp FileMaker Pro, ClarisDraw, ClarisWorks, ClarisImpact, MacPaint, MacWrite, and From Alice to Ocean. ☎→*dial* 408-987-7421 ✓**AMERICA ONLINE**→*keyword* claris ✓**COMPUSERVE**→*go* claris ✓**EWORLD**→*go* claris ✓**INTERNET**→*www* ftp://ftp.claris.com/...→*www* http://www.claris.com/

Clark Development Corp USR-PC board software. ☎→*dial* 801-261-8976

Clear Software Fishbone, allClear, and Bug. ☎→*dial* 617-965-5406 ✓**COMPUSERVE**→*go* grvenc→Messages *and* Libraries→Clear Software

Clippers Databases. ✓**COMPUSERVE**→*go* clipper

CNET Full line of token rings, ethernet cards, and ARCnet NICs. ☎→*dial* 408-954-1787

Coconut Computing Inc. CocoNet. ☎→*dial* 619-456-0815

Coda Music Software Finale. ✓**AMERICA ONLINE**→*keyword* coda ✓**COMPUSERVE**→*go* midibven→Messages *and* Libraries→Coda Music

Codenoll Full line of ethernet cards and FDDI cards. ☎→*dial* 914-965-1972

Colorado Memory Systems Memory systems. ☎→*dial* 303-635-0650 ✓**COMPUSERVE**→*go* pcvenf→Messages *and* Libraries→Colorado Memory Sys

Colorocs Color printers. ✓**INTERNET**→*www* http://www.nav.com/colorocs.colorocs.html

Colossal Graphics, Inc. Peace in the Streets. ✓**EWORLD**→*go* colossal

Columbia Data Products SCSI drivers for WD-7000 FAST. ☎→*dial* 407-862-4724

Commsoft Full line of genealogy software. ☎→*dial* 707-838-6373

Compaq Computer Systems Contura PCs, Concerto PCs, LTE PCs, Desktop Pro, Presario, Prolinea, Mini Tower, ProLiant, Prosignia, NetFlex, and Pagemarq. ☎→*dial* 713-378-1418 ✓**AMERICA ONLINE**→*keyword* compaq ✓**COMPUSERVE**→*go* cpqforum ✓**PRODIGY**→*jump* compaq ✓**INTERNET**→*www* http://www.compaq.com/

Compex Inc. Readylink and a full line of internet hardware accessories. ☎→*dial* 714-630-2570

Compton's NewMedia CD-ROM publisher including Compton's Encyclopedia. ✓**COMPUSERVE**→*go* cdven→Messages *and* Libraries→Compton's NewMedia ✓**IN-**

Net Tech 297

Company Support

TERNET→*www* http://www.comptons.com

CompuAdd 425C Laptop, 450CS Floppy Drive, 425 CXL, 425TFX Modem, 386SX hard drive, and CompuAdd TV card. ✓**COMPUSERVE**→*go* compuadd

ComputaLabel Label Designer, MacBARCODA, and MacThermal. ✓**EWORLD**→*go* computalabel

Computer Associates dBFast, Realia, Realizer, C++, CommonView, RET, Visual Express, and Visual Realia. ☎→*dial* 516-434-1753 ✓**COMPUSERVE**→*go* caidev ✓**INTERNET**→*www* http://www.cai.com/

Computer Peripherals, Inc. Modems. ☎→*dial* 714-470-1761 ✓**AMERICA ONLINE**→*keyword* comp-peripherals ✓**COMPUSERVE**→*go* vivamodem→Messages *and* Libraries→Computer Periph.

Computer Software Management, Inc. PC Manager. ✓**INTERNET**→*www* http://www.cm-soft.com/cms

Computone IntelliServer, IntelliPort, IntelliCluster, ValuPort, and MPA2. ☎→*dial* 404-343-9737 ✓**INTERNET**→*www* http://www.computone.com/

Comtrol Multiport boards. ☎→*dial* 612-631-8310

ConJelCo MacIntosh software and gambling games including Blackjack Trainer. ✓**INTERNET**→*www* ftp://ftp.conjelco.com/ ...→*www* http://www.conjelco.com

Connectix QuickCam, Maxima, CDU, RAM Doubler, CPUs, On The Road, InfoLog, Virtual, HandOff II. ✓**AMERICA ONLINE**→*keyword* connectix ✓**COMPUSERVE**→*go* macaven→Messages *and* Libraries→Connectix ✓**EWORLD**→*go* connectix

ConnectSoft, Inc. E-Mail Connection (EMC). ✓**COMPUSERVE**→*go* winapb→Messages *and* Libraries→ConnectSoft ✓**INTERNET**→*www* http://www.connectsoft.com/

Convex Computer Corporation Computer products including Exemplar, CX Soft software, and the C series. ✓**INTERNET**→*www* gopher://gopher.convex.com/ ...→*www* http://www.convex.com

Corbis Media Fine imagery software. ✓**AMERICA ONLINE**→*keyword* corbis

Core International Legato, Unipress, Pronto, NetManage, WRQ, and Pictronix. ☎→*dial* 407-241-2929 ✓**EWORLD**→*go* core ✓**INTERNET**→*www* http://www.corsys.com/core/

Corel Corp. CorelDraw, PhotoPaint, CorelFLOW, Ventura, SCSI, and Corel Gallery. ☎→*dial* 613-728-4752 ✓**AMERICA ONLINE**→*keyword* corel ✓**COMPUSERVE**→*go* corel ✓**INTERNET**→*www* http://www.cybergate.com/~compugrf/corel/index.html ...→*www* http://www.corel.ca

Cornerstone Piccolo and DynaAcess. ☎→*dial* 408-435-8943 ✓**INTERNET**→*www* http://www.corsof.com/

Corvus System, Inc. Neady Net. ☎→*dial* 408-972-9154

CoSA After Effects, AfterImage, and Hitchcock. ✓**AMERICA ONLINE**→*keyword* cosa

CoStar Corporation AddressMate, LabelWriter, Trackball, and AddressWriter. ☎→*dial* 203-661-6292 ✓**AMERICA ONLINE**→*keyword* costar ✓**COMPUSERVE**→*go* maccven→Messages *and* Libraries→CoStar ✓**EWORLD**→*go* costar

CP/M Decision Mate V and KAYPRO. ✓**COMPUSERVE**→*go* cpmforum

Cray Research, Inc. Research computer systems including CRAY T3D, CRAY C90; the massively parallel processing system (MPP), parallel-vector supercomputers, large memory systems including CRAY J90 series, and more. ✓**INTERNET**→*www* http://www.cray.com/

Creative Labs Video Blaster Series and ShareVision series. ☎→*dial* 405-742-6660 ✓**COMPUSERVE**→*go* blaster ✓**EWORLD**→*go* creativesolutions ✓**INTERNET**→*www* http://www.creaf.com/ ...→*www* ftp://ftp.creaf.com/pub/welcome.html

CrossTies Corp. CrossTies. ✓**COMPUSERVE**→*go* winapg→Messages *and* Libraries→CrossTies Corp.

CrystalGraphics Flying Fonts and Topas Pro. ✓**COMPUSERVE**→*go* graphbven→Messages *and* Libraries→CrystalGraphics

CTOS/Pathway ATE, SG series, Cluster Cards, Fasport, R:Base, OFIS, and NT S3 Driver. ✓**COMPUSERVE**→*go* ctos

CTX International Full line of monitors. ☎→*dial* 909-594-8973

D

D-Link Systems, Inc. LANsmart network and internet hardware accessories. ☎→*dial* 714-455-1779

Company Support

DAB Engineering, Inc. (a.k.a. Aerospace) DAB Ascent and DAB Orbit. ✓ **INTERNET**→www http://www.isso.org/Industry/DAB/DAB1.html

Dallas Semiconductor Silicon timed circuits, CPU supervisors, digital potentiometers, thermal products, microcontrollers, and telecommunication products. ✓ **INTERNET**→www http://www.dalsemi.com/

Dancing Rabbit Series of Hyper-Card educational programs. ✓ **AMERICA ONLINE**→keyword dancingrabbit

Dariana Technology Group FloppyDriver. ☎→dial 714-236-1388

Darwin Systems Custom software packaging. ☎→dial 301-251-9206 ✓ **INTERNET**→www http://www.deltanet.com/users/darwin/

Data I/O TaskLink, PromLink-6, ChipLab series, and ProMaster series. ☎→dial 206-882-3211 ✓ **INTERNET**→www http://www.data-io.com/

Data Technology USR HST series. ☎→dial 408-942-4010

DataEase DQL, DE, Express, and Dialogue. ✓ **COMPUSERVE**→go dataease

DataPak Software Word Solution Engine, Luster Pic, Matrix Engine, and Mem Manager. ✓ **AMERICA ONLINE**→keyword datapak

Dataproducts Corp. Full line of printers and printer utilities. ☎→dial 818-887-8167 ✓ **COMPUSERVE**→go dtpbven→Messages <and> Libraries→Dataproducts ✓ **INTERNET**→www ftp://ftp.dpc.com/

DataWatch Virex, ScreenLink, Citadel, and Shredder. ☎→dial 919-549-0042 /508-988-6373 ✓ **AMERICA ONLINE**→keyword datawatch

Davidson & Associates MathBlaster, Alge-Blaster, Kid CAD, Kid Phonics, Kid Keys, Kid Works, The Cruncher, Spell It, and Word Attack. ✓ **AMERICA ONLINE**→keyword davidson

Dayna Communications SafeDeposit, DaynaSTAR, DaynaPORT, DaynaFILE, and Etherprint. ☎→dial 801-269-7398 ✓ **AMERICA ONLINE**→keyword dayna ✓ **INTERNET**→www http://www.dayna.com/ ...→www ftp://ftp.dayna.com/

DayStar Digital MHz Turbo, Apple Adaptors, PowerPro 601, PowerCard 601, Turbo 601, Universal PowerCache, Universal Turbo 040, and Photomatic. ☎→dial 404-967-2978 ✓ **AMERICA ONLINE**→keyword daystar ✓ **COMPUSERVE**→go macaven→Messages and Libraries→DayStar Digital ✓ **EWORLD**→go daystar

Deadly Games Bomber, Battle of Britain II, U-Boat Aces, M4, and other games. ✓ **EWORLD**→go deadly

DEC PC Support Hinote, IDE, LA75, DSP3105s, SVGA, DECpc320P, and XL590. ☎→dial 508-496-8800 ✓ **COMPUSERVE**→go decpc

Dell Computer Corp Dimension, Latitude, PowerLine, Dell SCSI Array, EMS-1434 External Media System, UltraScan monitor, VS14 and VS15 monitors, and OmniPlex. ☎→dial 512-728-8528 ✓ **AMERICA ONLINE**→keyword dell ✓ **COMPUSERVE**→go hardware support bb→Choose a Topic→Dell Computer ✓ **PRODIGY**→jump dell ✓ **INTERNET**→www http://www.es.dell.com/ ...→www ftp://dell1.dell.com/dellbbs

Delrina Technology, Inc. Delrina WinFax PRO series, Fax Broadcast, Fax Mailbox, WinComm PRO, Communications Suite package, and PerForm. ☎→dial 416-441-2752 ✓ **AMERICA ONLINE**→keyword delrina ✓ **COMPUSERVE**→go delrina ✓ **INTERNET**→www http://www.delrina.com/ ...→www ftp://ftp.delrina.com/pub

Delta Drawing Today Delta Drawing Today. ☎→dial 800-395-5009 ✓ **AMERICA ONLINE**→keyword industryconnection→Companies D-H→Delta Drawing Today

Delta Tao Software WonderPrint, Color MacCheese, Monet, Polly MacBeep, Eric's Ultimate Solitaire, Spaceward Ho!, and Strategic Conquest. ✓ **AMERICA ONLINE**→keyword deltatao

DeltaComm Development Telix. ☎→dial 919-481-9399

DeltaPoint, Inc. DeltaGraph, FreezeFrame, and Animated Desktop. ✓ **AMERICA ONLINE**→keyword deltapoint ✓ **COMPUSERVE**→go winapd or macaven→Messages and Libraries→Delta Point ✓ **EWORLD**→go Deltapoint

Deneba Software Canvas, Spelling Coach, UtraPaint, and Big Thesaurus. ✓ **AMERICA ONLINE**→keyword daneba ✓ **COMPUSERVE**→go macbven→Messages and Libraries→Deneba Software ✓ **EWORLD**→go deneba

DeScribe DeScribe. ☎→dial 916-929-3237

DesignWare MyHouse. ✓ **COMPUSERVE**→go graphbven→Messages

Company Support

and Libraries→Designware

Diamond Multimedia Systems Video Star, Stealth, Speedstar, Viper, FastBus, Sonic Sound, and Video Card. ✓**AMERICA ONLINE**→*keyword* diamond ✓**COMPUSERVE**→*go* graphbven→ Messages *and* Libraries→Diamond ✓**INTERNET**→*www* http://www.diamondmm.com/ ...→*www* ftp://ftp.diamondmm.com/

DigiBoard/DigiCom Systems PC/Xe and MC/Xe systems, C/X system, EPC/X system, Acceleport C1 & C2, and ISDN LAN adapters. ☎→*dial* 612-943-0812 ✓**INTERNET**→*www* http://www.digibd.com/

Digidesign Sound Designer, Pro School, PTII-III, and other digital audio recording products. ✓**COMPUSERVE**→*go* mididven→Messages *and* Libraries→Digidesign

Digital Communications Irma and 10Net products. ☎→*dial* 513-433-5080

Digital Eclipse Software, Inc. Defender, Robotron, Joust, DiskMaster, OTA, Zounds. ✓**AMERICA ONLINE**→*keyword* digitaleclipse ✓**COMPUSERVE**→*go* macdven→Messages *and* Libraries→Digital Eclipse

Digital Equipment Corp Full line of software, personal computers, storage products, networking products, including: HiNote, Digital Venturis, Celebris, Prioris, Remote Server Manager System, DECwriter, DEClaser. ✓**AMERICA ONLINE**→*keyword* digital ✓**INTERNET**→*www* http://www.digital.com/info.html ...→*www* http://www.dec.com/

Digital Ocean, Inc. Tarpon Groupers. ✓**EWORLD**→*go* digocean

Digital Vision, Inc. ComputerEyes and TelevEyes. ☎→*dial* 617-329-8387 ✓**AMERICA ONLINE**→*keyword* digitalvision ✓**COMPUSERVE**→*go* digvis

Digitool, Inc. MCL (MacIntosh Common Lisp). ☎→*dial* 617-576-7680 ✓**INTERNET**→*www* ftp://ftp.digitool.com/ ...→*www* http://www.digitool.com/

Direct Software SecureInit, NetLook, and HeapSizer. ✓**AMERICA ONLINE**→*keyword* direct

Distributed Processing Tech. Full line of cache controllers. ☎→*dial* 407-831-6432

Don Johnston, Inc. Jokus, Kenx, TalkAbout, and WriteOutLoud. ✓**EWORLD**→*go* johnston

Dream Maker MacGallery and Cliptures. ✓**EWORLD**→*go* dreammaker

Dreamworld DuelTris, DreamVoir, DreamGrafix, and View 32. ✓**AMERICA ONLINE**→*keyword* dreamworld

DSP Solutions Video boards. ☎→*dial* 415-494-1621

Dubl-Click Software Corporation ClickChange, ClickTrax, GoFigure, Icon Mania, MenuFonts, WetPaint, WetSet, MacTut, and ProGlyph. ✓**AMERICA ONLINE**→*keyword* dublclick ✓**EWORLD**→*go* dublclick ✓**INTERNET**→*www* http://empnet.com/dublclick/ ...→*www* ftp://empnet.com/pub/DublClick/

Dudley Software DOORWAY. ☎→*dial* 615-966-3574

DYA/Digisoft Innovations Twilight II, YouDrawIt, and DyaExibit A. ✓**AMERICA ONLINE**→*keyword* industryconnection→Companies D-H→DYA/Digisoft

Dynamic Microprocessor pcAnywhere and ASCOM IV. ☎→*dial* 516-462-6638

Dynaware USA, Inc. Ballade, DynaPerspective, GS/SC7 Controller, Jigsaw It!, Kirei!, and Super MIDI Player. ✓**AMERICA ONLINE**→*keyword* dynaware ✓**INTERNET**→*www* http://www.dynaware.com/~dynaware/

E

Eastman Kodak Co. Digital imaging products including full lines of scanners, printers, workstations, and much more. ✓**AMERICA ONLINE**→*keyword* kodak ✓**COMPUSERVE**→*go* kodak ✓**INTERNET**→*www* ftp://ftp.kodak.com/ ...→*www* http://www.kodak.com/

EBBS PlanetBashers, Pigskin, and Crypto. ✓**AMERICA ONLINE**→*keyword* ebbs

Edmark Corporation Bailey's Book House, Imagination Express, KidDesk, Millie's Math House, Sammy's Science House, Thinkin' Things, and Touchwindow. ✓**AMERICA ONLINE**→*keyword* edmark

EFI Power Protection Full line of PC surge protectors. ✓**INTERNET**→*www* http://www.icw.com/efi/efi.html

Eidetic, inc. Notion. ✓**EWORLD**→*go* eidetic

ELAN Software GoldMine. ✓**COMPUSERVE**→*go* winapa→Messages *and* Libraries→ELAN Software ✓**INTERNET**→*www* http://www.elan.com/

Electric Image Electric Image and Mr. Font. ✓**AMERICA ONLINE**→*keyword* electricimage

Electronic Arts Games including

Company Support

Tony LaRussa III, NBA Live, Magic Carpet, PGA Tour Golf, and NHL 95. ✓**COMPUSERVE**→*go* gamapub→Messages *and* Libraries→Electronic Arts ✓**INTERNET**→*www* http://www.ea.com/

Electronic Courseware Toon Up, Note Speller, Musicus, Lime, and Musique. ✓**AMERICA ONLINE**→*keyword* courseware

Ellery Systems, Inc. FastLane. ✓**INTERNET**→*www* http://www.esi.com/esi/index.html

Emerald Systems Disk and tape storage systems. ☎→*dial* 619-673-4617

Emigre Fonts Hundreds of font types. ✓**AMERICA ONLINE**→*keyword* emigre

Enable Software Grammatik IV and Enable. ☎→*dial* 518-877-6316 ✓**COMPUSERVE**→*go* pcvena→Messages *and* Libraries→Enable Software

Encore Computer Corporation Infinity 90 mainframe series and Infinity SP storage products. ✓**INTERNET**→*www* http://www.encore.com/

Ensoniq Synthesizers and Soundscape line of PC sound cards. ✓**COMPUSERVE**→*go* mididven→Messages <and> Libraries→Ensoniq ✓**INTERNET**→*www* http://www.cs.colorado.edu/~mccreary/vfx/ ...→*www* http://www.ensoniq.com

Envisions Twain Driver, Envision It, TextBridge, and 3000C Scanner. ✓**COMPUSERVE**→*go* grvenc →Messages *and* Libraries→Envision

Epson America, Inc. Impact printer, PX/HX series, image scanners, ActionNote, a complete line of inkjet and laser printers, fax machines, modems. ☎→*dial* 310-782-4531 ✓**COMPUSERVE**→*go* epson

Equilibrium DeBabelizer. ☎→*dial* 415-332-6152

Equinox Systems, Inc. Megaport. ☎→*dial* 305-746-0282

eSoft Inc. TBBS system and IPAD. ☎→*dial* 303-699-8222 ✓**INTERNET**→*www* http://www.esoft.com/

Exabyte Full line of tape drives. ☎→*dial* 913-492-8751

Excel Software MacAnalyst, MacDesigner, and MacA & D. ✓**EWORLD**→*go* excel

Expert Software, Inc. Astronomer and Color Paint. ✓**AMERICA ONLINE**→*keyword* expert ✓**COMPUSERVE**→*go* pcvenh→Messages *and* Libraries→Expert Software

EZX Publishing EZ-Forms. ☎→*dial* 713-280-8180

F

Farallon Computing StarController, Starlet, MicroSCSI, LocalPath, and PhoneNET. ☎→*dial* 510-865-1321 ✓**AMERICA ONLINE**→*keyword* farallon ✓**COMPUSERVE**→*go* pcvene *or* maccven→Messages *and* Libraries→Farallon Computing ✓**EWORLD**→*go* farallon ✓**INTERNET**→*www* ftp://ftp.farallon.com/pub/ ...→*www* http://www.farallon.com/

FarPoint Tech. Tab/Pro, Professional ToolBox, Aware, Spread VBX, and more. ✓**COMPUSERVE**→*go* winapf→Messages *and* Libraries→FarPoint Tech

Focus Enhancements System 7.5, L-TV Portable, EtherLAN, TurboStar, TurboNet. ✓**AMERICA ONLINE**→*keyword* focus ✓**COMPUSERVE**→*go* macdven→Messages *and* Libraries→Focus Enhancements ✓**EWORLD**→*go* focus ✓**INTERNET**→*www* ftp://ftp.netcom.com/pub/fo/focus/

FontBank Hundreds of type faces. ✓**AMERICA ONLINE**→*keyword* fontbank ✓**COMPUSERVE**→*go* dtpaven→Messages *and* Libraries →FontBank

Foresight Technology, Inc. Drafix and Planix. ✓**COMPUSERVE**→*go* pcvena→Messages *and* Libraries→Foresight Corp. ✓**INTERNET**→*www* http://www.fsti.com ...→*www* ftp://ftp.fsti.com

Fourth World SuperCard and SCAuthor. ✓**EWORLD**→*go* 4w ✓**INTERNET**→*www* ftp://ftp.cts.com ...→*www* ftp://192.188.72.27

Fractal Design Poser, Painter, Really Cool textures, Dabbler, and Sketcher. ✓**AMERICA ONLINE**→*keyword* fractal

Frame Technology FrameMaker. ☎→*dial* 408-975-6729 ✓**COMPUSERVE** *go* dtpaven→Messages *and* Libraries→Frame Technology ✓**INTERNET**→*www* ftp://ftp.frame.com/ ...→*www* http://www.frame.com/

France & Associates Instant Math, Fastball Fractions, WorldCap, and the Early Learning series. ✓**AMERICA ONLINE**→*keyword* france

Franklin Quest Company Values Quest and Ascend. ☎→*dial* 801-977-1991 ✓**AMERICA ONLINE**→*keyword* franklin ✓**COMPUSERVE**→*go* oavendor→Messages *and* Libraries→Franklin Quest

Freedom Software Freedom

Company Support

Desktop. ✓**INTERNET**→*www* http://freedom.lm.com/freedom.html

FreeMail, Inc. FreeMail and CallHome. ✓**AMERICA ONLINE**→*keyword* freemail

Fujitsu Hundreds of consumer electronic and computer products. ✓**COMPUSERVE**→*go* pcvenj→Messages *and* Libraries→Fujitsu ✓**INTERNET**→*www* http://www.fujitsu.com/

FullWrite FullWrite. ✓**AMERICA ONLINE**→*keyword* fullwrite

Funk Software Proxy and Wanderlink. ✓**COMPUSERVE**→*go* pcvenf→Messages *and* Libraries→Funk Software

Future Domain Full line of SCSI adaptors. ☎→*dial* 714-253-0432

Future Labs, Inc. TALKShow. ✓**AMERICA ONLINE**→*keyword* futurelabs

FutureSoft Engineering DynaComm series. ☎→*dial* 713-588-6870 ✓**COMPUSERVE**→*go* winapa→Messages *and* Libraries→Future Software Engr ✓**INTERNET**→*www* http://www.fse.com/

Futurus Corporation Email software. ✓**COMPUSERVE**→*go* pcveng→Messages *and* Libraries→Futurus Corporation

FWB Software, Inc. SledgeHammer. ✓**EWORLD**→*go* fwb

G

Galacticomm Major BBS, Galactibox, Major Gateway, and GalactiBoard. ☎→*dial* 305-583-7808 ✓**AMERICA ONLINE**→*keyword* galacticomm ✓**COMPUSERVE**→*go* pcvenj→Messages *and* Libraries →Galacticomm

GameTek Bureau 13, Brutal, Saturday Night Live, Quarantine, Star Crusader, and several Nintendo titles. ✓**AMERICA ONLINE**→*keyword* gametek

GammaLink MS-Mail, GammaLink, and GammaPage. ☎→*dial* 408-745-2216 ✓**COMPUSERVE**→*go* pcvend→Messages *and* Libraries →GammaLink

GAP Development Company GAP BBS software. ☎→*dial* 714-493-3819

Gateway 2000 Liberty, ColorBook, Family, 4DX2-66, P4D-66, and P5 series. ☎→*dial* 605-232-2224 ✓**AMERICA ONLINE**→*keyword* gateway ✓**COMPUSERVE**→*go* gateway ✓**PRODIGY**→*jump* gateway 2000 bb ✓**INTERNET**→*www* http://www.mcs.com/~brooklyn/home.html …→*www* ftp://ftp.sei.cmu.edu/pub/gateway2000

Gateway Communications Token rings. ☎→*dial* 703-960-8509

GCC Technologies BLP Elite, Business LaserPrinter, Personal LaserPrinter, WideWriter, WriteImpact, ColorFast, Utrasave, and UltraDrive. ✓**AMERICA ONLINE**→*keyword* gcc ✓**COMPUSERVE**→*go* macbven→Messages *and* Libraries→GCC Technologies

GDE Systems, Inc. SOCET Set. ✓**INTERNET**→*www* http://www.gdesystems.com/

GDT Softworks, Inc. PowerPrint, StyleScript, PLOTTERgeist, and PowerPlot. ✓**AMERICA ONLINE**→*keyword* gdt

General DataComm Ind. ATM software. ☎→*dial* 203-598-0593 ✓**INTERNET**→*www* http://www.gdc.com/

General Magic Magic Cap and Telescript. ✓**AMERICA ONLINE**→*keyword* generalmagic

GeneXus GeneXus. ✓**COMPUSERVE**→*go* pcvenc→Messages *and* Libraries→GENEXUS

Genicom Full line of printers. ☎→*dial* 703-949-1576

Genoa Systems Genoa 8500 and Phantom 64. ✓**COMPUSERVE**→*go* graphbven→Messages *and* Libraries→Genoa Systems

GeoClock GeoClock. ☎→*dial* 703-241-7980

Geoworks Backgrounds, Bindery, GeoCalc, GeoComm, GeoDraw, GeoFile, and GeoWrite. ✓**AMERICA ONLINE**→*keyword* geoworks

Gibson Research Disk utility software. ☎→*dial* 714-362-8848

GigaTrend, Inc. Series of high capacity tape drives. ☎→*dial* 619-931-9469

Global Village Communications OneWorld, TelePort series, FaxWorks, TP Gold, PP Merc, and GlobalFax. ✓**AMERICA ONLINE**→*keyword* globalvillage ✓**COMPUSERVE**→*go* modemvendor→Messages *and* Libraries→Global Village Comm ✓**EWORLD**→*go* global ✓**INTERNET**→*www* http://info.globalvillag.com/welcome.html …→*www* http://ftp.globalvillag.com/

GoldDisk Multimedia software. ☎→*dial* 905-602-7534

Graphic Simulations Corporation F/A-18 Hornet, Korean

Company Support

Crisis, Hellcats Over the Pacific, Missions at Leyte Gulf, and other games. ✓**AMERICA ONLINE**→*keyword* graphicsimulations ✓**INTERNET**→*www* http://www.computek.net/graphsim/gsc.html ...→*www* ftp://ftp.computek.net/graphsim/

Graphisoft US, Inc. ArchiCAD. ✓**AMERICA ONLINE**→*keyword* graphisoft

Graphsoft, Inc. MiniPascal, MiniCad, Azumuth, and Blueprint. ✓**AMERICA ONLINE**→*keyword* graphsoft

Greenleaf Software Commlib, FoxPro, and other database software. ✓**COMPUSERVE**→*go* pcvenb→Messages *and* Libraries→Greenleaf Software ✓**INTERNET**→*www* http://www.transformation.com/foxpro/index.html

Ground Zero Software Partware and Critical Mass. ✓**EWORLD**→*go* groundzero

Gryphon Software Corporation Morph, Colorforms Computer Fun Set, Gryphon Dynamic Effects, Batch It!, and GDE. ✓**AMERICA ONLINE**→*keyword* gryphon ✓**INTERNET**→*www* http://www.gryphonsw.com ...→*www* ftp://ftp.gryphonsw.com

Gupta Corporation SAL, SDK, DLLS, Quest, Ranger, Solo, SQL Base, and SQL WIndows. ✓**INTERNET**→*www* http://www.gupta.com/

GVC Technologies LANode workstation and modems. ☎→*dial* 201-579-2380 ✓**PRODIGY**→*jump* hardware support bb→Choose a Topic→Maxtech/GVC

H

Hash, Inc. Animation Master. ☎→*dial* 206-574-5619 ✓**AMERICA ONLINE**→*keyword* hash ✓**COMPUSERVE**→*go* anvena→Messages *and* Libraries→Hash, Inc. ✓**INTERNET**→*www* ftp.netcom.com/pub/ga/gavingav/

Hayes Microcomputer MacIntosh software, OPTIMA series, Smartcom series, and ULTRA series. ☎→*dial* 800-874-2937 ✓**INTERNET**→*www* gopher://gopher.almac.co.uk/11/business/comms/hayes

hDC Corporation First Apps, hDC Express Meter, and hDC Windows Express. ☎→*dial* 206-869-2418 ✓**AMERICA ONLINE**→*keyword* hdc ✓**COMPUSERVE**→*go* winapa→Messages *and* Libraries→hDC

HDS Computer terminals and software including ViewStation Xcelerator LX, FX, Ultra, and Dual series. ✓**INTERNET**→*www* http://www.hds.com/

Heizer Software Hypercard. ✓**INTERNET**→*www* http://www.webcom.com/~heizer

Helios USA PCShare, EtherShare, and netOctopus. ☎→*dial* 408-864-7976 ✓**AMERICA ONLINE**→*keyword* helios

Helix Software Netroom (a memory manager for PCs) and Multimedia Cloaking. ✓**COMPUSERVE**→*go* pcveng→Messages *and* Libraries→Helix Software

Helix Technologies Helix, Helix Express, NetRoom, and other software. ✓**COMPUSERVE**→*go* macdven→Messages *and* Libraries→Helix Technologies ✓**EWORLD**→*go* helix ✓**INTERNET**→*www* http://www.mcs.net/~skeller/

Hercules Graphite Power, Stingray VLB, and Dynamite Pro. ✓**COMPUSERVE**→*go* graphbven→Messages *and* Libraries→Hercules ✓**INTERNET**→*www* http://www.dnai.com/~hercules/

Hewlett Packard Computers, networks, printers, scanners, plotters, faxes, and much more. ☎→*dial* 208-344-1691 ✓**AMERICA ONLINE**→*keyword* hp ✓**COMPUSERVE**→*go* hpsys ✓**INTERNET**→*www* http://www.hp.com/ ...→*www* ftp://ftp-boi.external.hp.com/

Hilgraeve KopyKat and HaWin. ✓**COMPUSERVE**→*go* pcvenf→Messages *and* Libraries→Hilgraeve

Hitachi Instruments, Inc. Full line of mainframe computers, storage systems, open systems hardware and software, and services. ✓**INTERNET**→*www* http://www.hii.hitachi.com/

Honeywell, Inc. Full line of computer and electronic products. ✓**INTERNET**→*www* http://www.iac.honeywell.com/

Houston Instruments Plotter series. ☎→*dial* 512-873-1477

HSC Software Kai's Power Tools, Convolver, and Bryce. ✓**AMERICA ONLINE**→*keyword* hsc ✓**COMPUSERVE**→*go* graphbven→Messages *and* Libraries→HSC Software (PC) <and> HSC Software (Mac) ✓**EWORLD**→*go* hsc ✓**INTERNET**→*www* ftp://ftp.netcom.com/pub/hs/hsc/

Hybrid Networks, Inc. Remote Link Adapter and Moder 110. ✓**INTERNET**→*www* ftp://hybrid.com/ ...→*www* http://www.hybrid.com/

Net Tech 303

Company Support

Hyperbole Quantum Gate CD-ROM. ✓**COMPUSERVE**→*go* hyperbole

I

IBM Complete personal and business computer systems. ☎→*dial* 905-316-4244 (Canada)/919-517-0001 ✓**AMERICA ONLINE**→*keyword* ibm ✓**COMPUSERVE**→*go* ibm ✓**PRODIGY**→*jump* ibm ✓**INTERNET**→*www* http://www.ibm.com/ …→*www* ftp://software.watson.ibm.com/pub

IBVA Technolgies IBVA Developer and NuBus. ✓**AMERICA ONLINE**→*keyword* ibva

id Software, Inc. Doom, Doom2, Heretic. ☎→*dial* 508-368-4237 ✓**INTERNET**→*www* http://ftp.idsoftware.com …→*www* ftp://ftp.idsoftware.com

IKOS Systems Voyager series and NSIM Hardware Accelerator. ✓**INTERNET**→*www* http://www.ikos.com/

Image Club Graphics Art & Type, ArtRoom, and LetterPress. ✓**EWORLD**→*go* icg

IMC Networks Full line of network hardware and ethernet cards. ☎→*dial* 714-724-0930

imMedia Several custom icons, including iContraption. ✓**AMERICA ONLINE**→*keyword* imMedia

Impediment Memory products. ✓**INTERNET**→*www* http://www.impediment.com/

IMSI Software Menu Direct and Backup Direct. ☎→*dial* 415-454-2893

Industrial Innovations Data-Hand. ✓**INTERNET**→*www* http://www.cis.princeton.edu/grad/dwallach/tifaq/keyboards.html

Informix Databases. ✓**INTERNET**→*www* http://www.informix.com/ …→*www* ftp://ftp.informix.com

Ingres Databases. ✓**INTERNET**→*www* http://www.adc.com/ingres/ing-top.html

Inline Design 3 in Three, Mutant Beach, Swamp Gas USA, Tesserae, and Darwin's Dilemma. ✓**AMERICA ONLINE**→*keyword* inline ✓**COMPUSERVE**→*go* maccven→Messages *and* Libraries→Inline Design

Innovative Data Design, Inc. TCXL, TPrint, CAM, and TTSR. ✓**COMPUSERVE**→*go* pcvenc→Messages *and* Libraries→Innovative Data

Innovative Quality Software SAMM, SAW, and other sound products. ✓**COMPUSERVE**→*go* midicven→Messages *and* Libraries→Innovative Qual SW

Insignia Solutions, Inc. SoftWindows, SoftPC, AccessPC, Rapid CD, and MacDisk. ✓**AMERICA ONLINE**→*keyword* insignia ✓**COMPUSERVE**→*go* macven→Messages *and* Libraries→Insignia Solutions ✓**INTERNET**→*www* http://www.insignia.com/ …→*www* ftp://ftp.insignia.com/

InstallSHIELD InstallSHIELD. ✓**COMPUSERVE**→*go* winapc→Messages *and* Libraries→InstallSHIELD

Intel Pentium processors, Pentium OverDrive, IntelDX4, and ProShare. ☎→*dial* 916-356-3600/503-264-7999 ✓**AMERICA ONLINE**→*keyword* intel ✓**INTERNET**→*www* http://www.intel.com/

Intellimation Shakespeare's Life & Times CD-ROM, Teaching, Learning & Technology CD-ROM, Easy Grade Pro, and Chemical Bonding series. ✓**AMERICA ONLINE**→*keyword* intellimation

Interactive Image EWB. ✓**COMPUSERVE**→*go* pcvenc→Messages *and* Libraries→Interactive Images

InterCon Systems Corporation InterPrint, NFS/Share, Planet X, TCP/Connect, TCP/Toolz & Toys, UUCP/Connect, Watchtower, and WorldLink. ☎→*dial* 703-709-5538 ✓**AMERICA ONLINE**→*keyword* intercon ✓**EWORLD**→*go* intercon ✓**INTERNET**→*www* ftp://ftp.intercon.com/

Intergraph Personal workstations, graphics accelerators, servers, workstation furniture, InterPro/CLIX, software, and much more. ✓**INTERNET**→*www* http://www.ingr.com/

InterPlay Productions Two Towers, Out Of This World, Track Meet, Lexicross, Dvorak Top 30, Neuromancer, and other games. ☎→*dial* 714-252-2822 ✓**AMERICA ONLINE**→*keyword* interplay ✓**COMPUSERVE**→*go* gambpub→Messages *and* Libraries→InterPlay ✓**INTERNET**→*www* http://www.interplay.com/website/homepage.html

Intuit TurboTax, Quicken, and QuickBooks. ✓**AMERICA ONLINE**→*keyword* intuit ✓**PRODIGY**→*jump* intuit

Iomega Corp. ZIP Drive, Bernoulli 230, and Iomega Drivers. ☎→*dial* 801-392-9819 ✓**AMERICA ONLINE**→*keyword* iomega ✓**COMPUSERVE**→*go* pcvene *or* macven→Messages *and* Libraries→Iomega Corporation ✓**INTERNET**→*www* http://www.iomega.com/

Company Support

IQ Software Laptop-To-Lan, and token rings. ☎→*dial* 206-821-5486

IS Robotics Corp. Genghis, Pebbles, Hermes. ✓**INTERNET**→*www* http://isr.com/~isr

ISIS International ISIS Notes, Flash-Data, System 7, Antwerp, Construction, Architrieve, Dental, Graphic Bid, Hathor, Horus, Medical, and PrIntelligence. ✓**AMERICA ONLINE**→*keyword* isis ✓**INTERNET**→*www* ftp://ftp.netcom.com/pub/is/isis/

Island Graphics Corporation IslandTrapper and IslandChecker. ✓**AMERICA ONLINE**→*keyword* island

J

JDR Microdevices VESA local buses and a series of motherboards, monitors, and modems. ☎→*dial* 408-494-1430 ✓**COMPUSERVE**→*go* jdr

Jetfax Fax software. ☎→*dial* 415-324-1259

JetForm JetForm. ☎→*dial* 613-563-2894

JL Cooper data9PIN, dataMaster, dataSYNC, CS-Edit, AVSIX, PPS series, SoftMix, and MSB PLUS. ✓**AMERICA ONLINE**→*keyword* jlcooper

JP Software TCMD and 4DOS. ✓**COMPUSERVE**→*go* pcvenb→Messages *and* Libraries→JP Software

JPEGView JPEGView. ✓**AMERICA ONLINE**→*keyword* jpegview ✓**INTERNET**→*www* http://www.med.cornell.edu/jpegview.html

K

Kaleida Labs Media Player and ScriptX. ✓**INTERNET**→*www* http://www.kaleida.com/

KAOS AntiVirus KAOS. ✓**COMPUSERVE**→*go* antivirus

KAT, Inc. Sound products. ✓**INTERNET**→*www* http://mozart.mw3.com:80/kat/

Keep It Simple software Solar powered add-ons for PCs. ✓**EWORLD**→*go* kiss

Kensington NoteBook Traveler, MicroSaver, Expert Mouse, Turbo Mouse, Masterpiece Plus, Power Backer Plus, and Power Traveler Adaptor. ✓**AMERICA ONLINE**→*keyword* kensington ✓**EWORLD**→*go* kensington

Kent Marsh, Ltd. FolderBolt, Cryptomatic, NightWatch II, and QuickLock. ☎→*dial* 713-522-8921 ✓**AMERICA ONLINE**→*keyword* kentmarsh ✓**EWORLD**→*go* kentmarsh ✓**INTERNET**→*www* ftp://ftp.neosoft.com/pub/kentmarsh/

Keytronics Full line of keyboards. ☎→*dial* 509-927-5288

Kingston Technology Memory chips. ☎→*dial* 714-435-2636

Koala Acquisitions MacVision Digitizer. ✓**AMERICA ONLINE**→*keyword* koala

Korenthal Associates PhDBase and 4Print. ✓**COMPUSERVE**→*go* pcvenb→Messages *and* Libraries→Korenthal Assocs.

Kurta Corp. Drawing tablets. ☎→*dial* 602-243-9440

Kurzweil Music Systems K2000, Micropiano, Mark series, RG100, RG200, MASS, K2500 series, and DMTi. ✓**AMERICA ONLINE**→*keyword* kurzweil

L

L & L Productions GBBS Pro. ✓**AMERICA ONLINE**→*keyword* industryconnection→Companies I-M→l&l Productions

Lanark Technologies Pythia Web browser. ✓**INTERNET**→*www* http://pythia.com/

Landmark Research WinProbe. ✓**COMPUSERVE**→*go* pcvenh→Messages *and* Libraries→Landmark Research

LandWare, Inc. MoonLight, PhotoShow, StartUpScreenManager, NewsHopper, and EasyTyper. ✓**EWORLD**→*go* landware ✓**INTERNET**→*www* http://www.planet.net/landware/

Language Systems LS FORTRAN, LS Object Pascal CD-ROM, Math77, Source Code Analyzer, TSiGraphics, SuperPlot, and SoftPolish. ☎→*dial* 703-709-0134 ✓**AMERICA ONLINE**→*keyword* langsys ✓**EWORLD**→*go* languagesystems ✓**INTERNET**→*www* ftp://cais.com/

LANSource Tech. WinPort, ViaFax, and FaxPort. ✓**COMPUSERVE**→*go* lanven→Messages *and* Libraries→LANSource Tech

Lapis L-TV Interface. ✓**AMERICA ONLINE**→*keyword* lapis

Lari Software LightningDraw GX. ✓**INTERNET**→*www* ftp://ftp.cybernetics.net/pub/users/lari ...→*www* http://www.cybernetics.net/pub/users/lari

Laser Master High-end laser printers. ☎→*dial* 612-835-5463

LaserTools Printer software. ☎→*dial* 510-420-1942 ✓**COMPUSERVE**→*go* winape→Messages

Net Tech 305

Company Support

and Libraries→LaserTools

Lattice CCompiler/Library and Secret Disk II. ☎→*dial* 708-916-1200

Lawrence Productions Trolls, Dragons & Mechanics, Mathology, Word Wizards, The Lost Tribe, Nigel's World, Discovering America, and other games. ✓**AMERICA ONLINE**→*keyword* lawrence

Leader Technologies PowerMerge. ✓**AMERICA ONLINE**→*keyword* leader ✓**COMPUSERVE**→*go* macdven→Messages *and* Libraries→Leader Technologies

Leading Edge CPC-52xx, MT6000, CPC series including WinTower and Fortiva, DC series, and the LEP series. ☎→*dial* 508-836-3971 ✓**AMERICA ONLINE**→*keyword* leadingedge ✓**PRODIGY**→*jump* hardware support bb→Choose a Topic→Leading Edge

Lexmark Full line of printers including the Optra series, MarkNet series, ValuWriter series, and the Execjet. ☎→*dial* 606-232-5238 ✓**INTERNET**→*www* http://www.lexmark.com/

Lind Portable Power Lind batteries, power packs, and power adaptors. ✓**AMERICA ONLINE**→*keyword* lind

Link Technologies Full line of terminals. ☎→*dial* 510-623-6680

LinksWare, Inc. AppleWorks, AppleWriter, Mouse Text, Mouse Graphics, Apple//cc monitor ROM, ProDos, LookUp, ThunderScan, CAMS, DPS, Word Benders, Escape from the Logic Spiders, and LinksWare. ✓**AMERICA ONLINE**→*keyword* linksware

Logic eXtension Resources LXR*TEST and InterActive. ✓**EWORLD**→*go* lxr

Logitech Full line of hardware. ✓**COMPUSERVE**→*go* logitech

Lotus Development Corp. Lotus 1-2-3, AmiPro, Lotus Organizer, Lotus Approach, cc: Mail, and Lotus Notes. ☎→*dial* 404-395-7707/617-693-7001 ✓**COMPUSERVE**→*go* lotus ✓**INTERNET**→*www* http://www.lotus.com/

LucasArts Entertainment Indy Desktop Adventures, Full Throttle, Dark Forces, Defender of the the Empire, TIE Fighter, Sam & Max Hit the Road, Rebel Assault, Day of the Tentacle, and other games. ☎→*dial* 415-257-3070 ✓**AMERICA ONLINE**→*keyword* lucas ✓**COMPUSERVE**→*go* gamapub→Messages *and* Libraries→LucasArts ✓**INTERNET**→*www* ftp://ftp.lucasarts.com/

Lumina Decision Systems, Inc. Demos. ✓**INTERNET**→*www* ftp://ftp.rahul.net/pub/lumina/...→*www* http://www.lumina.com/lumina/

Lunar Productions Edit-16, NiftyList, GSBug, NameOBJ, and Foundation. ✓**AMERICA ONLINE**→*keyword* industryconnection→Companies I-M→Lunar Productions

M

MacroMedia SoundEdit, Fontographer, Freehand, Illustrator, Director, Script X, and Fontographer. ✓**AMERICA ONLINE**→*keyword* macromedia ✓**COMPUSERVE**→*go* macromedia ✓**EWORLD**→*go* macromedia

Madenta Communications Telepathic, ScreenDoors, PreDict-ate, Revolving Doors, and PROXi. ✓**EWORLD**→*go* madenta

Madge Networks Token rings. ☎→*dial* 408-955-0262 ✓**COMPUSERVE**→*go* pcveng→Messages *and* Libraries→Madge Networks

Magee Enterprises, Inc. Automenu. ☎→*dial* 404-446-6650 ✓**COMPUSERVE**→*go* pcvena→Messages *and* Libraries→Magee Enterprises

Magnetic Technology QIC series. ✓**INTERNET**→*www* http://argus-inc.com/MagTech/MagTech.html

Magnus Computing, Inc. Unitools. ✓**INTERNET**→*www* http://www.magnus1.com/magnus/about.html

Mainsoft Corporation MAINWinCDK. ✓**INTERNET**→*www* http://www.mainsoft.com/

Mainstay Phyla, MacFlow, WinFlow, Plan & Track for Mac and Windows, MarkUp, MarcoPolo, VIP-C, VIP-BASIC, VIP Database Manager, and Captivate. ✓**AMERICA ONLINE**→*keyword* mainstay ✓**COMPUSERVE**→*go* macaven→Messages *and* Libraries→Mainstay

Management Science Association ALLright and COPYright Pro. ✓**AMERICA ONLINE**→*keyword* msa

Manhattan Graphics Corporation Ready, Set, Go! ✓**AMERICA ONLINE**→*keyword* manhattangraphics

Mannesman Tally Printers. ☎→*dial* 206-251-5513

Mansfield Software Group KEDIT and KEDITW. ☎→*dial* 203-429-3784 ✓**COMPUSERVE**→*go* pcvena→Messages *and* Libraries→Mansfield Software

Company Support

Manzanita Software Systems BusinessWorks and Flexware. ☎→*dial* 916-791-2061 ✓**COMPUSERVE**→*go* accounting→Messages *and* Libraries→Manzanita Software

Mark/Space Softworks Products include: Communicate Lite, Mark/Space ZModem Tool, and PageNOW! ☎→*dial* 408-293-7290 ✓**INTERNET**→*www* ftp://ftp.netcom.com/pub/ms/mspace/

MarketMaster MarketMaster. ✓**AMERICA ONLINE**→*keyword* marketmaster

Martinsen's Software Packit!, Wallpaper Manager, and INI Manager. ✓**AMERICA ONLINE**→*keyword* martinsen

MathSoft MathCad and MathBrowser. ✓**INTERNET**→*www* http://www.mathsoft.com/

MathWorks, Inc., The Engineering software including MATLAB, and SIMULINK. ✓**INTERNET**→*www* ftp://ftp.mathworks.com/ …→*www* http://www.mathworks/com/

Matrox Graphics Inc. Quick Access, IlumFast, and Millinium. ☎→*dial* 514-685-6008 ✓**COMPUSERVE**→*go* graphbven→Messages *and* Libraries→Matrox

Maximum Computer Technologies, Inc. DoubleVision. ✓**INTERNET**→*www* http://www.maxtech.com/

Maximum Strategy, Inc. Gen 5 series and ProFILE series. ✓**INTERNET**→*www* http://www.maxstrat.com/

Maxis Software A-Train, Coral Reef, Daring To Fly, SimCity, Doodle-mation, El Fish, Gift Maker, Kid's Studio, Klik & Play, Print Artist, RedShift, RoboSport, Rome, Unnatural Selections, Warplanes, Widget Workshop, Wrath of the Gods, and other games. ☎→*dial* 510-254-3869 ✓**AMERICA ONLINE**→*keyword* maxis ✓**COMPUSERVE**→*go* gambpub→Messages *and* Libraries→Maxis ✓**INTERNET**→*www* http://www.maxis.com/maxhome.html

Maxtor/Miniscribe High capacity disk drives. ☎→*dial* 303-678-2020

Maynard Electronics Tape backups. ☎→*dial* 407-263-3502

McAfee Associates Scan, VShield, NetShield, Sentry, ProView, NetRemote, HelpPlus, and more. ✓**AMERICA ONLINE**→*keyword* mcafee ✓**COMPUSERVE**→*go* virusforum ✓**INTERNET**→*www* http://www.mcafee.com/ …→*www* ftp://ftp.mcafee.com/

MDL Corporation Full line of storage products, backup products, and EISA workstation products. ✓**INTERNET**→*www* http://www.halcyon.com/mdlcorp/

MECC Educational software such as Addition Logician, Arithmetic Critters, Backyard Birds, and the Conquering Math series. ✓**AMERICA ONLINE**→*keyword* mecc ✓**INTERNET**→*www* http://www.mecc.com/

Media Vision ☎→*dial* 510-770-0968 ✓**COMPUSERVE**→*go* mediavision ✓**INTERNET**→*www* http://www.mediavis.com/

Mediatrix Soundboards. ✓**INTERNET**→*www* http://www.fmmo.ca/mediatrix

Megahertz Corp. Modems and ethernet connectors. ☎→*dial* 801-320-8840 ✓**COMPUSERVE**→*go* modemvendor→Messages *and* Libraries→Megahertz

Mergent International PC/DACS, NetDACS, SSO/DACS, SiteDACS, and DomainDACS. ☎→*dial* 203-257-4305 ✓**INTERNET**→*www* http://www.mergent.com/

Meridian Data, Inc. Optical drives for LANs and CD-ROM drivers. ☎→*dial* 408-439-9509 ✓**AMERICA ONLINE**→*keyword* meridian ✓**COMPUSERVE**→*go* meridian

Merisel Netra, Solaris, and SPARC storage systems. ☎→*dial* 508-485-8507 ✓**INTERNET**→*www* http://esat.meriselpd.com/

Merit Software Entertainment software. ☎→*dial* 214-702-8641 ✓**COMPUSERVE**→*go* gamapub→Messages *and* Libraries→Merit Studios

Mesquite Software, Inc. CSIM17. ✓**INTERNET**→*www* http://www.mesquite.com/

Metricom STRATA3. ✓**AMERICA ONLINE**→*keyword* metricom

Metrowerks QuickView and CodeWarrrior. ✓**AMERICA ONLINE**→*keyword* metrowerks ✓**EWORLD**→*go* metrowerks ✓**INTERNET**→*www* ftp://www.iquest.com/pub/fairgate …→*www* http://www.iquest.com/~fairgate/cw/cw.html

Metz Software Metz series including Lock, Task Manager, Widget, Desktop Manager, Phones, Dialer, Time, FreeMem. ☎→*dial* 206-644-3663 ✓**AMERICA ONLINE**→*keyword* metz ✓**COMPUSERVE**→*go* winapc→Messages *and* Libraries→Metz Software

Micro J Systems, Inc. PCHunter RMS, MacHunter RMS, and MPP. ✓**AMERICA ONLINE**

Net Tech 307

Company Support

→*keyword* microj

Micro Solutions Parallel Part, Uniform PC, and a line of CD-ROMs. ☎→*dial* 815-756-9100

Microchip Technology, Inc. Full line of microcontrollers, EPROMS, peripherals, and software. ✓**INTERNET**→*www* http://www.ultranet.com/biz/mchip/

Microcom Full line of MacIntosh and PC software. ☎→*dial* 617-255-1125 ✓**AMERICA ONLINE**→*keyword* microcom

Microedge Software SlickEdit. ✓**COMPUSERVE**→*go* pcvenf→Messages *and* Libraries→Microedge Software

MicroFrontier, Inc. Color It!, Enhance!, Paint It!, and Pattern Workshop. ✓**AMERICA ONLINE**→*keyword* microfrontier ✓**COMPUSERVE**→*go* grvenc→Messages *and* Libraries→Microfrontier

Micrografx ABC FlowerCharter, Picture Publisher, Micrografx Designer, Crayola Art Studio, and Crayola Amazing Art Adventure. ✓**AMERICA ONLINE**→*keyword* micrografx

MicroMat Computer Systems PrintShuttle, MicroProbe, and Mac EKG. ✓**AMERICA ONLINE**→*keyword* micromat ✓**COMPUSERVE**→*go* macaven→Messages *and* Libraries→MicroMat ✓**EWORLD**→*go* micromat

Microplex Systems, Ltd. M200, M202, M204, and M212. ✓**INTERNET**→*www* ftp://ftp.microplex.com/ ...→*www* http://www.microplex.com/

Micropolis Corp PC drives. ☎→*dial* 818-709-3310 ✓**COMPUSERVE**→*go* pcvend→Messages *and* Libraries→Micropolis Corp.

MicroProse Magic: The Gathering, Master of Magic, Colonization, XCOM:UFO Defense, and other games. ☎→*dial* 410-785-1841 ✓**AMERICA ONLINE**→*keyword* microprose ✓**COMPUSERVE**→*go* gambpub→Messages *and* Libraries→MicroProse ✓**INTERNET**→*www* http://www.microprose.com/website.html ...→*www* ftp://ftp.microprose.com/

MicroRim r:BASE and r:PORT. ✓**COMPUSERVE**→*go* microrim

Microsoft Windows products. ☎→*dial* 206-936-6735/905-507-3022 ✓**AMERICA ONLINE**→*keyword* microsoft ✓**COMPUSERVE**→*go* microsft ✓**PRODIGY**→*jump* microsoft ✓**INTERNET**→*www* http://www.microsoft.com/ ...→*www* ftp://ftp.microsoft.com/

Microspeed Ticac and Trackball. ☎→*dial* 510-490-1664

Microsystems Software Calendar. ☎→*dial* 508-875-8009

MicroTek Lab True Image and Color scanners. ☎→*dial* 310-297-5102

Mindscape AV/PowerMac, MegaRace, San Diego Zoo, Newsweek Interactive, Mavis Beacon Teaches Typing!, Chessmaster 3000, Mario is Missing, Wing Commander, The Animals!, Loom, The Secret of Monkey Island, Miracle Piano Teaching System, Word for Word, Life and Death, and other games. ☎→*dial* 415-883-7145 ✓**AMERICA ONLINE**→*keyword* mindscape ✓**COMPUSERVE**→*go* gamapub→Messages *and* Libraries→Mindscape

MIPS Technologies, Inc. R4000, R4200, R4400, R4600, and R8000 series. ✓**INTERNET**→*www* http://www.mips.com/

Mirror Technologies PowerVision, PixelView, ProView, 600 and 800 series, M series, and RM series. ✓**AMERICA ONLINE**→*keyword* mirror ✓**COMPUSERVE**→*go* maccven→Messages *and* Libraries→Mirror Technologies ✓**EWORLD**→*go* mirror

Mitsubishi Electronic Research Labs Expanding software line compatible with their semiconductors. ☎→*dial* 714-236-6286

MMB Development Corporation TEAMate. ✓**INTERNET**→*www* http://teamate.mmb.com/

Molecular OptoElectronics Corporation Morning Star SecureConnect, Morning Star Authentication Server, Morning Star PPP, Morning Star Express Router Family, including the Express, the Express Office, and the Express Plus. ✓**INTERNET**→*www* http://www.morningstar.com/

Molex, Inc. Full line of connectors, switches, and cable systems. ✓**INTERNET**→*www* http://www.molex.com/

Morgan Davis Group MicroEMACS, CRC, RADE, QInit, Clear Backup Bits, fGrep, File Fixer, and Stream Editor. ✓**AMERICA ONLINE**→*keyword* morgandavis

Multi-Tech Systems ZDX, MT2834ZDXKi, and MT2834LT. ☎→*dial* 612-785-9875 ✓**COMPUSERVE**→*go* modemvendor→Messages *and* Libraries→Multi-Tech Systems

Mustang Software Off-Line Xpress, QmodemPro, and WILDCAT. ☎→*dial* 805-873-2400 ✓**AMERICA ONLINE**→*keyword* mus-

Company Support

tang ✓**COMPUSERVE**→*go* pcvena→ Messages *and* Libraries→Mustang Software

Mylex Motherboards and SCSI host adapters. ☎→*dial* 510-793-3491

Myxa Corporation Custom programs for DOS, Windows, and OS/2. ✓**INTERNET**→*www* http://www.myxa.com/

N

National Semiconductor TyIN cards, InfoMover, and modems. ☎→*dial* 408-245-0671 ✓**COMPUSERVE**→*go* modemvendor→Messages *and* Libraries→National Semiconductor ✓**INTERNET**→*www* http://www.nsc.com/

NCR 3270 Connectivity. ☎→*dial* 719-596-1649

NEC Technologies MultiSync, MultiSpin, Versa, Riscstation, SilentWriter; desktop computers including 486es series, Ready ES series, RISCstation 2000, Versa, and the SX-4 Supercomputer. ☎→*dial* 508-635-4706 ✓**AMERICA ONLINE**→*keyword* nec ✓**INTERNET**→*www* http://www.nec.com/

NeoLogic NeoAccess. ✓**AMERICA ONLINE**→*keyword* neologic ✓**INTERNET**→*www* http://www.neologic.com/~neologic/

Neon Software LANSurveyor, NetMinder, RouterCheck, and TrafficWatch. ☎→*dial* 510-283-4802 ✓**EWORLD**→*go* neon ✓**INTERNET**→*www* ftp://ftp.neon.com/

Netscape Comunications Corporation NetScape. ✓**INTERNET**→*www* ftp://ftp.netscape.com/ …→*www* http://home.netscape.com/

Network and Communications Managemwnt, inc. G3 TCP Gateway. ✓**INTERNET**→*www* http://www.ncm.com/

Network Appliance Corporation FAServer 450 and FAServer 1400. ✓**INTERNET**→*www* http://www.weaver-gw.netapp.com/productInfo/ …→*www* http://www.netapp.com:80/

Network Computing Devices, Inc. Mariner and Z-Mail. ✓**INTERNET**→*www* http://www.ncd.com/IP/mariner.html

Network Products Corp Asynchronous communications servers. ☎→*dial* 818-441-6933

Network Systems Corporation BorderGuard, DPF, PCF/BCF, ERS, 6000 series, PS32 switch, ES-1 switch, Interface card series, and much more. ✓**INTERNET**→*www* http://www.network.com/

NetWorks, Inc. . NetWare. ✓**INTERNET**→*www* http://www.i-link.com/

Networks Northwest, Inc. Breeze series. ✓**INTERNET**→*www* http://networksnw.com/breeze

New Media Graphics TV cards and multimedia software. ☎→*dial* 714-453-0214

New World Computing Celebrity Poker, Empire Deluxe, Hammer, Hereos of Might & Magic I-IV, Inherit the Earth, Iron Cross, Macintercomm, Vegas Games, and World of Xeen, and other games. ☎→*dial* 818-899-5684 ✓**AMERICA ONLINE**→*keyword* newworld ✓**COMPUSERVE**→*go* gambpub→Messages *and* Libraries→New World Computing

Newbridge VIVID line system managers, route servers, network interface cards, and switches. ✓**INTERNET**→*www* http://www.vivid.newbridge.com/

NewGen TurboPS. ☎→*dial* 714-641-3869

neXT NEXTSTEP, NeXT Cube, and TAZ. ✓**COMPUSERVE**→*go* nextforum ✓**INTERNET**→*www* http://www.next.com/

NICE Technologies TagWizard. ✓**INTERNET**→*www* http://infolane.com/infolane/nice/nice.html

Nikon Electronic Imaging E2, CP-10 Coolprint, AX-1200 Scantouch, LS-10, LS-3510AF, CP-3000 printer, NT-3000, and HQ-1500 Digital Still Camera. ☎→*dial* 516-547-8367 ✓**AMERICA ONLINE**→*keyword* nikon ✓**COMPUSERVE**→*go* imgaven→Messages *and* Libraries→Nikon

Niles and Associates EndNote and EndLink. ✓**AMERICA ONLINE**→*keyword* niles ✓**INTERNET**→*www* ftp://magic.ucsb.edu/pub/EndNote/

Nine To Five Software Co., Inc. Office Patch, Contact Log Converter, PaperLess, and Future Contact Reports. ✓**AMERICA ONLINE**→*keyword* industryconnection→Companies I-M→Nine To Five

Nisus Software QUED/M, Nisus Writer, and Easy Alarms. ✓**AMERICA ONLINE**→*keyword* nisus ✓**COMPUSERVE**→*go* macaven→Messages *and* Libraries→Nisus Software ✓**EWORLD**→*go* nisus ✓**INTERNET**→*www* ftp://ftp.nisus-soft.com/pub/nisus/ …→*www* http://www.nisus-soft.com/~nisus/

No Hands Software Magnet. ✓**AMERICA ONLINE**→*keyword* nohands ✓**EWORLD**→*go* nohands ✓**IN-**

Company Support

TERNET→*www* ftp://ftp.netcom.com/pub/no/nohands/

Northern Telecom Meridian, Magellan, Norstar Key System, DMS SuperNodes, PersonalExpress, GSM 900, PCS 1900, CDMA 1900, SONET, SDH, and ICN Video. ✓**INTERNET**→*www* http://www.nortel.com/

Norton-Lambert Closeup. ☎→*dial* 805-683-2249 ✓**COMPUSERVE**→*go* pcveni→Messages *and* Libraries→Norton-Lambert

Novell, Inc. NetWare operating systems, UnixWare servers, QuatroPro, WordPerfect, Perfect Office, Envoy, Presentations, DR DOS, DR Multiuser DOS, and FlexOS. ☎→*dial* 801-429-3308 ✓**AMERICA ONLINE**→*keyword* novell ✓**COMPUSERVE**→*go* novell ✓**INTERNET**→*www* http://www.novell.com/

Now Software Now Up-to-Date, Now Contact, Now Utility, Now Compress, and Now Fun. ✓**AMERICA ONLINE**→*keyword* now ✓**EWORLD**→*go* now

Nu-Mega Tech. Bounds-Checker, Watcom, and DOS Soft-ICE. ✓**COMPUSERVE**→*go* winapb→Messages *and* Libraries→Nu-Mega Tech

NUIQ Software Inc Powerboard BBS software. ☎→*dial* 914-833-1479

Number Nine High resolution graphics adapters. ☎→*dial* 617-862-7502 ✓**COMPUSERVE**→*go* grvenc→Messages *and* Libraries→Number Nine

O

Object Factory Object, GENERALizer, and Working Class Library series. ✓**AMERICA ONLINE**→ *keyword* object factory

Objects, Inc. Layout and LayWin. ✓**COMPUSERVE**→*go* pcvene→Messages *and* Libraries→Objects Inc.

OCCAM Research Corporation MUSE. ✓**AMERICA ONLINE**→ *keyword* industryconnection→Companies N-R→OCCAM Research

Ocean Isle Software Reach-Out. ☎→*dial* 407-778-2407

Okidata Full line of printers and error correcting modems. ☎→*dial* 609-234-5344

Olduvai Software ArtClips, ArtFonts, Icon-It!, MultiClip, MasterFinder, Magic Typist, VideoPaint, and READ-IT OCR. ✓**AMERICA ONLINE**→*keyword* olduvai ✓**COMPUSERVE**→*go* macbven →Messages *and* Libraries→Olduvai Software

Olicom Ethernet adapters, bridges, and wiring products. ☎→*dial* 214-422-9835 ✓**COMPUSERVE**→*go* lanven→Messages *and* Libraries→Olicom ✓**INTERNET**→*www* http://www.olicom.dk/

Olivetti Corporation Active Badges, Release I, and other banking software. ✓**INTERNET**→*www* http://www.spk.olivetti.com/

Omen Technology Telebit modem and DSZ. ☎→*dial* 503-621-3746

ON Technology DaVinci Email, Notework Email, AuditTrack, Meeting Maker XP, SofTrack, and Instant Update. ✓**AMERICA ONLINE** →*keyword* on ✓**EWORLD**→*go* ontech

OnTrack Computer Systems Disk Manager. ☎→*dial* 612-937-0860

Onyx Technology QC. ✓**AMERICA ONLINE**→*keyword* onyx

Opcode Systems, Inc. Allie's Activity Kit, Audioshop, Claire, Easy Music, Edit One, EZ Vision, Galaxy Plus, MAXplay, Musicshop, OMS, Overture Notation, Studio 4-5LX, Studio Vision, Translator Pro, and Vision. ✓**AMERICA ONLINE**→*keyword* opcode ✓**COMPUSERVE**→*go* macbven <or> midiaven→Messages *and* Libraries→Opcode Systems ✓**INTERNET**→*www* http://www.rahul.net/opcode/ ...→*www* ftp://ftp.rahul.net/pub/opcode/

OptImage Interactive Systems OptImage, Delta V, MediaMogul, CD-IT!ALL, and the Compact Disc series. ☎→*dial* 515-225-1933 ✓**AMERICA ONLINE**→ *keyword* optimage

OPTIMAS SnapShot and OPTIMATE. ✓**AMERICA ONLINE**→*keyword* optimas

Oracle RDB. ✓**INTERNET**→*www* http://www.oracle.com/index.html

Orchid Technology Full line of motherboards and peripherals. ☎→*dial* 510-683-0555

Origin Systems BioForge, Super Wing, Wing Commander series, Wings of Glory, System Shock, Ultima series, Pacific Strike, The Book of Orbs, and other games. ☎→*dial* 512-328-8402 ✓**AMERICA ONLINE**→*keyword* origin ✓**COMPUSERVE**→*go* gamapub→Messages *and* Libraries→Origin

OS/9 OS/9 6000 series. ✓**COMPUSERVE**→*go* os9

Otter Solutions QuickCapture, SCION, GPIB, Serial, and MacPhase. ✓**AMERICA ONLINE**→ *keyword* industryconnection→Com-

Company Support

panies N-R→Otter Solutions

Outland, Inc. Games such as Hearts, Reversi, Galley, Go, Chess, and Backstab. ✓ **INTERNET**→*www* ftp://ftp.outland.com/pub/ …→*www* http://www.outland.com/

Output Enablers Zippy Clip, Jet Clip, Jiffy Clip, Turbo Clip, AV-Rocket, Rocket Clip, AV-Terburner, Granny Smith, and the PowerClip series. ✓ **INTERNET**→*www* ftp://io.com/pub/oenabler/ …→*www* http://www.io.conm/user/oe/index.html

P

PaceMark Technologies, Inc. IIeasy printers and Super ram cards. ✓ **AMERICA ONLINE**→*keyword* pacemark

Pacific Data Products Custom database systems. ☎→*dial* 619-452-6229 ✓ **INTERNET**→*www* http://www.pdm-inc.com/

Packard Bell Full line of desktops, laptops, notebooks, modems, and monitors. ☎→*dial* 801-250-1600 ✓ **PRODIGY**→*jump* packard bell ✓ **COMPUSERVE**→*go* packardbell

Packer Software DownToBusiness and Small Business Partner. ✓ **AMERICA ONLINE**→*keyword* packer

Pages Software, Inc. WebPages. ✓ **INTERNET**→*www* http://www.pages.com/index.html

Palindrome Archivist software. ☎→*dial* 708-505-3336

Palm Computing PalmConnect and Graffiti. ✓ **AMERICA ONLINE**→*keyword* palm

Panasonic Full line of computers and printers. ☎→*dial* 201-863-7845 ✓ **INTERNET**→*www* http://www.mitl.research.panasonic.com/ …→*www* http://www.mei.co.jp/

PandaSoft Screen Saver series. ✓ **AMERICA ONLINE**→*keyword* pandasoft

Pantone Print, textile, and plastics color systems. ✓ **COMPUSERVE**→*go* dtpbven→Messages *and* Libraries→Pantone

Paper Clip Products GraVu, The DEAL, and FaxMajik. ✓ **EWORLD**→*go* paperclip

Papyrus IndyCar Racing, NASCAR, and other games. ☎→*dial* 617-576-7472 ✓ **AMERICA ONLINE**→*keyword* papyrus ✓ **COMPUSERVE**→*go* gamcpub→Messages *and* Libraries→Papyrus Software ✓ **INTERNET**→*www* http://yarrow.wt.com.au/~sjackson/racing.html

Paradise Systems Multimedia custom software for video conferencing and virtual meetings. ☎→*dial* 714-753-1234 ✓ **INTERNET**→*www* http://www.paradise.com/

ParaSoft Corporation Insure++ and Fortran90. ✓ **INTERNET**→*www* http://www.parasoft.com/

ParcPlace VisualWorks, ObjectWorks, and SmallTalk add-ons. ✓ **COMPUSERVE**→*go* winape→Messages *and* Libraries→ParcPlace Systems ✓ **INTERNET**→*www* gopher://parcbench.parcplace.com/

Passport Designs Alchemy, Master Tracks Pro, MusicTime, Encore, Trax, SCORE, and NoteWriter II. ✓ **AMERICA ONLINE**→*keyword* passport ✓ **COMPUSERVE**→*go* midibven→Messages *and* Libraries→Passport Designs

Patton & Patton Software Flow Charting. ☎→*dial* 408-778-9697

Peachtree Software Complete Accounting, Bank Account Manager, Contact & Account Manager, First Accounting, Peachtree, and Client Write Up. ☎→*dial* 404-564-8071 ✓ **AMERICA ONLINE**→*keyword* peachtree ✓ **COMPUSERVE**→*go* pcvenf *and* winapd→Peachtree Software

Pearl Pearl Scripter. ✓ **COMPUSERVE**→*go* pearl

Pegasus Imaging Corp. Imaging technology products and services including PIC's IMPAC software series. ☎→*dial* 407-380-1701 ✓ **AMERICA ONLINE**→*keyword* pegasus ✓ **COMPUSERVE**→*go* grvenc →Messages *and* Libraries→Pegasus

PelicanWare, Inc. QuickFigure Pro and NewtCase. ✓ **INTERNET**→*www* http://www.teleport.com/~bettes/index.html

Pentax Technologies Flatbed scanners and printers. ☎→*dial* 303-460-1637

Peripheral Technology Group, Inc. Firefox and Frontier Technology series. ✓ **INTERNET**→*www* http://www.ptgs.com/

Persoft Software Intersect and SmarTerm420. ☎→*dial* 608-273-6595

Personal Bibliographic Software, Inc. ProCite and BiblioLink II. ✓ **INTERNET**→*www* http://argus-inc.com/pbs/pbs.html

Personal Computer Peripherals NetStream, HFS, JetStream, and DATStream. ✓ **AMERICA ONLINE**→*keyword* pcpc

Personics Corporation Monarch. ✓ **COMPUSERVE**→*go*

Net Tech 311

Company Support

pcvenb→Messages and Libraries→Personics

Philmont Software Mill Symposuim and Interaction of Color. ✓**EWORLD**→go philmont

Phoenix Technologies, Ltd. NoteBIOS, PhoenixPICO, and PhoenixCard Manager Plus. ✓**INTERNET**→www http://www.ptltd.com/

Pick Systems Databases. ✓**INTERNET**→www http://www.picksys.com ...→www ftp://ftp.picksys.com/

Pinnacle Publishing Parse-O-Matic, Sapphire, ForAge, G, and many others. ☎→dial 206-251-6217 ✓**COMPUSERVE**→go pcveng→Messages and Libraries→Pinnacle Publishing ✓**INTERNET**→www http://www.cam.org/~pinnacl/

Pinpoint Publishing Full line of cooking software. ☎→dial 707-523-0468 ✓**COMPUSERVE**→go winapc→Messages and Libraries→Pinpoint Publishing

Pioneer Software Q and E Query. ☎→dial 919-851-1381

Pixar Typestry, Showplace, 128 CD, and NetRenderMan. ✓**AMERICA ONLINE**→keyword pixar

Pixel Resources, Inc. Joy of Pixels and PixelPaint Pro. ✓**AMERICA ONLINE**→keyword pixel

PKWare PKZip and PKUnzip. ☎→dial 414-354-8670 ✓**COMPUSERVE**→go pcvenc→Messages and Libraries→PKWare

Polaris Software PackRat series. ☎→dial 619-738-8640 ✓**COMPUSERVE**→go polaris

Polaroid Corp. SprintScan series. ✓**COMPUSERVE**→go imgaven→Messages and Libraries→Polaroid Corp.

Portfolio Software Day-To-Day, DynoPage, and Dyno Notepad. ✓**COMPUSERVE**→go macaven→Messages and Libraries→Portfolio Software ✓**EWORLD**→go portfoliosw

PowerCerv Corporation PowerTOOL, Xceed, Response, PowerMAN, PowerTEXT, and FLOWBuilder. ✓**INTERNET**→www http://www.powercerv.com/

Powercore, Inc. Orpheus and CarbonCopy. ☎→dial 815-468-2633 ✓**COMPUSERVE**→go pcvenb→Messages and Libraries→Powercore, Inc.

Powersoft PowerBuilder and InfoMaker. ✓**COMPUSERVE**→go powersoft ✓**INTERNET**→www http://www.powersoft.com/

Practical Peripherals, Inc. MacClass, MiniTower, MicroBuffer, Mac Pocket Modem, Practical FaxMe, and full line of modems. ☎→dial 805-496-4445 ✓**AMERICA ONLINE**→keyword ppi ✓**COMPUSERVE**→go ppiforum

PrairieSoft Alarming Events, DateView, DiskTop, and In/Out, and InTouch. ✓**AMERICA ONLINE**→keyword prairiesoft ✓**EWORLD**→go prairiesoft

Process Software Corporation Purveyor, NFSware, and a complete line of TCPware. ✓**INTERNET**→www http://www.process.com/

Procom Technologies SCSI drives, hard drives, telecommunication software, and other PC hardware and peripherals; CD-ROM recording and storage systems, and LANforce series storage system. ☎→dial 714-852-1305 ✓**COMPUSERVE**→go pcvend→Messages and Libraries→Procom Technologies ✓**INTERNET**→www http://www.procom.com:80/

Prograph International, Inc. Prograph series. ✓**AMERICA ONLINE**→keyword prograph ✓**INTERNET**→www ftp://ftp.iup.edu/

Prometheus Products, Inc. MaxFax and Promodem. ☎→dial 503-691-5199 ✓**COMPUSERVE**→go modemvendor→Messages and Libraries→Prometheus

Proteon Full line of Internet hardware including token rings, NICs, bridges, and routers. ☎→dial 508-366-7827

ProVUE Development Panorama. ✓**AMERICA ONLINE**→keyword provue

PureData Network hardware, ethernet cards, and fax/modems. ☎→dial 214-242-3225 ✓**COMPUSERVE**→go pcvenf→Messages and Libraries→PUREDATA Fax/Modem

Q

QMS, Inc. Printers and software. ☎→dial 205-633-3632 ✓**COMPUSERVE**→go dtpaven→Messages and Libraries→QMS, Inc. ✓**INTERNET**→www http://www.qms.com/ ...→www ftp://gatekeeper.imagen.com/

QQP ZigZag, Perfect General III, Pure Wargame, and other games. ✓**AMERICA ONLINE**→keyword qqp ✓**COMPUSERVE**→go gamcpub→Messages and Libraries→QQP

Quadram Accessory boards.

Company Support

☎→*dial* 404-564-5678

Qualcomm Eudora, OmniTRACS, LEO, and CDMA. ✓**INTERNET**→*www* http://www.qualcomm.com/ …→*www* ftp://ftp.qualcomm.com/

Qualitas, Inc. 386MAX 7, RAMEXAM, and Dispatch. ☎→*dial* 301-907-8030 ✓**AMERICA ONLINE**→*keyword* qualitas ✓**COMPUSERVE**→*go* pcvena→Messages *and* Libraries→Qualitas

Quality Computers Smart Match. ✓**EWORLD**→*go* qualitycom

Quantum Storage products and tape drives. ☎→*dial* 408-894-3214 ✓**INTERNET**→*www* http://www.quantum.com/

Quark, Inc. QuarkXpress. ✓**AMERICA ONLINE**→*keyword* quark ✓**COMPUSERVE**→*go* quark ✓**INTERNET** →*www* ftp://ftp.telalink.net.pub/quark

Quarterdeck Office Systems Quarterdeck Mosaic, WebAuthor, Internet Toolbox, WebServer, and DESQview. ☎→*dial* 310-314-3227 ✓**COMPUSERVE**→*go* quarterdec ✓**INTERNET**→*www* http://www.qdeck.com/

Quasar Knowledge systems, Inc. VisualAgents and SmalltalkAgents. ✓**INTERNET**→*www* http://www.qks.com/ …→*www* ftp://ftp.qks.com/

Quercus Systems REXX. ☎→*dial* 408-867-7488 ✓**COMPUSERVE**→*go* pcvena→Messages *and* Libraries→Quercus Systems

R

Rabbit Software 3270 Gateway. ☎→*dial* 508-264-4345

RAD Technologies, Ltd. PowerMedia, ScreenPlay, and MediaViewer. ✓**INTERNET**→*www* http://www.batnet.com:80/RAD/

Radius-SuperMac Telecast, VideoVision, Studio Array, Spigot-Pro, Video Fusion, QuickFLIX, Thunder, Precision Color, Color-Composer, Super Match, IntelliColor, PhotoEngine, and FireStorm. ✓**AMERICA ONLINE**→*keyword* radius ✓**COMPUSERVE**→*go* macbven→Messages *nad* Libraries→Radius-SuperMac ✓**EWORLD**→*go* radius ✓**INTERNET** →*www* ftp://ftp.radius.com/

Raven Systems, Ltd. BBEdit Extensions, Frontier Droplets, GEnieNav, MiniApps Pack, and Color Floppy Maker. ✓**INTERNET**→*www* ftp://ftp.eskimo.com/ravensys/

Ray Dream, Inc. Ray Dream Designer 3, addDepth, and the JAG series. ✓**AMERICA ONLINE**→*keyword* raydream ✓**COMPUSERVE**→*go* grvenc→Messages *and* Libraries→ray dream ✓**EWORLD**→*go* raydream

Reactor Spaceship Warlock and Virtual Valerie. ✓**AMERICA ONLINE**→*keyword* reactor

ResNova Software NovaLink Professional and MacKennelx. ☎→*dial* 714-379-9004 ✓**AMERICA ONLINE**→*keyword* resnova ✓**INTERNET**→*www* http://www.resnova.com/

Rhintek RhinoCom and Warp. ✓**COMPUSERVE**→*go* pcvenc→Messages *and* Libraries→Rhintek

Rockland Software Buttons, BP70LIB Pascal Library, Tank, Global War, SIMSpace, Seige!, Mordorventure, Armies of Steel, Combat Zone, and GAMMAWing. ☎→*dial* 301-868-8381 ✓**AMERICA ONLINE**→*keyword* rockland

Rockwell Software WINtelligent software products. ✓**COMPUSERVE**→*go* winapf→Messages *and* Libraries→Rockwell Software

Rocky Mountain Digital Peeks CD-ROMs such as Earth Observatorium, Calculated Beauty, Virtual Landscape I, Rocky Mountain Wildflowers, and Magnificent Rocky. ✓**INTERNET**→*www* ftp://ftp.csn.net/rmdp/

Rocky Mountain System Design, Inc. Full line of Internet support and Pascal software. ✓**INTERNET**→*www* http://www.rmsd.com/

Roger Wagner Publishing StudioWare. ✓**AMERICA ONLINE**→*keyword* rogerwagner

Roland Corp. Sound cards and MIDI products, including the Roland SoundCanvas. ✓**COMPUSERVE**→*go* midiven→Messages *and* Libraries→Roland Corp. ✓**INTERNET**→*www* http://www.imagic.be/roland/ …→*www* http://www.eeb.ele.tue.nl/midi/scgroup/index.html

RSA Data Security, Inc. MailSafe, RSA Secure, CIS, TIPEM, B SAFE. ✓**INTERNET**→*www* http://www.rsa.com/

Rupp Corporation Winlynx and Rupplynx. ✓**COMPUSERVE**→*go* pcvenc→Messages *and* Libraries →Rupp Corporation

RYBS Electronics Hicard 2 and ATLast!. ☎→*dial* 303-443-7437

S

Saber Software Slipstream, Saber 5 Net, and Reachout.

Company Support

☎ →dial 214-361-1883 ✓ **COMPUSERVE**→go pcvena→Messages and Libraries→Saber Software ✓ **EWORLD**→go saber

Samsung Info Systems PCTerminal/286 and the 386AE file server. ☎→dial 201-691-6238 ✓ **INTERNET**→www http://www.samsung.com/

SAS Institute On Location and Meeting Maker. ☎→dial 919-677-8155

Seagate Hard drives such as Decathalon, Marathon, Medalist; software marketed by the subsidiaries Crystal Services, Dragon Systems, Network Computing, Inc., and Palindrome Software. ☎→dial 408-438-8771 ✓ **COMPUSERVE**→go seagate ✓ **INTERNET**→www http://www.seagate.com/ ...→www ftp://www.seagate.com/

Searchlight Software Searchlight BBS software. ☎→dial 216-631-9285

Sega Full line of games, gear, and gaming equipment. ✓ **COMPUSERVE**→go sega ✓ **INTERNET**→www http://www.segaoa.com/

SemWare Qedit and TSE. ☎→dial 404-641-8968

Serif Serif PagePlus. ✓ **INTERNET**→www http://www.serif.com

Serius Corporation Workshop and Developer Pro. ✓ **AMERICA ONLINE**→keyword serius

Seven Hills Software Spectrum, At Home, Driver Clean Kit, and Funny Fruit Faces. ✓ **COMPUSERVE**→go apiiven→Messages and Libraries→Seven Hills ✓ **EWORLD**→go sevenhills

Shana Corporation Informed Designer and Informed Manager. ☎→dial 403-462-8365 ✓ **EWORLD**→go shanacorp ✓ **INTERNET**→www http://www.shana.com/

Sharp Full line of laptop computers. ☎→dial 404-962-1788 ✓ **COMPUSERVE**→go sharp

Shaw Technologies, Inc. Designer 21xx. ✓ **INTERNET**→www http://www.teleport.com/~sti/

Shiva Corporation LanRover/T series, LanRover/E, EtherGate, TeleBridge, and FastPath 5/5R. ☎→dial 617-273-0023 ✓ **AMERICA ONLINE**→keyword shiva ✓ **COMPUSERVE**→go lanven→Messages and Libraries→Shiva Corporation ✓ **INTERNET**→www http://www.shva.com/

ShowCase Corporation VISTA series. ✓ **COMPUSERVE**→go winapg→Messages and Libraries→ShowCase Corp. ✓ **INTERNET**→www http://www.millcomm.com/showcase/

Siemens Nixdorf RM1000, BS2000, BEETLE, CALYPSO, POSition, UNIPOS, NAMOS series, and peripherals. ✓ **INTERNET**→www http://www.sni.de/

Sierra Online Space Quest, Gabriel Knight, Quest for Glory, Police Quest, Goblins, King's Quest, Lost In Time. ☎→dial 209-683-4463 ✓ **AMERICA ONLINE**→keyword sierra ✓ **COMPUSERVE**→go si

Sigma Designs Video monitors and video cards including ReelMagic. ☎→dial 510-770-0111 ✓ **COMPUSERVE**→go dtpaven→Messages and Libraries→Sigma Designs

Silicon Graphics, Inc Full line of custom graphics and software. ✓ **INTERNET**→www http://www.sgi.com/

SmartDisk Security Corporation SmartDisk systems. ✓ **INTERNET**→www http://infolane.com/infolane/smrtdisk/

SMS Technology USR HST series. ☎→dial 408-954-8231

SofNet FileFax. ☎→dial 404-984-9926

Soft-Tek Grafsman. ✓ **COMPUSERVE**→go grvenc→Messages and Libraries→Soft-Tek

SoftArc Inc. FirstClass. ☎→dial 905-415-7070 ✓ **AMERICA ONLINE**→keyword softarc ✓ **EWORLD**→go softarc

SoftEasy Software SoftFoot, PowerNotes, and QuickNote. ✓ **EWORLD**→go softeasy

SoftKlone Mirror III and TAKEOVER. ☎→dial 904-878-9884

Softlogic Solutions Full line of utilities software. ☎→dial 603-644-5556

Software AG The Natural series, the Entire series, and the Adabas series. ✓ **INTERNET**→www http://www.demon.co.uk:80/web/natinfo.html

Software Products Intl. WindowBase and Meta-Index. ☎→dial 619-450-2179 ✓ **INTERNET**→www http://www.cts.com/~spi/

Software Ventures Snatcher and the MicroPhone series. ☎→dial 510-849-1912 ✓ **COMPUSERVE**→go macbven→Messages and Libraries→Software Ventures ✓ **INTERNET**→www ftp://ftp.svcdudes.com/

Company Support

Softway Pty. Ltd. SoftQ, SHARE II, Hibernator, Secure-It, and Secure-It Firewall. ✓INTERNET→*www* http://www.softawy.com.au/

Solectek Accessories Laptop NICs. ☎→*dial* 619-450-6537

Sony Electronics Full line of computers and electronics. ☎→*dial* 408-955-5107 ✓INTERNET→*www* http://www.sony.com/

Sophisticated Circuits Desktop Dialer, PowerKey, and PowerPad. ✓AMERICA ONLINE→*keyword* sophcir ✓COMPUSERVE→*go* maccven→Messages *and* Libraries→Soph.Circuits ✓EWORLD→*go* sophcir

Sound, Studio & Stage Proton, GrooveStation, WaveKey, Ultimate Guitar Lesson series, GeneralMusic series. ✓AMERICA ONLINE→*keyword* sss

Spectrum Holobyte Falcon, Operation: Fighting Tiger, Tetris, and other games. ☎→*dial* 510-522-8909 ✓AMERICA ONLINE→*keyword* spectrum ✓COMPUSERVE→*go* gambpub→Messages *and* Libraries→Spectrum Holobyte

Specular International Infini-D, BackBurner, TextureScape, Collage, LogoMotion. ✓AMERICA ONLINE→*keyword* specular

SPRY, Inc. AIR series, Internet in a Box, Mosaic in a Box, Safety Web. ✓INTERNET→*www* http://www/spry.com/

Spyglass Plot, Transform, and Dicer. ✓INTERNET→*www* ftp://spyglass.com/ ...→*www* http://www.spyglass.com/

STAC Electronics Reachout and Stacker. ☎→*dial* 619-431-5956 ✓AMERICA ONLINE→*keyword* stac

Standard Microsystems Corp. SMC9000 series, ethernet products, ARCNET LAN devices, and I/O products. ☎→*dial* 516-434-3162 ✓INTERNET→*www* http://www.smc.com/

Star Micronics Printers. ☎→*dial* 908-572-5010

StarNet Communications Corporation Micro X series. ✓INTERNET→*www* http://www.starnet.com/

StarNine Technologies, Inc. WebStar, ListStar, and OmniStar. ✓INTERNET→*www* ftp://ftp.starnine.com/ ...→*www* http://www.starnine.com/

STB Systems Accessory boards. ☎→*dial* 214-437-9615

Sterling Software ObjectView, FileSets, and ZIMWin. ✓COMPUSERVE→*go* pcveni→Messages *and* Libraries→Sterling Software

STF Technologies PowerFax and FaxSTF. ☎→*dial* 816-463-1131 ✓AMERICA ONLINE→*keyword* stf ✓COMPUSERVE→*go* macbven→Messages *and* Libraries→STF Technologies ✓EWORLD→*go* stf

Storm Software, Inc EasyPhoto, Apple PhotoFlash, and Kid's Studio. ✓INTERNET→*www* ftp://ftp.stormsoft.com/companies/storm/ftp/ ...→*www* http://www.stormsoft.com/storm/

Strata StudioPro, MediaPrint, Instant Replay, StrataVision, Texture & Shapes, StrataVirtual, RenderPro, Fractal Terrain Modeler, MediaForge, Visual FX. ✓AMERICA ONLINE→*keyword* strata ✓EWORLD→*go* strata

Strategic Simulations Renegade Legion Intercepter, Buck Rogers:Countdown to Doomsday, Second Front, Medieval Lords, Carrier Strike, Cyber Empires, Summoning, Champions of Krynn, Strategic Simulations, Eye of the Beholder, and other games. ☎→*dial* 408-739-6623/408-739-6137 ✓AMERICA ONLINE→*keyword* strategic ✓COMPUSERVE→*go* gamapub→Messages <and> Libraries→strategic simulations

Sun Microsystems SPARCstation series, Netra I, Wabi, Classic X, Netra S, and more. ✓INTERNET→*www* http://www.sun.com/

Sunburst Communications Educational software, CD-ROMs, and more. ✓AMERICA ONLINE→*keyword* sunburst

Sunrise Software ezX GUI. ☎→*dial* 404-256-9525

SunRiver Fiber optics. ☎→*dial* 512-835-8082

Supermac Software Spectrum/24 series. ☎→*dial* 408-541-6190

Survivor Software MacMoney, InvoicIt, and TaxMatch. ✓AMERICA ONLINE→*keyword* survivor ✓COMPUSERVE→*go* macaven→Messages *and* Libraries→Survivor Software ✓EWORLD→*go* survivor

Sutton Designs NetSavers, RemoteUPS, and MM-Series - All-Net. ✓COMPUSERVE→*go* lanbven→Messages *and* Libraries→Sutton Designs

Swan Technologies Swan Palette Plus, Swan EISA cards, and other PC hardware and peripherals. ☎→*dial* 814-237-6145 ✓COMPUSERVE→*go* pcveng→Messages *and* Libraries→Swan Technologies ✓INTERNET→*www* http://www.tisco.com/swan/

Net Tech 315

Company Support

Sybase Databases. ✓INTERNET→*www* http://www.sybase.com

Sydex Shez. ☎→*dial* 503-683-1385

Symantec Norton Speedrive, Norton Commander, THINK Products, Justwrite, Norton antiVirus, and Norton Utilities. ☎→*dial* 503-484-6669 ✓AMERICA ONLINE→*keyword* symantec ✓COMPUSERVE→*go* symnet ✓INTERNET→*www* ftp://ftp.symantec.com/public ...→*www* http://www.symantec.com/

Synex Systems Label Press, Waterworks, MacEnvelope, MacPhonebook, and Bar Code Pro. ✓AMERICA ONLINE→*keyword* synex ✓COMPUSERVE→*go* oavendor→Messages *and* Libraries→Synex Systems

Synopsys Complete line of computer design and IC products including PCI Design Kit, ModelSource 3000, and Smart Model Library. ☎→*dial* 408-970-3719 ✓INTERNET→*www* http://www.synopsys.com/

Syquest Syquest disks. ☎→*dial* 510-656-0473

Systems Compatibility Writer's utility software. ☎→*dial* 312-670-4239

Systems & Computer Technology Corporation BANNERQuest, IA-Plus, and EDI.Smart. ✓INTERNET→*www* http://www.sctcorp.com/

T

T/Maker VroomBooks series, ClikArt series, and SnapArt series. ✓AMERICA ONLINE→*keyword* tmaker ✓COMPUSERVE→*go* macdven→Messages *and* Libraries→T/Maker

Tactic Software Corporation nuBASE Pro. ✓AMERICA ONLINE→*keyword* tactic ✓COMPUSERVE→*go* macbven→Messages *and* Libraries→Tactic Software

Taligent, Inc. CommonPoint System. ✓INTERNET→*www* http://www.taligent.com/

Tandem Computers NonStop Kernel, Syshealth, PowerExec, PSX series; full lines of software for other desktop systems. ✓INTERNET→*www* http://www.tandem.com/

Tandy Full line of hardware and electronics. ✓COMPUSERVE→*go* tandy

Tangram Enterprise Solutions AM:PM, Open Advantage series, Merlin, FileWizard, FileAuditor, and NLMAuto. ✓INTERNET→*www* http://www.tesi.com/

Tatung Company Full line of faxes, minicomputers, printers, and workstations. ✓INTERNET|→*www* http://www.tatung.com/tatung/homepage.html

Technology Works GraceLAN, TechWorks LAN series, and ThunderBolt buses. ✓AMERICA ONLINE→*keyword* techworks

TechWorks GraceLAN and TechStar. ✓EWORLD→*go* techworks

Tecmar Memory and tape backup systems. ☎→*dial* 216-349-0853

Teknosys Help! series. ✓AMERICA ONLINE→*keyword* teknosys ✓COMPUSERVE→*go* macdven→Messages *and* Libraries→Teknosys ✓EWORLD→*go* teknosys

Tektronix Phaser printers. ☎→*dial* 503-685-4504 ✓AMERICA ONLINE→*keyword* tektronix ✓EWORLD→*go* tektronix ✓INTERNET→*www* http://www.tek.com

Telebit NetBlazer, NASI, QBlazer, FastBlazer, and WorldBlazer. ☎→*dial* 408-745-3861 ✓COMPUSERVE→*go* modemvendor→Messages *and* Libraries→Telebit ✓INTERNET→*www* http://www.telebit.com/ ...→*www* ftp://ftp.telebit.com/

Teledyne Brown Engineering TIE-Net, Data Aquisitions, and a series of control systems. ✓INTERNET→*www* http://www.tbe.com/

Tenon Intersystems MachTen, X Window, and MachTen. ✓INTERNET→*www* ftp://ftp.tenon.com/ ...→*www* http://www.tenon.com/

Tera Computer Company MTA computer series. ✓INTERNET→*www* http://www.tera.com ...→*www* http://204.118.137.100/

Texas Instruments TravelMate notebook computers, CD-ROM docking system, TI microLasero, ATB printers, TI 201 printers. ☎→*dial* 817-774-6809 ✓AMERICA ONLINE→*keyword* texasinstruments ✓COMPUSERVE→*go* tiforum

Thinking Machines Corp. Programming languages and libraries including CM Fortran C*, the CMSSL library, the CMMD library, and Connection Machine (CM-5) supercomputer. ✓INTERNET→*www* http://www.think.com/

Thomas Conrad ARCNET and token ring series. ☎→*dial* 512-836-8012

Thought I Could CAL and Wallpaper. ✓EWORLD→*go* tic

Three-Sixty Pacific Victory at Sea and Harpoon II. ✓AMERICA

316 Net Tech

Company Support

ONLINE→*keyword* threesixty ✓**COMPUSERVE**→*go* gamapub→Messages *and* Libraries→Thrity-sixty Pacific

ThrustMaster Flight Control System, Weapon Control System, Rudder Control System, U-Prom, Thrustmaster Cockpit, and other games. ✓**AMERICA ONLINE**→*keyword* thrustmaster ✓**COMPUSERVE**→*go* gamdpub→Messages *and* Libraries→ThrustMaster ✓**INTERNET**→*www* http://www.caprica.com/thrustmaster/

Thunderware ThunderScan Plus and the Lightning Scan series. ✓**AMERICA ONLINE**→*keyword* thunderware

Tiara Computer Systems 10net series. ☎→*dial* 408-496-5480

Time Warner Interactive CD-ROMs, Aegis, Chuck Jones, Clinton:Portrait of Victory, Desert Storm, Flash Traffic:City of Angels, Funny, Kurt Vonnegut's Slaughterhouse Five, the New Family Bible, and many others. ✓**AMERICA ONLINE**→*keyword* twi

TimeSlips Corporation Time & Expense, TimeSheet, Timeslips, and LapTrack. ☎→*dial* 508-768-7581 ✓**AMERICA ONLINE**→*keyword* timeslips ✓**COMPUSERVE**→*go* timeslips

Timeworks Publish It, Word Writer, Data Manager, and Swift-Calc. ✓**AMERICA ONLINE**→*keyword* timeworks ✓**COMPUSERVE**→*go* dt-paven→Messages *and* Libraries→Timeworks ✓**EWORLD**→*go* timeworks

TMS Peripherals Storage and memory products. ✓**AMERICA ONLINE**→*keyword* tms ✓**COMPUSERVE**→*go* apiiven <or> maccven→Messages *and* Libraries→TMS Peripherals

Toshiba Printer Products Printer series. ☎→*dial* 714-837-4408 ✓**COMPUSERVE**→*go* toshiba

TouchStone Software CheckIt series. ☎→*dial* 714-969-0688

Traveling Software Lap Link. ☎→*dial* 206-485-1736

Trident Microsystems TVGA 8916. ☎→*dial* 415-691-1016

Trio Information Systems Fax and scanner software. ☎→*dial* 919-846-4987 ✓**COMPUSERVE**→*go* winapf→Messages *and* Libraries→Trio Info Systems

TripleSoft TripleSoft. ✓**EWORLD**→*go* triplesoft

Triton Technologies Co/Session. ☎→*dial* 908-855-9609

Tru Image Audio MacSpeakerz. ✓**AMERICA ONLINE**→*keyword* macspeakerz

Truevision/RasterOps TARGA 2000 and PaintBoard Prism. ☎→*dial* 317-577-8777 ✓**AMERICA ONLINE**→*keyword* truevision ✓**INTERNET**→*www* ftp://ftp.truevision.com/ …→*www* ftp://ftp.rasterops.com/

Tseng Labs ET1000, ET2000, ET3000, and ET4000 computer chips. ☎→*dial* 215-579-7536 ✓**AMERICA ONLINE**→*keyword* tseng ✓**COMPUSERVE**→*go* graphbven→Messages *and* Libraries→Tseng Labs

Turtle Beach Maui, MultiSound MPC, and other MIDI products. ☎→*dial* 717-767-5934 ✓**COMPUSERVE**→*go* midiaven→Messages *and* Libraries→Turtle Beach

U

UnderWare, Inc. Track Record. ✓**COMPUSERVE**→*go* winapg→Messages *and* Libraries→UnderWare, Inc.

US Robotics Full line of modems including Sportster, Courier, WorldPort Modems, Rack Mount, and Shared Access. ☎→*dial* 708-982-5092 ✓**COMPUSERVE**→*go* modemvendor→Messages *and* Libraries→US Robotics ✓**INTERNET**→*www* ftp://ftp.usr.com/ …→*www* http://www.primenet.com/usr/

Userland Userland Frontier series. ☎→*dial* 415-326-7793 ✓**AMERICA ONLINE**→*keyword* userland ✓**INTERNET**→*www* ftp://ftp.netcom.com/pub/us/userland/ …→*www* http://www.hotwired.com/userland/

V

Ven-Tel Series of error modems. ☎→*dial* 408-922-0988

Verity, Inc. Topic series. ✓**INTERNET**→*www* ftp://ftp.verity.com/ …→*www* http://www.verity.com/

Vermont Microsystems Automate Pro. ☎→*dial* 802-655-7461

Vertisoft Emulasr and DoubleDisk. ✓**AMERICA ONLINE**→*keyword* vertisoft ✓**COMPUSERVE**→*go* pcveng→Messages *and* Libraries→Vertisoft

Viacom New Media Shadowgate, Lenny's Music Toons, MTV's Club Dead, Are You Afraid of the Dark, Nickelodeon, and other CD-ROMs. ✓**AMERICA ONLINE**→*keyword* viacom ✓**COMPUSERVE**→*go* winapa→Messages *and* Libraries→Viacom New Media

Videodiscovery, Inc. Laserdiscs

Company Support

and CD-ROMs including Anatomy and Physiology, Atoms to Anatomy, Bio Sci II, Cell Biology I, Death Trap, Evolution, MediaMAX, Math Sleuths, Life Cylces, Physics of Sports, Pollination Biology, STS Science Forums, Science Discovery series. ✓**AMERICA ONLINE**→*keyword* videodiscovery ✓**INTERNET**→*www* http://www.videodiscovery.com/vdyweb/ ...→*www* ftp://ftp.videodiscovery.com/local/vdy/

VIDI VIDIxpress and VIDI Presenter. ✓**AMERICA ONLINE**→*keyword* vidi

Viewpoint DataLabs Evan Ricks, Entire World, Imagination Works, Indy Car, Motion Data, Motorola, and Real Time. ✓**AMERICA ONLINE**→*keyword* viewpoint

ViewSonic 8514/A monitors. ☎→*dial* 909-468-1241

Virtual Reality Labs, Inc. Formbuster, Cyberflight, Vistapro, Makepath Flight Director, Distant Suns, Mars Explorer. ✓**AMERICA ONLINE**→*keyword* industryconnection→Companies S-Z→Virtual Reality Labs ✓**COMPUSERVE**→*go* VRLI

Virtual Technologies Virtual BBS software. ☎→*dial* 210-787-8974

Virtus Corporation Alien Skin Textureshop, Virtus Galleries, Virtus Player, Virtus VR, Virtus Walkthrough Pro. ✓**AMERICA ONLINE**→*keyword* virtus ✓**COMPUSERVE**→*go* maccven→Messages and Libraries→Virtus Corp.

Visionary Software First Things First, Lifeguard, ErgoKnowledge, Serial Number Checking, MindSet, Synchronicity. ✓**AMERICA ONLINE**→*keyword* visionary

Visual Software DesignCAD, Simply 3D, VR, and other animation products. ✓**COMPUSERVE**→*go* anvena→Messages and Libraries→Visual Software

Volante PC Prime Time. ✓**COMPUSERVE**→*go* graphbven→Messages and Libraries →volante

The Voyager Company CD-ROMs such as For All Mankind, If Monks Had Macs, P.A.W.S., Puppet Motel, This Is Spinal Tap, Truths and Fictions, American Poetry, Baseball's Greatest Hits, Cinema Volta, Dazzeloids, and hundreds of others. ✓**AMERICA ONLINE**→*keyword* voyager ✓**COMPUSERVE**→*go* multiven→Messages and Libraries→Voyager ✓**INTERNET**→*www* http://www.voyager.com

Voyetra Technologies MIDI Orchestrator Plus; MIDI interfaces such as VP-11 Parallel Port, V-22, and the V-24 series. ✓**AMERICA ONLINE**→*keyword* voyetra

W

Wacom Technology Series of digitizing tablets including the ARTZ-SERIAL and the SD-#10E series. ✓**AMERICA ONLINE**→*keyword* wacom

WAIS, Inc. Online publishing tools including WAIS Server, Gopher Gateway, WAISgate, Cutom Parser toolkit , and more. ✓**INTERNET**→*www* ftp://ftp.wais.com/pub/ ...→*www* http://www.wais.com/

Walker Richer & Quinn, Inc. Reflection. ✓**INTERNET**→*www* ftp://ftp.wrq.com/ ...→*www* http://www.wrq.com/

Wall Data Rumba. ☎→*dial* 206-814-4361 ✓**COMPUSERVE**→*go* winapc→Messages and Libraries →Wall Data

Walt Disney Software Aladdin Print Kit, Coaster, Disney Animation Studio, Dick Tracy Crime Solving Adventure, Duck Tales, Heaven and Earth, Disney Sound Source, Mickey's ABCs, Mickey's 1-2-3, The Rocketeer, Stunt Island, and others. ☎→*dial* 818-567-4027 ✓**AMERICA ONLINE**→*keyword* disneysoftware ✓**COMPUSERVE**→*go* gamapub→Messages and Libraries→Disney/Buena Vista

WaveMetrics Igor, Igor XOP Toolkit, and Igor Filter Design Lab. ✓**AMERICA ONLINE**→*keyword* wavemetrics ✓**INTERNET**→*www* ftp://d31rz0.stanford.edu/ ...→*www* http://www.wavemetrics.com/

Weigand Report Network Calendar, Golden Rectangles, Tabs and Rules, Fountain Pen, and TWR Address Book. ✓**AMERICA ONLINE**→*keyword* weigand

Western Digital Caviar, Caviar-Lite, Paradise graphic accelerator cards, and the Enhanced IDE product series. ☎→*dial* 714-753-1068 ✓**AMERICA ONLINE**→*keyword* wdc ✓**INTERNET**→*www* http://www.wdc.com/ ...→*www* ftp://ftp.wdc.com/

Westwood Studios Legend of Kyrandia series, Duneseries, Lands of Lore, Young Merlin, The Lion King, and other games. ☎→*dial* 702-368-2319 ✓**AMERICA ONLINE**→*keyword* westwood ✓**COMPUSERVE**→*go* gambpub→Messages and Libraries→Westwood Studios ✓**PRODIGY**→*jump* westwood support

WexTech Systems Doc-To-Help. ✓**COMPUSERVE**→*go* winapd→Messages and Libraries→Wex-

Company Support

Tech Systems

WH Networks Communications products. ✓**INTERNET**→*www* http://www/whnet.com/wolfgang

White Pine Software DataSheets. ✓**EWORLD**→*go* whitepine ✓**INTERNET**→*www* http://www.wpine.com/ ...→*www* ftp://wpine.com/

Williams & Macias myDiskLabeler, SlapSticks, and Sicky Business. ✓**EWORLD**→*go* wmi.tech

Willow Peripherals Toner cartridges. ☎→*dial* 718-993-2066

Wilson WindowWare WinEdit, Address Manager, Command Post, File Commander, Windows Reminder, WinBatch. ✓**AMERICA ONLINE**→*keyword* wilson ✓**COMPUSERVE**→*go* winapa→Messages *and* Libraries→Wilson WindowWare

Word Perfect Corporation WordPerfect and add-ons. ☎→*dial* 801-225-4444 ✓**AMERICA ONLINE**→*keyword* wordperfect ✓**COMPUSERVE**→*go* Wordperfect *and* wpuser ✓**INERNET**→*www* ftp://ftp.wordperfect.com/ ...→*www* http://www.wordperfect.com/

Working Software Toner Tuner, Spellswell, Last Resort, Findswell, Lookup, QuickLetter, and Dictionary series. ✓**AMERICA ONLINE**→*keyword* working ✓**COMPUSERVE**→*go* macbven→Messages *and* Libraries→Working Software

X

Xaos Tools NewTek, Xaos Tools, Fresco, Terrazzo, Pennello, and Paint Alchemy. ✓**AMERICA ONLINE**→*keyword* xaos

Xceed ColorFusion and Mac Video cards. ✓**AMERICA ONLINE**→*keyword* xceed

Xerox Imaging systems, color copiers, software, and other office computer hardware. ✓**COMPUSERVE**→*go* xerox ✓**INTERNET**→*www* http://www.xerox.com/

Xilinx, Inc XC7200A, XC7300, XC4000, XC4010D, and many others. ✓**INTERNET**→*www* http://www.xilinx.com/

Xircom ThinkPads and Xircom PE3. ✓**COMPUSERVE**→*go* pcvenh→Messages *and* Libraries→Xircom

Xylogics, Inc Annex and Remote Annex. ✓**INTERNET**→*www* http://www.xylogics.com/

Z

Zedcor, Inc. DeskGallery CD-ROMs, DeskPaint, DeskDraw, and FutureBasic. ✓**AMERICA ONLINE**→*keyword* zedcor

Zelos Shoot Video, 3-D Tutor, and Escape from Management Hell. ✓**EWORLD**→*go* zelos

Zenographics SuperPrint fonts, Mirage, ImPort, ArtPack II, SuperQueue. ☎→*dial* 714-851-3860 ✓**COMPUSERVE**→*go* zeno→Messages *and* Libraries→Zenographics

Zeos Workstations, network file servers, notebook computers, and other PC hardware. ✓**COMPUSERVE**→*go* pcvene→Messages *and* Libraries→Zeos

Zero Surge Full line of surge suppressors. ✓**INTERNET**→*www* http://www.targetus.com/

Zilog Z8 series and other mass storage controllers. ✓**INTERNET**→*www* http://www.zilog.com/zilog/

ZipIt Zipit. ✓**INTERNET**→*www* ftp://ftp.awa.com/pub/softlock/mac/products/zipit/ ...→*www* http://www.awa.com/softlock/zipit/zipit.html

Zoom BitFax and the Zoom series. ☎→*dial* 617-423-3733 ✓**COMPUSERVE**→*go* modemvendor→Messages *and* Libraries→Zoom

Zoomer PDAs. ✓**INTERNET**→*www* http://www.eit.com/mailinglists/zoomer/zoomer

Zsoft Publishers Paintbrush and the Soft Type font series. ☎→*dial* 404-514-6332

ZyXel Software and a full line of external, internal, and portable modems. ☎→*dial* 714-693-0762 ✓**COMPUSERVE**→*go* modemvendor→Messages *and* Libraries→ZyXel ✓**INTERNET**→*www* http://www.zyxel.com/

Internet Providers

Internet Providers
by region and state

National

Alternet (UUNET Technologies, Inc.)
703-204-8000 (vox)

America OnLine
800-827-6364 (vox)

CompuServe
800-848-8199 (vox)

Delphi
800-695-4005 (vox)

GEnie
800-638-9636 (vox)

Global Connect, Inc.
804-229-4484 (vox)

MindVox
800-646-3869 (vox)

NETCOM On-Line Communications Services
800-501-8649/408-554-8649 (vox)

Prodigy
800-776-3449 (vox)

YPN
800-638-1133 (vox)

Regional

Digital Express Group, Inc.
301-847-5000 (vox)

Internet Express
800-592-1240 (vox)

Interpath
800-849-6305 (vox)

New Mexico Technet, Inc.
505-345-6559 (vox)

Alabama

Community Internet Connect, Inc.
205-722-0199 (vox)

db Technology
205-556-9020 (vox)

interQuest
205-464-8280 (vox)

WSNetwork Communications Services, Inc.
800-463-8750/334-263-5505 (vox)

Arkansas

Cloverleaf Technologies
903-832-1367 (vox)

Sibylline, Inc.
501-521-4660 (vox)

Arizona

Crossroads Communications
602-813-9040 (vox)

Internet Direct of Utah, Inc.
602-274-0100 (vox)

Opus One
602-324-0494 (vox)

Primenet
800-463-8386/602-870-1010 (vox)

RTD Systems & Networking, Inc.
602-318-0696 (vox)

Systems Solutions Inc.
602-955-5566 (vox)

California

Access InfoSystems
707-422-1034 (vox)

Aimnet Information Services
408-257-0900 (vox)

Beckmeyer Development
510-530-9637 (vox)

BTR Communications Company
415-966-1429 (vox)

CC NET
510-988-0680 (vox)

CineNet
310-399-4421 (vox)

Cloverleaf Communications
714-895-3075 (vox)

CONNECTnet Internet Network Services
619-450-0254 (vox)

CRL
415-837-5300 (vox)

CTS Network Services
619-637-3637 (vox)

Cybergate Information Services
209-486-4283 (vox)

The Cyberspace Station
619-634-2894 (vox)

Delta Internet Services
714-778-0370 (vox)

DigiLink Network Services
310-542-7421 (vox)

Internet Providers

Direct Net Access Incorporated
510-649-6110 (vox)

Directnet
213-383-3144 (vox)

Earth Spirit Online
310-264-4785 (vox)

EarthLink Network, Inc.
213-644-9500 (vox)

Electriciti
619-338-9000 (vox)

HoloNet Information Access
510-704-0160 (vox)

Infoserv Connections
408-335-5600 (vox)

INTERNEX
415-473-3060 (vox)

ISP Networks
408-653-0100 (vox)

KAIWAN Internet
714-638-2139 (vox)

LanMinds, Inc.
510-843-6389 (vox)

Lightside, Inc.
818-858-9261 (vox)

LineX Communications
415-455-1650 (vox)

NetGate Communications
408-565-9601 (vox)

Northcoast Internet
707-443-8696 (vox)

Primenet
800-463-8386/602-870-1010 (vox)

QuakeNet
415-655-6607 (vox)

Regional Alliance for

Information Networking
805-967-7246 (vox)

Scruz-Net
800-319-5555/408-457-5050 (vox)

SenseMedia
408-335-9400 (vox)

Sierra-Net
702-831-3353 (vox)

SLIPNET
415-281-3132 (vox)

South Valley Internet
408-683-4533 (vox)

ViaNet Communications
415-903-2242 (vox)

The WELL
415-332-4335 (vox)

West Coast Online
707-586-3060 (vox)

WombatNet
415-462-8800 (vox)

zNET
619-755-7772 (vox)

Zocalo Engineering
510-540-8000 (vox)

Colorado

Colorado SuperNet, Inc.
303-296-8202 (vox)

Community News Service, Inc.
719-592-1240 (vox)

CSDC, Inc.
303-665-8053 (vox)

ENVISIONET, Inc.
303-770-2408 (vox)

Indra's Net, Inc.
303-546-9151 (vox)

Old Colorado City Communications
719-528-5849 (vox)

Rocky Mountain Internet
800-900-7644 (vox)

Stonehenge Internet Communications
800-786-4638 (vox)

Connecticut

CONNIX
203-349-7059 (vox)

Futuris Networks, Inc.
203-359-8868 (vox)

I-2000, Inc.
516-867-6379 (vox)

Paradigm Communications
203-250-7397 (vox)

District of Columbia

CAPCON Library Network
202-331-5771 (vox)

CharmNet
410-558-3300 (vox)

Genuine Computing Resources
703-878-4680 (vox)

Internet Online, Inc.
301-652-4468 (vox)

usNet, Inc.
301-572-5926 (vox)

Delaware

SSNet, Inc.
302-378-1386 (vox)

Net Tech 321

Internet Providers

Florida

Acquired Knowledge Systems Inc.
305-525-2574 (vox)

CocoNet Corporation
813-945-0055 (vox)

CyberGate, Inc.
305-428-4283 (vox)

East Greenwich
401-885-6855 (vox)

The EmiNet Domain
407-731-0222 (vox)

Florida Online
407-635-8888 (vox)

Intelligence Network Online, Inc.
813-442-0144 EXT.22 (vox)

InternetU
407-952-8487 (vox)

MagicNet, Inc.
407-657-2202 (vox)

MetroLink Internet Services
407-726-6707 (vox)

PacketWorks, Inc.
813-446-8826 (vox)

Polaris Network, Inc.
904-878-9745 (vox)

PSS InterNet Services
800-463-8499 (vox)

SatelNET Communications
305-434-8738 (vox)

SymNet
904-385-1061 (vox)

Georgia

Internet Atlanta
404-410-9000 (vox)

MindSpring
404-888-0725 (vox)

Prometheus Information Network Group, Inc. (PING)
800-746-4835/404-399-1670 (vox)

Hawaii

Hawaii OnLine
808-533-6981 (vox)

LavaNet, Inc.
808-545-5282 (vox)

PACCOM
808-956-3499 (vox)

Pacific Information Exchange, Inc.
808-596-7494 (vox)

SenseMedia
408-335-9400 (vox)

Idaho

Micron Internet Services
208-368-5400 (vox)

Primenet
800-463-8386/602-870-1010 (vox)

Transport Logic
503-243-1940 (vox)

Illinois

American Information Systems
708-413-8400 (vox)

INETDOM
800-463-8366 (vox)

InterAccess Co.
800-967-1580 (vox)

MCSNet
312-248-8649 (vox)

netILLINOIS
708-866-1825 (vox)

Open Business Systems, Inc.
708-250-0260 (vox)

Ripco Communications, Inc.
312-477-6210 (vox)

Sol Tec, Inc.
800-765-1832/317-920-1832 (vox)

Tezcatlipoca, Inc.
312-850-0181 (vox)

WorldWide Access
708-367-1870 (vox)

Indiana

Evansville Online
812-479-1700 (vox)

HolliCom Internet Services
317-883-4500 (vox)

IgLou Internet ServiceS
800-436-4456 (vox)

IQuest Network Services
317-259-5050 (vox)

Metropolitan Data Networks Limited
317-449-0539 (vox)

Net Direct
317-251-5252 (vox)

Sol Tec, Inc.
800-765-1832/317-920-1832 (vox)

World Connection Services
812-479-1700 (vox)

Kansas

DATABANK, Inc.
913-842-6699 (vox)

Internet Providers

Interstate Networking Corporation
816-472-4949 (vox)

Primenet
800-463-8386/602-870-1010 (vox)

SouthWind Internet Access, Inc.
316-263-7963 (vox)

Kentucky

IgLou Internet ServiceS
800-436-4456 (vox)

Lousiana

Communique Inc.
504-527-6200 (vox)

I-Link Ltd
800-454-6599 (vox)

NEOSOFT
800-438-6367/713-684-5969 (vox)

Maine

Internet Services
207-947-8248 (vox)

Maine.Net
207-780-6381 (vox)

Maryland

CAPCON Library Network
202-331-5771 (vox)

CharmNet
410-558-3900 (vox)

CLARK
410-995-0691 (vox)

FredNet
301-698-2386 (vox)

Genuine Computing Resources
703-878-4680 (vox)

Internet Online, Inc.
301-652-4468 (vox)

jaguNET Access Services
410-931-3157 (vox)

Softaid Internet Services Inc.
410-290-7763 (vox)

SURAnet
301-982-4600 (vox)

usNet, Inc.
301-572-5926 (vox)

Massachusetts

CENTnet, Inc.
617-492-6079 (vox)

FOURnet Information Network
508-291-2900 (vox)

info@millcomm.com
508-363-2413 (vox)

The Internet Access Company
617-276-7200 (vox)

The Internet Access Company
617-275-2221 (vox)

intuitive information, inc.
508-342-1100 (vox)

Mallard Electronics, Inc.
413-732-0214 (vox)

North Shore Access
617-593-3110 (vox)

Pioneer Neighborhood
617-646-4800 (vox)

SCHUNIX
508-853-0258 (vox)

ShaysNet.COM
413-772-2923 (vox)

StarNet (Advanced Communication Systems
508-922-8238 (vox)

TerraNet, Inc.
617-450-9000 (vox)

UltraNet Communications, Inc.
800-763-8111/508-229-8400 (vox)

Wilder Systems, Inc.
617-933-8810 (vox)

The World
617-739-0202 (vox)

Wrentham Internet Services
508-384-1404 (vox)

Michigan

Branch Information Services
313-741-4442 (vox)

IACNet
313-998-0090 (vox)

ICNET / Innovative Concepts
313-998-0090 (vox)

Innovative Data Services
810-478-3554 (vox)

Isthmus Corporation
313-973-2100 (vox)

Msen, Inc.
313-998-4562 (vox)

RustNet, Inc.
810-650-6812 (vox)

Minnesota

InforMNs
612-638-8786 (vox)

Internet Connections, Inc.
507-625-7320 (vox)

Internet Providers

Millennium Communications, Inc.
612-338-5509 (vox)

Red River Net
701-232-2227 (vox)

StarNet Communications, Inc.
612-941-9177 (vox)

Missouri

INETDOM
800-463-8366 (vox)

Interstate Networking Corporation
816-472-4949 (vox)

NEOSOFT
800-438-6367/713-684-5969 (vox)

THOUGHTPORT
314-474-6870 (vox)

Montana

Montana Online
406-721-4952 (vox)

North Carolina

CONCERT
919-248-1999 (vox)

FXNET
704-338-4670 (vox)

Red Barn Data Center
910-750-9809 (vox)

SunBelt.Net
803-328-1500 (vox)

Vnet Internet Access
800-377-3282/704-334-3282 (vox)

North Dakota

Red River Net
701-232-2227 (vox)

Nebraska

Internet Nebraska
402-434-8680 (vox)

Synergy Communications, Inc.
800-345-9669 (vox)

New Hampshire

Destek
603-635-7263 (vox)

info@millcomm.com
603-635-3857 (vox)

MV Communications, Inc.
603-429-2223 (vox)

NETIS Public Access Internet
603-437-1811 (vox)

New Jersey

Carroll-Net
201-488-1332 (vox)

Castle Network, Inc.
800-577-9449/908-548-8881 (vox)

The Connection
201-435-4414 (vox)

Fry
201-455-3505 (vox)

I-2000, Inc.
516-867-6379 (vox)

INTAC Access Corporation
800-504-6822 (vox)

InterCom Online
212-714-7183 (vox)

Internet For 'U'
800-638-9291 (vox)

Internet Online Services
201-928-1000 ext. 226 (vox)

K2NE Software
609-893-0673 (vox)

New Jersey Computer Connection
609-896-2799 (vox)

New York Net
718-776-6811 (vox)

NIC - Neighborhood Internet Connection
201-934-1445 (vox)

Planet Access Networks
201-691-4704 (vox)

New Mexico

Computer Systems Consulting
505-984-0085 (vox)

Southwest Cyberport
505-271-0009 (vox)

ZyNet SouthWest
505-343-8846 (vox)

Nevada

Great Basin Internet Services
702-348-7299 (vox)

InterMind
702-878-6111 (vox)

NevadaNet
702-784-4827 (vox)

Sierra-Net
702-831-3353 (vox)

wizard.com
702-871-4461 (vox)

New York

Blythe Systems
212-226-7171 (vox)

Internet Providers

Cloud 9 Internet
914-682-0626 (VOX)

Computer Solutions by Hawkinson
914-229-9853 (VOX)

Creative Data Consultants (SILLY.COM)
718-229-0489 EXT. 23 (VOX)

E-Znet, Inc.
716-262-2485 (VOX)

East Greenwich, Rhode Island
401-885-6855 (VOX)

Echo Communications Group
212-255-3839 (VOX)

escape.com - Kazan Corp
212-888-8780 (VOX)

I-2000, Inc.
516-867-6379 (VOX)

Ingress Communications Inc.
212-679-2838 (VOX)

INTAC Access Corporation
800-504-6822 (VOX)

InterCom Online
212-714-7183 (VOX)

Internet For 'U'
800-638-9291 (VOX)

Internet Online Services
201-928-1000 EXT. 226 (VOX)

Interport Communications Corp.
212-989-1128 (VOX)

LI Net, Inc.
516-265-0997 (VOX)

Maestro
212-240-9600 (VOX)

Mnematics, Incorporated
914-359-4546 (VOX)

Moran Communications
716-639-1254 (VOX)

Network Internet Services
516-543-0234 (VOX)

Network-USA
516-543-0234 (VOX)

New York Net
718-776-6811 (VOX)

NY WEBB, Inc.
800-458-4660 (VOX)

NYSERNet
315-453-2912 (VOX)

Panix
212-877-4854 (VOX)

PHANTOM (MindVox)
212-989-2418 (VOX)

The Pipeline Network
212-267-2626 (VOX)

SERVTECH
716-546-6908 (VOX)

TZ-Link
914-353-5443 (VOX)

WestNet Internet Services
914-967-7802 (VOX)

Wizvax Communications
518-273-4325 (VOX)

Ohio

APK Net, Ltd
216-481-9428 (VOX)

The Dayton Network Access Company
513-237-6868 (VOX)

EriNet
513-436-1700 (VOX)

Exchange Network Services, Inc.
216-261-4593 (VOX)

IgLou Internet ServiceS
800-436-4456 (VOX)

Infinite Systems
614-268-9941 (VOX)

Internet Access Cincinnati
513-887-8877 (VOX)

Local Internet Gateway Co.
510-503-9227 (VOX)

NACS Networking
216-524-8388 (VOX)

New Age Consulting Service
216-524-3162 (VOX)

Oarnet
800-627-8101/614-728-8100 (VOX)

Oklahoma

Galaxy Star Systems
918-835-3655 (VOX)

Internet Oklahoma
405-721-4861 (VOX)

Questar Network Services
405-848-3228 (VOX)

Oregon

Data Research Group, Inc.
503-465-3282 (VOX)

Europa
503-222-9508 (VOX)

Hevanet Communications
503-228-3520 (VOX)

Open Door Networks, Inc.
503-488-4127 (VOX)

Net Tech 325

Internet Providers

Structured Network Systems, Inc.
800-881-0962/503-656-3530 (vox)

Teleport, Inc.
503-223-4245 (vox)

Transport Logic
503-243-1940 (vox)

Pennsylvania

City-Net
412-481-5406 (vox)

King of Prussia, PA 19406
610-337-9994 (vox)

Microserve Information Systems
800-380-4638/717-779-4430 (vox)

OASIS
610-439-8560 (vox)

PREPnet
412-268-7870 (vox)

PSCNET
412-268-4960 (vox)

SSNet, Inc.
302-378-1386 (vox)

Telerama Public Access Internet
412-481-3505 (vox)

YOU TOOLS Corporation
610-954-5910 (vox)

Rhode Island

East Greenwich
401-885-6855 (vox)

South Carolina

A World of Difference, Inc.
803-769-4488 (vox)

Global Vision Inc.
803-241-0901 (vox)

SIMS, Inc.
803-762-4956 (vox)

South Carolina SuperNet
803-748-1207 (vox)

SunBelt.Net
803-328-1500 (vox)

Tennessee

The Edge
615-455-9915 (vox)

GoldSword Systems
615-691-6498 (vox)

ISDN-Net Inc.
615-377-7672 (vox)

Magibox Incorporated
901-757-7835 (vox)

Preferred Internet Services
615-323-1142 (vox)

The Telalink Corporation
615-321-9100 (vox)

The Tri-Cities Connection
615-378-5355 (vox)

Texas

The Black Box
713-480-2684 (vox)

Cloverleaf Technologies
903-832-1367 (vox)

DFW Internet Services, Inc.
817-332-6642 (vox)

Electrotex, Inc.
800-460-1801/713-526-3456 (vox)

I-Link Ltd
800-454-6599 (vox)

Illuminati Online
512-462-0999 (vox)

Internet Access of El Paso
915-533-1525 (vox)

Internet Connect Services
512-572-9987 (vox)

NEOSOFT
800-438-6367/713-684-5969 (vox)

Real/Time Communications
512-451-0046 (vox)

Sesquinet
713-527-4988 (vox)

@sig.net
512-306-0700 (vox)

Texas Metronet, Inc.
214-705-2900 (vox)

THEnet
512-471-2444 (vox)

USiS
713-682-1666 (vox)

Zilker Internet Park, Inc.
512-206-3850 (vox)

Utah

DATABANK, Inc.
913-842-6699 (vox)

Infonaut Communication Services
801-370-3068 (vox)

Internet Direct of Utah, Inc.
801-578-0300 (vox)

XMission
801-539-0852 (vox)

Virginia

CAPCON Library Network
202-331-5771 (vox)

Internet Providers

CharmNet
410-558-3900 (vox)

CLARK
410-995-0691 (vox)

DATABANK, Inc.
913-842-6699 (vox)

Genine Computing Resources
703-878-4680 (vox)

Genuine Computing Resources
703-878-4680 (vox)

Internet Online, Inc.
301-652-4468 (vox)

usNet, Inc.
301-572-5926 (vox)

Widomaker Communication Service
804-253-7621 (vox)

Washington

Cyberspace
206-281-5397 (vox)

dBUG
206-932-6369 (vox)

Eskimo North
206-367-7457 (vox)

GemStar Iformation Services
206-539-1257 (vox)

Halcyon
206-455-3505 (vox)

Internetworks, Inc.
206-576-7147 (vox)

Network Access Services
206-733-9279 (vox)

NEXUS
206-455-3505 (vox)

NorthWest CommLink
360-336-0103 (vox)

Olympus
206-385-0464 (vox)

Pacific Rim Network, Inc.
360-650-0442 (vox)

Pacifier Computers
206-254-3886 (vox)

Seanet Online Services
206-343-7828 (vox)

Seanews
206-747-6397 (vox)

SenseMedia
408-335-9400 (vox)

Skagit On-Line Services
360-755-0190 (vox)

Structured Network Systems, Inc.
800-881-0962/503-656-3530 (vox)

Teleport, Inc.
503-223-4245 (vox)

Townsend Communications, Inc.
360-385-0464 (vox)

Transport Logic
503-243-1940 (vox)

WHIDBEY
360-678-0262 (vox)

WLN
800-342-5956/360-923-4000 (vox)

Wisconsin

Exec-PC, Inc.
800-393-2721/414-789-4200 (vox)

FullFeed Communications
608-246-4239 (vox)

MIX Communications
414-351-1868 (vox)

NetNet, Inc.
414-499-1339 (vox)

WiscNet
608-262-8874 (vox)

West Virginia

WVNET
304-293-5192 (vox)

Wyoming

wyoming.com
800-996-4638/307-332-3030 (vox)

Canada

CCI Networks
403-450-6787 (vox)

Communication Accessibles Montreal
514-288-2581 (vox)

Debug Computer Services
403-248-5798 (vox)

Information Gateway Services
613-592-5619 (vox)

Island Net
604-727-6030 (vox)

HookUp Communications
905-847-8000 (vox)

Okanagan Internet Junction
604-549-1036 (vox)

Sunshine Net, Inc.
604-886-4120 (vox)

Shareware BBSs
by area code

201

Boss BBS
568-7293
Bytes 'n Bits BBS
437-4355
Evergreen BBS
398-2373
Golden Dane BBS
338-5265
Hard Drive Cafe BBS System
790-6300
Jezebel's Parlour
927-2932
NJPCUG
835-3122
TIMBBS
224-2688

203

Cygnus X-I Opus BBS
628-9702
The Power House BBS
268-1275

204

Info-Source Canada
667-0899

205

Po' Boy's BBS
271-3545
Razz-Ma-Tazz
859-5459
SFE Systems BBS
650-0107

206

A to Z Tech Line
432-4732
Game room
698-1052

Sales Automation Success!
392-8943
Starlight
782-3221
Ten Forward
452-7681
The Beacon BBS
839-9062
The Shareware Store
531-3022

208

Valley Network
788-0703

210

Last Chance TBBS
822-4050

212

Invention factory
274-8110
Rael Exposure
376-4444
Red Phone Info System
924-1138

213

Mr. Wonderful's Lair
261-8055
ThunderVolts BBS
225-5474

214

Collector's edition
351-9859
Garbage Dump
644-6060
Hogard software Solutions
641-6292

Puss N Boots
437-0688
UT Dallas Undergraduate
883-2168

215

Diretc Connect
535-1917
National Cheese Emporium
673-0261
Newtown Express BBS
943-6806
SataLink Info Systems
364-3324
Storm Front BBS
788-4662
WinConnect BBS
542-9059

216

G-Net BBS
755-0843
HoneyRun Valley BBS
674-7809
Multiverse
241-0076
PC-Ohio
381-3320
Rusty-N-Edie's BBS
726-2620

217

Koeltz Scientific Books
355-4532

218

Bertha BBS
924-2060

Shareware BBSs

219

GeoFract BBS
484-9740
KSI Public BBS
626-2150
Networking BBS
288-1402

301

BlockBuster Bulletin Board
831-9942
Capitol Area Network
499-4671
File Exchange BBS
890-5678
HUG & Lincoln Software
733-6456
T.I.F.S.D.B.
975-9794
World Data network
654-2554

302

DTEL
739-2818

303

Aspenwoods BBS
388-0336
Boardwatch Magazine
973-4222
C.C.N.
477-0356
Colorado Connection
423-9775
Dart Board RBBS
882-2360
File Bank Inc.
534-4646
Global-Link Network
680-4563
Long's Peak BBS
772-7921
Microlink D
237-8575
Stoic Financial BBS
238-0588
System design
421-6368

304

Cat Eye
592-3390

305

Miami PC Users Group
680-9481
Ram BBS
258-1844
Shadows Palace BBS
895-4688
WinCrew BBS
253-9598

306

Business Solutions BBS
653-1664
SkyWatch
569-0581

308

LoperNet BBS
234-2247

310

Link BBS
459-1264
Sable Online
768-8362
Why Not RBBS-PC
436-9008

312

OnLine Resource BBS
631-7191

313

Gateway Online
291-5571
HAL 9000 BBS
663-4173
mAp/LZ
563-8940
The Unstoppable Dragons BBS
697-0609

Toledo's TBBS
854-6001

314

Bob and Joe's
351-3551
Mill Dog BBS
240-7545
St Louis Users Group BBS
878-7614

315

Dimensional Rift BBS
789-1061
Nite-Air BBS
339-8831

316

Linker BBS
321-5410

317

Delaware Online services
741-8631
Mail Room BBS
644-5029
RoadHouse BBS
784-2147
Sudden Impact
457-5957
Trader's Connection
359-5199

318

DataExchange BBS
239-2122
PUMA Wildcat!
443-1065
Small Circle BBS
662-3328

319

Crawdad's World
377-3084
The Lower Level
373-5852

Shareware BBSs

334
DFG Financial BBS
745-0579
Out-Post RBBS
774-6989
The Shareware Exchange
809-0270

401
Playtime Computer BBS
724-1864
Prime Cut BBS
334-3096

402
Hawg Wild!
493-2737

403
BorderQuest BBS
262-5095
Nucleus Information Service
531-9353
T-8000 Info system
686-6336

404
Express Net
410-9139
INDEX Systems
924-8472
Serious Fun
433-8213
Thompson Towers BBS
941-0746
Wesley's window
522-9240

405
Car 54 BBS
372-1421
Games 'R Us
447-7954
Sandbox
737-9540
Tranquility Base BBS
682-2352

407
Black Cauldron BBS
699-6613
$ensible $oftware
298-5830
FABulous BBS
834-6466
Jupiter BBS
575-3853
Round Table Software
740-8353

408
Globalnet
439-9367
Mainstreet online
224-7523

409
Motherboard III
441-2939
Tech Resource
892-1977

410
BorderTown BBS
876-5101
HouseNet
745-2037
Upper Limits BBS
860-0212
V-I-S-I-O-N
750-3800

412
Dew Drop Inn
854-0619
JBJ System PCBoard BBS
341-9323
MetroPitts BBS
487-9222

413
The BMB Software BBS
731-1155
The X-Sight BBS
664-6501

414
Chip-N-Disk BBS
862-6221
Exec-PC
789-4210
The Back Door BBS
744-6003
The Crystal Barrier
457-8399

415
Gateway software BBS
885-1392
Space BBS
323-4193
Window World BBS
931-0649

416
ComputerLink
233-5410

417
Alpha-Omega
862-5584
Computer matrix
862-8910

419
Menagerie BBS
935-0245

501
Arkansas River Valley
968-1931
Conway PC Users Group BBS
329-7227

502
File World BBS
867-0062

503
Event Horizons
697-5100

Shareware BBSs

504
Southern Star BBS
885-5928

505
Albequerque ROS
296-3000
Construction Net #6
662-0659
Garbage Dump
294-5675
Zia Software BBS
336-4360

506
BlueMax BBS
382-9220
Digital Acces BBS
277-1122

507
PC-MONITOR
373-1100

508
Archives BBS
995-0085
Crystal Mountain BBS
249-9778
Electric Connections BBS
485-6440
Nordic Enterprises EDMS
356-1166
Software Creations
365-2359
TechNet BBS
366-7683
Xanadu BBS
995-9876
xevious BBS
788-6951

509
Night Voyager BBS
926-1686
Sigma Iotia RBBS
966-2023

510
MindWare Online
843-8071
Tiger Team Buddhist
268-0102
VisionBytes!
355-0968

512
CCAT
242-2206
CompuBasix
994-8300
Computer Data Services
887-0787

513
Multisystems TBBS
231-7013

514
ToToche BBS
326-8363

515
Computer Support Hotline
288-9601

516
America's Suggestion Box
471-8625
L.I.N.E.
261-9701
Mistral BBS
921-6806
The Moon Base
395-1315
The Nut House
862-2274
The Ultimate BBS
488-1828
Time Slice BBS
266-5182

517
CRIS
895-0510
I-Star Computer
739-2841
Jackson Area PCUG
789-7556
PJ Systems
451-2072
Wolverine BBS
695-9952

519
Knightec BBS
940-0007
Late Nite Diversions
332-0241
Online Systems of Canada
642-0700
UpAllNite BBS
351-4364

601
Afetr Hours BBS
371-0423
OMEGA-ONE BBS
287-1336
Psychobabble
332-9453

602
At The Mountain
981-3591
Pinnacle BBS
242-9226
Rock Garden
220-0001
The Arizona Speed Trap
768-6584
The Code-3 BBS
686-3575

603
BotNay Bay
431-7090
Nor'Easter Premium
886-7072

Net Tech 331

Shareware BBSs

604
AIS Multiline
489-4206
Deep Cove BBS
536-5885
Trade Link
768-0988

605
Capitol View BBS
224-0982

606
Bluegrass RBBS
272-0499
Peace Connection
439-1734
PROF-BBS
269-1565
The Midiland BBS
324-3917
Vampirella's Crypt
327-6605

607
Destination CPU
737-6901
EmmaSoft Shareware Boards
533-7072

608
Boardwalk BBS
257-0486
JADE
757-3000

609
Casino Bulletin Board
485-2380
NJ Computer Connection
895-0398
Radio wave BBS
764-0812
Wall BBS
758-1991

610
Black Bag BBS
454-7396
Del Ches Systems BBS
363-6625
DreamLine II BBS
279-2760
Mystic Mansion in Lehigh Valley
691-1254
RunWay BBS
534-3082

612
Top City BBS
225-1003

613
Silicon Tundra
838-5341
V-Net Online Services
723-1740

614
Vault BBS
387-2762
VICOM Information Service
775-7083
Wizard's Gate BBS
224-1635

615
Bill's BBS
694-8757
Comunique
885-9792
Sounds of Silence
449-5969
Tennessee connection
781-8636
Trader's Connection
883-4700
Your Personal enrichment BBS
833-6018

616
8-Bit Corner
755-3013
Alien Space ship
275-7000
Cherry capital Playground
929-0905
Evans BBS
754-6180
The Gateway BBS
422-2877
Vision Quest
725-8566

617
Argus Computerized Exchange
674-2345
Flix, Pages & Tunes
235-0789
Mass online - The XTC Zone
582-2223
StarSoft
545-0669
TessHeder/Brian Miller
354-3230

618
Ace Online
942-2218
Ace Online
942-2218
C'Mon Inn BBS
948-0952
Omega Line
392-4607

619
Classified Connection
566-7347
File Bank
728-7307
Global Cyber-media BBS
280-5309
Lakeside Wildcat! BBS
390-7328
MARS Station
254-3012
Pacific Rim Information

332 Net Tech

Shareware BBSs

278-7361

701
Node Dakota
224-1431

702
Charleston Communications
386-7979
Eagle's Nest BBS
853-4703
InterComm
359-2666
M.I.A. BBS
423-6675
Planet One Systems
738-2378
QuickSilver
384-8503

703
Break RBBS
680-9269
Contraxx BBS
573-5255
Jon Larimore
578-4542
Nexus BBS
898-7205
The Communique Capsule
490-4184
Va Shareware Network
730-8731
Window Shop
878-2989
World Data network
620-8900

704
Big Byte
279-2295
Cliffside BBS
657-4154
Mind's Eye
322-1681
Transporter Room
567-9513

706
Country Store
561-7359
INDEX Systems
613-0566

707
BBS Express
571-7526
Electric Grapevine
257-2338
Philosopher's Stone
464-8722
Sigma Industries BBS
263-8581
The Information Exchange
542-7901

708
Age of Information
301-6465
Chicago Syslink
795-4442
Horse feathers
587-9214
Lambda Zone BBS
827-3619
Mortgage Market On-Line
834-9734
NAFI On-Line
885-9305
RadioComm
518-8336
Resting Place BBS
786-6240
Sportsman's Plus
516-8953
Sunset Ridge BBS
636-0971
Wild Onion!
993-0461

713
Atomic Cafe BBS
530-8875

714
Liberty BBS
996-7777
The Amazons Arena
840-145
The Quest Online
693-2480
Vivid Image BBS
669-8823

715
Cutting Edge
333-2007
Family Room
355-8311
Point BBS
345-1327
Rapid River BBS
435-3855
Twilight Zone
652-2758

716
PC3
723-8489
Pier Exchange
875-0283

717
Cyberia
840-1444
Pennsylvania Online!
657-8699
Stimpy's Sandbox
730-8504

718
Apartment 2
347-1075
Berkshire Tool Company
321-0678
Consultant BBS
837-3236
Jim's PC Paradise
458-0502
Kitty's Cafe! BBS
352-1720

Net Tech 333

Shareware BBSs

Rama One BBS
366-6165
The Electric Line BBS
822-6997

719
Electro-Technika
380-0541

800
Liberty BBS
474-1818

801
Privy Ledged BBS
966-6270
Rocky Mountain Software
963-8721
The OutWest BBS
250-5029
The Windows Source BBS
532-3716

802
The Particle Board
864-0250

803
Crossroads BBS
957-7077
Night Vision BBS
654-2945

804
Blue Ridge Express
790-1675
Club PC BBS
357-0357
Intercity BBS
353-4160
Pistonhead
288-8416
Richmond Connection
740-1364
RiverCity BBS
965-9739

Servant of the Lord
590-2161
Virginia Data Exchange
877-0407

805
Beyond The REALM
987-5506
Board
579-9082
CD-ROM Multimedia & Specialties BBS
373-2965
Grinder
583-5833
Seaside
964-4766

806
Windmill Company BBS
792-6116

807
Acumen BBS
626-9339
Superior Shareware
475-3099

810
Advantage Business Forum
781-8601
FireBox Express
826-9411
Techno-Babble
737-2912
Wishing Well BBS
754-6731

812
Good News BBS
335-3575
Magpie BBS
793-2537
The Top of the Hill BBS
824-8682
Ya! WebeCad! BBS
428-0267

813
Bayline Online
661-0903
DataWave
665-5694
ENIAC BBS
853-4883
Margaritaville
939-3009
Mercury Opus
321-0734
MicroMetric Support
371-2490
Southeast Data Link
954-3282
TNT Online
337-5999

816
Cypress Corners BBS
7967078
E.A.
767-1811
The Haven BBS
322-2032

817
Trojan Horse
346-8382

818
A Community BBS
358-3811
Ace-Station-BBS
891-0397
Hottips BBS
248-3088
Ledge PCBoard
896-2007
Mog-Ur's EMS
366-6442
Prime Time BBS
982-7271
SouthWest BBS
285-8684
Sports Club BBS
792-4752

Shareware BBSs

819
Synapse BBS
561-4321
X-CONNECTIONS BBS
776-0088

901
Smart Move BBS
632-1947

902
ATAB BBS
435-0751

904
Dr. Sned's BBS-In-A-Box
325-6558
Land of the Lounge Lizards
645-3846
Panama Shareware
235-3634
Steve's Place
874-2821
Toy Shop
688-9124
WINGIT
386-8693

905
Alpha City BBS
579-6302
French Connexion
632-5653

906
Colligatarch Authority
265-0037

907
Dagan Software BBS
248-8130
The Highland BBS
376-0894

908
Computer Junction
354-6979
Data-Base BBS
735-2185
Dataland! BBS
572-5762
Just Programs BBS
298-9098

909
Attention to Details
681-6221
Library! BBS
780-6365
Locker Room
270-5278

910
Cape Fear BBS
270-3178
Tarheel Connection
643-9570
Treasure Chest
922-1047

912
Coastal Communications
353-8014
Darton Connection
430-3007

913
Computer Users Exchange
267-1903
North Star BBS
888-9848
The Military Connection
784-3575

914
Johnny Boy's PC-Mania
733-5697
Laser BBS
734-7045

916
24thStreet exchange
448-2483
Racer's Net
546-2095

918
Black gold BBS
272-7779

919
Entertainment Club BBS
544-7811
Late-Nite BBS
776-2368
Micro message service
779-6674
Seascape!
726-9364
The BC BBS
217-9540

Net Tech 335

netspeak™

@	Separates the **userid** and **domain name** of an Internet address. Pronounced "at."
anonymous FTP	Method of logging in to public file archives over the **Internet**. Enter "anonymous" when prompted for a **userid**. See **FTP**.
Archie	A program that lets you search **Internet FTP** archives worldwide by file name. One variant is called **Veronica**.
ASCII	A basic text format readable by most computers. The acronym stands for American Standard Code for Information Interchange.
bandwidth	The data transmission capacity of a network. Used colloquially to refer to the "size" of the Net; some information transmittals (e.g., multitudes of graphic files) are considered to be a "waste of bandwidth."
baud	The speed at which signals are sent by a **modem**, measured by the number of changes per second in the signals during transmission. A baud rate of 1,200, for example, would indicate 1,200 signal changes in one second. Baud rate is often confused with **bits per second (bps)**.
BBS	"Bulletin-board system." Once referred to stand-alone desktop computers with a single modem that answered the phone, but can now be as complicated and interconnected as a commercial service.
binary transfer	A file transfer between two computers that preserves binary data—used for all non-text files.
bits per second (bps)	The data-transfer rate between two **modems**. The higher the bps, the higher the speed of the transfer.
bounced message	An **email** message "returned to sender," usually because of an address error.
bye	A log-off command, like "quit" and "exit."
carrier signal	The squeaking noise that modems use to maintain a connection. See also **handshake**.
cd	"Change directory." A command used, for example, at an **FTP** site to move from a directory to a subdirectory.
cdup	"Change directory up." Can be used at an **FTP** site to move from a subdirectory to its parent directory. Also **chdirup**.
chdirup	See **cdup**.
client	A computer that connects to a more powerful computer (see **server**) for complex tasks.
commercial service	General term for large online services (e.g., America Online, CompuServe, Prodigy, GEnie).
compression	Shrinkage of computer files to conserve storage space and reduce transfer times. Special utility programs, available for most platforms (including DOS, Mac, and

Net Speak

	Amiga), perform the compression and decompression.
cracker	A person who maliciously breaks into a computer system in order to steal files or disrupt system activities.
dial-up access	Computer connection made over standard telephone lines.
dir	"Directory." A command used to display the contents of the current directory.
domain name	The worded address of an **IP number** on the **Internet**, in the form of domain subsets separated by periods. The full address of an **Internet** user is **userid@domain name**.
email	"Electronic mail."
emoticon	See **smiley**.
FAQ	"Frequently asked questions." A file of questions and answers compiled for **Usenet newsgroups**, **mailing lists**, and games to reduce repeated posts about commonplace subjects.
file transfer	Transfer of a file from one computer to another over a network.
finger	A program that provides information about a user who is logged into your local system or on a remote computer on the Internet. Generally invoked by typing "finger" and the person's **userid**.
flame	A violent and usually *ad hominem* attack against another person in a **newsgroup** or message area.
flame war	A back-and-forth series of **flames**.
Free-Net	A community-based network that provides free access to the **Internet**, usually to local residents, and often includes its own forums and news.
freeware	Free software. Not to be confused with **shareware**.
FTP	"File transfer protocol." The standard used to transfer files between computers.
get	An **FTP** command that transfers single files from the **FTP** site to your local directory. The command is followed by a file name; typing "get file.name" would transfer only that file. Also see **mget**.
GIF	Common file format for pictures first popularized by CompuServe, standing for "graphics interchange format." Pronounced with a hard *g*.
gopher	A menu-based guide to directories on the **Internet**, usually organized by subject.
GUI	"Graphical user interface" with windows and point-and-click capability, as opposed to a command-line interface with typed-out instructions.
hacker	A computer enthusiast who enjoys exploring computer systems and programs, sometimes to the point of obsession. Not to be confused with **cracker**.
handle	The name a user wishes to be known by; a user's handle may differ significantly from his or her real name or **userid**.
handshake	The squawking noise at the beginning of a computer connection when two modems settle on a protocol for exchanging information.
Home Page	The main **World Wide Web** site for a particular group or organization.
hqx	File suffix for a BinHex file, a common format for transmitting Macintosh binary files over the **Internet**.
hypertext	An easy method of retrieving information by choosing highlighted words in a text on the screen. The words link to documents with related subject matter.
IC	"In character." A game player who is IC is acting as his or her **character**'s persona.
Internet	The largest network of computer networks in the world, easily recognizable by the format of Internet **email** addresses: **userid**@host.

Net Speak

Internet provider	Wholesale or retail reseller of access to the **Internet**. YPN is one example.
IP connection	Full-fledged link to the **Internet**. See **SLIP**, **PPP**, and **TCP/IP**.
IP number	The unique number that determines the ultimate **Internet** identity of an **IP connection**.
IRC	"**Internet** relay chat." A service that allows **real-time** conversations between multiple users on a variety of subject-oriented channels.
jpeg	Common compressed format for picture files. Pronounced "jay-peg."
ls	"List." A command that provides simplified directory information at **FTP** sites and other directories. It lists only file names for the directory, not file sizes or dates.
lurkers	Regular readers of messages online who never post.
lynx	A popular text-based **Web browser**.
mailing list	Group discussion distributed through **email**. Many mailing lists are administered through listserv.
mget	An **FTP** command that transfers multiple files from the **FTP** site to your local directory. The command is followed by a list of file names separated by spaces, sometimes in combination with an asterisk used as a wild card. Typing "mget b*" would transfer all files in the directory beginning with the letter *b*. Also see **get**.
Net, the	A colloquial term that is often used to refer to the entirety of Cyberspace: the **Internet**, the **commercial services**, **BBSs**, etc.
netiquette	The rules of Cyberspace civility. Usually applied to the **Internet**, where manners are enforced exclusively by fellow users.
newbie	A newcomer to the **Net**, to a game, or to a discussion. Also called **fluxer**.
newsgroups	The **Usenet** message areas, organized by subject.
newsreader	Software program for reading **Usenet newsgroups** on the **Internet**.
port number	A number that follows a **telnet** address. The number connects a user to a particular application on the telnet site. LambdaMOO, for example, is at port 8888 of lambda.parc.xerox.com (lambda.parc.xerox.com 8888).
posting	The sending of a message to a **newsgroup**, bulletin board, or other public message area. The message itself is called a **post**.
pwd	A command used at an **FTP** site to display the name of the current directory on your screen.
real-time	The **Net** term for "live," as in "live broadcast." Real-time connections include **IRC** and **MUDs**.
remote machine	Any computer on the **Internet** reached with a program such as **FTP** or **telnet**. The machine making the connection is called the home, or local, machine.
RL	"Real life."
server	A software program, or the computer running the program, that allows other computers, called **clients**, to share its resources.
shareware	Free software, distributed over the **Net** with a request from the programmer for voluntary payment.
sig	Short for **signature**.
signature	A file added to the end of **email** messages or **Usenet** posts that contains personal information—usually your name, email address, postal address, and telephone number. **Netiquette** dictates that signatures, or **sigs**, should be no longer than four or five lines.
SLIP and PPP	"Serial line **Internet** protocol" and "point-to-point protocol." Connecting by

Net Speak

	SLIP or PPP actually puts a computer on the Internet, which offers a number of advantages over regular **dial-up**. A SLIP or PPP connection can support a graphical **Web browser** (such as Mosaic), and allows for multiple connections at the same time. Requires special software and a SLIP or PPP service provider.
smiley	Text used to indicate emotion, humor, or irony in electronic messages—best understood if viewed sideways. Also called an **emoticon**. The most common smileys are :-) and :-(
snail mail	The paper mail the U.S. Postal Service delivers. The forerunner of **email**.
spam	The posting of the same article to multiple **newsgroups** (usually every possible one) regardless of the appropriateness of the topic (e.g., "Make Money Fast").
sysop	"System operator." The person who owns and/or manages a **BBS** or other **Net** site.
TCP/IP	The "transmission control protocol" and the "**Internet** protocol." The basis of a full-fledged Internet connection. See **IP Connection**, **PPP**, and **SLIP**. Pronounced "T-C-P-I-P."
telnet	An **Internet** program that allows you to log into other Internet-connected computers.
terminal emulator	A program or utility that allows a computer to communicate in a foreign or nonstandard **terminal mode**.
terminal mode	The software standard a computer uses for text communication—for example, ANSI for PCs and **VT-100** for UNIX.
thread	Posted **newsgroup** message with a series of replies. Threaded **newsreaders** organize replies under the original subject.
timeout	The break in communication that occurs when two computers are talking and one takes so long to respond that the other gives up.
URL	"Uniform resource locator." The **World Wide Web** address of a resource on the **Internet**.
Usenet	A collection of networks and computer systems that exchange messages, organized by subject in **newsgroups**.
userid	The unique name (often eight characters or less) given to a user on a system for his or her account. The complete address, which can be used for **email** or fingering, is a userid followed by the @ sign and the **domain name** (e.g., Bill Clinton's address is president@whitehouse.gov).
Veronica	See **Archie**.
VT-100 emulation	Widely used terminal protocol for formatting full screens of text over computer connections.
WAIS	"Wide area information server." A system that searches through database indexes around the **Internet**, using keywords.
Web browser	A **client** program designed to interact with **World Wide Web servers** on the **Internet** for the purpose of viewing **Web pages**.
Web page	A **hypertext** document that is part of the **World Wide Web** and that can incorporate graphics, sounds, and links to other **Web pages**, **FTP** sites, **gophers**, and a variety of other **Internet** resources.
World Wide Web	A **hypertext**-based navigation system that lets you browse through a variety of linked **Net** resources, including **Usenet newsgroups** and **FTP**, **telnet**, and **gopher** sites, without typing commands. Also known as WWW and the Web.
zip	File-compression standard in the DOS and Windows worlds.

Index

1995 International BEAM Robot Olympics, 229
#2600, 239
3-D Mac Games Homepage, 160
386-Users, 70
3D Rendering Resource Center, 189
4DOS, 79
4th Dimension, 144
8-Bit FAQs, 99

A

A & M Networking Inc., 46
A2Z Multimedia SuperShop, 46
AApex Software Corporation, 221
ABC (programming lang.), 164
ABCs (kids' software), 152
About the Clipper Chip, 235
Academic Press, 35
Access Market Square—Computer Stuff, 48
Access-L, 147
Acer Computers, 75
ACM Press, 36
ACM SIGMOD, 244
Acorn Computers, 102
    games 158
ACT, 221
Ada (programming lang.), 164
Adobe, 186-187
Adobe Illustrator, 186
Adobe PageMaker, 131
Adobe Photoshop, 186
Adobe Type Manager, 129
Advanced Gravis Forum, 205
Aeon Technology On-Line, 27
AfterDark Modules for the Macintosh, 177
Age of Sail Clip Art, 193
AI
    see artificial intelligence
AI-Nat, 224
AirMosaic Express 1.1, 289
Albion Books, 36
Alf MIDI Site, The, 200
Alias Alian Nation, 46
Alife, 224-FUT02
Aliweb, 281
All-in-One Search Page, 278

Almac BBS, 270
Alpha Books, 36
alt.2600, 238
alt.aldus.pagemaker, 131-132
alt.aol-sucks, 258
alt.bbs, 268
alt.bbs.ads, 269
alt.bbs.allsysop, 270
alt.bbs.first-class, 270
alt.bbs.gigo-gateway, 270
alt.bbs.internet, 268
alt.bbs.lists, 269
alt.bbs.majorbbs, 270
alt.bbs.pcboard, 270
alt.bbs.renegade, 270
alt.bbs.tribbs, 270
alt.bbs.unixbbs, 270
alt.bbs.waffle, 270
alt.bbs.watergate
alt.bbs.wildcat, 270
alt.binaries.clip-art, 130
alt.binaries.multimedia, 216-217
alt.binaries.multimedia.erotica, 217
alt.binaries.pictures*, 180, 189
alt.binaries.sounds.cartoons, 198
alt.binaries.sounds.d, 198
alt.binaries.sounds.midi, 202
alt.binaries.sounds.misc, 198
alt.binaries.sounds.mods, 205
alt.binaries.sounds.movies, 198
alt.binaries.sounds.music, 198
alt.binaries.sounds.tv, 198
alt.binaries.sounds.utilities, 197
alt.binaries.startrek, 189
alt.cad, 188
alt.cad.autocad, 188
alt.cobol, 166
alt.comp.compression, 173
alt.comp.databases.xbase.clipper, 142
alt.cyberpunk.tech, 225-226
alt.dcom.telecom, 253
alt.folklore.computers, 243
alt.graphics.pixutils, 184
alt.hackers, 238
alt.hypertext, 209
alt.internet.access.wanted, 257
alt.internet.media-coverage, 277
alt.irc*, 271, 272
alt.lang.basic, 164

alt.music.makers.synthesizers, 200
alt.music.midi, 200
alt.newbie, 276
alt.newbies, 276
alt.online-service, 257
alt.online-service.america-online, 258
alt.online-service.compuserve, 259
alt.online-service.delphi, 259
alt.online-service.freenet, 258
alt.online-service.genie, 259
alt.online-service.imagination, 260
alt.online-service.prodigy, 260
alt.politics.datahighway, 243
alt.privacy, 233
alt.security.misc, 233
alt.security.pgp, 236
alt.sex.sounds, 198
alt.sources.amiga, 95-96
alt.sources.mac, 54-55
alt.sys.amiga.demos, 96
alt.sys.pc-clone.dell, 76
alt.sys.pc-clone.gateway2000, 76
alt.sys.pc-clone.zeos, 78
alt.usenet.culture, 282
alt.winsock, 265
alt.wired, 240-241
alt.www.culture, 280
Ambrosia Times, 59
America Online (AOL), 2, 5, 12-13, 258, 274, 289
    browser, 289
    games, 156
AmeriCom Long Distance AREA DECODER, The, 255
Amiga, 94-97, 274
    basics, 95
    CD-ROM, 30
    communications, 248-249
    FAQs, 95, 248
    games, 158
    graphics, 181-182
    hardware, 95
    networking, 248
    news, 95
    programming, 96
    software (business), 135
    software (general), 34, 95-96
    software (Net), 265
    sound, 195, 197, 205

Index

users, 97
utilities, 174
vendors, 96
Aminet software archives, 34, 96, 158, 197, 205, 248
AmiPro, 123
AmiTCP Networking Software, 265
AmiTCP/IP FAQ, 265
AMOS, 164, 207
Analogue Heaven, 200
Anarchie, 286
Andataco On-the-Net, 41
Animal Sounds, 198
animation, 215-216
Annex On-Line, The, 270
anonymity and privacy online, 233-234
Anonymous FTP FAQ, 284
Anonymous FTP Site List, 284
Anonymous Remailer FAQ, 234
Ansi C, 165
Anthony's Icon Library, 128
Anti-Virus Resource Center, 237
Apache Digital Corporation, 39
APL, 164
Apocalypse 2000, 239
Apple, 50-51, 66-67, 166
    internet providers, 260
    news, 50-51
    Newton, 114-116
    programming, 63, 67
    technical support, 51
    vendors, 67
Apple II, 66-67, 274
    communications, 249
    compression, 174
    education, 151
    games, 158-159
    graphics, 182
    programming, 67
    software, 34, 66-67
    sound, 195
    utilities, 174
    vendors, 67
Apple III, 67
Apple's Dylan Page, 166
Apple's QuickTime Online, 216
Applied Cryptography, 239
Archie, 285, 286
archives
    See software
Archive Films Forum, 217
Archive Photos Forum, 190
AREXX, 170

ARI Virtual Reality Research, 226
Arizona Macintosh Users Group, 64-65
Arrick Robotics, 229
Art Crimes: The Writing on the Wall, 193
Art on the Net, 191
Artech House, 36
artificial intelligence, 224-225
artists, 191
ArtServe, 191
ASCII graphics, 191
askSam Systems Home Page, 142
Association of LISP Users, 167
AST Forum, 112
Astronomy Pretty Pictures, 193
AT&T, 47, 77-78, 255, 256
    shopping, 47
AT&T 800 Directory, 255
AT&T-GIS Information Server, 77-78
Atari, 98-100, 159
    2600, 99-100
    8-bit, 99
    communications, 249
    compression, 174
    desktop publishing, 126
    FAQs, 249
    games, 159
    graphics, 182
    Jaguar, 99
    magazines, 99
    networking, 249
    programming, 100
    software, 100
    sound, 195, 200
    ST, 99
    utilities, 174
    vendors, 100
Atari Ghostscript, 100
Atari ST SLIP FAQ, 249
ATI Technologies, Inc., 45
Atlanta Windows BBS, 270
Audio Engineering Society, 194
Audio FAQ, 196
Audio File Formats FAQ, 197
Audio Virtual Library, 194
Australian Acorn Page, 102
Australian National Botanical Gardens' Bird Sounds, 198
Australian Telerobot, 229
Autodesk AutoCAD Forum, 188
Autodesk Multimedia Forum, 188, 218
Autodesk Showcase Forum, 218

AWARE—Authorware Mailing List, 218-219
Awesome List, The, 282
Axcess Magazine CD-Rom Reviews, 33-34

B

Back Alley BBS, 270
Balthazar 1.5.1, 207
BASIC, 164
BBSs, 268-270
    FAQs, 270
    lists, 269-270
    news, 269
    software packages, 270
BC Gopher, 287
BCTEL, 256
Beastie Delux, 178
Beavis & Butt-head Screen Saver, 178
Beginner's Guide to Effective email, A, 280
Bell Atlantic, 256
Bell Canada, 256
Bellcore, 256
BellSouth, 256
Benjamin/Cummings Publishing Co., Inc., 36
Berkeley Mac User Group BBSs, 65
Berkeley OS/2 Users' Group, 92
BETA, 164
Bishop University's OS/2 Site, 91
bit.listserv.ibmtcp-l, 265
bit.listserv.pagemakr, 132
bit.listserv.quarkxpr, 130
bit.listserv.win3-1, 82
bit.mailserv.word-mac, 124
bit.mailserv.word-pc, 124
Bits and Bytes, 19
Black Gold BBS, 270
Blackberry Creek, 153
BMUG (Berkeley Mac User Group), 48, 65
Boardwatch Magazine, 269
Boatanchors List, 24
books and booksellers, 35-38
Borderware-Internet Firewall Server, 234
Borland, 163
    C++, 165
    dBASE, 143
    Delphi, 169
    Paradox, 149
Boston University, 231

Index

Bottom Line Distribution, 41
Branch Mall, The, 40-41
Brian's Repository of Macintosh Information, 52
Brief Introduction to the Internet, A, 276
British Telecom, 256
BrowserWatch, 280
Bulletin Board Systems Corner, 268
Burn This Flag BBS, 270
business & finance, 133-137
    office automation, 133-134
    software, 135-137
    software support, 134-135
    workgroups, 135
Buyer's Assistant, 61-62
Buying and Selling Macintosh Computers, Software, and Peripherals, 41

C

C and C++, 165
C= Home Page, The, 96
C-IBM-370, 165
c2man, 165
C64 Emulators, 96
CA Visual Objects Forum, 163
CA-Clipper Forum, 142
CAD Resource Center, 188
CAD/CAM, 188-189
CAD/Draw/Plot/Engnr, 188
Cakewalk Home Page, 203
Calamus, 132
Calc/Stats/Clocks, 119
calculators, 118-119
    Hewlett-Packard, 118-119
    shareware, 119
    Texas Instruments, 118
calendars & PIMs, 135-136
California Institute of Technology, 231
California State University at Hayward PC Clubhouse, 74
CallAmerica, 256
CalTech Robotics Laboratory, 231
CalTech's OS/2 Site, 88
Cambridge University Speech Vision Robotics Group, 231
Canberra PC Users Group, 74
Canon Support Forum, 27
Capital PC Users Group (Washington, D.C.), 74
Cappella Sistina: the Extended Tour, 191-192
Cardiff VR Pages, 226
Carl & Gary's Visual Basic Home Page, 171
Carlos' Coloring Book Home Page, 153
Catalink Direct, 41
Catalog.com, 39
Catalog of Free Database Systems, 150
CB Bands, 273-274
CD Publishing Corp, 36
CD-I FAQ, 30
CD-ROM, 30-31, 215
    Amiga, 30
    FAQ, 30
    news, 34
    shopping, 44-45
    reviews, 33-34
    vendors, 30
CD-ROM Today, 34
Cello, 289
Cellular One Mobile Communications, 256
Center for Automation Research (CAR), 231
Center for Computer Research in Music and Acoustics, 206
Central Atari Information Network, 98
Central Kentucky Computer Society, 74
Ceram Incorporated, 41
Champaign-Urbana Commodore Users Group, 95
Channel 1, 270
Charles River Media, 37
Charm Net Personal IP Page, 264
chat (on the Net), 271-274
Checkpoint, 235
Children's Software Company, 151, 221
Chiplist, 72
CICA Shareware Archive, 34, 84
clari.nb.apple, 51
ClarisDraw and ClarisImpact, 187
Claris Macintosh Forum, 55
Claris Support Forum, 143-144
Claris TechInfo Database, 144
Classic Movie Posters, 192
Classical MIDI Archives, 202
CLBV Digest, 171
Clearinghouse for Subject-Oriented Internet Resource Guides, 278
Cleveland OS/2 User's Group, 92

Cliff Stoll's Performance Art Theater and Networking Security Revue, 232
clip art, 130, 193
Clipper (database), 142
Clipper Chip, 235-236
Closer to Home Atari Archive, 99
CMP Publications, Inc., 19
CMU Artificial Inteligence Repository, 225
CMU Common LISP Repository, 167
COAST Project, 232
Coast-to-Coast Software Repository, 86
Cobb Group, 19-20
Cobol, 166
Coca Cola Screen Savers, 178
CoCo—The Tandy Color Computer List, 103
Colin's FoxPro Page, 144
College Email Address FAQ, 279
Color Computer Forum, 103
Colorado State Entomology, 193
Colorocs, 27
Commerce, 235
commercial service chat, 273-274
commercial services & internet providers, 257-260
CommNet for Windows, 288
Commodore 64 & 128, 96-97
    games, 158
communications, 246-251
    see also telecommunications
    Amiga, 248-249
    Apple II, 249
    Atari, 249
    DOS, 250-251
    faxing, 247, 250
    Macintosh, 249-250
    news, 247
    Windows, 250-251
    wireless, 247-248
CommunicationsWeek, 247
comp.ai*, 225
comp.apps.spreadsheets, 138
comp.archives.msdos.announce, 79
comp.archives.msdos.d, 79-80
comp.bbs.majorbbs, 270
comp.bbs.misc, 268
comp.bbs.tbbs, 270
comp.bbs.waffle, 270
comp.binaries.apple2, 67
comp.binaries.mac, 55
comp.binaries.newton, 114

342 Net Tech

Index

comp.cad.autocad, 188
comp.cad.cadence, 188
comp.cad.compass, 188
comp.cad.pro-engineer, 188-189
comp.cad.synthesis, 189
comp.client.server, 140
comp.compilers, 166
comp.compilers.tools.pccts, 166
comp.compression, 173
comp.compression.research, 173
comp.databases, 140
comp.databases.informix, 145
comp.databases.ingres, 146
comp.databases.ms-access, 147
comp.databases.object, 147
comp.databases.oracle, 148
comp.databases.paradox, 149
comp.databases.pick, 149
comp.databases.rdb, 148
comp.databases.sybase, 150
comp.databases.theory, 140
comp.databases.xbase.fox, 144
comp.databases.xbase.misc, 140
comp.dcom.fax, 247
comp.dcom.isdn, 267
comp.dcom.modems, 28
comp.dcom.telecom, 253-254
comp.dcom.telecom.tech, 254
comp.dcom.videoconf, 272
comp.emulators.announce, 21
comp.emulators.apple2, 67
comp.emulators.misc, 21
comp.fonts, 129
comp.fonts FAQ, 129
comp.fonts Homepage, The, 129
comp.graphics, 181
comp.graphics.algorithms, 215
comp.graphics.animation, 215
comp.graphics.avs, 189
comp.graphics.data-explorer, 189
comp.graphics.explorer, 189
comp.graphics.gnuplot, 189
comp.graphics.opengl, 189
comp.graphics.packages.alias, 215
comp.graphics.packages.lightwave, 215
comp.graphics.raytracing, 189
comp.graphics.rendering.renderman, 189
comp.graphics.visualization, 189
comp.groupware.lotus-notes.misc, 146
comp.infosystems.gopher, 285
comp.infosystems.wais, 285
comp.infosystems.www*, 280
comp.internet.net-happenings, 278

comp.lang.ada, 164
comp.lang.apl, 164
comp.lang.basic.misc, 164
comp.lang.basic.visual, 171
comp.lang.basic.visual.3rd-party, 171
comp.lang.basic.visual.announce, 171
comp.lang.basic.visual.database, 171
comp.lang.beta, 165
comp.lang.c, 165
comp.lang.c++, 165
comp.lang.clipper, 142
comp.lang.cobol, 166
comp.lang.dylan, 166
comp.lang.eiffel, 166
comp.lang.forth, 166
comp.lang.forth.mac, 167
comp.lang.fortran, 167
comp.lang.icon, 167
comp.lang.idl, 167
comp.lang.idl-pvwave, 167
comp.lang.lisp, 168
comp.lang.lisp.franz, 168
comp.lang.lisp.mcl, 168
comp.lang.lisp.x, 168
comp.lang.logo, 168
comp.lang.misc, 162
comp.lang.ml, 168
comp.lang.modula2, 168
comp.lang.modula3, 168
comp.lang.oberon, 168
comp.lang.objective-c, 169
comp.lang.pascal, 169
comp.lang.perl, 169
comp.lang.pop, 169
comp.lang.postscript, 169
comp.lang.prograph, 170
comp.lang.prolog, 170
comp.lang.python, 170
comp.lang.rexx, 170
comp.lang.sather, 170
comp.lang.scheme, 170
comp.lang.scheme.c, 170
comp.lang.smalltalk, 171
comp.lang.verilog, 171
comp.lang.verilog archive, 171
comp.lang.vhdl, 171
comp.mail*, 278-279
comp.multimedia, 214
comp.org.eff.talk, 242
comp.os.cpm, 104
comp.os.geos, 74
comp.os.linux*, 107
comp.os.misc, 103
comp.os.ms-windows.advocacy, 81

comp.os.ms-windows.announce, 83
comp.os.ms-windows.apps.comm, 250
comp.os.ms-windows.apps.financial, 136
comp.os.ms-windows.apps.misc, 84
comp.os.ms-windows.apps.utilities, 174
comp.os.ms-windows.apps.word-proc, 122
comp.os.ms-windows.misc, 81
comp.os.ms-windows.networking.tcp-ip, 265
comp.os.ms-windows.nt.misc, 86
comp.os.ms-windows.nt.setup, 86
comp.os.ms-windows.programmer.controls, 85
comp.os.ms-windows.programmer.drivers, 85
comp.os.ms-windows.programmer.graphics, 85
comp.os.ms-windows.programmer.memory, 85
comp.os.ms-windows.programmer.misc, 85
comp.os.ms-windows.programmer.multimedia, 219
comp.os.ms-windows.programmer.networks, 86
comp.os.ms-windows.programmer.ole, 86
comp.os.ms-windows.programmer.tools, 86
comp.os.ms-windows.programmer.win32, 86
comp.os.ms-windows.programmer.winhelp, 86
comp.os.ms-windows.setup, 81
comp.os.msdos.4dos, 79
comp.os.msdos.apps, 80
comp.os.msdos.programmer, 79
comp.os.msdos.programmer.turbovision, 79
comp.os.os2.advocacy, 89
comp.os.os2.announce, 89
comp.os.os2.apps, 90
comp.os.os2.beta, 90
comp.os.os2.bugs, 89

Net Tech 343

Index

comp.os.os2.games, 161
comp.os.os2.misc, 89
comp.os.os2.multimedia, 214
comp.os.os2.networking.tcp-ip, 267
comp.os.os2.programmer.misc, 91
comp.os.os2.programmer.oop, 91
comp.os.os2.programmer.porting, 91-92
comp.os.os2.programmer.tools, 92
comp.os.os2.setup, 89-90
comp.os.os2.utilities, 176
comp.os.os9, 103
comp.periphs.printers, 27-28
comp.periphs.scsi, 27
comp.protocols.ppp, 264
comp.protocols.tcp-ip, 264-265
comp.protocols.tcp-ip.domains, 265
comp.protocols.tcp-ip.ibmpc, 265
comp.publish.cdrom.hardware, 30
comp.publish.cdrom.multimedia, 215
comp.publish.cdrom.software, 34
comp.risks, 234
comp.robotics, 229
comp.robotics FAQ, 229
comp.security.announce, 234
comp.security.misc, 234
comp.security.unix, 234
comp.society, 241
comp.society.cu-digest, 244
comp.society.development, 241
comp.society.futures, 241
comp.society.privacy, 234
comp.soft-sys.powerbuilder, 147-148
comp.sources*, 32
comp.sources.postscript, 169
comp.sys.acorn, 102
comp.sys.acorn.advocacy, 102
comp.sys.acorn.games, 158
comp.sys.acorn.tech, 102
comp.sys.amiga.advocacy, 95
comp.sys.amiga.announce, 95
comp.sys.amiga.applications, 96
comp.sys.amiga.audio, 195
comp.sys.amiga.datacomm, 249
comp.sys.amiga.games, 158
comp.sys.amiga.graphics, 181-182
comp.sys.amiga.hardware, 95
comp.sys.amiga.introduction, 95
comp.sys.amiga.marketplace, 41
comp.sys.amiga.misc, 95
comp.sys.amiga.multimedia, 214
comp.sys.amiga.programmer, 96
comp.sys.amiga.reviews, 96
comp.sys.apple2, 67

comp.sys.apple2.comm, 249
comp.sys.apple2.gno, 67
comp.sys.apple2.marketplace, 41
comp.sys.apple2.programmer, 67
comp.sys.apple2.usergroups, 67
comp.sys.atari.8bit, 99
comp.sys.atari.advocacy, 98
comp.sys.atari.announce, 99
comp.sys.atari.programmer, 100
comp.sys.atari.st, 99
comp.sys.atari.st.tech, 99
comp.sys.cbm, 97
comp.sys.handhelds, 113
comp.sys.ibm.pc.demos, 72
comp.sys.ibm.pc.digest, 70-71
comp.sys.ibm.pc.games.action, 160
comp.sys.ibm.pc.games.adventure, 160
comp.sys.ibm.pc.games.announce, 160
comp.sys.ibm.pc.games.flight-sim, 160
comp.sys.ibm.pc.games.misc, 160
comp.sys.ibm.pc.games.rpg, 160
comp.sys.ibm.pc.games.strategic, 160
comp.sys.ibm.pc.hardware.cd-rom, 31
comp.sys.ibm.pc.hardware.chips, 72
comp.sys.ibm.pc.hardware.comm, 28
comp.sys.ibm.pc.hardware.comm, 250
comp.sys.ibm.pc.hardware.misc, 72
comp.sys.ibm.pc.hardware.storage, 72-73
comp.sys.ibm.pc.hardware.systems, 73
comp.sys.ibm.pc.hardware.video, 27
comp.sys.ibm.pc.misc, 71
comp.sys.ibm.pc.soundcard.advocacy, 205
comp.sys.ibm.pc.soundcard.games, 205
comp.sys.ibm.pc.soundcard.misc, 205
comp.sys.ibm.pc.soundcard.music, 206
comp.sys.ibm.pc.soundcard.tech, 206
comp.sys.ibm.pr.rt, 77
comp.sys.ibm.ps2.hardware, 77
comp.sys.laptops, 110
comp.sys.mac.advocacy, 53
comp.sys.mac.announce, 59
comp.sys.mac.apps, 55
comp.sys.mac.comm, 249
comp.sys.mac.databases, 140-141
comp.sys.mac.digest, 59
comp.sys.mac.games, 159
comp.sys.mac.graphics, 182
comp.sys.mac.hardware, 58
comp.sys.mac.hypercard, 210
comp.sys.mac.misc, 53

comp.sys.mac.oop.macapp3, 63
comp.sys.mac.oop.misc, 53
comp.sys.mac.portables, 111
comp.sys.mac.programmer.codewarrior, 64
comp.sys.mac.programmer.help, 64
comp.sys.mac.programmer.info, 64
comp.sys.mac.programmer.misc, 64
comp.sys.mac.programmer.tools, 64
comp.sys.mac.scitech, 53
comp.sys.mac.system, 54
comp.sys.mac.wanted, 41
comp.sys.ncr, 78
comp.sys.newton.announce, 114
comp.sys.newton.misc, 114
comp.sys.newton.programmer, 114
comp.sys.next*, 107
comp.sys.next.marketplace, 41
comp.sys.palmtops, 113
comp.sys.powerpc, 62
comp.sys.sgi.graphics, 184
comp.sys.sinclair, 101
comp.sys.tandy, 103
comp.text.desktop, 127
comp.text.frame, 131
comp.unix.admin, 106
comp.unix.advocacy, 106
comp.unix.amiga, 106
comp.unix.dos-under-unix, 106
comp.unix.mist, 106
comp.unix.pc-clone.16bit, 106
comp.unix.pc-clone.32bit, 106
comp.unix.questions, 106
comp.unix.questions, 276
comp.unix.shell, 106
comp.unix.wizards, 107
comp.virus, 237
comp.windows.garnet, 104
comp.windows.interviews, 104
comp.windows.misc, 105
comp.windows.news, 105
comp.windows.open-look, 105
comp.windows.suit, 105
comp.windows.ui-builders, 105
comp.windows.x, 104
comp.windows.x.announce, 104
comp.windows.x.apps, 104
comp.windows.x.i386unix, 104
Compact Disk Formats, 31
Compaq, 75
compilers, 166
Complete FTP Servers List, The, 32
compression, 173
Compromised Security FAQ, 234

Index

Compton's New Media, 44
Compubooks, 36
CompuServe, 2, 5, 13, 259, 273-274
COMPUTE Magazine
    See I-WIRE
Computer Ailments, 22
Computers and Communications
    Page, 246
Computer Associates, 163
Computer Basics, 23
Computer BB, 19
computer bookstores, 35-38
    reviews & lists, 35
Computer Buyer's Guide, 48
Computer Center, 18
Computer Conversions, 48
Computer Corporations, 21
Computer Currents, 154
Computer Data Archival Services
    (CDAS), 44
Computer Database Plus, 23
Computer Express, 39
Computer Gaming World, 157-158
Computer Graphics and Visualization, 188
Computer History Association of California, 24
Computer Industry Almanac Online, 25
Computer Library Online, 23
Computer Life, 154
Computer Lingo, 24
Computer Literacy Bookshops Information, 36
Computer Management Software, Inc., 41-42
Computer Marketplace, Inc., 39
Computer Professionals for Social Responsibility, 242-243
Computer Recyclers, 39
Computer Security Research Lab, 232
Computer Shopper BBS and Users Groups, 269
Computer Shopper, 20
Computer Technologies Security Center, 232-233
Computer User Groups on the Web, 22
Computer Users of Baltimore (CUB), 74
computer vendors, 292-319
Computer Viruses & Security, 237
Computer White Pages, 21
computers, 1-335

Computers and Society ARPA Digest, 241
Computers and Society Articles Collection, 242
Computers at Large, 221
Computers/Technology, 18
Computing Print & Broadcast, 20
Computing WWW Virtual Library, 18-19
Concise Guide to Unix Books, A, 35
Config.Sys, 44
Conlang, 162
Connect, 277
Connectsoft, 286
Consummate Winsock Apps List, The, 265
Contemporary Motion Images Forum, 217
Cook Communications, 256
Cool Site of the Day, 282
Cool Software for Kids, 151-152
Corel, 187
    CorelDRAW, 187
    Ventura, 187
Cornell CSRVL, 231
Cowles/SIMBA, 20, 247
CP/M, 97, 104
Creative Labs, Inc., 206, 221
CRISP Directory, 257
Crypto Anarchist Manifesto, The, 244
cryptography, 239
CSUSM Library Technical Services
    Windows NT Archive, 86
CU-SeeMe, 272
Cuban Music Samples, 198
CUSI, 281
Cute FTP, 287
CWarrior, 166
Cyber Forum, 226
cybercafés, 262-263
Cyberian Outpost, 42
Cyberlaw/Cyberlex, 244
Cybermind, 226
Cyberpunks, The, 233
Cybersight: Real-Time Conversations, 273
CyberWarehouse, 40
CypherWonks, 239

D

Dalco Computer Electronics, 40
Dallas Museum of Art Online, 192
Damark International, Inc., 42

Daniel's Icon Archive, 128
Dartmouth College Macintosh Software, 55
Data Based Advisor Forum, 141-142
Data Fellows Ltd., 237
databases, 140-150
    4th Dimension, 144
    askSam, 142
    Clipper, 142
    conferences, 141
    DB2, 142
    dBASE, 143
    FAQ, 140
    FileMaker Pro, 143-144
    FoxPro, 144-145
    Informix, 145-146
    Ingres, 146
    Lotus Notes, 146
    MS-Access, 147
    news & magazines, 141-142
    object-oriented, 147-148
    Oracle, 148-149
    Paradox, 149
    Pick, 149-150
    shareware, 150
    SQL, 150
    Sybase, 150
DB2, 142
dBASE, 143
DBMS Forum, 142
DBMS Magazine, 142
DEC, 75-76
    See Digital Equipment Corporation
DECRDB List, 148
Delft Digital Picture Archive, 190
Dell, 76
Delphi, 259
Delphi Development, 169
demos, PCs, 72
DeskMate Forum, 103-104
Desktop Internet Reference, 276
Desktop Publisher's Journal, The, 128
desktop publishing, 126-132
    clip art, 130
    FAQs, 128
    fonts, 129-130
    FrameMaker, 131
    icons, 128
    news & magazines, 128
    PageMaker, 131-132
    professionals, 132
    QuarkXPress, 130-131
    vendors, 130

Index

Desktop Video Forum, 212
Deutsche Telekom, 256
Developer's Resources, 162
Digital Currency, 214
Digital Equipment Corporation, 75-76
    shopping, 42
Digital Guitar Archive, 200
Digital Media Research & Development Center, 212
Digital Press, 36
Discovery CD-ROM, 44
Disk-O-Tape, 47
Disney Software, 156
Documentation Page, 97
Doran's Mudlist, 272-273
DOS, 79-80
    4DOS, 79
    communications, 250-251
    programming, 79
    software (general), 79-80
    software (Net), 265-266
    utilities, 174-176
DOS Internet Kit, The, 265-266
Down to BASIC, 164
Download Superstore, The, 43
Downloadable Files for the PC, 80
downloading, 12-15
Dr. Dobb's Journal, 162
Dragon's Eye Software, 177
Dragon's Lair BBS, The, 270
Drive and Controller Guide, 26
DTE Homewise, 154
DTF.WWW, 156
DTP
    See desktop publishing
Due North Multimedia, 221
Dylan (programming lang.), 166
Dylan's Windows 95 Home Page, 87

E

E-Mail Web Resources, 279
E-Privacy Home Page, 235-236
E-Znet's Winsock Archive, 266
Easy Mosaic and Introductory Web Surfing, 280
Eddie New Shareware Archive for HP 100/200 LX, 116
educational resources, 151-153
    ABCs, 152
    foreign languages, 152-153
    multimedia, 152-153, 216
EFF
    See Electronic Frontier Foundation
EFF's Extended Guide to the Internet, 276
Eiffel (programming lang.), 166
Einet Galaxy, 281
EINet winWais, 289
EkBackup, 174
electronic activism, 242-243
Electric Bookstore Inc., The, 37
Electronic and Computer Music FAQ, 196
Electronic Commerce Standards for the WWW, 233
Electronic Frontier Foundation, The, 243, 276
Electronic Music Software Price Guide, 203
Electronic Newsstand, 45
Elsevier Science (The Netherlands), 37
Emagic Logic, 100
Emagic Users Page, The, 203
email, 6, 8-9, 278-280
    basics, 278-279
    client software, 286
    e-style, 280
    mailing lists, 279-280
    remailers, 280
    searching for people, 279
EMASHE/Establishing Multimedia Authoring Skills in Higher Education, 219
emulators, 21
EMUSIC-L Home Page, 200
Encyclopedia of Virtual Environments, The, 226
Entering the Worldwide Web: A Guide to Cyberspace, 280
entertainment, 156-161
    See also games
    shopping, 45
Entertainment Drive Forum, 217
Entertainment Drive: Multimedia and More, 217
Entry Level Internet, 276-277
Epson, 76
Epub Center, The, 209
erotic graphics, 192-193
Erotic Photography Index, 192
Escher Gallery, The, 192
ESO/ST-ECF Sybase Archive, The, 150
Essential Utilities, 174
Ethan Brodsky's Home Page/Learn about About Programming, 200

EtherPPP, 266
Ethics-L, 242
ETHZ—Institute of Robotics, 231
Eudora, 286
Eurobots, 229-230
Event Horizons BBS, 270
EWAN, 288
eWorld Web Central, 260
Excel, 138-139
Exec-PC, 270
Exec/Direct, 42
Eye Contact, 270

F

family computing, 154-155
Family News Product Reviews, 48
Family PC, 155
FAQs, 284
    hacking, 238
    Ada, 164
    America Online, 258
    Amiga, 95, 248
    APL, 164
    artifical intelligence, 224, 225
    Atari, 99, 249
    audio, 196
    BBS, 270
    CD-ROM, 30
    Clipper, 142
    Cobol, 166
    CompuServe, 259
    computers & society, 241
    CP/M, 104
    cryptography, 239
    databases, 140
    databases, object-oriented, 147-148
    desktop publishing, 127-128
    DOS programming, 79
    DOS software, 79
    Dylan, 166
    Eiffel, 166
    faxing, 247
    fonts, 129
    Forth, 167
    Fortran, 167
    FoxPro, 144
    FrameMaker, 131
    games, Macintosh, 159
    games, PCs, 160
    Gateway 2000, 76
    gopher, 285
    Hewlett Packard calculators,

Index

118
HP 100/200 LX, 116
Icon, 167
Informix, 145
Ingres, 146
internet providers, 257, 260
IRC, 271
Linux, 107
LISP, 168
LOGO, 168
Lotus Notes, 146
Macintosh, 54, 249
Microsoft Windows, 82-83
MIDI, 200, 202
ML, 168
MOD, 205
modems, 29
Modula2, 168
Modula3, 168
MS-Access, 147
newsgroups, 283, 284
Next, 107
Oberon, 169
Objective-C, 169
Oracle, 148
OS/2, 90
PageMaker, 132
PCs, 73
Perl, 169
Pick, 149
PostScript, 170
privacy, 233, 234
Prograph, 170
Prolog, 170
Python, 170
REXX, 170
robotics, 229
Scheme, 171
SCSI, 27
security, 234
security, PGP, 236
security software, 235
Smalltalk, 171
sound, 196
sound cards & boards, 206
sound formats, 197
SQL, 150
surfing, 265, 266, 267
telecommunications, 253-254
Unix, 106, 107
Verilog, 171
videoconferencing, 272
virtual reality, 227-228
viruses, 238

Visual Basic, 171
Web, 280
Web browsers, 289
Windows, 104, 105
faxing, 247
Fetch, 286
Few Useful Utilities, A, 174
FidoNet Archive, 270
Fight for Your Right to Electronic Privacy!, 236
FileMaker Pro, 143-144
finance
    See business & finance
fine art, 191-192
firewalls, 234-235
FIRST, 233
First Course in X Windows, 104
First Guide to PostScript, A, 169
FMPRO-L, 144
fonts, 129-130
FOOTAGE.net, 217
foreign languages, 152-153
Forth, 166-167
Fortran 77, 167
Fortune Cookie, 178
Four11 Directory Services (SLED), 279
FoxPro, 144-145
Fractal Movie Archive, 217
Frame Technology Corporation, 131
FrameMaker, 131
France Telecom Network Services, 256
Frank's Windows 95 Page, 87
Free Agent, 288
Free On-Line Dictionary of Computing, 24
freenets, 258, 261
Fry Multimedia, 220
FTP, 12-13, 32, 46, 284-285, 286-287
    Archie, 286
    client software, 286-287
Funet Amiga Archive, 34, 96
Funet Clip Art Collection, 130
Funet Software Archives, 32
Future Music, 200
Fuzzy-Mail, 225

G

G-Web, 215
Gadget Mania, 226
games, 156-161

    Acorn, 158
    Amiga, 158
    Apple, 158-159
    Atari, 159
    Macintosh, 159-160
    news, 157-158
    OS/2, 161
    PCs, 160-161
Garbo FTP Archive, 32
Garbo PC Archive, 34, 80
Gateway 2000, 28, 76
Gateway to Free-Nets and Community Networks via the World Wide Web, 258
Geekgirl, 244
General Audio Information, 197
General DOS Game Programming Material/Directory, 219
GEnie, 259-260
Geographical Amiga Users Home Page Internet List, 97
Georgia Tech Mobile Robot Laboratory, 231
GEOS, 74
Gerben's Acorn Page, 102
Get Info, 128
Get Warped with OS/2!, 91
GFX-94 Family of Internet Firewalls, 235
GIFs at UIUC, 190
Glamour Paintings and Illustrations, 192
Global Village, 28
Globetrotter, 277
Go Digital, 214
Go Graphics, 180
gopher, 13, 285
    client software, 287
    FAQ, 285
Gopher Surfer Lite, 287
Graphic Art using Photoshop, 186
graphics, 180-193
    Adobe, 186-187
    Amiga, 181-182
    Apple II, 182
    artists, 191
    ASCII, 191
    Atari, 182
    bizarre, 193
    CAD/CAM, 188-189
    Claris, 187
    Corel, 187
    erotic, 192-193
    fine art, 191-192

Index

horror, 193
image compression, 186
Macintosh, 182
maps, 193
newsgroups, 189
PC, 182-184
pop culture, 192
Print Artist, 187
raytrace & rendering, 189
science, 193
ships, 193
shopping, 45
Silicon Graphics, 184
space, 193
travel, 193
vendors, 188
viewing programs, 184-186
Grotesque in Art, 193
GTE Laboratories, 256
Guide to Select BBSs on the Internet, 269

H

H-MAC History and Macintosh Society, 59
hacking, 24, 238-239
Hands on with ZiffNet/Mac, 55
HARC-C Compression Technology, 173
hardware, 26-31
    See also peripherals
    See also under specific manufacturers' names
        Amiga, 95
        Macintosh, 58-59
        PCs, 72-73
Harmony Central, 200-201
HarperAudio!, 198-199
Harvard Computer Review, 20
Harvard Robotics Lab, 231
Harvest Homepage Broker, 281
Hayden Books, 37
Hayes Online Forum, 28-04
health, computing, 22
Heizer Software, 210
Helsinki Telephone Company, 256
HENSA/Micros IBM PC Section, 71
Heriot-Watt University —Ocean Systems Lab, 231
Hewlett-Packard, 31, 77
    calculators, 118-119
    HP48, 118, 274
    HP 100/200 LX, 116-117

Omnibook, 112
peripherals, 31
HGopher, 287
High Performance Cartridges, 28
Historic Computer Images, 25
Historical Map Exhibit, 193
Historical Speeches, 199
history, computing, 24-25, 105
Hobbes OS/2 Software, 34
Hollywood Online Forum, 217
Home and Hobby Helpers, 155
Home Office Computing, 133
Home PC, 155
Homebrew-VR Homepage, The, 226-227
Homer, 287
Horror Graphics Archive, 193
HotWired, 241
How Can I Send a Fax from the Internet?, 247
How to Find People's E-mail Addresses, 279
How to Make MPEG Movies, 215
How to Select an Internet Provider, 257
How to Upgrade to ISDN, 267
HSC Software Mailing List, 219
HT_Lit, 209
humor (computer), 243
Hyper Magazine, 34
Hyperbole, 211
HyperCard, 210-211
Hyperedu, 209
Hyperlinked Visual Tour of Windows 95, A, 87
hypermedia, 209-211
    history, 210
    HyperCard, 210-211
    software, 211
    terminology, 210
hypertext
    See hypermedia

I

I Hate Windoze, 82
I-Comm, 289
I-TV List, 272
I-WIRE (formerly *COMPUTE* Magazine online), 20
I-Wire Software, 71
Ian's REXX Home Page, 170
IBM, 69, 77, 136
    See also OS/2

See also PC clones
    data storage, 73
    DB2, 142
    ImagePlus, 31
    languages, 164
    PS/1 and Aptiva, 77
    PS2, 77
    shopping, 42
    software, 71
    ThinkPad, 112
ICMA Software Library, The, 197
ICON (programming lang.), 167
icons, 128-129
id FTP Site, 161
IDL (programming lang.), 167
IDOL (programming lang.), 167
Image Compression Information, 186
Imagen, 28
Imagine, 187-188
ImaginEngine, 153
Imaging Resource Center, 180-181
Imazine, 95
Impediment, Inc., 27
In, Around and On-Line, 277
Independent Nation, 239
Index—OS/2 User Groups from Around the World, 92
Index to Multimedia Information Sources, 212
Indiana University UCS Knowledge Bas, 23
Industry Connection, 21
Industry Insider, 20
industry profiles (computer), 25
Info-Fibers List, 254
Info-IBMPC, 71
Info-Mac Archive, 34, 55
Info-Mac Communications Directory, 249, 267
Info-Mac Digest, 55
Info-Mac Productivity Applications, 136
Info-Mac Screen Saver Archive, 177-178
Info-Mac Sound Archive, 195
Info-PGP, 236
Info-Robo, 230
InfoNet, 256
Information about Hypermedia, 209
Information About Standard ML, 168
Information Inc.'s Microindustry News Briefs, 20
Information Sources: the Internet and Computer-Mediated Commu-

348 Net Tech

Index

nication, 246
Information Systems MetaList, 141
InformationWeek, 20, 240
Informix (database), 145-146
InfoSeek, 281
InfoWorld, 240
Ingres (database), 146
Inland Empire OS/2 Users, 92
insurance, computer, 45
Intel, 27, 73
Inter@ctive Week, 247
Interact Multimedia, 220
Interactive Age, 247
Interactive WWW Games List, 157
InterCon Systems, 46
Interior Alaska Windows NT, 86
International Aerial Robotics Competition, 230
International E-mail Accesibility, 280
International Free-Nets Listing, 258
International PGP Home Page, The, 236
Internet
   See Net, the
Internet Access Provider FAQ, 260
Internet Access Providers List, 257
Internet Adapter, The, 46-47
Internet Cafe, 275
Internet Connection, The, 275-276
InterNet Directory, 267
Internet Fax Server, The, 247
Internet Files and Utilities, 276
Internet Font Archive, The, 129
Internet Foreplay, 277
Internet Index, The, 285
Internet Mall - THIRD FLOOR: Computer Hardware and Software, 40
Internet MIDI Archives, 201
Internet PostScript Resources, 169
internet providers, 257-258, 260, 320-327
Internet Scheme Repository, The, 170
Internet Security Firewalls Tutorial, 235
Internet Services, 276
Internet Shopping Network, 40
Internet Tools and the Mac, 267
Internet Underground Music Archive, 199
Internet Underground, The, 233
Internet World, 277
Internetwork Mailguide, The, 280
Intro to Sybase, 150

Introduction to C Programming, 165, 166
Introduction to Object Oriented Programming Using C++, 166
Introduction to PC Hardware, 69
Introduction to Prograph CPX, An, 170
Introduction to TCP/IP, 265
Introduction to Lotus Notes, An, 146
Intuit, 134
IRC, 271-272, 274
   client software, 287
   FAQ, 271
   Undernet, 271
IS Robotics Corporation, 230
ISDN, 267
It's Your Money, 20
ITU WWW Server, 255
IVI Publishing, 221

J

Jaguar Info, 99
Jaron Lanier's Homepage, 227
JCC's Oracle Rdb Home Page, 148
JDR Microdevices, 42
Jef's Nude of the Month, 193
Jeff Sawdy's HP Pages, 118
JEM Computers, 47
Jerry's World, 129
Jim Brain's CBM 8-bit Computer Home Page, 97
John Lueders's Home Page, 119
John Wiley & Sons, 37
John's Boxing Page, 239
Johns Hopkins Robotics Lab, 231
Journal of Artificial Intelligence, 225
Journal of Computer-Mediated Communication, The, 247
JPEG, 185
JPL Robotics/NASA, 230
JPL Telerobotics, 231
Junior's Clippin' Pages, 142
JUTASTAT, 221

K

K-Sculpt, 100
Kaleida Labs, 221
KAT Home Page, The, 203
KDD, 256
Keith O'Brien's Telecom Info Home Page, 252
Keith's Best Of List of Winsock Apps, 266
KILL File FAQ, 282-283
Kim Komando's Komputer Kling, 20
Knowledge in Motion, 37
Kodak CD Forum, 31
Kodak Sample Digital Images, 190
Korea Telecom, 256

L

Lang-Lucid, 168
Language List, The, 162
Larry Majid on PCs, 69
Las Vegas PC Users Group, 74
law (computer-related), 243-244
LDC Word Processing Forum, 123
LDDS Communications, 256
Lemur Gallery, 193
Leonardo da Vinci Museum, 192
Lexicor Graphics Support List, 188
Library Solutions Institute and Press, 37
Linda (programming lang.), 167
Line-Link Mailing LIst, 29
Linux, 34, 107, 274
   sound, 206
Lips' List of IAP's Internet Access Providers Around the World, The, 257
Liquid Mercury Soap, 244
LISP (programming lang.), 167-168
List of Lists, The, 279
List of USENET FAQs, 284
Listing Lists of Internet Providers, 257-258
Livermore Software, 235
LNotes-L, 146
LOGO (programming lang.), 168
Long Island PC Users Group, 74
Long-Distance Digest, 254
Look Software, 237
Lotus, 139
   Lotus Notes, 146
   shopping, 45
   spreadsheets, 139
   word processing, 123
Lovelace Ada Tutorial, 164
Low End User, 59
Lucid (programming lang.), 168
Lycos, 281

M

Mac Bible, 53

Net Tech 349

Index

MAC Home Journal, 59
Mac Net Journal, 59
Macintosh, 52-65, 274
    BBSs, 268-269
    calculators, 119
    communications, 249-250
    compression, 176
    cryptography, 239
    databases, 141
    desktop publishing, 127
    education, 152
    FAQs, 54
    file formats, 59
    fonts, 129
    games, 159-160
    graphics, 182
    hardware, 58-59
    history, 59
    HyperCard, 211
    hypertext, 209-210
    instruction, 53-54
    magazines, 59-61
    multimedia, 212, 213
    news, 59-61
    operating systems, 54, 57
    portables, 111
    PowerBook, 111
    PowerMac, 62-63
    printers, 28
    programming, 63-64
    screen savers, 177-178
    scripting, 64
    security, 234, 239
    shopping, 42, 43
    software (business), 133, 136
    software (general), 54-58, 60, 136, 176, 197-198
    software (Net),267, 289
    sound, 195, 196, 201
    spreadsheets, 139
    user groups, 64-65
    utilities, 174-176, 198
    vendors, 21, 61-62
    viruses, 237
    word processing, 122
MacLinux, 107
MacMania FreeWare and ShareWare, 176
Macmillan Computer Publishing Forum, 37
Macmillan Spreadsheet Library, 138
Macmillan USA Information SuperLibrary, 37
MACMULTI, 214

MacPing, 288
MACPPC-L, 62
MacPPP, 267
MacProducts USA, 42
Macromedia Director, 219
MacSense, 60
MacShareNews, 57
MacTech Magazine, 60
MacUser, 60-61
MacWAIS, 289
MacWarehouse, 42
MacWatcher, 288
MacWeek, 61
MacWorld, 48, 62
MacWrite, 123-124
Madonna Screen Saver, 178
magazines
    See news & magazines
Magic Link, 117
Magic World of ABC's, The, 152
MagNet, 20-21
Magnet Interactive Studios, 220
MAIL-IT, 286
mailing lists, 11-12, 279
Major Apple 2 Archives, 34, 67
Major Commodore FTP Site, 97
Male Box BBS, The, 270
map graphics, 193
Mathematical Introduction to Robotic Manipulation, A, 229
McAfee Associates, 237
McCaw Cellular, 256
McGraw-Hill Online, 37
MCI, 255, 256
Mdeiatrix, 27
MECA Forum, 134
MediaPro, Inc., 153
MediaTools Online, 221
MediaVision Forum, 206
MEGAzine & *MegaZone*, 158
Melbourne PC User Group, 74
Member List, 279
memory products, 27
Mercury News, 283
Mercury Robot, 230
Metalogic, 44-45
Metrostar Computer Center, 47
MFS Datanet, 256
MG's Fabulous News Page, 283
Michael Wolff & Company, Inc., 37
Micro Machines, 47
microchips, 27
Microsoft & Microsoft Windows, 81-87

    See also PC
    antipathy, 82
    communications, 250-251
    databases, 150
    education, 152
    extensions, 85
    FAQs & info, 82-83
    fonts, 129
    games, 161
    graphics, 128-129, 183-184
    Knowledge Base, The, 23, 83
    Microsoft Press Bookstore, 38
    MS Access, 147
    MS BASIC Forum, 164
    MS Desktop, 130
    MS-DOS, 79, 80, 174-175
    MS Excel, 138-139
    MS FoxPro & FoxBase, 145
    MS Home, 155
    MS Office, 135
    MS Publisher, 132
    MS SQL, 150
    MS Windows AV, 213
    MS Word, 124-125
    MS Workgroups, 135
    multimedia, 219
    news, 83-84
    programming, 85-86, 163
    screen savers, 177
    software (business), 133-135, 137
    software (general), 34, 84-85, 137, 198
    software (Net), 251, 265-266, 286-289
    sound, 196, 198, 207
    user groups, 82
    utilities, 137, 175
    vendors, 87
    Windows '95, 87, 266
    Windows NT, 86-87
    word processing, 135, 137
MicroWarehouse, 42
Mid-Atlantic OS/2 User Group, Virginia Beach, VA, 92
MIDI, 200-203
    clips, 202-203
    FAQ, 200
    players, 208
    tools, 202
    vendors, 203-205
Millenium Communications, 220
Mind Logic, 47
Ministry of Posts and Telecommunica-

Index

tions, Japan, 255
MinitelWeb: France Telecom Intelmatique, 256
MiNTOS Distribution and Information Page, 100
mIRC, 287
misc.books.technical, 35
misc.books.technical FAQ, 35
misc.forsale.computers.discussion, 40
misc.forsale.computers.mac-specific.cards.misc, 42
misc.forsale.computers.mac-specific.cards.video, 42
misc.forsale.computers.mac-specific.misc, 42
misc.forsale.computers.mac-specific.portables, 42
misc.forsale.computers.mac-specific.software, 42
misc.forsale.computers.mac-specific.systems, 42
misc.forsale.computers.memory, 47
misc.forsale.computers.modems, 47
misc.forsale.computers.monitors, 47
misc.forsale.computers.net-hardware, 46
misc.forsale.computers.other.misc, 40
misc.forsale.computers.other.software, 40
misc.forsale.computers.other.systems, 40
misc.forsale.computers.pc-specific.audio, 42
misc.forsale.computers.pc-specific.cards.video, 42
misc.forsale.computers.pc-specific.misc, 43
misc.forsale.computers.pc-specific.motherboards, 43
misc.forsale.computers.pc-specific.portables, 43
misc.forsale.computers.pc-specific.software, 43
misc.forsale.computers.pc-specific.systems, 43
misc.forsale.computers.printers, 47-48
misc.forsale.computers.workstation, 43
misc.security, 234
Mission Control Software, 45
MIT Distrubution Site for PGP, 236
MIT FAQ Repository, 284
MIT Scheme Hubsite, 170
MIT's OS/2 Site, 88-89
Mjolner Beta System Home Page, 165

ML (programming lang.), 168
MMDEVX, 219
Mobidata: An Interactive Journal, 110
Mobile and Wireless Computing, 110, 247-248
Mobile Computing and Personal Digital Assistants, 113
Mobile Office, 110-111
MOD, 205
  players, 208
modems, 28-30
  archive, 30
  FAQ, 29
  tutorial, 29
  vendors, 29
Modula2 (programming lang.), 168
Modula3 (programming lang.), 168
Monash Archive for the HP 100/200 LX., 117
Monet: the Cyberspace Gallery, 192
monitors, 30
Montreal FoxPro User's Group, 145
Morgan Kaufmann, 38
Mosaic, 289
Motorola Envoy, 117
Mountain Lake Software, 153
Movie Sounds, 199
MP2 Audio Playback, 207
MPEG, 215-216
MPEGAud 1.0a7, 207-208
Mr. Upgrade, 43
MSU Catalog, 45
Mucho Newton Stuff, 114
MUDs, 272-273
MultiDialog, 100
multimedia, 212-221
  animation, 215-216
  CD-ROMs, 215
  clips, 216-218
  education, 153, 216
  MPEG, 215-216
  news, 214-215
  production companies, 220-221
  programming & authoring, 218-219
  QuickTime, 216
  shopping, 46
  software, 221
  vendors, 220
MultiMedia World, 46, 213, 214
Museum of HP Calculators, The, 119
music
  See sound

N

NASA Telerobotics Program, 231
NASA VR lab, 227
NASA's Web Stars, 227
Nathan Mates' Apple II Resources, 66-67
National Telecommunications & Information Administration, 252
Navigating the Net: Let's Go Gopherin', 285
Navy Multimedia Page, 213
NCC Blackwell, 38
NCR/AT&T, 77-78
NCSA InfoSecurity Forum, 237-238
NCSA Telnet, 288
NCSA Virtual Reality Lab, 227
NCSA Virus Vendor Forum, 238
Net Day, 277
Net, the, 2
  See also email; FTP; gopher; Net software; newsgroups; telnet; WAIS; World Wide Web
  access providers, 6-8, 320-327
  getting started, 4-8
  navigating, 275-285
  news, 277-278
.net—The Internet Magazine, 277-278
Net software, 264-267, 285, 286-289
  Amigas, 265
  DOS, 265-266
  FAQs, 265, 266, 267
  ISDN, 267
  Macintosh, 267
  OS/2, 267
  Windows, 265-266
NETcetera, 286
NetGuide, 278
Netizens and the Wonderful World of the Net: An Anthology, 242
NetLib Scientific Computing Repository, The, 162
NetManage, 46
Netpages, 279
Netscape, 46, 235, 289
NetSearch, 281
Netsurfer Digest, 278
Netsurfer Tools, 285
Network Payment Mechanisms, 235
Neural Net FAQ, 225
New Media Associates, 220
New York Macintosh Users Group, 65
New York PC Users Group, 74

Index

news
    Amiga, 95
    Apple, 50-51
    BBSs, 269
    communications, 247
    databases, 141-142
    desktop publishing, 128
    games, 157-158
    general, 19-21
    information age, 240
    Macintosh, 59-61
    Microsoft Windows, 83-84
    multimedia, 214-215
    Net, 3, 277-278
    PCs, 69-70
    telecommunications, 254-255
news.admin.hierarchies, 283
news.admin.misc, 283
news.admin.net-abuse.announce, 283
news.admin.net-abuse.misc, 283
news.admin.policy, 283
news.admin.technical, 283
news.announce.important, 283
news.announce.newsgroups, 283
news.announce.newusers, 283
news.answers, 283
news.groups, 283
news.groups.questions, 283
news.groups.reviews, 284
news.lists, 284
news.misc, 284
news.newusers.questions, 276
news.newusers.questions, 284
news readers, client software, 287-288
news.software*, 284
Newsbytes, 21
newsgroups, 10-11, 282
    client software, 287-288
    FAQs, 283, 284
    newsreaders, 10-11
NewsWatcher, 287
NewsXpress, 288
NewtNews, 114
Newton, 114-116
    programming, 114
    news & reviews, 115
    vendors, 115
Newton Medical Applications, 115
NeXT, 107
NIH, 185
Nomadic Computing, 111
North American CAD, 45
North Carolina State University State University Walking Machine Project, 230
North Suburban Chicago-Area OS/2 Users' Group (NSCOUG), 92
Northern California Windows NT Users Group, 86
Northern New Jersey TEAM OS/2 Web Server, 92
Novell Inc., 125, 139
Now Hear This! 2.1 for the Mac, 207
Now Utilities 5.0, 176
NPTN Free-Net List, The, 258
NS-Lookup, 288
NSTN Cybermall—Computer Services
NTT (Nippon Telegraph and Telephone Corporation), 256
Nude Images, 193
Nude Pictures of Women, 193
Nuntius, 288
NYU Center for Digital Multimedia, 216
NYU's LabCam, 230

O

O'Reilly, 38
Oak Software Repository, The, 32
Oberon (programming lang.), 168-169
object-oriented databases, 147-148
Objective-C (programming lang.), 169
Obsolete Computer Museum, 25
office automation, 133-134
office supplies, 47
Official Windows Sockets Web Page, The, 266
Online Bookstore, 38
Online Today, 278
Online World, The, 277
Opcode, 203
Open Virtual Reality Testbed Home Page, 227
operating systems, Macintosh, 54
Optimus, 221
Opus, 270
Oracle (database), 148-149
Oracle Magazine, 149
OS9, 103-104
OS/2, 88-92, 161, 274
    FAQ, 90
    games, 161
    programming, 91-92
    software (general), 90-91
    software (Net), 267
    sound, 195-196
    support & info, 89-90
    user groups, 92
    utilities, 176
    vendors, 92
    WARP, 91
OscarNet, 192
OTIS, 191
OTS Mac Software Archive, 57
Ottawa OS/2 User's Group, 92
Output Enablers, 43

P

Pacific Bell, 256
Pacific Hi-Tech Corp., 221
Pacific Northwest OS/2 Users Group, 92
Pacific Telesis, 256
Packard Bell Online, 78
Packard-Bell, 78
PageMaker, 131-132
palmtops
    See PDAs
Paradon Computer Systems, 40
Paradox, 149
Parallel Tools Consortium, The, 105
Pascal (programming lang.), 166, 169
PBS Applications Forum, 32
PBS Arcade Forum, 161
PBS Business Forum, 136
PBS Education Forum, 153
PBS Home Forum, 155
PBS Screen Savers, 177
PBS Studio Forum, 127, 183
PBS Utilities Forum, 172
PC, 68-92
    See also DOS; PC clones; Microsoft Windows
    BBSs, 269
    calculators, 119
    communications, 250-251
    compression, 175
    databases, 141
    demos, 72
    desktop publishing, 127
    FAQ, 73
    games, 160-161
    GEOS, 74
    graphics, 182-183
    hardware, 72-73
    multimedia, 213
    news, 69-70
    novices, 69

352 Net Tech

Index

programming, 162
resellers, 73-74
security, 233
shopping, 40, 41-44, 48, 74
software (business), 136
software (general), 71-72
sound, 196-197, 206
spreadsheets, 139
tutorials & info, 69
user groups, 74
utilities, 175
vendors, 74
word processing, 122-123
PC911/First Aid, 80
PC-Mac TCP/IP & NFS FAQ List, The, 265
PC Magazine, 69-70
PC News, 70
PC clones, 75-78
    Acer, 75
    Compaq, 75
    DEC, 75-76
    Dell, 76
    Epson, 76
    Gateway 2000, 76
    Hewlett-Packard, 77
    NCR/AT&T, 78
    Packard-Bell, 78
    75-78
    Texas Instruments, 78
    Toshiba, 78
    Zenith, 78
    ZEOS, 78
PC Week, 70
PC World, 70
PDAs, 113-117
    HP 100/200LX, 116-117
    Magic Link, 117
    Newton, 114-116
    shopping, 48
    Zoomer, 117
PDP-8 Lovers, 105
Pegasus Mail, 286
Pen Technology Forum, 31
Penthouse, 193
PenWorld-Personal Electronics News, 116
People Connections, 274
Performa Resource Center, 59
peripherals, 26-31
    CD-ROMs, 30-31
    Hewlett-Packard, 31
    memory products, 27
    microchips, 27

modems, 28-30
monitors, 30
printers, 27-28
scanners, 27
SCSI, 27
shopping, 47-48
video, 27
Perl (programming lang.), 169
Personal Finance Software Forum, 136-137
Peter W. Huber Home Page, 254
PGP—Pretty Good Privacy, 236
Photo Gallery Forum, 190
PHOTO-CD, 31
Photos to Go, 190
Photoshop, 186-187
PHP (Lahti Telephone Company), 256
Phrack, 239
#phreak, 239
Pick Systems Home Page, 149-150
PIM/PhoneBk/Dialers, 137
Ping client software, 288
Planet Earth, 190-191, 281
Playboy, 193
Pop, 169
pop culture graphics, 192
portable computers, 110-112
    shopping, 48
Porting to Power PC, 62
Post & Telecom Iceland, 256
PostScript, 169-170
Power Macintosh, 62-63
    See also Macintosh
PowerBooks, 111-112
    See also Macintosh
PowerBuilder Home Page, 148
PowerGlove FAQ, 227
Powersoft Home Page, 148
PPP
    See Net software
PPP FAQ, 265
Practical Peripherals Forum, 29
Preparing Media for Director, 219-220
Print Artist, 187
Printer Works, 28
printers, 27-28
privacy, 233-234
    See also security
    FAQs, 233, 234
Pro-CD, 221
Prodigy, 3, 6, 260, 274
Product Query Form, 87

product reviews, 48
Programmer University, 162-163
programming, 162-171
    abc, 164
    Ada, 164
    Amiga, 96
    AMOS, 164
    APL, 164
    Apple, 67
    Atari, 100
    BASIC, 164
    BETA, 164-165
    Borland, 163
    C/C++, 165
    Cobol, 166
    compilers, 166
    Computer Associates, 163
    DOS, 79
    Dylan, 166
    Eiffel, 166
    Forth, 166-167
    Fortran, 167
    Icon, 167
    Linda, 167
    LISP, 167-168
    LOGO, 168
    Lucid, 168
    Macintosh, 63-64
    Microsoft, 163
    Microsoft Windows, 85-86
    ML, 168
    Modula2, 168
    Modula3, 168
    multimedia, 218-219
    Oberon, 168-169
    Objective-C, 169
    OS/2, 91-92
    Pascal, 169
    Perl, 169
    Pop, 169
    PostScript, 169-170
    Prograph, 170
    Prolog, 170
    Python, 170
    REXX, 170
    Sather, 170
    Scheme, 170-171
    Smalltalk, 171
    Verilog, 171
    VHDL, 171
    Visual Basic, 171
    Watcom, 163
Prograph (programming lang.), 170
Prolog (programming lang.), 170

Index

Pronto IP, 286
PTC Web!, 255
Public Ada Library, 164
Publicly Accessible Mailing Lists, 279
Publish It!, 132
Python (programming lang.), 170

Q

QMS, Inc., 28
QNews, 288
QRZ (Ham Radio CD-Rom, Beer CD-Rom, etc.), 221
QuarkXPress, 130-131
Quattro Pro, 139
Queens University (Ontario) —Robotics and Perception Lab Index, 231
Query Interface to the PC Software Harvest Broker, 72
Quick Guide to NEXTSTEP Information on the Internet, 107
Quick Pictures Forum, 191
Quicken Support, 135
QuickTime, 216
 FAQ, 216
QWS3270 Extra, 288

R

Radius, 30
Random House Electronic Publishing, 38
raytrace & rendering, 189
RBBS-PC, 270
Reading Usenet News, 284
Real Audio, 207
real-time chat, 271-274
Redgate Online, 21-22, 48, 62
Remailer List, 234
Remailers!!!, 280
repairs, 3
resellers, PCs, 73
Resolution Business Press, 38
Reveal, 46
REXX (programming lang.), 170
Road Warrior Outpost, 48, 111
Rob's Mac Page, 52
Rob's Multimedia Lab, 218
Robert Lentz's Macintosh Resources, 53
Robert Lentz's Programming Resources, 64
robotics, 229-231

Rocket Science, 221
Rockwell Telecommunications, 29
Rocky Mountain Digital Peeks Home Page, 221
Rocky Mountain FoxPro Mailing List, 145
Rocky Mountain NT Users Group, 86
Roland SoundCanvas Products Compared, 204
root, 274
Rosenthal on Mac, 61
Rosenthal on Multimedia, 214
RTFM Mail Server, The, 279
Rune Stone, 239

S

S/KEY, 236
Sachi's Icons, 153
Safeware Computer Insurance, 45
San Diego County Windows Users Group, 86
Sandra's Clip Art Server, 130
Sather (programming lang.), 170
scanners, 27, 128
Scarecrow's WWW Link, 191
SCDI's HP48 Calculators Department, 119
Scheme (programming lang.), 170-171
sci.crypt, 239
sci.crypt.research, 239
sci.virtual-worlds, 227-228
Science Fiction Sound Clips, 199
science graphics, 193
screen savers, 177-178
 Macintosh, 177-178
 Windows, 177
 single-module, 178
Screening Room, The, 218
SCSI, 27
searching for people, 279
security, 232-239
 Clipper Chip, 235-236
 cryptography, 239
 FAQs, 234, 235
 firewalls, 234-235
 hacking, 238-239
 PGP, 236
 privacy, 233-234
 S/KEY, 236
 software, 235
 viruses, 237-238
Sega, 221
Seinfeld: The Sounds, 199

SEL-HPC Article Archive, 225
Serif PagePlus, 132
shareware BBSs, 328-335
Shareware Club, 40
Shareware Depot, 40
Shareware Discuss, 32
shareware/freeware
 See software
ship graphics, 193
shopping, 3-4, 39-48
 CD-ROMs, 44-45
 computer insurance, 45
 entertainment, 45
 graphics & video, 45
 Lotus, 45
 magazines, 45-46
 multimedia, 46
 networking, 46-47
 office supplies, 47
 PCs, 41-44
 PDAs, 48
 peripherals, 47-48
 portables, 48
 reviews, 48
Short History of Hypertext, A, 210
Short Introduction to the ABC Language, A, 164
Sierra Vista IBM PC Users Group, 74
Sight and Sound Forum, 194
Signature, Finger, & Customized Headers FAQ, 280
Silicon Graphics, 184
Silicon Surf, 184
Simon Net, 117
Simply, 135
SimTel Animation Utilities, 215-216
SimTel Calculators, 119
SimTel Communications Programs, 251
SimTel dBASE Directory, 143
SimTel Desktop Publishing, 130
SimTel DOS Graphics Viewer, 183
SimTel Education Software, 152
SimTel Encoding Software, 175
SimTel Finance Software, 137
SimTel Foreign Language Software, 152-153
SimTel Hypertext Software, 210
SimTel MS-DOS Archive, 34
SimTel MS-DOS Archive, 80
SimTel Multimedia Directory, 221
SimTel PC Databases, 150
SimTel Windows Archive, 84-85
SimTel Windows Education Software,

Index

152
SimTel Windows Graphics Viewers, 183
SimTel Windows Screen Savers, 177
SimTel WindowsNT Software, 86-87
SimTel Word for Windows, 124-125
SimTel WordPerfect Software, 125
Sinclair, 101-102
Singapore Telecom, 256
Sites with Audio Clips, 199
SLIP
　See Net Software
Slipknot, 289
Slovenian Telekom, 256
Sly Stone—Images of the Past, 192
Small Computer Book Club, 38
Smalltalk (programming lang.), 171
Snake Oil, Miracle Cures and Monitors, 26-27
SNC International, 47
soc.net-people, 279
society, 241-242
Society For Electronic Access, The, 242
Softdisk Superstore, 40
Softkey Forum, 125
Softpro Books, 38
software, 2-3, 32-34, 48
　　Amiga, 34, 95-96
　　Apple II & III, 34, 66-68
　　Atari, 100
　　business, 134-137
　　calculators, 118
　　databases, 150
　　DOS, 79-80
　　hypermedia, 211
　　Macintosh, 54-58
　　Microsoft Windows, 34, 80, 84-85
　　multimedia, 221
　　Net, 285
　　OS/2, 90-91
　　PCs, 71-72, 136
　　programming, 163
　　security, 235
　　shareware BBSs, 328-335
　　spreadsheets, 139
software.net, 40
Software Phone Directory, 22
SonicNet, 270
Sony Magic Link, 117
Sony Music Clips, 199
sound, 194-208
　　clips, 198-200

editors, 207-208
FAQs, 196, 197, 202, 205, 206
formats, 197
MIDI, 200-202
MIDI clips, 202-203
MIDI players, 208
MIDI vendors, 203-205
MOD, 205
MOD players, 208
players, 207
sound cards & boards, 205-206
utilities, 197-198
Sources of Information About X, 104
Sources of Smalltalk Information, 171
Southwestern Bell, 256
SOX10 (SOund eXchange), 208
space graphics, 193
Space Images at Indiana University, 193
Spectrum Forever, 101
Spider's Pick of the Day, 282
spreadsheets, 138-139
　　Excel, 138-139
　　Lotus, 139
　　Quattro Pro, 139
　　shareware, 139
Sprint, 255, 256
Spry Mosaic-CompuServe Edition, 289
SQL (programming lang.), 150
SRI Artificial Intelligence Center, 225
ST Beermat, 99
Stanford Aerospace Robotics Laboratory Home Page, 231
Stanford Dextrous Manipulation Lab, 231
Stanford Netnews Filtering Service, 284
Stanford Robotics Laboratory, 231
Stanford University, 231
Staples—The Office Superstore, 47
Star Trek Pictures, 192
Starting to Use the WWW, 280
Starwave, 221
State of the Art Review on Hypermedia Issues and Applications, 210
Statistics on Internet Usage, 285
Stepwise Server, 107
Steve and his Sony Magic Link, 117
Stiquito Colony, 230
Stock Solution, The, 191
Straight To The Source, 62
Stupid OS/2 Tricks, 92
Sugar Screen Saver, 178

Sun Site Sound Files, 199
Sun-Sounds Movie Themes Page, 199
Sunet Pictures, 190
Sunsite Multimedia Information, 218
Sunsite Pictures, 191
supercomputers, 105-106
SuperDOS, 80
Support Directory, 22
Support On Site, 24
Survival Research Lab, 230
Swiss PTT Telecom, 256
Sybase, 150
Symantec AntiVirus Forum, 238
Symantec Central Point Software DOS Forum, 175
Symantec Central Point Software WinMac Forum, 172
Symantec Norton Utilities Forum, 172
Synapse—Multimedia Journal of the Eclectic, 215
sysop info, BBS04

T

talk.politics.crypto, 239
Talker, 273
Tampere Telephone Company (Finland), 256
Tandy, 103-104
　　Model 100, 112
　　sound, 196
TAP: The Ada Project, 244
Teach Yourself Ingres, 146
Team OS/2 Online, 92
Tech Museum of Innovation, The, 25
Technology Review, 45, 240
{Tele}Communications Information Sources, 252
Telecom Eireann, 256
Telecom Finland, 256
Telecom Information Resources on the Internet, 252-253
Telecom Regulations, 254
telecommunications, 252-256
　　FAQ, 253-254
　　news & reference, 254-255
　　services, 255
Teleglobe, 256
Telekom Malaysia, 256
Telephone Industry Information Page, 253
Telkom (Indonesia), 256
telnet, 11-12

Index

client software, 288-289
Telos, 38
Telstra, 256
Terisa Systems, 235
terminology, computing, 24
Texas Instruments, 78, 118
Texas Metronet PERL Archive, 169
Text Processing Directory, 123
They May Be Beautiful or Ugly—They Are on IRC, 272
Think-C, 166
ThinkPad 750 List, 112
Thor's Newton Nonsense, 116
TidBITS, 61
TidBITS Guide to MIDI and the Macintosh, The, 202
Tile.Net ListServ Lists, 279-280
Tile.Net News, 284
tile.NET Vendors, 22
Time Warner Interactive, 220
Timeslips Forum, 135
Timestream, 221
Timex/Sinclair, 102
Tips for Access Database Users, 147
Today's Cryptography, 239
Tokyo PC Users Group, 74
ToolBook Mailing List, 220
Tools For Windows Vendor, 87
TopSoft, 64
Toshiba, 78
Trailblazer Utilities, 172
Travels with Samantha, 193
Triangle Virtual Reality, The, 231
Trilogy Online Service, 270
Trumpet Archie, 286
Trumpet News, 288
Trumpet Ping, 288
Trumpet Telnet, 288
Trumpet Winsock for Windows, 266
Turbo Gopher, 287
TurboPascal, 169
TurboVision, 166
Turku Telephone Company (Finland), 256
tutorials, PCs, 69
Typing Injury and Keyboard FAQ, 22
Typography and Type Design List, 127

U

UCLA Mobile Robotics, 231
UFO Images, 193
UIUC OS/2 Site, 89
UK Communications Forum, 246-247
U.K. Computing Forum, 19
UK PC Users Group, 74
U.K. Shareware Forum, 33
U.K. Telecom FAQ, 255
U.S. Internet Service Providers List, 258
Ultimate Collection of Winsock Software, 266
Ultimate Software Home Page, 178
Ultra Recorder 2.1 for the Mac, 207
Ultralite List, 112
UMich Atari Software Archive, 100
UMich Software Archive, 33
UNC Multimedia Archive, 218
Undernet Directory, The, 272
Understanding C++: An Accelerated Introduction, 166
Underworld Sound Links, 199
Unisys History Newsletter, 25
Univ. of Delaware—Rehabilitation Robotics Program, 231
Univ. of Kentucky Atari Archives, 100
Univ. of Tokyo Jouhou System Kougaku Laboratory, 231
University Ingres, 146
University of Amsterdam Robotics and Neurocomputing, 231
University of Genova—Laboratory for Integrated Advanced Robotics, 231
University of Illinois Sound File Archive, 199-200
University of Illinois UC Robotics and Automation Laboratory, 231
University of Karlsruhe Windows NT Support Center, 87
University of Maryland at College Park: Autonomous Mobile Robots Lab, 231
University of Massachusetts Laboratory for Perceptual Robotics, 231
University of Michigan Macintosh Archive, 34
University of Michigan Macintosh Screen Saver Archive, 178
University of Michigan Newton Archives, 116
University of Rochester Micro-Mouse Robot Contest, 230
University of Utah—Robotics, 231
Unix, 106-107, 274
FAQs, 106, 107
vendors, 107
UnixWorld, 107
Unofficial Acorn Home Page, 102
Unofficial Internet Book List, The, 35
Unofficial Windows 95 Software Archive, 87
Upside Online, 240
URouLette, 282
US West, 256
USA New Gear Price List, 204
Usenet, 10-11, 284
user groups, 22, 65
Amiga, 97
Macintosh, 64-65
OS/2, 92
PCs, 74
utilities, 172-176
Amiga, 174
Apple II, 174
Atari, 174
compression, 173
DOS, 174-176
Macintosh, 176
OS/2, 176
sound, 197-198
Windows, 174-176
UUdeview, 173
UUNet Archive, 33
UUNET's List of Newsgroups, 284
UWTerm, 289

V

Vancouver PC Users' Group, 74
Vatican Exhibit, The, 192
Vektron Online, 44
vendors, 21-22, 292-319
Amiga, 96
Apple, 67
Atari, 100
desktop publishing, 130
graphics, 188
Macintosh, 61-62
Microsoft Windows, 87
MIDI, 203-205
OS/2, 92
PCs, 74
Verilog (programming lang.), 171
Veronica, 285
VHDL (programming lang.), 171
Vibe Online Helper Applications, 198
VibeLine, 200
Vicious Book of BBS's, The, 269-270
video, 27, 213-214

Index

shopping, 45
videoconferencing, 272
Viewer Resource Center, 185-186
viewing programs for graphics, 184-185
Village, The, 29-30
Vincent Voice Library at Michigan State University, The, 200
vintage computers, 105
Virtual City Network Project, 228
Virtual Computer Library, 19
Virtual Computer Library, 22
Virtual Environments Research at Delft, 231
virtual reality, 225-229
Virtual Shareware Library, 33
Virtual Vegas, 157
viruses, 237-238
VISION OS/2 Gopher, 91
Visual Basic (programming lang.), 171
Voyager, 45, 221
VR at Banff, 228
VR Metropolis, 229
VR World, 229
VR-SIG, 229
VX-REXX, 170

W

W3 CUI Search Engine, 281
WAIS, 285
    client software, 289
#warez, 239
WARP, 91
Watcom, 163
    C/C++, 166
Wavestation Home Page, The, 204-205
WaveWindow v2.5, 208
Wayne's HP48 G/GX Calculator Resource, 119
Web
    See World Wide Web
Web HotSpots: No 404's!, 282
WebChat, 273
WebCrawler, 281-282
WebMuseum Network, The, 192
Webster's Dictionary of Computer Terms, 24
WebWeek, 278
Welcome to MUDdom..., 273
Well Connected Mac, The, 53
WFW-L: Microsoft Windows for Workgroups, 135

WH Networks Communications Archive, 300
WHAM (Waveform Hold and Modify), 208
What's Going On, 21
What's Hot and Cool, 282
Whole Internet Catalog, The, 282
Wierenga Coloring Programs, 153
WilTel, 253, 256
Windows
    See also Microsoft Windows
    other windows, 104-105
    Windows '95, 87, 266
    Windows NT, 86-87
    X Windows, 104
Windows Magazine, 84
Winjammer V2.30, 208
WinQVT 16-bit, 289
#Winsock, 266
Winsock-L, 266
WinVN, 288
WinWeb, 289
WinZip Home Page, 176
Wired, 240-241
wireless communications, 247-248
women and computing, 244
Word Perfect Magazine, 125
word processing, 122-125
    AmiPro, 123
    MacWrite, 123-124
    MS Word, 124-125
    WordPerfect, 125
    WriteStar/WriteNow, 125
WordPerfect, 125
workgroups, 135
World Arts Resources, 192
World List of Desktop Publishers and Freelancers, 132
World of Audio, 194-195
World of Audio MIDI Page, 202
World of Newton, 116
World Wide Web, 9-10, 274, 280
    basics, 280
    browsers, 9-10, 289
    directories, 281
    FAQ, 281
    picks, 282
World Wide Web Worm, The, 282
World's Atari Archive, The, 100
World-Wide Web Tools, 280-281
Worldwide Index of Commodore Users Groups, 97
Worldwide Yellow Pages, 282
WPCorp Files Forum, 125

WriteStar/WriteNow, 125
WS Archie, 286
WS Gopher, 287
WS-FTP, 287
WS-FTP 32 Bit, 287
WS-IRC, 287
WS-Ping 16-bit, 288
WSN-FTPC, 287
Wuarchive Graphics Archive, 191
Wuarchive Image Finder, 191
Wuarchive MS-DOS Site, 80
Wuarchive Software Archive, 33
WWW
    See World Wide Web
WWW Virtual Library, The, 282
WWW Virtual Library's Computer Programming Languages, 163
WWW-Security, 233

X, Y, Z

X Windows, 104
X-Rated Star Trek Archive, 193
XBase Applications and Programming, 141
Xerox Link, The, 31
Xerox Office Solutions Forum, 134
XFerIt, 286
XPresso Bar, The, 131
Yahoo, 282
Your Privacy, 234
YPN—Your Personal Network, 282
Zarf's List of Interactive Games on the Web, 157
ZD Europe, 240
ZD Net, 70
Zen and the Art of the Internet, 277
Zenith, 78
ZEOS, 78
Ziff Davis Publishing, 38, 45-46
ZiffNet, 68-69
ZiffNet Free Utilities Forum, 176
ZiffNet Reviews Index, 48
ZiffNet/Mac, 57
ZiffNet/Mac Download Software And Support Forum, 58
Zip.Com, 117
ZMac, 61
Zoomer, 117
ZyXEL Home Page, 30

Michael Wolff & Company, Inc.

Michael Wolff & Company, Inc., digital publisher and packager, specializing in information presentation and graphic design, is one of the leading providers of information about the Net. The company's book *Net Guide*, published with Random House, has spent almost a year on bestseller lists, and is now a monthly magazine published by CMP Publications.

MW& Co., and its team of Net surfers, is embarked upon a project to map all corners of the Net. This means that the growing community of Net adventurers can expect a steady flow of new Net baedekers. *Net Guide* has now been joined by *Net Games*, *Net Chat*, *Net Money*, *Net Trek*, *Net Sports*, and *Net Tech*, and will shortly be followed by *Net Guide, 2nd edition*, and *Net Music*. MW&Co.'s online service, YPN—Your Personal Network (http://www.ypn.com/), features a hypertext version of the entire series. It is the most comprehensive Net source available anywhere.

Among the company's other recent projects are *Where We Stand—Can America Make It in the Global Race for Wealth, Health, and Happiness?* (Bantam Books), one of the most graphically complex information books ever to be wholly created and produced by means of desktop-publishing technology, and *Made in America?*, a four-part PBS series on global competitiveness, hosted by Labor Secretary Robert B. Reich.

Kelly Maloni, who directed the *Net Tech* project, is the executive editor of MW&Co. Managing editor Ben Greenman has written pop-culture criticism for many publications, including *Miami New Times*, the *Chicago Reader*, the *Village Voice*, and *Rolling Stone*, and has taught in the English department at Northwestern University. Jeff Hearn has served as art director for *Net Chat*, *Net Money*, *Net Trek*, and *Net Sports* and has been a desktop-publishing consultant for several publications, including *Spy*.

Websight

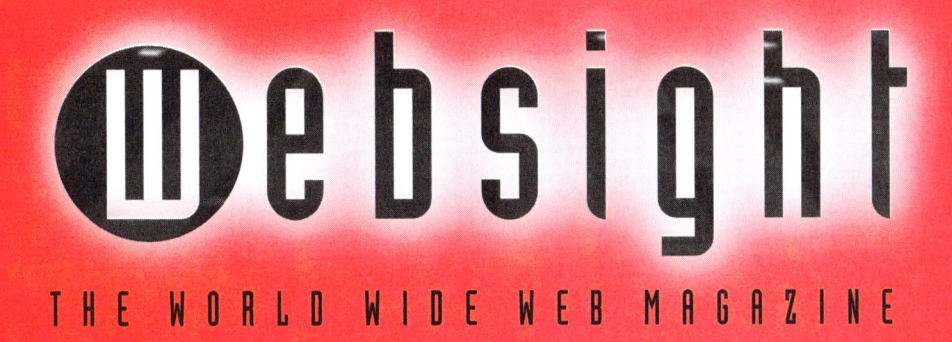

THE WORLD WIDE WEB MAGAZINE

Websight Magazine helps you explore the vast, uncharted World Wide Web.

As our title implies, Websight focuses exclusively on the Web. We bring you feature articles from the foremost authorities on the Web. Think of us as your travel magazine or "T.V. Guide" to the virtual Web wilderness.

Plus, our WebGuide section features hundreds of the best sites on the Web, sorted by subject!

http://websight.com

RESERVE YOUR NAME ON THE INTERNET.

(stop using names like xyz@aol.com)

identity ▸ john@xyzcorp.com

Having your own domain name on the internet gives you or your company an online identity. It is no longer necessary to use your service providers address as your own. You can register a recognizable phrase or name that ties in with who you are. Making it easier for clients and friends to get in touch.

a simple solution

YOURNAME.COM will take care of everything. We will register the personal domain name of your choice and forward all your e-mail to your present online account.

fee

$29.95 for registration
$10 a month for mail forwarding

YOURNAME.COM

phone 1 800.577.5443   e-mail info@yourname.com   web site www.yourname.com

Macintosh Users:
Want to connect to CompuServe directly over the Internet ?

Call us today for details about TCPack at (408) 725 4242 or try downloading our TCPack Demo from our anonymous FTP site, ftp.ascus.com

About Software Corporation is one of the premier Macintosh developers, doing Communications Toolbox (CTB) applications and tools for the MacOS.

TCPack is a CTB TCP/IP connection tool that allows users to connect applications across the Internet. TCPack has been licensed for use with AOL and eWorld. We provide a version that will allow you to get the same direct Internet access to CompuServe.

We also publish 5PM Internet and 5PM Term, two application suites for doing internet Mail, Gopher, FTP, Newsreading and Web Browsing, along with top quality telnet support for PC-ANSI, VT220, VT420, TN3270, TN5250, HP 700/98, VIP7800, UNISYS T27 & UTS 20-100. Applications are Native Power Macintosh. Connect to our FTP site today and try out some of our software.

About Software Corporation
10601 S. De Anza Blvd., Suite 105; Cupertino, CA 95014
Tel: (408) 725-4242   Fax: (408) 725-4243
Internet: info@ascus.com   FTP server: ftp.ascus.com

ASC

BBS

THE BULLETIN BOARD SERVICES MAGAZINE

We Battle Beta

(so you won't have to)

BBSs

World Wide Web

Consumer Online Services

Annotated BBS List

Netlaw

Macintosh

Shareware

Sysops

Insider Buzz

Hardware

BBS Magazine— Get the latest version

800.822.0437 ($30/12 issues U.S.) Or check your local newsstand.

This green slopes down toward the east.

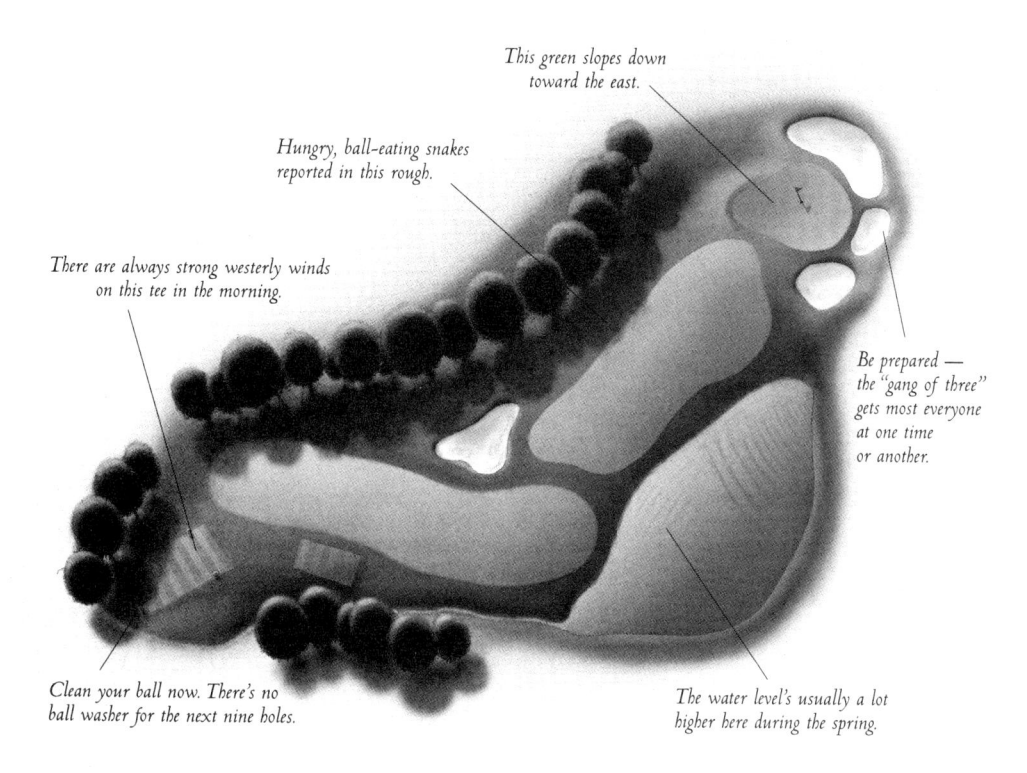

Hungry, ball-eating snakes reported in this rough.

There are always strong westerly winds on this tee in the morning.

Be prepared — the "gang of three" gets most everyone at one time or another.

Clean your ball now. There's no ball washer for the next nine holes.

The water level's usually a lot higher here during the spring.

CompuServe. Because the smallest details can make the biggest difference.

CompuServe is the world's largest computer information service, with more than 3 million members. You can get information on better than 13,000 different golf courses all over the world from CompuServe. You can learn what goes into the design of a good course. We have services to help you check out the resorts, or even plan your whole golf vacation. The latest golf news is available on CompuServe, too.

Plus, all of the thousands of other golfers online will be more than happy to provide you with any and all advice you might need for your next game.

Like how to steer clear of those ball-eating snakes.

Free Membership Kit*

Join CompuServe now. Call **1 800 487-0588**, and ask for your *Net Sports* representative. You'll receive:
1) **A free membership kit.** CompuServe Information Manager software for DOS, Macintosh, Windows, or OS/2.
2) **One free month** of over 120 popular services, a $9.95 value.
3) **$25 usage credit** to explore other extended services.

CompuServe®
The information service you won't outgrow.

* New members only, please. All names listed are proprietary trademarks of their respective corporations.

NOT YOUR TYPICAL
INTERNET MAGAZINE...

INFOBAHN
the MAGAZINE of INTERNET CULTURE

http://www.postmodern.com/

✓ **YES!** Send my <u>FREE</u> issue of INFOBAHN immediately! If I like it, I'll get a years worth (6 issues in all) at the special introductory rate of $19.95. That's a savings of 33% off the cover price. If I'm not completely satisfied, I'll write "cancel" on my invoice. I will owe nothing at all, and the free issue is mine to keep.

Name
Address
City   State   Zip   +4   Country
Telephone
E-mail (Please. No spam, we promise!)

FREE!

SEND NO MONEY NOW — NO COST & NO OBLIGATION!
Canadian subscriptions are US$29.95 (GST included). Foreign subscriptions are US$39.95, prepaid only.

clip coupon & MAIL to: INFOBAHN Magazine, PO Box 4216, Foster City, CA 94404
OR FAX to: (415) 286-9518 OR E-MAIL info to: subscriptions@postmodern.com
OR for QUICKEST response, visit our WEB site: http://www.postmodern.com/

The Date – Friday, July 14th, The Place – The Internet, The Site – Computer Currents Interactive http://www.ccurrents.com/cc

Products & Services

Use our exclusive Product/Service Locator button to find exactly what you want and who's got it, especially the computer store down the block. And, to shop the easiest way of all, click our NetQuote button to have qualified vendors at your bidding.

Information

Computer Currents Interactive puts the full text of *Computer Currents* at your fingertips – including months of back issues searchable by keywords. Vital information from the industry's most respected writers, reporters and analysts – Bajarin, Magid, Holsinger, Weibel, Spector and more.

Resources

Whether it's a local calendar of events, user group connections, classifieds, or local sources of supply, Computer Currents Interactive's got it.

The Online Source for Real World Computing

On July 14th...computing in the real world comes a lot closer.

For advertising information:

Call Eric Bergman at 1-800-365-7773, or e-mail ccadvertise@ccurrents.com.

Computer Currents Interactive http://www.ccurrents.com/cc

What do you get when you cross Bill Gates with a Slinky?

We'll leave the answer to your imagination, but if you're looking for fascinating tidbits about Gates and other industry pioneers, you'll find it in *Hoover's Guide to Computer Companies*. You'll learn how he and other leaders built their companies, trounced their competitors, and continue to pave the road to the 21st century.

It's packed with useful and entertaining information on more than 1,000 top companies, including such industry leaders as **Apple**, **Compaq**, **Logitech**, **Machines Bull**, **Microsoft**, **NEC**, **Nintendo**, **Novell**, and **Packard Bell**, and such up-and-coming pioneers as **Acclaim Entertainment**, **Delrina**, **Knowledge Adventure**, **Madge NV**, **Netscape Communications**, and **Zoom Telephonics**. Within its pages you'll find:

- An overview of the industry by the editors of *Upside* magazine, a list of *Upside*'s top 200 companies, and *Upside*'s "Who's Who in the Computer Industry"

- In-depth profiles of 250 computer companies, including operations overviews, company strategies, histories, up to 10 years of key financial data, lists of products, executives' names, headquarters addresses, and phone and fax numbers – plus web site addresses

- Capsule profiles of over 1,000 of the largest public and private computer industry companies, including headquarters addresses, phone and fax numbers, key officers' names, industry and product specialties, stock symbols, sales growth figures, and employment data

- A **FREE** software edition on disk, loaded with an easy-to-use Windows program that allows users to search the company information in the capsule profiles, export data to other programs, and create mailing lists from the companies listed in *Hoover's Guide to Computer Companies*

Produced in a joint effort with *Upside* magazine, this valuable book/software set is ideal for anyone investing in, selling to, buying from, interviewing with, or researching top computer companies. **Order yours today for only $34.95 (plus $3.50 shipping and handling) by phone 800-486-8666, fax 512-454-9401, e-mail refpress6@aol.com, or at our store on the Internet http://www.hoovers.com.**

Only $34.95

COVERS OVER 1,000 KEY COMPUTER COMPANIES

While you're on the Net, get all your company information from

HOOVER'S Online
http://www.hoovers.com

The Ultimate Source for Company Information

BOARDWATCH MAGAZINE
Guide to Electronic Bulletin Boards and The Internet

STAY UP-TO-DATE
On The Internet & World Wide Web, Product Information and Reviews

40% DISCOUNT

Subscribe Now By Calling
1-800-933-6038

and receive a 40% discount off our newsstand price for a 1 year subscription of only $36 (regular newsstand price - $59) or save even more off our 2 years subscription for only $59 (regular newsstand price $118) when ordering please have your MC/VISA ready.

"TechnologyReview, MIT's remarkably understandable and often artful, and therefore highly regarded magazine"
—The Washington Post

WE MAY NOT BE WIRED, BUT WE'RE ADMIRED!

http://web.mit.edu/techreview/www/

In covering its beat of ``technology and its implications,'' Technology Review is unique in that it addresses the practical applications of science, emphasizing policy issues rather than nuts and bolts.

GET A FREE ISSUE!

Send your name, mailing address, and the words *"free issue"* to:

techreview@mit.edu

When your issue arrives, enjoy it thoroughly with our compliments. Then decide whether or not you wish to maintain your association with MIT and Technology Review. If so, you'll receive 7 additional issues for only $19.95. If not, simply mark "cancel" on the form we'll send. You'll owe nothing and you may keep your FREE, no-obligation issue.

The ultimate online navigation tool!

Explore Cyberspace

with the new monthly guide to the online world of information and entertainment!

What's new online? Which Internet newsgroups, chat lines, and bulletin boards are hot? Where's the online action—and how do I get there?

Find out with NetGuide, the first-ever program guide to Cyberspace!

There's never been a magazine like NetGuide! Every month NetGuide points you to the best and brightest places to be and things to see online—more than a hundred listings <u>broken down by areas of interest</u> for quick and easy access.

- News, Arts & Entertainment! • Sports!
- Business & Finance! • Travel! • Reference Sources! • Science & Technology!
- Computers & Software! • Games!
- Romance • Lifestyles! • Politics!
- The Media! • And much more!

These aren't ordinary listings — they're reviews.
Before we publish them, our expert staff researches each listing. How easy is it to access? If it's a bulletin board, is the line always busy? How expensive is it? Is it worth the cost?

Navigate like a pro...
NetGuide isn't only a "where to" guide. It's also a "how-to" manual. You'll learn how to get around cyberspace and valuable techniques to make you a more cost-effective explorer on the information superhighway.

Charter Offer 3 FREE ISSUES!

Be one of the first to try NetGuide!
Call 1-800-336-5900.

OFFER: You will receive a COMPLIMENTARY 3 ISSUE TRIAL SUBSCRIPTION to NetGuide. We will also send a Charter discount invoice for 12 additional issues (15 issues in all) for only $14.97 — less than a dollar an issue, and a Charter savings of 65% off the newsstand rate. If you aren't *amazed* by what NetGuide shows you, return the invoice marked "cancel." You will owe nothing and your three free issues will be yours to keep.

MAC HOME
NO JARGON

FREE!

MACINTOSH USERS! For help to get beyond the infohighway hype. From getting started to what's hot once you're there, **MacHome Journal** is your practical guide to the ever-expanding resources of the Net —

SO GET THE FAQ'S!*

— on everything you do with your Mac! We'll send you the latest issue FREE! Fill out the card to the left or call our toll-free number: **800.800.6542.**

*Answers to Frequently Asked Questions

SUBSCRIBE NOW!

EACH MONTH:

Best Education Software

New Owner Tips

Home Office Musts

Games To Die For

Cloning Around

Multimedia How-Tos

Reviews, Reviews & More Reviews

Do-It-Yourself Graphics

Troubleshooting Solutions

NO JARGON — JUST THE FAQ'S

BUSINESS REPLY MAIL
FIRST-CLASS PERMIT NO. 124 MT MORRIS, IL 61054

POSTAGE WILL BE PAID BY ADDRESSEE

MAC HOME
JOURNAL
**P.O. BOX 469
Mt. Morris, IL 61054**

NO POSTAGE
NECESSARY
IF MAILED
IN THE
UNITED STATES

MacHome Journal

Your #1 Personal Macintosh Magazine

Every issue is packed with groundbreaking coverage of Education, the Information Superhighway, Home Office, Entertainment, Multimedia and beyond! In addition to plain-English articles and product information, MacHome Journal provides straightforward reviews of the best learning software (<u>and</u> what to avoid!)

To order please call
800.800.6542
and mention code TNBB65

E-Mail: **subscribe@machome.com**
Subject: NetBooks
Body: Full Name & Address

▶ *For work, play or education*
MacHome Journal — exclusively for Mac owners

Simply cut along this line and mail card below. No postage necessary!

TRY US OUT FOR FREE!
Receive the latest issue of MacHome Journal, Free!

☐ **YES!** Send me the latest issue FREE with absolutely no obligation. If I agree that MacHome Journal is the magazine for me, I will receive 11 more issues for only $23.95 (Canada & Mexico, US $35.95; Overseas, US $41.95). If not, I will simply write "No Thanks" across the invoice.

Name: _____
Address: _____
_____
Signature: _____ Date: _____

**NO COST. NO OBLIGATION.
100% GUARANTEED.**

MAC HOME™
JOURNAL   TNBB65